The Whole Horse Catalog

Revised & Updated

Steven D. Price, *Editorial Director*

Barbara Burn, Gail Rentsch, and David A. Spector

Illustrations by Werner Rentsch

A Fireside Book

Published by Simon & Schuster

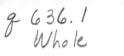

FIRESIDE
Rockefeller Center
1230 Avenue of the Americas
New York, NY 10020

This Fireside Edition 1998

FIRESIDE and colophon are registered trademarks
of Simon & Schuster Inc.

Designed by JUDITH STAGNITTO ABBATE

Manufactured in the United States of America

10   9   8   7   6   5   4   3   2   1

Library of Congress Cataloging-in-Publication Data
The whole horse catalog / Steven D. Price,
editorial director . . . [et al.] ; illustrations by Werner Rentsch.—
Rev. and updated.
p.   cm.
Includes bibliographical references and index.
"A Fireside book."
1. Horses.   2. Horsemanship.   I. Price, Steven D.
SF285.W63   1998
636.1—dc21   98-39589
CIP
ISBN 0-684-83995-4

Acknowledgments

In addition to the many individuals and organizations we've thanked in previous editions of *The Catalog,* our gratitude for their help in this go-round goes to:

Don Treadway of the American Quarter Horse Association, Lesli Groves of *America's Horse,* Lilly Golden of The Lyons Press, Bill Cook of the International Museum of the Horse, Sam Slater of Hunt Cup Productions, Martha Hall of the EMO Agency, Marty Bauman of Classic Communications, Boots and Dave Wright, Ann E. Weiss, Liz Dickmann, Joan Brierly, Mary Hazzard, Myron Weiss, Fred Sagarin, Marie C. Lafrenz, Steven H. Simenowitz, Mary D. Midkiff, Laura Rose of the National Sporting Library, and Mel and Bayard Fox of Bitterroot Ranch and Equitour.

Contents

Preface

———— ∩ ————

The year was 1975, almost a quarter of a century ago, and catalog sourcebooks were still very much a force in book publishing. To that point, however, no one had compiled one on equestrian products, services, and organizations: something that would present the basics of owning, looking after and using horses, together with leads as to where to find more detailed information. Well, I asked myself, why shouldn't I put

such a book together? After all, I was a writer by profession and a recreational rider by avocation. . . . why not combine the two?

In those days (and now, too) anyone in search of intelligent feedback on any horse-book idea could do no better than to ask Bill Steinkraus, the United States Equestrian Team mainstay and all-around polymath.

Bill, who had just moved to Simon & Schuster as an editor, responded in something of a good news/bad news way. The good news was that he found the concept eminently viable. The not-so-good news (or so it seemed to me) was that the project was far too massive for one person—namely, me—to do alone.

Fortunately, help was close at hand. A number of New York book-publishing types who were also avid riders thought the idea was worth getting involved with—and so they did.

Barbara Burn had introduced herself several years earlier as "the girl who outfitted the shed in the backyard for the horse my parents never bought me." Barbara, who had edited two of my books, chose the areas of apparel and horse health, the latter as if anticipating her marriage to a veterinarian who, among his other duties, looked after New York City's Mounted Police horses.

Gail and Werner Rentsch were and are, respectively, a publicist and an artist. They kept horses on

their farm in upstate New York, so who better to compile the chapters on stable construction and management and tack (Gail) and to provide the book's illustrations and layout (Werner)?

Although a stockbroker by profession, David Spector had written several books on horse-related subjects and was active in equestrian organizations. David chose equestrian activities as his area of primary responsibility.

Since I was involved in equestrian tourism, I chose to write the chapter on horseback holidays. I also picked organizations and, even though I'd never had the occasion to buy a horse, I knew where to find out about the selection process.

So we rolled up our sleeves and set to work.

Fade out 1975 . . . fade in 1997 . . .

As you might deduce from the volume you hold in your hands, *The Whole Horse Catalog* remains very much alive and well. Strong initial response was followed by steady annual sales, to rank the books among the all-time best-selling equestrian titles worldwide. One aspect of which we're especially proud is its adoption as a textbook in equestrian studies programs at many schools and colleges.

Equally gratifying has been the reaction of the book's users (they're more than just readers). Many have written or told us how helpful they found *The Cat-*

alog, adding "Why don't you include . . ." or "Hadn't you better update . . . ?"

They were right. Twenty years is a long time, and even though the basic product (the horse) hasn't changed very much over that time, just about everything surrounding the animal has. Products that existed twenty years ago have been improved or dropped; organizations have moved, merged or disbanded. New items and services have arisen. There was plenty that could be added or deleted.

Nothing succeeds like success, and convincing the publisher that *The Catalog* needed substantial updating that went far beyond the cosmetic changes we had made in previous editions was less of a chore than anticipated. The extent to which we were allowed to make changes, however, took a bit of negotiating. If we had our druthers, we would have been able to revise far more than Simon & Schuster allowed us to, but that's the difference between authors and publishers when it comes to cost-consciousness.

Making the changes and additions gave us an opportunity to investigate many of the ways in which the horse world has changed. Some breeds and types of horses, especially the European warmbloods, have become immensely popular in this country. Dressage, competitive endurance riding, cutting and team penning lead the list of growth sports. Even when urban encroachment is reducing the amount of recreation land, trail riding for pleasure is another activity that's experiencing a burst of interest and energy.

When it comes to new products, even such conservative bastions as the show ring and foxhunting field recognize that safety and comfort are the order of the day. No matter what the type of riding or driving, helmets with chin straps are no longer considered icky or wussy, but as an essential way to reduce the possibility of head injuries. Flack-jacket vests are a similar requirement for the cross-country phase of combined training's horse trials and events (many rodeo riders use them, too, although ten-gallon hats haven't given way to harder headgear). Comfort begins with stretch fabrics used in clothing for a variety of disciplines and climates, with bright colors and patterns particularly visible in endurance riding and dressage warm-up wear. Although traditionalists may decry their use, durable fabrics have become substitutes for leather in saddles, bridles, halters, and other equine wear.

The new age has reached the horse world in the form of alternative therapies and medications. Massage, acupuncture and other types of physical manipulation, as well as herbal and other natural remedies, may have been initially viewed with skepticism, but now they are widely accepted as preventive and curative tools.*

New technologies have affected the way we get our information. Often as important in research as books and magazines, computers give us access to the Internet, which, in turn, has opened up a worldwide network of resources. To learn about training techniques, to find horse show results, or vacation possibilities, or to join in conversations in chat rooms, just log on to the Web.

New approaches have even changed the way we buy and receive products. When this book was assembled more than twenty years ago, resources included only a handful of tack-shop catalogs because, as nearly as we compilers could discover, that's all there were. Now hundreds of stores present their wares that way, and some have begun to do so via the Internet. Thanks to overnight shipping services, catalogs are a very popular way to get tack, apparel and other supplies. There's also been an increase in shops that offer their own brands or better-known items at discount prices. In short, contemporary merchandising techniques have hit the horse world.

One area that hasn't expanded as rapidly as predicted (or perhaps just hoped for) is the amount of equestrian coverage on television. A network channel devoted to horse sports and allied activities has failed to materialize, at least as of now. With the notable exceptions of the American Quarter Horse Association's *America's Horse* series and ESPN's coverage of American Grand Prix Association show jumping, horses on the tube are pretty much relegated to racing and cowboy movies.

This revision of *The Whole Horse Catalog* reflects these changes and innovations. In response to other suggestions, we've also added new minichapters and fillers dealing with horse-related matters (some might say "trivia"). All, we hope, meet with the reader's— um, make that user's—approval.

---

* Confession time: I admit I had my doubts about the efficacy of equine manipulation until someone worked on an elderly arthritic mare at the barn where I ride. Thereafter, or at least for the next few hours, the old gal was able to do flying changes of leads for the first time in a very long while.

To end on personal notes, the past score of years finds us Catalogers still very much involved in equestrian activities. Barbara Burn finally got that horse she wanted. The Rentschs still keep horses on their farm, while Werner now serves as president of the American Academy of Equine Artists. David Spector has hung up his tack, but continues to appear at horse shows. And as for me, I continue to ride whenever and wherever I get the chance, while my editing and writing assignments led to western breeds and activities.

As we've done in the prefaces to previous editions, my colleagues and I wish you every possible enjoyment and success in your own involvement with horses.

Happy trails,

STEVEN D. PRICE

chapter 1

Selecting a Horse

The process of selecting a horse should be simplicity itself. You determine what kind you want, take a look at what's available, and then choose the best animal you can find. Although this process seems easy on paper, unfortunately horses aren't found on paper. They're obtained from breeders, race tracks, dealers, and private owners under a variety of conditions. Moreover, animals come in all kinds of shapes and sizes, ages and conditions, genders and temperaments. Cost, too, must be taken into account.

No one goes into the business of selecting a horse completely blind,* at least to the extent of not having any idea why he wants an animal. You will know ahead of time whether you plan to do pleasure riding, ranch work, or distance riding. Perhaps you're interested in driving, combined training, or some other form of competition, and if so, you'll already have some idea in what classes you'd like to show—such as hunter/jumper, saddle seat, or Western stock seat. Whatever the case, your choice of activity has both pointed you toward certain breeds and types (e.g., Thoroughbreds, Trakeheners, or Hanoverians for dressage) and eliminated others (a Hackney is as unlikely for three-day eventing as a Clydesdale would be for cutting cattle).

But since there's such a wide range of horses suitable for so many equestrian purposes, your first step in deciding what kind to look for would be to gather some information. Start with what you already learned as a participant and spectator; then talk to owners and, in the case of competition horses, exhibitors.

With regard to printed matter, breed registries and associations will supply material ranging from pro-

fessionally prepared brochures to handwritten letters (depending on the organization's size and financial resources). Keep in mind that registries and associations are in the business of singing their animals' praises. Most emphasize versatility, from excellence in the show ring to a flair for differential calculus, so read these publications critically.

General books tend to go into a breed's history and present activities in greater detail and with a little less hype.

Chapter 7 of this book has sources for further information about a host of equestrian sports, where you'll find references to the breeds and types used in particular activities. In addition, your favorite Internet search engine will lead you to useful sites; see pages 335–340 for site-specific suggestions.

Breeds, Types, and Other Choices

Don't be dismayed by the fact that there are more than 150 different breeds and types of horses and ponies. As already suggested, the breed or type you'll want to consider will mainly be governed by the activity in which you and the horse will take part. You should know enough about the activity—dressage, cutting, jumping, endurance riding, or whatever—to know

---

* Some people have selected completely blind horses, but we'll show you how to minimize that possibility.

American saddlebred

Appaloosa

Draft horse

which breeds or types are the best at it (and if you don't, please consider deferring buying a horse until you've done more homework).

Registries and associations are in the business of promoting their particular breed or type.* They're a good source of basic information: a letter or phone call will produce brochures and other literature about the breed's history, talents, and accomplishments. Lists of the individual breeders and other association members will show you how to get in touch with them, while the same information appears in organization magazines and newsletters.

We're not going to list the approximately one hundred breed and type organizations (you'll find them all in *The Horse Industry Directory,* published by the American Horse Council, 1700 K Street, NW, Washington, DC 20006). Here, however, are some of the country's most popular:

APPALOOSA

Distinguished by hindquarters marked with distinctive spots or oval patterns, Appaloosas are used primarily for Western competitive and general pleasure riding.

The Appaloosa Horse Club, Box 8403, Moscow, ID 83843 (telephone: (208) 882-5578), publishes the *Appaloosa Journal* and the *Appaloosa Trail Riders News.*

ARABIAN

Adherents of this oldest of breeds extol Arabians' fine features, versatility, and hardiness (the last quality has led to unparalleled success in endurance and competitive trail-riding competitions).

The Arabian Horse Registry, 12000 Zuni Street, Westminster, CO 80234 (telephone: (303) 450-4748) publishes *Registry News.* The International Arabian Horse Association, 12000 Zuni Street, Westminster, CO 80234 (telephone: (303) 450-4774), publishes *Inside International.*

CONNEMARA

Connemara ponies, which resemble miniature Thoroughbreds, are used primarily for English-style show riding.

* A breed is a group of animals that can genetically reproduce its collective characteristics; a type is a group of horses that share certain characteristics that may or not be reproducible.

The American Connemara Pony Society, 2360 Hunting Ridge Rd., Winchester, VA 22603 (telephone: (540) 662-5953) publishes *The American Connemara*.

DONKEY AND MULE

Donkeys and mules (the offspring of donkeys and horses) are used for riding, driving, plowing, and as pets.

The American Donkey and Mule Society, 2901 N. Elm St., Denton, TX 76201 (telephone: (817) 382-6845), publishes *The Brayer*.

DRAFT HORSES

These "gentle giants" are used almost exclusively for heavy transportation and agricultural work and competition.

The Draft Horse and Mule Association of America, Rte. 1, Box 98, Lovington, IL 61937 (telephone: (217) 864-5450), will provide information on the Belgian, Clydesdale, Percheron, Shire, and Suffolk breeds.

HACKNEY

These high-steppers appear in horse-show fine harness and roadster classes and in coaching competition.

For information, contact The American Hackney Horse Society, 4059 Iron Works Rd. #A, Lexington, KY 40511-8462 (telephone: (606) 255-8694).

HANOVERIAN

A German warmblood, the Hanoverian is especially adept at dressage, eventing, and coaching.

The American Hanoverian Society, 4059 Iron Works Pike, Bldg. C, Lexington, KY 40511 (telephone: (606) 255-4141), publishes *The American Hanoverian Newsletter*.

MISSOURI FOX TROTTING HORSE

This breed, noted for its distinctive pace, is especially popular in the Midwest.

The Missouri Fox Trotting Breed Association, P.O. Box 1027, Ava, MO 65608 (telephone: (417) 683-2468), publishes the *Missouri Fox Trotting Journal*.

MORGAN

Originating in New England in the late 18th century, the Morgan is prized for its versatility as a riding and driving horse.

Hanoverian

Morgan

Paint

Palomino

Standardbred

Thoroughbred

The American Morgan Association, P.O. Box 960, Shelbourne, VT 05482 (telephone: (802) 985-4944), publishes *The Morgan Horse.*

PAINT

Technically speaking, only a Quarter Horse or a Thoroughbred that is marked with two colors, one of which is white, qualifies as a Paint. The "tobiano" marking scheme features a primarily white body, while the "overo" is primarily dark.

The American Paint Horse Association, P.O. Box 961023, Fort Worth, TX 76161 (telephone: (817) 439-3484), publishes the *Paint Horse Journal.*

PALOMINO

Distinguished by its golden color, the Palomino is most closely identified with Western-style riding.

Palomino Horse Breeders of America, 15253 East Skelly Drive, Tulsa, OK 74116 (telephone: (918) 438-1234), publishes *Palomino Horses.*

PINTO

A Pinto is a horse of any breed with markings of two colors, one of which is white (see Paint above).

The Pinto Horse Association of America, 1900 Samuels Ave., Fort Worth, TX 76102 (telephone: (817) 336-7842), publishes *The Pinto Horse.*

QUARTER HORSE

The most populous breed in this country and the "classic" Western horse, the American Quarter Horse is used in a wide range of activities, from Western ranch and competition work to hunter/jumper classes, and in sprint racing.

The American Quarter Horse Association, P.O. Box 200, Amarillo, TX 79168 (telephone: (806) 376-4811), publishes *The Quarter Horse Journal* and *America's Horse.*

SADDLEBRED

These high-steppers are best known as three- and five-gaited saddle and fine-harness driving horses.

The American Saddlebred Horse Association, 4093 Iron Works Pike, Lexington, KY 40511 (telephone: (606) 259-2742), publishes *The American Saddlebred.*

SHETLAND

These shaggy, hardy ponies are used in a variety of disciplines.

The American Shetland Pony Club, P.O. Box 3415, Peoria, IL 61614 (telephone: (309) 691-9661), publishes *The Pony Journal.*

STANDARDBRED

Created for harness racing, the Standardbred is most often seen in trotting or pacing events and in coaching competitions.

The United States Trotting Association, 750 Michigan Ave., Columbus, OH 43215 (telephone: (614) 224-2291), publishes *Hoof Beats.*

TENNESSEE WALKING HORSE

Exhibiting a comfortable "running" walk and a rocking-chair canter, the Tennessee Walker is found primarily in the show ring.

The Tennessee Walking Horse Breeders' and Exhibitors' Association, P.O. Box 286, Lewisburg, TN 37091 (telephone: (615) 359-1574), publishes *Voice of the Tennessee Walking Horse.*

THOROUGHBRED

Elegant and athletic, Thoroughbreds are widely used for flat and steeplechase racing and in hunter/jumper, dressage, and combined training events.

Thoroughbreds, especially those that are intended to be raced, are registered with The Jockey Club, 821 Corporate Drive, Lexington, KY 40503 (telephone: (606) 224-2700).

TRAKEHENER

Originating in East Prussia (in the modern-day Russia and Poland), the Trakehener has found a niche in dressage and combined training.

The American Trakehener Association, 1520 W. Church St., Newark, OH 43055 (telephone: (614) 344-1111), which recognizes only those horses whose ancestry can be tracked back to Polish stock, publishes *The American Trakehener.* The North American Trakehener Association, 1660 Collier Rd., Akron, OH

44320 (telephone: (216) 836-9545), which has no such restriction, publishes *Trakehener Tails.*

WELSH

These hardy ponies are used in a variety of ways, especially English-style showing.

The Welsh Pony and Cob Society of America, P.O. Box 2977, Winchester, VA 22601 (telephone: (703) 667-6195) publishes a newsletter.

CROSSBREDS

Crossbreds exist in just about every combination of breed and type, created to blend particular aesthetic or athletic qualities. Some crossbreds, such as the Morab (Morgan-Arabian) and the National Show Horse (Saddlebred-Arabian) have acquired legitimate breed status within the horse industry.

GRADES

The "mutts" of the horse world, so-called grade horses and ponies come in all shapes, sizes, and colors. They're all over the place too—just take a look at any riding academy, dude ranch, or summer-camp string. Because their heritage is such a hodgepodge, accurate predictions about performance or temperament are impossible, although almost every rider has a warm spot for a grade horse that has figured prominently in his or her life.

A Note About Registries

A certificate from a recognized breed registry is essential before the animal can compete in certain kinds of events (e.g., Thoroughbred and Standardbred racing, and horse-show breed events), and it may be needed to authenticate pedigree for breeding and/or sales purposes.

Although breed and type organizations can be useful when it comes to marketing their particular kind of animal, whether you will need—or even want—to register your horse with some groups is a different matter. Unlike some highly selective and authoritative registries, others eagerly welcome any animal whose colors, markings, athletic propensities, or vague ancestry meet rather loose criteria. In some instances more than one organization claims to be "the" registry.

The point is that some registries are more useful

Warmbloods

—— ∩ ——

THE MOST IMPORTANT CHANGE in the competitive horse world, at least in the Olympic disciplines of show jumping, dressage, and three-day eventing, has been the ascendancy and dominance of European warmblood horses.

Hot bloods are those breeds descended from the Arab—most notably, the Thoroughbred. Their speed and their high-spirited temperament are legendary. The term *cold blood* refers to breeds that trace their ancestry to the medieval Great Horses that carried armored knights into battle. Coldbloods are characterized by their large size, great strength, and more placid disposition (if this sounds to you like a description of a draft horse, you're right).

Europeans had been breeding what came to be called *sport horses* even before the existence of Olympic-discipline sports. Cavalry officers wanted mounts with the speed and agility of a Thoroughbred, but also with a cold-blood's stamina and more stable disposition. The result of such crossbreeding came to be known as the Warmblood, the name based on the simple equation *hot + cold = warm.* Within this broader classification, European warmbloods were identified by geography, from the Irish hunter and England's Cleveland Bay to the continent's Swedish and Dutch warmbloods and France's *Selle Français.* Germany produced a host of these types of horses, classified by province or state: for example, Hanoverian, Oldenburg, Holsteiner, and Trakehener (which is actually in Poland, but that part of Poland spent so much time under German rule that the horses are considered German).

Until the 1970s, few warmbloods were seen in competition on this side of the Atlantic. America had long used Thoroughbreds, primarily because of our English-style hunter tradition, and there were plenty of Thoroughbreds to be used. As horse racing grew into a year-round industry, fewer and fewer Thoroughbreds were sold off the track, and those that were tended to lack the physical or mental attributes needed for jumping, eventing, or dressage success.

Enter the warmblood. When our riders, trainers, and owners saw the quality of the animals against which our horses were competing, they began to purchase the best the Europeans had to offer. Americans scoured the European countryside the way they once beat the Virginia and Kentucky bushes in search of Thoroughbred show prospects—and when Europeans saw the size of American bankrolls, the best that they offered was very good indeed.

Thoroughbreds have now become the American show ring and arena exceptions. All the horses ridden by our 1996 Olympic show jumping and dressage squads were warmbloods (many eventers still prefer Thoroughbreds for their cross-country speed). Warmbloods dominate the Grand Prix show-jumping world as they do the dressage arena at all levels.

You'll hear much debate among warmblood fanciers as to which breed is best, whether the Trakehener is better than the Hanoverian, the Swedish warmblood versus the Oldenberg. However, some commentators take the position that the names refer more to marketing ploys than to actually specific breeds: a group of breeders from Hanover, for example, got together and started a registry, and then began to hype the "unique" qualities of their breed. There's no refuting that breed registries police their breed's bloodlines, but whether breeds based on European geopolitical distinctions are any more distinct than the difference between, say, a Kentucky Thoroughbred and a Pennsylvania Thoroughbred is a question that's still being debated.

Suffice it to say that wherever they're from, warmbloods are here to stay. ∩

---

than others. We suggest that you first investigate a registry, then use common sense in determining whether a certificate from a particular organization will have any more value than the fancy paper it's printed on.

Colors and Markings

In the course of your research and observation, you'll come across a veritable Joseph's coat of equine hues and markings. Some colorations define particular breeds or types, while others can be found in many breeds.

COLORS

albino   A pure white coat, genetically a result of a mutation. (As with mice and other species, equine albinos have blue or pink eyes.)

appaloosa   Characterized by a large light-colored patch (or blanket) on the hindquarters on which

Akhal Teke, Haflinger, New Forest, Konik, Knabstrup . . . these are just a few of the planet's more exotic breeds and types. If you'd like to expand your knowledge in this area, delve into *Horses: The Visual Guide To Over 100 Horse Breeds From Around The World,* by Elwyn Hartley Edwards (Dorling Kindersley). In addition to its panoramic nature, the book traces the development of the breeds and describes their uses.

are darker markings. A *leopard* appaloosa is light gray with dots of one or two darker colors all over the body—something of an equine Dalmatian.

bay A brown coat with black mane and tail.

black A solid black coat with or without white markings.

brown A coat that is darker than chestnut. (If there is any doubt in distinguishing color, as between, for example, chestnut and brown or brown and black, the color of hairs on the horse's muzzle controls.)

buckskin A tan to light-brown coat with a black stripe along the spine.

chestnut A reddish-brown coat with mane and tail of the same color. A *flaxen* chestnut has a lighter mane and tail.

dun A tan to light-brown coat; a buckskin without the dorsal stripe.

gray A mixture of black and white hairs. A *dapple* gray has mottled markings of a darker shade.

palomino A coat of yellow with a white mane and tail over a black skin. The most prized palominos, such as Roy Rogers' Trigger, approximate the color of a newly minted gold coin.

pinto (or paint) A coat with patches of white and another color. *Piebald* describes a black-and-white combination; *skewbald* is brown and white. Another distinction is *overo* (a darker coat with white patches), as opposed to *tobiano* (white with colored patches).

roan A coat composed of white and colored (any but black) hairs. *Strawberry roan* is a combination of chestnut and white; *blue roan* is dark gray and white; and *bay roan* is dark brown and white.

sorrel A Western term for chestnut.

white Properly, the word is "albino." It is also something of a shorthand word for light gray, as in describing a piebald as a horse with a black-and-white-patched coat.

MARKINGS

This denotes certain white patterns, most often on blacks, browns, bays, and chestnuts.

bald A facial patch covering one or both eyes.

blaze A marking starting on the forehead and extending down the muzzle.

girth mark A spot behind the foreleg.

saddle mark A spot behind the withers.

snip An isolated spot near the nostril.

sock A marking from hoof to fetlock.

star A mark on the forehead.

stocking A marking from hoof extending to the knee.

stripe A narrow band extending the length of the face.

further information: *The Color of Horses* by Ben K. Green (Northland), opinionated and often plumb wrong, is always lively. Doc Green was a Texas veterinarian who did a considerable amount of research into coloration and conformation. A colorful, crusty man, Green wrote several books about buying and selling horses full of anecdotes about the shady side of horse tradin'. Although they're out of print, search out *Horse Tradin', More Horse Tradin', Wild Cow Tales,* and *Village Horse Doctor* at libraries and secondhand-book stores. All were published by Knopf.

Other Factors

Now we move to more general factors in selecting a horse. Much of this category relates to personal considerations in terms of what you'll need in the way of an animal.

SIZE

A small child on a horse 16+ hands high or a tall adult on a pony will feel as awkward as they look. Horses and ponies to be used under saddle should be well matched to their riders. In the case of youngsters, our British cousins start them off on ponies. Then as the kids grow, they are moved up to horses.

GENDER

A horse's sex (or lack thereof) directly affects its temperament and, accordingly, its performance. Stallions (also known as studs) are characteristically testy, the reason why female riders and drivers have traditionally been barred from showing them in certain classes. Mares can be equally difficult when they go into heat (every twenty-one days is the cycle), and if there's a stallion, the mutual urge to go tandem can prove overpowering.

Geldings are males that have been altered—an operation that produces equine equanimity. Most colts are gelded almost as a matter of course just because people tend to want horses with stable temperaments. Of course, if you're planning to breed your horse, it will need its faculties unimparied, and a stallion's bloodlines will be a strong factor in the decision to cut or not to cut. (See page 140 for more information on the gelding procedure.)

AGE

One of the great rewarding joys of the horse world is to "bring along"—to break and school—a young horse. On the other hand, unless you have the time, facilities, and know-how, an older animal will be a better choice. As with other species, age brings with it a certain maturity of termperament (unless the animal has been mistreated or is a congenital rogue). A horse that's too old, however, has its future behind it, and you shouldn't consider asking one over the age of twenty to perform strenuous tasks.

Unless valid registration papers accompany a horse, the way to determine age is by examining teeth. The following chart and illustrations show how to do it.

5 years   *7 years*   *20 years*

"Bishoping" (probably named after an unscrupulous horse trader) is the process of altering teeth to try to make the horse look younger. The equivalent of turning back a car's odometer, bishoping can involve the use of a hot iron or drill to recreate incisor cups or to stain the cups (often using apple juice and peels) to obtain an appropriate color.

Age	Characteristics of Teeth
2½ years	Permanent central incisors appear.
3½ years	Permanent second incisors appear.
4½ years	Permanent third incisors appear; canine teeth (in males and some females) appear.
6 years	Cups (indentations) in central incisors disappear.
7 years	Cups of second incisors disappear.
8 years	Cups of third incisors disappear.
9–10 years	Tops of central incisors appear rectangular.
11–12 years	Tops of central incisors appear oval.
13–14 years	Tops of central incisors appear triangular.
15 years	A groove ("Galvayne's groove") appears in the third incisor.
17 years	The groove extends halfway down the third incisor.
20 years	The groove extends the length of the third incisor.

EXPERIENCE

Age is just one small factor in this area, since an older horse hasn't necessarily had the training and opportunity to perform to qualify it as "experienced." Again, some people will want to bring a green horse along, but others will want to buy a "made" animal.

If the latter is your goal, especially for a competition horse, you can check blue-ribbon lists or observe the animal in action during a polo match, calf-roping event, or driving trial. Then approach the horse's owner with an offer. You should realize, of course, that you'll be paying top dollar for a top horse, and the purchase price will include what his owner could make in the future with the animal as well as the time and expense invested in the horse's training.

A horse's experience can also work against him in another discipline, even though the animal comes with ribbons, pedigree, and letters of recommendation that would impress a Rhodes Scholarship committee. Just a few case histories will make this point clear. One horse was purchased from the show ring to be used as a pleasure horse. The several months required to teach the animal to negotiate unlevel terrain weren't much of a

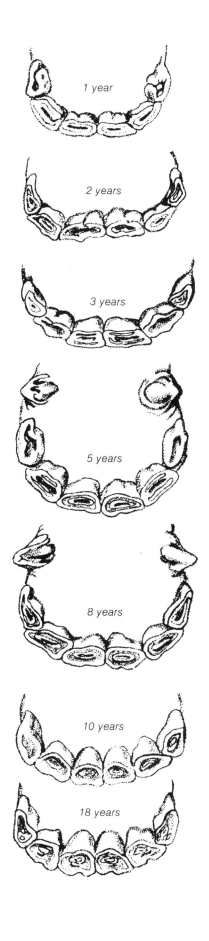

1 year

2 years

3 years

5 years

8 years

10 years

18 years

pleasure. Another, trained as a cow pony, had been taught never to cross a fence. When sent East and asked to jump even a low fence, the horse refused. And refused again, almost requiring a lobotomy to overcome his basic training. Moral: You can lead a horse to a new activity, but he may take a while—if not forever—to respond.

A Note About Experts: Now that you're about to go out in search of a horse, it's time to spend a few moments assessing your own capabilities in that area. Although it's one thing to be able to distinguish a hock from a hip, relying on limited knowledge is quite another. That is, unless in all candor you feel thoroughly confident about your knowledge of horseflesh (based on experience), you'd do well to enlist the services of an expert. That person might be a riding instructor, a stable manager, another kind of professional, or anyone else who's been around horses for a long time. An expert is *not*, however, someone who rides only once a week or who has never had a horse of his own to care for. In addition to an experienced eye, the expert should have a realistic understanding of your needs and complete objectivity (the latter criterion means no incentive to persuade you to buy a horse in order to receive a kickback from the seller). With regard to money, some experts may accompany you as a favor, while others will require a fee. In the case of a professional's judgment, it's money well spent.

A necessary expert is a veterinarian—a doctor who is thoroughly familiar with horses and not one who specializes in small animals. You can learn the name of one from horse owners in your area, and as you talk to him, be sure to explain how you plan to use your purchase so that the vet can examine it in that light. If the vet doesn't accompany you when you scour the highways for horses, he'll look at any possible prospects soon after you locate them.

Where to Look

Armed with background information and accompanied by an expert, it's time to go out in search of a horse. Here are the likeliest sources.

BREEDERS
Organizations listed later in this chapter will be delighted to refer you to members who have animals for

sale. These people also advertise in equestrian journals, especially those devoted to particular breeds. Since many breeders are also exhibitors, their horses range from top show horses to "culls" (culls are non-show-quality animals). Breeders tend to have young animals—foals and yearlings.

Speaking of yearlings, yearling sales are auctions to which breeders bring their colts and fillies. We've all seen newspaper accounts of astronimical sums some of these animals have brought, but it's also possible to pick up a well-conformed and otherwise attractive youngster for less than what Secretariat's get-set fetches.

AUCTIONS

If yearling sales are auto shows, livestock auctions are used-car lots, and they tend to be classic examples of "You pays your money and you takes your chance." Horses sold at auction are seldom salable under better conditions, whether because they aren't terribly attractive or sound or because their owners don't want to put more effort into their disposition. However, more than a handful of equine nuggets have been located in this fashion. One that appealed to Rodney Jenkins and Bernie Traurig turned out to be hell on wheels to load into a trailer after he was purchased. Never losing his bad temper, Sloopy went on to international stardom on the United States Equestrian Team. More often than not, however, auction horses are candidates less for the Olympics than for dog food.

Auctions seldom allow much opportunity for testing a horse, but that procedure is essential anywhere and especially here. Show up early to look over the lot. If any strike your fancy, arrange to try them out, if only by trotting once around the parking lot. (A few bucks slipped to an auction's stable hand will facilitate matters.) If you continue to like what you see, and your expert agrees, make a bid. Return privileges depend on the auction's policy. Usually there's none, unless you can subsequently produce a vet's certificate saying the purchase is diseased or unsound.

RACETRACKS AND TRAINING CENTERS

Many Thoroughbreds, Standardbreds, and American Quarter Horses have been reclaimed from racing and gone on to successful careers in other disciplines. The best method to explore this source is through a trainer. He'll know what animals are for sale, and he may also

be candid about their injuries and other problems (since it's possible to race horses at many tracks and in the cheapest of company, animals for sale in this way are usually beset by all sorts of wind, leg, and other disabilities). Racers also need to be acclimated to civilian life, as in the case of one man who started buying Thoroughbreds off the track to turn them into hunters and jumpers. Without realizing that racehorses are trained to break from the starting gate when they hear the bell, he installed a telephone in one of his barns. At the first phone call, the barn's occupants, in a response that would have made Pavlov grin from ear to ear, crashed through their doors and hightailed it across the countryside.

DEALERS

Dealers specialize in buying and selling horses. They either own the animals or act as brokers for those who do. You'll find their names in magazine advertisements and telephone directories, as well as by inquiry at public and private stables, tack shops, and feed stores, and at rodeos, horse shows, and other events.

A telephone call in advance will set up an appointment and will also alert a dealer to your requirements. Tell him about your past and present equestrian career, hopes, and more mundane matters such as what you can afford to spend. Even if the dealer doesn't have a likely prospect in his barn, he may be able to get one on consignment or refer you elsewhere (he'll receive a finder's fee in the event a sale is made).

Horse dealers don't always enjoy the world's best reputations. Their daily bread comes from turning over a supply of merchandise, so be prepared for a hard-sell approach. Restrain your enthusiasm, heed your expert, and generally conduct yourself in a businesslike manner

PRIVATE SALES

Hundreds of thousands of horses change hands every year through nonprofessional deals. Sources include conversations with veterinarians, blacksmiths, and feed dealers (who may be familiar with an animal's condition, temperament and abilities). Other ways to learn of available animals are newspaper and magazine advertisements and signs on stable or tack-shop bulletin boards. We've all seen them: "OWNER GOING TO COLLEGE," "HORSE SADLY OUTGROWN," or "MOVING TO

ANOTHER CITY." But the fact that you might be buying from a nonprofessional shouldn't mean that you can be unprofessional. Don't be led on by a low price without the same kind of assessment you'd give to a prospect being sold by a dealer.

A Note About Gift Horses: What if Uncle Charley wants to give the kids a Christmas present in the form of a real live horse, or those nice people down the road are willing to give away their family's equine pet? The offer may be tempting, but look such gift horses in the mouth as well as all over. An animal that isn't suitable will be a liability, not an asset, no matter how little it costs. In the case of Uncle Charley, let him read this book: perhaps a piece of tack or a scholarship for riding lessons would be a better present. Your neighbors should understand enough about horses to accept a firm but polite "No thank you" as a response if their animal isn't what you're looking for.

Gift horses are sometimes available from urban and county police departments. Mounted units occasionally give away retired animals, and a letter to the departments will put you on their lists. Police horses are put up for adoption when they're about twenty years old, and if your facility is approved, you'll be the recipient of a well-schooled, savvy animal not suitable for hard work but excellent for safe pleasure riding.

Assessing Individual Horses

The way to judge specific candidates is in terms of conformation, temperament, movement, and condition.

CONFORMATION

This word describes how an individual horse compares with certain ideal physical standards that characterize a particular breed or type. The process is more than a beauty contest; in the course of seeing how an animal is "put together," you'll be able to estimate how its features (and combinations of features) will influence its performance. Although precise points vary from breed to breed, all well-conformed horses share certain attributes.

• The *head* should be well formed, with responsive eyes and ears. Although a Roman nose (convex between eyes and nostrils) is a feature of mustangs and several draft breeds, some people deem it a mark of stupidity. Wide nostrils permit unimpeded breathing. A horse with extended upper incisor teeth is said to have a "parrot mouth," extended lower teeth mark a "salmon mouth," and neither is terribly attractive. A rogue or sluggard is somehow betrayed by its expression, so look for an overall impression of alertness and intelligence.

• Since the *neck* is used for balance, one too long or too short will impair optimum performance at extended gaits or in jumping. A "ewe neck," one wider at the poll than at the withers, forces a horse to carry its head at an awkward angle and makes collection difficult.

• Among parts of the *forequarters*, the shoulder is a most important factor. A sloping, powerful shoulder is the mark of a good galloper; a straighter one (less than 45 degrees) is preferred for Western and harness horses. Well-defined, prominent withers allow a suitable length of shoulder muscles. If the withers are too low, keeping a saddle in place will be difficult. If they are too high, fitting a saddle will be a problem, and the horse may be prone to sores. A large chest and rib cage in proportion to the animal's size provide room for healthy lungs and a "big" heart.

• *Hindquarters* should be rounded and well muscled. Long backs afford more comfortable rides under saddle, but short backs are the mark of greater power. In either case, the coupling (the space between the last rib and the point of hip) should be short. A swayback, usually a sign of age, interferes with fluid movement and makes a saddle difficult to fit.

• *Legs* should be tapered and free of blemishes. Forearms and gaskins should be wide, and cannons and hocks should be solid. Pasterns absorb shock, so they should be neither too straight nor too sloping (as a rule of thumb, pasterns should be at the same angle as the shoulder).

• Good *feet* are extremely important, since they bear the brunt of any kind of performance. The soles of forefeet should be round and flat, while those of hind feet should be slightly elliptical. The outsides of the hooves should be smooth and resilient, firm enough to retain shoes.

How individual features stand in relation to others is of equal importance. For example, when the horse is viewed from the front or rear, its legs should be well set apart so that the animal is standing squarely.

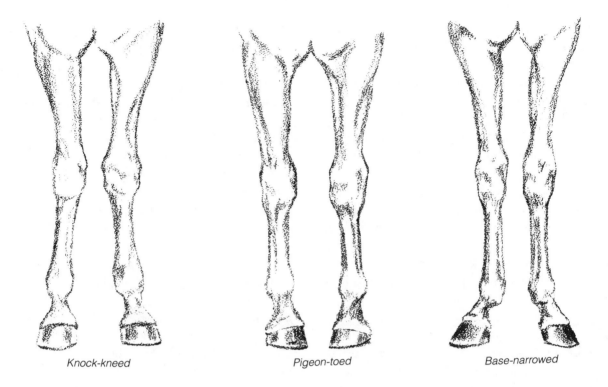

Knock-kneed　　　　　*Pigeon-toed*　　　　　*Base-narrowed*

"Cow" hocks bend toward each other, "sickle" hocks show an excessive angle when viewed from the side, and neither permits a horse to carry weight to best advantage. Standing "over at the knee" is preferable to "back at the knee," yet a horse whose legs hang down well is best of all. Good proportion is most highly prized, with no feature standing out as a glaring fault.

A NOTE ABOUT CONFORMATION

This side of the Platonic ideal of the horse, perfectly conformed animals are few and far between. Most have at least one imperfection, if not an outright deformity, and many are collections of conformation faults.

When asked when conformation faults become rejectable disabilities, several big-league riders and trainers were agreed: only when they affect performance. Then too, it's a matter of degree. One sickle hock, a bit of a Roman nose, or pigeon toes or paddle feet aren't grounds on which to dismiss a horse completely, except perhaps for model-conformation classes. There's no hard-and-fast formula—there are just rules of reason and good sense. To complicate matters, the experts referred to horses that had overcome faults and problems, going on to great success. Forego, the great racehorse, has the legs of a Joe Namath, yet emulating the football player, the animal has achieved the equine equivalent of Super Bowl fame. Several open jumpers and Olympic show-jumping mounts aren't much to look at, but they get the job done.

There's a considerable difference between assessing a green horse and assessing one that's already performing. Untried prospects are unknown quantities, so textbook conformation considerations become important indications of future success. On the other hand, one trainer pointed out that "I'll look at any horse that's been winning consistently, even if it has three legs and the heaves." The statement may be a bit extreme, but the implication is clear: overcoming handicaps is always a possibility.

Further information:

The Anatomy of a Horse by Robert F. Way and Donald G. Lee (Lippincott).
The Affordable Horse by Sharon B. Smith (Howell/ Macmillan).
The Horsemaster's Notebook by Mary Rose (Half Halt Press).

TEMPERAMENT

Start evaluating this factor as soon as the horse is led into view. How does it react to contact with humans

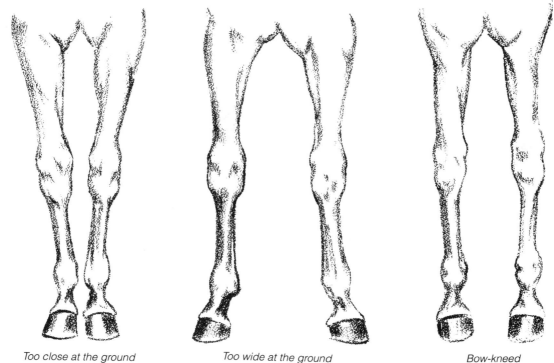

Too close at the ground   Too wide at the ground   Bow-kneed

Good leg   Over at knee   Back at knee

Shakespeare on the "perfect" horse:

"Round-hoof'd, short jointed, fetlocks shag and long,
Broad breast, full eye, small head, and nostril wide,
High crest, short ears, straight legs and passing strong,
Thin mane, thick tail, broad buttock, tender hide:
Look, what a horse should have he did not lack,
Save a proud rider on so proud a back."

Venus and Adonis

and its surroundings? Any biting, kicking, shying? Does the animal stand quietly yet alertly while its conformation is being assessed, appearing like neither a candidate for a straitjacket nor a basket case? Experienced horsemen can cope with tough customers, while other people want a more mannerly animal.

Check the horse's stall to look for cribbing (biting on wooden fixtures), kicking, and other indications of an unhappy lodger. Cribbing may be a consequence of boredom, but it can also be the sign of a horse with serious respiratory problems.

MOVEMENT

A horse in action provides a way to learn about its attitude as well as its athletic ability. Watch how it goes in hand. Does it move easily and in a workmanlike fashion? As it trots, look to see whether it interferes (bumping forelegs or hind legs) or forges (striking a foreleg with a hind leg).

As the seller tacks up and mounts the horse, watch to see how the animal responds to the process. As you ask the seller to work the horse at all gaits and in both directions, confer with your expert. Does the horse move freely and respond to simple aids? Then as you

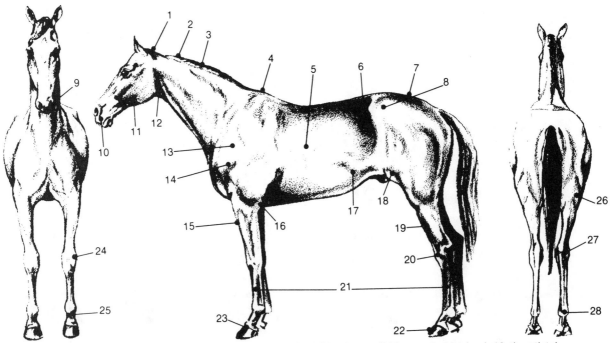

1. poll 2. mane 3. crest 4. withers 5. ribs 6. loin 7. croup 8. point of hip 9. nostril 10. muzzle 11. cheek 12. throatlatch
13. shoulder 14. point of shoulder 15. forearm 16. point of elbow 17. flank 18. stifle 19. gaskin 20. hock 21. cannon
22. hoof 23. coronet 24. knee 25. pastern 26. thigh 27. point of hock 28. fetlock

climb into the saddle, confirm your preliminary reactions. Depending on the animal's training, how does it respond to your aids? Do you like its gaits? Any doubts can be resolved by your expert companion, who should be willing to try out the horse while you observe and heed his reactions.

Special requirements mandate specialized testing. A horse to be used for jumping should be tried over a few fences, while draft and driving candidates need to be assessed in harness. Don't expect the world from a green horse, but also don't settle for any animal that shows no aptitude for what you want.

A Note on Testing a Horse: One expert reminded us to mention that the testing process should include an opportunity for a horse to demonstrate what it doesn't know as well as any temperament flaws. The expert suggested beginning the test by riding passively, or "like a dummy." "I look to see whether the horse will wait for my cues or whether it will start meandering around," he said. "Then I give it conflicting cues to see whether it becomes confused in the course of testing. I'll ask someone to throw a wad of newspaper or a towel in the horse's path—I hope it won't spook or buck me off, but I'd rather learn about such

problems before I buy an animal. I'll also give a horse the chance to run away and to rub me off against a tree."

CONDITION

The best judge of a horse's condition is a veterinarian, but a layman can spot certain signs of an unhealthy animal. Obvious medical problems include runny eyes, a runny nose, and heaving flanks, although a certain amount of the last can be expected from a physically unfit horse after unaccustomed exercise. Sores and subdermal lumps may indicate the presence of secondary infections.

Particular attention should be paid to scars for several reasons. First of all, they are unsightly, but more important, they can indicate that the animal is a fighter. Scars on the lower leg may be the result of the firing process used to cure tendon problems. Sometimes firing can be successful, but often it's a process that must be repeated throughout the horse's working career.

A healthy, "blooming" coat is one sign of a healthy horse. Adding small doses of arsenic to a thin animal's diet was (perhaps it still is) an old horse trader's trick;

the chemical would cause the horse to "flesh out," at least temporarily—but once deprived of the arsenic, it would return to a scarecrow state. Horse dealers and auctioneers, who have never enjoyed reputations for great honesty, still include among their number people who will resort to tricks to make their wares more attractive than would normally be the case. Tranquilizers will turn a congenital rogue into a veritable Emily Post, at least until the drug wears off (that is after the sale has been concluded). We're not saying that all dealers and auctioneers are unscrupulous—merely that the professional services of a veterinarian are an essential element in the selection process.

Purchase Price

The answer to the question "how much will a horse cost?" is a seemingly cynical but quite accurate "as much as its seller can get." Like paintings, houses and other unique items, horses do not carry manufacturer's suggested retail price tags; accordingly, marketplace laws of supply and demand apply. A seller's asking price reflects an animal's breeding, breeding potential, age, soundness, manners and education.

As a prospective purchaser, you'd be well advised to enlist the aid of an expert, a person who not only knows horses but also is experienced in the fine art of horse tradin'. Negotiation is never considered bad form, and even before getting down to dollars and cents over an animal that's caught your eye, the expert will

> *Modern civilization started out as a horseless society, even though horses had been on earth for millions of years, evolving right alongside Homo sapiens. Babylonia, for all its sophistication and wisdom, had no horses, and Egypt managed to build its pyramids without any help from equines.*
>
> *Even the Arabs didn't use horses until after the beginning of the Christian era. It wasn't until the barbaric tribes of Persia invaded the plains of Mesopotamia on horseback and drove out the inhabitants that civilized Babylonians became aware of the advantages of using "asses from the east."*

know whether the asking price is reasonable or so far out of line that any dealing with the seller is likely to be a waste of time.

For your part, establishing your own price range should be your first step. That way you won't waste anyone's time—yours, the seller's or your expert's. You can get a fair assessment of what's available within your range by scanning advertisements in equestrian magazines and local newspapers, talking to horse owners and, most easily, merely by telling the expert about your requirements and then listening to his or her reply.

Joint Ownership

Perhaps you can't afford to own a horse by yourself, or one of your friends has persuaded you to become a

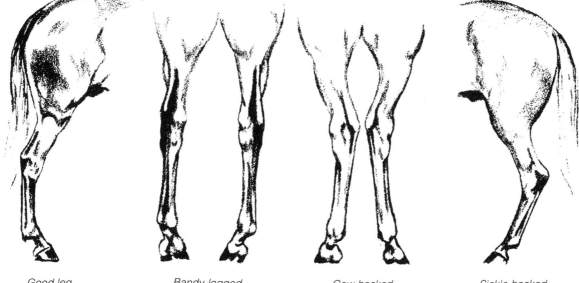

Good leg   Bandy-legged   Cow-hocked   Sickle-hocked

Horse Ownership and the Law

—————————— Ω ——————————

by Ann E. Weiss, Esq.

Even though the horse in your backyard is, in your eyes, just a "pet," the pleasure of ownership carries with it potential situations that may require the services of (or at least a consultation with) an attorney.

The legal consequences of ownership begin with the acquisition of your horse. First, and most obvious, you'll want to protect your interest in a sales transaction. Whether you're the buyer or the seller, you should use a contract of sale, unless you are involved in a warrantyless, cash-on-the-barrelhead, as-is sale of the animal.

Most buyers, however, agree to transactions subject to such contingencies as a veterinary examination or a short trial period in which to determine whether a horse is suitable for a particular discipline. All the particulars of the agreement must be spelled out in a contract, which can take the form of a simple letter agreement. You do not want to be caught as buyer in a situation where, for example, the horse passes the vet's exam only to become injured prior to the transfer of ownership. If your only contingency was veterinarian approval, you may be forced to accept damaged goods. Other items to be considered from a buyer's perspective are that the sale is subject to the approval of the buyer's trainer; and that after a satisfactory prepurchase exam, the buyer shall be entitled to use the horse on a one-week trial basis, after which any sale shall be subject to the buyer's approval of the animal's performance during that trial period.

Elements of a sales agreement that a seller should consider are that the choice of veterinarian for a presale exam be subject to the seller's approval; that the horse must be removed from the seller's premises within three days of the satisfactory prepurchase exam; that payment must be in the form of a certified check, cashier's check, or money order; and that in the event the buyer takes the horse for a trial, the buyer bears the risk of loss, including the value of the loss of use of the animal for any period greater than three days.

You as buyer should always receive a bill of sale, a receipt indicting the dollar amount that you have paid. In the event—unlikely as it might be—the horse is sold for a profit in the future, you will need to establish your basis for tax purposes and claim the gain on your income tax return.

Any backyard-horse owner will need to consider the matter of liability insurance (the subject of equine insurance is covered in another essay in this chapter). Most homeowner policies will defend and indemnify the insured for accidents or injuries that occur when the homeowner owns up to three horses. One common type of accident that would be covered would involve a neighbor's child who, without your knowledge, walked into your horse's paddock and was kicked or trampled. Even situations involving inadvertence or carelessness, known legally as *negligence,* on your part should be covered too. Simply put, negligence consists of a duty of care followed by a breach of that duty that results in an injury. For example, you fail to shut and latch the paddock gate, and as a result your horse escapes and kicks someone. In such a situation, even though the responsibility and the fault were clearly your doing, your homeowner's insurance policy should provide payment for the damages incurred.

Gross negligence, however, is a different category, and one that may not be covered by a homeowner's insurance policy. An example would be allowing a young child or inexperienced rider to mount your unbroken three-year-old horse. Such action arguably shows a conscious disregard for the person's safety that is well beyond a failure to use ordinary care. Another type of action which would not allow you to collect under your homeowner's policy comes from malicious or intentional conduct, such as purposely letting your horse run across an adjoining property because you were angry with your neighbor.

You should always be aware that liability extends beyond your property line. It should go without saying that you need to be cautious around other people and their property, but that often isn't the case. Make sure you know where horses are and are not welcome: crossing posted land without permission can expose you to a claim of trespass (or even arrest for criminal trespass if it can be proved that you intentionally entered upon the premises).

Many foxhunting clubs and other organized riding associations require that their members sign liability waivers as a prerequisite to riding over other people's land. While in situations involving hidden nuisances, such as animal traps, the waiver may not be enforceable, most jurisdictions are beginning to recognize that those of us who choose to ride must bear the risk of injury. In fact, some states have legislation recognizing that involvement with horses is inherently dangerous; in those states civil actions resulting from horse-related injuries is limited under a legal doctrine known as "assumption of risk" (loosely translated as "you take your chances").

Owners who attempt to treat their horse affairs as a business and thus deduct all horse-related expenses should be warned to approach with caution. Although the Internal Revenue Code does not require business horse owners to turn a profit, there nevertheless must be evidence of an effort to be profitable. Such evidence includes breeding and/or selling horses, the taxpayer's principal participation in everyday operations (as distinguished from absentee management), and separate checking accounts for horse-related expenses. Under no circumstances should personal and horse-business funds be commingled.

Depending on the extent of your horse-business activities, you may be eligible in some states for an agricultural exemption on your property taxes. In many localities, even a modest amount grossed from breeding and/or sales entitles the horse-related land and structures to qualify for an agricultural exemption. Check with your local tax assessor to determine the criteria in your area. ∩

Ann E. Weiss, Esq. is a former horse-show rider who trained with Rodney Jenkins, George Morris, and the Leone brothers. She currently resides, rides, and practices law in New York's Mid-Hudson Valley.

partner in an animal he or she already has. Such an arrangement can be perfectly satisfactory, but only if you and the other person have a realistic understanding of what it entails.

An important consideration is how you both plan to use the horse. One person's wanting to compete the horse in dressage while the other wants an animal for distance riding will create problems. Similarly, before the purchase is made, the breed or type, size, and amount of training should be a matter of mutual agreement or at least compromise. Another series of questions to be dealt with in advance is who does and pays for what. For example, who gets to ride the animal when (don't forget that the animal will need rest periods too)? Who will do the feeding, grooming and mucking out, if performing such chores yourselves is necessary? What if (perish the thought but recognize the possibility) one of you is responsible in a situation in which the horse is fatally injured or must be put down? We suggest that you and your prospective partner discuss all possible costs, schedules, and contingencies. Then too, consider the mechanics of someone's wanting out of the arrangement, such as in the event of moving away or merely losing interest. Decide whether one partner will buy out the other or whether the horse will be placed for sale.

Once you've pondered and resolved these and any other contingencies that come to mind, set them down on paper. Many lovely friendships have disintegrated faster than a plastic hoof pick over "But I never agreed to that" reactions.

Another joint-ownership situation involves a "silent partner" who foots all or part of the finances in order to participate in a horse's show career. You may not be good enough to campaign a horse from the saddle or driver's seat, yet you can go into partnership with an exhibitor. Typically, you'd pay all the bills and be entitled to any trophies and prizes, although your rider or driver colleague might be expected to pay entry fees or transportation to and from events. Decide who contributes how much, and get it in writing.

Basic Questions and Answers about Equine Insurance

by MARTHA A. HALL

Q. Who among horse owners should carry equine insurance?

A. Anyone who cannot afford to replace his or her animal, or who chooses not to replace it.

Q. Which are the most common types of policies?

A. Equine mortality, which is term life insurance for the horse; care, custody, and control liability for the owner of a commercial operation that cares for other people's horses; and private horse owner liability for people who may not have coverage on their home-owner's policy. In addition, various endorsements, or riders, may be attached to equine mortality policies.

Q. What type of policy or endorsement should a non-professional backyard owner have on a not-very-expensive horse?

A. Equine mortality and, if the animal's value is at least $5,000, major medical endorsement. A private horse owner liability policy is also recommended.

Q. Explain the major medical endorsement.

A. It may be applied to a full mortality policy when the animal is valued for a minimum of $5,000. This pays for medical expenses including surgery up to a $5,000 annual limit. The procedures are for life-saving and enhancement; elective procedures are never covered, nor are such routine treatments as worming and vaccinations.

Q. What would such a policy and endorsement cost?

A. It depends upon which insurance carrier writes the policy. For example, the cost might be $150 per year, with a deductible of $200 per claim. Therefore, the cost to the insured is $350 before the first claim dollar is paid.

Terms vary. One carrier does not charge a deductible for colic surgery; it also offers a $2,500 surgical umbrella for horses evaluated in excess of $7,500.

Q. Is the horse's health also relevant?

A. Sometimes a horse may have too many pre-existing conditions to be eligible for a major medical endorsement that does include surgical coverage, but that horse can qualify for a surgical endorsement with a full mortality policy. The terms of the full mortality policy require that the owner do everything possible to maintain the health of the horse and to act on the attending veterinarian's recommendations (for example, colic surgery if needed).

Q. Suppose a horse becomes permanently incapacitated?

A. A loss of use endorsement, which is very expensive, pays only 50 percent to 60 percent of the horse's value in the event the animal becomes permanently unable to perform the intended use for which he was originally insured. The reason for the loss of use must be related to a external injury. This endorsement can be added only to a full mortality policy.

Q. Who determines a horse's value for insurance purposes? What are the criteria for value and for premium cost?

A. The insurance agent or company underwrites the value based on the purchase price and any show record of performance. In the case of my agency, we serve as appraisers or field underwriters. Criteria for determining the cost of premiums are the animal's breed, age, use, and value.

Q. How does the policy holder go about filing a claim?

A. Claim notification procedures are outlined on claim cards that are attached to the insured's policy jacket. The number and the effective date of the policy should be written on one of two cards, with one card given to whomever is in charge of the horse's care. Any questions about when to notify the insurance company should be taken up with your veterinarian or your insurance agent. ∩

Martha A. Hall is a vice-president of The EMO Agency, Inc., an insurance agency that specializes in equine-related coverage.

The Horses of Nineveh

———— Ω ————

by DAVID A. SPECTOR

FOR THOUSANDS OF YEARS mankind has been excited about horses. And what excites us soon shows up in art. From early days, there have been depictions and representations of horses, whether as Grecian temple friezes or Roman statuary. But some of the earliest equestrian drawings and sculptures have appeared in ancient Babylon, now modern Iraq.

Some of the finest statues, chiefly gigantic winged bulls, and mythological gods were dragged across the deserts of the Middle East using relatively primitive engineering methods, and now repose in museums throughout the world. The best examples may be found at the British Museum in London, and at New York's Metropolitan Museum of Art.

The various kingdoms of the area, generally bounded by the Tigris and Euphrates river valleys, were lost to history for millennia; only in the last century were they rediscovered. This is a continuing process, as excavating the mysterious *tells,* or mounds, are going on to this day, though greatly slowed by the intrusion and interference of modern political realities.

Foremost of the early adventurer-excavators was the intrepid young Englishman, Austen Henry Layard. Sporadically educated, he left his study of law to travel through the Ottoman Empire to reach India. However, he was captivated by Mesopotamia, and eventually excavated for the British Museum, whose trustees were notoriously frugal in underwriting expeditions. His great works were crudely excavated and recorded by modern standards, but he was far more than a mere treasure hunter. He achieved renown as "Layard of Nineveh," retired, and eventually became Her Majesty's ambassador to Turkey and Spain, and ended as a Member of Parliament.

He published his discoveries in the mid-nineteenth century; one of his travel volumes was *Monuments of Nineveh* (1853). It is Plate 7, "Led horses from a passage in the Palace of Kouyunjik," that merits our attention.

My original plate measures 15″ high by 22$\frac{1}{2}$″ long, and shows six horses being led by seven attendants across two registers. It is generally in a sepia tone; these were prepared from Layard's original sketches of the wall bas-reliefs.

The attendants are almost exactly the same; the only variance is the hand positions grasping the lead shank. The visages are identically stern and purposeful, and all attire is identical, except some wear sandals and others are barefoot. One man holds a stave, which is perhaps a sign of office, making him the chief groom.

The horses are presented in the same sterile composition with the exception of the first, which is leaping forward. These are tall, powerful animals broad of chest and strong of leg. Ideally they would be used with chariots, not ridden. The only tack is the braided lead shank caught around the lower jaw, for control. Indeed horses of this period were never ridden, and there existed no saddles, stirrups, or other equipment needed for riding to war. This would be consistent with the time of the palace, approximately 700 B.C. The only other ornamentation on the steeds is a wrapping about midway down the length of the tail. The horses are all stallions with roached manes.

It is impossible to more clearly identify the breeding of the animals, except to note if drawn to scale against their handlers, they loom quite large. The horses are unshod, and the sculptor took great pains to show the musculature and attenuation, particularly in the legs.

It is through Layard's careful copy of the palace wall decorations that we are able to get a glance at what role horses played so early in the history of mankind. Even at this early age, horses and equestrian activities played an important part in the development of the human race. Ω

chapter 2

Stabling

Most horses do very well pastured the year around with only a minimal structure for protection against wind and flies. Others need large and heated stalls. Between a remuda—a band of cow horses left loose to graze overnight—and a stable with crystal chandeliers and carpeted alleyways, however, are numerous methods for adequate horse-keeping. The remuda is practically a relic of our past, now found only in a few sparsely populated areas where hobbled horses aren't likely to go grazing through prize suburban petunia beds. At the other end of the spectrum, the befountained architectural complexes that are being featured these days in the "house and garden" sections of horse magazines are not appropriate for most backyard horses either. Obviously, the choice of stabling depends on the kind of horse or horses you have, the number you will want to keep, the type of work you will ask your horse(s) to do, and your finances.

What Kind of Horse-Keeping Arrangement Is Right?

- You have one or two horses you enjoy saddling up and taking over the trails. But other commitments, such as a job or school or a busy household to manage, prevent you from taking long, strenuous rides or even from tacking up as often as you would like. We recommend a pasture as your best horse-keeping solution. You probably have access to a pasture, either part of your own backyard or one rented from a neighbor. The area should be large enough for the horses to move about freely and graze, and there should also be trees, brush, or even a rock outcropping for shade and protection from the summer flies and winter winds.

- You own one or more horses kept out the year around, but unfortunately the pasture has no natural protection from the elements. You also need a place to confine your horse on the morning of a planned ride and to protect its feed from wind and rain. We recommend a three-sided or open-door free-access shed as a solution.

- You own one or two horses and rent space at the local stable; and as often as you've dreamed of caring for the horse yourself, it is not possible. We recommend you read this section and the one on Stable Management with special care.* Ask questions in your stable, and if the answers are not to your liking, look around for another. Remember, if you have a horse you will have to spend some money to keep it properly, and a bargain is rarely a good deal. There's an old horse saying, "I've spent weeks training my horse to go without food, and now that I've got him trained to do it, the s.o.b. ups and dies on me."

- You have just acquired a trail horse and you anticipate spending more and more time schooling the

---

* Unfortunately, as of this writing, there are few laws governing standards for commercial stables; anyone can open a stable and run it pretty much the way he wants. Several people in California are attempting to write a state law to impose standards on commercial stables—so far, unsuccessfully. There is a strict law in Maryland which tackles the problem.

animal and yourself. Perhaps you can also foresee having more than one horse to care for and your access to additional land is severely limited. You have looked over the old toolshed out back and decided for any number of reasons (the structure is unsound, the ground too damp, it's needed for other storage) that it is unsuitable. Now is a good time to consider building a small stable.

• You have one or more horses in a pasture with access to a shed, but you've improved your horsemanship to a point where you're ready to travel to some shows. Suddenly the long winter coat that begins growing as early as late August—and right in the middle of the show season—is most undesirable. You want to eliminate your horse's grass belly by cutting back on its time in pasture. You need a better grooming and tack area. The farrier, in order to shoe properly, needs to watch the horse as it stands on firm, level ground in a well-lighted area. You need access to electricity to use clippers. You want to blanket your clipped horse to protect it from drafts. You want to condition your horse in the ring and turn it out into the paddock for short, regulated periods. And you've sworn that the last stone bruise on your show prospect's withers received from rolling on hard ground was absolutely the last one. It will come as no surprise to hear that we recommend you give up the shed in favor of a stable.

• You are an experienced horseman with a few good broodmares and a desire to invest more energy and money in breeding, showing, and selling. In all likelihood, your goals have outgrown your existing facilities and you need to make additions. You know your limitations and have figured out just how large an operation your resources, the operation's potential, and local zoning regulations will allow. If you go all the way, you can build a stabling complex that includes broodmare barns, a stallion barn, foaling stalls, living quarters for the help, a barren-mare shed, a stud yard or barn, an isolation barn, offices, lounges, pastures (several), paddocks (many), and everything else such a massive operation requires (for example, its own waste-removal system, advertising and public relations, offices, accommodations for trainers and grooms, one or more tracks, or arenas, etc., etc.). On a less grandiose scale, you can also run a breeding farm in one barn with provisions for a stud stall, a breeding area, foaling stalls, a special pasture for the weanlings, and extra stalls for mares waiting to be covered.

• You are an experienced horse manager who wants to open a commercial stable. Obviously, you have given careful thought to what the market and your finances will bear. Your plans probably include a stable complex with roomy box stalls (some for boarding animals, some for schooling animals), a grooming area, a large tack room, an indoor arena, outdoor rings, trails for hacking, paddocks, offices, lounges, bleachers for audiences at your shows, parking facilities, and everything that goes along with establishing an attractive, profitable stable. If your plans are less ambitious, a stable with straight tie stalls situated near public riding trails—city or county ordinances permitting, of course—may be adequate. You will also need an outdoor ring for giving lessons and testing green riders before sending them off on their own.

The Remuda

The band of saddle horses used by cowboys working on open land is known as the remuda on the Southern ranges and in Texas and cavvy, from the Spanish word *caballada*, in the northwest ranges. The size of a remuda depends on the number of cowboys working; usually each cowboy has from nine to twelve horses in his personal string. Customarily two wranglers are assigned to a "horse block." It is their duty to get up early, saddle up their night horses which have been hobbled or staked nearby, find the remuda, and bring it in. The horses are driven into a corral made of rope, and the seasoned individuals move to the outside as the younger horses mill around in the center. The foreman does the roping as each cowboy calls out the name of the horse he wants for that day. The horses tend to stay calm during all this, since with so many horses in

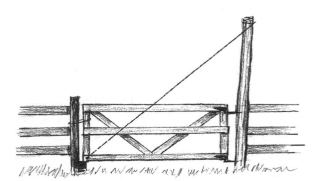

Wooden gates often need cable support to prevent sagging.

each cowboy's string, most of them are released more often than they are ridden.

Field Keeping

Individual horses of hardy breeds may be pastured the year around in most climates. It is a low-cost, easy-maintenance solution to keeping a horse that's worked infrequently, especially during the winter months. The pasture should be large enough to prevent the horse from overgrazing it or from easily reinfesting itself with parasites. (A full discussion of what makes a good pasture begins on page 65.) What the novice horseman needs to be aware of is that a field-kept horse has a few basic but essential needs: fresh, available water and minerals; shelter from wind and flies; a dry, soft area to bed down; and food. Pasturing a horse the year around is certainly closest to a natural situation, and for most horses it is the healthiest one as well.

The advantages of pasture-keeping a horse are that the animal will develop a warm winter coat as protection from severe temperatures; it will not suffer the changes in temperature experienced by those horses taken from a warm barn and worked outside in cold weather; it will be receiving natural nutrients and minerals from the grasses; it will be getting some regular exercise; it will be less prone to the leg and foot problems associated with various stable floorings; and it is less likely to become bored and develop such stable vices as cribbing, weaving, or windsucking.

But there are also disadvantages to pasturing a horse the year around. Because the horse acclimates so well to its environment, in winter it will have grown a long, unattractive, and difficult-to-clean woolly coat, causing it to lather up quickly when worked on all but the coldest of days; the horse may be difficult to catch and manage if it is permitted to run wild with only minimal handling; the horse will not be in condition to do anything more than the lightest of work unless it is ridden (or lunged) and grained regularly; it will be subject to bruises, sores, or cuts caused by rolling on stones or being bitten by the "boss horse" for an infraction of the rules. Some horses' extreme temperaments, be they the meek or the bully, do not permit satisfactory pasturing with others: the meek will be chased away from the food, while the bully will become too fat from eating

everyone else's portion. Horses fed from the ground, a common procedure with pasture-kept horses, run the risk of ingesting dirt and developing sand colic or becoming reinfested with parasites.

Horses turned out to pasture require anywhere from $1^1/_2$ to 3 or more acres per animal. The size depends on the quality of the grasses and the amount of supplemental feed you are willing to buy. And unless the pasture is well cared for, you should expect to have to add some food to your horse's diet, at least during certain seasons of the year.

Horse owners who grain more than one horse in a pasture usually hang out a separate grain manger for each animal, situating them far enough apart so that one bully cannot dominate them all. Other horsemen prefer to build open stalls—which are like straight stalls but divided by single planks or pipes rather than walls. This arrangement forces each horse to enter a stall where it can eat its grain and hay without intimidation.

Pastured horses that are not grained regularly are usually given hay, at least part of the year. If a number of horses are pastured together, a covered hay bunk made of wood slats and a peaked roof is a good apparatus. The most common type is V-shaped with the point of the bunk raised off the ground. The openwork slats keep the bunk clean and allow hay dust to fall to the ground as the animals pull the hay through. The eaves of the roof extend for at least a foot beyond the bunk for added protection against rain. These eaves are rarely less than 6 feet high at their lowest point. In drier climates, such a roof may not be necessary and hay may simply be loaded into uncovered bunks. For a smaller herd, hay nets may be preferable. While nylon nets are now stronger and longer-lasting than their cotton prototypes, they do tend to shred after a few months of being chewed and exposed to the weather. They are, however, easy to handle, fill, and hook onto a fence post.

Unless your pasture has a proper supply of all the minerals a horse needs (and few pastures do), mineral or salt blocks should be available at all times. Since these blocks will "melt" in the rain, many horsemen prefer to simply put one or two blocks in the bottom of the hay bunk. Some mineral blocks are made with a small hole molded into the bottom and are designed to be balanced atop a pipe driven into the ground. This works until the block is nearly used up. Then you (and the horses) are faced with a piece of metal sticking up from the ground—a potential source of danger. Setting it inside an old rubber tire provides better visibility and some protection from being kicked about.

If an adequate and constant supply of fresh water is unavailable in the pasture, you will have to provide one. For a few horses, simply putting out a water container to be filled daily and drained regularly is sufficient. For years, old bathtubs with rounded edges have served as troughs. To clean them out daily, one need only pull the drainage plug, wipe out any accumulated organic matter, and refill. Most horsemen prefer to use automatic water containers designed to release fresh water when the horse activates it by sticking its nose against the valve. For larger herds this device can save a lot of work. Steel or concrete tanks are often set into a fence line; if the fencing, however, is electric (or worse still, barbed wire), select another spot. The trough should be about 30 to 36 inches high; you can figure out the size needed by calculating one linear foot per five horses. The automatic tank should be equipped with a float valve, a cleanout drain, and, in colder climates, an electric thermostat to prevent freezing. Over the years, the manufacturers of automatic water troughs have developed and improved them until they are now nearly foolproof.

All water troughs should be situated on ground that has good natural drainage. In lush pastures, put the trough on a bed of stones or gravel extended for about 10 feet beyond the trough. Keep in mind that all the horses will be visiting the trough at least twice daily, so the gravel may help to prevent the surrounding area from turning into a mudhole. Where pastures are dry for a good part of the year, a mudhole may be just what is wanted; the mud makes an excellent treatment for dry and cracked hooves. Paint the trough white. It will look neater during the day—but more important, it will be more visible to you and the horses at night.

Sheds and Free-Access Shelters

In pastures where natural shelter is unavailable, a shed is a good addition. It has a number of distinct advantages and few of the disadvantages commonly associated with stables. Only the simplest of structures is needed: An old toolshed, for instance, can easily be converted into an outdoor stall. The stall area should be at least 10 feet square for each animal—large enough to turn around in comfortably and safely, with space for the feedbox and water trough. Figure on approximately 144 square feet per horse—the equivalent of a 12 x 12-foot stall. The shed may have only three walls, or it can have four walls with an open doorway at least 4 feet wide and 8 feet high. The shed should be large enough to accommodate *all* the horses. A three-sided shed is advisable for more than one or two animals since, invariably, all will head for the opening at the same time, and if the doorway is one horse width too narrow, you can count on a dispute and possible injuries.

When picking a site for the shed, look for the highest point in the pasture—which will usually be the driest spot as well. Take into account whether it will be accessible to you when it comes time to feed and water. Depending on the region in which you live, face the opening of the shed toward the mildest prevailing winds—in the Northeast, that means south; in the South, that means northeast. The shed floor should have excellent drainage and never be damp or, even worse, wet. The base of some sheds is first covered with 6 to 8 inches of gravel, then covered with dirt or with a heavy bedding material such as tobacco stems or wood chips. (A light bedding will blow away in the first breeze.) Some horse owners prefer to store the hay and bedding in the end of the shed that faces inclement weather. Separated from the horses by a sturdy partition, the hay not only is accessible at feed time but will insulate the shed as well.

A shed provides several benefits to the horse owner as well as to the horse. For one thing, it affords a covered, protected area in which to feed hay and grain. And for another, while the advantage of protecting the feed from the elements is readily apparent, the savings from avoiding waste is often worth the price of shed lumber. One design we've seen has hay racks that run along the back wall but only halfway along the two side walls. This designer anticipated the likelihood of the horses bunching up at the entrance instead of moving inside to the back wall. The shed floor was covered with compacted gravel extending some 15 to 20 feet beyond the entrance. This extra gravel kept the highly trafficked area in front of the shed dry.

Sheds are particularly useful for tying or simply enclosing a horse. This is desirable on the morning of a planned ride, the day the farrier is due, the night a sick

Free-Access shelter

animal needs nursing, or the weeks a foal is being weaned from its dam.

Stables

A stable arrangement may vary from a simple structure organized to house one or two horses to a large, elaborate structure with indoor ring facilities designed for more than a hundred. Obviously the style chosen will depend on the horse owner's needs and finances. Many available plans for horse barns are adaptable to various regions and climates, but all share common principles of stable design. All stable buildings satisfy three basic needs of the horse owner: they confine the horse, they control its environment, and they provide storage areas for feed and tack. Some stables, however, cope with these needs better than others.

WHERE TO BUILD A STABLE

It is worth considering a site that is relatively flat, since the less grading needs to be done, the lower the cost. However, site selection depends on several other considerations as well, and you may have to concede one aspect to find the best overall site. A low, level piece of ground will not drain as regularly as higher ground, while cold and frequent winds may make a hilltop site less than ideal. A stable should be accessible to delivery of construction materials and, more important, for later regular deliveries of feed and bedding. If the stable will not contain living quarters, it should be close enough to the house for someone to

sense when there is trouble. On the other hand, since flies and horses have a relationship that is difficult to discourage, a barn built too close to the house will make commuting an easy matter for these insects.

Zoning regulations may be a major factor in the choice of the site or may not affect you at all. It obviously depends on the laws in your county or township and on what you are planning to build. We can't go into the many zoning regulations, since they are often set on a local level, and each may require different variances from its neighbor—and invariably does. So we caution the potential horse-keeper to check with his county agent to be certain the zoning laws permit keeping "livestock" (a horse), and if they do, what regulations you must follow. Often zoning boards require that a stable be so many feet from boundary lines and be equipped with approved "sanitation facilities" (meaning manure removal). By all means, do your homework. It is expensive to build a stable; it is more expensive to build or renovate a stable and then tear it down for noncompliance with existing zoning laws.

BUILDING A STABLE

Where to begin? We suggest you first look around at other stables in your area to see what they look like and how they are built. Inquire to find out who built them. Chances are the stables you are looking at were constructed either by a company that specializes in prefabricated buildings or by local talent using standard stable plans. There is also the possibility that some were custom-designed. We suggest you be most cautious about getting involved with this type of struc-

Automatic Water Trough. This automatic waterer won't freeze or break. Made of galvanized steel, it is weather-resistant and fully insulated and has a heating unit that is thermostatically controlled. It can easily water two horses at one time and will fit nicely in a fence line between two separate paddocks. From Ritchie Industries, Conrad, Iowa 50621.

Portable and Permanent Horse Stalls. This stall is made of welded square tubular steel. It comes 10 × 12 feet square and 7 feet high with 4-foot-high wood panels. Each panel opens 90 degrees for cleaning. The sliding front gate features a safety latch. Available from Scranton Manufacturing Co., Scranton, Iowa 51462.

ture. Unless you know a great deal about horse management and can recognize a genuine improvement upon traditional techniques, as opposed to a newfangled approach that sounds great in theory but fails dismally when put to the test, we recommend you let someone else experiment with his or her money, not with yours.

After inspecting your neighbors' accommodations, take another good look at your site. If it is near an existing building, such as a toolshed or even a garage, it may be worthwhile attaching the new stable to this building. It may cut your building costs, since you need not worry about insulating the connecting wall.

One horsewoman moved from a large farm into a small house on one acre of land. She bought a prefabricated two-car garage, or at least the shell of one, and built two large stalls inside. one for her mare and one for her filly. Her reason for choosing a garage was a good one. When she put her house up for sale, as she intended to do in the not-too-distant future, it would be a simple matter to convert the stable back into a garage, something more desirable in that community than a horse barn would be. The remainder of the space in the garage/ stable was used to store tack, feed, bedding, and other horse necessities. Two paddocks,

neither on a particularly grand scale, were situated on either side of the stable. But the cleverest stabling arrangement was for a stallion she also owned: a large box stall in the house's basement garage, next to the family laundry room. The stallion quickly learned to look forward to the sound of the washing machine, since it usually meant company and sometimes even a carrot. The area just behind the house was his paddock, which he seemed delighted to share with the children of the house. All three horses were exercised regularly—often by lunging in the small area that was the front lawn. The flower beds may have suffered, but the horses didn't.

MATERIALS

Choosing building materials involves considering cost, durability, amount of maintenance needed, fire resistance and attractiveness. The most commonly used materials are wood, plywood, metal, masonry (concrete, brick, cinder block, pumice block or stone) and plastic. Wood-sided buildings are most people's favorite. Wood is attractive and is a naturally good insulator. But a quality wood is probably the most expensive material available today, with the cost of lumber per board foot climbing regularly. Wood also requires annual maintenance, which must be calculated into the general cost of the building. Treated plywood, while not as

Building a stable in which to house your horse is solving only part of your horse-keeping problems. Horses in the wild travel light, domesticated horses that are asked to perform specialized tasks need accoutrements. And the new horse owner about to build a small stable or convert an existing structure needs to go through a mental checklist before setting a plan to paper—not to mention a signature to a builder's contract. These questions must be asked and be reasonably answered:

- Is there an area nearby for pasturing or exercising a horse, either in a ring or on public or private trails?
- Does my plan include storage areas for feed, hay, bedding, tack, assorted stable supplies, manure?
- Is the location accessible to deliveries of supplies?
- Is the site well drained the year around?
- Is the design compatible with that of surrounding buildings, or will mine be an eyesore?
- Is there flexibility in the design for future expansion or conversion to another use in case I must move and sell my property?
- Is there access to electricity and water hookups?
- Do the materials being used minimize the risk of fire?
- Is the environment controllable (i.e., have I planned for proper ventilation)?
- Will the structure be easy to clean and maintain?
- Does my plan meet zoning regulations?

aesthetically pleasing as planking, is also somewhat expensive. However, it has several attractive properties: it is very strong, it will not warp, it will not split, it will not shrink; it requires less maintenance than board lumber, and it can be stained.

Steel buildings are somewhat less expensive than wooden ones, and they practically need no upkeep. They are, however, cold in winter and hot in summer and so require extra insulation. One alternative to the all-steel barn is a steel structure with a composition or plastic exterior which changes the look and adds insulation. Masonry, either concrete, cinder block, brick or stone, is less commonly used today. While the materials may be equivalent in price range with the other materials discussed here—and possibly even lower—the cost of labor is an important and most expensive factor. Added to the costs of masonry is the cost of digging a poured foundation or concrete slab. Masonry stables, while sturdy and requiring little maintenance, can be damp and cold.

It is worth considering using fireproof materials when you are planning a new stable and especially when you are converting an old existing structure into a stable. Obviously, steel and concrete-block exteriors are impregnable and will contain a fire, preventing it from spreading. Fire-conscious horsemen store hay and bedding in a separate fireproof room or shed. One large stable stores hay in an open nook separated from the stalls by a heavy steel overhead door programmed to shut tight (much like an automatic garage door) as soon as the fire-detection system relays a signal. Fire starting in the hay area would thus be contained, while a conflagration elsewhere would starve from lack of fuel.

Until this century, almost all barns stored hay in a loft, where it helped to insulate the building. Today, asbestos-covered insulation materials are preferred, with the hay stored away from the stalls. Another material finding popularity among stable designers is fiberglass, used most often to replace conventional glass windows. Fiberglass has a higher resistance to heat than regular glass, and it will not explode during a fire as glass will. Its durability is important in maintaining an airtight, fire-retentive environment, so that fire fighters can have added time to get a blaze under control.

There are a number of fire-detection systems available. While somewhat expensive to install, they will quickly prove their value if you are confronted by fire. Certain ones are designed to detect smoke, even at the first stages of a smoldering fire, while others are designed to react to heat above 135 degrees. Firefighting systems work on the same principle and activate an automatic sprinkler installed in the ceiling.

Even if your stable does not have such a system, it should not be without at least one easily accessible fire extinguisher that is checked monthly to make sure it is working properly. It's always a good idea to hang several extinguishers around the stable, especially near where hay is stored.

Types of Buildings

The pole building is the most popular type of construction for building stables and particularly arenas. It eliminates the need for vertical support beams in the center of the building and, most welcome in this day of rising costs, eliminates the need for a poured foundation and the expensive digging such a foundation requires. The pole building is supported by wooden posts sunk 4 feet below ground level and fixed into concrete. Posts are spaced at 16-foot intervals. Trusses instead of beams support the roof. Boards treated to prevent rotting are nailed to the support posts at ground level. Usually the topsoil surrounding the building is graded up against the "foundation" boards for insulation. The outside of the building can then be finished in metal (usually steel) or wood (often rough-cut lumber pretreated against fire). The pole building is ideal for arenas as well as large stables. For an arena, the structure is simply finished with kickboards around the lower inside of the building. For stables in colder climates, the shell is insulated and then finished with heavy oak lumber for the stall area and paneling or wallboard in the tack room.

Barns and stables may be classified by their roofs. The shed roof is recommended for small stables and for freestanding open-sided buildings in the pasture. This design also works best when an addition is attached to an existing building. The gable roof is a popular design which offers flexible layout possibilities. The monitor roof has been adopted by many of the large stall manufacturers. In milder climates, stables are made from several prefabricated stalls placed side by side in two facing rows with each row covered by a long shed roof. The alleyway formed between these two sheltered rows is capped by a short gable roof that overhangs each of the shed roofs. Together, these three roofs form an attractive and efficient structure. Often the spaces under the gables are kept open for access to air and light.

ENVIRONMENT

A stable creates an artificial environment for horses. Taking a horse out of the cold also removes it from such natural elements as sun, water, fresh air, soft ground to lie on, and well-drained ground to stand upon. In the stable the horse is forced to rely upon you for all its needs. So consideration must be given to each seemingly minor equine requirement.

Temperature and Humidity

Horses do better in a controlled temperature and a controlled humidity. In such an environment their me-

---

Fire Prevention Checklist

* **Keep such debris as loose hay, scrap wood, and any flammable item from the inside of the barn and the area around the building. Pay particular attention to the storage of any flammable liquids.**
* **Store hay and straw on pallets in an area where air can circulate. In addition, the hay should be well cured, which reduces the chance of spontaneous combustion.**
* **Electrical wiring belongs inside conduits or metal casings that rodents can't chew through. Lighting fixtures should include wire cages, so that bulbs are protected from breaking.**
* **Electric appliances should be turned off (unplugged is even better) when not in use. Make sure switches and wiring are in good repair. Those appliances and other electrical equipment that can be grounded should be grounded.**
* **One fire extinguisher for each room in the barn is not too many. Extinguishers must be readily accessible, and kept in up-to-date working condition.**
* **Smoking in or around barns should be prohibited. No exceptions.**

If you're planning to build a stable or arena, shop around for a builder by contacting some of the following companies:

American Building Systems, Inc.
10 La Crosse St.
Hudson Falls, N.Y. 12839

Bonanza Buildings, Inc.
P.O. Box 9
Charleston, Ill. 61920

Brooks Built Company (plans only)
P.O. Box 39
Grover, Mo. 63040

Butler Manufacturing Company
Angri-Products Division
7400 E. 13th Street
Kansas City, Mo. 64126

Cuckler Building System
P.O. Box 438
Monticello, Iowa 52310

Cuckler Building System
P.O. Drawer 1028
Turlock, Ca. 95380

Lehigh Pole Building
6410 Airport Road
Bethlehem, Pa. 18017

Lester's Inc.
Lester Prairie, Minnesota 55354

Morton Building, Inc.
Box 126
Phillipsburg, N.J. 08865

OK Corrals & Equipment
25852 Springbrook Avenue
P.O. Box 184
Saugus, California 91350

People's Building & Supply Co.
761 North Main Street
Hubbard, Ohio 44425

Star Building Systems
Box 94910
Oklahoma City, Oklahoma 73109

V.I.P. Builders, Inc.
201 East Street
Southampton, Massachusetts 01073

For further information, you can order a book, *Horse Handbook: Housing and Equipment*, published by Midwest Plan Service, Iowa State University, Ames, Iowa 50010.

tabolism is more stable, and they will therefore make more efficient use of their feed and water.

The ideal temperature for most horses is somewhere between 45 and 75 degrees Fahrenheit, with 55 degrees best and for a newborn foal between 75 and 80 degrees.

The ideal humidity for horses is somewhere between 50 and 75 percent, with 60 percent humidity best. The average 1,000-pound horse breathes 2.1 gallons of moisture into the air each day. So, quickly figuring out the numbers, if the stable holds 40 horses, you come out with 84 gallons of moisture *per day*. If the moisture has no place to go, you end up with a damp, moldy, smelly stable and horses that will continually suffer from respiratory ailments, stiffness, and mushrooms growing in stall corners. During the mild seasons of the year, simply opening the stable doors will usually draw the moisture out. But during the nontemperate times of the year, when the snow threatens to cover the windows or the blazing sun threatens to burn everything it touches, open doorways are no longer a solution. Good ventilation must be designed into the original stable plans. High ceilings, vents, or windows that open encourage the air to circulate freely. Occasionally, efficient ventilation must be helped along by strategically placed fans and blowers. Needless to say, the larger the stable and the more horses there are in an area, the better the ventilation system must be.

TYPES OF STABLE ROOFS

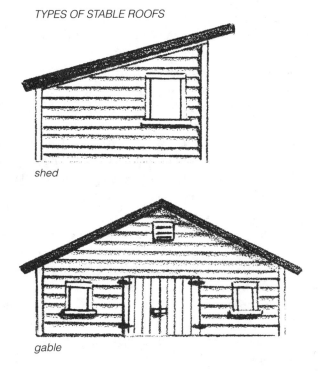

shed

gable

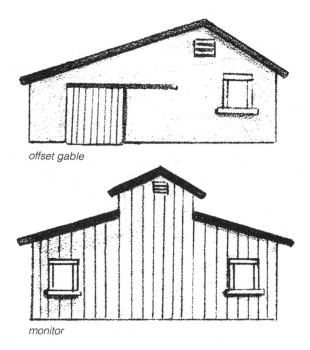

offset gable

monitor

While many large horse barns have built-in fans, few have heaters for the stall areas. Even in the coldest of climates (where, by the way, few commercial horse farms are found), removal of excessive heat is usually more of a problem than excessive cold. Good insulation and even warm blankets—sometimes as many as three piled one on top of another—will keep a horse warm enough. And since horses do give off heat, their collective b.t.u.s will make a difference inside the stable. We noted in one barn during a particular cold spell when the temperature failed to rise above zero that the temperature in the area surrounded by six stalls failed to

drop below 26 degrees. The horses survived quite well with only blankets.

Light

There are some needs a horse has that a stable manager cannot replace artificially. Horses must be allowed some access to sunlight, for instance—an important source of Vitamin D. Obviously, a light bulb will not do the job, nor will a window or skylight replace the sun. But windows, skylights and artificial lights are important to a horse's well-being.* Horses like to see what is going on about them. A window in each box stall lets in natural daylight and allows the horse to look outside. But in many new stable designs such an arrangement is impractical or simply too expensive.

Of the books on planning and constructing a facility, *Complete Plans For Building Horse Barns Big And Small* by Nancy W. Ambrosio and Mary Harcourt (Breakthrough) leads the way with eighteen plans that can be used as depicted or modified. The authors also discuss such essential topics as complying with zoning regulations, dealing with suppliers and contractors, and remodeling existing structures.

Designs and other advice can also be found in *Horsekeeper On A Small Acreage*, by Cherry Hill (Garden Way Publishing) and *Roofs And Rails*, by Gavin Ehringer (Western Horseman/ Mountain Press Publishing).

For adding ventilation to a barn, the Port-A-Stall Company features four different accessories—Continuous Ridge, Stationary Ridge, and Rotary Ridge ventilators, and a cupola. The cupola with weather vane and fan section (fan not included) is about $200.00

---

* Some stables that specialize in showing breeds supposed to exhibit "fire" and "spirit" will keep their horses in darkened stalls so that when they are brought out into the sunlight their eyes seem to flash. Actually, these poor animals are simply dazzled by the sudden bright light.

Windows are often replaced with translucent Filon or fiberglass panels built into the structure in the form of skylights or strips under the eaves of the roof. These attractive translucent panels let in a soft, diffused light that is bright but not glaring. If the stable is lit by natural light during the day, then artificial light is needed only at night. A recessed or protected light bulb in each stall is recommended, with brighter fluorescent fixtures for alleyways and tack and feed rooms. If the stable or arena ceilings are high, fluorescent lights can be replaced by mercury-vapor lights, several times brighter than fluorescent lights. They do cost more to install initially, but they are more efficient. Because they are so bright fewer fixtures need be installed, thus reducing electricity bills. Ceilings should be at least 16 feet high for mercury-vapor lights to diffuse evenly.

Flooring

Most stable designers pay a great deal of attention to flooring, especially the flooring beneath the stalls. To say that each horseman has an opinion about which type of flooring is best is to understate the case. And to do less than stress the importance of good flooring also drastically understates the case. In its natural environment, a horse will not stand in one place for hours at a time, especially in conditions that are less than ideal. So for flooring to be good it must have certain basic characteristics: it should have some "give" to reduce strain on the horse's tendons or feet, it should be absorbent, easy to clean, nonslippery, non-odor-retentive, and free of dampness. The flooring materials most commonly found under stalls are dirt, concrete, wood, clay, sand, asphalt, and brick. And not one of these materials is perfect.

Dirt, so it would seem at first thought, is the one material that most closely resembles the footing in a pasture and is therefore the best flooring choice. True, it is highly absorbent, nonslippery, and easy on a horse's legs. But such flooring is not always the ideal solution. Although it is porous, soil does not dry out quickly and can retain dampness and odor. It is easily pawed and must be replaced often. Dirt floors are also difficult to muck out and in cold climates may freeze hard.

Concrete is increasing in popularity. Most horse owners appreciate its good qualities and feel they can bury the disadvantages under a thick layer of bedding. What is good about concrete? It is hard-wearing, easy to clean (especially if poured at a slight inclination to encourage drainage), rodent-proof, and difficult for a horse to damage. Concrete's disadvantages are that it is nonporous, cold, and nonelastic, the last meaning it can be particularly hard on a horse's legs.

Wood should be at least two inches thick, preferably rough oak. Once common for stall flooring, wood is now avoided by most modern stables. We suspect the primary reason is that good oak planking is prohibitively expensive. Also, its disadvantages as flooring outweigh the good points. What are they? The good news is that wood is springy and easy on a horse's legs, it keeps the stall warmer in cold weather, and most important, the horse will not have to stand on a cold surface, which can cause stiffness of muscles and joints. But there is bad news too. Wood tends to become slippery when wet; it is difficult to clean and disinfect; it retains odors; and it must be checked often for signs of wear, then replaced immediately with treated planks.

Clay is easy on the horse's legs, and if it covers a base of crushed stone, it can be highly absorbent. Its major drawbacks are that it does not hold up well under constant pawing, thus needing replacement every few years, and it can remain damp for longer than is desirable.

Sand is highly absorbent and makes a soft surface for the legs. However, it does have a number of disadvantages most horsemen find difficult to overcome. Sand has a drying effect on the hooves, and it is not unusual for hoof walls to become cracked or split. Occasionally the sand will work its way behind the walls of the foot, where it can cause severe problems. Sand is also easily pushed about by the horse and must be raked flat daily.

Asphalt is inexpensive to lay, relatively porous, and easy to clean. While it has slightly more give and therefore is not as hard on a horse's legs as concrete, it also does not hold up as long and must be replaced after several years of wear. In hot weather asphalt can become sticky; when cold it may become brittle and crack.

Brick, we must admit, looks terrific around a stable. But we have seen few recently renovated or newly built stables make use of it. For one thing, brick is incredibly expensive to lay, mostly because labor is so costly. Aside from that, brick does not have many advantages to offer the horse-owner and, in fact, is usually uneven to walk on, slippery when wet, and difficult to clean and disinfect.

ELECTRICITY AND WATER

Both electricity and running water are necessities. Where to put them is something each horseman must weigh against costs and climate. We can see no reason why electricity should not be available to every area of the stable, and we recommend that it be generously allocated in the basic plans. Conduit (BX cable) wiring is a must; all electric wires are threaded through metal or hard-rubber pipes so that they are virtually impervious to rodents' gnawing teeth. The stable should have its own fuse box to prevent overloading of circuits. Wiring for stalls should be run behind the walls or in the ceiling—out of reach of horses' teeth or inquisitive lips. Light switches and fixtures also should be out of reach or protected by bulb guards. Most horses will not disturb the light bulb in their stall, but occasionally a frisky or shying head will hit the fixture. We know of one young, impish colt that would grab at the light bulb with its teeth, pulling until the bulb and its guard were totally wrecked. Now its stall is the only one in the stable without a light. If anyone asks why, the horse's owner will gladly explain how his horse eats light bulbs for breakfast.

In the planning of a stable, it is often difficult to anticipate exactly how much electricity you will eventually want to use. Possible needs may include electric heaters, electric clippers, an electric burner for cooking mashes, a heater cable or thermostat for the hydrants, a vacuum groomer, heat lamps for foals or sick animals, plus any number of added luxuries such as a radio or a refrigerator. True, you needn't have all these energy-consumers, but it is a good idea to wire as if you (or a future owner) might. Overloaded wiring is stupid, and extension cords are the playthings of fools. Statistics show that faulty wiring is the single largest cause of fire, and simple precautions and intelligent planning will help to keep that risk to a minimum. Of course, the decision about how to wire may be completely determined by the electric company and/or local building codes. If you run electricity into your stable, you may be required to follow their dictates with no alternatives available. So before you attempt to do the wiring yourself (something only an experienced electrician should do), check local building regulations.

Easily accessible water is essential to every stable. If you live in a region where freezing is not a problem and water is plentiful, we recommend you have water tapped into several parts of the stable. Obviously, the first requirement is to water the horses. Automatic waterers are a good solution. There are many kinds available, some with thermostats for those climates where temperatures go well below freezing. However, we know one cavalry remount veteran who scorns automatic waterers. He prefers to water his horse from a bucket three times a day in order to know exactly how much water is consumed. If the amount increases or decreases appreciably, he'll find out why. It's not surprising that because of such careful observation, his horses are rarely sick. Still, we recommend you provide a constant supply of clean water to each stall. If you choose one of the automatic troughs, make sure there is provision for turning it on and off easily, a necessity for those times (before worming, for instance) when you need to deprive the horse of water. Other logical places for faucets include the tack room, the grooming area, the feed room and the stable yard. The tack room is an excellent place for a sink or simply a hydrant and drain for cleaning saddles and bridles. A faucet in the grooming area is useful for filling a wash bucket or for attaching a hose or spray to rinse the horse down. There should of course be a drain in the floor to carry off the waste water. Water on tap in the feed room helps to clean out feed buckets, mix

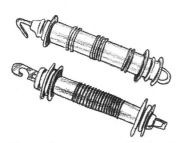

Electric fence gate handles

Fence pliers

boiling mashes, and generally keep the room clean. Plan also on installing an outside faucet either in the stable yard or near the paddock. It will quickly change from a luxury to a how-did-we-ever-do-without-it necessity for general bathing of horses in warm weather, for hosing lame legs, for cleaning equipment, and for running water into nearby paddocks.

All water pipes leading to the stable should be buried 3 feet underground, or more in climates where the frost line is deeper. Try to avoid having the pipes laid underneath driveways where heavy trucks will be delivering feed and bedding. The weight of these trucks may be enough to snap the pipes and necessitate some expensive repairs. All drains should lead directly to a dry well or to a leach field made from perforated pipes. Zoning laws may require a separate septic system for sinks or that the waste water hook into the local waste-disposal system. Here, again, is where a quick trip to your local county agent's office can save much later grief and wasted money.

ORGANIZING THE STABLE

Assuming you've decided on the best type of structure for your needs, you must then design an interior. We remember being asked as children to design a house

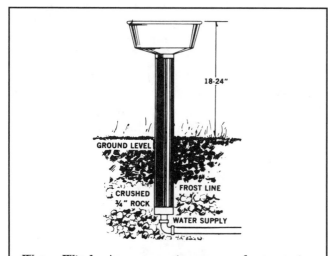

Water Witch. An automatic waterer that remains frostless without electricity or propane. The valve mechanism is located at the base of the column below the frost line. When the horse has finished drinking, an automatic drain-off feature slowly removes water from the basin before it can freeze. From Farnam, installation kit additional.

on paper, and while we had vociferous convictions about where things should go, we discovered that turning the ideal into the pragmatic was more difficult than anticipated. The novice stable manager should take another tour of neighborhood facilities. Check out what others have done; interview them about what they like and dislike about their setups. With tactful prodding most horsemen are willing to admit their stable problems as they proudly point out the good features. Sources for plans are listed on p. 41; we suggest you look into several of them and follow up on any ideas our listing may suggest to you.

Probably the most commonly visualized type of stabling is a long, single-floor structure with side-by-side stalls. Each stall door opens out into a stable yard, an alleyway created by the roof overhang, or directly into individual runs or a communal paddock.

There is also an arrangement that provides for a number of stalls situated side by side along opposite stable walls. These two rows of stalls are separated by a wide alleyway which, depending upon the width, can be used for tying, grooming, saddling up, and even cooling out hot animals. This setup allows the horses to see one another if wire or openwork pipe or wood is used on the top part of the stalls. An alternative layout that benefits the bigger stables (it can be found in the barns at Belmont racetrack) is the "Island" design. It features two rows of side-by-side stalls that back each other. The stall doors open into an aisle which completely encircles the island. This outside aisleway can be used for cooling out a horse and, if the ceilings are high enough, for exercising it during bad weather. It does use up space other designs would allocate to more stalls or a larger tack room, but if you don't give a hoot about things like square-foot ratios and maximum efficiency quotients, this design may appeal to you.

One particularly imaginative stabling arrangement designed by a Connecticut breeder of Morgan horses began with an Agway pole barn. Translucent fiberglass panels inserted under the eaves let in natural daylight, thus reducing the need for artificial light during the day. The stalls lined opposite sides of the building, with two stallion stalls in the corner of a third wall. The front of each stall was heavy gauge wire, with wooden supports that permitted easy viewing of the stalls' occupants.

Perhaps most innovative was the center of the barn: a sizable dirt-floor arena that allowed schooling or lunging a horse in bad weather. The space was also used as a turn-out area for foals: The breeder tied the mares in their stalls, then let the foals out for communal "play dates," and to be exposed to the many visitors to the farm. After such socialized foalhoods, none of the young horses showed any reluctance when it came to being gentled.

Stalls

Until well into this century, most horses in this country were used for transportation. Few, if any, needed box stalls or turn-out paddocks at the end of the day: the horses got all the exercise they needed from their long hours of work. All they needed in the way of lodging was a quiet place to rest, eat their feed, and drink their water. In such cases, a straight stall was perfectly adequate: Being tied by a rope to their halter in the eight- to ten-foot long and five- to six-foot wide space allowed the horses to eat and sleep (lying down if that was the way an individual slept), but not to turn or back out of the stall.

Nowadays, straight stalls are occupied almost exclusively by hack or school horses at commercial stables. The rest of the equine population, whether boarders or privately owned in public or private establishments, live in box stalls.

The most typical size for a box stall is 12-feet square, with 10-feet square accommodating ponies, and 15 feet for stallions and draft breeds. The criterion is that the space is large enough to allow the occupant to turn around easily and comfortably and to lie down and then get up without becoming *cast* (the term for rolling into such a position that the horse cannot get his legs under itself and rise without human assistance).

Although a large stall may make a horse owner feel that he or she is giving the horse the gift of plenty of space, there are certain disadvantages. Cleaning a large box stall is more difficult and time-consuming than dealing with a straight stall; a large stall permits a horse the freedom to develop such bad habits as stall-walking and weaving; and it also allows the animal to expend energy instead of standing quietly. Of course, many of these problems arise not because of the stall size but from the animal's boredom: Horses that are not given enough exercise (whether by being worked or by turned out in a paddock or field) or lack interesting things to see, hear, or smell will develop stable vices no matter where they live.

Horses are herd animals, happiest when they can see their stablemates. It is not uncommon for horses stabled next to each other to become devoted buddies, pairing off together in the pasture and whinnying when separated. Stalls are usually designed to allow the horses to see one another. Stalls should be solid, light, well ventilated and draft-free. Most 8-foot-high stalls use 4-foot-high walls made of 2-inch-thick hardwood lumber (oak has been found to be the sturdiest of the woods) that has been treated with a creosote-type substance to discourage chewing. The top of the stall is often encircled by about 4 feet of vertical metal piping or wood slats (spaced about 4 inches apart), or 2-inch wire mesh. Metal is stronger and will last longer. Almost any building-supply outlet will sell piping ($\frac{1}{2}$-inch iron piping is good), and you can easily do your own assembling. If construction is not your forte, however, we have listed a number of builders on this page who will do the job.

Wood used for stalls should be treated with a nontoxic preservative to prevent it from rotting or splintering. Some horsemen install metal strips along the wooden ledges surrounding the grillwork to discourage chewing. If a horse is particularly unruly or a confirmed masticator, an electrified wire strung around the inside of the stall will usually keep it standing center stage.

Stall doors are normally made of solid wood, part wood and part grillwork, or (occasionally), all grillwork. Be it of a Dutch, swinging, or sliding design, it must be strong, yet balanced for easy opening. The Dutch door, able to be opened in separate halves, is the type of stable doorway most people think of first. In those sections of the country where stall doors can lead directly to a paddock or run, it is at once a door and,

---

For portable or ready-to-assemble stalls:

Farnam Companies, Inc.
2230 East Magnolia Street
P.O. Box 21447
Phoenix, Arizona 85036

Port-A-Stall
P.O. Box 447
Mesa, Arizona 85201

Scranton Manufacturing Company, Inc.
Scranton, Iowa 51462

Stall Matting
————⋂————

THERE ARE SEVERAL ADVANTAGES to having a layer of rubber matting in stalls. It provides an extra layer of comfortable cushioning to a horse's feet, so less bedding is required. The result is less dust and a saving in money. There's also better traction, especially with grooved or raised patterns. From a health and stable management viewpoint, matting keeps urine moisture from seeping into flooring, which means a drier, less odoriferous environment. The rubber layer also reduces wear and tear, as well as preventing divots in soil or clay flooring caused by horses' pawing.

The most efficient way to insure a waterproof floor is by a wall-to-wall installation. Because a single sheet that's the size of an entire box or straight stall would be difficult to manage, matting is sold in pieces that range from one by five feet to four by six feet. The better ones have interlocking edges that insure a tight-seal fit. Another benefit of the virtual seamlessness is that cleaning the stall doesn't involve catching any edges with manure forks or brooms.

For further information:

Protector Mats
Summit Rubber Products Ltd.
4820 Old LaGrange Rd.
Buckner, KY 40010
(800) 782-5628

LokTuff Mats
Humane Manufacturing Co.
805 Moore St.
Baraboo, WI 53913
(800) 369-6263

Black Beauty Mats
Caple-Shaw Industries
1112 N.E. 29 St.
Ft. Worth, TX 76106
(800) 969-3234 ⋂

when the bottom section is latched closed, a window to the world outside. Dutch doors are less efficient for stable interiors, where many horsemen find it awkward to have a door open into an aisle trafficked by other horses. Nor is it pleasant when a horse can easily reach over the top of its door to nip any equine or human passerby (a bad habit that, unfortunately, can quickly develop). A Dutch door left open as a window encourages a horse to lean over and against the bottom door. Weeks of such weighty leaning is bound to bend almost any hinge or, at the least, alter the balance of the bottom door as it swings. A heavy-duty screen installed inside the frame of a regular one-piece door is a better solution. The screen is usually about 4½ feet high and is set about 2 feet off the ground, a height that can vary according to individual animals. Few horses can lean over the top or stretch out to nip at unsuspecting passersby, but they can have access to additional fresh air and a good view of the stable.

Doors that swing open should always be hung to swing out, never into the stall. Besides a strong lock, the door should have a separate hook to hold the opened door from swinging closed or into an entryway and blocking the area. Few of the newer stables make use of the full-size swinging door, preferring a sliding door made of 2-inch hardwood with open grillwork at the top. The sliding door, when properly hung from a top track, easily slides back against the outer wall of the stall and can be opened full width or less if desired.

Door latches should be accessible from the inside as well as from the outside of the stall. Now, obviously, you know enough not to lock yourself into the stall. But we can't remember an occasion when a visiting youngster didn't find it wonderful fun to lock the stall door when we were inside.

Door latches must be horseproof—something easier said than achieved, since many horses are Houdinis about opening locks. It is difficult to judge what kind of latch is really horseproof. The horse that picks locks is usually spending hours and hours researching the problem and using that scientific method known as trial and error. Some horses get to be pretty good at it. For those individuals, and you will quickly discover which ones they are, we recommend that you use two locks on the stall door—one at normal height and the other at floor level where it can be fastened with your foot.

Several types of locks that are sold for horse barns are perfectly fine. But remember, it does not pay to scrimp when it comes to buying hardware for a stall. Heavy-gauge steel is a must; a lightweight material will

Tying a Horse

A log-and-rope arrangement is a proven method for tying a horse in its stall. It permits the horse enough rope to lie down comfortably while preventing the animal from becoming tangled in the rope's slack. One end of the rope is attached to the horse's halter. The other end is passed through an eye hook or through a hole drilled into the edge of the feed trough at about two-thirds the height of the horse at the withers. The rope should be about 3½ feet long, the length between the top of the manger and the floor. A doughnut-shaped wooden ball, hung from the bottom of the rope, is held in place by a simple knot. The ball acts as a weight, holding the rope taut at all times, taking up slack when the horse lowers its head and giving it sufficient length when the animal lies down. You can understand the value of this method when you hear a story, as we did, about a young horse incorrectly tied in its stall that got caught in the loose rope, panicked, and broke its neck. The cavalry always tied its horses (except those of the officers, who had box stalls for their mounts) into straight stalls. Instead of a wood ball, the cavalry used a variation on the hangman's knot which, when properly tied, was heavy enough to weigh down the rope but could not bruise the horse if the end swung into a knee.

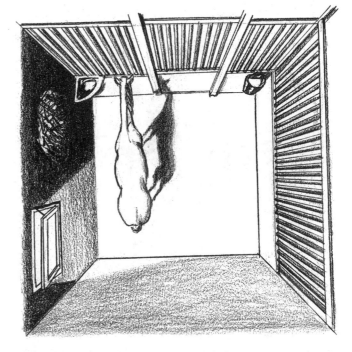

A good stall

inevitably prove true the maxim that cost is what cost does. Even the most mild-mannered animal will lean against its door, kick to tell you that it's feeding time, or rub its backside during the shedding season. Good locks and hinges will hold up without difficulty, but thin ones will snap at an inopportune moment.

There is one basic latch style—a simple and strong latch (see illustration next page) which we recommend, but with some reservations. We know of one young horse cross-tied parallel to the front of its stall that panicked and pulled back. It broke the cross ties and landed on the protruding 1-inch edge of the latch. One hundred and twenty stitches later, the horses' owner replaced that latch with one that had no protruding edges. However, we should point out that despite

rare exceptions, the horse latch is efficient. When the bolt slides into the clamp, the shaft automatically slides down to hold it securely in place. Even with methodical and vigorous kicking and shaking, the bolt cannot be knocked loose. That is not true for other bolt-action locks. We recommend that you install the horse latch with an improvement: either recess the latch into the wall and the door, or add wood blocks above and below the latch (essentially replacing the metal protrusion with wooden ones), or cap the sharp edges with strips of hard rubber. This last solution sounds the best, but unfortunately it is difficult to keep the strips in place under constant use.

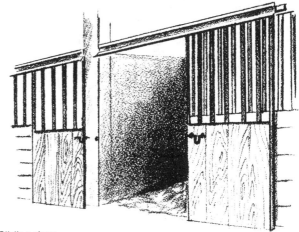

Sliding door

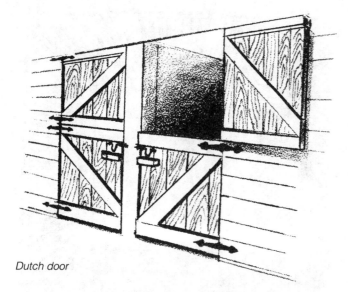

Dutch door

Inside the stall is one place where decorating should be nonexistent. The interior of the stall must be free of any jutting edges and furnished with only the bare necessities. Basically, the horse requires only a feed manger and a water basin. For some horsemen even a hay rack is optional equipment.

The food manger should be hung in a corner, preferably one that is convenient for you to reach when filling it. A hole large enough to accommodate a scoop of grain cut into the stall wall directly above the feed basin saves time and labor. Most feed containers are large enough to hold from 16 to 20 quarts of grain. Pony feed boxes are somewhat smaller, in scale with their users' size. If you are planning to build your own manger, the dimensions are approximately 12 by 24 by 8 inches deep. While earlier mangers were made of ei-

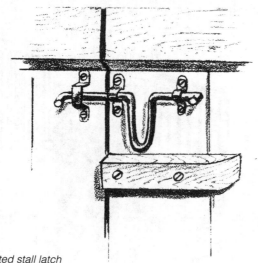

Protected stall latch

ther wood or galvanized iron, neither material is popular now. Wood was always difficult to clean, tended to splinter, and was easily chewed by the impatient horse thinking that feeding time was close. Galvanized iron basins were heavy and therefore difficult to lift out to clean. Even less desirable, the iron had hard edges that often caused severe cuts. Almost all horsemen appreciate the advantages of hard-plastic or heavy-rubber feed mangers. Nearly indestructible, they have a smooth, nonabsorbent surface that is easily wiped clean. The biggest single advantage, however, is that while these containers are almost impossible to kick apart, they will yield to pressure without causing any harm to the horse. We highly recommend these materials for feed mangers, water buckets, and any other containers you need around the stable. Hard-rubber water buckets that are misshapen by ice can be pounded with a hammer; as soon as the block of ice is crushed, the bucket regains its original shape.

Before World War II, most stable managers adhered to the theory that the manger should be set low so that

Wood, a Tasty Subject for Horses

A test of eight different kinds of woods was conducted by the North Central Forest Experiment Station of the Forest Service of the U.S. Department of Agriculture and the School of Agriculture of Southern Illinois University at Carbondale to discover what woods were most durable and safe for horse stalls. Yellow poplar, elm, ash, red oak, beech, soft maple, hickory, and southern yellow pine were assessed. After seven years of testing, it was found that although none of the untreated parts decayed, the southern pine panels splintered and shelled more than the hardwoods but did not split or warp. Minor splitting occurred in soft maple and pine panels. Elm did not wear smoothly where horses' necks rubbed the door parts, while the hickory, beech, oak, and ash were rubbed smooth. Kicking and chewing damage was most obvious in the softest woods (southern yellow pine, yellow poplar, soft maple, and elm), while red oak, beech, and hickory were the least damaged.

the horse had to bend its neck downward to eat, simulating the posture necessary in pasture. These same people hung the hay racks up high so that the horse could reach up to pull at the hay but not risk catching its legs in the rack if it reared or kicked. The theory of furnishing a stall is quite different today. The grain box is normally hung at about two-thirds the height of the horse. For most horses that is between 38 and 42 inches from the ground, and for ponies from 28 to 32 inches high. Hay racks, on the other hand, either have been eliminated or are hung so that the bottom of the rack is the same height as the horse's withers. The rationale behind this change in theories, especially when it comes to the feeding of hay, is this: when the horse must reach up to pull down its hay, it will also pull down hay dust. This dust can easily lead to respiratory problems and eye infections. For this reason, many horsemen prefer to simply put the hay directly on the floor. Others object to that method, claiming it increases the chances for parasite reinfestation, as well as being wasteful. These horsemen, who have returned to the hay rack or hay net, hang it lower than did their predecessors. They use rubber, fiber, or plastic instead of metal or wood. These new materials ensure that if a horse does kick the rack, he will be less likely to be hurt.

Hay racks or nets should be large enough to hold between 25 and 30 pounds of hay for the average-size horse (between 10 and 15 pounds for ponies).

The other piece of equipment that is essential to every stall is the water trough. It may be a pail, preferably one that holds about 3 gallons, hanging at about the same height as the grain feeder. This bucket should be easily removable for at least twice-daily cleaning and refilling. Invariably, or at least it seems that way, many horses will dump their hay into the water bucket, making it more difficult to clean out. Planning where to put the stall equipment should be determined with your convenience in mind. But sometimes you will have to accede to the horse's occasionally pointed likes and dislikes. We know of one animal that consistently dropped a load of manure into its water bucket. The solution was, of course, quite simple. After cleaning out the bucket for the third day in a row, the owner realized the only way to win this decorating disagreement was to give in. He moved the water bucket to the other side of the stall, and it has remained free of manure ever since. It's harder to make such adjustments with automatic water containers, but that is only a minor disadvantage when you consider all the good points such equipment has. True, it is more expensive to install, but it also guarantees that clean water will always be available. And since horses require about 12 gallons of water per day, you can readily see that the automatic waterer provides a huge saving in labor. In some stable designs, one automatic water container is installed in between two stalls to service two horses. This arrangement can nearly halve installation costs. The only problem is to be certain you have compatible animals. If one tends to be bossy or possessive and the other meek and acquiescent, a shared water trough will not work. Also, be aware that when two horses share a common feed utensil, they are more likely to transmit harmful bacteria.

Ideally, a horse's drinking water should not be colder than 40 degrees Fahrenheit or warmer than 75 degrees. Water that is above or below that range may cause digestive problems or simply fail to cool the horse's body in the summer or heat it in the winter. In parts of the country where the temperature rarely goes below freezing, automatic water containers are ideal. For colder climates, you will need a heating unit for the pipe that leads directly to the container. In climates with fairly severe winters and cold periods that last for several months, automatic waterers need to be chosen with special care or they may prove themselves more of an inconvenience than a help.

A piece of equipment you may want to add to the stall is a container for holding a salt and/or mineral block. (The necessity for regular access to minerals and their availability in a variety of forms are discussed in the following chapter.) If you provide minerals in the form of a block, there is a holder made for that purpose. An alternative is to set it on a small raised platform directly beneath the feedbox or, as one old horseman we know prefers, you can put a large chunk into the feedbox. This latter method requires the horse to eat slowly, pushing the block around to reach all the grain. The

Flexi lunge retractable lunge line

mineral blocks, of course, can be eliminated entirely if you add the proper minerals to each day's feed.

Cross ties complete a well-furnished stall. They are handy for tying the horse while you muck out the night's bedding or for brushing it when the grooming area is already in use. When you want to deny the horse water, tying it away from the automatic waterer may be preferable to turning off the faucet and thus depriving a number of other horses. (This might be necessary to do after a horse returns from a heavy workout and, although cooled out, should be prevented from gulping water for about an hour.) Cross ties are easy to install. All you need is two No. 0 screw eyes and two strong beams on opposite walls. The screw eyes should be placed at about the same height as the horse's head. We recommend using a stout cord or rope for the ties themselves—something that is strong but will, with exceptional pulling or with the stroke of a penknife, break loose. Chain is stronger than rope, but we've seen too many horses panic and so tighten the chain that it could not be unhooked before the horse had done a great deal of damage to itself. Quick thinking, a rope, and a ready penknife would have saved the situation.

Alleyways

Unless your stable is so designed that each stall opens out into a paddock, there will be an alleyway in front of the stalls. This aisle should be a minimum of 8 feet wide to allow swinging doors (which are, you remember, 4 feet wide) to open without blocking the passageway and to allow the horse to be turned around with ease. We know of one old converted stable with an aisle only 4 feet wide. When a door to a stall is opened, guests must stand aside. None of the horses can be turned around in the aisle, and as they are led past the other

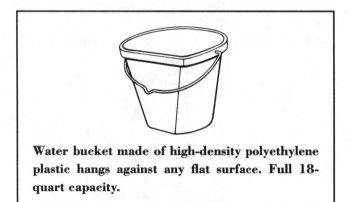

Water bucket made of high-density polyethylene plastic hangs against any flat surface. Full 18-quart capacity.

stalls, there is invariably much squealing and kicking. Leading a belligerent horse down such an alleyway can make even an experienced horseman apprehensive.

Aisles that are wider than 8 feet may be necessary in those stables where tractors deliver feed and pick up manure. Aisles that are wider still can be used for exercising or cooling out the horses. (At some point an aisle may be classified as a center ring, but we will refrain from committing ourselves to deciding when.) In the aisle, directly outside each stall, should be hooks for hanging halters and lead ropes. It may seem a convenience, but it is also an essential safety precaution ensuring that each horse has a halter and lead rope always available. For in case of fire, the tack room, however close by, will be too far away for you to quickly find the headgear needed to lead the horse from danger. Try not to put the halter near the grillwork of the stall; it is an easy game for a horse to pull the halter into the stall and then treat the leather as if it were chewing gum. Although horses rarely get sick from this game, you may when you make an unexpected payment to your tack shop.

With the addition of cross ties, alleyways can be used for grooming and washing a horse. In a small stable, that is an efficient use of the space. In a larger stable, tying a horse in the aisle will probably block the flow of traffic.

The flooring in the aisle can be the same as that used in the stalls. Because the area is put to more diverse uses, however, you may find you have different requirements for its flooring. It is not uncommon for a stable to use concrete or asphalt, or even indoor/outdoor carpeting over concrete, for the alleyways or even in the tack, feed, and grooming rooms. Basically, the floor in the aisle must be skidproof, easy to sweep clean, and fireproof.

Feed Room

The feed room of a small stable needn't be particularly large, but it must be separated from the stall area by a sturdy partition and a horseproof lock. Horses are naturally grazing animals; in the wild they spend their time carefully clipping each blade of grass slowly and systematically. A horse's natural inclination is to eat as much as it can get, and when confronted with 100 pounds of grain, it will eat itself literally to death or, at least, to lameness (founder). Ideally, the feed room must have a solid rat- and mouse-proof flooring (concrete is best and easiest to clean). The room should also be accessible to delivery areas.

Many small stables find that aluminum or hard-plastic garbage cans with tightly locking lids are excellent for storing feed. We find that one large-size (about 30 gallons) can will hold 100 pounds of corn, while two cans are needed to hold 100 pounds of crimped oats. One horse owner, while reconverting an old barn into a stable for his mare and her foal, found the old grain-storage bin still intact. It was made of beautifully antiqued wood perforated along the bottom with a series of equally antique mouseholes. Determined to restore the grain bin, he discovered upon inquiry that the local newspaper was delighted to sell used tin plates, sheets about 24 x 30 inches, for very little money. He bought enough of the sheet metal to line the grain bin completely. We know of another horseman who acquired an old dairy barn equipped with an all-metal cooler that had been used to store cans of milk. The barn was easily converted to accommodate horses, but the milk room was left intact. It was found that the milk cooler would hold as many as six 100-pound bags of grain safely out of reach of rodents. Some horse owners with limited space prefer to store their grain in large wooden boxes kept in a combination feed and tack area. If it is accessible to horses, stand the box against a wall where it will be impossible for even the most determined animal to kick it over.

Larger stables store their feed in special metal grain bins designed for that purpose. These bins are often built on the roof of the stable, connecting to the feed room by a chute that empties into a container or feed cart. Although an excellent arrangement for the larger stable that has the equipment to load the feed and unload it into the storage bin, it is totally inefficient for a smaller stable. In fact, it is unwise to attempt to store large quantities of feed that will not be used quickly. For even though

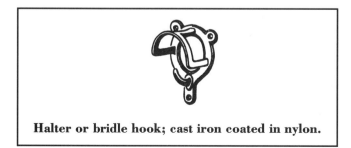

Halter or bridle hook; cast iron coated in nylon.

> Sunbeam makes several models of portable hanging scales that feature a straight spring balance that comes with top and bottom hooks. Marked in one-pound increments, it is available in a model that weighs up to 25 lbs. or up to 200 lbs. Farnam makes a Scale Scoop that holds up to 7¹/₄ pound capacity and allows you to adjust the amount of feed as you scoop out each horse's ration.

buying feed in large quantities seems economical, it is anything but when the feed begins to mold.

Hay and bedding to be stored in the feed room require extra space. It is usually more economical to buy hay and bedding during a particular season—either during harvest time or, in the case of sawdust, during the mill's busiest period—and you may want to store a year's worth in the feed room. Most stables, however, simply do not have the space and order their hay in smaller batches.

Hayloft

Some stable designs include a loft for hay storage; others provide for a separate floor. This latter arrangement worked well for centuries. In old walled cities in Bavaria, for instance, are houses over nine hundred years old that were originally designed with the ground floor for the livestock, the two middle floors for the family, and the top floor for hay. They knew that hay insulated the building to keep it warm in winter and cool in summer. But hay also has another inherent quality that is important to keep in mind: it is highly flammable. Many stable designers opt for safety, storing hay away from the stall areas in a fireproof room or even in a separate structure.

Tack Room

More horses require more tack and, therefore, a larger tack room. Tack should be kept out of the stall area in a well-lighted room tightly closed against stable dust. In a one- or two-stall stable, a small area away from the horses' reach or from the direct line of traffic is satisfactory.

The tack room can be as large as requirements and

Hay Fever: How To Know When You've Got It

Hay, especially when it is damp, is a major source of spontaneous combustion. When buying newly baled hay, check to be sure it was properly cured. All newly baled hay should be watched for the first few weeks for signs of heating; good ventilation is essential during this period. A damp surface appearance or a fruity smell is a sign of excessive heating. Take the temperature by forcing a pipe into the hay for several feet from the top. Then drop a thermometer down the pipe on a string. Wait a few minutes before pulling the thermometer up. If the temperature is above 160 degrees, cut open the bales and let the air circulate to cool the hay.

finances dictate. For some stables, it serves not only as a storage room for saddles and blankets but also as a workroom (and a social area for swapping horse tales). It is not uncommon to find a couch, a refrigerator, a bar, and a wall decorated with ribbons or photographs in this room.

The tack room needs to be large enough to accommodate a rack for each saddle and bridle. Racks are necessary for several reasons: they help maintain the shape of the saddle; they organize the equipment so that it is accessible; they keep it off the floor where it might otherwise be dumped to become damp, dusty, mouse-trodden and generally unusable. Racks are sold at tack shops, and you can also make your own quite easily and inexpensively. A clean 20-gallon oil drum bought from a local gas station and bolted to a tack-room wall is an excellent size for holding the saddle's shape (and for storing such equipment as spurs, ropes, and extra bits in the opening beneath). A small coffee can or cat-food can mounted on a wall is a good shape for holding bridles and halters, and you need only raid the kitchen garbage to find one.

Grooming Area

It is a good idea to situate the tack room near the grooming area. This spot can, again, be a separate room or simply part of the aisle outside the stalls. The grooming area should have firm, nonskid flooring, a high ceiling, drainage, electrical outlets for grooming equipment, and a storage shelf or cabinet for grooming supplies and the first-aid kit. One stable included a 10 x 12-foot wash room painted with marine enamel to protect the wood. The poured cement floor was scored to prevent slipping and sloped toward a drain in the center of the room. As soon as the horse had been washed and hosed down, it was moved directly under a small radiant heater that hung from the ceiling. Capable of heating the area within its range to about 70 degrees, it would quickly dry the wet horse, even when the temperature was below freezing.

Tool Storage

Every stable needs certain tools for maintaining the building. A separate room isn't necessary for these supplies, yet you will have to give some thought to where they will be stored. First, let's list the items: a broom; a 4- or 5-tined manure fork (with several extra for company); a shovel; a wheelbarrow, cart or basket for carrying the manure to the manure pit; a basic tool kit that will include a screwdriver, pliers, wire clipper, hammer, and nails; a supply of disinfectant such as lime; and a fly repellent for spraying the stable in summer. Many horsemen hang forks and shovels from hooks in one corner of the feed or tack room. The only requirement is that the tools be out of the way of the horses, so that a horse standing on cross ties, for instance, cannot accidentally back into a manure fork propped against the wall.

Tack trunk. The perfect solution for the small stable that does not have a separate tack room. This trunk holds up to four English saddles or one Western saddle as well as bridles, halters, and grooming aids. Rodent- and dustproof.

Infrared heaters can be used in the tack room, to eliminate mildew and dampness; in foaling stalls, where they can give quick warmth for the newly dropped foal; for the horse needing therapeutic heat treatments; and for slicking up coats before a show. Infrared heaters virtually eliminate the danger of fire. It is necessary to determine the height and location of heaters before ordering and then to follow the manufacturer's watt density recommendations which will take into account the type of building (either insulated wood frame, metal shell, etc.) and the floor coverage.

Manure Disposal

To pit, to pile, to raise mushrooms, that is the question. Mushroom growers love it, and avid gardeners appreciate a free supply, but few horse-owners know how to deal with it successfully. We are talking, of course, about manure. One 1,000-pound horse will produce 10 tons (yes, *tons*) of manure per year. Fortunately, only 20 percent of horse manure is urine; the rest is dry. (Hog

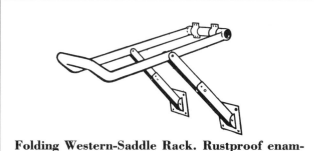

Folding Western-Saddle Rack. Rustproof enameled-steel rack attaches to any wall and will support up to 250 pounds. When not in use, it folds out of the way; especially useful in trailers and tight storage areas.

English-Saddle Bracket. Made of iron covered with brightly colored plastic for a smooth, non-rust surface over a strong brace.

manure, for instance, is about 40 percent urine.) Horse manure can, therefore, be handled with forks as a solid rather than with shovels as a liquid. Even if you have only one or two horses, the accumulation of manure can become a growing and unending problem. Large stables find it economical to install automatic gutter cleaners for carrying the manure through the barn and into a dump truck, a manure spreader, or a manure pit. Such equipment, while expensive to install, saves on labor. One or two people can quickly go through each stall and shovel the day's manure onto the gutter cleaners, usually located in an alleyway off the stall or along a wall behind the stall. Some stables prefer to fork the manure into the alley, where a scraper and power loader drives through and cleans up the area.

For the small stable, however, such equipment is incredibly costly. The alternatives are to arrange for daily removal of the waste, to dig a manure pit, or simply to make a pile. If you live in a strictly zoned area (regulated as to how many birdhouses permitted per tree), then consult local experts about waste storage. If you are permitted to store waste on your property, you should apply certain standards to the area as well. A manure pile or pit has certain requirements. It should be accessible to the stalls for easy filling each day. It should also be accessible to the trucks that regularly cart it away. And, since manure piles are rarely pleasing to the eye, it should be kept out of sight and out of smell. Remember that manure attracts flies, that it has a bad odor as it composts, that it is filled with the parasites eliminated by the horse (the best reason why it should never be located within a pasture or corral), that it may smoke as it composts, and that its ammonia content may be damaging to foundations. The last two points are sound reasons for locating the manure pile a distance from the stable walls. The least objectional method for dealing with manure is to dig a pit about 4 feet square and 4 feet deep. This pit can be covered with a perforated top that will keep the pit out of sight, and prevent children and other animals from falling through, but will also allow the fumes caused by the composting process to escape. Some horsemen prefer to build a concrete platform that slopes slightly to one side to encourage drainage. Manure piled on the platform for storage is scraped off with a tractor plow when enough has accumulated.

LARGE STABLE FACILITIES

Another book can be written about how to organize facilities for the large breeding or training stable. We will simply outline what some of those needs are and offer suggestions about where to get more information. Even if you do not intend to build a stabling complex in your backyard, you may find some ideas that can easily adapt to your small stabling needs.

The largest breeding farms will often have separate areas (either barns, sheds, or simply pastures) for broodmares about to foal, for mares waiting to be covered by a stallion, for weanlings of various ages, for stallions, for breeding, for isolation. Broodmare barns are normally built close to living quarters (or vice versa) and often provide a place for the attendant groom to keep watch during the foaling season. A stall for a large, blooded animal (usually the only kind of horse to merit such a setup) is 16 feet square. It is well lighted and usually includes a heat lamp for the newly born foal. Soon after the foal is born, the mare and her youngster are turned out to pasture with other broodmares and their young. When the weather is too severe for the foals, they will be brought in at night (however, rarely is a large and profitable breeding complex situated in a region where the climate normally requires such additional housing).

Stallion barns in the large establishments are based on two theories: one says that the stallions ought to be kept away and upwind from the broodmares; the second theory says that stallions are herd animals that like to see other horses, even if only at a distance. Some breeders find that allowing a stud to run in pasture with two or three mares in foal keeps him quiet and content. What is obvious to anyone who keeps a stallion (something we believe should not be done unless you have both an animal with particularly good qualities that you intend to use for breeding and the facilities to keep him properly) is that extra attention must be given to his facilities. A

stud stall should be fairly large—most breeders prefer a stall about 14 feet square—with its own paddock. The paddock fence should be strong and a minimum of 6 feet high, and double fence should separate nearby stallion paddocks. Many local zoning laws have restrictions against keeping stallions or may require that you obtain a special permit after passing an inspection of your facilities. And if your stallion manages to break out of his paddock to cover your neighbor's mares, don't expect to collect stud fees, no matter how valuable your horse. Do, however, expect a visit from the local police and your neighbor's attorney. The saying "Good fences make good neighbors" still holds true.

Some breeding establishments have a separate barn, shed, or other area for the actual breeding. Normally it is a roofed area about 24 feet square and may include a stall for prepping the mare (for such things as bandaging her tail, hobbling her legs, or padding her hind feet), a small stall for restraining her foal, and often a breeding rail over which the mare may first be teased. This breeding shed, usually located near the stallion barn, may even be a part of that barn.

Large establishments will also maintain a separate barn for isolating sick animals or for keeping newly arriving horses for a short quarantine period. This isolation barn should have its own watering and feeding equipment and its own waste-removal system. Manure and waste bedding from it should not be added to the regular pit if that pit is anywhere near the other barns.

Rings and Arenas

Commercial suburban and urban stables usually provide their boarders with the use of outdoor and indoor ring facilities. Some horsemen are finding it beneficial to join with others to build cooperative facilities. The type of ring that will be built is often determined by the type of riding most of the people using the facility will be doing. A jumping arena for a large horse show is usually 150 x 300 feet with straight sides of 200 feet. Many commercial establishments function quite well with rings only 125 x 250 feet. If the stable is quite small, then 80 x 150 feet may be sufficient.

Rings' three basic shapes are each adapted for a specialized kind of work: rectangular, rectangular with rounded edges, and oval. Rectangular "rings" are preferred by dressage riders, who will use the corners for

Cavalletti

───── ∩ ─────

by Catherine McWilliams

CAVALLETTI ARE AN EXTREMELY valuable aid in the training of horses and riders. In addition to their use in improving the horse's way of going on the flat, they are especially helpful in training over jumps. The cavalletti, or ground rails, are wooden poles raised from 4 to 20 inches off the ground. They are spaced in various patterns that require the horse to step over them in normal gaits of walk, trot, and canter.

Many riders use ordinary jumping rails laid flat on the ground as cavalletti. These lack many of the advantages of properly built cavalletti. In addition, they could cause an accident by rolling under a horse's foot.

The most useful cavalletti consists of one rail supported by an attached X-shaped frame at either end. If the X is constructed so that one pair of legs is longer than the other, the resulting cavalletti can be set up at three different heights.

Aside from the obvious advantage of a choice of three heights, cavalletti of this type are easily portable and can be stacked one upon another to make a jump of any desired height and spread.

In schooling, cavalletti can largely replace the traditional standards and poles, as they require less space to store, fewer materials to construct, and less effort to set up and adjust.

The most common application of cavalletti is in the regulation of the horse's stride at the trot. Three to six cavalletti, placed in a straight line $4\frac{1}{2}$ to $5\frac{1}{2}$ feet apart, accommodate the stride of most horses. Experimenting will

determine the exact distance for each horse. In its effort to step over the rails and place its feet on the ground between them, the horse's concentration and way of moving are both improved.

Placing cavalletti before a fence will make the jump easy for the horse, as its speed, length of stride, and straightness are all determined by the ground rails. The distance between the fence and the closest cavalletti should be twice the distance between adjacent cavalletti.

A thorough treatise on the use of cavalletti for training dressage horses as well as jumpers is *Cavalletti* by Reiner Klemke, J. A. Allen & Co., London. ∩

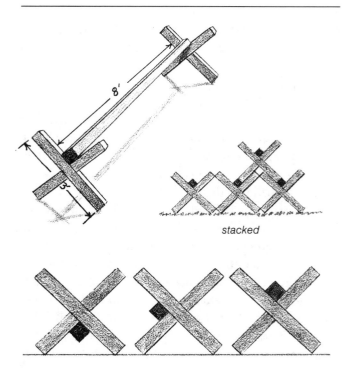

stacked

teaching the horse to bend correctly. The rounded-ends "ring" is preferred by horsemen who jump their animals (and many stable managers are finding it an easier shape for their tractors to disk). Oval "rings" that can be banked along the sides are preferred by horsemen who work their horses with buggies and other wheeled vehicles.

For both indoor and outdoor rings, good footing is the single essential ingredient for success. And good footing depends, as do so many other things, on what kind of work you are asking your horse to perform. If you are interested in jumping, then you will want a ring with a fairly deep and soft surface to help cushion the

horse's legs. If, however, you are interested in speed events, such as barrel racing or rodeo eventing, a firmer surface would be more desirable. For work that requires high collection and a high-stepping gait, you will want a springier surface that is neither too deep nor too hard. Footing in a ring also depends on drainage, and it is essential that the ring be located in a high area that is naturally dry. Many arenas' bases are stone, covered by gravel and then clay. On this surface are laid any number of materials for the desired footing: manure mixed with sand; tanbark or soil about 6 to 8 inches deep; shavings or sawdust mixed with soil; 18 to 24 inches of sand; or shredded rubber.

Rings also require regular maintenance. They should be gone over with a chain harrow before each show and in between major events or each morning before regular workouts. They should be watered or coated with a thin layer of oil to keep down dust. Surfaces mixed with soil are dustier than others, and the amount of watering needed will vary accordingly. It is usually necessary to redo the surface of a ring each year. A dirt-based outdoor ring should be disked under. To prevent the ground from freezing in winter, rock salt or calcium chloride may be added to the composition.

Outdoor rings should be enclosed by painted fencing that is sturdy and solid-looking, of wood plank or even of pipe. Either fencing will discourage a horse from bursting through, and it will not harm the animal when you intentionally turn it into the rails for schooling purposes. With regard to gates, if the ring is occasionally used as a paddock, then a horseproof latch is essential. A good ring, however, should be used only for working. It is more convenient to install a gate latch that can easily be opened by the rider while on horseback. Many Western pleasure-riding classes, of course, require the rider to do just that.

Pole-constructed indoor arenas are often finished with a rim of lumber about 4 feet high. This resilient kickboard protects the horse in case it kicks out or cuts too close to the edge of the inner wall. It also encloses the steel beams that would otherwise protrude into the ring. Many stable managers wrap the exposed steel beams with a quilted material (much like the kind used by professional moving men) to protect the riders from injury if they are accidentally thrown against the beam.

Fencing

Fences work two ways. They are necessary for keeping your horses in. They are also necessary for keeping your neighbors out. The latter problem may not seem an important one unless you live in a residential sec-

The horse owner throughout history has always held a position of social esteem. In the European languages, for example, cavalier in English, chevalier in French, caballero in Spanish, Ritter in German—all designations for aristocrats—originally simply meant "horseman."

Some Famous Horses of Myth and History

Bavieca. El Cid's horse, which survived its master by two and one-half years. The horse was buried in front of a monastery in Valencia, Spain, where two elm trees were planted to mark the grave.
Bucephalus. Alexander the Great's horse. The emperor was the only person who could ride the horse, which, according to history, always knelt down when Alexander mounted.
Copenhagen. The mount of the Duke of Wellington during the Napoleonic Wars.
Incitatus. The horse prized by the Roman emperor Caligula, who had the animal named a priest and consul. (Some people say that was the first time an entire horse was a politician.)
Lamri. King Arthur's mare.
Marengo. Napoleon's favorite horse, the white Arabian stallion that he rode at Waterloo.
Traveller. Robert E. Lee's horse.
White Surrey. Richard III's horse, for which he cried, according to the Shakespearean play, "A horse! A horse! My kingdom for a horse!"

tion where children and dogs are attracted, like flies, to horses. Then you must consider them seriously. For the law says that if an accident occurs on your property, you are responsible. And if negligence can be proved (for example, if an electric wire is lying loose and shocks a child, causing him to fall and hurt himself), then insurance may not protect you from loss.

Every horse magazine and book includes a photograph of a farm or ranch crisscrossed by a grid of white fences. This beautiful white-painted post-and-board fencing means horses. Always beautiful and strong (and we recommend it highly), it has also become terribly expensive to install and maintain and is now often used for small pastures. It is ideal for outdoor rings, for

"Martha Carleton, a student at Michigan State University, has filed a paternity suit in Walled Lake, Mich., District Court against the Colonial Acres Hunt Club in South Lyon, Mich., charging that Martha's mare was unwillingly forced into a romantic affair by a stallion and as a result the mare gave birth to a colt. Martha seeks damages under an 1867 law holding stable owners responsible for such equine dalliance."
The Boston Globe
November 1976

paddocks, and for fencing a highly visible front stretch of a pasture. For the back part of that pasture, however, or even for alternative fencing for the front, there are several kinds that are effective. The following chart includes several fencing materials, with the advantages and disadvantages of each listed.

FENCES

Types	Advantages	Disadvantages	Suggestions
CHAIN-LINK (all-metal links, 2-4-inch gauge. Supported by metal vertical and horizontal pipe)	highly effective; recommended for stud paddocks; excellent for keeping out small people and dogs and for keeping in foals; low maintenance	expensive; may stretch when horse leans against it.	use for difficult-to-keep horses or in highly developed residential areas
POST-AND-BOARD (2 × 4-inch cedar or locust posts; 2-inch hardwood lumber; 2, 3, or 4 boards)	good-looking; increases value of property; safe for horses	expensive; requires preservative or painting; can be chewed or kicked apart; horse can loosen posts by constant pushing against boards (as he leans to eat grass on other side); not long-lasting	to keep horse away from fence, run an electric wire along inside of top board; mow a strip of grass around the border of the paddock; place boards on inside of posts except at corners; paint boards with a chewing preventive or nail metal strips along the top of the board
POST-AND-RAIL (2 × 4-inch cedar or locust posts; 4-inch-diameter poles)	good-looking; safe for horses; need not be painted	expensive, although less than boards; same disadvantages as boards	
PIPE (prejobbed sections; rustproof metal; posts sunk into concrete)	strong; safe; maintenance-free; long-lasting	initially expensive to install	excellent for paddocks and for difficult horses
WIRE-MESH (wood or metal posts and horizontal bracing; 2–4-inch mesh)	inexpensive; will keep small animals out	wire gives easily and must be restretched often; must must be braced at top and bottom to prevent curling or stretching; can rust	not recommended for difficult-to-keep horses
RUBBER-RAIL (wood or metal posts)	safe for horses; excellent for training rings; low maintenance	initially expensive	

ELECTRIC WIRE
(wood or metal posts; 2- or 3-strand 10-12-gauge wire; 115-volt pulsating current)

inexpensive; good for fence training young horses

difficult to see; not recommended for populated areas; wire stretches easily and can be broken by deer and other animals; electric flow can be easily shorted by high-growing weeds or fallen branches; must be accessible to power or battery; must be maintained; not particularly attractive

good when used with board fence; recommend medium-light-gauge wire that will break in an emergency; tie white strips of cloth to wire to increase visibility; attach gate handle to the dead end of wire so that you aren't handling a live end when the gate is open

---

BARBED-WIRE
(wood or metal fence posts)

inexpensive

barbed wire can tear horses up so severely that they must be destroyed; it stretches; it is difficult to handle in installing or restretching

not recommended

ROSA MULTIFLORA
(living hedge fully grown can be 10-15 feet wide, 8-10 feet high)

attractive

requires good soil and climate; takes up some space from the pasture; takes three years to reach fence size; should be pruned and fertilized annually for good growth

---

PLASTIC
durable, maintenance-free (no need to paint), made from recycled materials

initially expensive

but ultimately no more expensive than wood because maintenance-free

chapter 3

Stable Management

Good stable management doesn't come out of a book. True, you can outline all the procedures that are necessary for seeing that horses are well cared for, and we intend to some degree to do that here. But the best stable manager we know combines years of experience, ever-observant senses, and pure common sense to manage his horses, and they are rarely sick or troubled with such ailments as lameness, colic, heaves, or

thrush. This old horseman knows even before he opens the stable door whether one of his horses is in trouble—if its nose is running, or if it is becoming constipated and in need of some bran. How does he do it? It's not something that can be explained—it's a talent either you have or you don't. It is a talent for observation, for empathizing with the animals, and for being deeply concerned for their well-being. Obviously it is not a talent that is easily taught, but nonetheless it is one that people who care for horses should concentrate on developing.

There are two essential reasons for being concerned about good management: for the safety of the horse and the safety of the horseman. A stable manager must apply his intellect to anticipate what a horse will do under any number of situations and even to anticipate the impossible (which, to every horseman's surprise, inevitably happens). In any stable there is always one animal that, when brought into the established routine, quickly finds the flaws in that routine and makes the most experienced horseman sigh in disbelief. Stating the obvious, a horse is a big animal, outweighing most horsemen by some 800 pounds. Fortunately, no one has told the horse about this. But because the horse doesn't know its own size, it is also capable of getting itself into trouble. Being a genetically flighty animal, it will normally attempt to sprint

away when confronted with the unusual. Running in the face of danger has done wonders for the preservation of the species; however, when that instinct meets up with modern stabling, it can be a dangerous trait. So the contemporary stable must be analyzed and made as free as is possible of any faults potentially harmful to the horse or the horseman. For example, we know of one older and wiser gelding who had never heard live band music before, a fact that the owner did not hold against it. But one spring, the town fathers organized a parade and chose the road in front of the stable to gather the band and start them off on the right foot. The drums rolled, the cymbals clashed, the band marched off and that normally quiet old gelding quivered, reared, and bucked. And, its kicking found the one weakness in its stall—the latch on the swinging stall door. The latch, it seems, was put on with ³/₄-inch screws instead of bolts, and while the screws looked sturdy, one well-motivated kick proved they weren't. Even more frightened than before, the horse ran up and down the stable aisle exciting all the other horses. The owner, who only moments before had thought he had the stable well organized and safe, was confronted with a crazed horse needing to be gentled and led to safety.

Accidents or health problems caused by poor management are more common than one might think, and one minute of carelessness can easily make a valuable horse worthless and a much-loved pet into food for the dogs. Horsemen tell stories that prove beyond doubt (or logic, for that matter) that it is invariably the refined, well-bred horse that pulls a stifle en route to the stable yard while its coarser, less well-put-together counterpart will trip over the door ledge, for instance, and go down in a spectacular and terrifying spill, only to gallop off with never a pulled ligament to show for his clumsiness. We know of several coarse, perfect glue-factory candidates pastured in an area surrounded on three sides by downed barbed-wire fencing. The fourth side of the pasture has no fencing, but the ground is littered with every conceivable obstacle. With open mouths we would watch these horses trot and gallop through the center of this minefield, tangle in the loose wire, and blithely kick themselves free. We can only guess that there is special attention from above for animals asked to endure such hardships. The purpose of this story is not, by any means, to encourage sloppiness in caring for horses; it is intended to assert that even though there are occasionally some horses that can survive anything, it is never your own animal.

Basic Care

Whether your horse is the star of the National Horse Show or a green-broke grade pastured outside the year around, it has certain basic needs you will have to see to. And failure to fulfill any of these basic needs almost certainly will end in equine health problems or even in the horse's death.

The first concern for any horse is a clean, adequate supply of water. Nothing, short of a shotgun, will kill a horse quicker than lack of water. Few people deny the substance to their horses intentionally, but occasionally water is absent through negligence. Automatic waterers, even though they have been improved over the years and are now generally reliable, can clog, freeze, or simply break. Therefore, it is a basic rule of horse care that the waterer be inspected daily. Neglect of the automatic waterer for just two or three days could be fatal. If you rely on a pond, stream, or spring-fed trough for your horse's water supply, it too should be inspected daily. Besides its possibly freezing, or unexpectedly drying up at the source, there is always the possibility that a small animal could drown in the

water supply and contaminate it. The automatic water troughs inside the stalls also need to be checked for cleanliness. Some horses periodically drop their feces into the trough and then refuse to drink the polluted water. When traveling from one area to another, be sure to check to see that your horse is drinking its regular amount. Often a horse will refuse water that tastes unfamiliar, as can happen when chlorinated or fluoridated water is introduced or withdrawn. We know of one old gelding that would go without water for almost two days when first brought in from summer pasture. Used to drinking from a clear, spring-fed pond, the old fellow had developed the taste buds of a gourmet, and he made it quite clear that the metallic-tasting water from the faucet just would not do. His owners learned to anticipate the problem and now add a small amount of molasses to the water bucket, reducing the amount each day until no molasses is needed.

The second most important need every horse has is adequate feed. Again, few horse owners intentionally deny feed to their animals. Malnutrition is usually due to ignorance (for example, the pasture that seemed so green may in fact have been depleted of any nutritional grasses or legumes). The malnourished horse has a low resistance to disease and is more likely to die from a respiratory ailment than from lack of bulk food. Even stall-housed horses fed daily rations may be malnourished, so it is essential that the horse owner remain alert to the possibility. Check and clean out the feed manger daily and note when the horse is off its feed, an important sign that it is sick. Also inspect the horse's feces. If you notice a quantity of grain in the manure, call the vet to check the horse's teeth. There are terrible stories about the person (we can't call him a horseman) who, in order to economize on feed, adds sawdust for bulk. Bulk it may be, but good horse care it sure isn't.

Most feeding problems stem from overfeeding rather than underfeeding. In this country of plenty we sometimes blindly follow the unstated concept "More is better." Often we overfeed ourselves but the effects on our health of the extra weight may not show up for forty or fifty years. However, a horse that is overfed, either with too much or with too rich a feed, can let us know immediately by going lame (founder). It is important to recognize the symptoms and to anticipate the problem by checking your horse's condition daily and asking, and taking, the advice of your veterinarian.

All horses need a certain amount of exercise. The necessary amount, like food requirements, depends on the individual animal. However, it is unusual to find privately owned horses that are over-exercised. Usually it is the other way around. Horses need exercise to keep their systems functioning properly, to keep up and develop muscle tone, and to stay in good spirits. (Horses rarely develop depression as we know it in humans; they do, however, develop bad habits—vices—that once learned are rarely forgotten.)

There are certain basic rules that every horseman learns and follows closely. And just a moment's deviation from these rules can often cause severe problems. For example, an experienced horseman knows that putting a lathered horse into its stall invites such problems as colic, founder, or respiratory ailments. Lathered or hot horses should not, for the same reason, be permitted to drink until they are sufficiently cooled out. A good horseman will also see that the horse is not asked to begin hard work abruptly without a short period of warm-up. (One old horseman refers to this warm-up as "getting the farts out.") Inexperienced horsemen will, in their enthusiasm, occasionally ask their horse to do more than it is conditioned to do. This is a serious fault and can lead to many problems. Some horses when pushed beyond their capability—and a horse's capability often depends on its conditioning—may lose their will (sense of self, heart, call it what you want).

Experienced horsemen will also groom their animals daily. During this ritual—and properly done, it becomes just that—the horseman will remove all obvious clumps of dirt from the horse's coat, taking particular care to see that the part of the back where a saddle will sit and that part of the belly where the girth fits is altogether clean and free of sores or bruises. During the daily brushing, he will be on the lookout for cuts or bruises that need first-aid attention and for heat in the legs indicating fever, checking at the same time for running eyes or nose and whether the eye has a bright and alert look instead of a dull and cloudy one (a sign of some disorder). While cleaning the horse's feet, he will also check to see that the shoes fit firmly and that the hoof is adequately trimmed, the frog firm and pliant, and the hoofs without cracks or splits.

Feeding

Although any feeding program is part of stable management, the subject is so large and yet so often given short shrift that we debated whether it should be given a section of its own under the general heading of "Animal Health." We concluded, however, that it is, after all, part of what most horsemen mean when they talk about "stable management," even if it can also be described as "preventive medicine." Many ailments result from poor nutrition, and since digestive problems are not uncommon in equines, every horse owner must determine his animal's needs and fulfill them as satisfactorily as possible.

The daily food, or ration, given a horse must satisfy many requirements, summed up briefly as palatability, quantity, and quality. A horse that won't or can't eat its food, even though it contains all the appropriate nutrients, won't benefit from it. The animal may suffer from too little food, or too much, or from improperly scheduled feedings. And of course, if the quality of the food is substandard, the animal will not receive the nourishment needed to remain healthy. All of these aspects of horse nutrition are interrelated, and a working knowledge of the animal's digestive system will be a good first step in arriving at a sensible, effective feeding program.

Horses are by nature grazing animals, eating fresh grass on a relatively constant basis throughout the day. Their stomachs are fairly small (about 4 gallons in capacity) and cannot handle the daily ration all at once, as can the stomachs of many other animals. Their digestive tract, therefore, must continuously empty the stomach even as the horse eats, processing the food materials through its long (about 100 feet) series of intestinal organs until the waste is eliminated. This is why knowledgeable horsemen feed stabled horses two to three times daily. A side benefit of such multiple

* Storing grain in covered, rodentproof containers prevents contamination that will result in feed having to be thrown away (it also can prevent you from inadvertently feeding soiled and spoiled feed to your horse).
* Add $1/_2$ tablespoon of table salt to one feed a day, a far more economical way to provide salt than in block form.
* Buy bedding in quantity. You may get a better price if you buy it loose and bag it yourself.
* A bar of saddle soap lasts longer if you cut it in half and use one half at a time. Save the small pieces when the bar is almost gone; when you have enough, melting them down creates another bar.
* Burlap feed sacks make good grooming clothes.
* Use old hand and bath towels for bandages or cleaning cloths.
* Tack, blankets, and other items that show initial signs of wear and tear won't heal themselves—get them fixed before the problem gets worse.
* By the same token, keeping tack, apparel, and other items clean and in good condition prolongs their lives. Making sure they're clean is also a way to make sure they're in good repair (see above).

feedings is that it helps prevent boredom and attendant stable vices.

Many horses will do well on good pasture grass. Some, ponies, for example, are best maintained on hay alone, provided they are not heavily worked and the hay is of high quality. But because fields are often overworked and depleted of nutrients, the average horse needs concentrated feed in the form of grains and even supplementary vitamins and minerals. The pelleted feeds manufactured and sold as "complete foods" are, for the most part, nutritionally complete, but for horses that cannot forage, hay or grass is necessary to relieve boredom and to keep the animal from feeling hungry.* Also, a horse receiving only one or two feedings of concentrated food a day will tend to bolt its food, losing much of the nutritional value in the process. Therefore, it is always preferable to give some of the hay ration first to take the edge off an appetite. Even better is water, if the animal does not have constant access to it, ahead of or directly after the hay. This is to prevent the horse from gulping water after eating grain, which can cause the grains to swell up in stomach and produce digestive upset.

Horses do not vomit the way humans do; instead, they may choke or cough up food that is still in the esophagus. (It will come out the nose rather than the mouth because of the way in which the pharynx—the tube connecting mouth and esophagus—works as a safety valve.† Because of the peculiar nature of equine digestion, therefore, ailments such as colic (a catchall word indicating a stomachache but with many different causes and effects) are both common and difficult to cure; so prevention is the name of the game. Proper schedules and amounts of food are essential considerations, but perhaps the most important of all is that of quality.

Food begins to lose what nutritive value it has the moment it is harvested. Careless purchasing and storage can increase deterioration and even make foods harmful. Drying is the most common way of retaining nutrients in horse feed. To prevent loss of quality, dry foods must be stored in cool, dark, well-ventilated areas that are free of pests. If grains have been crushed, however, their storage life is shortened. Saving money by buying such feed in larger quantities than can be used up in a month is risky, for it will soon turn moldy and worthless. Hay is at its best when green, leafy, and harvested when relatively young. If stored when wet, it will become moldy and perhaps combustible; on the other hand, if too dry, it may become brittle and dusty. Most of the large feed companies are reliable about producing quality feeds, but

---

* Sixteen pounds of good hay, for example, will provide 6 to 7 pounds of digestible nutrients, appropriate for a 1,000-pound animal worked two to three hours a day, whereas 10 to 12 pounds of oats will provide the same quantity of the nutrients. But the bulk of hay, its 14 pounds of dry material, will help keep the horse contented and full, which the lesser quantity of oats cannot accomplish.

† Horses that do vomit stomach contents, which is rare but not unknown, are showing very serious symptoms, usually of a rupture or acute dilatation, and death may be imminent.

problems may arise in distributors' handling, so you should always check any feed before accepting it. One usually reliable feed supplier we know sold us some oats with stones mixed in—no disaster for cows, but a real threat to horses. Hay, whether from your own field or from a local supplier, should also be checked carefully for presence of mold, dust, or dirt. Once hay has entered your barn, it must be kept well ventilated, free from contamination by rodents and other pests, and protected from exposure to moisture or the elements. At feeding time, check the food again. Each flake of hay should be shaken as it is removed from the bale so that all dusty particles are blown away before they can do damage to a horse's eyes or respiratory tract. Dusty hay can sometimes be improved by sprinkling with water (use a coffee can with a perforated bottom). Foods such as carrots, potatoes, grass, and clover should, of course, be clean, fresh, of good general quality, and washed free of poisonous contaminants like insecticides. They should not be broken up so small that horses will be tempted to swallow the chunks without chewing.

NUTRITION IN HORSES

Before we discuss in detail the various types of feed available for horses, let's look at the animal's nutritional requirements in order to design a well-balanced ration. Requirements depend on the horse's size, age, use, and general condition, and some horses can vary considerably as individuals—"easy" or "hard" keepers—but research has shown that all horses need certain nutrients in a particular balance. The chart on the following page, based on data furnished by the National Research Council, is a good guide. Please keep in mind that the figures given are minimums—many horses will need more than these amounts. Your veterinarian will be the best source of advice for your animal, so feel free to ask his help in establishing the best feeding program.

The basic components of food digested and used by all animals are protein, carbohydrate, fat, vitamins, minerals, and water, and some understanding of the relative properties is basic to good horse management.

Proteins, complex organic compounds made up chiefly of amino acids, are used primarily to build and repair tissue. Most foods contain protein in one form or another, but some are richer than others; grains, protein-rich pellets or food supplements, and good young hay (alfalfa, which is a legume rather than a grass, is higher in protein than timothy, for instance) contain more protein than fresh, succulent foods such as carrots and potatoes. As important as protein is, however, we tend to overrate it, taking in more than we can use, with excess protein not required for cell building utilized as energy (a fairly expensive way of providing it). Most mature horses, regardless of how much they are worked, need only 10 to 12 percent of their ration in crude protein; young horses and pregnant and lactating mares will need more. Too much protein can cause real problems, the most common being laminitis (or founder). Protein deficiency is also dangerous, resulting in poor growth, loss of weight, lack of stamina, poor hoof and hair-coat development, irregular estrous cycles, and poor milk production in mares.

Carbohydrates, such as cellulose starch or sugar, furnish the horse with heat and energy. The source of the carbohydrates is not important as long as the energy level remains the same when sources are changed. Carbohydrates make up about three-fourths of the dry matter in plants, the horse's chief source of food. The more exercise a horse is given, the more energy it will need—up to twice the energy needed to be maintained at rest. The usual way to increase energy is to feed more grain and less roughage, since grain is concentrated and takes less time to consume. Growing grass, fresh or dried, is richer in energy than the more fibrous mature grass or hay and is somewhat easier to digest; young animals and those worked strenuously must therefore have their carbohydrates low in fiber. Roughage, however, is important, for its bulk keeps the intestinal tract active, and should not be overlooked or omitted from the ration.

It has been found that horses can tolerate relatively high levels of fat in their diet—even as high as 10 percent of the daily ration when an increase in energy is required. (Fat yields more than twice as much energy as carbohydrates.) Fat may also increase the palatability of food for some horses, and it is believed to aid in the conditioning of the animal's skin and hair coat. Grains, such as corn and oats, are good sources of fat.

Vitamins, normally present in good grain and hay, are readily lost with poor harvesting and storage, and because vitamins do play a significant role in all body functions, supplements may be necessary. Vitamin A is particularly important. Deficiency may result in reproductive failure, nerve degeneration, night blindness, respiratory infections, and poor hair coat and hoof development. Green pasture grass is the best source of

MINIMUM NUTRITIONAL REQUIREMENTS FOR HORSES

Type of Horse	Crude Protein (in grams and % of daily ration)	Energy (calories)	Vitamin A	Calcium (International Units)	Phosphorus
Mature animal at rest 900 lbs.	505 gr (10%)	13,860	10,000	16,000	12,000
1100 lbs.	597 gr (10%)	16,390	12,500	20,000	15,000
Mature animal at light work 900 lbs.	672 gr (10%)	18,360	10,000	16,000	12,000
1100 lbs.	803 gr (10%)	21,890	12,500	20,000	15,000
Mature animal at moderate work 900 lbs.	871 gr (10%)	23,800	10,000	17,200	13,000
1100 lbs.	1,047 gr (10%)	28,690	12,500	21,200	16,000
Mares in last 90 days of pregnancy 900 lbs.	613 gr (11.5%)	14,880	20,000	19,500	15,000
1100 lbs.	725 gr (11.5%)	17,350	25,000	24,000	18,000
Lactating mares 900 lbs.	1,181 gr (13.3%)	24,390	20,000	42,000	35,600
1100 lbs.	1,317 gr (13.1%)	27,620	25,000	47,000	38,600
Foals (3 months) 1100 lbs. mature	834 gr (19%)	12,070	4,400	30,500	19,100
Weanlings (6 mos.) 1100 lbs. mature	800 gr (14.3%)*	15,400	9,000	46,000	28,700
Yearlings 1100 lbs. mature	750 gr (12.3%)	16,810	11,000	26,000	17,400
18-month animals 1100 lbs. mature	700 gr (11.3%)	17,160	16,000	23,000	16,000

* Experts believe that rations for foals should include at least 18% protein until the animal has reached 6 to 8 months; 16% to 2 years; 14% to 3 years; and 10–12% thereafter.

carotene, which is readily converted by the horse into vitamin A. Hay kept under ideal conditions will retain its vitamin A constituent for six to 12 months, but it is quickly destroyed by oxygen and light. The vitamin A requirement for horses has been established at 1,000 to 2,000 International Units daily for every 100 pounds of body weight—the higher figure for pregnant and lactating mares. Ten times this amount can be toxic, however, so don't assume that more is necessarily better

(the symptoms of toxicity are similar to those for vitamin A deficiency). Vitamin D, sometimes known as the sunshine vitamin, has an important role in the conversion of calcium and phosphorus to use in the body, necessary for good bone formation. It is produced in the skin by the solar rays. Horses without access to the outdoors can get their vitamin D from sun-cured forage or vitamin supplements; 200 to 500 I.U. daily for every 100 pounds of body weight is the recommended amount. Vitamin E seems to be good for young, rapidly growing horses, and it may (or may not) play a part in reproduction. Although its exact requirements are not known, 20 I.U. per 100 pounds is recommended. Vitamin C (ascorbic acid) may help wounds to heal and prevent nasal hemorrhage; the recommended dosage is 100 milligrams per 100 pounds daily. Both vitamins E and C are found in good feeds and in good-quality hay. Vitamin K, which preserves the clotting power in the blood, is synthesized in the gut, and supplements are not necessary. The vitamin B complex, which includes thiamine (B_1), riboflavin (B_2), niacin, pantothenic acid, and cobalamin (B_{12}) are necessary for good appetite, growth, and reproduction. Varying amounts of each are thought to be necessary (20 mg thiamine, 1.5 mg of riboflavin, .5 mg of niacin, 2 mg of pantothenic acid per 100 pounds body weight); but since all the B vitamins must work together and the exact requirements are not known, one can be safe by simply adding 1 percent brewer's yeast to the daily grain ration or checking the ingredient list on pelleted foods.

Minerals are inorganic elements, which, like vitamins, are needed in small amounts even though their exact requirements and uses are not fully known. The minerals of primary concern for horses are sodium, chlorine, calcium, and phosphorus. Sodium chloride, better known as common table salt, helps transfer nutrients to the cells and remove waste materials; hence the need for constant access to a salt block or the daily addition of salt to the feed. Most horses need about 3 ounces of salt a day; deficiency produces poor appetite,

> "A horse soldier took the utmost care of his charger. As long as the war lasted, he looked upon him as his fellow-helper in all emergencies, and fed him carefully with hay and corn. When the war was over, he only allowed the horse hay and chaff to eat, made him carry heavy loads of wood, and subjected him to slavish drudgery and ill treatment. When war was again proclaimed, the soldier clad himself in his military trappings and heavy coat of armour. When he mounted his charger, the horse fell down under the weight. No longer equal to the burden, the horse said to his master 'You must now go to war on foot. You have transformed me from a horse to an ass, and how can you expect that I can return again at a moment's notice from an ass to a horse?'"
>
> Aesop's Fables

rough coat, reduced growth in young animals, and decreased milk production in mares. Calcium and phosphorus together are the major components of bone and tooth, and a deficiency of them may result in unsoundness and may retard conception in mares. In the adult animal, bone contains three parts calcium to one part phosphorus; in the young growing horse, their ratio is about equal. Most roughage is relatively high in calcium and low in phosphorus, which can be found in grains. Other minerals are needed in smaller quantities (trace minerals); these include iodine (for the thyroid gland, which controls metabolism), iron and copper (to form hemoglobin for the blood to supply oxygen to the cells), cobalt (important in food digestion and in synthesizing B vitamins), and sulfur (an essential part of most proteins and certain vitamins). Manganese, magnesium, selenium, and potassium are also required by all horses in small amounts. These can be supplied in mineral supplements or in blocks similar to (and perhaps attached to) the salt blocks in a stall or paddock.

Water is the cheapest and perhaps most important constituent of all diets. The body of a mature horse is composed of about 80 percent water, and fluids must be supplied on a constant basis. Fresh grass contains a good deal of water, but horses consume at least 5 gallons and as much as 15 gallons daily (an average of $\frac{1}{2}$ gallon for each pound of dry food), and it must be supplied separately from food. Ordinary drinking water (cool, clean, and fresh) can perform miracles; it dissolves nutrients and carries them throughout the body via the circulatory system, picking up waste materials and eliminating them through the urine. Water also acts as a temperature control; when the horse is overheated, evaporation will cool it while watery tissues will absorb heat in cold weather. Horses deprived of water for some time can become intoxicated by it; therefore horses worked strenuously should be cooled before being allowed free access to water.

TYPES OF FOOD

A well-balanced ration of hay or grass, grains or concentrated foods, and water should provide all the nutritional requirements, with occasional or regular supplements if the foodstuff is of relatively poor quality. The following descriptions of the major sources of nutrients for horses will enable you to determine the best proportions and types of food to fit your horse's own needs.

Pasture grass of high quality is the most natural

and one of the best foods for a horse. Major horse farms have fine pastures that are well fertilized, drained, and kept free of weeds. Some horses will do well on pasture alone, and even horses that are confined most of the time should be allowed short periods on grass; not only is young, growing grass high in nutrition, but the horse will have a chance to relax and to exercise at will. Horsemen can save a good deal of money as well, since hay and grain rations can be cut back if a horse is getting sufficient nutrition from forage. Don't, however, suddenly turn a hay-fed horse out to graze for long periods. Rich grasses can easily founder a horse. Herbage should not be allowed to grow too high or be clipped too short; high mature grass is less nutritious, and overgrazed land may breed parasites. For that reason, both pasture rotation and fertilization are recommended. Legumes, such as alfalfa and clover, and grasses, such as timothy and Kentucky bluegrass, are both excellent pasture feeds. Some grasses may have a laxative effect at certain times of the year, probably when animals are turned out after a period of confinement and the diet is suddenly richer. This is troublesome for heavily worked horses, but excellent for broodmares and young horses. Temporary pastures of young, growing oats, rye, wheat, or barley can provide a welcome change when the regular pastures are dormant. Cattle can improve horse pastures by fertilizing the soil and keeping the grass cropped, allowing the horse to consume the easily digestible and more nutritious young grass.

Everyone knows that hay is for horses. Although it isn't a horse's only fuel, it is the most important of the harvested roughage that horses eat throughout the temperate zones of the world, especially where growing grass is not available the year around. Absolute requirements have not been established for hay, but the intake of about 1 to $1\frac{1}{4}$ percent of the horse's body weight daily seems desirable for horses that are worked. Mature, idle horses can be maintained on good-quality hay alone, though broodmares or growing or heavily worked animals will need supplementary grain to provide sufficient proteins and vitamins. The quality of hay is directly influenced by the way in which it is harvested. Grasses should be cut when the head is just beginning to grow, and when cured, the heads of timothy should be about $1\frac{1}{2}$ inches long; alfalfa should be cut at the bud to early bloom stage. Rapid curing is essential if the nutrients are to be pre-

served; dust and mold are signs of badly cured hay and may be harmful to horses. Good hay can be provided on a free-choice basis (as much as horses will eat); distended "hay bellies" are caused by overly mature hay, not by overconsumption.

As with forage there are two basic kinds of hay—legume and grass. Each type has its own qualities, and mixtures are often fed. Even in dried form legumes are richer in protein, calcium, and vitamins A and D, though they are not rich in phosphorus. The important legumes used for forage are alfalfa, red clover, and other clovers; grasses include timothy, prairie grass, bromegrass, orchard grass, Bermuda grass and Kentucky bluegrass.

Many people believe that alfalfa, the most widely grown tame hay in the United States, should be limited in use, with not more than 1 pound per day allowed for every 100 pounds of body weight. Most problems from feeding alfalfa, however, are the result of putting horses on it too suddenly, and two weeks of gradual conversion from timothy to alfalfa, for instance, should prevent any difficulties. Increased urine production, due to increased excretion of nitrogen, is common with alfalfa and not harmful.

Red clover, often grown in combination with timothy, is second only to alfalfa in food value, containing about two-thirds as much digestible protein. It does furnish more total digestible nutrients than alfalfa, however, and thus exceeds it slightly in net energy.

Timothy is the most important hay grass in the country, especially in the Northern states. It is usually freer of dust and mold than legume hay and is standard roughage for mature horses, whose need for protein, calcium, and vitamins is not so high as that of broodmares and growing horses. Wheat grasses, buffalo grass, and bluestem are leading native grasses used for hay in the Western states, though their value depends on climate and soil, the best (those equal to timothy) being grown on mountain meadows and upland prairies. Bermuda grass is the most important pasture grass of the South, but will not grow in a severe climate. It is about equal to timothy in value. Horsemen in the Central states find that orchard grass (grown in partial shade and often seeded with red clover), bromegrass (which is very palatable), and others are good, especially when mixed with legumes for higher nutritional value. Kentucky bluegrass is probably the

1892

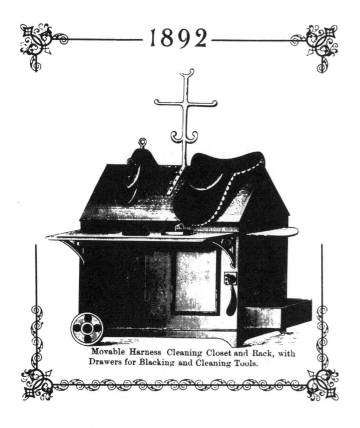

Movable Harness Cleaning Closet and Rack, with Drawers for Blacking and Cleaning Tools.

roughages, the nutrients are stored in large amounts as the plants mature, usually in the form of seeds.

Oats, the most widely used grain, are the standard by which other grains are judged. Although oats are not necessarily the richest grain, they are one of the safest, since because of their hulls they form a relatively loose, digestible mass in the stomach, unlike heavier corn and barley, which tend to pack. Oats weigh about 32 pounds or more per bushel and may be purchased whole, crimped, or crushed—the last two preferred for animals that tend to bolt their grain or for those with poor or developing teeth. New or mushy oats should never be fed to horses, for they may cause colic.

Wheat bran, the outer coating of the wheat kernel, is twice as bulky as oats, is richer in phosphorus and niacin, and has a better-quality protein than corn, although some experts believe it has been overrated as a food for horses since it is low in calcium and vitamins A and D. Nevertheless, because it is bulky and mildly laxative, as well as palatable, it mixes well with oats (two parts oats to one part bran) for feeding hardworking, hard-fed animals on their idle days to prevent tying up from an overproduction of lactic acid (a description of the ailment azoturia follows). Bran is also an excellent additive to the rations of breeding stock and foals. Constipation can be relieved if bran is fed wet; it is more laxative in this state than when dry and mixed with other feed. Pour hot water over the bran and let it stand for approximately a half hour before feeding. Wet mash should be given at night preferably before a day of rest. A mash made of 1 pound of bran mixed with warm water, 2 tablespoons of salt, and a cup of mineral oil may also be used to relieve colic.

Sorghum grains are popular in some areas, but the protein is not of good quality. The small seeds must be crushed or rolled to permit easy chewing and mixed with bran, barley, or oats if they are to be fully digested. Other meals such as soybean or linseed meal

best hay of all, being high in protein (up to 20 percent) and retaining it when cut before it heads out in the spring.

Corn silage and straw are also considered roughage suitable for horses, though most horsemen dismiss straw (the mature stems and leaves of any forage plant) as suitable only for bedding because of its lack of nutritional and digestive qualities. Corn and other fodder can be substituted for timothy if they are of good quality. Silage can be used only if it is perfectly free of decay and mold, for horses are far more susceptible to poisoning than cattle or sheep. Silage should not be the only roughage, but it may replace one-third to one-half the hay ration. Other roughages include low-grade milling by-products such as oat hulls, ground corncobs, and cottonseed hulls, but these are not particularly suitable—or palatable—to horses.

Concentrated foods are low in fiber (18 percent or less) but high in nutrients. This category includes grains and high-grade by-products such as hominy feed, wheat bran, cottonseed and linseed meal, and corn-gluten feed, with protein content up to 16 percent (a substance with more than 16 percent is considered a protein supplement). In concentrates, unlike most

> "In enclosing a pasture for mares and sucklings care must be taken to place the bottom rail or plank close to the ground; otherwise the foal is likely to be down by the fence and get up on the opposite side, much to the frantic dismay of all concerned."
>
> PEGGY JETT PITTENGER
> The Back-Yard Foal

Recommended Daily Rations

Mature horse at light work (1 to 3 hours daily):
$\frac{1}{2}$ pound grain mix and $1\frac{1}{4}$ to $1\frac{1}{2}$ pounds hay (or pasture equivalent) per hundred pounds of body weight. (A good ration for a pleasure or show horse might be, for a 1,000-pound animal, 5 pounds oats or mixture of 4 parts oats to 1 part corn or barley and 12 to 15 pounds hay.)

Mature horse at moderate work (3 to 5 hours daily):
1 pound grain mix and 1 to $1\frac{1}{4}$ pounds hay per hundred pounds of body weight

Mature horse at heavy work (5 to 8 hours daily):
$1\frac{1}{4}$ to $1\frac{1}{2}$ pounds grain mix and 1 pound of hay for every hundred pounds of body weight

Stallions
breeding: 1 to $1\frac{1}{2}$ pounds alfalfa; $1\frac{1}{4}$ pounds grain mix per hundred pounds of body weight
idle: $\frac{3}{4}$ to $1\frac{1}{2}$ pounds alfalfa and $\frac{3}{4}$ pound grain per hundred pounds of body weight

Broodmares
early pregnancy: $\frac{1}{2}$ to 1 pound grain and $\frac{3}{4}$ to $1\frac{1}{2}$ pound hay per hundred pounds of body weight
late pregnancy: 1 to $1\frac{1}{2}$ pounds grain and $\frac{3}{4}$ to $1\frac{1}{2}$ pounds hay
lactating: $1\frac{1}{2}$ to 2 pounds grain and 1 to $1\frac{3}{4}$ pounds alfalfa

Suckling foals:
$\frac{1}{2}$ to $\frac{3}{4}$ pound grain mix per hundred pounds of body weight

Weanlings:
1 to $1\frac{1}{2}$ pounds grain and $1\frac{1}{2}$ to 2 pounds hay per hundred pounds of body weight

Yearlings:
$\frac{1}{2}$ to $1\frac{1}{2}$ pounds grain and $\frac{1}{2}$ to $\frac{3}{4}$ pounds hay per hundred pounds of body weight

A good grain mix for breeding stock is 35 percent rolled barley, 30 percent rolled oats, 10 percent rolled corn, 10 percent linseed or soybean meal, 7 percent molasses, 6 percent calf manna or bran, 1 percent iodized salt, 1 percent bone meal.

are so high in protein that they are considered protein supplements rather than basal concentrates. Also very heavy, they must be mixed with bulkier grains to avoid packing up in the stomach. It's not a good idea to feed them in quantities of more than a pound a day, and they should be incorporated gradually into the ration to avoid digestive upset. Young horses should not be fed linseed meal, since it is higher in fiber and lower in quality and digestibility than soy meal.

Linseed meal is sometimes used as a supplement to improve hair coat, but the addition to the feed of polyunsaturated fat (corn or other vegetable oil) in small (2-ounce) doses can be more effective. Moreover, it does not adversely affect the protein supply by adding more than you want to the grain ration. Molasses is a useful supplement to grain because it is highly palatable, has a slightly laxative effect, and will bind together any dusty particles in grain. Succulent, fresh foods, such as root vegetables (carrots, potatoes) or apples, traditional treats for horses, provide some vitamins (though not many) and are highly palatable.

Most of the large feed companies produce prepared horse feeds, usually called "sweet feed," which are combinations of oats, corn and molasses fortified with alfalfa, linseed, salt, vitamins, and minerals. These feeds will often be accepted by fussy horses and are easier on the owners, since they need no preparation and take up less storage space. Similar mixtures are also available in nondusty dry pellet form, which horses may or may not like. Because the companies must maintain steady nutrient levels and because grains may vary in quality over a period of time, manufacturers may not always give exactly the same proportion (or weight) of grains in these prepared products. Therefore, a new bag should be opened before the old bag is empty and incorporated into the ration gradually rather than presented all at once. Feeding instructions accompanying these products can be very useful indeed. For horse owners who prefer to mix their own feed, the general suggested rations above are offered.

Horses and poets should be fed, not overfed.
CHARLES II OF ENGLAND

Caution should be taken in feeding grains, straight or in combination. Whole grains, especially if they are bolted by a hungry or greedy horse, can pass undigested through the system; crushing, rolling, and crimping will make grains more readily digestible, though ground grain is not always palatable because it tends to be dusty. Some people go so far as to cook or steam ground grain into mashes, although experts feel that if water is readily accessible, mashes are neither practical nor particularly desirable, since the grains lose nutritional and even digestive value. Nevertheless, as we pointed out earlier, wet bran is somewhat more effective than dry bran as a laxative and has been the traditional late supper for a hard-working horse facing a day of rest. Those who cook mashes do so to try to avoid azoturia, or Monday-morning sickness, once common among workhorses and not uncommon among high-performance animals today. It results when a heavily worked and heavily grained horse is allowed to be idle for a day and is then put back to work. The overproduction of lactic acid causes legs and hindquarter muscles to tie up and become rigid; the horse sweats profusely, and death can be the unhappy result if the animal is not treated immediately with complete rest, warmth, and the elimination of grain from the diet. Most cases can be prevented by good management—avoiding overworking a horse that is not in top form, not overfeeding grain, and exercising on a daily basis.

POISONOUS PLANTS

Because treatment for plant poisoning is not usually effective, prevention is the best, if not the only way to control this problem. Although few poisonous plants taste good to horses, animals will eat them when very

Although horses can be inoculated against Lyme disease (there's no such vaccine as yet for humans), the manager of a leading show barn suggests one method of repelling the deer ticks that carry and spread the disease. She adds several cloves of garlic (a "clove" is a portion of the garlic head) to her horses' feed on a daily basis. The smell is emitted through the horses' skin and, according to the manager, "ticks and other insects find garlic as offensive as vampires do."

A lot of horsemen find it easier to use a volume measure—usually a 2-pound coffee can—than to weigh out grain for their animals. This method is fine for oats, of which about 2 pounds will fill the 2-pound can. Some grains are heavier than oats, however, and unless one takes this fact into account, you may end up giving Dobbin a serious overdose without realizing it. Corn, for instance, has a reputation for causing horses to get fat, hot, or colicky, but if it were measured out properly, by weight, problems resulting from overfeeding would not occur. Grains even of the same variety don't always weigh the same from bag to bag, and crimping and rolling will affect weight considerably. Weigh each bag of grain as it is delivered, and adjust your feeding measure accordingly. Be sure too that you get a full measure when you dip the can into your grain bin.

A 2-pound (or 1-quart) coffee can will hold approximately:

2 pounds of oats
2 pounds of some sweet feeds
$2^3/_4$ pounds of pellets
$3^2/_5$ pounds of corn
1 pound of wheat bran
$2^1/_5$ pounds of linseed meal
3 pounds of barley
$3^2/_5$ pounds of sorghum grain
6 pounds of molasses
$3^4/_5$ pounds of whole wheat

hungry, when the plants or seeds are mixed in with grain or hay, or when plant clippings are placed where horses normally eat. If certain plants in a pasture look at all suspicious, either dig them up, kill them with chemicals (and be careful of that stuff, too!), mow them down before they go to seed, or move the animals out of the pasture at the time when the poisonous plants are particularly toxic. Some plants with a salty taste may be palatable to a hungry or young horse that may not be particularly discriminating. Occasionally such plants as oleander, which in large amounts can cause poisoning, are mixed in with hay; horse owners should therefore check new shipments of hay carefully.

Three different kinds of plants cause similar symp-

One of the most imaginative and informative books in the stable management part of the pasture is the *Ultimate Guide To Pampering Your Horse* by June V. Evers (Horse Hollow Press). The range of suggestions from the author and other horse owners covers such subjects as bathing and grooming (your barn becomes a spa), toys, and even costume parties—anything and everything to make a fuss over your horse.

In the extensive chapter on food are recipes for salads, bran mashes, and some dishes, like this one, that are fit for man (or woman) *and* beast:

APPLE SPICE MUFFINS

1 cup flour
1 cup wheat germ
$1/_2$ teaspoon cinnamon
$1/_2$ cup sugar
$1/_2$ teasoon salt
3 teaspoons baking powder
1 egg
$2/_3$ cup milk
$1/_4$ cup corn oil
1 cup Macintosh apple, chopped

Preheat oven to 400 degrees. Grease muffin tins and set aside.

In a large bowl, mix dry ingredients and set aside. In a separate bowl, mix the remaining ingredients thoroughly, including the apples. Pour the liquid ingredients into the dry ingredients. Mix until everything is moistened. Scoop into muffin tins and bake 15–25 minutes. Serve cool to horses and warm to people.

(If your idea of pampering begins and ends with food, June V. Evers is also the author of *The Original Book Of Horse Treats* [Horse Hollow Press]).

---

toms, each producing cirrhosis of the liver: *Amsinckia intermedia* (fiddleneck, tarweed, fireweed, buckthorn, and yellow burr weed), found in the West, where it is a common weed of wheat and other grain crops; *Senecio jacobaea* (ragwort, groundsel, and "stinking Willie"), found in the West and Midwest; and *Crotalaria spectabilis* and *C. sagittalis* (rattlebox, rattleweed, and wild pea), common in the Southeast. The *Senecio* species caused walking disease (also called hard liver disease or Walla Walla walking disease). All of these plants affect the liver, causing a dysfunction of the central nervous system with symptoms including staggering, aimless walking, incoordination, mania, or delirium, often accompanied by severe intestinal irritation along with diarrhea and signs of colic. When the liver has been sufficiently damaged, loss of condition and death result, and there is no cure or treatment once the liver has been damaged. Since other causes for these symptoms, however, are rabies, abscesses,

brain tumor, encephalitis, and meningitis, don't assume poisoning unless you are convinced the animal had access to any of these plants.

Ricinus communis (called the castor bean, castor oil plant, and palma christi), common in the Southeast and Southwest, is the source of castor oil (which, if we remember our childhoods correctly, tastes bad but is terribly good for you). Actually, the plant is beneficial, but the seeds, if ingested, are highly toxic, causing both humans and horses severe irritation in the intestinal tract. In addition to the plants' use in commercial production of castor oil, they are sometimes grown for ornamental effect around barns or corrals where horses—young, inquisitive ones for the most part, since the older ones are sensible enough to know that what tastes bad *is* bad—can eat them. As few as 7 grams of the seeds may be fatal to a horse. Severe enteritis is the characteristic sign; at first the horse is rather dull, then uncoordinated, and then very sweaty.

Spasms may be apparent, and watery diarrhea, plus other colicky symptoms, will appear. Eventually the horse goes into convulsions and dies.

Nerium oleander is also grown as an ornament in the South and in California, where it has been known to poison people who used the sticks of the plant for food skewers. Lawn clippings or bales of hay containing oleander leaves are the usual source of the poisoning in horses, since they will rarely eat the shrub itself. It can be lethal; 40 to 50 grams of the green or dried leaves will kill a 1,000-pound horse. Profuse diarrhea, abnormal heartbeat, and chilled extremities are progressive signs of the poisoning, with the pulse eventually becoming imperceptible and death following shortly thereafter. If the dose was small and nonfatal, treatment must involve removal of the contents of the intestinal tract and maintenance of general good nursing care.

Bracken, or brake fern, is common in woodland areas all over the United States, and some species of the genus *Pteridium* can poison cattle and horses, with different reactions—the latter suffering disorders of the central nervous system. Since bracken stays green into the fall, animals may begin to eat it after pasture grass has browned, even cultivating a taste for it, and bracken sometimes shows up in hay. Animals must eat bracken over a period of time (one or two months) before showing such symptoms of toxicity as loss of weight, unsteadiness, swaying, and staggering. If the animal falls, it may not be able to get up.

"Chewing disease" is the colloquial term for yellow star thistle poisoning, from the plant *Centaurea solstitialis*, which grows throughout the West and is often found along roadsides and dumps. It is an attractive, yellow-flowered annual, a member of the sunflower family. As with bracken, this thistle must be consumed over a long period before signs of poisoning appear, but once they do, death is probable. A victim will have difficulty in swallowing, and food may be spat out or become lodged in the mouth; the horse will probably be unable to drink and may develop a wooden facial expression as muscles around the mouth and tongue become paralyzed. If not helped, it will die of starvation, but in any case functional recovery is unlikely even if the animal responds to treatment.

The short, sharp prickles of yellow bristle grass (*Steraia glauca* and *S. lutescens*) cause ulcers in the stomach and irritation in the tongue and lips. Once the source is removed, healing is rapid. Many other plants, such as thistles, cacti, and thorny shrubs, will cause puncture wounds or cuts.

Some lupines are toxic, some not, and it is difficult to tell the two types apart. Poisoning occurs usually in the fall or winter in the form of gastric irritation and diarrhea, and acute poisoning will cause depression, weakness, and coma. Loco-weed disease, which is caused by some species of the genus *Astragalus*, causes horses to stagger, wander in circles, act depressed, and then fall into convulsions. Some species of the same genus (woody aster, prince's plum, and "golden weed") will cause selenium poisoning, which affects the central nervous system; it also causes feces to become dark and fluid and an occasional fever to flare. The horse may die within a few hours or may linger for a few days. Other plants absorb selenium to a toxic level, causing chronic poisoning, sometimes called alkali disease. Losses of hair and hooves are characteristic, and victims become emaciated and lame. Oats, barley, and wheat grown in selenium-rich soil may be the villains here, but treatment involves simply removing the animal from the area or the feed from the animal.

There is no treatment or cure for nicotine poisoning, but you needn't keep the animal from smoking, only from eating plants of the wild tobacco family. Normally paralysis precedes the death. *Lathyrus* is another genus of poisonous plants; they are now rare, but there was an outbreak in 1969 affecting horses. Signs involve stiff hindquarters, unbalanced walking, and difficulty in rising. Removal of the plant (in the 1969 epidemic it was in baled hay) will relieve the symptoms.

Avocados are a delicacy for humans, but their stalks, leaves, and bark can be just the opposite. Severe mastitis and lack of milk production in mares result. Other plants, rarely eaten by horses but poisonous to them, include oak, ergot (a fungus), *Datura*, poison hemlock, and perhaps water hemlock.

FEED SUPPLEMENTS: NECESSARY OR NOT?

Horses, like all living creatures, need vitamins, minerals, proteins, carbohydrates, and the rest of the nutritional components to remain healthy and maintain their weight and condition. But not all horses need anything beyond their daily ration, except a mineral

A horse shut in a stall for hours at a time can develop bad habits. Try some of the following to keep the horse interested and alert:

- *Exercise it regularly.*
- *Allow the horse to watch other horses.*
- *Provide a window with a view.*
- *Keep a radio tuned to soothing music.*
- *Get the horse a pet; donkeys, goats, chickens, ducks, dogs, and cats (even mice) are acceptable.*
- *Provide toys in the stall; a rubber tire, hanging tether balls, or a large plastic bottle (a Clorox bottle is good) suspended from the ceiling makes an excellent punching bag.*

block. Most tack shops and catalogs offer a wide array of feed supplements, so many that the average horse owner can become confused or feel guilty about not buying at least something, but often these products are as unnecessary as they are expensive. In fact, the best thing any horse owner can do is to provide the finest hay or grass available, supplemented by grains or concentrate when a horse is growing or doing heavy work, carrying or nursing a foal, or losing condition because of low-quality hay or grass, or cold weather.

If you are concerned that your horse is too thin or out of condition, the first step is to determine the horse's weight by using a weight tape. Increase or improve the hay or grass in his diet and, if he shows no improvement within two weeks, increase the ration of grain or concentrate by about 25 percent. After a couple of weeks more, use the tape again to determine the horse's weight gain. Make the changes gradually and keep good records, giving the horse at least two weeks to show a difference after you make the changes. Only after you have worked with balancing the basic diet should you consider adding a feed supplement if the horse is still lacking in energy or losing weight, or if the condition of the coat or hooves remains poor. Call your veterinarian or an equine nutritionist first, however, as these symptoms may be a sign of illness, intestinal parasites, or some other problem unrelated to nutrition.

Report to your vet exactly what your horse has been eating, and how much and what kind of work the horse is doing. The vet will analyze the horse's condition and make an appropriate suggestion. If a feed supplement is recommended, find out what type you need. Don't just run out and buy whatever looks good or costs least or works for your neighbors. If the quality of your hay or pasture is poor, as is the case in many parts of the country, there may be a protein or vitamin deficiency to correct. If the horse is young, pregnant, or nursing, additional protein or calcium may be necessary. If the weather is hot and the horse is working hard, perhaps all that is necessary is an occasional (not regular) dose of electrolytes to compensate for the loss of minerals through sweat; a hardworking horse may also need additional energy. If the horse's hooves are dry or cracked, the vet might suggest a supplement designed to promote hoof growth and repair damaged hoof tissue.

There are several different categories—and many hundreds of brands, too many to list here—of supplements available, ranging from all-purpose products combining vitamins and minerals in a filler base, some of them pure (or nearly so) ingredients, some of them herbal or natural, some designed for specific purposes (such as hoof or coat care), and some of them verging on the medicinal, such as calmatives. Before you buy any product, read the labels very carefully. You may find that in order to get the ingredients you need, you are being asked to pay for a great deal of filler material or processing to make the basic ingredients palatable. Also keep in mind that many of the heavily advertised, widely available products are designed for use throughout the country, where soil may be rich in minerals or seriously depleted. Any all-purpose product will probably not contain a very high level of anything just to avoid overdosing, which means that it may not serve your particular needs very well. These products also contain vitamins C (not necessary as horses produce their own), A, and D (which are important for pregnant mares and growing horses but can be toxic in the average horse). Also, some vitamins, such as the B complex, become inactive at temperatures over 120 degrees F., so that the B vitamins in pelleted feeds are probably not of any value at all. You may find it more effective and less expensive to buy a pure ingredient (vitamin E, protein-rich soybean meal, B-complex vitamins) and mix your own supplement suited to your horse's own needs and taste buds. Again, however, feed your horse only what is absolutely necessary: Too much iron and too much vitamin A or D or other fat-soluble vitamins can be dangerous, while too much of the B complex, which are water-soluble, may simply end up creating expensive urine.

Most all-purpose vitamin-mineral-protein supplements are mixed with fillers that add considerably to the price, but increase the palatability of the active ingredients they contain. As noted above, they probably won't do any harm but they may not be necessary unless the quality of your hay or grass is poor. Liquid or blood tonics (*hematinics*) are recommended only for heavily worked or anemic horses, as they are very rich in iron and copper and other vitamins and minerals that are probably present in the basic diet of the average horse and may prove toxic. Natural products that are designed for all-purpose use include bee-pollen powder, wheat-germ oil, and soybean oil.

Some products are advertised as coat conditioners, but most all-purpose supplements will have some positive effect on the coat. A basic diet and regular grooming care, however, are the best way to insure a healthy, shining coat.

Supplements designed to improve hoof growth and to repair damaged hoof tissue usually contain biotin and methionine with fillers to make them palatable. Check with your farrier as well as your veterinarian before investing in these relatively costly products and, if you use them, be patient. It may take as long as a couple of months for any improvement to become noticeable.

Electrolytes are the mineral salts in body fluids such as sodium, potassium, chloride, calcium, and magnesium that are necessary for the body to function properly in generating and using energy and eliminating waste. When these minerals are out of balance, the result can be exhaustion and even shock, but the horse's body compensates by maintaining a constant balance of minerals and water, either by conserving electrolytes when sweat loss is great or by increasing water when the electrolyte level is high. Most experts do not recommend feeding electrolytes as a regular supplement, as it may interfere with the horse's natural ability to deal with stress. When stress is great (caused by illness, overwork, extreme changes in temperature, humidity, living conditions, or altitude), a horse may not be able to get sufficient electrolytes in water to make up for loss through sweat. The ideal remedy is to give the appropriate dose before or at the time of the stressful situation—before and during an endurance ride, for example.

Calmative supplements are rather controversial, because their use in subduing or relaxing a nervous or hyperactive horse may only mask an environmental, medical, nutritional, or genetic problem that might be better dealt with in another way. A good, basic diet should provide appropriate amounts of magnesium, L-tryptophan, and thiamine, which are known to affect nerve function; excessive amounts of these substances may create imbalances and other undesirable effects. The actual effectiveness of various herbs has not been measured scientifically, but many enthusiasts count on such products as valerian root, ginseng, hops, and passionflower for their sedative qualities. Three cautionary notes regarding the use of calmative drugs, natural or otherwise: don't use these drugs as a regular supplement but search for the real reason a horse may be difficult to handle; be aware that the use of these drugs may be considered illegal in the show ring; and don't take risks by riding a drugged horse at speed or over fences.

Exercising

There are many ways to ensure that the horse gets a good daily dose of exercise. The most common method is to turn the animal out into a pen or a paddock where it can run, kick, buck, and generally provide a wonder-

A Supplement Worth Its Salt

Aside from clean fresh water, good-quality hay, and enough concentrate to maintain weight, a horse needs very little by way of nutrition, aside from an easy-to-reach salt block that contains trace minerals. A horse that sweats from heat or hard work will lose minerals that may not be replenished in its daily diet. Salt may be added to the diet or fed in crystals, but a salt block mounted on a special holder in the stall (not simply left in the feed tub) is all that most horses will require. Heavily worked horses may need to have electrolytes added to their feed (not water) to prevent the loss of precious minerals, but electrolytes should be given only when the horse is worked, not as a regular part of the diet. There is some evidence that the regular use of these supplements weakens a horse's ability to respond to stress.

fully picturesque show. Sometimes, however, this is not sufficient. Certain horses, like some people, are lazy. They may not want to move about, and the longer they go without proper exercise, the more their muscles will atrophy and the harder they will be to recondition. Mares in the later months of pregnancy are sometimes loath to move about and may need encouragement in the form of a rider, a lead rope, an automatic walker, or a lunge line. Obviously, the best way to exercise saddle horses is to work them under saddle. Twenty minutes of concentrated effort at all the gaits (or even at only the walk or trot) will do wonders to exercise the animal, building and developing its muscles, wind, balance, and general conditioning. We know of one pastured horse that developed its own program of daily exercise. About eleven o'clock each morning the family dog arrived in the pasture, where it began to bark at the horse. The two friends took off across the field, the horse in the lead and the dog following at its heels. When this odd couple reached the opposite fence, they turned and reversed the order of the chase, with the dog in the lead and the horse, head low to the ground, close behind. The scheduled chase always began on time, ended about fifteen minutes after starting time, and occurred every day—winter and summer.

HOT-WALKERS

Large breeding and training stables are finding hot-walkers a most useful device for cooling out, exercising, or conditioning their stock, since the apparatus frees the often overworked staff for other necessary chores. They're also good for showing a horse "who's boss." One arrogant horse used to getting its own way changed its attitude after finding that its antics could not alter the patience and persistence of the hot-walker.

The hot-walker may be housed in a separate shed or under a tent, or in the center of a paddock. The arms of the hot-walker extend about 16 feet, thus requiring an area that is about 40 feet in diameter when it is in use. When not in use, many models feature arms that fold up out of the way.

The standard hot-walker is powered by a $1/2$ to 1-horsepower electric motor that uses normal household 110/115 AC current. For many stables, a hot-walker is an essential part of their management. But it is occasionally abused by its users, and it does have certain inherent disadvantages. Horses hooked up to a hot-walker tend to become easily bored; they may be

asked to trot or even canter in circles too tight for their abilities; the machines that work in only one direction can badly overdevelop a horse's muscles on one side while the other side remains sadly underdeveloped. An automatic hot-walker will walk either two, four, or six horses at one time. Most machines have four forward and four reverse speeds. Four-speed walkers allow adjustment to approximate a slow and a fast walk and a slow and a fast trot. Some of the more expensive models permit adjustment of the speed to match the horse's natural gait instead of demanding that the animal adjust its stride to the predetermined speed of the machine.

Bedding

In their natural state, horses will rarely lie down to sleep; when they do, they will look for a soft, dry area clean of any excrement and protected from direct winds. Stalled horses haven't such choice, nor obviously, are their needs the same as those of the horse running free. However, the addition of good bedding is necessary to make most stall flooring (discussed in Chapter 2) more comfortable for the horse. Indeed, there are a number of reasons why a thick layer of bedding is important. Clean bedding keeps the horse cleaner and drier (a clean coat is less prone to skin infections); it encourages the horse to lie down (resting the muscles and tendons in delicate legs); it makes it easier to muck out the manure; it cushions the horse's legs against a solid, unyielding floor (eliminating such problems as capped hock or elbow); it absorbs moisture; it cuts down the smell of fresh manure and urine; it helps to prevent reinfestation with parasites; and it cuts down the chance for disease bacteria to multiply and spread.

The average 12×12-foot box stall requires anywhere from two to four bales of fresh bedding per week. The quantity depends upon the type of material used, the weight of the horse, and the time of year. If your horse is heavier than most, you will need more bedding to settle it comfortably; if the weather is cold, you will need additional bedding to bank around the sides of the stall, preventing drafts and insulating the bottom of the stall walls as well as the floor.

There are a number of kinds of bedding that are perfectly acceptable and will do a decent job. The kind you choose most likely will depend on its availability

Farnam features a horse walker for which it makes a number of claims that permit its model to be compared to others for shopping purposes. Many other companies, claim Farnam, use transmission parts taken from junk cars, which, when used on the walkers, will break down, and replacement parts will be difficult to find. Farnam uses a one-horsepower electric motor, adaptable to either 120- or 240-volt input, that is counter-balanced, making speed changes simple, fast and trouble-free. It is cabled to an industrial gearbox, not automotive rear-end gears, and is connected to the drive assembly by heavy wall pipe that helps to eliminate rocking often found in other walkers.

The Farnam "Real Tough Walker" model is a 4-speed machine that permits starting horses out on a slow or normal walk or a slow or normal trot. Speeds range from 2 to 12 rpm. Its clutch design provides a constant amount of pull at all times, eliminating jerking, which can often cause a horse to fight the lead. This 4-horse walker with 8-foot-high arms and a 28-foot diameter includes a one-year guarantee against defective parts and workmanship

in your area, the cost, and the season. A discussion follows of the different types of bedding, with their good points and bad. Do keep in mind that if you live in an area of the country where your horses are plagued with a very wet pasture, then a bedding that tends to dry out horse's hooves may be preferable. If, on the other hand, your pasture is extremely dry, you should avoid using any of the materials that will promote further drying of the hoof.

Straw (wheat, rye, or oat) is a light, absorbent, generally available material for bedding that is preferred by most horsemen. It does not dry horse's hooves, and it fluffs dry quickly. Straw manure is highly prized by gardeners and mushroom growers, so much so that you may be able to sell used bedding for a small profit or, better still, prove yourself a generous neighbor. Unfortunately, straw is also appetizing for many horses, which will often eat it when fresh hay is not available. The best way to break your horse of that habit is to change the kind of bedding used.

Wood shavings are usually easily accessible, and few horses find them particularly appetizing. They provide a comfortable, springy surface and act as a good deodorant. Wood shavings may be drying on a horse's hooves, and we recommend you avoid using oak shavings, since the tannic acid in that wood tends to heat the hooves and cause discomfort.

Sawdust, like wood shavings, is usually easily available and is nonedible, but it does have some disadvantages that should be acknowledged. For instance, it may be dusty and when inhaled, cause respiratory problems; it can sift into areas such as drains where it will clog the pipes; and it tends to cake into the feet, where it can cause irritation or simply draw out all moisture from the hoof. Note: It should go without saying, but we will say it anyway, that wood shavings or sawdust must not come from wood that has been treated with toxic materials of any kind. Be sure your supplier understands the use you intend to make of the shavings or sawdust.

Peat moss is a highly absorbent bedding that can be expensive and hard to find in certain areas. However, its public relations potential is great in suburban areas especially, and we recommend it highly. Peat moss is terrific for gardens, and you will find your neighbors begging to be the next to haul away your manure pile, especially during the spring and fall. Peat moss also has a pleasant deodorant effect and is not drying on hooves.

Stazdry (or Stae Dri or Scravell or Bagass) is a specially prepared bedding made from dried sugar cane. Usually available in bales, it is easy to store and to handle. Horses won't eat Stazdry, making it easier to keep under the animal than straw.

Peanut hulls are probably difficult to find in many parts of the country, but where they are available they are worth considering. However, they have disadvantages. You'll need a lot of peanut hulls to make a comfortable bed. They tend to pile up in one part of the stall, making it difficult to keep uniform bedding under the horse. Hulls are small and difficult to handle and will fall through the tines of a manure fork (an advantage when you are simply cleaning out the previous night's droppings, but disadvantageous when you are cleaning out the entire stall).

MUCKING OUT

Novices, in their concern for keeping the horse clean, usually remove too much dry bedding, while their only slightly more experienced and perhaps soured counterparts may delay the mucking-out process longer than is healthy for the horse. Removing too much bedding is uneconomical and exhausting; failing to remove the wet manure is courting such problems as thrushy hooves, skin infections, and parasite infestation.

As with many procedures, there is a secret to good mucking. First, either turn the horse out into a paddock or pasture or tie it on cross ties. Take a six- or eight-tined manure fork that will balance comfortably in one hand when held near the center of the handle. Begin mucking by scooping up the top of any obvious pile of manure and loading it into the manure wagon. Then dig down into the bedding and thoroughly shake it out. The heavier wet bedding and manure will fall to the bottom of the pile, while the lighter, cleaner bedding will be on top. Scoop off the top layer and pile it to one side of the stall. Scoop up the bottom layer of wet

muck and remove. Continue doing this throughout the stall until the wettest (usually the center) part of the stall is bare. Scrape the floors clean with a shovel and disinfect regularly with lime. Spread the clean bedding, now piled in one corner, throughout the stall, adding fresh bedding to replace the amount removed.

Grooming

Proper grooming may take only ten minutes per day per horse, it may take one hour per day per horse, or it may take eight hours a day per horse—it all depends on what you want from your horse and the conditions under which the animal is kept. To realize why grooming is important for all horses, it is necessary to understand what hides under that hair coat. The horse has two layers of "skin," known as the dermis, the layer that is not immediately visible, and the epidermis, which is actually the outer "skin" we would call by such names as hair or hoof. The dermis is porous and eliminates sweat, which is water and waste matter (much the same as urine) excreted through the pores of the skin. This waste

The Art of Making a Muckheap

A British-style muckheap is neat, tidy, compact, fast-rotting, less odorous, inhibiting to the growth of flies and parasites—almost a thing of beauty. It is slightly more time-consuming to build than an ordinary manure pile (but so is any artistic creation). Start by choosing a site that is a little way from the horses' stalls. Mark out a square about 6 feet by 6 feet. Fill the square area with dirty straw and manure until it covers the entire area to a depth of about 1 foot. Pound it down flat with a heavy shovel, or turn the kids loose to stomp it down with their feet. Pile another layer and pound that one down. Continue piling and pounding, making sure each layer covers the square area and is flat. To trim and finish the muckheap, use a pitchfork. With the tines pointed down, begin combing the sides of the heap, starting from the top. This will take out lumps while flattening and straightening the sides. Work on all sides until the heap is perfectly square. Remove the excess loose material that has accumulated around the base and place it around the top of the heap to form a ledge about one foot wide. You are now ready to take photographs of your work of art before calling in someone to remove it.

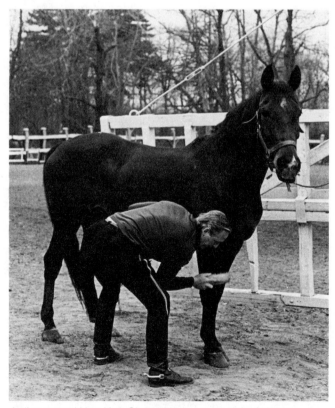

A dismounted New York City policeman grooming his horse.

STABLE MANAGEMENT | 77

matter is normally absorbed by the dandruff in the epidermis (hair), where it remains unless brushed or washed out. If excess sweat is permitted to remain in the hair, it can eventually clog the pores, causing skin infections, or even block the excretion of the sweat, allowing toxic waste matter to accumulate in the horse's system. A horse that is stabled, clipped, and blanketed needs daily grooming, and removal of the dust is an essential part of the grooming reason and ritual. Pastured horses permitted to retain long, woolly coats should not be heavily groomed, however—at least, not in winter. Instead, they should receive a light brushing that removes obvious clumps of dirt from the coat. This should be done to keep the hair free of lice, to prevent mud fever from developing, and to clean the saddle-pad and girth areas. The "grease" and dust in the coat, however, should be left as a natural insulation and protection; this scruff and dust forms a layer which effectively keeps the horse warm and dry. Pastured horses will usually roll and scratch themselves on branches, rocks, or brush, a motion that stimulates the skin and keeps the pores open and functioning. They will also roll in mud, writhing in pleasure; and like the famous mud facials Victorian ladies paid great prices to secure, the mud hardens to absorb and draw out the sweat and impurities from the skin, cleansing the pores while stimulating the circulation of blood.

For stabled and blanketed horses, grooming not only makes them look better; it actually keeps them healthy. The massaging motion of the grooming tools, like the good hearty roll on firm ground, stimulates the glands that lie just beneath the skin to secrete a fluid that can keep hair soft and glossy. At the same time, the massaging motion helps to tone muscles and to stimulate blood circulation, increasing the quantity of blood carried to the coat and bringing with it additional nutrients that make a horse's coat shine.

Stabled horses need more grooming attention and plain hard rubbing than their pastured brothers, and horses about to enter the show ring need still more care, with conscientious attention given to every small detail that can turn a turkey into a triumphant trophy collector.

On the following page is a list of tools needed to do a good, basic grooming for any horse.

Further Reading
The following are recommended by Janet Blevins of Knight Equestrian Books:

A Horse of Your Own by M. A. Stoneridge (Doubleday).
Basic Horse Care by Prince & Collier (Doubleday).
Backyard Horseman by Ron Rude (Mountain Press).
Horse Keeping on Small Acreage by Cherry Hill (Gardenway Publishing).
The Horse, 2nd edition by J. Warren Evans (W. H. Freeman).
Happy Horsemanship by Dorothy Pinch (Simon & Schuster).
Feeding, Grooming and Handling by Jane Kidd (Howell Book House).
Safe Horse Safe Rider by Jesse Haas (Storey).

Mane and Tail Styling*

In one of the books on horses there are two drawings, the first showing a girl clad in clean jeans and blouse confronting a dirt-encrusted horse, the second drawing depicting a clean, shiny, well-groomed show horse standing beside a dirt-encrusted girl. The real joke of the drawings is, it's true! For many horsemen, a quick shower, a brush to their teeth, and a comb through their hair are usually adequate grooming to spend the rest of the day brushing, massaging, combing, clipping, pulling, and wiping horses.

Actually, for most horses, a brush or comb through the mane and tail is all that is necessary to remove caked-in dirt and keep it free of tangles and burrs. In fact, horses pastured even for a few hours during the summer depend on their long, natural manes and tails to swat away the irritating and ever-present flies. Often a herd of horses will line up side to side facing head to tail to head to tail and so on, swatting their neighbor's face in mutual cooperation.

The shape and length of natural manes and tails vary quite a bit with each breed or type. Morgans, for instance, grow manes that reach to the bottom of their thick necks, with a forelock that can touch the tip of their nose and a tail that dusts the ground as they move. Quarter Horses, on the other hand, have naturally thin, short manes and tails that rarely reach the hock. Clydesdales, which do everything in a big way, not only grow abundant manes and tails, they also have long, thick "feathers" on their fetlocks, which are simply brushed and left unclipped.

* This section was written with the assistance of Jamye Peters.

GROOMING EQUIPMENT

Tool	What It Is	Used for	How to Use It
Currycomb	hard rubber, plastic, or metal with serrated edges and a hand strap	to remove excess mud and to loosen matted dirt; to groom horses that have long, thick coats; to clean body brush	use gently in circular strokes; don't use on fine-skinned horses, or horses just clipped, or below knees or hocks
Dandy Brush or Mud Brush	wood block with strong, stiff fibers usually 2 inches long	to remove mud, caked-on dirt and sweat, and sweat marks; to brush mane and tail	vigorous brushing at caked-on dirt; brush in circular motion
Body Brush	usually made of wooden block with nylon, rice-root, or natural bristle	used from head to tail to reach through the skin, massaging and removing dirt and loose hair	brush firmly and vigorously in circular motion
All-Purpose Brush	medium-firm fibers	for removing stable dirt when a thorough cleaning is not needed; for bathing	brush all over in the direction in which the hair lies
Finishing Brush	soft bristles	to lay the horse's coat after grooming and take up dust	brush gently with the lie of the hairs
Sponge	natural or synthetic	to wipe horse's eyes, inside of ears, and nostrils; clean under tail; wipe sheath or udders	dampen sponge and wipe gently
Stable Rubber	soft rag of tightly woven linen or silk	for a final polish to bring out the shine and catch any remaining dust	wipe in direction in which the hair lies
Sweat Scraper	a long metal scoop	to remove excess sweat or water after bathing the horse	hold the side against the horse and slide downward, forcing the water to slide off
Hoof Pick	a hooked implement best made from a stout metal; comes in plastic	to clean out the feet and remove stones and caked-in dirt from the frog	see "How to Clean a Horse's Feet"
Mane Comb	aluminum, hard rubber, or plastic	for combing mane and tail for silky, flowing look	don't use on heavily matted or tangled hairs; tends to break hairs, causing frizzles
Cactus-Cloth Wisp or Burlap	hand-woven tough fiber; woven straw or feed sack	use for hearty massaging; to absorb sweat or rain; to stimulate circulation of blood to skin	apply with elbow grease in circular motion
Hand Clippers or Shears	scissor-action clipper with narrow head; scissor with curved blades	use for trimming and clipping horse's fetlock, mane, and head	clip against the lie of the hair
Power Clippers	electric or battery-powered; various blades	use for trimming or for full clipping of body hairs	for full clip, start with head, work against lie of hair; maintain even pressure to avoid lawnmower stripes

A widely distributed vacuum for stable use, the Decker Curry Vac has a 1.5-horsepower industrial power motor that cleans, blows, dries, and picks up water. The model shown comes with a round-tooth curry nozzle for removing mud and massaging the skin, a saw-tooth curry nozzle for removing dirt, loose hair, and dandruff, a hard-tooth round brush for combing matted hair, and a soft-tooth round brush for blow-drying the coat.

Natural manes and tails suit the majority of horses that hack along trails. But for some owners who have the time and energy to spend grooming their horses, there are a number of reasons to trim, or pull, or braid. Thinning and shortening the mane and tail, for instance, make them easier to clean, since they are less

Hoof Black comes in an applicator bottle similar to shoe polish felt tip types. Its water base formula shines without drying the hoof and it all washes off with soap and water.

likely to tangle in brush or brier, burrs being particularly difficult to remove and capable of causing skin irritations if ignored. We know of one luxuriantly maned horse that returned to the stable each day with a forelock so full of burrs it looked like a 1940s high pompadour hairstyle. Many horsemen pull the hairs near the lock for a neater tail appearance that will not look raggedy even when the horse rubs against a tree, fence, or manger. Other horsemen shear a "bridle path" along the upper portion of the mane to prevent the bridle from becoming entangled in hairs. Roaching or hogging the mane is a sure way to prevent hairs from catching in a wrangler's rope or polo player's mallet. Sometimes specialized grooming greatly enhances the horse's conformation, for example, a horse with a thick neck often looks better in a hogged mane because it makes the neck appear less deep; a thin-necked animal looks better wearing a full mane. Of course, certain breeds have a "look" that can be further exaggerated by grooming, as in the case of the Arabian, normally groomed with a bridle path that emphasizes the graceful arch of the neck and clean throatlatch while at the same time displaying the full, flowing mane that is one of the hallmarks of the breed. Finally, in showing a horse there are often rules or perhaps only recommendations for specialized grooming, and before entering a horse into competition it is a good idea to check the regulations set forth by the horse show or as stated in the *Rule Book* of the American Horse Shows Association.

Following are some of the ways in which the mane and tail can be worn:

Natural: The style worn by most backyard horses and trail horses. Usually the mane grows or is trained to be carried on the right side of the neck, although stock horses will wear their mane on the left side, out of the rope's way. The horse wearing its hair natural should always appear well groomed with the hairs brushed clean, free of tangles, lying flat, smooth, and silky.

Pulled (plucking): The grooming technique preferred for Quarter Horses among others. It is accomplished by pulling a few hairs at a time along the edges of the upper tail to give the tail a neat, slim appearance; pulling longer, wispy hairs from the bottom of the tail so that the hair hangs just above the hock; and pulling long hairs from the mane so that the finished mane is about 4 to 6 inches long.

Banged: The banged tail (never mane) worn by

A good number of grooming aids on the market are intended to improve your horse's appearance, especially when showing. For instance, there are shampoos with moisturizers to soften the hair coat, others with medication to reduce bacterial skin conditions, and others with lanolin to reduce dandruff. Conditioners are available to soften and brighten the coat and some include fly repellents as well. For horses with dull coats due to bleaching from the sun's rays, you can find a sun-screen, often combined with a hair polish that also helps to prevent grass and manure stains. For last-minute grooming touchups, there are sprays that add luster to the coat and make wiping off dust easier. While many of these are not particularly high-ticket items, they are often packaged in small quantities, and when the cost is totaled at the end of the year may be surprisingly expensive to the horse-owner using many of them regularly.

How to Clean a Horse's Feet

Horses like routine, even when it comes to cleaning their feet. If the horse has been handled by one person, then watch to see how he approaches the animal. Most handlers start cleaning the feet by asking for the near (or left) foreleg, then moving to the left rear leg, then to the right foreleg and ending up with the right hind leg. Some horses couldn't care less on which leg you start, while high-strung types may insist you follow procedure to the letter. So after you've determined how to start off on the right foot, here is the method to follow.

Facing the horse's rear, place your shoulder against the horse's shoulder and run your hand nearest the horse gently down the shoulder to the fetlock. Say "feet," or "lift," or "give," or even "come on" and a well-trained horse should lift its foot. If you do not get a response, gently pinch the tendons with your thumb and fingers just above the fetlock and at the same time press your shoulder more firmly against the horse's shoulder. Again give the voice command. Be firm and patient, and eventually even the less well-educated horse will respond to the pressure. When the horse lifts its foot, hold the front of the hoof in the palm of the hand closest to the horse and take the hoof pick in the other hand. Starting from the heel of the foot, pick around the inside of the shoe or, if the horse is unshod, along the rim of the foot. Remove all mud and other matter from the sole of the foot. Then find the two valleys formed by the frog and, always working from the heel toward the toe, clean out these valleys, making certain that no stones remain. By stroking away from you toward the toe you avoid accidentally pushing any foreign matter into the heel of the frog, where it might become embedded. When the frog grooves are clean, gently run the flat edge of the hoof pick over the frog to check for lodged stones, cuts, or bruises and to remove excess mud. Lightly tap the frog with the side of the hoof pick, and if the horse flinches or reacts, check carefully for reasons why. If the frog looks soft and somewhat mushy in texture, lean down and sniff. If what you smell is acidic and foul, you are probably smelling the distinctive odor of thrush, and you must take measures to cure it and to prevent its recurrence. (A discussion of thrush and how to cure it can be found in Chapter 4). Before putting the foot down, check the shoe to be sure it is firmly attached to the wall of the hoof and that there are no loose or missing nails. If a nail has worked its way loose, pull it free before it snaps off, leaving a small piece of metal that could work its way from the wall of the hoof into the bone and cause severe damage. Finally, look at the hoof wall. It should be solid, free of cracks, splits, chips, or rings, the last indicating founder or fever. If the hoof walls are dry, apply a hoof conditioner, and if they continue to worsen, consult your farrier.

The entire process of cleaning a horse's feet should take just minutes. During those minutes, however, experienced horsemen will not only use their hands for picking; they will use all of their senses for observing the condition of the horse's feet and anticipating problems before they occur.

TAIL STYLES

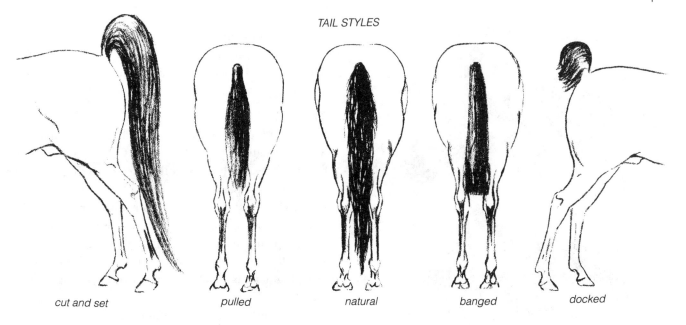

cut and set   pulled   natural   banged   docked

hunter types is the only kind of trimming that requires scissors. The long hair of the tail is chopped straight across the bottom in a blunt cut so that the end falls even with the hock.

Roaching (hogging): This term applies to the mane only. It is normally found on stock horses but required on Three-Gaited Saddle Horses (but not on Five-Gaited ones, which must wear their manes long). Actually, the terms hogging and roaching have slightly different meanings, although they are often used interchangeably. Hogging means that the mane is clipped flat to the neck, while roaching means that the center mane hairs are left slightly longer, forming a herringbone pattern. Whether hogged or roached, a handhold (a wisp of hair at the withers) and the forelock are usually left unclipped.

Bridle Path: This style of mane, commonly worn by certain breeds such as Arabians and Morgans, is becoming popular on other breeds as well. The bridle-path area, from the poll down to about one-third of the mane, is hogged to prevent hairs from tangling in the bridle and to show off the animal's wide, arching neck. The remainder of the mane is worn at its natural length.

Braiding: This specialized hairstyle is used on both the manes and tails of hunters. It is also useful for training any horse's mane to lie flat. A braided mane is normally accompanied by a braided tail and may be required for certain shows. The number of braids tied is sometimes dictated by tradition. In England, for example, no more than eleven braids are acceptable. In

some parts of our country mares are shown in an odd number of braids and geldings in even numbers, while in other regions mares are required to wear even and geldings odd numbers. More often, the number of braids tied into a mane or tail is determined by the horses' conformation. Many small braids make a short neck appear longer, while fewer braids make a long neck appear shorter; and fine tail braids can make a large, heavy rear end look slimmer, while fewer, thicker braids make a thin rear end look wider. Hunters' braids are usually tucked under and finished in a heavy thread of the same color as the horse's coat. Braids on ponies' manes and tails are normally sewn with a bright-colored yarn. Five-Gaited Saddle Horses, Tennessee Walking Horses, harness horses and some ponies are always shown in a braided forelock and three fine, long braids (all with a ribbon in the stable colors woven in) at the beginning of a loose, flowing mane. A utilitarian rather than decorative braid is a style called a "mud tail"—basically a single, thick tail braid that is tucked under and held in place by elastic. This style is used on hunters for wet, muddy days.

Cut and Set: Found only on fine Harness Horses, Three-, and Five-Gaited Saddle Horses, and Hackney Ponies. These animals' tails are surgically cut and then put into a tail set to heal in an artificially upright position. Often the surgical procedure must be repeated several times before the ideal set is attained. Hackneys wear their tails clipped short, about a foot from the root, and Three- and Five-Gaited Saddle Horses wear

MANE STYLES

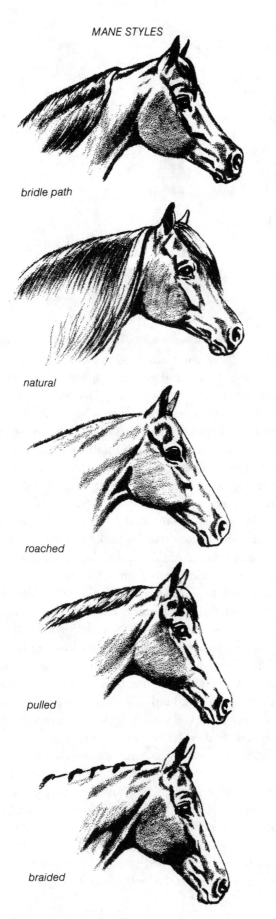

bridle path

natural

roached

pulled

braided

their tails full and long. Owners of these horses will often set the tail in curlers for a fluffed effect, or they may even add a switch (or chignon) for extra fullness.

CLIPPING

Clipping off a horse's winter coat should be considered when the natural protective quality of the long coat interferes with the horse's ability to work efficiently. For those animals pastured throughout most of the year, a long coat is just that—a coat to keep warm. For within the coat's long hairs is a thick layer of grease and dust that helps to insulate the skin against rain, snow, and winds. But for horses that are stabled and worked regularly, that coat is a liability and clipping becomes a necessity.

Most horsemen's first reason for clipping their animals is to improve the appearance, since those with a horse of any quality enjoy riding a well-turned-out mount. The clipped horse is also far easier to clean and keep clean—certainly a plus for any horseman eager to tack up and go. Aside from the cosmetic reasons, taking a clipper to the coat has distinct advantages for the horse. For instance, a shorter coat cools out faster, permitting the sweat to evaporate more quickly and thus keeping the horse's internal temperature level. Removing the excess hair also eliminates dry ends that otherwise dull the coat's finish. And if the horse is to be shown, clipping is essential, since no judge would consider a scruffy, long-haired horse for the blue ribbon, no matter what its breeding or performance. But surely the most important reason to clip a stabled horse is to prevent it from sweating quickly and profusely when being worked, to prevent it from becoming overly fatigued faster, and to quicken the cooling-out process, thereby preventing a propensity to chilling.

Most owners of hot-blooded horses need to clip

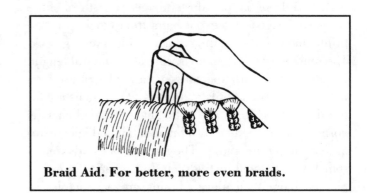

Braid Aid. For better, more even braids.

Trace clip   Hunter clip

their animals only twice a year, usually in late October and again in January. Cold-blooded horses (those with draft breeding in their ancestry) need to be clipped more often; Shetland ponies sometimes need to be clipped as often as twice a month during the winter. How often to clip the horse depends on why you are clipping. If the horse will be traveling on the show circuit and judged on appearance, then regular and frequent clipping will be necessary. On the other hand, hunting or hacking horses may need only the minimum number of clippings. It is a good idea to cease clipping as the horse begins to shed late in the winter, since the clipper is likely not only to remove the dead winter coat but to clip off the tops of the fine summer coat growing in underneath. Trimming that coat may cause

it to grow in with bristled ends, which can make the summer coat shaggy rather than sleek and smooth.

Three basic styles of clips are used on most horses today: the full cut, the hunter clip, and the trace clip. Certainly the full cut is the most attractive and therefore the most popular, although it may take several hours to accomplish. The full clip is easy to describe: all the long hairs except for the mane and tail are cut as close to the skin as possible. Horses that are fully clipped must be blanketed during cool weather, with at least one blanket when indoors and sometimes as many as three blankets when outdoors. In the hunter clip, preferred by many horsemen who hunt or hack, the legs are left unclipped for protection against rough and briered terrain. The rest of the coat is clipped clean,

"In India the practice among native grooms is to hold an earthen pot under the horse or gelding, and behind the mare, so as to catch the urine the moment they see the animal stretch itself out. The same custom is observed in some places on the Continent, where a pot with a long handle is used. I do not like this plan, because horses which are accustomed to it are apt, if the groom does not hold the vessel for them, to abstain from staling for a long time."

M. HORACE HAYES, F.R.C.V.S.
Stable Management and Exercise, 1900
Sixth edition revised by
Colonel Sir Andrew Horsbrugh-Porter
Arco Publishing Co., Inc., 1969

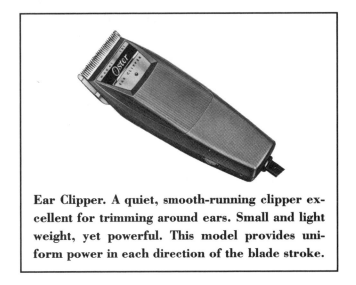

Ear Clipper. A quiet, smooth-running clipper excellent for trimming around ears. Small and light weight, yet powerful. This model provides uniform power in each direction of the blade stroke.

except, occasionally, that the saddle-pad area is left long. When not being used, hunter-clipped horses must be blanketed in cool weather. The trace clip is less frequently seen, since it is unacceptable for show animals and not especially attractive, but a horse clipped in such a way need not be blanketed—a decided advantage, saving both labor and clothing. In the trace clip, hair is removed from the areas of the body where the horse sweats most profusely: from under the neck, under the chest and belly, across the arm and stifle, along the buttock, and up around the dock. The trace clip is fine for horses that are hunted or hacked during the winter, and it is preferable to not clipping at all when you're trying to groom those areas where mud and manure tend to cling most tenaciously.

Before electric clippers were available, horsemen would clip their animals with razors (a time-consuming job), singe the long hairs with a candle or gas lamp (both time-consuming and dangerous), or use hand-cranked clippers. Today, wide head clippers are available in electric, battery-powered, and manual styles with a variety of blades, each designed to best handle a particular part of the horse's anatomy.

Horseshoeing

By JERRY TRAPANI

All horse owners and riders know—or should know—why horses need shoes. The primary reason is to protect their feet. Hooves are hard and strong, but not strong enough to withstand the wear and tear of rough, unyielding terrain and the work demanded by riding or driving. Another reason for shoeing is corrective. Many hoof and foot problems can be ameliorated, if not cured, by blacksmiths.

The word "blacksmith," by the way, means a worker in iron, one of the "black" metals (tin, on the other hand, is a "white" metal). Another name for my profession is "farrier," from *fer,* the French word for iron. Iron horseshoes, however, were not always used. The first shoes were made of leather, strapped like boots over the feet. They didn't last very long. Egyptians were the first to nail shoes to hooves: first wooden footware, then shoes made of iron.

What, then, does a blacksmith do when he pays his periodic call? After removing worn-down shoes, he

must make sure the horse's foot is properly trimmed and balanced. Yes, balanced, just as a car's tires are. A horse that isn't standing straight and square will be subject to strains all the way up its leg. Sometimes imbalance can so affect a horse's stride that it will appear to be lame or interfere in its action.

As I trim a hoof, I cut away the dead sole and clean the frog. Only a small amount of frog is trimmed, since that fleshy part of the foot is very important to the animal's performance. The frog pumps blood throughout the foot and acts as both a shock absorber and a lever to cushion and spread the foot at each stride. In that regard, a foot should never be allowed to dry out and lose this important flexibility.

As I go about this process, I remove loose tissue and overlaps to prevent dirt and manure from being trapped in the foot. Then the wall is cut down until it is level, to eliminate hills and valleys so that the foot rests flush on the ground. The surface is smoothed with a rasp.

I ask myself several questions during this process. How should the horse stand on the ground? Is its toe too long? Are its heels too high? Are the forefeet and the hind feet matched? A well-trimmed foot needs to by symmetrical and level, and balance is determined by the angle of the foot. A straight line drawn from the point of the shoulder through the knee to the center of the foot is what a well-conformed horse should show. When a heel is too low, a horse will stand "in front of itself." Heels too high and toes too short force an animal to stand "under itself." These conformations will also affect the foot in action. A low-heeled foot tends to move close to the ground, inviting stumbling, while a high-heeled foot makes for short, choppy strides.

A horse's foot must also be balanced laterally. As viewed from the front or rear, the animal should stand straight, neither toed in nor toed out. I recommend starting early to prevent these problems. A foal's feet grow incredibly fast and need to be trimmed at least every three weeks. If a foal's feet present problems, it's fairly easy to correct them at this stage, since bones and joints are not fully developed.

A warning sign of a poorly shod horse is contracted heels. Chronic contracted heels are a conformation fault, but in the majority of cases, the condition is created by humans. Shoes that are too tight won't allow feet to expand. A foot trimmed too low at the toes, with heels left too high, will prevent weight from being

HOOF

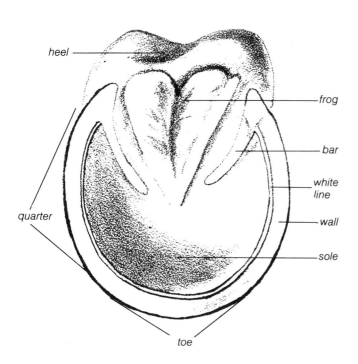

heel

frog

bar

white
line

quarter

wall

sole

toe

carried on the frog. The result will be contracted heels.

Now comes the matter of the kind of shoes your horse should wear. Human activities call for a variety of footgear, from boots and dress shoes to sneakers and bedroom slippers. Depending on what your horse will be asked to do, durability and comfort are equally important criteria. Shoes won't turn a loser into a winner, but they will enable a horse to give its best possible performance. For example, imagine two horses in a hunter class that are equal in performance, manners, and conformation. As the judge asks them to jog in hand, he sees that one is a superb mover, while the other lacks the first's brilliance. Perhaps there's too little knee action—the horse not reaching out as it should. Perhaps it might be a wrong combination of horseshoes. The owner should know that there's a wide range from which to choose.

Jumpers need a special shoe for their job, which includes quick turns, bursts of speed, and the impact of landing off big fences. Shoes must be heavy enough to prevent slipping or wilting, yet light enough not to restrict or tire the animal. Most jumpers wear either steel or aluminum wide-webbed shoes with holes for screw-in caulks, which can be easily changed according to the footing condition of the arena.

Shoeing a show hunter aims at affording graceful

movement. Wide aluminum shoes without caulks are most usual. Hind shoes are flat so that the horse will move as naturally as possible.

A field hunter needs more substantial shoes, since its work includes a variety of terrain ranging from mud to unyielding roads. Field-hunter shoes need welded-on borium studs. Borium is an extremely hard metal; when applied, the studs form small crystals that act like snow tires for grip. These horses are often fitted with pads under their front shoes to protect against stones and other cross-country hazards.

Aluminum shoes used by jumpers and hunters should not be confused with the racing plates worn by racehorses. Those are much more fragile and have a toe grab to enable the horse to dig into a track's surface. If such spikes were used on jumping horses, landing on them would produce leg injuries.

Jumpers and hunters wear aluminum shoes that are more substantial, up to $3/8$" thick and $1^{1}/_{4}$" wide (aluminum absorbs concussion better than steel does).

Polo and barrel-racing horses wear rimmed and relatively lightweight shoes. When the rim fills, the friction of dirt against dirt provides an excellent grip.

Gaited and Walking Horses, with their very long toes, have pads inserted in their heavy shoes to increase their high-stepping action.

Draft horses are able to carry weight both behind and below, so they wear shoes that are relatively heavy and resilient.

Distance and endurance horses that travel over varied and demanding terrain need lightweight protection and durability in their footwear. An alloy or lightweight steel work well.

Reining horses require a very wide, smooth shoe on their hind feet to allow a long and smooth sliding stop.

Now I'd like to add a few words about the care and treatment of blacksmiths. We're a rare breed, in the sense that there are more horse owners than farriers, so we can afford to be influenced by how you people treat us. We're busy, so make appointments well in advance. Set up a schedule, whether every six weeks or two months and we'll be there on time. Since our job shouldn't include racing around a field to help you catch a recalcitrant horse, please be sure our client (equine variety) is ready to be treated. Have a clean, dry area for us to work in: there's nothing worse than having to shoe a horse under pouring rain or freezing to death. We'd like your assistance to hold the animal and

HORSESHOES

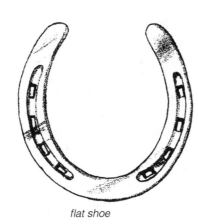

flat shoe

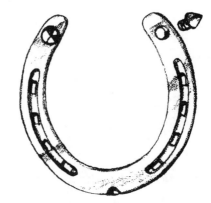

screw-in calks

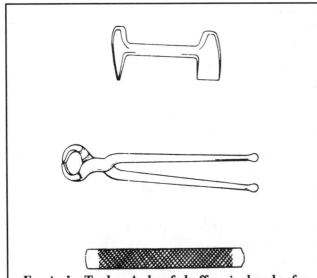

heels

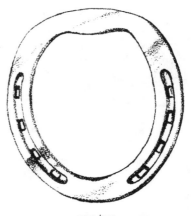

egg bar

Farrier's Tools: A hoof buffer is handy for clinching nails in removal of shoes. A shoe puller can not only pull shoes but cut nails as well. A rasp files rough edges.

keep it calm. Blacksmiths regard with favor a horse that submits to being handled, an attitude you can facilitate by examining its hooves before and after riding and by using a hoof pick to remove small rocks and other foreign matter.

Although I don't recommend that anyone but the most experienced horseman try to shoe his own horses, there are a few steps you can take in the event your horse has a loose shoe. Remove the shoe if it's still attached to the hoof, using a pair of shoe pullers. First file the remaining clinch smooth with a farrier's rasp; then carefully pull off the shoe. Start at the heel and work forward. Always pull toward the center of the foot; pulling toward the outside may rip the hoof's walls. Then rasp the edges of the hoof to prevent the chance of its splitting. If your horse has torn its foot, apply a poultice and wrap the foot in a burlap bag, leaving it on until professional assistance is available. It goes without saying—but I'll say it anyway—that a shoeless horse shouldn't be worked.

———— 1892 ————

Ice Creepers for Horses,

Sand cracks: These are sometimes described by their placement (a toe, quarter, or bar crack) and usually are caused by dry and brittle hoofs. For a mild crack, the farrier can cut a half-moon in the hoof wall at the base of the crack and then use a regular shoe with clips. In addition, he may use a hot iron to burn ridge lines horizontally over the crack to relieve stress. Depending on how far the crack has advanced up the hoof wall it may take as much as a full year to grow out. For severe cracks, the farrier will use the same methods mentioned and, in addition, will shoe the horse with a bar shoe.

Thrush: For horses that develop thrush on their frogs, the farrier can cut out the infected area and treat it with a drying agent such as Kopertox.

Oats—a grain which in England is generally given to horses, but in Scotland supports the people.
SAMUEL JOHNSON, LD.D.
Dictionary of the English Language

Earlier editions of *The Whole Horse Catalog* contained a list of farrier schools. Because the lifespan of many such institutions is short, we now recommend as a good source of information (including the names and addresses of schools the organization recognizes) the American Farriers Association, 4059 Iron Works Pike, Lexington, KY 40511-8434. (606) 233-7411. Fax: (606) 231-7862.

Two Websites on the subject can be reached at www.horseshoes.com (lots of product information, articles, and a chat room), and www.hoofcare.com.

So You Want To Be a Blacksmith

——— Ω ———

by JERRY TRAPANI

A LOT OF PEOPLE—young boys, usually—tell me, when they see me working, that they would like to be farriers too. I always ask them why. Is it for the money? Is it because you can be your own boss? Or is it because you care about craftsmanship and take pleasure in a job well done? I always hope it is for the last reason, although I have to admit that there are many people in the horseshoeing trade because they can make a decent living without the hassle of getting a license or permit and without laying out tremendous amounts of capital.

Horseshoeing is one of the few businesses in which you can get started for only a few hundred dollars. Some people shoe on a part-time basis while holding other jobs. In several states, including New York, there is no regulatory agency governing farriers. Anyone who wants to can read a book or two, buy some tools, and go out and try to shoe horses.

However, if you are serious about a career in this field, there is much more to it than that. Many schools in this country offer courses in shoeing or even specialize in it. Check through horse publications; write the Veterans Administration (if you qualify), or your county extension office. (Most schools today are accredited, but the Veterans Administration schools are usually the most reliable ones.) Compile a list of likely-looking schools, then check into them. Write to see if any of their graduates work in your area; either write to or visit a few of them. If possible, go to the school yourself.

The old apprentice tradition has pretty much disappeared now, mainly because the horseshoer has taken to the road to call on his customers rather than running a forge in town where people bring their horses. In the old shops, there were always tasks to be done, so that boys could get jobs and work their way up the ladder. Occasionally, you can find a farrier now who does hire a regular helper. Many states have organizations or associations of professional farriers, and you may get a lead on a job through one of those groups.

Although many tack shops carry some equipment for farriers, most professionals buy their tools from wholesale farrier suppliers. Aside from a truck, a forge, and an anvil—the most expensive items—a farrier will need in his basic bag of tricks at least the following: a set of shoe pullers, a set of hoof nippers, two knives (wide-blade and narrow-blade), two rasps (one for the foot and one for finishing), a driving hammer, a clinch block, a clinching tool, a farrier's apron, fire tongs, a ball-peen hammer, and a rounding hammer, as well as assorted shoes and nails.

The work itself is hard, but very rewarding. You can take a great deal of pride in the craft, but there are many problems you will be called upon to solve, not all of them having to do with horses' feet. In some cases you may be the closest thing to a veterinarian the horses will ever see. In the very old days, veterinary medicine began in blacksmith shops, since sick and lame animals were often taken there for complete tune-ups. Today life is somewhat easier, especially now that most shoes come ready-made and one needs only to trim the foot properly, adjust the shoe, and then nail it on. That sounds easy enough, and it looks easy when a professional does the job. But many inexperienced people who buy the equipment and go into business do not realize until they have been at it for a short while that shoeing horses is hardly a simple matter. Even though shoes are ready-made, there is a real art to choosing the right one and to trimming the foot in the best way. Time is the best teacher, but it helps to start out on the right foot and get as much knowledge as you can at the outset. Ω

You and Your Farrier

—————— ∩ ——————

by RICHARD MASSIMI

OVER YEARS OF HORSE-owning a special relationship will develop between you and your farrier. Good farriers have the ability to get along with people and with horses, referring to the latter as their "clients." Often much in demand, like any other businessman they have tight schedules, so once you have found a farrier you like it is advisable to make regular appointments for trimming and shoeing.

What You Can Expect from Your Farrier:

* For regularly scheduled appointments, expect the farrier to be there the day of the appointment and within several hours of the agreed time.
* Expect shoes to last about six to eight weeks, depending on your horse's history of shoeing and use. If your horse loses a shoe between visits many farriers will re-shoe without charging extra.
* Expect the farrier to examine the horse's shoes on each visit and recommend when worn shoes should be replaced. Even a shoe that does not appear worn may have enlarged nail holes that will cause the shoe to loosen prematurely. Many farriers will use a small nail in new shoes and then use progressively larger nails as the holes widen. This is an accepted practice to a point, for most horses up to a size six nail. Larger nails can cause splitting of the hoof wall and should be avoided.
* Expect the farrier, particularly on the first visit, to inspect your horse's feet carefully, analyze the way the horse stands and its flight pattern, and assess any need for corrective shoeing. The owner should also discuss any problems he or she has noticed before the farrier goes to work.
* If your horse is disobedient, you can expect the farrier to take mild disciplinary action. (See box on page 91 for types of acceptable disciplines.)
* After the farrier has shod a horse that was free of problems, expect the horse to move freely at all gaits, to pick up its feet without stumbling, to have shoes that fit tightly, to stand straight-legged when squared, and to maintain an elastic frog.

What Your Farrier Expects from You:

* If this is the first visit for the farrier, he expects the owner or an experienced horseperson to be present and to know about the horse's particular shoeing needs.
* Farriers appreciate owners who schedule regular appointments at six- to eight-week intervals. They are not eager to be called to shoe a horse that has developed hoof problems because of neglect.
* They appreciate owners who make appointments in advance and are understanding of their tight schedules.
* Have a clean place to work and level ground on which to stand the horse. Do not expect a farrier to enjoy working while standing in a stall filled with manure or in a muddy paddock.
* Working on a clean horse is also welcome. If your horse's legs are matted with mud or manure, wash them down and dry them well before the farrier arrives. And, while you're at it, you'd be doing everyone a favor to clean the entire animal, not just the parts the farrier will be working on.
* Have the horse caught, haltered, and waiting in a stall or paddock before the farrier arrives.
* Have cross ties available or, if your horse balks at them, a person who can hold the horse while the farrier is working.
* Try to keep dogs out of the farrier's way. Many dogs love to eat hoof trimmings and will literally get underfoot.
* The farrier expects your horse to be trained to stand quietly and to lift its foot on command.
* Be prepared to show your horse on a lead at the walk and trot so the farrier may evaluate flight patterns and possible corrective shoeing needs.
* Pay your bill on time. ∩

Custom-Fitting Horseshoes

by RICHARD MASSIMI,
edited by JERRY TRAPANI

WITHIN THE RANGE OF normal shoeing, some types of shoes enhance the horse's natural ability while others correct problems.

Once you and your farrier have settled on the type of shoe that best suits your horse, there are several options with regard to modifications.

The most commonly used shoe is the plain, flat, fullered shoe. This shoe encourages good balance and gives good traction. For those horses that go up and down hills, a heeled shoe tends to give a better grip, especially while descending. However, since most horses are naturally more secure going uphill, caulks often prove to be an unnecessary addition.

If your horse is frequently worked on roads or, in winter, on ice and snow, adding borium or studs will give better traction than does a plain shoe.

For horses that are heavy on the forehand, your farrier may advise rolled toes on the front shoes. Horses that tend to "work" their hind feet may need side clips. Both toe and side clips keep the shoe from shifting or sliding by securing the shoe to the hoof wall (clips also reduce wear on nail holes in both the shoe and the hoof wall).

Pads come in several styles. Those that cover the entire bottom of the hoof are used on show horses to protect them against cuts. U-shaped rim pads leave the sole and frog uncovered; they help lessen the severe impact that fast riding on hard surfaces may have on feet and legs.

Corrective shoeing

Farriers whose expertise includes corrective shoeing should advise the horse owner about which steps would be appropriate and useful. Among the problems that corrective shoeing may be able to correct or cure are:

- Navicular disease: Although a farrier cannot cure the disease, proper trimming and shoeing may make the horse usable. The farrier will trim the hoof wall and sole to make them lower at the toe, then use degree pads (which are thicker at the heel) under an egg-bar shoe. The combination of the slope and the shoe's bar across the heel elevates the heel to take pressure off the navicular bones.
- Contracted heels: A problem often created by shoes that are too small, lack of regular trimming, or severe drying, contracted heels occur when the frog dries out. Elasticity is lost and, with it, the ability to take pressure. One form of correction is a beveled heart-egg-bar shoe that puts pressure on the frog and, over time, spreads the heels. If the problem is a dry frog, the farrier will apply hoof dressing, and perhaps a full pad with packing treated with a moisturizer such as pine tar, oakum, or a product called *Hoof Packing*.
- Founder: Although a farrier cannot cure this disease, the use of a heart-bar or egg-heart-bar shoe to support the coffin bone will make the horse more comfortable. Ω

Disciplinary Methods Common to Farriers

———————— ∩ ————————

by RICHARD MASSIMI

FROM THE FIRST WEEKS of a foal's life, it should be taught to stand while held and to calmly pick up its feet. Foals and mature horses can become fidgety while being shod and the farrier should patiently encourage the horse to remain quiet. However, there may be a point at which the farrier is put into a dangerous position and needs to take disciplinary action. Following are some of the problems farriers encounter and the generally accepted steps they may take.

Rearing

Place a chain or rope shank through the halter rings and around the nose, pulling in jerking motions until the horse stands quietly; have the handler apply a twitch.

Backing Up

Back the horse into a corner and shoe it there.

Kicking

Have the handler apply a twitch; use a hobble or leather strap around the hind pastern and secure the leg by means of a short rope.

Striking

Have the handler apply a twitch; tie front leg with a hobble or leather strap.

A farrier should never hit a horse with tools, although sometimes striking a horse with the hand will settle the animal. Occasionally a horse will give one farrier a hard time and be a perfect angel for another. If this is the case, change farriers. But if you find your horse is regularly difficult to shoe, seek help from a professional trainer. ∩

Do-It-Yourself Emergency Shoe Repair

———————— ∩ ————————

by RICHARD MASSIMI

A CLICKING SHOE, LOOSE nails, or a missing shoe are not uncommon happenings and, eventually, most horse owners will be faced with these problems. When you first notice a loose shoe, call your farrier and make an appointment for a re-set. It is best to wait for your farrier to arrive before taking matters into your own hands. Simply put the horse in its stall or paddock and wait. However, if your farrier can't come within a few days, here are some measures you can take.

If the problem is a matter of a loose nail, don't do anything. If you notice that one or two nails are sticking out of the bottom of the shoe, you can pull the nails out from the bottom using a shoe puller or pliers.

If the shoe is loose, you can hammer the nail heads and then use clinchers, placing the flat surface on the nail head and the curved part on the hoof wall over the clinch, squeezing to tighten.

If the shoe is flopping to the point that it will soon fall off by itself, then remove the shoe. To do this, it is *essential* that you first rasp or cut the clinches along the hoof wall. With a rasp, work the rough side across the clinch until it is gone or cut the clinch with the edge of a nail cutter or by hammering down on the clinch with a shoe buffer. Once the clinch is gone, use a shoe puller, starting at the outside heel and then the inside heel, pulling each nail loose as you work toward the toe and pulling the toe nails last. If the hoof is cracked or ragged, do not attempt to rasp it smooth yourself but keep the horse in its stall and wait for the farrier.

Duct tape can be used safely and easily to secure or protect the hoof. To secure a loose shoe, pull off or tamp down any loose nails, then wrap several layers of duct tape in a figure-eight pattern around the hoof. If a shoe has already come off and the foot is tender, place a four-inch-square gauze sponge over the sole and wall border and then wrap with duct tape. The horse can then be let out of his stall until the farrier arrives.

Generally, the rule about riding a horse with a missing shoe is, don't. However, if you won't be working the horse at fast gaits or where top performance is required you can ride if you use an Easyboot over the shoeless foot. Easyboots slip over the hoof and are held by cables that encircle the hoof wall. They are relatively secure when properly fitted. If the missing shoe is a rear one, you can pull the other shoe so that the horse stands evenly but then only work the horse lightly on grass or soft dirt, never on a hard surface. Do not attempt to use a horse that is barefoot in front. ∩

This is the way the Easyboot should look when properly fitted. The dotted line indicates where the boot trims down. This may be necessary to prevent any chafing above the hairline. Easyboots are something every horseman should know about. Made of urethane, they slip on the foot (even over metal shoes) and are useful for parades, shipping, medication, and riding. With Easyboots, the horse can go barefoot in pasture and shod under tack. The boot gives protection, traction, and cushioning on hard pavement and rocks; it prevents the horse from sliding on slippery streets; it prevents "snowballing" and provides traction on snow and ice; and it protects the sole and frog. Easyboots, so the manufacturer claims, "outwear metal shoes by over a three-to-one ratio." And the claims go on: Easyboots can prevent or alleviate hoof cracks, contracted heels, corns, navicular disease, thrush, excessive hoof wear, and impact-caused hoof and leg injuries, and they are also useful for treating nail punctures, abscesses, and other hoof wounds. Available in natural, black, red, and blue in widths from 4 to $5^1/_4$ inches, with pony sizes and extra-large sizes available by special order.

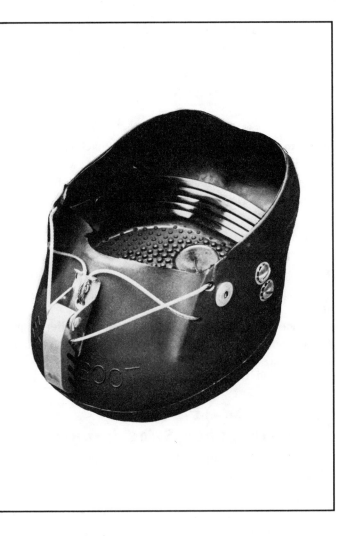

chapter 4

Horse Health

No one would dispute the statement that the best horse is the sound horse, yet it is surprising how little is known by the average horse owner about equine health. Too often we rely on the once-a-year visit of the veterinarian, or his help in emergencies, to keep our horses in working order, but the old saying "An ounce of prevention is worth a pound of cure" is as true for horses as it is for people. We cannot stress enough the

importance of good management, sensible nutrition, and regular veterinary care in preventing illness. We must also emphasize the necessity for each horse owner to learn as much as possible about equine health to catch trouble before it becomes serious and to know about the handling of animals in distress before the veterinarian arrives. This chapter will deal not only with aspects of good management as they apply specifically to health, but also with various preventive measures that the owner can and should take on a regular basis. Your veterinarian will be of invaluable help in establishing good programs and assisting in serious problems, but it is up to the individual to be sure that he is fully equipped with information, in the form of good references and well-kept records, and with various items that can be used in examining, restraining, and medicating animals at home. See the sample chart on page 96 and adapt a similar record for each horse you own.

Soundness in Horses

The first step in learning about equine health is to determine what are the normal signs in a healthy horse. The following section will act as a guide, but keep in mind that each horse can vary a bit from the norm, depending on its conformation, the way in which it is used,

and its general condition. Therefore, it is always best to examine your own horse on a regular basis, daily if possible during the grooming session, and make notes of its individual peculiarities—temperature and other vital signs, appetite, and behavior. Pick a time when the horse has been at rest (exercise can increase the normal rates of respiration and pulse) and set up a routine. The veterinarian will benefit from your records and from the way in which the horse accepts the examination procedure. And you will be able to tell at a glance when something is amiss and take steps to prevent anything serious from developing. (See the section beginning on page 114 for first-aid remedies.)

HOW TO EXAMINE A HORSE

Respiration

Using a clock with a second hand, count how many times the horse's flanks rise and fall in 30 seconds. Double the number to find the respiration rate per minute. Note whether the breathing is regular or not. In a horse at rest, the frequency should be between 8 and 16 breaths a minute; the younger the horse, the greater the rate (up to 30 a minute for foals). If the horse is lying down, the rate will be higher than normal. Increased rates may also be caused by exercise, stress, excitement, high temperature, or a health problem.

Temperature

Coat a rectal thermometer with a lubricating jelly and shake it down to below 96 degrees; insert it into the horse's rectum, rotating it gently, and leave it in place for at least one minute. To avoid losing the thermometer, either in the horse or in the bedding, tie a string to it with a clip that may be attached to the horse's tail. Normal temperature for an adult horse can range from 100.4 degrees to 100.8 degrees; a foal's normal temperature is 99.5 to 101.5 degrees. Temperatures may vary according to time of day (the highest is in late afternoon), sex (mares are usually lower than horses except when in heat, when the temperature may be 2 degrees above normal), age (young and old horses may be 1 degree higher than others), exercise, stress, environmental temperature, and disease. Thoroughbreds have higher temperatures than most other breeds, and violent exercise in hot weather can increase temperature 4 or 5 degrees. Well-fed horses have higher temperatures than poorly fed ones.

Pulse

Using a watch with the second hand, feel for the horse's pulse at one of the major arteries—either in the girth area behind the elbow or underneath the lower jaw, a little in front of the fleshy region of the cheek. Normal pulse for an adult horse at rest is 30 to 40 beats a minute, though variations may be normal depending on the horse's age, sex, and size (the smaller and younger, the higher the rate—foals having a range of 50 to 70 beats a minute), and the climate and stress mentioned above. Note any irregularities in the beat

This heavy-duty thermometer, 5 inches long, has a stubby tip and a ring top to which a string may be attached. Thermometers of this type are usually made of glass, although more expensive metal ones are also available. Electronic digital thermometers produce a reading in less than 45 seconds with no risk of broken glass. Special skin thermometers are also made for diagnosing areas of inflammation. The stainless steel back is placed in contact with the skin and the dial top registers temperature (between 70 and 110 degrees F.).

and mention them when the veterinarian visits next, unless the abnormality is accompanied by other abnormal signs, in which case a special call might be in order.

Eyes and Nose

Although a small amount of clear discharge from either eyes or nose is perfectly normal, any sign of pus, heavy mucus, or blood should be considered an indicator of possible trouble. The mucous membranes inside the nostrils and the eyelid lining should be pink, the same color as the gums (nostril lining will be bright red after exercise), and the third eyelid (inside corner of the eye) should be white to pink with visible blood vessels. Using a penlight, examine the pupils of the eyes, which should constrict within 1 to 2 seconds. Note any abnormal conditions such as cloudiness or discoloration in the cornea, which overlies the iris and pupil, or spots that may be in the center of the pupil—all of which are abnormal.

Ears

Check for any swelling or heat at the base of the ears. Look for any irritation or growth inside the area if the horse is unusually sensitive in that area. Ear mites are not uncommon and may give rise to secondary infections without treatment. Using your penlight, check for unusual reddening, bleeding, or other abnormalities.

Teeth

Familiarize yourself with the tooth structure of horses (see section on aging horses by teeth on page 21), and periodically check the horse's mouth for any problems, such as broken teeth, irregular growth, or sharp edges and points that may need filing. Gums should be pink, not whitish or yellow, and the horse's breath should smell sweet.

Neck and Back

As you groom, check for any swelling or tenderness, sores, or scars that may be signs of old sores caused by saddles or harness. Swollen glands and lymph nodes can be detected by feeling in the throatlatch region for signs of heat or sensitivity when pressure is applied. Look also for any signs of external parasites, such as ringworm, botfly eggs, and skin disorders, as well as abscesses, ulcerations, scaliness, loss of hair, and other abnormalities. The coat (except in winter) should be fine, smooth, and glossy, and the skin relatively soft and resilient. A dry coat or a hard skin may indicate nutritional deficiency, the presence of internal parasites, or disease. Check under the tail for swellings or lumps in the anal and vulvar region; if the animal has been rubbing its tail, indicating possible parasites, the hair in this area will be worn. Check the overall condition of the horse's barrel area; if ribs, backbone, and hip bones are at all prominent, the animal may not be getting sufficient rations.

Abdomen

If the horse is particularly sensitive in its nether region and is not calmed by regular handling or soothing noises, be alert for swellings, lesions, or sores of any sort. A horse suffering from abdominal pain will often look around at its sides or kick up. Any continued behavior like this (more than an hour) should be reported immediately to the vet.

Legs

Run your hands carefully over all parts of the legs and feet, watching for any excessive heat, pulse, or swelling. If you find some irregularity in one leg, check the other side for symmetrical similarities. Become familiar with common ailments, such as splints, bog spavin, and capped hocks, and ask the vet to recommend suitable treatment. (See pages 119–126 for detailed information about these conditions.) Flex the horse's legs at each joint to check for any sensitivity or restricted movement—signs of developing lameness; then note the feet for cracks, wounds, and thrush (which can also be detected by smell). See that the feet are cleanly and evenly trimmed and that the shoes are in place and evenly worn.

Stool and Urine

When you clean the horse's stall, note the condition of the bedding for any unusual coloration or texture. Urine is light yellow in color and a bit cloudy; a horse normally excretes between four and seven quarts of urine a day, five or more times. A horse moves its bowels, or makes manure as some like to put it, anywhere from four to eight times daily. Normal droppings are brown, mucus-free, and firm in texture. Whole grains visible in manure will indicate a digestive problem. Sometimes you may notice a looser, somewhat green stool after a horse has been turned out to graze for the first time in the spring. This is not necessarily serious, but if diarrhea continues, call the vet. Incontinence or retention of urine or droppings may indicate the presence of a disease process. If the vet wishes to examine a stool or urine sample, or if you feel that an examination is indicated (by other symptoms of internal parasites), place samples in clean plastic containers with tight lids and deliver them fresh to his office, or store temporarily in the refrigerator. Mark the containers carefully with the name of the horse and the date to avoid confusion to the vet and unpleasant surprises for the rest of the family. While you are checking the stall, look at the salt block and note whether the wood of the stall has been chewed. If so, the horse may be overly nervous or bored, evidenced by wind sucking or cribbing.

Behavior

Since each horse has its own personality, every owner should become aware of normal behavior so that irregular activity can be noted as a sign of something amiss. A sudden display of bad temper may be the result of pain, not vice, and any change in normal eating habits may indicate a serious problem. When you are using the horse, keep an eye out for any signs of unusual movement—shying, lameness, or uneven gaits. Have someone else ride or lead the horse at the trot so that you can inspect its movement. Any deviation from symmetrical motion or an irregular gait should be sufficient reason for further investigation. (See page 122 for a detailed explanation of lameness diagnosis.) Heaving, or heavy breathing, after exercise is not normal in the conditioned horse, and coughing fits may indicate respiratory disease. If a horse's shoes have been unevenly worn, keep a watch for interfering hooves or cross firing when the animal is moving, and report it to your blacksmith when he next visits.

Routine Preventive Care

Once you know what is normal for your horse and have set down records for your veterinarian to check, you can begin to establish regular routines for care, based on good management, sound nutrition, and regular veterinary attention. Horses are creatures of habit, and any dramatic change in routine can cause stress and

Sample Health Chart

Animal's name: _____ Sire: _____

Birthdate and place: _____ Dam: _____

Breeder (or previous owner): _____ Date purchased: _____

Color and markings: _____

Height at the withers: _____

Normal weight: _____

Normal respiration (at rest): _____

Normal pulse (at rest): _____

Normal estrous cycle (for mares): _____

Ration in hay: _____ Pasture (number of months): _____

Ration in grain: _____ Feed supplier: _____

Vitamin/mineral/protein supplements: _____

Farrier (name, address, dates of visits, and notes about unusual hoof problems, corrective shoeing, and/or treatments): _____

Worming Program (dates and medication used; how dosed): _____

Medical history (illnesses, accidents, treatments, and dates; medications used and dosages; special notes about behavioral peculiarities and whether tranquilizers are necessary for examination): _____

Inoculations (dates and vaccinations used): _____

Coggins Test (dates): _____

Breeding history (gelded when; bred when, with names of mates and get): ____

Name and telephone number of veterinarian: _____

Emergency vets (names and telephone numbers): _____

even illness, so one should take care to see that routines, once set up, are adhered to with great consistency.

STABLE MANAGEMENT

One of the most effective ways to prevent trouble is to see that the stable in which a horse or horses are kept is run efficiently. The chapter on stable management contains the basic information about routines and equipment that make up any good stable-management program, but we would like to make special note here

> "Horses should be washed with warm water which has been laced with some sort of body wash containing a little oil and only when they are hot. A horse should be sweating before you wash him. If a horse comes in and he's just a little sticky under a saddle or at the girth, wipe him with a damp sponge but don't automatically wash him. It's the surest way to kill a coat I know."
> From "J. Arthur Reynolds: Showing on the Line"
> Practical Horseman, *June 1976*

of routines that should be developed for good health care.

Cleaning

We have already mentioned the advisability of regular examinations during the usual grooming and stall-cleaning sessions. Any knowledgeable owner is already aware of the beneficial effects of a good cleaning program for both horse and surroundings—not only for appearance but also for the sake of health. Skin and coat will be kept healthy and glossy by strong, vigorous grooming, which helps stimulate circulation of the blood and removes excess dirt and oils that may attract flies, lice, and other external parasites. Special coat and hoof dressings improve appearance, though their regular use is not recommended without a vet's supervision, since poor coat and dry hooves may be symptomatic of ill health; the dressings may serve cosmetically, but they do not cure the underlying problem. Hoof dressings, for instance, help to retain moisture in the hoof, but they will not provide it; horses bedded on dry wood chips, sawdust, or shavings must be given extra moisture through the use of soaking swabs, or their hooves will become dried out. Poor skin or coat condition may be caused by internal parasites (worms) or a nutritional deficiency, and no amount of cleaning or special dressing can improve the situation on any permanent basis. Regular cleaning of the stall and pasture area is also essential to health, not just to improve the pleasantness of the environment but also to help eliminate parasites and the possibility of diseases, such as thrush, caused by the presence in the cleft of the frog of moist, decomposing organic material. Fresh bedding and daily hoof cleaning should prevent this condition; in fact, we will even go so far as to say that thrush should never be present in any self-respecting horse owner's stable.

Feeding

A good feeding program should be established with the help of the veterinarian, who will know the nutritional requirements of the individual horse, based on weight, age, general condition, and use. (See pages 61–65 for detailed information about nutrition in horses.) The selection, purchase, and feeding of hay and grains are an integral part of preventive medicine. Check all supplies as they are delivered, and again before feeding, to be sure that weight and quality are controlled. See that feed is given under hygienic circumstances: grain and water should be fed in clean containers, and hay should—if possible—be presented away from soiled bedding, to avoid recycling parasites. Many people believe that hay should be placed on the floor of the stall. This enables the horse to eat in a more natural way and reduces the risk of irritation from dust. Nevertheless, ingestion of bedding materials and the parasites present in manure is always a risk with this kind of feeding, and good hay, properly cured and stored, should be free of dust and other foreign particles. If horses are allowed to graze, the pasture should be kept clean, with regular removal of feces, although pasture rotation (at least every two months) is more practical. Harrowing and liming pastureland after rotation are also beneficial, especially if the ground is naturally moist. (Research has shown that wet pastureland is far more likely to harbor parasites than dry land, and that warmer regions are worse than cold ones.) Poisonous plants should be avoided (see page 69) or removed from pastureland, and good, nutritious grass should be available, with fertilization and replanting programs undertaken on a regular basis. Naturally grazing horses will nibble as they move around, getting exercise and keeping busy as they take in nourishment. Horses that are confined to the stall are obviously members of the same species and deserve special attention to keep them fit and occupied. Several feedings a day are superior to one or two feedings, and constant access to hay and water will prevent the animal's developing nervous habits out of boredom. Overfeeding is as dangerous as underfeeding, however, so be sure to keep close track of the amount of food an animal takes in, and see that the horse is worked accordingly. Heavily worked animals deserve days of rest like everyone else, but azoturia (or Monday-morning sickness), in which a horse ties up (its muscles become rigid) and, if not treated, may die, should be prevented by special feedings the night before a day off. Bran mashes are traditional, and their use is recommended (see page 67). Other special feeds—such as those designed for broodmares, growing foals, and animals in need of supplements—are discussed in Chapter 3 and should be fed only under a veterinarian's supervision.

Exercise

Wild horses get natural exercise while grazing, as they wander from one feeding area to another. Domestic horses need the same, whether it is the exercise they get on their own in a pasture or the work they are made to do carrying riders or pulling plows, carts, or large coaches. Ideally, all horses should get a minimum of exercise a day; without it, their systems may go awry—not only the muscular but also the digestive, cardiovascular, and respiratory—and their psychological makeup may be affected as well. Bored horses with little to occupy them often take to bad habits, such as cribbing, digging into the floors of their stalls, and weaving. Common sense applies here, as in most other aspects of horse-keeping. A horse that is fed lightly should not be overexercised unless its diet is increased proportionately; a horse that has not been exercised heavily should not be expected to undertake a long, strenuous siege of work without proper conditioning. Even a heavily worked horse that suddenly faces a day of rest should get some light, laxative bran mash the night before to adjust its system to inactivity. If one is unable to ride or drive, the animal should at least be lunged.

When horses are conditioned to moderate work

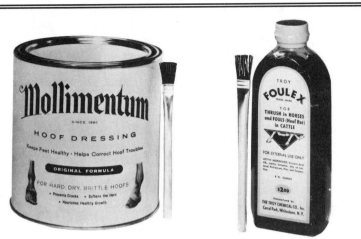

Hoof Dressings and Conditioners

Polishes and brighteners are discussed in the stable-management chapter, since they are primarily cosmetic in use, bringing out a high gloss on the hoof wall. Special dressings have more therapeutic uses, since they are richer in lanolin and other oils, which are intended to prevent or treat dry hooves. Some products contain antiseptic and fungicidal ingredients as well. There are many hoof products on the market and, while many successfully prevent the loss of moisture in the hoof, they do not provide it. Some will help promote healthy growth if applied with massage to the coronary band (where the hoof originates), but good nutrition and the advice of a well-informed farrier may be more effective.

Liquid conditioners are designed to penetrate the hoof wall and moisturize the hoof without clogging pores; they are usually applied with a brush. Ointments and pastes, with or without grease, do not penetrate as well, but form a protective outer coating to retain moisture in the hoof and are preferred for use on the sole, frog, heel, and coronary band. Aloe vera, biotin (a B-complex vitamin), and vitamin E are more commonly used now than traditional pine tar and turpentine; the overall effectiveness of these ingredients on hooves may be relatively slight in comparison to that of general good health and nutrition, but they have the additional benefit of improving the condition of the horse owner's fingernails.

The most popular liquid conditioners are:
- **Absorbine Liquid Hooflex (W. F. Young)**, a liquid form of the original Hooflex ointment, which contains neatsfoot oil, lanolin, petrolatum, turpentine, and pine tar.
- **Corona Hoof Dressing**, available in both liquid and paste.
- **Fiebing's Hoof Dressing**, another old timer, which contains soy oil, liquid petrolatum, tar acid, and gilsonite.
- **Hoof-It**, a combination of various oils, pine tar, turpentine, fish oil, and amino acids fortified with biotin and vitamin E.

- **Rain Maker Hoof Dressing** is now the most popular hoof dressing from Farnam.

Some of the ointment or oil-based paste conditioners are:
- **Absorbine Hooflex Ointment**, a popular product for more than 85 years, contains the same ingredients as Liquid Hooflex with the addition of aloe vera and paraffin.
- **Mollimentum Hoof Dressing (Y-Tex)** is a traditional product that contains cottonseed oil, rosin, beeswax, paraffin, and turpentine.

The most appealing hoof dressings these days seem to be the greaseless lotions that are pleasant to handle, increasing the likelihood that the coronary band will get the massaging it needs:
- **The Hoofmaker (Straight Arrow)** is a condensed cream designed to soften hoofs and stimulate growth.
- **Hoof-Saver** also contains no pine tar but is like a hand cream, with aloe vera, glycerin, vegetable oil, and other easily absorbed ingredients.
- **Hoof Quencher** is Absorbine's nongreasy vitamin-enriched cream that is pleasant to use.

Hoof packing is generally prescribed for specific ailments, such as soreness of the sole and frog caused by stone bruises, and it may be applied with or without the use of shoe pads to keep it in place when the horse is shod. Pine tar is the traditional material, but commercial medicated packings are available, such as Fiebing's Hoof Packing and Forshner's Hoof Packing.

Other special hoof medications are designed to treat thrush, foot rot, ringworm, and superficial wounds of the sole and frog. In addition to the usual oils, these generally contain aromatics (such as camphor) to eliminate odor, and iodine and turpentine, which will act on bacteria and fungus and afford a moistureproof coating to protect the affected foot. The best-known brands are Foulex (Y-tex), Kopertox (Franklin), Thrush-XX (Farnam), and Absorbine Thrush Remedy (W.F. Young).

Some products are available to patch or fill cracked hooves; these are best used on the advice of your farrier or veterinarian.

(from one to three hours a day), they should be walked for the first few minutes and walked home for the last ten or fifteen. This will cool them out, and one should take note of their condition before putting them back into the barn or pasture. If the coat is wet, the horse should be walked until it has dried off. If work has been strenuous, water should be withheld until the animal is thoroughly cool.

While riding or driving, take care to avoid gaits faster than the walk on hard surfaces, such as tarred roads and frozen ground, or on areas with sharp stones or other objects that may injure the feet. Any horse unaccustomed to trail riding shouldn't be expected to pick its way sensibly through woods and streams, and riders should be careful to avoid allowing the animal to get itself into trouble. Leaning forward while riding up and slightly back going down hills will help the horse maintain balance and increase its traction.

Stable Construction

Chapter 2 covers most of the potential dangers that can lead to illness or accident, but it doesn't hurt to repeat the cautions here. Stalls should be large and free of any protuberances that a horse could run or get into—loose wiring, unprotected light bulbs, rough edges of wood or metal, uncovered windows, low ceilings, narrow doorways, badly stored hay and grain, high sills, and partitions that are not sufficiently solid. Even stall latches and bolts that are not flush with the wall can cause tears as nasty as those caused by protruding nails, and buckets and tubs should be attached to the wall so that the horse can't get its feet tangled. Many injuries have been caused by the tops of Dutch doors that swing inward or that are not latched securely whether open or shut. The bottom part of a double stall door should be at least four feet high to discourage escape and, like the top, should be secured whether open or not. Pastures and corrals must also be free of dangerous elements, and fencing should be as safe as it is sound. Barbed wire can injure high-strung or inquisitive horses, and bales of loose wire should be removed to prevent horses from getting caught.

Isolation of Newcomers or Sick Horses

If you have a stableful of healthy horses, it behooves you to be careful when any new horse arrives on the scene or when one of the residents becomes ill. Coggins tests and fecal examinations may clear your conscience about swamp fever and parasites in a newcomer, but many horses can carry infectious diseases that may not become evident for a matter of days. Although inoculating the residents will help prevent the spread of a disease, the least expensive and most sensible arrangement is simply to isolate a new horse in a stall or paddock away from the others. (Such an area is also useful for an injured or diseased animal, for purposes of treatment.) The newcomer should remain in quarantine for at least two weeks until your veterinarian gives it a clean bill of health. During this period, be sure that manure and horsehair are not transferred from one horse to another—whether by pitchfork, wheelbarrow, or grooming tools or by your own shoes or clothing. If a newcomer (or a horse undergoing rest and recuperation) can be kept in sight of the other horses, so that they are aware of its presence, introduction (or reintroduction) into the herd may cause fewer problems. It is fascinating to observe horses pastured together, trying to figure out the pecking order or the relative dominance of the animals. But the arrival of a newcomer may throw the order out of whack for a while, until the head horse establishes its dominance, and equine fisticuffs may result. A gradual introduction will keep disaster to a minimum, although it might also be practical to remove hind shoes from any horse you suspect of hostile behavior.

"You hear of the city feller who wanted to board his horse and he asked his friends what he ought to pay and they said, 'The price ranges from one dollar a month to fifty cents to two-bits, but whatever you pay, you're entitled to the manure.' So this city feller goes to the first farmer, and the farmer says, 'One dollar,' and the city feller says, 'But I get the manure?' The farmer nods, and at the next place it's fifty cents, and the city feller says, 'But I get the manure?' and the farmer nods. At the third farm two-bits and the same story, so the city feller says, 'Maybe I can find a place that's real cheap,' and he goes to a broken-down farm and the man says, 'Ten cents a month,' and the city feller says, 'But I get the manure?' and the farmer says, 'Son, at ten cents a month there ain't gonna be any manure.'"

JAMES MICHENER
CENTENNIAL

Stable Medicine Chest

Any kind of stable, whether it is a one-horse shed or a twenty-horse barn, should not be without a cabinet or box containing medical supplies for use in emergencies or in treatments of problematical situations. The container should be kept within easy reach, but locked or otherwise inaccessible to children. Items to be kept in the chest at all times—and promptly replaced as they are used—are suggested below. Keep a list of the contents in the chest and check periodically to see that none is missing. Include on that list the names and telephone numbers of at least two veterinarians for handy reference, as well as the name of the local farrier. Familiarize yourself, under a veterinarian's guidance, with the use of each of these items and with proper first-aid procedures. Be sure to leave some extra space in the chest for medications that the veterinarian may leave with you, such as worming medicines. And remember to keep a separate medicine chest in the horse van or in your tack trunk for use on the road, at horse shows, or at stables where your horse may be boarding. Do not rely on other owners or grooms to have these things on hand, but see that you do. The methods of applying internal and external medications are described later on in this chapter.

Antibiotic powder (as your veterinarian recommends) for treating superficial wounds to prevent infection

Antibiotic ointment (prescribed by the vet) for covering open wounds

Bandaging materials: 1 large roll cotton, 1 roll 2-inch gauze; 1 roll 2-inch adhesive tape, 1 elastic bandage, 1 set leg bandages and pads; 1 package sterile gauze sponges; Vetrap tape

Boric acid, for use in solution for treating eyes

Instant cold pack (or soaking tub and access to hose), to reduce swelling

Dosing syringes, 12-cc and 35-cc sizes

Epsom salts

Fly repellent, stick or spray form, for use around eyes and wounds (as well as for general use)

Hoof dressing, to keep walls pliable

Hydrogen peroxide

Laxative and diuretics (prescribed by the vet)

Liniment, for soothing sore muscles after heavy exercise

Measuring cup and spoons

Mineral oil, for use in treating colic

Ophthalmic ointment, for use in the eyes

Penlight, for examining eyes and ears

Petroleum jelly (Vaseline) or lubricant (K-Y Jelly)

Poultice—hot pack for relief of swelling

Prep pads

Rasp (for feet)

Rubbing alcohol

Salt, to make a saline solution for flushing out wounds and for treating colic

Scissors

Shoe remover

Tincture of iodine (or another disinfectant recommended by the vet)

Towels (cotton)

Twitch, for restraint

Veterinary thermometer

Witch hazel

Wound dressing, for minor abrasions

Zinc oxide (powder or ointment)

HEALTH PRODUCTS

If your horse is sick or injured, your first step, of course, is to call the veterinarian rather than apply such home remedies, especially if you don't have much experience. The vet will have drugs, procedures, and equipment on hand to deal with most problems, and there are a number of equine centers that can handle more complicated cases requiring surgery and advanced techniques for treatment. Then why are there so many over-the-counter medications available for horses with old-fashioned names like liniment, poultice, blister, and such? Those methods went out of use years ago in human medicine along with bleeding and leeching. But look at your average drugstore—full of remedies for minor human ailments, such as coughs, colds, and stomachaches. None of these is particularly powerful, but some are sufficiently effective to bring relief unless the problem is serious enough to demand a physician's attention. And so it is with horses. Years ago, before there were veterinarians, horsemen kept their own animals reasonably healthy, sometimes relying on the farrier for help and sometimes on their own ingenuity in concocting preparations that seemed to work pretty well. Even when veterinarians did come along, there weren't very many of them that specialized in equine practice once the automobile became our major form of transportation. Nowadays, of course, there are perhaps ten million horses in the country, thanks to the boom in pleasure riding, and the number of veterinarians has also increased, if not at quite the same rate. Nevertheless, experienced horsemen who have learned to count on their own remedies still do so, and the products that are available to the public today are based in large part on those tried-and-true medications. Witch hazel, pine tar, glycerine, alcohol, and other ingredients that sound as though they came right out of a medieval herbal-medicine book are still used, along with more modern substances.

Most tack shops and feed suppliers carry a few of these products in stock or can order them from their wholesalers, although some products—such as prescription drugs—can be obtained only through a licensed veterinarian. Unless you know just what you are doing, the kind of medication you need and the way to apply it, you should probably check with your vet before investing in any for your first-aid chest. Over-the-counter products tend to be safe enough if used according to directions, but the size, age, and condition of any horse may require a slightly different product or application, and it pays to be sure. And speaking of paying, do not assume that a cheaper product is necessarily of a lower quality, or that a high price ensures greater effectiveness. Some suppliers charge very different prices for the same item (since overhead costs

vary considerably), and in some cases it does pay to shop around.

In addition to checking the horse catalogs, tack shops, and your veterinarian, you might also subscribe to one of the veterinary-supply catalogs. Not only are their prices usually reasonable, but they also tend to carry a wider range of equipment for breeders and farm animals.

A number of companies specialize in horse products and have entire lines of medications and equipment. If you find that you like a certain product from one manufacturer and are unable to get others in its line, you can always write the company directly for a descriptive brochure and for a list of its retail distributors. Because of space limitations, we cannot list all of these companies (nor can we illustrate or describe all of the health products available), but we have attempted to select the most comprehensive well-established firms that exist in all parts of the country. Where special items are mentioned and the manufacturer is not listed below, we have included the address in the description of the product.

Miles Agri/Bayer Corp., P. O. Box 390, Shawnee Mission, KS 66201 (Anti-inflammatory drugs)

Bickmore, Inc., P. O. Box 279, Hudson, MA 01749 (Gall salve, poultice, liniment, wound dressing)

The Farnam Companies, Inc. (Horse Health Products) P. O. Box 12068, Omaha, NE 68112 (Coat and hoof dressings, cough medicine, eye-care products, insecticides, liniment, oitments, supplement, wormers)

Fort Dodge Laboratories, 800 Fifth Street NW, Fort Dodge, IA 50501 (Wormers, feed supplements)

KV Vet Supply, P. O. Box 245, David City, NE 68632

Merck & Co. Inc., (Top Form Products), P. O. Box M. Rahway, NJ 07065 (Coat dressings, supplements, hoof-care products, insecticides, medications, vitamins, wormers)

Pfizer Inc., P. O. Box 747029, Pittsburgh PA 15274 (Repellents, medications)

Straight Arrow Inc., 2020 Highland Avenue, Bethlehem, PA 18017 (Coat dressings, hoof-care products, leg bandages, repellents)

Thoroughbred Remedy Corp., 251 Hempstead Turnpike, Elmont NY 11003 (Coat products, disinfectant, supplements, hoof dressings, wound dressings)

United Vet Equine, 14101 West 62nd Street, Eden Prairie, MN 55346

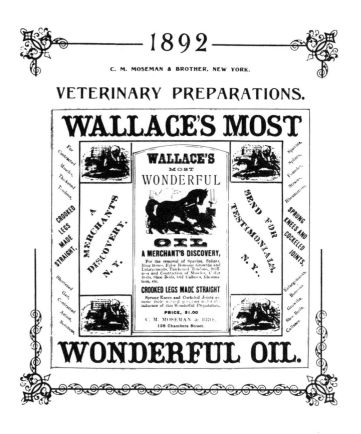

Vita-Flex Nutrition Co. Inc., P. O. Box 070140, Staten Island NY 10307 (Anti-inflammatory medications, supplements)

W. F. Young (Absorbine Products), P. O. Box 14, Springfield MA 01102 (Hoof-care products, liniments, insecticides)

Once you have selected the item you want and determined the manufacturer and/or distributor, the next step is to figure out how much to buy and in what sort of container. Many medications, liniments, and such are available in giant economy sizes, just like soap, but until you know how often you will use something (which may not be much at all if the animal doesn't respond well), stick to the smaller, easier-to-store sizes, even though they may be more expensive on a unit-cost basis. Keep in mind, too, the fact that some liquids may be less economical than ointments because of the loss caused by pouring or brushing the material onto the horse. We tend to disapprove of aerosols for atmospheric reasons, and horses often react badly as well, just because they hate the sound of the spray; this supposedly efficient method of applying a substance may not be so effective after all.

Except for mentioning the names of some worming medicines and a few drugs in the text, we have not gone into much detail about the products sold by ethical-drug companies, since they can be purchased only through a licensed veterinarian—who should also be the only person to use them or supervise their use. Only when a vet leaves medication with you and specific instructions should you attempt to give a horse any of these prescription products.

Some of the many products available over the counter should be part of each stable first-aid kit and some are to be considered optional, depending on the horse. We have been highly selective because of the limitation of space, choosing to mention and illustrate only the most popular or readily available or particularly effective brands.

VETERINARIANS

Although you may see the veterinarian only once or twice a year, he or she can be your best friend when you are in need—not just during emergencies but on a steady basis, helping you establish good management and feeding programs and giving your animal regular

A Veterinarian Speaks Out

Somehow, when some people buy a horse they fail to consider that they will have to spend quite a bit of money for routine medication. They forget that food is not the only thing that is important to a horse. A horse needs foot care. It needs routine dewormings. It needs help against the "dangers" that sometimes mark its outdoor life: Give me a horse and give me a small nail in a pasture fence and I will make an even bet that nail and horse will find each other—even if the pasture covers three acres.

More important, some people are seldom prepared for the "catastrophic" medical problems that can afflict horses. Thus, when faced by a four-hundred-dollar operation to save a colicky horse, some owners, forced by financial considerations, choose to put the animal to sleep.

For many race-horse owners, the animal is no more than a living racing machine. Often, when the horse breaks down, it is just patched up—even if the patchwork will enable the horse to run no more than one additional race. If a horse suffers a minor injury—to the knee, for example—it often should be laid up for a month. But to retrain a horse after a month's lay-off can cost thirty dollars per day or more for still another month. Many race-horse owners are not willing to spend that much more time and money on a minor knee injury. Instead, they ask the attending veterinarian to inject cortisone in the affected joint and keep the horse running until it finally can no longer compete and must be put out to pasture or put down.

I just like horses too much to find real pleasure practicing a medicine dictated by economic necessity.

Lucas Younker, D.V.M.
Animal Doctor

Gentlemen don't fall off their horses; they are thrown.
ANONYMOUS

examinations, inoculations, and worming medications as preventive measures. Every horse owner should use a vet who is familiar with the horse in its normal condition and who specializes in equine work. Because small-animal practitioners will not often handle them, horses in suburban areas may not have the advantages of their country cousins, who can benefit from the presence of a large-animal vet who routinely cares for farm animals. Nevertheless, in areas where horses are kept in any number, veterinarians can usually be found without too much difficulty, even if they have more clients than they can fit into a 9-to-5 working day. Because they must go to their patients rather than work out of a clinic or hospital setup, they are not always easy to reach, but many now have effective telephone, beeper, or CB radio systems in their vehicles and can be contacted within an hour or less. There are also equine centers, sometimes connected with racetracks or veterinary colleges, where information about practitioners in certain areas can be obtained or where horses needing specialist care can be shipped for treatment or diagnosis. New owners can usually find a veterinarian through the animal's previous owner, while newcomers to an area can check the Yellow Pages or call local breeding farms or stables for recommendations. Because the veterinarian you select may not always be available when emergencies arise, or because you may want to get a second opinion on a particular question, it is always a good idea to have one or two names in reserve.

Before we talk about what you can expect of a veterinarian, let's discuss what a vet will require of you. In addition to fees, which vary widely from one part of the country to another depending on many factors, he will expect that you keep good records in addition to the one he keeps for himself. He will also want you to establish and implement on a routine basis a good management program. He will expect you to keep careful watch on your horse's general condition and behavior, to catch signs of trouble as early as possible to make effective treatment possible. Sensible observation and notation of irregularities in feeding, elimination, action, and the condition of feet, coat, eyes, and so on will be valuable bits of information in diagnosis; and, of course, good follow-up care is only common sense. If you have questions about anything that a vet says or recommends, be sure you ask them. Experienced

horsemen are familiar with various ways of dosing an animal or bandaging or treating its feet, for instance, but the neophyte shouldn't be expected to do so without expert instruction. Don't rely entirely on friends who claim superior knowledge. Although they may know what they are talking about chances are that the vet has more up-to-date and certainly more professional information at his command. It bears repeating that it is unwise to take chances when it comes to equine health. Don't count on your feed store or supplier to give you good advice about patent medicines, worming dosages, or food supplements. Always check with your horse doctor first.

In addition to giving you advice about your horse's daily care—feed ration, capability for work, and other aspects of management—the veterinarian can be expected to perform any number of other services. When you are considering the purchase of a new animal, ask your vet to join you and comment about the horse's conformation, state of health, and general condition. Later, he can help you break the animal into a new regimen of feeding and exercise, if necessary, as well as providing medical attention.

A thorough examination by a veterinarian once if not twice a year is the least you owe any horse in your care. A careful look at the animal's eyes, teeth, nose, ears, feet, legs, back, coat, and general appearance will give him a good idea of the animal's condition as well as whether it needs supplementary food, corrective shoeing, or any other special care on a regular basis.

At the same time, the doctor will inoculate the animal for any diseases that may be prevalent in your area and take a fecal sample to examine for the presence of internal parasites. (Some vets will do this on the spot; others will take the specimen back to their office for microscopic examination and call you—or ask you to call them—about the results and recommended treatment.) Since few horses are free of parasites, the question is not usually whether you will need to have your animal wormed, but what kind of medication will take care of the problem and how and when it should be administered.

A yearly Coggins test to determine the absence (we hope) of equine infectious anemia (swamp fever) will be necessary in most areas; this involves the taking of a blood sample for analysis in an authorized laboratory. If the horse is to be shipped out of state, federal law says that you must have proof that the animal was free of the disease within no more than a year of the shipping date. Some states have made it illegal to trailer a horse off your own property without a negative Coggins test within the year, but laws aside, if you plan to move your horse into any location where other horses are to be present, a Coggins test is a good idea. (Also determine, if you are moving your horse to another stable, that the horses there have been tested.) For a discussion of EIA and the Coggins test see page 113.

As to specific problems the vet might encounter, broken teeth or teeth that are unevenly worn will need to be filed down with a dental float, with a speculum used to hold the horse's mouth open. (Some brave men just pull the tongue to the side between the animal's teeth so that it is unlikely to bite, but high-strung horses aren't easy to handle, and floating isn't an easy job anyhow.) Keeping the teeth in good working order, and extracting any that may need it (such as the small wolf teeth, which are premolar vestiges and may interfere with biting), is an important routine, especially since horses with dental problems also tend to have di-

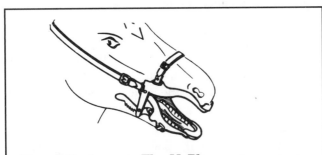

Dental Equipment. The McPherson-type speculum pictured contains two sets of plates for use on incisors or molars and is made of polished forged steel or aluminum with leather straps. (Available through some large tack shops and most agricultural catalogs.)

The dental float is a simple device, consisting of one handle to which is screwed a head that holds a rasp or file (or combination) attached to the head with two screws. Most floats are equipped with two heads, one straight and one angular.

gestive problems if they aren't able to eat properly. Although some horsemen are experienced enough to float their own horses' teeth, it is a tricky procedure. Unless you have received instruction and done the job in the presence of your vet, it isn't recommended for beginners.

Lameness is one of the most troublesome problems that can face the owner of a working horse, and vets pay particular attention to feet and legs. (See pages 119–126 for specific ailments and their symptoms.) An animal showing early signs of lameness, such as swelling, tenderness, heat, or irregular growth, will require an appropriate kind of treatment which you may be able to administer yourself. Hosing, soaking, and applying liniments, poultices, or other medications to a horse's legs are all effective in reducing inflammation, and the vet will tell you what he thinks is the best route to follow and which are the best medications to buy. (Blistering, firing, and surgical procedures are rigorous forms of treatment and must be left to professionals.) Ask the vet whether he recommends special leg boots or bandages, or whether hooves need special attention from the farrier on his next visit.

If any other ailments are visible—saddle sores, bruises, cuts, and so on—ask the vet for his recommended methods of treatment and types of medication to stock in your medicine chest. If because of either conformation or past history, an animal seems prone to any problems such as thrush, colic, lameness, or whatever, the vet will tell you if you should keep certain medications on hand in case of emergency.

Whatever the diagnosis and recommendations, for heaven's sake follow the advice you get. Don't assume the doctor is being too conservative, especially when you have your heart set on entering some kind of competition. If you feel you have good reason to disagree with or to disregard the vet's counsel, seek a responsible second opinion from another veterinarian. But don't take matters into your own hands unless you feel like risking your horse's health and perhaps causing the animal (and your pocketbook) a good deal of damage.

Before the vet leaves, write down everything he or she recommends in your record book or on the horse's chart. Make a note of the next visit, or a reminder to yourself to call at a suggested future date. And while we are thinking about the next visit, ask the vet if you should take any special precautions for the next examination. One should always make sure that the horse is in its stall or somehow conveniently confined when you expect the vet to call. (There's nothing more annoying or frustrating for both owner and vet than to have to recapture a loose animal that has somehow become aware of the fact that the doctor has arrived.) A difficult horse might have to be tranquilized ahead of time with some promazine obtained from the vet and sneaked into the morning feed on the day of the exam. Or you might have to learn how to use a twitch to keep the animal under control. If possible, have one or two other people on hand to help you hold the horse if it should get out of hand. And of course, be there yourself to calm the animal by steady chatter and whatever other sorts of soothing noises it might need. Most horses eventually become accustomed to regular handling during shoeing, veterinary examinations, and conformation classes at horse shows, but this kind of training takes time and practice. Those periodic checkups by the owner, as well as regular grooming, will help ensure a horse's good manners during these routines, as well as keep the owner alert to the animal's condition.

WORMING

Unless a horse lives alone at the North Pole or in the middle of the Sahara, it is a fact of life that it will have internal parasites of one form or another. Though they are all usually just referred to as worms, because it is the larval form of these parasites that uses the intestinal tract of the horse as a path toward maturity, there are actually many different species and stages of growth, some of which are more dangerous than others in terms of a horse's health. All can be controlled through medication and good management, but never completely eliminated. A horseman must always be on guard, especially when the animal is showing any of the following signs that can't be described to any other ailment:

- poor hair coat
- failure to gain weight in spite of increased rations
- listlessness

So You Want To Be A Veterinarian

Ω

by EMIL P. DOLENSEK, D.V.M.

LIKE ALL VETERINARIANS, I get many letters every year from young people asking me about the veterinary profession—what does it involve, how does one get into it, and may they work for me during their next vacation period. Needless to say, I can't hire all (or even a few) of them, and I have trouble finding time to answer all their questions, but it is possible to give some general advice to those who may be interested in a veterinary career. Many people do not realize that a veterinarian is a licensed medical professional with an extensive background in the field, including two to four years of undergraduate training in biology, chemistry, physics, and so on and four years of graduate study at an accredited veterinary school, followed by the completion of a state veterinary examination. All of that sounds difficult enough, but it is even more difficult in practice, for there are fewer than forty veterinary schools in the United States and Canada now (see list pp. 107–108), and these can accept only one of every ten students who apply.

My advice to young people, then, is to prepare yourself as well as possible, taking as many science courses as possible, even in high school, and making the best possible grade averages in all courses. During college, try to spend summers working with animals, at least one of them with a veterinarian, and work with both large and small animals. Remember that even if you plan to specialize in equine work, you must be equally proficient with all sorts of animals to become a vet—cats, dogs, sheep, cows, and others as well as horses. Then, after two or three years of college, apply to the veterinary school in your state. If there isn't one, write to the Board of Higher Education to ask whether your state partially supports a veterinary school in any other state; if it does not, apply to a number of schools. And keep your fingers crossed while you keep your hopes and your grades up.

Many people who do not have the time or money to invest in this extensive program choose instead the field of veterinary technology, which requires two to four years of undergraduate work in the veterinary or animal-technology department of any of several state universities. This field is also demanding, and requires proficiency in science and mathematics, but a certificate can open the door to becoming a veterinarian's assistant. Ω

* ribs showing with a big belly
* tail rubbing against the stall, trees, or fencing

Before the animal reaches that state, however, take some preventive measures: have the vet test the feces for the presence of parasites, and establish a regular program of preventive care. Some good health procedures include not feeding the horse on the ground, keeping the horse's manure away from the feeding area (or vice versa), cleaning out the pasture or paddock at least once a week, and not letting the horse out to graze in areas recently fertilized with horse manure. Lime stalls and grazing areas periodically, and rotate pastures every two months. (You can put cows and sheep into unused, or "resting," horse pastures, since they are not affected by equine parasites.) Mowing and harrowing pastureland frequently will diffuse droppings and kill the eggs by exposing them to sunlight.

Familiarize yourself with the various kinds of parasites that affect horses, the way they work to cause damage, and the means by which they may be controlled (see below).

Types of Internal Parasites

Botflies are unlike other internal parasites in that the insect, when mature, lives outside the horse's body; it is a parasite only during the larval stage. There are three species of bot that affect horses in the United States: *Gastrophilus intestinalis* (the common bot), *G. haemorrhoidales* (the nose, or red-tailed bot); and *G. nasalis* (the throat, or chin, bot): All three have similar life cycles and can be controlled in similar ways. The common botfly female, during a life span of a week or less in late summer, lays up to five hundred yellow eggs on a horse's forelegs, flanks, or forequarters, where they will remain for as long as two weeks. If the horse licks or bites them off, the eggs will stick to the tongue, hatch in the mouth, and eventually be ingested. After a month or so they arrive in the stomach, where they attach themselves to the wall and remain for nearly a year. Then they change from larvae into pupae and pass through the intestines, to be eliminated in the manure. After a dormant period of one or two months underground, the pupae become flies which will start the cycle all over again.

The nose botfly deposits her black eggs in the hairs of a horse's lips, where they hatch in two to four days into larvae that work their way into the inner membranes of the lip. After five or six weeks they migrate to the stomach, where they live the rest of their pesty lives much as the common bot does.

The eggs of the throat, or chin, bot, also yellow, are laid under the horse's jaw. They hatch by themselves, crawling eventually into the mouth, where they get into the gum tissue and continue the rest of the bot route into the stomach, where the damage they—like the other bots—can do may be considerable. Intestinal problems, including blockages that may result in colic and can be fatal, are inevitable if bots are allowed to multiply uncontrolled.

One way of eliminating the bot problem is to try to prevent their getting into the horse's system. Bot eggs are difficult to remove, but research into the curiously stubborn glue they possess has made possible the development of new products that will dissolve the substance that causes them to stick to the horse's coat. A traditional method has been to rub warm water into the area and scrape off the eggs in the hope that the heat, moisture, and friction will stimulate the eggs to hatch prematurely. This tiresome procedure is not one that most people would care to perform every day during the season. A more effective means of controlling bots is to kill them in the horse's stomach with ivermectin, which is also effective on 29 other parasites if given on a regular basis.

Large Strongyles (pronounced stron-jiles)

This group of bloodworms includes the most dangerous of all equine parasites: *Strongylus vulgaris*, also known as the red worm, as well as *S. edentatus* and *S. equinus*, which are to be taken seriously as well. Recent studies have indicated that strongyles are the culprit in many cases of colic; every horse owner should do his utmost to control the problem as effectively as possible. Unlike bots, strongyle adults are suckers that attach themselves to the walls or contents of the large intestines, where they lay their eggs, which pass out of the body with droppings. When the eggs hatch (after a day or so), the larvae attach themselves to blades of grass over the period of a week, and the horse can pick up thousands of them in a few bites. Once ingested, the larvae migrate throughout the body for at least six months, causing inflammatory arterial lesions, which may lead to thrombosis. (When a thrombus, or blood clot, is formed and dislodges, it can block the blood flow and cause sudden death.) Migrating strongyles

Schools/Colleges of Veterinary Medicine Accredited by the American Veterinary Medical Association

Auburn University
College of Veterinary Medicine
Auburn University, AL 36849
(205) 844-4546 (Administration)
(205) 844-4490 (Large Animal)
(205) 844-3697 (FAX)

University of California
School of Veterinary Medicine
Davis, CA 95616
(530) 752-1360 (Dean's Office)
(530) 752-6433 (Equine Research)
(530) 752-0290 (Large Animal Clinic)
(530) 752-2801 (Fax)

Colorado State University
College of Veterinary Medicine and
  Biomedical Sciences
Ft. Collins, CO 80523
(303) 491-7053 (Dean's Office)
(303) 221-4535 (Teaching Hospital)
(303) 491-1275 (Teaching Hospital
  Fax)

Cornell University
College of Veterinary Medicine
Ithaca, NY 14853
(607) 253-3000 (Administration)
(607) 253-3100 (Large Animal)
(607) 253-3708 (Fax)

University of Florida
College of Veterinary Medicine
Gainesville, FL 32610-0125
(904) 392-4700 (Administration)
(904) 392-4700, Ext. 4000 (Large
  Animal)
(904) 392-8351 (Fax)

University of Georgia,
College of Veterinary Medicine
Athens, GA 30602
(706) 542-3461 (Dean's Office)
(706) 542-6326 (Large Animal)
(706) 542-8524 (Fax)

University of Illinois
College of Veterinary Medicine
2001 S. Lincoln
Urbana, Il 61801
(217) 333-2760 (Administration)
(217) 333-2001 (Large Animal)
(217) 244-1475 (Large Animal Fax)

Iowa State University
College of Veterinary Medicine
Ames, IA 50011
(515) 294-1242 (Administration)
(515) 294-1500 (Large Animal)
(515) 294-8341 (Fax)

Kansas State University
College of Veterinary Medicine
Manhattan, KS 66506
(913) 532-6011 (Administration)
(913) 532-5700 (Large Animal)
(913) 532-5884 (Fax)

Louisiana State University
School of Veterinary Medicine
Baton Rouge, LA 70803
(504) 346-3200 (Dean's Office)
(504) 346-3131 (Large Animal)
(504) 346-5702 (Fax)

Michigan State University
College of Veterinary Medicine
East Lansing, MI 48824-1314
(517) 355-6509 (Dean's Office)
(517) 353-9710 (Large Animal)
(517) 336-1037 (Fax)

The University of Minnesota
College of Veterinary Medicine
St. Paul, MN 55108
(612) 624-9227 (Administration)
(612) 625-6700 (Large Animal)
(612) 625-7755 (Clinical and
  Population Studies)
(612) 624-8753 (Fax)

Mississippi State University
College of Veterinary Medicine
Mississippi State, MS 39762
(601) 325-3432 (Administration)
(601) 325-1498 (Fax)

University of Missouri
College of Veterinary Medicine
Columbia, MO 65211
(314) 882-3877 (Dean's Office)
(314) 882-3513 (Equine Hospital and
  Teaching Clinic)
(314) 882-5444 (Equine Hospital and
  Teaching Clinic Fax)

University of Montreal
Faculty of Veterinary Medicine
Veterinary Teaching Hospital
Large Animal Clinic
Saint Hyacinthe, QB CD J2S 7C6
(514) 773-8852 (Large Animal)
(514) 773-3807 (Large Animal Fax)

North Carolina State University
College of Veterinary Medicine
4700 Hillsborough St.
Raleigh, NC 27606
(919) 829-4200 (Switchboard)
(919) 821-9500 (Hospital)
(919) 829-4452 (Fax)

The Ohio State University
College of Veterinary Medicine
Columbus, OH 43210
(614) 292-1171 (Administration)
(614) 292-6661 (Hospital)
(614) 292-3530 (Fax)

Oklahoma State University
College of Veterinary Medicine
Stillwater, OK 74078
(405) 744-6648 (Dean's Office)
(405) 744-6656 (Large Animal)
(405) 744-6265 (Large Animal Fax)

University of Guelph
Ontario Veterinary College
Guelph, ONT, CD N16 2W1
(519) 823-8800 (Administration)

Oregon State University
College of Veterinary Medicine
Corvallis, OR 97331
(503) 737-2141 (Switchboard)
(503) 737-2858 (Large Animal)
(503) 737-0502 (Fax)

University of Pennsylvania
School of Veterinary Medicine
3800 Spruce Street
Philadelphia, PA 19101-6044
(215) 898-5438 (Administration)
(215) 898-9923 (Fax)

University of Prince Edward Island
Atlantic Veterinary College
Charlottetown, PEI CD C1A 4P3
(902) 566-0800 (Administration)

Purdue University
School of Veterinary Medicine
1240 Lynn Hall
West Lafayette, IN 47907
(317) 494-7607 (Dean's Office)
(317) 494-8548 (Large Animal
   Hospital)
(317) 496-1635 (Large Animal
   Hospital Fax)

University of Saskatchewan
Western College of Veterinary
   Medicine
Saskatoon, SASK CD S7N 0W0
(306) 966-7200
(306) 966-7129 (Fax)

University of Tennessee
College of Veterinary Medicine
Knoxville, TN 37901
(615) 974-7262 (Administration)
(615) 974-5701 (Large Animal)
(615) 974-8222 (Fax)

Texas A&M University
College of Veterinary Medicine
College Station, TX 77843-4461
(409) 845-5051 (Administration)
(409) 845-3541 (Large Animal)
(409) 847-8863 (Large Animal Fax)

Tufts University
School of Veterinary Medicine
200 Westboro Road
North Grafton, MA 01536
(508) 839-5302 (Administration)
(508) 839-5395, ext. 4840 (Large
   Animal)
(508) 839-7931 (Large Animal Fax)

Tuskegee University
School of Veterinary Medicine
Tuskegee, AL 36088

(205) 727-8461 (Large Animal)
(205) 727-8177 (Fax)

Virginia Tech and University of
   Maryland
Virginia-Maryland Regional College
   of Veterinary Medicine
Blacksburg, VA 24061
(703) 231-7666 (Switchboard)
(703) 231-4621 (Switchboard)
(703) 231-7367 (Fax)

Washington State University
College of Veterinary Medicine
Pullman, WA 99164
(509) 335-9515 (Administration)
(509) 335-0711 (Animal Clinic)
(509) 335-6094 (Fax)

The University of Wisconsin-
   Madison
School of Veterinary Medicine
Madison, WI 53706
(608) 263-6716 (Dean's Office)
(608) 262-7676 (Referral Services)
(608) 263-6573 (Fax)

have even been known to veer off into the brain and cause severe damage there. When the adult worms eventually arrive in the intestine, they feed on the intestinal lining, causing local irritation, tissue damage, and blood loss or even intestinal stoppage. These conditions can lead to colic, hemorrhagic enteritis, anemia, and general unthriftiness. After six to eight weeks, when permanent damage has been done, the female worms lay their eggs to begin the vicious cycle anew. Symptoms of strongyle infestation are constipation, loss of appetite, high fever, depression, and diarrhea as well as colic and anemia. The situation can best be prevented by stopping strongyles before they start—eliminating the adult population in the intestines before eggs can be laid. Because the larvae have already caused their part of the damage by this stage, a horse's condition, except its appearance, may not greatly improve, but one must start somewhere. Strongyles have become resistant to several of the medications that have been effective in the past—phenothiazine, piperazine, and thiabendazole—but ivermectin is considered the "miracle" drug for this group of parasites, which have not built up resistance to it. Since the migrating larvae will mature when they reach the intestine, in about six to eight weeks, worming every two months is recommended for at least a year, using different drugs each time, before a heavily infected herd and pasture can be considered under control. Pyramantel pamoate will suppress egg production for about twice as long as ivermectin.

Small Strongyles

There are many different genera and species in this group, of which *Strongyloides* (usually present only in foals), *Poteriostomum, Cylicobrachytus, Craterostomum, Oesophagodontus,* and *Cyathostomum* are the significant members. They all begin their cycles in the same manner as the large strongyles, but they don't migrate beyond the intestinal tract. There they may produce ulcers, but rarely blood loss in the small intestine. They aren't as harmful as the large strongyles, although they may accumulate in large numbers in the cecum and colon as well as in the small intestine, and they can cause diarrhea as a result. Young foals are particularly susceptible to small strongyles (getting them in mother's milk), which may result in weakness, emaciation, and anemia as well as digestive upset. Small strongyles have become resistant to thiabendazole, but for the most part they can be controlled, if not eliminated, by treatment with the same drugs as those used for the large strongyles.

Ascarids

The large roundworm *Parascaris equorum* can become as thick as a pencil and has been known to reach a length of fifteen inches. Mature roundworms breed in the horse's intestine, where thousands of eggs are laid, and then pass out with manure. After about two weeks on the ground they become infective, and horses will swallow them with grass, hay, or water that has become contaminated. The eggs hatch in the intestine and penetrate the wall, where they enter small blood vessels, traveling for a week or more through the circulatory system to the lungs. There they work or are coughed out into the trachea (windpipe), to be swallowed into the stomach. The larvae then move to the intestines and grow for a couple of months into breeding adults. The greatest danger caused by ascarids is usually in horses of up to two years (older horses develop a natural immunity), in which they can cause circulatory blockage; damage to liver, heart, and lung tissue; and most important, intestinal blockage, which may result

in rupture and a fatal case of peritonitis. Particular care should be taken to eliminate the pest in fillies destined to become broodmares, since ascarids can penetrate the muscles of young horses and later migrate through the placenta to infect foals. Effective medication includes ivermectin, pyrantel, mebendazole, trichloron, and piperazine with phenothiazine, or diathiazine iodide. These drugs will eliminate the adult worms in the intestine and should reach them before they begin to lay their eggs. Because the total cycle is about ten weeks, worming for two months in succession should greatly reduce the damage they can cause.

Pinworms

The two types of pinworms that affect horses to any degree are *Oxyuris equi* and *Probstmayria vivipara* (the minute pinworm), the latter of which is thought to be harmless. *Oxyuris equi* eggs are swallowed with contaminated grass, water, or dry food. The larvae hatch and mature in about seven weeks as they travel to the intestines. They breed in the colon, and both females and eggs are eliminated with manure, though some females may lay their eggs on the skin near the rectum, where they may be rubbed or drop off to the ground. One of the signs of pinworms is a horse rubbing itself against posts or other objects to relieve the intense itching, thereby causing hair loss, secondary infections, and further discomfort. This symptom is the best way to detect the presence of pinworms, which cannot be seen in usual fecal examinations (although they may be found in fresh feces). They do not require specific treatment, since nearly all the compounds effectively used on strongyles and ascarids will be effective against pinworms.

Stomach Worms

Three species of spirurids are found in the stomachs of horses, and the larvae may also invade skin wounds or abrasions, causing a condition referred to as "summer sores." Flies are the intermediate hosts for stomach worms, which can cause conjunctivitis in the eyes and pulmonary abscesses in the lungs. In the stomach one species, *Draschia megastoma*, lives in colonies, causing abscesses in the stomach wall. The two species of *Habronema* live in glandular areas of the stomach. The former can be treated with trichlorfon but resist carbon disulfide and dichlorvos, which are effective against the *Habronema*. The minute stomach worm

(*Trichostrongylus axei*) primarily affects cattle, sheep, and goats, and is usually light in horses, although heavy infections can cause gastritis. They can be controlled by the drugs that are effective against strongyles.

Tapeworms

One of the two tapeworm species found frequently in horses, *Anoplocephala perfoliata,* may result in severe ulcerations in the lining of the cecum. (Little research has been done toward eliminating them in horses, since heavy infestations are not common.) They are carried by orbatid mites which can live in pastures in some areas. When they are ingested, they reach maturity in about two months. Fecal examination will make detection possible. Pyrantel pamoate is effective in controlling tapeworms.

Worming Medications

In the good old days, horsemen used a number of tried (and perhaps not so true) methods of ridding their animals of parasites. One of them involved a monthly "feeding" of wood ash and tobacco, and it was supposed to be pretty effective. Nevertheless, modern medicine has come up with some superior products, and your veterinarian will be familiar with their use.

The easiest way to worm a horse successfully is to set up an effective program with your veterinarian, and be sure that the horse receives its medication properly. Gone are the days when one had to rely on the vet's visit every couple of months to tube worm or inject the horse and prescribe the appropriate medications for

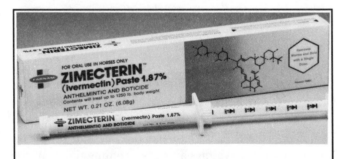

The "miracle" wormer ivermectin is available in paste form in an easy-to-use, disposable, one-dose syringe, under several brand names, including Zimecterin, Rotectin 1, Eqvalan, and Equimectrin.

dosing between visits. Tube worming directly into the stomach, while very effective in getting medication where it has to go, is a tricky business for a beginner; the principal danger in inserting the long tube is that one may run it down the trachea instead of the esophagus, and cause the animal to develop pneumonia. Happily, the pharmaceutical companies that produce dewormers package them in handy, disposable plastic syringes, which are a lot easier to use than such traditional devices as balling guns or metal syringes. You can buy these worming medications without a veterinarian's prescription, directly from most farm and tack shops or through most mail-order catalogs specializing in equine products.

In spite of the convenience of these over-the-counter medications, we still advise horse owners to consult their vets before simply assuming that a dose of the so-called miracle wormer ivermectin (available under several brand names, such as Eqvalan, Equimectrin, Rotectin 1, and Zimecterin) every two months will do the trick. Ivermectin is pretty amazing; it kills adult parasites (including bots), and most larvae, and so far worms have not developed resistance to its effectiveness. However, ivermectin does not kill encysted fourth-state larval worms, which can lay eggs and begin the life cycle within six weeks, and it does not affect tapeworms. Many vets recommend that to prevent drug resistance and to ensure that worms are eliminated at all life stages, other drugs be used in a regular rotation with ivermectin. Pyrantel pamoate (marketed as Strongid paste or pellets by Pfizer or as Rotectin 2 by Farnam) is very effective in suppressing parasite egg production temporarily and in killing tapeworms (but not bots). A recently introduced drug, moxidectin (sold by Fort Dodge as Quest), is in a new group of worming medicines called milbemycins, which effectively kill encysted larvae and suppress egg production for 12 weeks. Other drugs are also available—oxfendazole, fenbendazole, febantel, and so on—but many worms have developed a resistance to them, and some may even be toxic in pregnant mares.

Before you give your horse any drug, however, be sure you know the appropriate dosage for the animal's weight. In using paste wormers, be sure that the horse's mouth is empty, and that the syringe is pushed as far back in the mouth as possible, so that the chance of the paste being spit out is minimized.

VACCINATIONS

Unhappily, the three most troublesome equine ailments—colic, lameness, and swamp fever (equine infectious anemia)—cannot be prevented except by good management practices. Happily, however, there are a number of diseases that can be avoided by a regular program of vaccination. As more and more horses are shipped around the country to compete in races, shows, rodeos, trail rides, and other competitions, horse owners should take special precautions to prevent the following highly contagious diseases from affecting their own animals as well as causing widespread epidemics that have been known to break out in the not-so-recent past. Some of these ailments are more common in some parts of the country than others, so be sure to ask your veterinarian for advice not only about your own area but about other locations to which your horse might be shipped. Since some vaccinations take weeks to become effective, don't wait until the last moment to get the shots.

The following diseases can be controlled with vaccines; they are described in the order of significance for horse owners, from the most recommended vaccines to those only rarely recommended.

Viral Encephalitis

This group of diseases is far more serious than the relatively mild nonfatal equine influenza (see below), and vaccinations on an annual basis for the two most prevalent forms—Eastern and Western encephalomyelitis—are definitely recommended for most horses. Encephalitis was first isolated in horses during the 1930s, when hundreds of thousands of animals were lost, so it is described as an equine disease. However, horses do not cause it but are victims like many other species, including humans. The actual cause is a group of viruses carried by certain species of mosquitoes, and there is no cure. In addition to Eastern equine encephalomyelitis (also known as sleeping sickness or blind staggers) and Western equine encephalomyelitis (or Kansas horse plague) there is also a Venezuelan type, but this form is rare in the United States now, and vaccines are not routinely recommended, as they once were.

Foals can be vaccinated at three and four months; adult horses, including pregnant mares, should be vaccinated at least once a year, twice if mosquitoes are active all year. The most obvious signs of the disease are marked depression and high fever. Drooping of the lower lip, a reluctance to move, and lack of coordination are also characteristic; in the final stages, the horse is unable to stand up. The course of the disease is short, with death usually occurring in two or three days. Treatment, sometimes successful, consists of trying to keep fluid and electrolyte levels in balance, to reduce fever, and to keep the animal on its feet using boards, slings, or racks. However, horses that survive often suffer brain damage.

A similar disease in the Far East, known as *Japanese encephalitis,* is also spread by mosquitoes, and results in symptoms like the American versions of the disease. The mortality rate is much lower, but any imported animal suspected of the disease should be reported to local, state, or federal authorities.

Tetanus

Also known as *lockjaw,* this serious disease has been a major problem in horses for centuries. The bacterium *Clostridium tetani* exists worldwide, and every unvaccinated horse is susceptible. There is no known cure, although recovery is possible (if not likely) with the use of antibiotics and supportive therapy to keep the animal quiet, comfortable, and protected from injury. Particular care should be given to adequate nourishment and fluid balance. There is, happily, a highly effective vaccine—tetanus toxoid—which is given in two doses per month apart, followed by a booster shot nine to twelve months later, and annually thereafter. Broodmares should be vaccinated four weeks before foaling. There is also a tetanus antitoxin that supplies protection in the form of antibodies; because its effect is of short duration and it can cause liver problems in some animals, it is recommended only for immediate protection in wounded horses that have never received the tetanus vaccination.

Rabies

Although this well-known disease is not particularly common in horses, animals kept out in the open in localities where rabies has been prevalent in wild or farm animals should receive an annual preventive vaccination. An increasing number of skunks, raccoons, and other wild mammals have been found to be rabid in recent years, and dogs and cats that run free are at a much higher risk than horses, and should definitely be vaccinated regularly. The vaccine is also recommended for horses, however, if rabies exists in wildlife nearby. Symptoms of rabies are similar to those in other animals: aggressiveness, self-inflicted wounds, and eating of wood, straw, or other similar materials. Since there is no treatment for rabid horses, they should be destroyed right away, or isolated and reported to public health authorities.

Equine Influenza

This viral disease is not particularly serious, but it is becoming increasingly prevalent each year, affecting horses of any age, at any time, and in any area. Proper treatment involves complete rest and confinement for at least three weeks, so anyone with a horse on a rigorous training or competitive schedule should take the precaution of having the vaccine administered. Horses that are rarely in contact with other animals, or those for which a three-week rest would not be a serious interruption, need not have the inoculation, though owners should keep an eye out for symptoms. The first sign is a dry cough, which usually lasts for only two or three days but may continue for three weeks even with complete rest. Nasal discharge is watery at first, later developing into a thick mucus-like substance. Lymph nodes may be sensitive, and laryngitis may be present. Muscular weakness, soreness, and lack of appetite are other general signs, though in very young, old, or weak horses, there may be complications in the form of heart or liver damage, secondary infections, anemia, and such respiratory illnesses as bronchitis and emphysema.

Influenza vaccines were developed in the 1960s and are now available in combination with vaccines for rhino pneumonitis (see the following section). In foals the first injections should be given at three and four months; booster shots are recommended at one year and annually thereafter, more often if the horse travels for show, breeding, or racing purposes.

Rhino Pneumonitis

This viral disease, with at least two strains caused by equine herpes viruses 1 and 4, is best known for causing respiratory problems in horses and abortion in pregnant mares. It is spread by inhaling the airborne virus and, like the common cold, will spread rapidly from one horse to the next. Older horses tend to be re-

sistant to the virus but can still carry it, even if they show no symptoms. After a two- to ten-day incubation period, the first symptoms are high fever and nasal discharge, along with (but not always accompanied by) loss of appetite, depression, diarrhea, swellings in the legs, and mild congestion. All of these symptoms are exacerbated by exercise. Recovery is complete within two weeks if the animal is treated with complete rest, the only known effective treatment. Broodmares should be vaccinated at least twice a year, as well as one month before giving birth, and horses kept with them should be kept on the same schedule. Other animals should receive their first immunization with two injections a month apart, followed by a booster once or twice a year depending on exposure. Older horses that have little or no contact with other animals may not need to be vaccinated.

Strangles

This bacterial disease is caused by *Streptococcus equi*, which is transmitted through purulent discharges of infected horses. Infection can come about through direct contact or through contact with food, water, or objects that have been contaminated. Contaminated surfaces may remain a source of infection for a year or more. After infection, a horse will show signs of the disease within three to six days: a failure to drink, a high temperature (102 to 106 degrees Fahrenheit), and a nasal discharge. The bacteria induce abscesses in the lymph tissue of the pharynx, which cause the animal pain so that it becomes reluctant to swallow. The abscesses mature and drain quickly, and healing may occur in two weeks or so, but secondary infections are possible and complications may arise. Mortality is low, except among newborn foals, which may develop septicemia and die. Animals that recover are immune to the disease, and although they may become reinfected, the disease is then relatively mild and quick to disappear. Nevertheless, because strangles, once established among a group of horses, can last for years, it should be treated preventively by vaccination wherever it is known to exist. The vaccine, given in three doses at three-weekly intervals, is effective only in animals older than ten to twelve weeks; vaccination should be maintained on a six-month basis, with a single booster shot for all previously vaccinated horses. Only healthy horses should be vaccinated.

Potomac Horse Fever

This disease was identified in 1979 in the region of the Potomac River in Virginia but has spread to other parts of the eastern United States. The cause is *Erhlichia risticii,* but no one is certain how the organism is transmitted (possibly by insects); nevertheless, it seems to occur in warm weather near water, and its primary symptoms are diarrhea, fever, and colic. Some horses may simply go off their feed or become depressed; others show no symptoms at all. A vaccine may be given at three and four months and annually thereafter, but it is not entirely reliable and probably not necessary, unless the veterinarian recommends it because the disease occurs in the area.

Viral Arteritis

Like rhino pneumonitis, this infectious disease can also cause abortion in mares, and there seem to be varying responses in certain populations of horses. Standardbreds seem to have minor symptoms, whereas a 1984 outbreak in Thoroughbreds caused more severe symptoms with heavy losses in the breeding industry. There is in the United States an approved modified-live virus vaccine, which is used with stallions and unbred mares. Vaccination is recommended only when an outbreak is likely.

There are a number of other health problems in horses that can be prevented by vaccinations, such as clostridiosis (Shaker foal syndrome), anthrax, botulism, and endotoxemia, but vaccines should not be given routinely unless the diseases are common locally. Some vaccines are expensive or less than completely effective, with serious side effects and even transport restrictions. The vaccines used for viral encephalitis, tetanus, and usually rabies should be considered routine—and in fact are available in a combined dose—but the others may be necessary only if diseases exist in your area.

EIA and the Coggins Test Controversy

You will note that we recommend the Coggins test for equine infectious anemia (swamp fever) on a regular basis for every horse—whether or not the animal leaves home. The majority of states require proof of a negative Coggins test within six months or a year before the animal may be shipped interstate. This recommendation, however, is made not just to comply with applicable federal and state laws, but because the test is one of the only means now available to help control and eradicate this terrible disease. No vaccine has yet been developed to prevent EIA, which is caused by a virus and is transmitted by biting horse flies.

For years, there was not even an accurate way of detecting the disease, since the virus could not until recently be grown in the laboratory. Clinical signs are obvious in horses in an acute stage of EIA: high fever, weakness, anemia, depression, swelling of the abdomen and extremities (except in ponies), and death in 30 percent of the cases. But these signs may also indicate another disease process, and to complicate matters, not all horses with EIA show signs all the time. In chronic cases, horses may be symptomatic only intermittently and otherwise appear relatively normal; as the fever recurs, however, the horse's condition worsens, and death is probable. Latent EIA horses show no symptoms but are presumed to be carriers, since there are antibodies against the virus in their blood, which shows up positive on the Coggins test. In the early '70s, Dr. Leroy Coggins of Cornell perfected a test, which had first been tried in 1960, and he was able to report 95 percent accuracy for detecting EIA antibodies in horses. It is called an AGID test (agar-gel immunodiffusion) and involves the analysis of a blood sample taken from a horse. In March 1972 the U.S. Department of Agriculture initiated an EIA control program that includes the AGID test, which was declared the official USDA test in August of that year and can be performed by various official labs throughout the country. Horses that show positive reactions must be identified (with a brand) on the neck or a tattoo on the lip, and they cannot be moved across state lines except for purposes of slaughter or research. Owners have two choices: either to euthanize the positive horse or to quarantine him for life to prevent transmission of the disease. It is hoped, of course, that elimination of all diseased horses will eventually result in the eradication of the disease.

The Horse in Trouble: Problems and Treatments

So many books are available on the subject of equine health, some good and some not so good (see page 147), that there isn't much point in listing every disease and

Diseases Transmitted from Horses to Humans
———————Ω———————

BECAUSE HORSES LIVE LESS among people now than they did when we used them for transportation on a regular basis, the threat presented by diseases that can infect both horse and man is not now very great. Research and good management among horse owners have made it possible for us to prevent or control contagious diseases that affect both our species, and instances of horses causing human disease are quite rare. Nevertheless, it is interesting to learn what these conditions are, on the assumption that ignorance is not bliss and a little knowledge is not necessarily a dangerous thing. Horses are subject to various viral diseases, of which the best-known in terms of human illness is encephalitis, or sleeping sickness—the Eastern, Western, and Venezuelan varieties. In humans, symptoms can be fever, headache, drowsiness, gastric upset, lethargy, convulsions, and others. Eastern encephalitis is more serious for humans than the others, with a higher rate of fatality and permanent aftereffects for survivors. Though vaccination will build up antibody levels and prevent the disease in horses, epidemics can still occur in areas where vaccines are not used regularly, or where the disease has infected other animals from which the mosquitoes can carry the virus into humans. The other viral diseases common to man and horse are rabies (rare in horses now), vesicular stomatitis (common to many other animals as well, especially cattle, and not particularly serious), and equine infectious anemia. Human symptoms of the last-named disease, also called swamp fever, include fever, anemia, and diarrhea. Only a few human cases, however, have been reported and so swamp fever should not be considered serious except in horses.

Bacterial diseases affecting horses that man can catch are anthrax, brucellosis, glanders (now nearly extinct), hemorrhagic septicemia, listeriosis, meliodosis, tetanus, tuberculosis (the bovine type), and tularemia, but all of these could be considered of minor importance so far as horses are concerned. Cattle, cats, rabbits, and several other species are usually the source when these diseases infect humans. Leptospirosis is occasionally transmitted by both the horse and the donkey. Horses can carry both the bacteria that cause endemic relapsing fever and the ticks that transmit it, although the usual villains are wild rodents and birds.

There are several fungus diseases shared by man and horse, including a few kinds of ringworm, histoplasmosis, actinomycosis, and coccidiomycosis, among others. Equine parasites that may be significant for humans are rare in this country: sarcocystitis is rare in man, African trypanosomiasis is known only on that continent, and *Schistosoma japonicum* only in the Orient. The mite that causes sarcoptic mange is carried by the horse, as is the ox botfly, by which man may be infected. Ω

injury to which horses are susceptible. (There also isn't enough space, since that is a book in itself.) Nevertheless, the horse owner should be familiar with the obvious, serious symptoms that require veterinary attention, as well as some of the minor ailments or injuries and the measures to take until the veterinarian arrives.

If you are familiar with your horse's appearance and behavior during normal periods, any irregularity should attract your attention. Often there may be nothing to worry about, but try to find out the reason, if only because irregularity may be an early sign of something more serious in the offing. Some disease processes arrive suddenly and without apparent warning, while others come on gradually. The earlier you can see that there is a problem and the more detailed the information you can give the vet, the better your chances are for a quick and successful recovery.

Some problems, such as lameness and digestive ailments, may be chronic, requiring special preventive care or regular treatment. Since these are often congenital—caused by conformation defects—or brought about by poor care, anyone in the process of selecting a horse should take special precautions and get a veterinarian's opinion of the animal's condition. Even if an undesirable condition cannot be cured, there may be ways of treating it and allowing a horse to live a full useful life.

SYMPTOMS AND FIRST-AID PROCEDURES
The following symptoms should be considered deserving of a call to the veterinarian:

- refusal to eat or drink for twenty-four hours
- repeated coughing (more than twenty-four hours)
- high temperature (over 103 degrees Fahrenheit)

- shivering or excessive sweating for no obvious reason
- diarrhea or constipation for more than twelve hours
- frequent lying down or rolling, with or without moaning
- severe injury with obvious damage to skin, bone, or muscle
- persistent lameness

Any or all of these—in combination or singly—may indicate the presence of a serious disease or injury. Although many mild ailments or injuries can be diagnosed and treated at home without veterinary supervision, the inexperienced horse owner should not be encouraged to do more than exercise common sense, by calling the vet and applying some first-aid measures until he arrives or is able to give advice over the telephone. It is important to understand, however, why these symptoms—and less severe signs—are significant and what kinds of first aid are appropriate.

Refusal to Eat or Drink

Horses are creatures of habit, as we have said, and one of their fondest habits is eating. Refusal to do so should therefore be taken seriously. Before panicking, however, do make sure that there are no extenuating circumstances. Does the horse seem interested in food but unable to eat? There may be a mechanical blockage of some sort, not a disease process, and you might be able to deal with the situation yourself. Gentle massaging upward along the esophagus (left side of the neck) may bring up an object that is blocking the passage. Does the horse eat some but not all of its ration? You might be overfeeding or giving a new kind of feed that the animal hasn't grown accustomed to. See whether the horse will accept its usual ration instead. The problem may also be a dental one; taking great care, look inside the horse's mouth (holding its tongue between its teeth at the side of the jaw to keep your exploring hand from being bitten) for any broken or protruding teeth that may be causing the animal pain. If the mouth smells putrid, an abscess may be present. Chances are, however, that if the refusal to eat or drink is accompanied by other symptoms—sweating, lying down and rolling, high temperature, or diarrhea—a disease or colicky condition is causing the trouble, and immediate professional attention is required.

Repeated Coughing

This might be caused by a blockage (in which case the cough is really a choke); you can determine this by feeling the esophagus and massaging upward, as described above. If accompanied by heavy breathing, coughing may indicate emphysema (or heaves), which will require a vet's treatment. Rest the horse for a day, and if a bit of exercise brings on coughing or heaving again, call the vet. In addition to antihistamines, antibiotics, and rest (or occasionally, light work), the horse may be given a ration of special feed (with no hay), to eliminate irritating dust particles. Coughing may also indicate an upper-respiratory infection (the equine common cold), which will also involve some nasal dripping, keep the animal warm and isolated from others, put it on a soft diet (bran mash, for instance), and try a cough remedy recommended by your veterinarian. If the condition doesn't clear up within a day, call him again. Roaring—not coughing—is usually caused by paralysis of a vocal cord due to disease or a chronic condition that may be hereditary and is considered a fault.

High Temperature

This can be caused by a variety of problems and need not be serious unless it continues for a day or more, accompanied by sweating and excited behavior. Heat in the legs or feet indicates inflammation, which may be treated with anti-inflammatory treatments that will reduce the swelling. (See page 126). These include hosing with cold water and application of liniment or

A hunter recuperating from bronchitis with the help of an inhalator developed by the Delaware Equine Center, Cochranville, Pennsylvania.

Respiratory problems in horses can be mild or severe, temporary or chronic, but most of them will necessitate careful treatment under the supervision of a veterinarian, who may prescribe antibiotics, steroids, decongestants, or antihistamines. Horses with heaves, an equine form of emphysema that is not curable, will need special dust-free feed, and horses whose respiratory tracts produce blood during strenuous exercise (known as "bleeders") can benefit from the use of the drug Lasix, but there are also mechanical devices such as inhalators available to help relieve breathing problems. An effective device is Equi-Tech's Ultrasonic Nebulizer, which delivers vapor deep into the horse's respiratory system. This vapor can be simply a saline solution which has a cleansing effect for horses with allergies or an intolerance for dust-laden air, or it can carry drugs, such as Lasix or steroids, into the lungs to speed treatment. It is expensive, but for owners with several horses that are prone to respiratory ailments the investment may be a worthwhile one.

the various medications designed to cool the affected spot, so that healing may begin. If the condition persists and is accompanied by lameness, check the vet before taking more drastic measures. To treat high body temperature (over 103 degrees), keep the animal as quiet as possible, isolate it from other horses, and cover it with a blanket. Remove the usual ration, but provide plenty of cool water. If its temperature doesn't return to normal within 24 hours, call the vet.

Shivering or Excessive Sweating

Extreme cold, heat, and overexercise are obvious causes for these conditions. If none applies, you probably have trouble on your hands. Blanket the animal, isolate it, and keep it as quiet as possible. If the horse's muscles seem tight or hard, try feeding a bran mash. And go for the telephone.

Persistent Diarrhea or Constipation

Loose stool is not uncommon when an animal has had a sudden change of diet (grazing on young green grass is a common cause), but a distinctly liquid stool is a reason to alert a vet. Constipation may be treated

with a laxative medication or bran mash, but if relief is not evident within a few hours, call the expert in. Note whether the horse has been nibbling at its bedding and tell the vet, who may recommend that the animal be placed on wood chips rather than straw or whatever it is that is so appealing.

Frequent Lying Down and Rolling

This most obvious sign of colic, or intestinal trouble, requires immediate medical attention if the animal is to recover. There are many different kinds of colic—among them intestinal blockage, impaction, and torsion—and treatments vary. The first rule of first aid is to keep the animal on its feet and moving. Whether the activity actually helps to alleviate the problem or simply manages to distract the animal from its considerable pain is questionable. Keeping the horse from rolling, however, does help prevent injury and may keep the intestines from twisting and making matters worse. Ask the vet over the telephone if you should try to get some laxative into the horse. Mineral oil (through a syringe or stomach tube) is a possibility, or a mixture of bran (1 quart), mineral oil ($\frac{1}{2}$ cup), salt (2 tablespoons), and enough water to make a mash may be effective if the horse will ingest it. Your primary task, however, will be to keep the animal on its feet until the vet arrives. Horses cannot vomit as we do, so don't try any of your own remedies. The vet will probably give a muscle relaxant to promote defecation, or perhaps an enema, but that decision is best left to an expert.

Open Wounds

There are four general types of open wounds: abrasions (in which only surface layers of the skin are destroyed); incisions (produced by sharp instruments); puncture wounds (penetration of the superficial tissues); and lacerations (irregularly torn tissue). Wounds heal in one of two ways; either the sides of the wound,

Colic Remedies. There have always been a few commercial over-the-counter colic medications available, but we recommend that you ask your veterinarian's advice about products to keep on hand if your horse is prone to colic. Banamine, made by the Schering Company, is one of the excellent drugs available, through veterinarians only.

absent of infection, are kept close together (with or without suturing) so that cells grow quickly to bridge the gap, or granulation, the most common kind of healing in horses, takes place. Granulation involves the construction of new tissue growing upward from the depth of the wound and gradually filling in the gap from within until the wound closes. The presence of foreign bodies or contaminants in the wound will delay the healing process or even prevent it; the only way to avoid this problem is to remove the material. Irritation of a wound can also be caused by excessive movement of the affected area. Bandages may serve to immobilize the region of the wound, and horses may be restrained from bothering it through the use of cradles, side sticks, cross ties, or even a bit of red cayenne pepper on the bandage (not on the open wound, please!). The most common deterrent to healing is, surprisingly, the use of disinfectants, which may destroy surface cells and cause the granulating tissues to die and slough off rather than heal up. Instead of applying disinfectants, therefore, simply wash a wound with a mild salt solution (one teaspoon of salt in a pint of water) applied with cotton swabs. (The washing process will make it possible to see and remove any foreign bodies.)

If the wound is a superficial abrasion, it should heal quickly, without requiring veterinary attention. Wash the sore periodically with lukewarm water or a saline solution. Be sure that the stall and the horse are kept free of biting insects, and see that bedding is clean. Tack should be supple, soft, and well fitting, which should prevent saddle or girth sores to begin with—but if an abrasion exists, keep it free of all pressure from tack. (A piece of soft cloth or foam rubber may be used to pad the saddle.) Saddle and girth galls may develop if pressure on sore areas is allowed to continue for a long time, but if the owner is alert to the animal's condition, there is little possibility of things going that far. The skin of horses is very sensitive, especially during the shedding season, but sores need not be serious if treated properly. Witch hazel or zinc oxide can be applied lightly to soothe the irritation, but medication should not be necessary. If a sore does not heal quickly—within a few days—something is wrong, and the veterinarian should be consulted.

Skin eruptions may be caused by nervousness, allergies, dietary problems or infection, but these too are rarely serious. Keep the horse calm and well groomed, and put it on a light diet of bran mash and hay. Again,

if the situation doesn't clear up promptly, get expert advice before applying any medication.

If the horse suffers an injury of anything more than a superficial sort, remove it to a quiet spot, calm it down, and call the vet. You may clean the area with a mild salt solution, removing any foreign material as you go, but the horse may well need a tetanus shot and an antibiotic to prevent infection. Several effective antibiotic ointments are available to keep wounds covered and free of infection during the healing process, but these should not be used without supervision. Puncture wounds may heal superficially, but infections are all too likely to occur beneath the surface, causing abscesses. Incisions and most lacerations will probably require suturing to establish skin contact and promote healing, but punctures should never be sutured; drainage must be permitted to take place. Leg injuries may be treated with pressure bandages or casts, under which wounds will heal readily. Don't be disturbed by nasty-looking discharges from the top and bottom of the bandage; this is simply the sloughed-off tissue from the surface, under which the healthy granulating tissue is forming. Exposed joints require special care, flushing regularly with antibiotics as well as the use of bandages to inhibit movement and injected antibiotics as the veterinarian recommends. Some light exercise may be prescribed, since wounds will heal rapidly with complete rest but the scars that form are likely to break down and develop adhesions once the animal is allowed to move about.

If a wound is bleeding a great deal, you should try to stop the flow before the vet arrives by applying a pressure bandage (any piece of clean cloth will do) directly over the wound. Bright red blood spurting from the wound will indicate a severed artery, and no time should be lost in getting the bleeding to stop. Do not apply any medication yourself even after the bleeding stops unless you have instructions to do so; tranquilizers may only exacerbate the problem, especially if the animal is in pain.

Strains and Sprains

These words are often used interchangeably to refer to injuries that are neither bruises nor fractures, but some experts like to distinguish between damage to muscle alone (strain) and injury to the structures of the joint and its tendons or ligaments (sprain). Strenuous exercise will often cause mild strain, and most horsemen routinely treat their animals to a liniment or alco-

Wound Dressings

Many kinds of ointments, gels, liquid dressings, and powders are available for treating minor open wounds and abrasions, serving as disinfectants, antiseptics, and proud-flesh (or scar-tissue) deterrents. The products can be brushed, puffed, rubbed, sprayed, dabbed, or poured on wounds, and we recommend that you follow your veterinarian's advice as to their use. Many of them are excellent and will be necessary for certain situations but, in many cases, no medication at all will be necessary for prompt healing so long as the wound is kept clean. Disinfectants may, in fact, deter healing by damaging healthy tissue, and some ointments may have the same effect by keeping the wound covered when it should remain open. Preparations that deter infection and the growth of scar tissue are useful, because abscesses and overgrown scabs may have to be treated surgically if not prevented. A few of the most popular wound dressings—not all of them specifically intended for use on horses—are listed below.

Liquids:

Betadine Solution (Frederick Purdue Co.), which also comes as an ointment, is a disinfectant containing iodine and provides germicidal action.

Red-Kote (Dr. Naylor), a nondrying preparation that minimizes scar formation, keeps tissue soft and pliable and helps prevent infection.

Powders:

Cut-Heal Wound Powder for cuts promotes granulation (healing from the inside out) and reduces scarring, is available in a puffer bottle as well as in liquid, ointment, and aerosol forms.

Powders containing the antibiotic furazolidone, which is effective against many types of bacterial infection, include Topazone (Norden) and Furox Aerosol Powder (Farnam); available in aerosol cans

Nitrofurazone, another antibacterial agent, is contained in Bee Smart Fura-Aerosol (Farnam).

Wonder Dust (Farnam) is a caustic and drying agent for slow-healing cuts; prevents proud flesh.

Ointments:

A & D Ointment (Schering), which contains vitamins A and D, is a soothing, healing protective ointment for minor cuts and scrapes.

Aloe Vera Veterinarian Ointment Cream (Fiebing) is one of several products containing aloe vera, a soothing natural medication for healing minor cuts and abrasions.

Corona Ointment (Corona), enriched with lanolin, is a traditional product to restore dry or cracked hooves, also protects abrasions and irritations.

Neosporin (Warner Lambert) is a very effective product containing bacitracin-zinc, neomycin, and polymyxin B sulfate in cream form.

Nitrofurazone Dressing (Agrilabs) and Furacin are ointments containing nitrofurazone, an antibiotic that will attack various types of bacterial infection.

hol rub after work and put them in rest bandages, which will increase circulation. More severe strains and sprains, which may involve tendons and ligaments as well as muscles, deserve a great deal of care, however, and a call to the vet is usually in order. The affected area will be swollen or hot to the touch and must be cooled off before healing may take place. Once the spot has cooled and the swelling limited, heat treatments—or anti-inflammatory agents—will serve to restore circulation so that healing may take place. Since too much heat will slow down circulation and too little will have no effect at all, this process should be carried out with the utmost care. (See pages 126–31 for further information about medications and treatments for lameness.)

Bruises and Fractures

If a horse has suffered an injury—a kick or a fall or some other trauma—and there appears to be damage to muscle or bone, even though the skin has not been broken, your first task is to call the vet. Then move the animal to a place free of distraction and keep it as calm as possible under the circumstances, while you try to determine the location and source of the injury (if you didn't witness it yourself). A bad fracture may be obvious, but many times broken bones can be determined only by X-ray, so don't assume anything, especially if the injury is in the leg.

If you are, by some unhappy chance, out on the trail and the animal cannot or will not move on its own, you can try tying up the injured limb (if it's a leg that's affected) with a belt and getting it to move on three legs. If that does not work, your only path may be out of the woods to the nearest telephone. When you are riding with someone else, make sure one of you stays with the injured animal to keep it as calm as possible. Should you be several hours (or days) from help and the animal in great pain, you may find yourself in the unfortunate position of deciding whether it should be put out of its misery right there and then. Decisions about euthanasia are, of course, best left to a veterinarian—many advanced surgical procedures have been developed for saving badly injured horses—but if you feel that the situation is truly hopeless and the animal is suffering with a severe fracture, you may have to take matters into your own hands. There are several ways of putting a horse down, but the recommended method for nonexperts is a rifle or handgun, pointed directly between the eyes into the brain, taking care to avoid the possibility of ricochet. (Cutting the jugular vein or striking the head with a heavy club or stick is far too risky and will probably cause more pain and suffering than you would care to witness.) It goes without saying that anyone who rides out on the trail so far that help is unobtainable should carry a rifle or a so-called humane killer (which is a pistol that shoots a retractable bolt rather than a bullet and is recommended where the carrying of standard firearms is illegal).

Minor bruises or contusions, caused by a direct blow to bone or muscle, may clear up completely without even being noticed. If any blood vessels have been ruptured, however, and swelling takes place, the affected area should be hosed down or cooled until the hemorrhaging stops. Because bruises can be serious, a veterinarian should be called in.

Lameness

Almost any sensitive, observant person can tell when a horse is lame, whether the cause is pain or some mechanical defect, such as a congenital or acquired imperfection in the construction of the leg or foot. Painful lameness is the most common problem facing the owner of an otherwise sound horse, and in the pages that follow we will discuss many ailments that affect the equine foot and leg. Bruises, fractures, strains, and sprains may cause lameness, of course, but since it is not always easy to diagnose, sudden lameness should be treated as follows. Check each hoof to be sure that no foreign body has worked its way into the sole or frog. If the object is easily removed and seems to have caused no puncture, trot the horse for a few steps and be sure that no lameness persists. If there has been a puncture, check with the vet, who will examine the hoof and may wish to give a tetanus shot. If there is nothing visible in the hoof, run your hands over each leg for signs of heat, sores, or any other irregular condition. If after a few minutes of rest the animal still limps, call the veterinarian. The cause may be nothing more than a mild strain, which you can treat at home with applications of cold and heat (in that order, and not without reading up on treatments for inflammation), but any obvious lameness deserves professional attention, for without good care it may very well become a serious problem.

Eyes and Ears

Red, watery eyes may be flushed out with a warm solution of boric acid or treated with an ophthalmic ointment. Be sure that the stall is free of dust, pollen, or other foreign matter that may be affecting the eyes. If the wateriness is accompanied by swelling and accumulation of pus, the animal may be suffering from an infection—specifically, leptospirosis, of which this "moon blindness," as it is called, is a symptom. This will require veterinary treatment with antibiotics or corticosteroids. The ears are delicate instruments, and a horse suffering with an infection, an injury, or the presence of ear mites or a fungus growth will show sensitivity whenever its ears are touched. If you notice any sores, growths, or discharge, be sure to ask for veterinary advice. The condition may not be serious or require emergency attention, but if it is allowed to persist the animal may become difficult to handle during grooming or bridling or even at work.

FOOT AND LEG PROBLEMS

Because many horsemen would agree that at least 90 percent of a horse's problems are in the feet, it is worth

In spite of the widespread use of phenylbutazone (bute), corticosteroids, and other anti-inflammatory drugs, including aspirin, as well as various new treatments for lameness (see page 130), liniments of various kinds are still sold by the gallon to horse owners who believe in their soothing astringent value, and in their ability to reduce muscle soreness, stiffness, and minor swelling. Diluted in water, witch hazel or alcohol; liniments make good body washes; undiluted or in a strong solution, they are often called *braces* or *tighteners* and may result in temporary relief of soreness. However, any product labeled as a counterirritant, or containing iodine, should be used with care, and with a veterinarian's supervision. Masking chronic pain may cause more trouble in the long run than it solves in the short, and even over-the-counter products can cause damage if not used properly. Many liniment makers claim a certain amount of antiseptic effectiveness for their products (iodine), but most of their cooling, soothing effects are produced by such traditional ingredients as camphor, menthol, oil of spearmint, witch hazel, and so on, none of which are likely to cause harm—or bring permanent relief.

Absorbine Veterinary Liniment (W.F. Young) is still a best-selling product after over 100 years; the ingredients have changed only slightly, with acetone now removed; menthol, oil of wormwood, and iodine are still present. Also available in a gel form that contains a number of natural botanical extracts, such as echinacea, artemesia, and calendula.

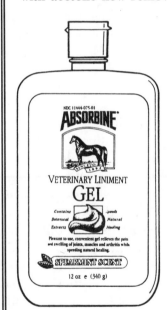

B.A.L. (Brace Antiseptic Liniment from Zirin) also contains aromatic oils that produce an astringent effect.

Bigeloil (Bigelow-Clark) is also full of menthol and camphor, with no iodine.

Equi-tite (Equi-Flite Technologies) contains the pepper extract capsaicin, and Boswellic acid, along with menthol, oil of rosemary, and other ingredients that produce a temporary topical relief when rubbed into the legs.

Mineral Ice (Straight Arrow) is gel that produces a cooling effect and acts as a therapeutic body wash in solution. Another Straight Arrow product is the slightly less expensive Icy Blue Liniment and a lotion, Heat Creme Liniment.

Tuttle's Elexer (Y-Tex) is an old-time product that contains ox gall, various oils, and pure-grain alcohol, which many trainers swear by as a cooling-off aid after exercise.

Vetrolin (Farnam) is another traditional concoction, which contains green castile soap along with the usual aromatic oils and camphor.

---

devoting a whole section to describe some of them briefly. Several disorders have common names, indicating that they are relatively common; others may be unfamiliar and not readily diagnosed by a nonexpert. All the more reason why any continued lameness should have the attention of a veterinarian—preferably sooner rather than later. Some lamenesses are caused by injury, and if this is the case, the horse may have to be given an injection of tetanus toxoid. Some may be caused simply by conformation defects, and others by bad care. Various ailments are curable, but others may be chronic and require regular attention and/or treatment.

Problems

Cracks in the horny wall of the hoof may start at the bottom and work up, or they may begin at the coronary band and work down. The latter are the result of an

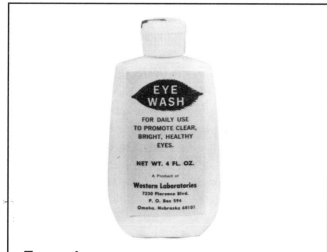

Eyewash

Many of the manufacturers of eye-washes recommend daily use of drops to prevent eye trouble, but we don't think that this should be necessary in a healthy animal. If a horse's eyes are not clear or are consistently red, with any unusual discharge, the veterinarian will undoubtedly prescribe an ophthalmic ointment. Eye-drop solutions are available, but a boric acid solution is perfectly safe and probably just as effective.

injury to the coronet which may result in permanent disruption of the hoof's growth. (A normal hoof grows $3/4$ to 1 inch a month.) When the crack begins at the bottom, the cause is usually drying of the wall or improper trimming. A hoof must be somewhat flexible and elastic, and this is controlled by moisture in the foot. (The wall contains about 25 percent water, the sole 33 percent, the frog 50 percent.) Cracks are identified by their location—toe, quarter, or heel, of which the last two are most serious. Sometimes treatment involves rasping a groove across the end of a crack to prevent its extending farther; toe clips may be applied to toe cracks, or proper trimming and shoeing may be enough to solve the problem. If the cracks are deep enough to reach the sensitive laminae beneath, it may be necessary to pare away the crack and fill it with plastic; this procedure often involves delicate dovetailing of the hoof wall and suturing with steel. Heel cracks are sometimes caused by injury; pressure bandages should be applied to stop any bleeding, and treatment may involve antibiotic ointments, bandaging, paring of the wall, and special bar shoes to protect the

heel. Drainage of abscesses is essential, and a poultice may be required to reduce inflammation. The foot should be bandaged until the draining has stopped and the wound is dry.

Keratoma is a rare tumorlike growth in the wall that causes lameness as it puts pressure on the sensitive laminae. The only treatment is surgical removal of the affected area.

A bruised sole may be caused by stones or an improperly fitting shoe, in acute cases producing inflammation and lameness. Cold packs or anti-inflammatory drugs (such as phenylbutazone) may be applied to reduce the swelling and a leather pad inserted between the shoe and the foot, to remain in place until the horse recovers from its lameness.

Bruised heels may develop lesions generally called corns, most commonly caused by incorrect shoeing. The shoes must be removed and the feet trimmed; the horse cannot be reshod until the bruise heals.

If the corn has become infected, it may be helpful to apply a poultice (see page 129) for a few days. After the infection has been controlled, the application of aureomycin spray may help harden the sole before shoeing. Your veterinarian can determine whether or not a metal plate will be necessary to protect the sole; the use of pads, once widely accepted, is now considered questionable, as they do not prevent concussion on the sole.

Puncture wounds in the sole may be caused by stepping on sharp objects, and lameness will result, but perhaps not immediately. A black dot or line in the sole will indicate a puncture, and the object may often be found embedded. If it is not found, pare away the sole and explore all black areas. Pain will stop once the abscess, if there is one, has drained. A tetanus shot should be given, and treatment for inflammation is indicated. Because complications are common, the vet should definitely be consulted. The frog may also be affected by puncture wounds similar to those of the sole, and they require the same sort of attention.

Thrush is usually caused by poor sanitation and improper trimming of the feet and, with some rare exceptions, should not be found in any horse kept, for whatever reason. It is a condition of the frog characterized by a fetid, blackish discharge in the sulci of the frog, caused by an infection by the organism *Spherophorus necrophorus*. The horse's feet will be tender and may even come up lame if the disease is allowed to progress. The condition can be prevented if the

Diagnosing Lameness at Home

Have someone trot the animal back and forth in front of you over a level area about 200 feet long, while you watch the motion of the horse's head, neck, and hindquarters. Most lamenesses affect only one foot, thus throwing the horse's symmetry off balance; the trot is the fastest of the symmetrical gaits and thus the easiest gait at which one can detect abnormal motion. (Of course, we are assuming that you know what normal motion is; if not, observe at least a dozen sound horses moving at the trot over the same ground, so that you will recognize irregular action when it occurs.) A sound horse will carry its head and neck relatively motionless at the trot while the croup will move up and down in a regular way as the animal springs off one diagonal and onto the other. If the head and neck movement is exaggerated during the trot, the lame leg is a foreleg. If the head and neck remain steady but the croup (or the hocks) rises and falls in an irregular pattern, a hind leg is the source of the problem.

In order to determine which of the two forelegs is lame, watch the position of the trot as the horse moves toward you. If the head lifts high above the normal level, the horse is supported at that point by the painful leg; the head will drop back to its normal position later in the stride, as the weight is borne by the healthy leg. If the head drops below normal during the stride, the pain may be caused during the break-over part of the gait, as the horse tries to transfer its weight as quickly as possible.

If the lameness appears to be in the hind legs, watch the horse trot away from you and observe the motion of the croup. One side will move perceptibly higher or lower than the other side. If one side regularly rises higher than the other, the pain is occurring as the horse shifts quickly from the bad leg to the good one or "hitches behind." If the croup on one side never rises to a normal height, the horse is delaying the break-over phase of the stride because that leg is painful. Another sign of hind-leg lameness is that the muscles on the painful side will tend to go slack within two or three days, this may not be noticeable at rest but will be so in motion.

This diagnosis should take only a few minutes for a horseman with a practiced eye. If you still can't be sure which leg is the bothersome one, make a careful examination of all four, feeling for heated areas, which indicate inflammation, and for irregular structure, obvious sores, or foreign bodies and lesions in the hoof. Another way of detecting areas is to tap lightly around the hoof with a small hammer. Flaky sole areas should be removed with a paring knife and all black spots or lines followed through to their depths. It is best to remove the shoe or shoes at this point (see page 86); if you expect to exercise the horse as described above to help in the diagnosis, remove both shoes front or back to maintain symmetry. The veterinarian can employ a number of devices to help in the diagnosis: hoof testers, which are used to compress the foot to determine pain; wedges, to accentuate lameness by applying pressure to a limited area of the foot; and nerve blocks, which anesthetize separate parts of the foot and leg.

stable is kept clean and the horse's feet cleaned and trimmed regularly. A horse with thrush should be kept on a dry surface and the affected frogs trimmed to permit drainage. Drying agents, such as formalin or Kopertox, may be applied in the early stages of the disease; an advanced case must involve soaking in a magnesium sulfate solution. A tetanus shot is also indicated.

Pedal osteitis is a term used to describe inflammation of the pedal bone (or distal phalanx), which shows up as lameness with foot pain and abnormal X-rays. This condition, for which there is little effective treatment, is difficult to diagnose—as many causes of lameness still are, in spite of advanced diagnostic techniques—and has a poor prognosis, as the bone abnormalities are permanent rather than temporary.

Contracted heels usually affect the forefeet and not just the heels. They result from improper pressure on the frog, due to neglect or a pathological condition, such as thrush or navicular disease. Contracted heels are seen often in Tennessee Walking Horses and American Saddlebreds, whose feet have been allowed to grow very long for show purposes. Heel contraction is a secondary condition, and the initial lesion or cause should be identified before treatment is given. Along with treatment, therapy for the heels should be provided to reestablish normal frog pressure by correct trimming, application of a hoof softener, or the use of corrective shoes.

Navicular disease (or podotrochleosis) describes a number of disease conditions affecting the distal sesamoid or navicular bone. The cause is not clearly defined; it may involve injury or conformation defects, but nutritional and hormonal influences may also contribute. In any event, it is a serious disease and an incurable one, although its effects may be alleviated by rest, corrective shoeing and trimming, and drugs, such as steroids, anti-inflammatory agents, and so on. The navicular bone is a tiny bone in the coffin joint, which rests on the deep flexor tendon; between bone and tendon is the navicular bursa, which contains a smooth lubricating substance. As weight is placed on the horse's foot, there is a certain amount of pressure of the bone on the tendon. Excessive friction will cause cartilage and tendon damage, and the bursa will become inflamed (bursitis). Eventually the bone itself will become deformed, and pain will result when the tendon moves over it. Horses with straight pasterns and shoulders or weak navicular bones may develop this disease, although horses of all ages and types may be affected, especially if they have been worked frequently on hard surfaces. Initially, the rider may notice a slight irregularity in gait, a stumbling or sloppy stride, which will disappear after rest and then recur. Eventually the lameness will become continuous, and secondary bursitis in the shoulder may result. Overworn toes of shoes, extended forelegs at rest, and short, square development of toes on barefoot horses are other signs, and an attempt at diagnosis should be made as soon as possible so that corrective measures may be taken, if the disease has not progressed too far, to relieve pain and lameness.

Laminitis (or founder) is an inflammation of the laminae of the feet, usually the front feet, and it appears in both acute and chronic phases. The acute stage involves extreme pain, warm feet, and a rapid pulse, while chronic laminitis (which may occur after an acute case) is indicated by intermittent lameness and a diverging ring around the hoof wall. Although many different causes have been listed, most cases originate from enterotoxemia—which results from overeating of grain or from a postpartum infection in broodmares—which causes the connective tissue in the coffin pedal joint to break down. The signs of laminitis develop quickly; feet will become hot because of increased circulation, and the pulse in the area will be very rapid. If only the forelegs are affected, the horse will try to support itself on the hind feet; if all four feet are affected, the animal may refuse to stand, and if forced to move it will make a shuffling, stumbling motion. Diagnosis is not difficult; lameness and a dropped (or flat, rather than concave) sole are common. In an advanced case, the coffin bone will rotate until it comes through the sole. There are many forms of treatment, the first one being to control the diet. Mineral oil can be used for laxative purposes and to prevent further absorption of the toxins. Nerve blocks, drugs, hormones, vitamin therapy, and soaking in warm water are other treatments, as are limited exercise, corrective shoeing, and the application of acrylic to affect the rotation of the coffin bone.

Sidebones is the common term for premature ossification of the lateral cartilages. This occurs primarily in the front feet, because of either conformation, concussion, or direct injury. As a horse ages, cartilage may normally ossify, or turn to bone, but the reason why this process may be hastened is not clear. Lameness is not common, but the foot cannot grow properly, and other disorders, such as corns, may result. If there is no pain or lameness, nothing need be done, unless one wishes to remove the calcified cartilage surgically for cosmetic reasons, since the affected foot may appear deformed.

Quittor is the common name for lateral cartilage necrosis, which is the destruction of tissue usually caused by deep puncture wounds above the coronary band, although punctures of the sole and an interfering gait may also result in necrosis. A painful swelling above the hoof is the first sign, with resulting lameness, which ceases when the lesion ruptures and drains. This draining does not cure the problem, which may require surgical removal of the affected cartilage. The long-term outlook is not good, because treatment and surgery are not always successful.

Ringbone is a term that refers generally to any bony enlargement below the fetlock, although there are different causes and types of affliction. True articular ringbone is a kind of arthritis or arthrosis affecting the pastern (high) or coffin (low) joint of the foot, usually caused by a sudden or chronic strain. A horse's conformation may make it susceptible to injury; a horse that toes in or out may be rotating the joint in such a way as to tear the ligaments. Forelegs are most commonly afflicted, and lameness may develop slowly or rapidly. Acute lameness accompanied by swelling in the affected joint is the usual sign; flexing of the limb to an extreme position may accentuate the tenderness. There is no cure, but the usefulness of a horse can be extended by good shoeing (or removal of shoes), trimming, and complete rest. Blistering, firing, X-ray treatment, and the use of anti-inflammatory drugs, such as bute, have been tried, with inconsistent success, for short-term relief, but none is reliable and some may even cause further destruction of the joint. Nonarticular ringbone, which looks like articular ringbone externally, does not affect the joints directly and may appear only as a blemish without accompanying tenderness; it is not as serious as articular ringbone but it is not curable. False ringbone, which can be diagnosed by X ray, looks like ringbone but does not usually cause lameness; this is an enlargement of the pastern joint caused by torn ligaments but not affecting the bone. It may be acute or chronic and can be treated with injection of steroids or radiation therapy, coupled with rest.

Osselets can be bony (true osselets) or they can involve no bony protuberance and be called "green." Either way, the condition involves a lesion affecting the fetlock joint, usually caused by a racing or training injury in which the fibrous joint capsule has been torn. The joint will be warm and swollen as a result, and lameness may occur. Rest with limited exercise is indicated until the inflammation has decreased; the traditional remedies are blistering, thermal cautery, and radiation therapy.

Osteoarthritis in the fetlock joint may be caused by excessive wear and tear (the condition is seen most often in racehorses), although many other causes have been described. Diet and general conformation should be evaluated and corrected; corrective shoeing, anti-inflammatory drugs, and other forms of therapy may bring only temporary relief.

Wind-puffs, or windgalls, are swellings of the joint capsule in the fetlock. There is no lameness, and treatment will vary according to the cause. Sometimes a horse that has been in heavy training will develop a wind-puff if it is suddenly not exercised; inadequate nutrition may also be the cause. An elastic wrap over a sweat, such as equal parts of glycerine and alcohol, will reduce the swelling temporarily; draining the joint capsule and injection of a corticosteroid may also improve the condition. Permanent correction may be impossible, but since performance is not affected, this is not necessary in any case.

Sesamoiditis is inflammation of the sesamoid bones, caused by a strain of the sesamoid ligaments during racing or jumping. The area around the fetlock joint may become enlarged or not, but there is sensitivity and in some cases acute lameness, in which case the joint must be immobilized in a cast or support bandage and treatment given to reduce inflammation. In chronic cases, the treatments described above for wind-puffs may be indicated. If there is a fracture, surgery may be performed, and the prognosis depends on the degree of the ligament tearing and the progress of the condition.

Bucked, or *sore, shins* means inflammation of the cannon bone (third metacarpal), seen most often in young animals trained for racing and rare in horses over three years old. Rest, reduction of inflammation, and other forms of therapy are recommended, after which time the animal may be returned to training.

Splints refers to the same condition in the splint bones (second and fourth metacarpals), usually caused by trauma and seen most often in horses with poor conformation whose knees are so badly aligned that the splint bones support more weight than they are designed to do. Lameness will result, along with inflammation, heat, and tenderness. After the acute phase, lameness will end, although the leg may be blemished. Rest and counterirritants are usually recommended to arrest the progress of the disorder, though surgery may be indicated in case of fracture.

Horses confined for a long time may come up lame with *ruptured knee tendons.* At extended paces the lameness will disappear, although the leg will be somewhat less efficient than a normal one. Surgery to reunite the ends of the tendon may be considered as treatment. Other tendons may become ruptured where surgery is not possible; rest, reduction or control of inflammation, and support of the limb are all one can do.

Contracted tendons in either forelegs or hind legs may be congenital or acquired, caused by either nutritional deficiency or injury. In foals, the leg may be splinted from foot to elbow as early in life as possible, so that tendons will relax enough to permit the leg to bear weight. In later life, the hooves should be trimmed and diet should be adjusted; at this point, prognosis is poor

Tendinitis (bowed tendons) is most often seen in horses that have been driven or ridden at a fast pace. The flexor tendon is strained or torn when exceptional stress is put on the leg, and when it is acute, the horse will feel extreme pain and come up very lame. The leg will be hot and swollen as a result of hemorrhage, and only the toe will rest on the ground when the animal is standing. Treatment of acute tendinitis requires controlling inflammation (cold-water packs do well) and supporting the leg with a cast or bandage. Steroids can be injected, and complete rest—for as long as a year—may be recommended. Chronic tendinitis, visible as a bulge behind the cannon bone, has been treated in many ways, but blistering and firing are not usually successful. Drugs and surgery are more effective, but general good care, involving applications of hot and cold (poultices and cold hosing), rest, and supporting bandages or massage will help relieve symptoms.

Capped knee refers to hygroma of the carpus (or knee), which is a swelling resulting from injury. (The knee joint in a horse's foreleg is comparable to the wrist joint in humans; both are referred to as the carpus.) The accumulated serum is removed and corticosteroids injected into the area, but most important is the use of an elastic bandage (for at least a week) to keep the swelling from recurring.

Carpitis is frequently seen in racehorses and is indicated by acute lameness (in the swinging phase of the gait). It is caused by injury, and fracture is often present as well. When there is no fracture, treatment may include rest, corticosteroids, or even surgery. If new bone growth takes place, the prognosis is poor, although pain can be relieved by the use of bute or other drugs.

Epiphysitis, or "big knee," is caused by compression of the epiphysis of the radial bone. It can occur in young horses, especially those that are overweight or that toe in as a result of too much exercise. Lameness does not always result, and the condition can be diagnosed only by X ray. The area will be hot to the touch, however, and sensitive to strong pressure. Rest and diet adjustment are the best forms of treatment.

Capped elbow and shoe boil refer to olecranon bursitis, an enlargement of the elbow following an injury, often by the horse's own shoes. The condition may require surgery, but usually the injection of corticosteroids will relieve the problem. If the condition persists, a round roll or sausage boot below the fetlock should be used to limit flexion of the damaging foot or an elbow.

Osteoarthritis of the shoulder joint is not common, but it should be taken into consideration when a horse comes up lame. Usually caused by some injury, it is often accompanied by a fracture. The horse will refuse to extend its foreleg fully, and flexing the shoulder and extending the elbow will cause pain. Treatment can be only temporary, through the use of a local anesthetic or an anti-inflammatory drug.

Trochanteric bursitis, often called "whirlbone" lameness, involves inflammation of the region between the greater trochanter and the middle gluteal-muscle tendon. It is usually secondary to other conditions, but is seen in show horses or racehorses (Standardbreds especially) that are turned frequently or forced to work often in a circle. The animal becomes lame behind and sore when palpated in the region of the swelling. Rest, heat, and massage of the muscles will help, as will corticosteroids and counterirritants.

Occasionally, accidents, falls, or other injuries may cause paralysis of various leg muscles and eventual atrophy (called "shoulder sweeney" when the shoulder muscles are affected). Good nursing care, including anti-inflammatory drugs, hosing the leg, and rest, will improve the situation, though complete recovery is not always possible.

Upward fixation of the patella, when the leg is locked in an extended position, is not uncommon in young horses and is most common in the Shetland pony, in which it is probably hereditary. It is quite painful, especially if both legs are affected, and may be confused with stringhalt (see next page), since it involves a sudden upward jerk in motion. The first time it is noticed, an attempt may be made to reposition the patella (you can do this by pulling the leg forward and pushing the patella upward and to the side, or by causing the animal to make a sudden movement). If it recurs, surgery may be necessary, for arthritis may follow.

Gonitis is the inflammation of the stifle joint, and it can be either very painful or a chronic problem with slowly developing lameness. Causes are numerous; the most common are strain and infection in the stifle following a wound. If infection is present, it must be identified so that it can be properly treated; drainage of the area is usually indicated, and rest and painkillers will help relieve symptoms.

Stringhalt (or springhalt) is a spasmodic flexion of one or both hind legs, seen more often in draft horses than in pleasure horses. The cause is not known, although the symptoms resemble those of other ailments—notably dermatitis, mange, and even thrush. Surgery will probably be required if a true case of stringhalt is diagnosed.

Spavin is lameness in the hock, and there are various different kinds; included are fractures and osteoarthritis, with new bone formation or with bone destruction. *Bone spavin* refers to bone destruction on the medial aspect of the hock, and it is not easy to diagnose. Lameness is most visible when a horse first gets up; at rest it will hold its hind leg slightly flexed, and in motion the lame leg moves with a jerky, stabbing movement. Pain occurs when the limb hits the ground, and the horse will try to lift it as quickly as possible. Because the degenerated tissue cannot be removed, treatment involves making the horse more comfortable through corrective shoeing in which the toe is shortened and rolled and the heel elevated. Firing and blistering have been traditional treatments, but there are more effective treatments now available, involving the destruction of cartilage in the affected joint.

Bog spavin usually results in a poorly conformed hock from strain on the tarsal joint. The horse is not usually lame unless the condition is complicated by arthritis or fracture. The blemish may remain, but if no pain exists, treatment may not be necessary. Blisters and liniments are not too effective; prolonged massage two or three times a day may bring down the swelling, and pressure bandages, if the horse will tolerate them, are also useful. The horse's diet should be reduced somewhat, especially the portion of grain.

Thoroughpin is a distention of the sheath of the deep flexor tendon at the hock, visible on the outside of the leg; the animal is not usually lame, but it is possible to reduce the swelling by removing the fluid from the area and applying a well-padded pressure bandage. Blisters and leg paints are not effective at all.

The above are the most common ailments affecting equine feet and legs; there are others, and there are many different ways in which the rest of the musculoskeletal system may be put out of commission. Readers are referred to any number of good medical books on the subject, most particularly *Equine Medicine and Surgery* (second edition), edited by E. J. Catcott, D.V.M. and J. F. Smithcors, D.V.M., Ph.D.; Wheaton, Illinois: American Veterinary Publications, 1972. See especially Chapter 18, by J. R. Rooney, J. L. Shupe, J. H. Johnson, and J. E. Bartels.

Treatments for Lameness

Special types of treatment are mentioned in the discussion of specific ailments and injuries, but we would like to give some attention to the methods and products involved in these treatments, so that nonprofessionals may be familiar with the procedures when their own horses are treated. Many over-the-counter products are available at tack and feed stores, as well as through catalogs, but because these are nonprescription agents, their effectiveness is relatively limited. Nevertheless, they should be used with care and—preferably—with a veterinarian's blessing, and they should not be substituted for a veterinarian's attention. Any injury deserves good care, and any prolonged condition involving lameness should not be allowed to go untreated by a professional.

The most effective treatment for lameness is complete rest, but because many trainers cannot afford to let their animals go unworked, they have devised many methods for treating mild injuries and other disorders. Some of these are today considered old-fashioned and not particularly effective, but you will see them still in use, as any tour around a racetrack stable will show.

Painful lameness in a horse is usually accompanied by heat and swelling in the affected area. This is usually caused by internal hemorrhage and inflammation, which must be arrested before healing can begin. The simplest way to do this is to cool the spot; hosing with cold water, soaking in a tub or whirlpool bath, and applying an ice pack or a bandage soaked in a cooling lotion are the most common methods. If you use a hose, make sure the flow of water is slow and the hose is laid against the affected part so that the water flows down in a sheet. Astringent lotions and cooling liniments are often used for rubbing on a horse's legs after strenuous exercise, but they are less effective than cold water for more serious inflammation, since for any long-lasting effect the lotion or liniment must be used to soak a cotton bandage, which is then wrapped on the leg, and when the liquid dries out the bandage will become hot and do more harm than good. It is probably the rubbing

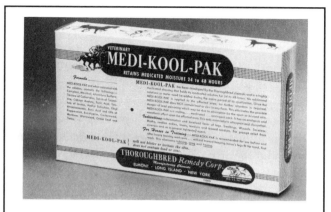

Cold water and ice are the cheapest ingredients for cold packs, and most veterinarians still recommend a good cold hosing (if you have the patience) or a bucket full of ice (if the horse does). Some clever devices have been developed to make the application of ice to a horse's legs somewhat easier for the owner and horse short on patience.

Hydro Therapy Boots attach to a garden hose and hold it in place to allow water to flow over the leg. The flow can be modulated and the water gradually released.

Canvas Ice Boots are a less expensive alternative, and are designed to hold ice in place against a horse's leg

The Hydro Therapy Leg Soaker is a hose device that encircles one or both legs in front or back, and allows cold water to be distributed on each in a more efficient way than with a handheld hose.

Temporary relief can be obtained with squeeze-activated cold packs developed for human athletes. These products stay in place with Velcro fasteners or cotton wraps and are easy to use and quick to apply in an emergency. Good for the first-aid box.

TTEAM

One of the pioneers in using manipulation techniques to work with difficult horses, Linda Tellington-Jones continues to spread the word on her Tellington-Jones Touch Equine Awareness Movement by publishing books, holding clinics to work with horses, and teaching others how to use the techniques she has perfected since 1975, when she began studying with Moshe Feldenkrais, an Israeli physicist whose work in body/mind integration enabled many humans to deal with pain and physical disorders. In 1977, Linda Tellington-Jones began to apply what she had learned about manipulating nerves and muscles to horses; since then she has been very successful rehabilitating animals that are sour, tense, and even unmanageable. Her training programs consist of exercises that the horse owner can perform at home. She considers her work a form of animal communication—a nonthreatening system of touch that can establish rapport between horse and human to build up self-confidence in each, as well as improving performance. For more information, call the TTEAM office at (800) 854-8326.

---

in any case rather than the liniment itself that has a therapeutic effect on the swelling.

The most effective anti-inflammatory agents are drugs that the veterinarian can provide. One of the most effective of these is phenylbutazone (Butazolidin, or "bute"), which has painkilling effects as well; it may be injected or applied directly to the affected joint or tissue. Because bute works so well to kill the pain, the temptation is to use this instead of proceeding with a treatment to eliminate the cause of the trouble. This is risky, of course, because the absence of pain (and subsequent lameness) does not mean that the condition no longer exists, and it may in fact be getting worse. A horse that feels no pain may injure itself again and the owner or trainer may not even notice. Also, recent research has shown that bute may not be such a miracle drug if used over an extended period of time; it is thought by some to affect bone marrow and the production of blood cells. Therefore, it is not recommended for use without expert veterinary guidance.

Corticosteroids are also effective anti-inflammatory drugs, but they too should not be overused, for horses treated with them have a lower general resistance to infection. Azium (which is dexamethasone) is the most common of these drugs; it may be injected or administered in food. Depomedrol is a useful and longer-acting steroid. Other treatments include the use of aspirin (which can also be administered for influenza, strangles, and pleurisy) and Vitamin E. Equiproxen, from Diamond Laboratories, is neither aspirin nor steroid but is an effective anti-inflammatory agent.

Once the inflammation has been reduced, circulation must be encouraged so that healing can take place. The application of heat or counterirritants of various kinds is the usual form of treatment at this stage. Some methods are relatively simple and some are drastic, the choice of method depending on the seriousness of the injury, the type of wound, the amount of time required for healing, the individual animal, its future use, and the availability of good nursing care. Counterirritants must not be used on acute injuries, since they may cause further damage to the tissue. The whole process of reducing inflammation must take place before heat or other circulation-stimulating methods may proceed.

One old-time means of promoting healing is the application of a poultice, which is a soft, moist dressing packed against the affected area, usually by a bandage of some sort to keep the material in place. This wet dressing is often an antiphlogistic—composed of glycerine, kaolin, and aromatics—and because it brings a certain amount of heat to the skin and muscles beneath, it may help in stimulating circulation. Therapy with hot water (about 120 degrees Fahrenheit) applied to the area for three or four minutes, alternating with a minute of cold water, may have the same effect if repeated three or four times—the whole procedure being performed several times a day. Obviously, this is not a very practical method for people without a lot of time on their hands. Gentle massage in the direction of the venous flow, radiation therapy, electrical stimulation, surgery, blistering, and firing are other counterirritant methods, but the use of these should, of course, be left to a vet's discretion.

Blistering, which many horsemen believe in, is a controversial method. A caustic agent is applied directly to the skin in paste or liquid form, either once or in several consecutive treatments. Active ingredients may be iodine, red iodide of mercury, muriatic acid, and coal oil, each requiring a different type of application and bandaging. The effect is the same, however: vesicles form, serum oozes, and the skin dries, becomes crusted, and eventually sloughs off. The procedure is painful, so that sedatives and twitches are often necessary, as well as some device to keep the animal from chewing on the blistered area. The acute pain may last from six to twenty-four hours, followed by a wet phase that can last up to four days. After a month or so, the dried material is shed and the limb begins to look normal. If reblistering is indicated, one must wait a week or so after this last stage. Aside from the painful and unattractive aspects of this practice, blistering is questionable for other reasons. For one thing, there is no way of stopping the blistering action once it has been applied. Soap and water or bandaging may help soothe the irritated tissues, but it is very difficult to control the results of the blister. Obviously, mild blisters applied in succession are to be preferred to one or two severe blisters, but many experts believe that the procedure shouldn't be used at all.

Leg painting is a more conservative method of applying the same principle. Leg paints—iodine in a glycerine or vegetable-oil base, turpentine with iodine and croton oil, kerosene and pine tar, red iodide of mercury with petroleum jelly, or some commercial preparations—are milder than blisters and less effective, but they don't necessarily involve the animal's stopping work entirely. Caustic agents may also be injected, with more immediate results and a shorter recovery time, but otherwise the risks are the same.

Firing is probably the most controversial form of treatment for lameness, and some people consider it unnecessary and cruel mutilation, while others still feel it is the most reliable treatment available for many common leg ailments. Briefly, firing involves the burning of the skin over an injured area—deeply or superficially—so that hardened scar tissue is formed and circulation is increased. Pin, or point, firing is the most common form, involving the application of individual puncture marks around the joints or over tendons. Line, or bar, firing means that lines are burned into the skin surrounding the flexor tendons, continuing at intervals for the length of the cannon bone. All types of objects have been used for firing: heated nails, pitchfork tines, and converted soldering irons; but rather more sophisticated tools have been developed, such as ether irons and electric cautery units, which are probably most commonly used today. Surgical conditions must be maintained during firing, including anesthesia, sterile cleansing of the area being fired, and postsurgical care, involving rest (sometimes for a long period) and painting or even blistering with counterirritants. Firing leaves a permanent scar, which may have the advantage of constantly reminding the trainer that too much work can cause the injury to recur,

Poultices

Like many other kinds of equine medication, a poultice is an old-fashioned remedy for inflammation and lameness. Many old-time horsemen prefer them to drugs or heated boots, because they are cheaper, time-honored, and at least partially effective as counterirritants in drawing heat and swelling out of injuries, tightening the skin, and cooling the area around an injury. Poultices contain such ingredients as clay (kaolin) to reduce swelling, glycerine to soften the skin and produce heat, wintergreen and eucalyptus oils to act as antiseptics, and *salicylic acid* (an antiseptic and antifungal agent found in aspirin). Poultices will not work unless they are moist, which makes them pretty messy to work with, and they must stay in place against the horse's injury, which requires the use of a poultice boot or wrap (see page 132). There are a number of poultices available, and they vary considerably in effectiveness and price.

According to *Michael Plum's Horse Journal*, the first two products listed here win the race hands down:

Antiphlogistine (W. F. Young) is probably the most expensive product, but it stays moist for over 24 hours and is very effective.

Uptite (Uptite Chemical Co.) is much cheaper and also stays moist for a long period with good effectiveness.

Reducine and **Phlogo** (Farnam) are old products in new packaging and, while they are effective, they are difficult to remove from the horse's leg.

Super H (Bickmore) is another familiar product, which must be diluted before application and is somewhat difficult to apply.

though it will make resale of the animal difficult and certain types of showing impossible (as in conformation or breed classes where soundness is essential.)

Tack-shop catalogues are full of different types of bandages for horses, and many horseowners are inveigled into buying them for many reasons, mostly having to do with tradition and misunderstanding of their use. Bandages for the average horse serve two primary purposes—to prevent injury during shipping and to protect wounds by holding dressings and keeping out foreign matter. Although some horses may need protection during exercise over rough footing or jumps and during a particularly fatiguing session of work, leg wraps or bandages are not recommended for simple support as a matter of daily care. In fact, the regular use of bandages for stabled horses, for horses with

DMSO

Although DMSO (Dimethyl Sulfoxide) is sold as a solvent with no instructions for its use as a preparation for equine leg injuries, many horsemen have found it to be a very useful product for stimulating circulation and speeding up the healing of various leg ailments. Developed by the paper company Crown-Zellerbach, it was originally used as a solvent because of its hydroscopic property (it dissolves in both water and oil), but some enterprising individual discovered that when applied to the skin, it seemed to stimulate the healing of injured tissue (as well as producing a distinct garlic flavor in the mouth). Since it has never been scientifically studied to the point where the U.S. FDA would allow it to be sold for medical purposes, DMSO continues to be sold as a solvent in various solutions, but this does not prevent horsemen from applying it to their lame animals, in whom they claim it produces miraculous effects as a topical swelling-reducer and pain reliever. It is available in an industrial solution as 99.5 percent DMSO (to be avoided) or in a liquid as a 50 percent or 90 percent solution. Ask your veterinarian which form, if any, he or she recommends. One danger with DMSO is a result of its apparent ability to be absorbed rapidity through the skin, into the blood stream, taking with it any compound that is applied in the same area. Although this might be useful in the absorption of cortisone, for instance, it can be dangerous since surface impurities may be absorbed as well.

Lameness Therapies

MOST OF US WHO HAVE horses know that sinking feeling when we lead Old Dobbin out of his stall and realize that he is noticeably lame. Once we have diagnosed the lameness (see page 122), there is nothing to be done but to set about treating it. The past 25 years have seen a number of revolutionary new treatments for this age-old problem, but a lot of the old-time remedies are still hanging around. Here are some of the best known treatments, tried, true, and unproven.

Rest. This is without question the best of the treatments, as it involves no expense, drugs, or special equipment. However, rest takes time and patience. Rest, coupled with controlled exercise, should nevertheless be the treatment of choice, if there is a choice. First-aid treatments are recommended, however, in case of an injury to reduce swelling and pain.

Cold water and ice packs. Unlike heat treatments, cold therapy is designed to bring down swelling or inflammation, as well as to reduce pain. Hosing an injury with cold water for short periods can be very therapeutic, and the use of ice packs immediately after an injury can help prevent swelling and keep pain under control. Many vets will recommend alternating hot and cold treatments to reduce swelling yet hasten healing and lessen pain.

Liniments, tighteners, braces, leg paints. When mixed in solution, these products make a soothing body wash after exercise; used pure or in a strong solution, they can help temporarily to relieve soreness, but they do not significantly affect the healing process. However, rubbing on a liniment can have its own therapeutic value in massaging the horse's legs and enabling the owner to detect any changes in condition.

Anti-inflammatory drugs. There are two principal types of drugs used to reduce inflammation, corticosteroids (adrenal hormones that affect cellular growth) and nonsteroidal anti-inflammatory drugs, also called *antiprostaglandins.* Dexamethasone and prednisone are synthetic steroids commonly used in horses to treat acute inflammation and shock; because they interfere with body functions and metabolism, there may be serious side effects, especially when used with other drugs, and should be used only under a vet's close supervision. Aspirin and phenylbutazone (bute) are relatively safe, commonly used nonsteroidal anti-inflammatory drugs that work by preventing the body from producing increased blood flow that will result in swelling, heat, and pain. Aspirin will lower fever and pain, though it may also thin blood and reduce blood clotting. Bute is effective in reducing joint and muscle pain and fever caused by infections and injuries.

Firing. This is without question one of the worst treatments, recommended by few veterinarians and no one of the humane persuasion. Firing involves applying a hot iron to an injured area and inducing a counterirritation (inflammation) to bring about a cure, as heat will increase the blood supply in the damaged area.

Blistering. Another old-fashioned and controversial treatment that involves rubbing a caustic counterirritant to the skin in the area of an injury. The blistering or heat-producing agent (such as menthol) must be strong enough to cause blisters on the horse's skin and presumably increase blood flow. As with firing, the pain is considerable and the effectiveness questionable.

Electromagnetic therapy. This therapeutic treatment is still in the development stages for its use on horses, but several products are already on the market. It involves the use of magnetic pads that create a weak electrical current (or a pulsing electromagnetic field) that dilates blood vessels and increases the flow of blood to stimulate healing. There is evidence that this treatment will stimulate bone repair, but its effect on slow-healing tendons has not been demonstrated.

Cold-laser therapy. Hot-laser surgery is used to remove tumors, cataracts, and so on, but cold lasers are still considered an alternative therapy. There is little scientific evidence of its healing powers beyond a temporary or superficial improvement in injured soft tissue, and it may be harmful in the long run if a horse with an unhealed injury is returned to work too quickly.

Acupuncture. After 3,000 years, this Chinese therapy is beginning to find support—at least for use on humans—from the National Institutes of Health and some insurers. Many veterinarians are convinced of its effectiveness in reducing pain in horses, at least temporarily, by stimulating the release of endorphins (which provide pain relief and increase general well-being), decreasing muscle spasms, and increasing blood circulation to an injured area. By stimulating acupuncture points, which are aligned along fourteen *meridians* (energy pathways) in the body, the acupuncturist is thought to be able to restore the body's balance and return the animal to a state of health. These points, according to holistic therapists, can also be stimulated by cold lasers and electrical currents, such as those used in the laser and electromagnetic therapies described above. ∩

Canvas ice boots

swollen (or filled) legs, or for animals doing heavy work may be harmful in the long run, since bandages may create new stresses and prevent a horse's tendons from developing properly. Protective bandages should be thick and well padded, and this padding may be built into the bandage itself or provided by a separate piece of material, a layer of sheet cotton, a quilted pad, elastic foam, synthetic fleece, or even a set of Pampers. The bandages come in several different forms, simple flannel, polo bandages (with Velcro closings), self-adhesive wraps, therapeutic wraps (lined with gauze containing poultice or cooling ingredients), and cold-water bandages (used on the racetrack for hosing, tail wrapping, or exercise). Because unnecesssary bandages or poorly wrapped bandages can be more harmful than useful, the average horse owner is advised to

Electro-therapeutic stimulation

We rarely quote from promotional copy, but we applaud the copywriter who included the following precautionary note in a brochure extolling the virtues of the liniment called Equitite: It is highly recommended if your horse has just "bowed," to rest the horse completely and apply ice to the injury until the swelling has subsided. THEN LAY THE HORSE OFF FOR AT LEAST THREE (3) MONTHS (we know you probably hate hearing this, but it is the absolute best thing you can do for the horse). After which time have your veterinarian evaluate the injury to see if you can resume training again. . . . : No amount of money, crying, blistering, pinfiring, yelling, screaming, or jumping up and down is going to heal that leg tomorrow. We all want the "quick fix" for bowed tendons, but there are some things in life that we can't have and this is one of them!

consult a veterinarian before using anything more complicated than a simple standing bandage. In any event, no bandage should be kept in place for more than a day, and special care should be taken with elastic bandages, since they will tighten as a horse's leg becomes swollen.

Great care must be used in wrapping leg bandages, to avoid providing too much pressure, insufficient support, or uneven pressure which may cause further damage, especially in the case of a bowed tendon. Since careful wrapping is an art requiring great skill, the procedure should not be attempted by anyone without careful supervision.

GIVING MEDICINE INTERNALLY

Whether it be worming medication or an antibiotic that the veterinarian has left with you, keep these two things in mind as you try to get whatever-it-is into the animal: a deft, confident approach on your part and a quiet, familiar environment for the horse. If you are inexperienced in giving medication, your vet can show you how or recommend the most effective method. Most important, be sure that the horse is not likely to become excited by too much restraint, nervousness on your part, or unnatural, unfamiliar conditions if you want the medication to be beneficial rather than harmful.

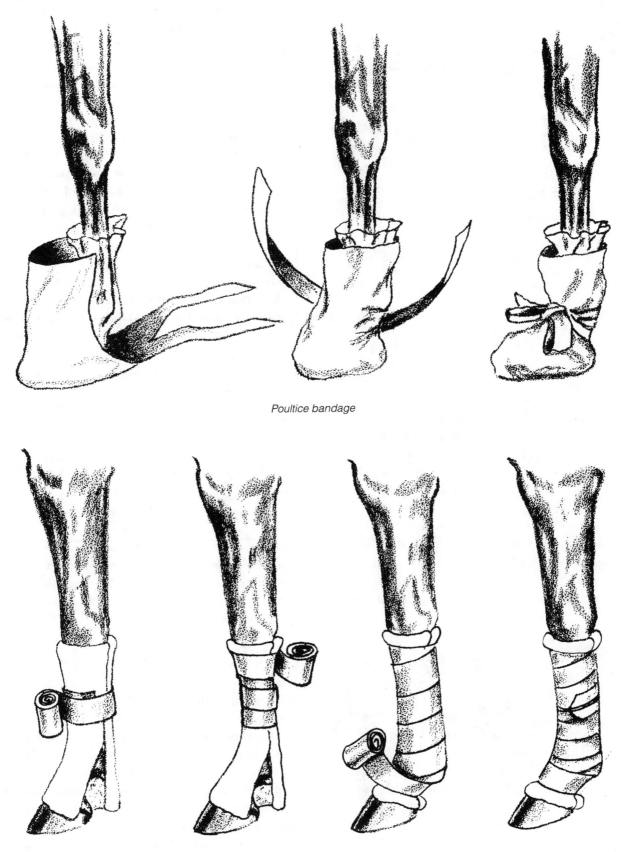

Poultice bandage

Standing bandage

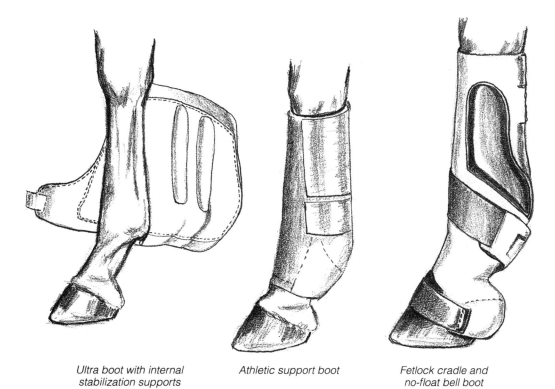

Ultra boot with internal
stabilization supports

Athletic support boot

Fetlock cradle and
no-float bell boot

Theoretically, the easiest way to dose a horse is to put medication into its water or food and let the animal treat itself. That's theory. In practice, however, horses tend to be pretty fussy about their food's smell and texture, and whatever isn't familiar will make them suspicious. Some medications are made to be palatable, but even these goodies will be rejected by some horses just because they are new and different. It is possible, however, to fool some of those horses some of the time. Try putting molasses into the feed to disguise the taste; horses love the sweet flavor and will usually lick the bucket clean. But untrusting animals will require the addition of molasses for a day or two before you put the medication in. An easy way of disguising scent is to rub a bit of Vicks VapoRub on the horse's nose before mealtime—the fumes should distract it from any medical aroma. Powdered medicine can be made into a sweet paste with corn syrup, honey, or molasses; liquid medications can be mixed with sugar. The paste can then be put on the tongue, teeth, or lips, and it should disappear pretty quickly. Nevertheless, one is never entirely sure just how much of the medication a horse takes, unless you watch the animal eat every bite. And not all medicines come in edible form, so the horse

owner will have to become familiar with other methods of dosing.

Drenching is a means of getting liquid medication into the animal's mouth by placing a syringe or a bottle into the interdental space in front of the first cheek tooth, pouring, and allowing the animal to swallow. This is not recommended for beginners, for the amount of medicine actually ingested is never accurate, and the risk of inhalation through the trachea is great.

Balls, pills, or capsules can be given either by hand or with a balling gun, though again great caution is required to avoid injuring the pharynx or lodging medicine in the esophagus. The smaller the horse, the greater the risk. To give a pill by hand, pull the tongue to one side between the upper and lower cheek teeth and place the pill, lubricated with mineral oil or glycerine, as far back on the tongue as possible. Hold the mouth closed until the horse swallows, and stroke the underside of the neck toward the stomach to encourage its passage into the stomach. The head should be held in a normal position. To use a balling gun, hold the tongue aside, insert the gun between the incisor teeth, and discharge it onto the base of the tongue. If it is "shot" too far back, the ball or pill may cause the horse to gag or cough it up. Care should be taken that the animal doesn't bite the end of the balling gun.

Stomach tubing is tricky for amateurs, but it is a good procedure to learn in case of emergency and vet-lessness. The tube should not be too large ($^3/_4$ inch in diameter for an adult horse; $^3/_8$ inch for ponies and foals) or too flexible, for it will curl or kink. (Tubes that seem too stiff, as in cold weather, may be softened by brief soaking in warm water.) The tube should have smooth edges at both ends and should be marked at intervals to indicate the distance from the nostril (where the tube enters) to the opening of the esophagus (about 16 inches) and then again for the beginning of the stomach, about $5^1/_2$ feet. Lubricate the tube's passage either by feeding the horse a little grain to stimulate saliva flow (if the horse will eat) or by rubbing the tube with petroleum jelly. Back the animal into a corner of the stall and have someone hold its head firmly with a halter lead and perhaps with a twitch as well. Violent movement of the head may cause the tube to damage the lining of the esophagus, so great care should be taken to prevent this from happening. The horse's head should be flexed, so that it will be easier for it to swallow when the tube touches the pharynx (the entry to the esophagus).

Holding the tube in your right hand, insert it into the animal's right nostril, placing your left thumb in the nostril so that you can feel the tube and keep it on the floor of the nasal passage. Work it into the nostril until it hits the pharynx, at which point the animal should swallow and admit it into the esophagus. Do not by any means try to force it at this point; just hold it firmly until it is passed into the esophagus. You can both see and feel it as it passes through, and if you are in doubt as to its exact location, withdraw the tube a few inches until you can do so. If it moves very easily, you may have inserted the tube into the trachea, which you can tell by hearing the tube rattle as you shake the animal's throat. Withdraw it and try again. Do not in any event put any medication into the tube until you are sure you have reached the stomach. One way of checking this is to blow into the tube; your assistant can hear bubbling noises in the horse's stomach. Once you are absolutely sure that the tube end is in the stomach (you can cause your horse to aspirate and choke to death if it isn't), pour in the liquid medication, using a funnel if neces-

sary. To be sure that the tube is thoroughly drained before you withdraw it, blow through it or hold a finger over the end as you pull it out. Again, exercise tremendous caution and manipulate the tube gently rather than forcefully.

Although we don't recommend that anyone without experience try to inject any medication into a horse, or that anyone do so at all without a veterinarian's advice, we would like to point out several basic warnings. The abuse of needles and syringes has caused trouble in the past, both to individual horses and to groups, as in the spread of EIA and other infectious diseases. *Always* use a sterile syringe and needle. (Disposable syringes are not expensive and always safe; if you reuse a syringe, make absolutely sure that it has been sterilized before use and kept in a sterile condition.) A needle that breaks under the skin or in a muscle, unless removed immediately, will travel and do damage internally. If the needle is too deep to remove by hand, the vet should be called right away for surgery or perhaps an X-ray. Don't bother to rub a horse's skin with alcohol before injecting the needle unless the spot is dirty. In any case, don't clip the area, for loose hairs may get into the skin. And be sure not to inject a needle where the harness or saddle touches the skin.

There are several kinds of injections: subcutaneous (usually into a fold of skin in the middle of the side of the neck), intravenous (into a vein, which is tricky unless you know exactly where the vein is), intradermal, intra-articular (into a joint), and intramuscular. For any number of good reasons, one should not attempt any of these without first receiving instruction from the veterinarian.

RESTRAINT PROCEDURES

It comes as no great surprise that the average horse is a fairly large animal with a great deal more muscle, weight, and power than the average human being. (Even ponies count here, especially when the owner is relatively small.) Happily, the human brain is somewhat superior to equine gray matter, so we have been able to develop various means of keeping the horse under control most of the time. Training—anything from gentle, constant handling to the finer points of equitation—is probably the most obvious, but even be-

Bandages

Standing bandages (used for shipping, as well as to immobilize an injured leg) may be made in several ways, but in essence the idea is to give a thick cushion to the leg and to secure it with a snug bandage (not too snug or circulation may be stopped). Sheet cotton is the traditional padding, but also available are washable self-adhering cotton wraps, washable quilted cotton wraps, or gauze-covered cotton sheeting. Bandage may be cotton web, flannel, nylon, or acrylic; some are equipped with sewn-on tie tapes or Velcro self-sticking tapes, while others require the separate purchase of pins, masking tape, or Velcro tapes. There are several lines of protective leg boots with support straps or built-in splints that offer considerable support.

Some bandages are now available that offer, or claim to offer, special therapeutic benefits, but they are expensive and should probably not be used without the advice of a veterinarian. *Sweats* that claim to reduce swelling and condition muscles are no substitute for medication and exercise. Boots with special insulation and pockets to hold ice or magnetic packs are useful alternatives to hosing with cold water. Norfields produces a line of wraps that contain bipolar magnets, believed to increase circulation and speed healing time. Respond also makes magnetic boots, plus blankets and wraps for the neck. Studies have proven the usefulness of these bandages, and it may well be that they shorten recovery time or reduce the incidence of chronic lameness, but one should be cautious in using them, since their pain-relieving properties may mask a serious injury without curing it.

Shoe-boil boots, or sausage boots, are made of lightweight chrome leather with canvas sides, and buckle around the horse's fetlock to prevent damage to kicked elbows.

fore halter breaking begins, humans have affected equine behavior by breeding in good temperament and breeding out the bad. Domestication of the horse has been a centuries-long process, during which the natural fears of the wild horse have been eliminated and a relative docility introduced. The horse's instinct to flee (or in mules and donkeys, to stop) or, when cornered or challenged, to attack is no longer "natural" in the domesticated breeds that we know today, except in those we call "feral" horses returned, like the American mustang, to a wild state. Even the most highly strung, badly behaved horse—whether it has been ill bred or badly treated—does not show the same characteristics as the zebra, for instance, or the Przewalski wild horse, neither of which can be successfully trained, no matter how effective gentle taming may be in reducing their fears.

The closest that the normal domestic horse comes temperamentally to the wild one is in times of extreme stress—not just when being cruelly treated, but when ill or injured. Pain creates panic along with discomfort, and even the mildest-mannered of creatures may become difficult, if not downright impossible, to handle even with more than one person present.

Several methods are available for handling an animal in trouble, both to make treatment possible and to prevent further damage. The best choice depends, of course, on the individual animal and its condition, available equipment and personnel, and general circumstances. We all remember Ruffian, that beautiful filly who was such a "bad patient" when she reacted violently in recovering from anesthesia, eventually making it necessary for the doctors to destroy her. Yet we also remember an unbeautiful grade gelding named Copperhead, who had the good sense when he sank up to his neck in a soft spot in the ground (a cesspool, if you must know) to keep his head and resist the impulse to struggle, thus managing to avoid slipping entirely out of sight. Horses differ, obviously, and the better you know your horse and what it is capable of doing in a bad situation, the better equipped you will be in dealing with it when trouble arises. The more highly trained an animal is, the more predictable its behavior. A green horse, although usually free enough of bad habits, may act unpredictably out of ignorance and be uncontrollable because it does not know enough to respond to certain commands or signals. A spoiled horse with bad habits is most difficult to handle, having un-

Alternative Medicine for Horses
——— Ω ———

TWENTY YEARS AGO, ALTERNATIVE medicine for horses according to most equine practitioners, was the kind practiced by horse owners who preferred to apply their own concoctions of pine tar, Epsom salts, and oil of peppermint than to wait for the vet to show up with expensive drugs and scientific treatments developed in laboratories rather than on the ranch. Nowadays, however, alternative medicine for horses—like that for humans—is a big, serious business, with books, magazines, Web sites, mail-order catalogs, and shops offering holistic advice, products, and therapies for the whole horse.

Many veterinarians, like their physician counterparts, are skeptical of alternative medicine, because conventional medicine tends to view health as a diseasefree state achieved by the pharmaceutical or surgical defeat of the chemical imbalances, bacteria, and viruses that cause illness. Practitioners of alternative medicine, on the other hand, view health from a completely different perspective, according to the principle of *holism*—the interrelationship of mind, body, and spirit, which, if out of balance, can result in illness. To combat disease caused by stress, imbalance, and a lack of well-being, the alternative approach must encompass the whole person—or horse—and recognize the importance of nutrition, physical fitness, and treatments that affect the entire system, not just the affected part or the obvious symptom.

Unfortunately, alternative medicine—though taken seriously now by many health-care professionals and even health management organizations—has become a grab bag of therapies, some of which have centuries of tradition to support their effectiveness (acupuncture, for example) and some of which teeter on the edge of fuzzyheadedness. No one will deny that many effective drugs had their origin in natural herbs and that the real value of many vitamins (such as E) remain unexplained, but many would question the usefulness of aromatherapy on a horse whose real problem may be masked by a strong scent. And, while herbs may be relatively safe to use, they, like other drugs, can be dangerous in the wrong dosage or combination. We find it exceptionally interesting that the tried-and-true medications of 100 years ago, such as Absorbine liniment, contained herbal ingredients along with the iodine and are still selling today, their manufacturers declaring proudly that they knew it all along. We find it amusing that aloe vera, ginseng, and yucca have crept into the horse catalogs along with ivermectin. We are happy to see horse trainers massaging more and blistering less. We are also gratified that along with laser and electromagnetic therapies, horse owners are also concerned with the preventive properties of sensible nutritional supplements and humane approaches to training that reward good behavior rather than punish mistakes. But, as authors of *The Whole Horse Catalog,* how could we behave otherwise?

If you need a bit more convincing, ask the American Association of Equine Practitioners to give you a veterinary opinion, write to 4075 Iron Works Pike, Lexington, KY 40511, and ask for a copy of *Therapeutic Options: Considerations for Horse Owners.* Ω

---

doubtedly learned too much with regard to outwitting people or pieces of equipment.

Certain kinds of equipment must always be on hand for use in emergencies: several yards of good, sturdy rope, a second halter and lead rope, and a twitch of some sort, as well as a good assistant. Other devices designed to deal with specific situations should also be considered if your horse is at all likely to require them. Most important is some self-restraint on your own part, to control the temper that an unruly horse can provoke. It is also essential that you become experienced in the correct use of the various restraint methods, since misuse of them can result in an angry horse and perhaps even further injury.

Physical Restraint

The most important first step in restraining a horse for whatever reason is to gain control of the head. A halter alone is not enough; a lead rope will give the handler greater control. If the horse refuses to move, a rope may be dropped around the hindquarters, crossed over the back, and passed up through the halter to encourage the animal to advance. (If this fails, the animal should be blindfolded.) The handler must remain alert at all times to the horse's behavior, standing on the same side of the horse that the vet (or whoever) is working on. His primary function, aside from keeping the animal from escaping, is to distract him from whatever is being done elsewhere. Reassuring noises often do the trick, but when the horse is still anxious, stronger measures will be necessary. One effective way of holding a horse's head is to keep one hand on the muzzle and the other on the nape of the neck, behind the ears. To keep the horse's head up, slip a thumb through the noseband of the halter; to keep it down, put pressure (not enough to compress the nostrils and prevent breathing) on the muzzle. The other hand will be free to grab the mane or an ear if necessary. Twisting the ear is often effective, but care should be taken to prevent the permanent condition of a fallen ear or a head-shy horse.

For especially spirited horses, a chain shank may be attached to the halter to slip over the muzzle, under the jaw, through the mouth, or over the upper gum. Never tie a horse with such a halter, however, or use it abusively. Other special halters include those used for holding a horse to an operating table and dental halters with a rigid loop of steel in the noseband, which provides space to open the jaws without affecting the cheeks. A war bridle, of which there are several variations, is a rope gag that is used in conjunction with a halter and lead to keep a horse from rearing.

One of the oldest and most common restraint devices is the twitch, which provides restraint by distracting the horse's attention. A simple twitching method, to grasp the upper lip between thumb and fingers and hold on, usually works for only a moment or so, but long enough to get a twitch device in place. This loop of small-linked chain or rope is attached to the end of a wooden stick about a yard long. The loop is applied to the lip (which is folded so that the mucosal tissue does not show), and the handle is twisted to tighten it. It is most effective at the beginning and loses effect as the lip becomes numb, so one should alternate the pressure, applying the maximum only when necessary. (One can also resort to the lower lip.) Some horses resent the use of a twitch and will fight it by pulling back, striking out with a foreleg, or rearing. The handler should be careful to keep a good hold on the end of the handle if this happens and to stand clear. A nose clamp, a type of twitch that can be attached to the halter to free the assistant's hand, takes time to apply and remove, and it may be impossible for a spirited horse. Humane twitches, ring twitches, and blanket clamps are other variations on the same theme.

METHODS OF RESTRAINT

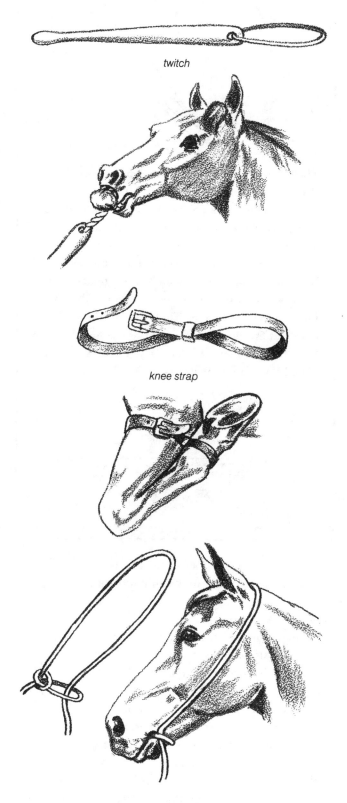

twitch

knee strap

emergency rope bridle

TWITCHES

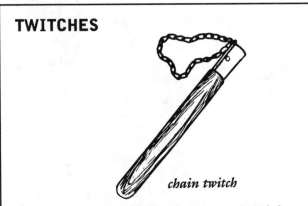

chain twitch

There are many different designs, most of them called humane and all of them painful to the horse. (They are probably called humane because they do not shut off circulation!) There are three common varieties: the nose or chain twitch, with a wooden handle and a nickel-plated brass nose chain; the screw twitch, made of polished aluminum; and the nutcracker style, which fastens to the halter. The first of these needs constant attention on the part of the handler, but the other two can be left in place and are thus called "one-man" twitches.

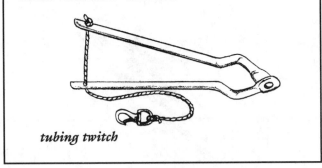

tubing twitch

Most of us know (or should know) how to pick up and hold a horse's feet for examination or cleaning. Restraining a horse by holding one or more legs is somewhat trickier, especially if the animal is not accustomed to frequent handling. The point is to keep the horse off balance to prevent kicking or striking. Therefore, in holding or tying a leg, be sure not to let the horse persuade you to carry part of its weight. If the vet or someone is working on a hind leg, lift the foreleg on the same side, tying it if necessary so that the rope or strap can be released quickly. Tying a hind leg will not permit close examination, but should discourage kicking. Rope burns can be prevented by the use of hobbles or bandages around the leg to be tied. Discourage a horse likely to strike with its forelegs by

grasping a roll of skin over the shoulders with two hands.

Tying the tail will also help prevent kicking and facilitate a rectal examination or treatment, although one may also simply hold the tail over the animal's back. Ponies or young animals are often restrained by a handler's holding both halter and tail. If the horse is relatively large or strong, it is a good precaution to stand the animal alongside a wall and lean against it. A young foal should be handled with special care. It is not a good idea to remove it from its dam, since it will probably become very much excited when left alone. If the foal is not broken to a halter, don't try to apply one now, but cradle the animal gently in your arms, one around the neck and the other around the rump.

Some barns are equipped with permanent stocks made of heavy wooden timbers or pipes, while temporary stocks may be made from rope. This type of restraint can be very useful for examining and treating standing horses; it can be dangerous, however, if a horse becomes unruly, and excitable horses should be tranquilized or sedated before being so confined. A heavy kickboard is a useful attachment (made to swing like a door at the back of the stock), and any surface that the horse may hit should be padded in some way. The horse's head should be cross-tied, and the ropes in front of and behind the horse should be secured in such a way that they can be released if the animal gets on top of one of them. A rope caught underneath a horse's tail will usually provoke a kicking fit, as most experienced horsemen know.

An effective rope stock—also called a hippoharness or Sigler's method—can be made with a single length of rope 30 to 40 feet long. Pass the center of the rope over the withers, making a half-hitch around each foreleg; pass the rope back to the hind legs, make another half-hitch, and cross the ends of the rope over the loins, pulling them tight and tying them (for quick release) or having them held by two assistants.

A drastic method of restraint—and one now virtually superseded by the use of tranquilizing drugs—is casting, or forcing a horse to fall and lie immobile, either by flexing the hind legs and setting the horse down before it is put on its side or by pulling all four legs until the animal falls over. Both can be dangerous, since the animal can become injured during the fall. You can cast a small horse or pony simply by pulling the halter to force the head around and pulling the animal's tail through its legs and out the opposite side; then, using the animal's body as a fulcrum, lift up and back until the horse can be lowered to the ground. Harnesses have been designed in various styles for larger horses, but are rarely used now without tranquilizers. Now most horses are cast by the use of drugs alone, harnesses being used merely for restraint or for holding certain limbs in position once the animal is down.

All of these methods are temporary, requiring the constant presence of a handler in addition to the vet or expert treating the horse, as well as being designed for use on standing animals. Slings can be very useful in helping a horse to its feet and then in keeping it in a standing position—either temporarily or over a period of time. A sling can be useful only if an animal can support its own weight, at least partially. (When a horse hangs in a sling, death is certain. Animals that can't support themselves are better off lying in a deep bed of straw or clean bedding and being turned from one side to the other at regular intervals.) Slings must be sturdy and custom-fitted to each animal. A sling is made up of a wide belly band, a breast collar (to prevent the horse from slipping forward), breeching (to prevent it from slipping back), a singletree (to keep the straps separated over the back and attached to the point of suspension), and a chain hoist firmly anchored in the ceiling of the stall. The hoist should be adjusted so that the animal can support itself without putting undue pressure on its belly, and feeding and watering containers must be placed conveniently nearby. A horse should be fully conscious when put into a sling, although tranquilizers may be necessary to prevent rearing or plunging. Once the horse has become accustomed to the confinement, a halter with a lead attached to the side of the stall should be used to keep the animal from swinging around in circles.

Many other devices have been developed to use on horses undergoing treatment. Protective hoods to prevent head injury, blindfolds to facilitate movement or recovery from anesthesia, and neck cradles to prevent the animal from licking a wound or dressing are just a few. Some horses learn to circumvent the cradle by raising a foreleg and propping it on the side of the stall until it can be reached with the mouth—in which case a leather bib under the halter will prevent chewing or licking. When a hind leg is involved, a stick may be attached from a side ring in a surcingle to the halter ring.

Cross tying may also be used, or a swivel tie, consisting of a rope dropped from the ceiling and attached to the noseband of the halter. Either method will discourage the animal from interfering with a wound or dressing.

Chemical Restraint

The following drugs should be used only by a veterinarian or under his or her supervision. Although research has made the development of various effective drugs possible, their use is nonetheless a risky business. Some horses may react in different ways from others, and highly dangerous or even fatal side effects may result if medications are not administered with utmost care and skill. Drugs used for restraint fall into three general categories: sedatives, narcotics, and tranquilizers. Used for quieting excitable animals for examination or as a preliminary step before surgery, they differ considerably from one another in effect.

Sedatives, administered most commonly to horses to quiet them before surgery in which a local anesthetic is used, allow for rapid recovery, so that the patient may walk immediately after the operation is over. They are also useful in procedures that require momentary pain, such as injection or certain kinds of treatment. Because most sedatives interfere with swallowing, horses should not be fed or watered for several hours after use. Chloral hydrate alone or in combination with other drugs reduces a horse's response to pain and makes it less likely to kick, strike, or try to escape. This drug may be given intravenously or orally in water in capsules. Injection is usually the method, for horses will not readily drink a chloral solution unless very thirsty. Drenching (by pouring down the throat) is not usually recommended for fear of irritating gums or inflaming alimentary or respiratory tracts. Oral doses, in any case, do not take effect for twenty to thirty minutes, and the degree of sedation is far more variable than it is with intravenous injection. Pentobarbital sodium in large doses may cause a horse to become overly excited, so slow, intravenous injection is preferred. Rompun (xylazine) is a sedative with analgesic (painkilling) properties; it is a potent, quick-acting sedative that can be administered intravenously, intramuscularly, or subcutaneously. Because it is efficient and relatively safe, Rompun is commonly used for loading horses prior to shipping; for clipping, shoeing, examination, or minor surgery; and as a preanesthetic drug. Horses will lower their heads and seem deeply drowsy, but they will remain steady on their feet and can even deliver a swift kick if so inclined. Recovery is generally smooth and quiet.

Narcotics are not widely used by veterinarians for horses except in severe cases of trauma or in combination with tranquilizers. Meperidine hydrochloride is the one most commonly used with horses, although most practitioners feel there is not sufficient need for narcotics to recommend their use. Methadone hydrochloride tends to cause excitement and is not recommended, nor is heroin, in spite of its former widespread use at the racetrack, which gave it the nickname "horse" and inspired the introduction of the saliva test.

Tranquilizers are good for controlling excitable animals when painful procedures are not intended. Although tranquilized horses seem to become sleepy and unresponsive, they may react more violently to pain than they would without the tranquilizer, which must not be used when an animal is in danger of shock. Unlike sedatives, tranquilizers may be fed orally as well as by injection; their effect is longer-lasting; and horses can eat and drink following their administration. Nevertheless, they are slower to work, and they may not work at all when an animal is excited; they also vary in their effect on horses, depending on breed, age, size, and temperament. The most dependable and safest tranquilizers are promazine and acepromazine, which have similar effects. Succinylcholine hydrochloride, a paralyzing drug, has been widely used in immobilizing horses, but it is risky, especially in animals that are malnourished, exhausted, excited, old, or suffering from cardiac or liver disease. Serpasil (reserpine) has also been widely used in horses because it produces a delayed reaction and may be effective up to seventy-two hours after administration (and undetectable by racing and show officials). But since it slows down the metabolic rate and the digestive process, colic and serious diarrhea may result, and since its effects on horses—as on humans—are quite unpredictable, it is not recommended by veterinarians if the horse's health is of any value.

Many of these sedatives and tranquilizers are used in combination for anesthetic purposes during surgical procedures, so that the animal does not perceive pain or respond reflexively to painful stimuli. Although it was once common to use only one drug for anesthesia, several drugs are now used in order to shorten recovery time and to widen the margin of safety. Intravenous drugs are generally used to induce anesthesia, usually after the administration of a tranquilizer and often accompanied by the use of a casting harness after the tranquilizer has taken effect. The safest way of maintaining anesthesia is then to use inhalation methods, with drugs such as halothane, methoxyfluorane, nitrous oxide, chloroform, ether, and cycloprone (these last three are seldom used now). There are many risks involved in the use of anesthetics in horses, such as respiratory obstructions, surgical shock, and cardiac arrest—one reason that local anesthetics are used whenever possible. These are applied as topical or surface agents, in the eyes and on the mucous membranes, as infiltration anesthetics (for suturing wounds or minor surgery), field blocks (somewhat deeper than infiltration), nerve blocks, and epidural blocks (in which the nerve roots from the vertebral canal are blocked). These can be used alone or in conjunction with a sedative, with the animal either standing or lying down.

Special Medical Problems

So far we have talked about care, treatment, and ailments that can apply to any horse, regardless of breed, color, or sex; but obviously there are situations in which a particular horse may require more than what we would consider routine medical attention. A bad fracture or other injury that might have meant certain death for a horse some years ago does not always mean the end nowadays. Valuable performing or breeding stock, or animals owned by people who care enough to spend the very best, can often be saved, thanks to advanced procedures that specialists in equine practice have developed. If your own veterinarian does not have the equipment or the know-how to deal with a problem, he will readily refer you to someone who does. Equine centers exist throughout the country—usually connected with veterinary schools or racetracks or in areas where horses are kept in substantial numbers—and these are equipped with specialized X-ray equipment, surgical apparatus, and specialist veterinarians to diagnose and treat difficult medical problems.

GELDING
Many minor forms of surgery may be done at home (or, rather, in your stable), since horses can be sedated and given local anesthesia from which they will re-

cover rapidly. In most of these cases, horses can even remain standing throughout the procedure. One example of this kind of surgery is gelding, or castrating, which is performed in most male horses before the age of two. In Europe, where breeding in many areas is strictly controlled, the decision whether or not to geld a horse is usually made by the organization or association supervising the improvement or continuance of certain breeds. In this country, the owner of the horse has the choice, both as to the surgery itself and as to the time when it is to take place. Most owners, unless they plan to embark on a breeding program—which can be expensive, time-consuming, and full of potential problems—prefer to keep geldings (or mares, of course) rather than stallions, since geldings are far easier to control. If a horse has particularly fine qualities that deserve to be passed along to future generations, there may be good reason to keep him whole, but even stallions with relatively quiet temperaments may not always behave calmly, regardless of how well trained they may be, especially if a mare in heat is anywhere nearby. Kelso, the famous money-winning racehorse, was gelded at two because his temperament was too much for the discipline of racing. When he turned out to be a fantastic performer, his owners undoubtedly regretted the fact that he had been gelded (an apocryphal story circulates to the effect that the owner said to the vet who did the deed: "I paid you fifty bucks to take 'em off; I'll pay you a million to put 'em back!"). Naturally, Kelso might very well not have been able to race at all if he had not been gelded, and his career certainly would not have been so spectacular if he had been retired to stud at four. And of course, it is always possible that he might not have been a good stud; many fine horses are not good breeders (though some can be trained) and their own traits and characteristics often fail to get passed along as planned by the owners. All of which simply goes to explain why breeding is such a risky and unpredictable business.

So, assuming that you have a young colt that shows promise as a riding or driving horse but isn't anything particularly special (and here's where sentiment must be firmly controlled), gelding is the usual course as the animal matures. This is a relatively simple surgical task, and the veterinarian may decide to do the surgery on the spot with the animal standing. Shetland ponies (for some reason), breeding stallions, and intractable

horses should not be gelded this way, for their surgery is more complicated and the risk to the veterinarian even greater than usual. (And no horse should be gelded at all if suffering from an infectious disease, anemia, or generally poor condition caused by parasites or malnutrition; the animal must be healthy before it is put through the stress that even minor surgery will bring on.)

If your horse is tractable, well trained (or readily handled), and young, the vet may very well decide to take the simplest route. This involves dosing with a sedative and applying a local anesthetic, cleansing the genital area, and removing the testicles with a emasculator. Procedures vary depending on the surgeon performing the task, but the effect is the same, and the animal can be put back to very light work the day after. Exercise for about twenty minutes twice a day is the usual prescription, with the time gradually increased over a period of a week until healing is completed. The wound should be kept clean and free of flies and other biting insects to avoid infection.

If you do not want to have your young stallion gelded and are willing to undertake the considerable responsibilities of dealing with him, and with the business of breeding, you should take the trouble to consult with experts, such as veterinarians and other breeders, and with good texts on the subject in order to determine whether your venture has a chance of success. This book is directed toward amateurs rather than professionals, and once you decide to get into breeding on any scale (which ownership of a stallion usually entails), you should be looking at other books than this one.

BREEDING A MARE
One way in which nonprofessionals get into the breeding business, without making it a business, is to own a mare and decide to have her bred. Some people we know have done so in order to get another horse without spending a whole lot of money, and all we can say to others considering the same route is: keep in mind the potential expenses of veterinarians, stud fees, and special feeds, to say nothing of the fact that the mare will be unable to work for a period of time and that the foal will require a great deal of handling, training, food, and time to grow up before it will be of any use. A good-looking, well-mannered mare of any quality might very well make a good mother, but she might not.

Horse Doping
———— Ω ————

THE FIRST SALIVA TEST for racehorses was introduced in 1933 at Gulfstream Park, Florida, to curb the widespread use of heroin and the fraudulent use of local anesthetics. At that time, racehorse doping was so common that the Thoroughbred breed in the country was in danger of being ruined, and federal narcotics agents began a campaign to eliminate the practice. Urine tests were then developed to supplement the saliva test, and strict regulations were adopted and enforced by the Thoroughbred Racing and Protective Bureau. Although it has never been possible to control the practice of doping entirely—Man O' War was known as the greatest hophead horse of all time—the campaign against it continues unabated. State racing associations have different rules pertaining to the use of drugs, but it is usually the first three horses in a race and the unexpected losers that are tested. Stimulants, depressants, and local anesthetics or painkillers are the primary targets for these tests, which now include the analysis of blood samples as well as of urine and saliva, but most racing associations also frown on antibiotics or anything else they consider "medicine."

Because racehorses must perform under particularly stressful conditions—hard tracks, daily exercise, and heavy racing schedules—unsoundness is a common occurrence among these young animals, whose musculature and skeletons are still in the process of growing. Veterinarians must therefore use drugs and other medical techniques to keep their patients as sound as possible under unnatural conditions. Therefore, in 1963, the American Association of Equine Practitioners offered suggested guidelines relating to the medication of racehorses in order to regulate the use of drugs and to encourage a more tolerant attitude toward their use. Most states have adopted these recommendations, which include the prohibition of stimulants, depressants, or local anesthetics if they may affect racing performance, or any drug that might screen or mask the use of a prohibited drug. No medications may be given on the day of a race without permission from officials (the "day" to be determined by those officials, according to the lasting effects of any drug). Accurate veterinary records must be made available to any official, and the use of any controversial medications must be reported so that it may be evaluated. Many states have gone so far as to allow the use of phenylbutazone ("bute"), since it is so effective in the treatment of lameness and since racing associations are as eager as anyone to increase the number of competitors, although this is still a highly controversial issue.

The American Horse Show Association also forbids the use of stimulants, depressants, tranquilizers, and local anesthetics that might affect a horse's performance, as well as any masking drugs, although it does permit "full use of modern therapeutic measures for the improvement and protection of the health of the horse including phenylbutazone," unless a drug might serve to stimulate or depress the circulatory, respiratory, or central nervous system. Dr. Joseph O'Dea, former veterinarian for the U.S. Equestrian Team, believes that bute or comparable medications should not be permitted in any class in which intrinsic physical soundness or conformation is a specification. He believes that it should be permitted, however, for working-hunter, jumper, and eventing competitions and racing, for it is safe and efficient when properly used, and its prohibition might bring on the use of more dangerous drugs that are less easily detected and controlled than bute.

But in spite of regulations, regular testing, and veterinary recommendations, doping will undoubtedly continue as long as new drugs are developed and new techniques for escaping detection are invented. Although it is not difficult to detect about forty of the traditional substances—amphetamines, cocaine, strychnine, heroin, promazine, and various other drugs—it is not always practical to search for the hundreds of others that might be used. This is unfortunate—and not just for the bettor or the honest competitor. The abuse of drugs, as we all know from their application in humans, can lead to dangerous and in some cases fatal situations. The effects of some drugs are unpredictable, and overdoses are highly possible; side effects can be damaging; and even the injection itself can be harmful. (A nonveterinarian might easily hit an artery instead of a vein, which may result in convulsions and death, and the use of unsterilized needles can spread infection.) Some trainers will always be able to come up with a new way of subverting the rules, but they always do so at the expense of their horses, to say nothing of the notion of good sportsmanship. Ω

The foal might be a disappointment, the mare might be physically or temperamentally unfit for the task, and there is, of course, the risk that the pregnancy and birth will do her irreparable harm, even cause her death. Raising a foal can be a wonderful experience for humans as well as horses, but it entails a lot of work and tender loving care, even at times when it does not seem to be convenient or even possible.

If you decide to have your mare bred anyway, be sure that you read the following bits of advice. Some friends of ours recently spent more than $1,500 to have their mare bred, and they ended up with no foal at all. First, if you don't know a stud in your area, check with several local experts (trainers, dealers, or stable managers) and sift their advice carefully. Go to see any stud who sounds promising, and be sure your veterinarian goes with you. There is hardly any point in breeding your mare to an animal whose traits—temperamental or physical—are not compatible with hers. This does not mean that the stud should be the same; many successful foals have been combinations of complementary rather than similar genes. If your mare is short and you want a tall offspring, a tall stallion might be the best choice; if color is important to you, you might do well to check the relative dominance of certain colors in the breed. (Chestnut is dominant in Thoroughbreds, for instance; gray in Arabs, and so on.) Keep in mind, however, that old story about George Bernard Shaw, who was approached by a beautiful woman with the suggestion that they "breed." He smiled and responded, "But my dear, what if the child has *your* brains and *my* looks?" Not all genetic mixes are successful, as any professional breeder (or racetrack tout) will tell you.

Once you find a stud who pleases you, and you are willing to take your chances, make certain that the financial arrangements are satisfactory, if not entirely in your favor. If your mare has not been bred before and if the stud is not proved, do not agree to pay a stud fee unless a live foal is guaranteed. Stud fees vary considerably, of course, depending on the area, the breed, the availability of local studs, and the stud itself; but anything over $100 should be considered an investment and must be taken seriously. (Unfortunately, the owners of mares cannot do what dog breeders do and offer the pick of the litter in lieu of a fee, since twins occur only once or twice per thousand foalings.)

Make sure that your agreement is in writing, and get a statement from your veterinarian about the state of health, general condition, and conformation of the stud. (The owner of the stud may very well demand the same information in the form of vet certificates about your mare, so be prepared to offer that too, along with any papers you have relating to her own family tree.) If the breeding, as it often does, involves the mare's being shipped to the stud, have your vet check into any infectious diseases that may be present in the stud's part of the world and have her inoculated, in addition to having a Coggins test performed. If at all possible, check ahead of time into the conditions of the stable where she will be kept, and be sure that a veterinarian (with whom your own vet will have talked) will be on hand for the breeding. We have heard altogether too many unhappy tales of undecipherable invoices for examinations, inoculations, and so on that were not anticipated by the eager foal-owners-to-be.

If your mare is being shipped away from home for the purpose of breeding, you may have to expect her to be gone for two or three months, especially if she is untried. Many mares are not always receptive to stallions, although they may be in heat (and even this is not always easy to detect). There have been drugs developed to determine (or to encourage) ovulation at any particular time during the estrous cycle, but even these are not foolproof, and it may take several breedings before a mare is actually impregnated. Most mares will show obvious signs in the presence of other horses when they are in estrus (arching the tail, moving it aside to display the vulva, and other generally flirtatious types of behavior); but some won't, and whether or not a single breeding will be effective is not easy to determine until long after the fact (at least 30 days by rectal palpation; 45 to 150 days for a urine test). Mares have a regular 21-day estrous cycle throughout the year, but cannot be bred successfully except perhaps three or four times of the year.

Estrus can take three different forms: the dormant phase (usually during fall and winter); the adjustment phase (late summer, early spring); and the true breeding period (March through July or August in Northern states). During the breeding period, estrous cycles may last five to seven days, with ovulation occurring during the second half of the cycle. The season for Thoroughbreds and most commercially important breeds can extend from mid-February until mid-June. The earlier in the year the better as far as Thoroughbreds being raised for the track are concerned, since each foal is given an official birth date of January 1 regardless of actual foaling. A well-developed two-year-old born in February, say, obviously has a distinct advantage over a two-year-old born in July or later. Gestation is normally eleven months (315 to 350 days, with 340 the average for Thoroughbreds). The deviation of a few days is not necessarily significant, but foaling two weeks or more before the calculated date must be considered premature; a foal that is three weeks early will need special intensive care to remain alive, and one born earlier than that will probably not survive. If it does, it will always be weaker than average.

If breeding is so chancy—with barrenness, pregnancy, and potency so difficult to determine at the breeding time—why don't horsemen employ artificial insemination regularly, as cattle breeders and even human physicians seem willing to do? They do, but because horse-breeding associations regulate against it, artificially inseminated horses cannot usually be registered. The Jockey Club, for example, limits the use of artificial insemination to the period immediately following natural breeding. Other organizations allow the practice but not the transport of semen, so that the stallion and mare must be on the same premises when the mare is inseminated. There are obvious advantages to the practice: it decreases the possibility of infection transmission, and it avoids the problems caused by animals that cannot physically perform for one reason or another. But according to the breed associations, it removes as well certain means by which breeding can be controlled and increases the possibilities for fraud and deception.

However you manage to get your mare bred, be sure that you get a breeder's certificate from the owner of the stallion at the time the mare is serviced.

Diseases may affect the pregnant mare, and in areas where these diseases are present, inoculations, if available, should be administered. Rhinopneumonitis or other viral diseases (see page 112) may be prevented in this way; other causes of abortion—bacterial infection, nutritional deficiency, bad condition generally, and genetic faults—may be avoided through good care and a sensible breeding program. Mares that seem likely to abort may be treated with hormones and the abortion prevented, but evidence indicates that the resulting foals are not particularly healthy, since they did not develop at a normal rate. Other inoculations may be indicated for the pregnant mare in order to immunize the foal against various diseases, such as tetanus, and of course, other good stable-management practices, including parasite control, are of the utmost importance.

Nutrition is another all-important consideration. Obviously, no broodmare should be too fat or too thin, since either condition can cause complications during pregnancy and foaling. During the first two-thirds of pregnancy, the mare needs no special diet, or any increase in her feed, since fetal development is slow at this stage. During the last four months, however, her protein and energy requirements will be greater, and special attention must also be given to vitamins A and D, calcium, phosphorus, and iodine. High-protein feeds, such as legume hay or protein supplements, should be fed (see pages 71–73). People living in areas where fescue grass (in pasture or as hay) is available should take note that this must not be fed during the last three months of pregnancy. Once the mare has foaled, she will need dietary supplements as long as she is nursing her offspring.

A heavily pregnant mare should be separated from other horses which might injure her or cause her stress and be given a place that will be suitable for foaling. A clean, small pasture free of steep hills, muddy areas, or piles of brush is ideal, as is a larger-than-average stall (16 feet square), in which bedding (straw rather than dusty chips) is kept clean and deep. The mare may be worked until the last couple of months, if the veterinarian approves, but should not be put under much stress at this time. Mares that are exercised regularly during pregnancy will probably have a much easier time foaling than unconditioned mares, but strenuous or risky exercise (such as jumping or cross-country work) should be avoided. Irregular exercise is probably worse, however, than none at all.

Most mares will foal in the dead of night without any trouble at all—and without giving their owners the thrill of seeing the foal's first few steps. Nevertheless, most owners will want to do everything they can to ensure the delivery of a healthy foal, and we recommend that one remain as alert as possible to the impending

Breeding Hopples (or Hobbles)

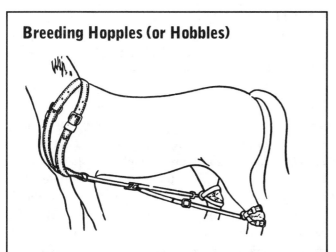

These are used to keep the mare from kicking the stallion and can be made of nylon or cotton rope or leather, with or without pulleys, quick-release straps, and copper rivets. The cheapest kind is made of cotton rope with hock straps and no pulley; the most expensive—and most durable—type is made of double-stitched leather straps with copper rivets, latigo-lined hock straps, and a pulley for control.

A general introduction to breeding is Handbook No. 394, "Breeding and Raising Horses," by M. E. Ensminger, published by the U.S. Department of Agriculture. In addition to information about breeds, care, and other aspects of horsemanship, the booklet contains a valuable sample breeding certificate. Write to the Superintendent of Documents, U.S. Government Printing Office, Washington, D.C. 20102. Two excellent books on the subject, available through tack shops or through Pegasos Press (Santa Fe, New Mexico 87501) are Phyllis Lose's *Blessed Are the Broodmares* (Howell) and *Breeding Management and Foal Development* by Equine Research Publications.

signs of delivery. The first sign is usually the development of the mare's udder, which can happen as early as eight weeks before delivery or as late as the day after. Most mares, however, "bag down" two to six weeks ahead of time, with a tight udder showing a day or two before foaling. Hair will drop out from the udder, and teats will fill out—probably four to six days ahead—

and "wax," or show a tiny drop of the yellowish colostrum, within forty-eight hours before foaling. Not all mares do wax or drip milk, however, so don't count on having a guaranteed signal. Other signs include a flabbiness around the root of the tail, which will be higher than normal with the tissues on either side relatively sunken in appearance, indicating that the pelvic canal is relaxing. The mare herself may become restless and move away from other animals she may be pastured with, eating little and perhaps even becoming somewhat unfriendly. At this point, a bran mash should be offered.

Labor has three stages, the first of which is signaled by uterine contractions and perhaps—but not always—the rupture of the water bag in which the fetus is contained. The mare may become more restless, getting up and down, twitching her tail, and becoming sweaty. Once the fetus begins to move into the birth canal, the second stage begins; at this point the mare may be lying down with her legs stretched, straining and pushing with each contraction. The foal's feet and nose should appear quickly (if they do not and the vet is not present, run for the telephone). After this point, labor—during which the foal will emerge entirely—should take no more than ten minutes to a half hour. Any deviation in this process should be considered an abnormality deserving of emergency treatment.

After foaling, the mare may lie quietly for a few minutes. Leave her alone, and do not under any circumstances assume the role of Mother Nature and cut the cord yourself (valuable nutrients and blood are still passing through the umbilical cord). Only if the foal's head is covered with membrane and it is unable to breathe should you attempt to interfere. The placenta and fetal wastes (or afterbirth) should be expelled within half an hour to three hours after birth, and if the material has not emerged by this time, the vet should be consulted. In any event, you should have on hand for the foaling at least two buckets of hot, clean water, soap, and some mineral oil, disinfectant, tail bandages, iodine (for the foal's navel), and a rubber tube or douche syringe in case the vet needs to give the foal an enema or a laxative. In most cases, and all normal ones, the foal should be on its feet and nursing within an hour or two. If it is weak and unable to stand, the vet should be called if not already on hand; artificial respiration (by clearing the tracheal passage, stimulating breath by rubbing and thumping the rib cage, mouth-to-mouth resuscitation, or an injection) may be required but should not be attempted by an inexperienced person.

Most foalings, happily, are uneventful and, less happily, unobserved. The foaling mare will obviously prefer to conduct her serious business when activity and stress are least apparent, and the eager owner is usually connected—in her mind, at least—with both. Nevertheless, every owner should be alert to the various signs and be ready with the telephone should anything seem out of the ordinary.

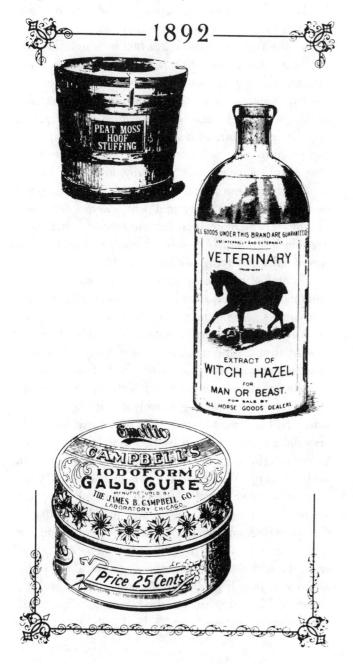

1892

PEAT MOSS HOOF STUFFING

ALL GOODS UNDER THIS BRAND ARE GUARANTEED
USE INTERNALLY AND EXTERNALLY

VETERINARY

EXTRACT OF
WITCH HAZEL
FOR
MAN OR BEAST.
FOR SALE BY
ALL HORSE GOOODS DEALERS

Emollio
CAMPBELL'S
IODOFORM
GALL CURE
MANUFACTURED BY
THE JAMES B. CAMPBELL CO.
LABORATORY CHICAGO.

Price 25 Cents

RAISING A FOAL

In the best of all worlds (and, luckily, in most cases), the mare will turn out to be an ideal mother, trying to get her offspring up as soon as she rises to her feet and urging it to nurse right away. If a foal is not nursing within two hours, the vet should be alerted to give it and the mare an examination. If the foal is not nursing at the end of three hours, hand rearing is probably indicated. This involves milking the mare and placing the colostrum into a bottle that can be fitted with a small nipple. Once the foal has managed to nurse from the bottle, it should be allowed to try nursing from its mother, but if this doesn't work (and restraint devices on an intractable mare that seems unwilling have no effect), the job will probably be yours from then on. Be patient, however, especially if this is the mare's first foal, and give her every chance. See that her udders are in good condition and can be milked freely with gentle massage. If she still refuses to allow the foal to nurse, make sure that you are there to get nourishment into the creature—at least every hour around the clock for the first week, and every two hours for a week after that. Warmed synthetic or simulated milk formulas may work satisactorily, but if it is possible to milk the mare, do so. By the time the foal is a month old, feedings can be reduced to four a day. If you are unable to get one of the simulated formulas, you can substitute 4 ounces of evaporated cow's milk, 4 ounces of warm water, and 1 teaspoon of corn syrup; the foal may consume as much as 8 ounces every hour. If diarrhea results, substitute limewater for the corn syrup. Orphaned or abandoned foals will probably require some antibiotic treatment for the first week, as well as a lot of company, human or otherwise. Warmth is important, of course, but most important is the mare's milk, which contains antibodies, and sufficient vitamins and other nutrients to ensure the foal's health.

By the time a foal reaches a month in age, solids—hay, grain, or a pelleted ration—may be introduced into its diet, which is called a "creep ration" since it is usually presented in a "creep," or a container to which only the foal has access. Ten to 12 pecent of the ration may be devoted to a supplement of some sort, such as Calf Manna, a pelleted high-energy, easily digestible feed developed by Carnation for feeding to slowly developing calves. Nutrition is extremely important during these crucial months if the foal is to develop into a healthy weanling.

Whether or not the foal is hand-reared, one should

Vet Books

There are many veterinary books around, some of them addressed to specialists, some to horse owners who simply need advice about when to call the vet or what to do until the vet comes. Any serious horse owner, however, should have at least a couple of good basic books on hand to consult in times of trouble, and most good tack shops and catalogues offer useful titles. The fourth edition of *Equine Medicine and Surgery* (1991) is one of the most thorough reference volumes, while the *Concise Guide* series to such individual problems as navicular disease or tendon problems are brief introductions to specific ailments and treatments. Three good general books are Tim Hawcroft's *A–Z of Horse Diseases and Health Problems*, Colin J. Vogel's *Illustrated Guide to Veterinary Care of the Horse*, and the 17th edition of *Veterinary Notes for Horse Owners* by Captain M. Horace Hayes, a basic text for more than 100 years. There are many books on specialized problems, such as lameness, injuries, nutrition, and specific therapies, and *Equus* (655 Quince Orchard Road, Gaithersburg, MD 20878) is a monthly magazine that focuses on horse health, from the latest theories to practical hands-on advice. A good on-line reference is http://www.horseadvice.com, a homepage operated by Dr. Robert N. Oglesby, a veterinarian who raises horses and offers information as well as a consulting service. *Healing Your Horse: Alternative Therapies* by Meredith L. Snader et al., is a useful guide to the confusing new world of holistic horse medicine; there are several magazines and journals devoted to the subject as well, including *The Holistic Horse* (20 Prospect Avenue, Ardsley, NY 10542 or on the Internet at http://www.holistichorse.com). Phyllis Lose's *Blessed Are the Brood Mares* (second edition), and *Blessed Are the Foals* are must reading for anyone who plans to breed horses.

always be sure to give a baby horse the most gentle and attentive of care—even if it involves only occasional (daily) handling. This will relax the mare and make the foal generally friendly toward humans, an invaluable first step toward successful training later on. Do not be overattentive—so that the mare becomes worried or nervous—and do not subject the foal to the stress of more than a few minutes of handling at a time while it is very young. But do make it aware of your existence and let it be sure from the start that you are a friend, someone that can be trusted. Some trainers like to halter a foal the moment it is born, to accustom the animal to the feel of a piece of equipment, but the first haltering can usually wait for a couple of months at least, even if you plan to show the baby or begin its training before it is weaned at about six months. Whatever you do, don't spoil the animal by presenting a treat each time you present yourself; a foal is not a pet in the usual sense, and bad habits—such as nipping and jumping up—can begin at any time during these first few months.

chapter 5

Tack

The making and selling of tack, or virtually anything a horse wears, has developed into a multi-million-dollar industry. While saddle making may not be the world's oldest profession, it has certainly been around for a number of centuries, changing slowly as new concepts of riding, new materials, and specialized breeding demanded. The American Plains Indian is known to have tied a strip of rawhide around the lower jaw of a horse, jumped on its bare back, and ridden off. Whether Plains Indians were, in fact, the precise horsemen that movies have made them out to be is something better left to historians. One can only speculate that without a saddle to help maintain a stable seat, control of the mount was often haphazard. Actually, the Indian rawhide bit was predated by the more sophisticated hand-forged bits found in the Bronze Age. The Greeks and Romans are known to have used both the snaffle and the curb. The Romans, along with the invention of gluttonous feasts, are credited with producing the first saddle, a high-peaked affair that most likely developed from the addition of rolls of padding to the basic saddlecloth. Later, medieval and Oriental saddles were developed with high backs to support the warrior as he charged with his lance. These chairlike saddles did not last long, however, for when the warrior was on the receiving end of the lance, he often discovered the high back might support him so well his spine would break before the saddle did. Jousting saddles without a back support followed, although by present-day standards the pommel and cantle were certainly high. The ladies' sidesaddle dates from approximately the twelfth century, and the Spanish saddles ridden by the Conquistadores, obvious ancestors of our Western saddle, date from about then as well.

The biggest revolution in tack came with the invention of the stirrup, a truly ingenious device believed to have been used first by the Huns. Superb equestrians and fierce fighters, the Huns no doubt owe their reputation as horsemen to their ability to turn in the saddle and shift their weight and balance.

Tack has changed relatively little over the centuries. Probably the newest revolution in horse equipment can be found in the last fifty years with the introduction of such new materials as nylon, stainless steel, plastic, fiberglass, aluminum, and plywood. One could speculate that the single thing future historians may find most interesting about our tack is its wide variety. That variety, of course, reflects the varied and specialized work we ask our horses to perform, such as dressage, cutting, jumping, flat racing, barrel racing, steeplechasing, endurance, driving, trotting, and bronc, park, pleasure, trail, and trick riding.

For each horseman there is a catalog that sells the equipment he needs. What we hope to do is describe what all of those items are, how they are used, how one item varies from another, and lastly, where hard-to-come-by items can be found. Despite protests from the committed, we strongly feel that all styles of riding are directly related and equipment used by one horseman may be the perfect solution for another. Therefore, we have not divided this section into the traditional "English" and "Western" categories. Instead, we hope the reader will find interest in all tack and attempt to understand the "how" and "why" of its use. The English rider may discover, for example, that the Western bosal used with a snaffle can be as effective as the English double bridle and under some conditions may have advantages the other does not. In other words, tack normally associated with one style of riding may be suitable for a horse being trained to another style. Many items of tack are based on tradition, often with good reason. Some, however, are adaptable and should be discovered wherever they fit an individual horse's or rider's needs.

Bits

It has been noted that one half of good riding is in the employment of the seat; the other half is in the employment of the legs. If that statement seems an odd way to begin a discussion of bits, we suggest you read on.

When you take reins and thus a bit into your hands, you are helping your seat and legs to achieve the head set basic to a well-balanced and well-trained animal. And if the head is set correctly (the "correct" head set will depend on the breed, the work you are asking the horse to do, and to some degree the horse's natural way of going), then such problems as evasion of the bit, improper turning, lack of suppleness, and difficulty of gait transitions can be avoided before they begin.

Bits can be grouped as follows: the snaffle, the gag, the curb, the Weymouth, the Pelham, the hackamore, and the spade. Within each of these groupings are many items, each having different emphasis.

To understand the action of various bits, it is necessary to understand that there are seven basic areas on the horse where the bridle is capable of applying pressure. These are the tongue, the bars (that area of the gum between the incisors and molars), the roof of the mouth, the lips, the chin (or curb groove), the nose, and the poll. Some bits exert pressure on only one or two of these points, while others bring pressure to bear simultaneously on a number of them. Nearly all bits work on the principle that a horse will move away from pressure or pain. For example, pressure on the poll will encourage a horse to lower its head, while an upward pressure on the lips will encourage the horse to raise

its head. Therefore, in choosing the proper bit for your horse (and learning how to use it), it is necessary to know what you will be asking the horse to do and then selecting the bit that best communicates that command.

In order for your horse to remain sensitive to the pressure of the bit, and therefore responsive to your commands, it is imperative that the mouth remain moist. A wet mouth stimulates and lubricates nerve endings near the surface, while a dry mouth has the opposite effect. Many bits encourage the horse to "play" with the mouthpiece, rolling the metal against its tongue and the roof of its mouth. Some training bits include "keys" (small pieces of metal that dangle from the center of the bit) for the young horse to tongue. Horsemen with access to older, hand-forged steel bits swear by them, claiming that the metal used has a sweeter taste and a more salutary effect on the horse. Others find that copper mouthpieces have an appealing taste which encourages the horse to salivate freely (some horses, however, reject the copper as strange and unpleasant).

Most bits are made of stainless steel, which is rustproof and practically nonbreakable; many bits come with stainless steel cheeks and copper mouthpieces or copper wire wrapped around the steel mouth. Also available, however, are chrome-plated or nickel-plated bits, many of them made from malleable iron. These are far stronger than the now-outmoded solid-nickel bit, which bends or breaks easily. Aluminum, which is marvelously lightweight when every ounce counts, is used on almost all racing bits and on many Western curb bits. Finally, you can also buy stainless steel bits with hard or soft rubber or nylon mouthpieces, materials often preferred for training a young, sensitive mouth.

Snaffle

Although the snaffle bit is associated with English-style riding, it is becoming more and more commonly used for Western training as well. The snaffle, by applying pressure to the tongue, bars, and lips, causes the horse to raise its head. Many horsemen use it along with a curb bit or with an auxiliary to the bit (such as a dropped noseband or a martingale) to obtain a flexion of the poll or tucking of the chin which a snaffle alone cannot produce.

Snaffle bits come in various shapes and forms. The

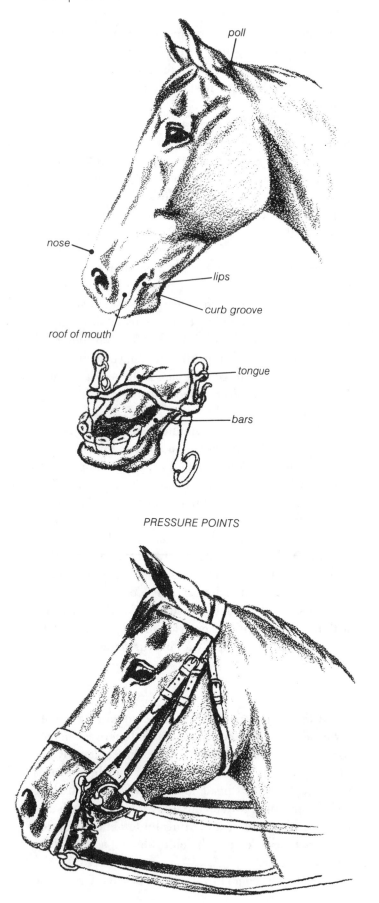

PRESSURE POINTS

mouthpiece may be either two short arms that are joined in the middle (the jointed snaffle) or one piece that may be either straight or half-mooned in shape (the mullen mouthpiece). The jointed mouthpiece causes a nutcracker effect on the tongue as the two arms are pulled back against the horse's lips, while the mullen mouthpiece has none of this effect.

The snaffle is generally considered one of the gentlest bits now available, but it can also be quite severe (severity often meaning the amount of pain inflicted upon the animal), with misuse resulting in an overflexed, cold-jawed, mean animal with no trust in or respect for its rider. In fact, few bits are severe in themselves; but when combined with heavy, jerking, pulling hands, any bit can become pure torture for the horse. However, there are several factors which can influence the amount of pressure a bit produces:

• thickness—a thin, slight-looking bit will cut into the mouth more sharply than a stout bit.

• the shape of the arms—a twisted mouthpiece has an effect much like that of a rough-toothed saw (the use of the twisted mouthpiece is banned in Maryland), and a chain-link mouthpiece can pinch the tongue and rub the bars raw.

• the flexibility of the joint—the looser the joint, the more pronounced its nutcracker effect upon the tongue; the tighter the joint, the less sharp the action. There is a variation known as a "Y" or "W" mouth snaffle, made of two sets of arms, jointed off-center to opposite sides of the mouth. When pulled back, the two arms hinge and pinch a wider surface of the tongue than the single-jointed mouthpiece, and its more severe action should be used only by experienced hands. For horses with sensitive mouths there is a jointed snaffle with the two arms linked by a small ring or connecting piece of metal. This added piece actually reduces the leverage of the joint and lessens the nutcracker effect.

• the shape and size of the rings—the larger the rings, the less likely the bit is to pull around and through the mouth. Many horsemen prefer loose-fitting rings which encourage the horse to play with the bit. Rings fixed onto the mouthpiece give greater pressure to the lips and bars, as well as giving the rider extra leverage to activate the nutcracker pressure on the tongue. While a loose-ring bit sits flat along the horse's cheek and produces a straighter and therefore less severe pull, particularly large or long bit cheeks may rub the sides of the horse's cheek. Some bits (or bit aids) feature an abrasive surface on one cheek to discourage the animal that continually runs out to that side. There is a nasty bit called a Scorrier, or Cornish, snaffle with bridle cheek rings fixed in slots within a twisted mouthpiece while an outside set of rings attaches to the reins. The bridle rings produce an inward squeezing action against the horse's lips, which in tandem with the twisted mouthpiece produces a sharp action.

Gag

Like the snaffle, the gag bit essentially raises the horse's head, but its more severe action should be used by experienced hands only. You can easily spot a gag bit; the bridle cheekpieces, made of rounded leather or rope, pass through holes in the top and bottom of the bit cheeks, and the reins attach to the bridle cheekpieces below the bit. It was originally developed for polo players and was used only recently on jumpers.

How does a gag bit work? As the reins pull back on the bridle, the bit slides upward along the rounded cheekpieces. The additional upward leverage brings pressure to bear on the lips and bars of the mouth. In theory, to escape this strong pressure, the horse immediately raises its head. But some horsemen dispute the

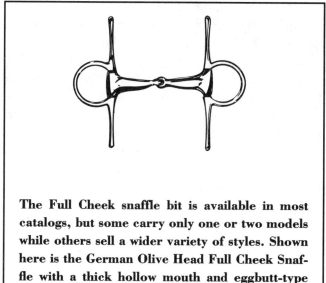

The Full Cheek snaffle bit is available in most catalogs, but some carry only one or two models while others sell a wider variety of styles. Shown here is the German Olive Head Full Cheek Snaffle with a thick hollow mouth and eggbutt-type attachment. Full Cheek Snaffles are also available in different mouth styles, including rubber, twisted wire, French snaffle mouthpiece, wire wrapped, and knife edge mouth.

gag's ability to raise the head pointing out that pressure is also applied to the poll. The hard-mouthed horse, therefore, will lower its head to avoid that downward pull.

Some horsemen will use two sets of reins with the gag bit, one set attached to the bridle rings and one set attached to the bit rings. Therefore, depending on the reining, the bit can work either as a plain snaffle or as a gag bit. A gag bit is sometimes used to replace the bradoon in a double bridle, and some riders use a gag bit with a martingale. (The action of the martingale, basically a downward-bearing one, is discussed on pages 163–64.) However, a martingale used along with a gag bit can be a severe means of control when you consider that the strong upward action of the gag is applied to a mouth held stationary by the martingale.

Curb

The American Plains Indians knew some of the principles of the curb when they tied rawhide around their mounts' lower jaw, and certainly heavy, high-ported curb bits were used in the Bronze Age. Like the Spaniards and knights before them, cowboys regarded their horses as beasts for work, and for the cow horse quick turns and sliding stops were essential for survival. So bitting for Western use quickly became more sophisticated, incorporating a large number of the basic pressure points as more specialized control was needed. While many people associate the curb primarily with Western reining, this bit is also an important element in English and dressage riding, and it is the basic bit for the high-strutting gaited show animals.

The curb is capable of applying pressure to as many as five of the seven basic pressure points: to the curb groove through the curb strap; to the poll via the bridle (the amount of pressure depending on the length between the mouthpiece and the bridle rings); to the bars; to the tongue; and, with the use of a bit such as the Half-Breed (a high-ported bit), to the roof of the mouth. All these pressure points ask the horse to lower its head and tuck its chin into its chest. By so doing, the animal is forced to arch its neck and flex at the poll. This reaction is ideal for the loose-reined cutting horse or calf roper required to perform sliding stops and rollbacks while balanced on its haunches and for the highly collected Walking Horse. Such a head carriage, however, would be less than ideal for the English rider about to attempt a jump or for the advanced-level dressage horse required to perform various exercises in collection and extension. These last two horses, therefore, would carry the curb along with a snaffle (the double bridle).

The curb bit comes with either a fixed or a sliding mouthpiece (either the fixed, or stiff-jaw, mouthpiece is bolted to the cheeks or the bit is molded all in one piece, while the sliding, or loose-jaw, mouthpiece can slide vertically when leverage is applied to the cheeks). The shape of the curb mouthpiece varies from the straight-mouth through numerous kinds of ports to a combination high-port and roller (either the Salinas or the Half-Breed bit).

The cheeks, or shanks, of the curb also vary greatly in overall length, from the Western reining bit, averaging approximately $7^1/_2$ inches long, to the Walking Horse bit, from 8 to as much as $11^1/_2$ inches long. The cheeks of the curb are either straight (as in the Weymouth, the Walking Horse, and numerous Western curbs) or curved back (as in the popular Grazing bit commonly used on cutting horses) or even curved back farther still to meet under the chin (as in the Roping

Curb straps

bit, designed to eliminate the chance of the rope's catching in the bit).

The curb strap attaches to the bit either at the bridle rings or through special curb loops. Curb straps are available in single and double-linked chain (the single is usually thinner and therefore sharper in action, while the double-linked chain lies flat and covers a wider surface); in a leather strap with adjustable buckles (often used on Weymouth bridles); in a combination of leather strap and chain link, with or without a rubber curb guard; in an elastic strap; or in a chain that features an oval metal centerpiece designed to fit in between the jaw bones (called a "Jodhpur," it is rarely seen nowadays).

Bit and Bradoon

The double bridle, also known as a Weymouth or bit and bradoon (bridoon), is used exclusively by English-style riders. It consists of a thin snaffle (the bradoon) and a curb bit. Each bit is attached to its own headstall and its own set of reins. The bradoon reins are slightly wider than the curb reins and are normally held on the outside of the pinky fingers, while the curb reins are held between the third and fourth fingers. Both reins then pass over the palm of the hands, where they are layered over the index fingers and held in place by the thumbs.

The bradoon, which can be jointed or mullen-mouth, is always finer than the snaffle, and its action is thus sharper. The mouthpiece of the curb (about $5^1/_2$ inches wide) is often the same as or only slightly shorter than the total length of the cheek. A mild bit known as a Tom Thumb has cheeks which seldom exceed $3^1/_2$ inches in total length. The Weymouth curb generally has a low-port mouth and straight cheeks. Unlike its Western counterparts, however, it has small loops halfway between the mouthpiece and the end of the cheeks to which a thin leather strap is attached. This lip strap, which attaches to the curb chain by means of a fly link, a small ring in the center of the curb chain, keeps the chain in the curb groove and prevents the bit from reversing in the horse's mouth.

The bit and bradoon is an advanced form of bitting combining the snaffle's ability to raise the horse's head with the curb's capacity to lower it and tuck the nose into the chest. The separate actions of the two bits give the experienced horseman additional means for control and a more precise vocabulary with which to communicate his commands. It is certainly easy to understand why the Weymouth is compulsory for horses shown at third-level and higher dressage tests.

Pelham

The Pelham bit, a combination snaffle and curb, has a set of rings connected to the mouthpiece and another set connected to the curb cheeks. The rider therefore uses two sets of reins and, by maintaining equal and steady contact on the reins, applies pressure to the horse's lips, bars, and tongue and to the curb groove simultaneously. Pelhams are available in a variety of mouthpiece styles, including a straight mullen mouth, in hard rubber or metal, a jointed mouthpiece, or a port. The cheeks of the Pelham are relatively shorter than those of Western and Walking Horse curbs, from the short-checked "Tom Thumb" style with cheeks under 4 inches long, to the "Hartwell" Pelham, about 6 or 7 inches long. Some Pelhams, such as the "Show Hack" or "Globe Cheek," are used with only one set of reins and in the cases just mentioned function essentially as mild curb bits. The "Kimblewick" Pelham calls for a single set of reins that attach to large Dee rings beginning a short distance above the mouthpiece and ending at the bottom of the horse's cheek. When this bit is properly used the rider can work the snaffle by raising his hands slightly higher than normal or switch to the curb by simply lowering his hands.

Mechanical Hackamore

Since it has no mouthpiece, the hackamore, or mechanical bit, is not literally a bit at all. Rather than applying pressure to the horse's lips, bars, or tongue, it instead affects the nose through the pressure of a covered metal noseband and the curb groove by the leverage of the long (usually 8 or 9 inches) free-swinging metal shanks. The curb strap is attached to a short metal shank that curves back from the end of the noseband toward the chin. To complete the hackamore, a metal chin, bar, or leather strap usually joins the two cheek bottoms to prevent the bit from swinging forward and up where it would be ineffective.

Hackamore bits are used for the particularly rough riding often required in rodeo roping, steer-wrestling, and barrel-racing events, and since there is no bit in the horse's mouth, it is impossible to injure that area with quick jerking motions. Hackamores are also an excellent—and sometimes the only—solution for riding an animal with a sore or spoiled mouth.

Spade

There are many for whom simply the mention of a spade bit causes eyes to narrow and lips to tighten in automatic signs of disapproval. In the hands of anyone but the most skilled equestrian, we must agree. But the spade bit, in highly competent hands and on an animal that has been slowly and painstakingly brought along to accept it, is capable of firmly setting the head and allowing the rider to communicate with only the lightest of touch. There is a wonderful Mexican performer named Antonio Aguilar who travels throughout North America singing and gesturing with gusto while his mount performs *haute école* dressage movements with equal enthusiasm and skill. The horse carries a spade bit, and Señor Aguilar cues for each movement. But watching them work together one feels that the rider needs simply think a cue and the horse, reading his mind, performs.

The spade was brought to this country by Spaniards and was later refined by the California Mission Indians, who were schooled in the art by the Franciscan Fathers. The Mission Indians, highly skilled craftsmen, created many beautifully engraved bits inlaid with silver and gold.

The spade bit comes in several traditional styles, but certain parts are basic to each. The mouthpiece is a straight bar with a port rising from its center. At the top of the port is a flat, shaped piece of metal (the spade), and within the port's arch there is often a "cricket" (a roller). "Keepers," two pieces of wire covered with copper wire or copper rollers, are attached to the bottom of the spade piece and to each cheekpiece. The entire length of the mouthpiece, from the tip of the spade to the bar, is between 3 and 5 inches. The mouthpiece is joined to the cheeks either by hinging (in which case the bit is known as a loose-jaw, or soft, bit), or by welding (a solid-jaw, or hard, bit).

The cheeks of the spade may be plain but are more often intricately carved with beautiful traditional designs. The cheeks of the spade are usually between 6 and 8 inches long and can be straight or curved back. Usually these cheekpieces are joined at the bottom by

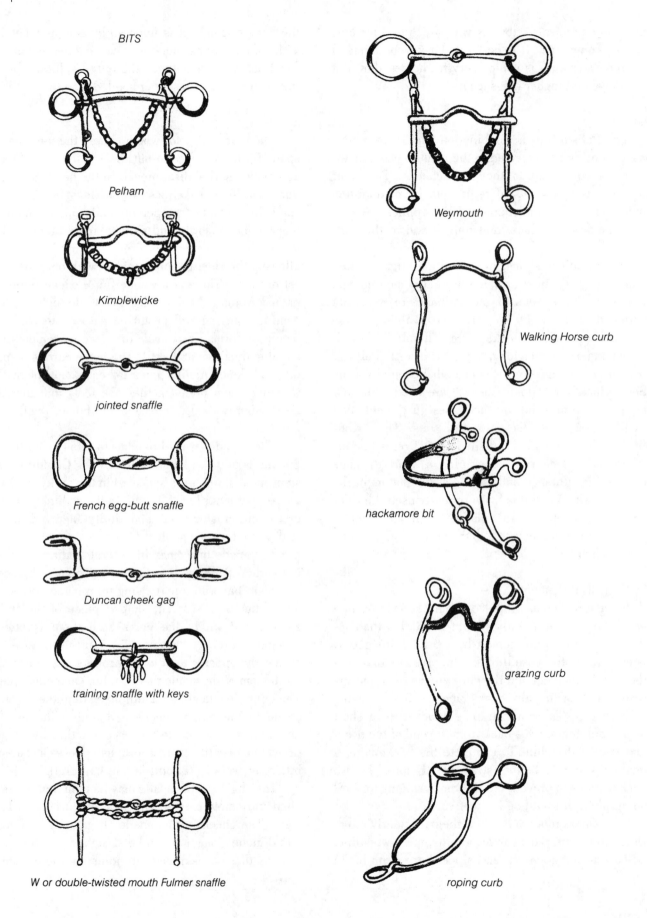

BITS

Pelham

Kimblewicke

jointed snaffle

French egg-butt snaffle

Duncan cheek gag

training snaffle with keys

W or double-twisted mouth Fulmer snaffle

Weymouth

Walking Horse curb

hackamore bit

grazing curb

roping curb

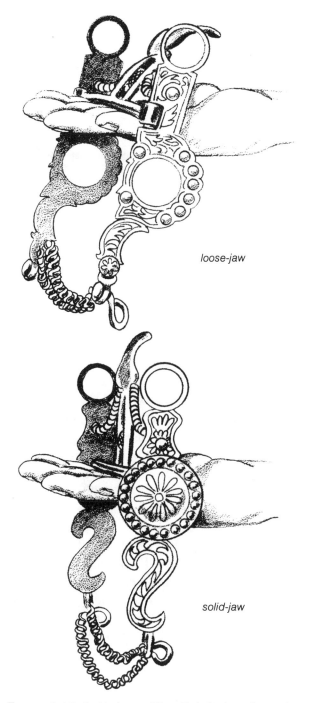

loose-jaw

solid-jaw

Two spade bits that balance differently in the horse's mouth

Some of the best-known styles include the Santa Barbara, a straight cheek on which can usually be found a pattern of a star or a large concho; the Las Cruces, usually a solid-jaw bit with a large concho on its straight cheeks; the Santa Paula, a loose-jaw bit with a large concho and narrow cheekpieces that sweep back toward the rider; and the Santa Susanna, sometimes called a "lay-back," which features a "D" shape on top of a concho and a cheek that curves back.

The mouthpiece of the spade is a large and imposing thing, and its action works primarily upon the roof of a horse's mouth. However, when the spade is carried by a wise, well-schooled horse, it rarely touches the top of its mouth at all. Instead, the horse is alert and sensitive to the other pressure points and responds to a warning action from the slightest rein movement. In fact, some spade-trained horses will work only off the cheekpieces.

The spade mouth is weighted and balanced to lie flat on the tongue when the horse holds its head properly. The bit's wide mouthpiece offers a large bearing surface, while the copper rollers—"crickets"—keep the mouth moist and produce a sound most horses find soothing. For the first several months and sometimes years of training, the horse carries the bit without reins. Initial training on a hackamore and then with the spade bit balanced in its mouth teaches a horse to tuck its head and flex at the poll, a position that when maintained prevents the spade from rising to hit the roof of the mouth. While playing with the bit the horse learns to keep the spade flat against its tongue at all gaits. Only when the hackamore control is discarded can the animal be considered a "straight-up spade horse."

The height of a spade mouthpiece has less to do with its effectiveness than the balance of the mouthpiece and the shape and leverage of the cheeks. The most demanding spade is a solid-jaw Santa Barbara cheek with a vertically balanced mouthpiece, which should be used only on a show horse required to perform with an exaggerated tucked head and arched neck. Such a bit is balanced to lie flat against the tongue when the horse holds its head directly perpendicular to the ground. A cutting horse that works with a low head and extended nose will more likely be found in a Santa Susanna or Santa Paula bit with a spade balanced for a more extended head carriage.

A spade bit, despite its torture-chamber reputation, is severe only in ignorant or evil hands (a razor in the

a solid bar or "slobber chains," which are important to the balance of the bit. The reins attach to weighted chains, normally about 8 inches long, which hang from the end of the cheekpiece, and these too play an important part in balancing the bit.

Spade bits are identified by their cheekpieces, which come in several classic patterns and shapes.

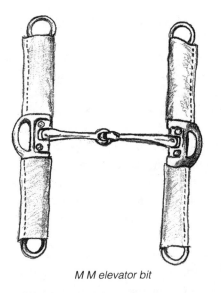

M M elevator bit

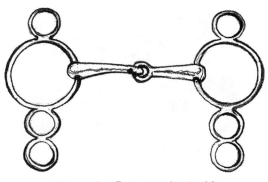

Loose ring European elevator bit

hands of a monkey, as the saying goes). The sensitive rider will never tie a spade-bitted horse by the reins, nor will he ever pull back or jerk the reins. When teaching the art of light hands, some spade-bit trainers will replace a portion of the reins with a light, easily breakable twine that will snap as soon as the student pulls back too hard. For above all else, the spade bit requires light, quiet hands and an easy, steady temperament to match.

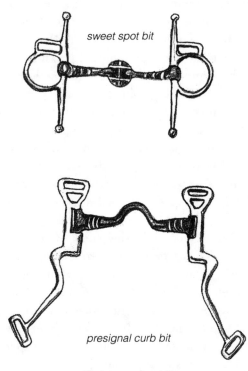

sweet spot bit

presignal curb bit

Resistance free bits

Bridles

The ideal bridle simply reaffirms what early training should have taught: the proper head set for the type of work the horse will be doing. For, so the theory goes, if the head set is correct, then control of the horse's speed and direction comes close behind. If this sounds simple, it isn't. The debates over proper bitting continue to rage.

A bridle is designed to hold a bit in the horse's mouth. Most bridles complement the action of the bit some supplement it, and some even replace it. All bridles share common parts, even though these parts may vary in form and in name. For example, every bridle has a headpiece, sometimes called the headstall—a piece of leather that lies across the poll. The headpiece frequently includes a throat-latch, an adjustable strap designed to prevent the bridle from slipping. When it

> *"I regard the spade bit as an archaic instrument that should be seen only in museums along with such similar relics of semibarbarism as chastity belts and brain squeezers. . . . I do maintain that any horseman whose firmness of seat and delicacy of touch enable him to get fair results with a spade bit should be able to achieve excellent results without the spade."*
>
> RICHARD YOUNG,
> The Schooling of the Western Horse
> *University of Oklahoma Press, 1954*

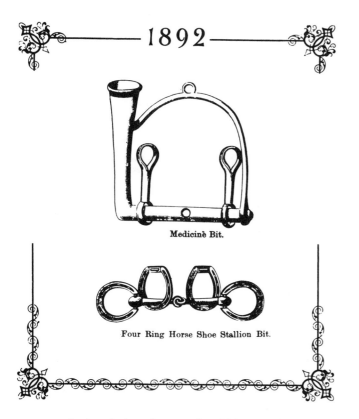

1892

Medicine Bit.

Four Ring Horse Shoe Stallion Bit.

is properly fitted, four fingers should be easily inserted between the strap and the horse's throat. Many Western headstalls feature a shaped split, or sliding earpiece that slips over the offside ear. The shaped earpiece is usually sewn into the headstall; the crown of the split-ear headstall is divided slightly to the right of center for about 12 inches, and the sliding-ear headstall has a separate piece of leather about 6 inches long which, true to its name, forms an adjustable loop. Although some Western bridles come with a fitted earpiece, English bridles are designed instead with a browband, a piece of leather that slips onto the headpiece and wraps across the animal's forehead. Both the fitted-ear and the browband serve the same function: to hold the bridle firmly in place.

Every bridle has a cheekpiece, usually two straps which buckle on to the headpiece at one end while the other end holds the bit in place. The cheekpiece should be adjustable on both sides of the head so that the bit can be set evenly at the proper height in the mouth.

Most bridles, including all English and many modern Western types, include a cavesson. Its primary function is to provide a place to attach a martingale or tie-down. A properly fitted cavesson should be loose enough to insert two fingers between it and the horse's

face, while permitting the horse to open its mouth and flex its jaw. Some trainers prefer to tighten the cavesson to the point where it prevents the horse from opening its jaw and getting behind the bit. The correct placement of a cavesson is halfway between the horse's cheekbone and the corners of its mouth. One that is fitted too low may interfere with the action of a snaffle bit and can cause pinching, especially if adjusted too tightly, while a too-loose-fitting cavesson looks ill-fitting and may cause unnecessary rubbing on the horse's face. The cavesson should not be confused with a noseband, a piece of equipment that has a specific and different function. (A discussion of nosebands can be found later in this chapter.)

English bridles may include a cavesson with bit keepers, small leather loops that extend from the cavesson cheekpieces and are designed to hold the top of the full-cheek snaffle bit in place.

If you are looking through tack catalogs, it will be readily apparent that bridles, even when labeled "English" or "Western," differ widely within each classification. And one of the major variations is the strength and weight of the materials. A hunting bridle, for example, will be a sturdy affair with the cheek about $^3/_4$ inch wide. A show bridle is usually thinner and lighter in weight than the hunt bridle, and its cheeks will average $^5/_8$ inch or smaller. A racing exercise bridle may be equally strong, while cheeks of actual racing bridles rarely exceed $^1/_2$ inch in width and will be used with lightweight rubber reins instead of leather ones for better grip. Most Western-style bridles are $^5/_8$ inch wide, and many feature a flared cheek bottom to accommodate a screw fastening.

Unless you are having a bridle made to order, you will have to specify Pony, Cob, or Full-Size. Determining these "sizes" is much like trying to describe one clothes designer's size 8 or 42—the answer lies somewhere between him and his cutter. The best way to anticipate this problem is to measure the distance from lip to lip across the poll and then find the size that most closely corresponds. Remember that bridles should be especially important for fitting the young, growing horse.

Single Bridle

As already described, this consists of a headpiece with a throatlatch, two cheekpieces, a browband (for

English bridles), and often a cavesson. Basic differences between the Western and English bridles can be found in the fitted-ear versus the browband and whether a cavesson is included or not. Many Arabian show bridles will include a decorative browband, but they omit the cavesson which would detract from that breed's beautiful dish nose.

Double, or Weymouth, Bridle

This bridle is designed to hold two separate bits in the horse's mouth. The bridle has two headpieces that pass through the loops of the browband and attach to two separate sets of cheekpieces. One cheek holds the bradoon bit while the other cheek holds the curb bit (Weymouth), which lies in the mouth directly below the bradoon. The actions of the bradoon and the Weymouth are controlled through separate sets of reins, permitting the rider a large reining vocabulary for communicating with his horse.

Gag Bridle

Similar to the basic single bridle, this differs in one small but important way; the cheekpieces are not attached to the bit, as usual, by the bit rings. Instead, the bridle cheeks pass through small holes in the top and bottom of the bit rings (or bit cheeks), ending in a ring that attaches to the reins. In other words, the reins

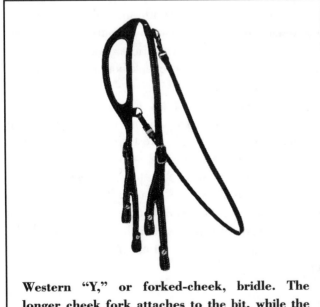

Western "Y," or forked-cheek, bridle. The longer cheek fork attaches to the bit, while the shorter cheek fork holds the tie-down at the correct height.

and the bridle cheeks form one continuous line, with the bit strung on the bridle leather like beads on a necklace. The bridle cheekpieces are normally made of leather that has been rounded onto a piece of cord or sometimes of braided rope, in either case made thin enough to pass through the small holes in the bit and made strong enough to stand up to the constant friction as the bit slides up and down the leather.

Hackamore

The bitless bridle, widely used by Western and occasionally by English trainers, is a useful tool for teaching the young horse proper flexion or simply for obtaining control. In Western-style riding, Texans use a full hackamore before advancing their horses to a curb bit, and Californians use it before, during, and even after putting their horse into a spade bit.

The hackamore—the name is from the Spanish word *jáquima*—applies pressure to the horse's nose, its chin, and sometimes just below its cheeks, to teach the animal to tuck its nose, flex at the poll, and come to a halt balanced on its haunches. The basic hackamore bridle is made up of three essential parts: the bosal (bo-sal'), the fiador (Americanized to theodore), and the mecate (Americanized to McCarty). The starting bosal is a thick, heavy, rounded noseband usually made of braided rawhide and sometimes reinforced with steel. For horses that are particularly difficult to break, a braided-horsehair bosal that has been soaked in water and permitted to stiffen is used. It usually takes only one or two days in such a bosal to bring any mount to attention. If the horse responds to the stout rawhide bosal, the trainer will replace it with a lighter one, progressing to a still lighter version as training continues. All bosals meet behind the horse's jaw in a large ball called a heel butt which is weighted to hang low. A simple leather headstall holds the bosal in place, and a rawhide button on either side holds the headstall in place. (Occasionally a bosal with abrasive rawhide buttons is used. The buttons rub the area below the horse's cheeks raw—an encouragement, some horsemen feel, to take turning cues more quickly.)

The fiador is a rope that passes over the poll and around the jaw, where it is knotted to hold the heel butt. The fiador is essentially a throatlatch keeping the headstall from slipping forward and off a stubborn, head-tossing youngster. The mecate is usually a long

BRIDLES

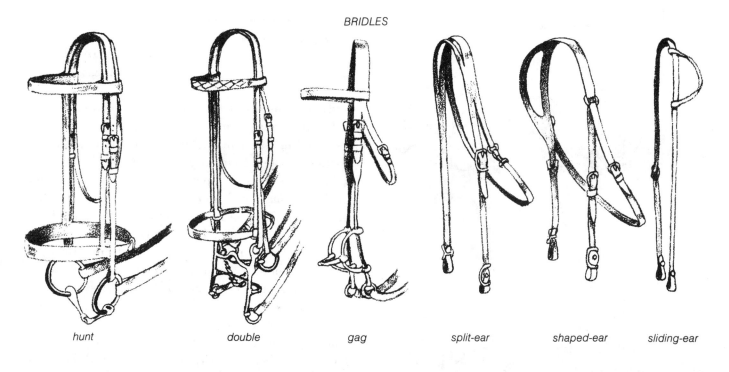

hunt   *double*   *gag*   *split-ear*   *shaped-ear*   *sliding-ear*

(about 24 feet), soft, flexible cotton rope that wraps around the heel butt in a series of precise knots—part of it to loop back to the saddle as reins, the extra length to tie around the horse's neck and available for use as a lead rope. Instead of the soft rope, some horsemen prefer a stiffer mecate made from horsehair.*

After the initial stages of hackamore training, the California horseman will introduce the spade bit. Depending on the animal's learning timetable, he eventually adds reins to the bit, replacing the training hackamore with a thinner bosal and eliminating the supporting fiador altogether. California-trained horses thus carry a lightweight bosal as an English-trained horse wears a cavesson; it is no ornament, however, but a necessary means by which to tie the horse. (The spade-bitted horse is never, but never, tied by its reins, only by the thin mecate attached to the bosal.) The curb-bitted Texas horse may carry a type of bosal that is actually a tie-down noseband. This thin noseband is often made from rawhide or flexible cabled steel covered with plaited rawhide, plain leather, or vinyl. The noseband attaches to a tie-down, a strap of leather connected to either the breastplate or the girth, and it

serves the same function as the standing martingale (see page 164).

The English-style bitless bridle works on the same principle as the Western hackamore. It consists of a headpiece, cheekpieces, a wide noseband, a backstrap to hold the noseband in place, and a set of reins which pass through the rings on either side of the noseband to join at a padded curb piece under the chin. Pressure is therefore applied to the curb groove and to the nose. After working a young horse in this bridle for a while, most trainers add a headpiece to which a mild snaffle is attached. For a period the horse does nothing more than carry this bit in its mouth while continuing to take its cues from the reins. Eventually, the trainer attaches a set of reins to the bit and begins to transfer the cues onto the snaffle while simultaneously lessening the use of the bridle reins.

REINS

Reins are essentially strips of material connecting our hands to the bit. They come in leather (either plain, plaited, rolled, or laced), rubber, web, nylon, cotton, or rope. In the plaited rein the leather is split into several strips of equal length and then braided. In the laced rein a piece of thin rawhide is "sewn" through the rein in such a way that it forms a V shape down the length. Rolled reins, usually $1\frac{1}{2}$ to 2 feet of rein on either side of the bit, involve leather rolled around a piece of cord

---

* If you come across one of the old, exquisitely made horsehair ropes, you will immediately appreciate the quality of workmanship that went into its creation and understand its coarse, irritating quality when stoutly tied under the horse's jaw.

TYING THE MECATE

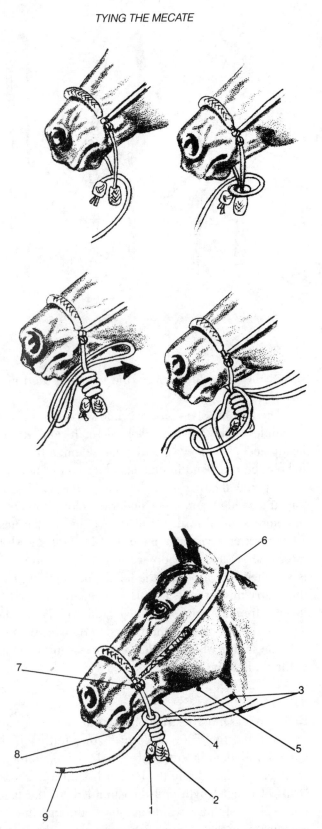

1. rope tassel 2. heel butt 3. reins 4. point of pressure 5. cheek 6. headstall 7. button 8. chin 9. lead rope

and sewn closed with the remainder of the rein left flat. All of these reins give excellent grip and are commonly used on English-style bridles. The normal English rein is approximately 5 feet long and generally $1/2$, $5/8$, $3/4$, or 1 inch wide. Show-jumping reins may be shorter and pony reins may be shorter still, down to $4^1/4$ feet. Each of these reins is open-style, joined at the ends by a buckle. It is customary when using a double bridle to use snaffle reins that are about $1/8$ inch wider than the curb reins for easy tactile differentiation.

Western-style reins are split into Texas and California schools, with further variations within each style. The Texan may use an open-ended rein, between 6 and 7 feet long, or a roping rein made from one uncut piece of leather, normally between 6 and 8 feet long from end to end. A distinctive feature of the roping rein is that one or both ends are nearly always attached to the bit by swivel snaps, good for quick release when needed. Texas-style reins are single-ply, plaited, braided, or double-stitched. Weighted leather (around 1 pound more or less) open-end reins are available for training the neck-reining horse.

California reins are closed (about 8 feet long from

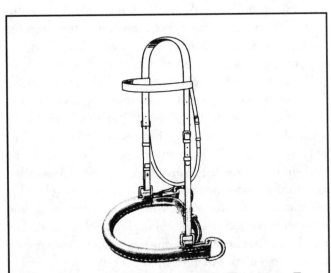

Jumping Hackamore Noseband. This is an English-style hackamore. The noseband is made of leather-covered rope with rings on the ends for attachment of reins.

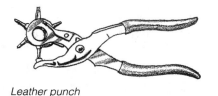

Leather punch

bit end to bit end) with a romal, a 4-foot piece of leather that attaches to a ring centered in the closed reins. The romal may include a popper, which is used much like a bat or noisy crop. It is not uncommon for California-style reins to have buttons, barrels, or knots, convenient for gripping and weighted for better spade-bit balance. The reins are $3/8$ or $1/2$ inch wide, with the corresponding romals $1/2$ and $5/8$ inch.

Supplements to the Bit

A mount, as any horseman will have noticed, does not always perform to cue. The horse occasionally needs to be reminded to balance itself properly, to stay under control, and to stop such tricks as evading the bit or throwing its head. Such maneuvers are at least frightening and usually dangerous, and danger is not what horsemanship should be all about.

Before any horseman turns to additional means for controlling any of the reactions described, he must in-

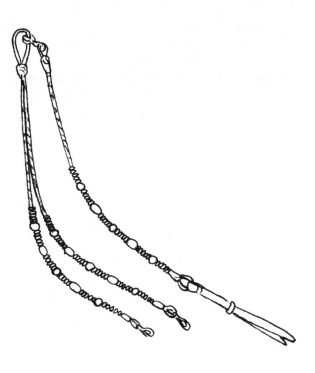

Seeing Strait

When amateur hunter rider Joan Ciampi had difficulty maintaining her horse's straightness and encouraging him to bend in his corners, she and her professional trainer, the well-known Jim Toon, came up with a solution. Their response was two lightweight tubes that fit over the reins and that rest along the animal's shoulders. Whenever the animal started to drift, the tubes prevented him from dropping his shoulder in or out. Ciampi and Toon named their invention "Strait Lines®."

Toon is quick to stress that the tubes are a training aid, not a cure-all. "But the nice thing about them is that unlike draw reins or side reins, they don't seem to be abusive," he points out. "Plus, rein stoppers near the bit keep the tubes from sliding up and hurting the horse's mouth."

Also, according to the trainer, the light weight of Strait Lines® means that a rider need not be an expert to use the device. "And many instructors have found that using the tubes helps students understand the concept of outside aids and bending."

Strait Lines® is available at many tack shops. For further information, contact Ciampi Ltd. at (918) 496-8696

vestigate the cause; more often than not the problem can be found in the bit already in use which is applying pressure the animal finds intolerable. A milder bit will often correct the problem. For those horses that go well in a particular bit most of the time but are also occasionally headstrong, something more may be necessary to maintain control consistently. Most such "extras" do not interfere with the horse when it performs well but will quickly and often forcibly come into play when the horse acts up. As with all tack, most of the adjuncts to the bit are designed for a particular purpose and must be used with understanding; an incorrectly adjusted standing martingale, for instance, can be fitted so tightly that it interferes with the horse's ability to balance itself, causing it to move improperly and even to endanger the rider.

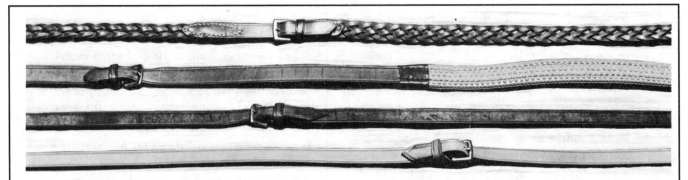

English-style reins. The reins pictured here are made in England of top-quality leather that has been hand stitched. They attach to the bit with hook studs. The plain leather reins come in width sizes $3/8$, $1/2$, $5/8$, $3/4$, and $7/8$ inch. The plaited reins (shown) and laced reins (not shown) come in widths from $5/8$ inch up to 1 inch. Rubber-covered leather reins, especially useful for hunting and jumping, are $5/8$ or $3/4$ inch wide.

Reins are normally sold with the bridle and they are a good deal less expensive if bought as part of the "package." The English imports lead the field as the most expensive all-leather item.

Western reins, when decorated with silver, will raise the price significantly, but a set of good quality utility roping reins are the most reasonable. Split reins will cost only slightly more. Four-plait hand-braided split reins with a 4-inch popper are in a pricier category.

Holding It All Together

Fastenings, the method by which the bit is attached to the bridle and to the reins, are available in a wide range of possibilities. Sewing is a traditional, neat, strong, and nonbulky means of attaching a bit to the bridle. However, opening the stitching and resewing the leather each time the bit needs changing is inconvenient, and it is also almost impossible to clean the bit thoroughly. The stud fastening is simply a small stud or hook that slips through a slit in the leather, with the downward pull of the bit holding it tightly in place.

The basic buckle, the first fastening that might come to mind, is, in fact, rarely used directly on the bit. Buckle tongues have a tendency to corrode, bend, and eventually break; a buckle can get caught up where it shouldn't, and it usually does. A rounded buckle known as a "fiddle buckle" is less likely than its square counterpart to catch in unwanted areas, but that too is seldom used at the bit. There is a "Conway" buckle which has become popular on Western-style bridles for many good reasons: it is strong, safe, and easy to open and clean. The Conway is a curved buckle with a stationary tongue that can protrude through the holes in a piece of leather that is folded back upon itself to form a loop. The Chicago screw, which was popular for a while and then unfashionable, has regained popularity in recent years. If tightened carefully with a screwdriver, the prethreaded screw will not loosen, and it is far less bulky than most of the previously discussed fastenings. Another common Western fastening for the bit or the tie-down is a self-locking swivel snap. Sometimes called a scissors snap (because of the action required to open it), it is strong, safe, and extremely easy to open in an emergency. Western catalogs also feature bridles with bit ends "to tie," which means that a piece of rawhide is pulled through punched holes and then tied on the outside. Although it may look authentic, and knowing how to make such a fastening in case of an emergency is useful, it has a tendency to work loose, and it is bulkier than many of the other fastenings.

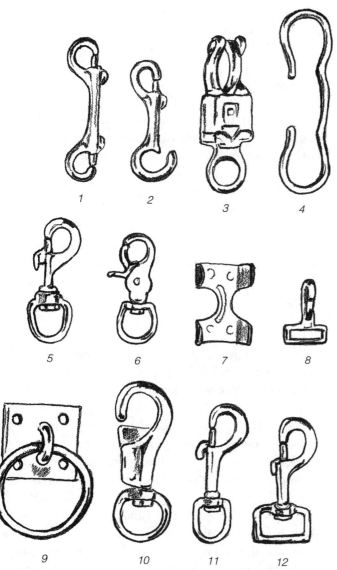

1. Double end snap 2. Clamp end trigger snap 3. Panic snap 4. Bucket hook 5. Swivel end snap 6. Swivel rein snap 7. Rope clamp 8. Rein snap 9. Tie ring plate 10. Bull snap 11. Brass swivel snap 12. Replacement lead snap

NOSEBANDS

One of the most commonly used adjuncts to the bit is the noseband. There are several styles including the dropped, flash, figure-8, kineton, and bosal, each having a slightly different emphasis in the way it functions. Dropped nosebands are designed to be worn $2\frac{1}{2}$ to 3 inches above the nostrils and when correctly fitted rest above the nostrils in the front and in the chin groove in back. When the noseband is adjusted tightly the horse can neither cross its jaw nor open its mouth wide in an attempt to evade the bit. However, care

should be taken to avoid pinching and preventing the horse from flexing its jaw. Western-style riders often use a bosal, a braided rawhide noseband, to achieve the same effect as the dropped noseband.

The flash noseband is composed of a cavesson to which diagonally crossed straps are attached to the top and fit in the chin groove in back. This is a useful noseband for riders who require a standing martingale in addition to a dropped noseband. Another option for riders who need both the dropped noseband and a standing martingale is the hinged dropped noseband. It can be bought separately and buckled onto an existing cavesson.

The figure-8 noseband resembles the number used to describe it, crossing on the front of the horse's face. The top part of the figure-8 buckles in the rear, halfway between the cheekbone and the corners of the mouth, while the bottom section fits in the chin groove. The effect of this noseband can be increased by raising the nosepiece.

The kineton is also known as an "antipulling" noseband, and its action is fairly strong since it puts pressure on the nose via the bit. A piece of leather-covered reinforced metal fits into the center of the nosepiece which is attached to two slanting U-shaped loops. The U sidepiece fits inside the rings of the bit and around the mouthpiece. The consequence of pressure on the bit forces the noseband down, occasioning the horse to lower its head in reaction. Like most tack, the kineton is useful in the right hands, painful to the horse otherwise.

MARTINGALES AND TIE-DOWNS

Fixing a horse's head at a particular height prevents the animal from throwing its head in an attempt to

Hinged Dropped Noseband. Buckles to regular cavesson but does not eliminate use of standing martingale.

evade the bit. Such restraint is also important for the rider who does not welcome the possibility of a broken nose as the horse suddenly tosses its head. For these reasons, a martingale or tie-down is a frequently necessary auxiliary to the bit. Several kinds are available, each having a slightly different emphasis.

English riders may use a standing martingale, basically a strap that fits around the horse's neck with a second strap crossing the first at chest center. This chest strap loops around the girth strap under the belly and attaches to the back of the cavesson at the other end. Buckles permit proper adjustment. The Western-style tie-down is a strap that hooks onto the rear of a thin rawhide or cable bosal at one end and whose other end snaps or hooks either onto the center ring on a breastplate or directly onto the cinch. When properly fitted, both the martingale and the tie-down restrain the horse from tossing its head or "stargazing."

Many Western as well as English horsemen prefer the running martingale for its greater versatility. It is similar to the standing type except that the upper chest strap forks for approximately 12 inches, ending in rings that slip onto each rein. These rings are held from slipping forward and into the horse's mouth by "rein stops"—pieces of leather or rubber which fit onto the reins about 10 inches above the bit. If set tightly, this martingale will also increase the leverage of the bit's action on the bars of the horse's mouth. The difference between the standing and running martingales is that as the animal attempts to raise its head, the standing martingale applies pressure to the horse's nose, while the running martingale applies a restraining pressure to the horse's mouth.

A bib martingale, as its name applies, is made from a triangular piece of leather sewn between the two forked chest straps and is occasionally needed to prevent high-strung horses from getting their feet caught in the tack; bibs are frequently worn by Thoroughbred racehorses during their morning workouts.

A Market Harborough, also known as an Olympic Martingale Rein Set, works on a principle similar to that of draw reins (reins attached to the girth which pass up and through the bit rings and into the rider's hands) but has replaced draw reins in popularity. A strip of rounded leather snaps onto each running-martingale ring, passes through the bit rings, and attaches to the rein about 10 inches beyond the bit. Its action is simple. If the horse carries its head properly, then the round straps are slack and inactive. When the horse throws its head, then the straps become taut, exerting a downward pull on the bit rings and producing pressure on the horse's lips, bars, tongue, and even poll.

Several types of martingales designed to teach the horse to lower its head carriage work their influence on the top of the horse's head or even combine poll pressure with nose pressure for added emphasis. Western catalogs offer a "training headstall" used primarily on cutting horses, who must carry their heads low. The headstall presses against the sensitive nerve endings around the ears, encouraging the horse to put its head down. To produce the same reaction, English-style trainers use Continental or Chambon martingales. In the Continental, one end of a strap attaches to the noseband in the normal way; the other end passes down through a single ring at the center of the breastplate and then up to another strap that crosses the poll to buckle firmly at the throatlatch. Simultaneous pres-

MARTINGALES

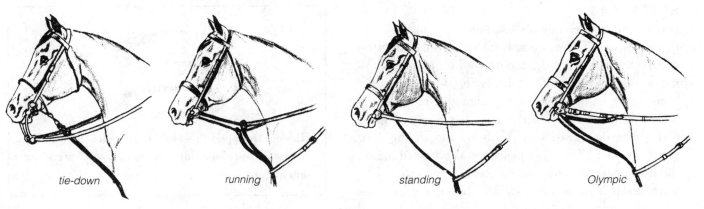

tie-down   running   standing   Olympic

sure on the nose and poll will provide a strong inducement to quickly lower the head. The Chambon martingale, on the other hand, applies concurrent pressure to the poll and to the lips. The ends of a strap attached at its center to a breastplate run up along both sides of the head to the poll, through the rings on either end of the pollpiece (a small strap which sits directly behind the ears), and then down to hook onto the bit rings. Therefore, a pulley effect is created; when the horse raises its head, the breastplate pulls the Chambon strap, which then pulls down on the headpiece and up on the bit rings. To escape this martingale's influence, the horse usually learns to hold its head at the correct level.

We should mention a sidecheck here, although it is not actually an auxiliary to the bit. Rather, it is a support for weak hands, most often found attached to the bridles of ponies. The singular purpose of the sidecheck is to prevent the horse from lowering its head to chomp grass. Called an "Antigrazing Sidecheck," it is simply a strap that attaches to the pommel and to the top of the cheekpiece on the bridle.

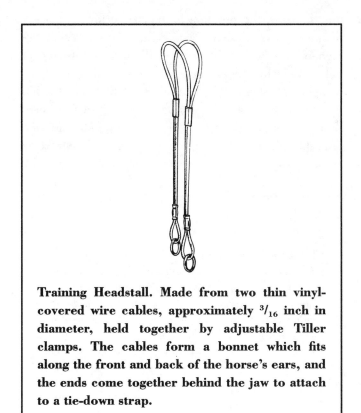

Training Headstall. Made from two thin vinyl-covered wire cables, approximately ³/₁₆ inch in diameter, held together by adjustable Tiller clamps. The cables form a bonnet which fits along the front and back of the horse's ears, and the ends come together behind the jaw to attach to a tie-down strap.

> *"As soon as the little fellow can be handled calmly, a light halter can be slipped on. Most colts are so constructed that when their heads are raised, the crownpiece of the halter slips back on the neck so far that when the head is put down to the ground the nosepiece and the crownpiece pull uncomfortably. To avoid this, a brow band must be added to the halter. I usually use a double strip of muslin."*
>
> LOUIS TAYLOR
> Ride Western
> *Wilshire Book Co., 1968, 1973 ed.*

We did not list the Irish martingale directly under the other martingales because it does not affect the horse's head carriage, as the others do. Basically, it is a short strap with loops at either end that slip onto the reins to keep them from flopping apart and may add enough weight to keep the bit properly balanced in the mouth.

MISCELLANEOUS SUPPLEMENTS

Fortunately, horses are animals with some minor degree of intelligence. But they do have a major capacity for asserting themselves (which leaves one wondering whether the first horse wrote it all down in what can only be the greatest horse-training manual of all time, even now being surreptitiously passed along from one stall to another).

Probably the single most common evasion occurs when the horse gets its tongue over the bit. By so doing, the animal disengages the contact points of the bit, essentially nullifying its action and any control the bit may have given the rider. As soon as a horse begins to evade the bit in this way, the trainer must first determine the cause. There are three reasons: the bit is too large and hangs too low in the horse's mouth; the bit pinches or is in some way uncomfortable to the tongue; and the horse is experiencing discomfort because of sores or tooth problems. Once you discover the cause of the problem, the cure may be easy. But there are horses for which this evasion has become a routine part of their repertoire. There may be no easy solution for these chronic evaders, and perhaps the trainer must use an alternative such as a bitless bridle. For other than the confirmed offender, there are several devices that have been found to work more often than not.

If the problem stems from a bit too large and too low-hanging, then replacement of this bit is required. The trainer may also want to add a rubber tongue port to his existing bit or turn to a "Nagbut" snaffle. The rubber tongue port is designed to slip over the mouthpiece of any bit and lie flat on the horse's tongue, facing toward the rear; the arms of the "Nagbut" snaffle are jointed onto a center tongue port which acts the same as the rubber tongue port. Both effectively present the horse with too large an object to lift its tongue over.

Racehorses that habitually get their tongue over the bit are often put into an "Australian checker," or as one catalog calls it, a "Sure-Win" bit holder worn by Seattle Slew when he won the Triple Crown. It is basically a flat leather or rubber strap that comes down from the crown of the bridle between the horse's eyes to fork above the nose into two doughnut-shaped pieces that attach to the mouth of the bit. Some racing trainers also make use of a device known as a tongue tie. A seemingly barbaric implement, it serves the double function of keeping the horse from getting its tongue over the bit and from swallowing its tongue, a not uncommon occurrence during a race. Although a tongue tie is certainly effective, it was designed for usage over short periods of time (such as during a race) and is not recommended for other types of riding.

For horses that evade the bit because it pinches the lips, there is a rubber bit guard—simply a doughnut-shaped piece of rubber or soft leather that fits around the mouthpiece.

Another problem not uncommon to racehorses and occasionally to jumpers is a tendency to pull to one side. The problem does not normally stem from the bit, but several bitting aids are available to help deal with this fault. There is a "brush picker" or "bit burr," a bristled piece of leather or rubber which attaches to the mouthpiece on the side to which the horse swings out. Because the problem is expensive for racehorses to have, there is also a whole line of racing bits designed to cope with it. Few of them are, however, of value to other than racehorse trainers. Sometimes something as simple as blinders—half-moon-shaped covers for horses' eyes—effectively correct the horse that lugs in or bears out by directing its attention straight ahead and eliminating many distracting sights.

The Collector was designed by a Pennsylvania horsewoman and it is an effective training device to reschool horses that try to evade the pressure of the bit. It attaches to the bit rings, crosses over the nose just under the cavesson, and works by raising the bit off the bars of the lower jaw, partially distributing the pressure across the nose. The Collector is effective with snaffle and Pelham bits or used in combination with a curb strap.

Bit Converters are useful for converting the Pelham from two sets of reins to only one set. Particularly good for people who have difficulty handling four reins but need more than a snaffle bit alone.

About Bits
direct from the horse's mouth

"Those who have never had a bit in their mouths cannot think how bad it feels; a great piece of cold hard steel as thick as a man's finger to be pushed into one's mouth, between one's teeth, and over one's tongue, with the ends coming out at the corner of your mouth, and held fast there by straps over your head, under your throat, round your nose, and under your chin; so that in no way in the world can you get rid of the nasty hard thing; it is very bad!"

ANNA SEWELL
Black Beauty

Saddles

The purpose of a saddle is to protect the horse's back and to aid the rider in maintaining a balanced seat, permitting him to shift his weight as needed. Most saddles allow the rider to remain in balance over the horse's center of gravity. Since the center of gravity varies according to the type of horse, the work it does, its gait, and its way of going, a large variety of saddles have been developed over the centuries.

The foundation of every saddle is the tree, usually made of beechwood for lightness, with metal (often steel) for reinforcement. Many trees today are made entirely of fiberglass or laminated Ply-Bond. The tree must be strong enough to withstand pressure, high enough to clear the horse's withers and backbone, and wide enough to rest on the muscle pads on either side of the backbone. The tree is often padded, usually with foam rubber, and then covered with leather. The kinds and quality of leather vary according to the type of saddle and the parts of which it is constructed. (For example, a soft, stretchable leather would be useless for billet or stirrup straps.) The quality of the leather is one of the major factors affecting the price of a saddle; other factors are the quality of materials used in making the tree and the overall workmanship in putting it all together. After that, the price varies with brand names and extra details.

SADDLE LEATHER

Most saddles produced in England and in most parts of Europe are made from top-quality cowhide, with pigskin often used for saddle seats and occasionally for flaps as well. Western saddles are normally made of bullhide- or rawhide-covered trees which are then covered with cowhide, either smooth-finished (later stamped or hand-tooled) or rough-out, with suede commonly used on the seat.

The leather in English- and European-made saddles (and many of the English-style saddles sold in the United States are either imported from those areas or made there for American companies) is normally tanned by one of two methods: bark tanning, which is preferable because it takes oiling and absorbs grease easily, and chrome tanning, a fairly recent process using chemicals, which does not have quite the grease-

absorbing capability of the bark-tanning process. Chrome tanning is recognizable by a gray-cream or greenish color, and sometimes a light tan to brown dye is applied to make it appear bark-tanned. Rawhide is nothing more than cowhide that has been tanned by a vegetable process. It is recognizable along the edge by a light-colored untanned center layer.

In piecing a saddle together, leather is culled from different parts of the animal hide; for instance, the butt (the section from the shoulder to the tail) is the most durable and least stretchable section and therefore preferred by saddlemakers. Stirrup leather especially should come from this section of the hide and not from more stretchable areas such as the belly. Before buying a stirrup leather, test the stretch by pulling it as hard as possible. If it gives more than a quarter of an inch, shop further. The shoulder section of the hide, while strong, tends to also be wrinkled and therefore visually less appealing. Shank or leg leather should be avoided, since it is hard and will crack easily.

Leather, like the meat we eat, is graded. And as you would prefer prime-cut steaks on the table, grade A leather is most desirable in your saddle. Obviously, though, such steak and leather are available only at a price. Grade A and B leathers most often come from the United States, England, and Germany, and saddles manufactured in those countries are normally made from these quality leathers, but not necessarily. And since there are no regulations requiring the leather be graded for the consumer, no guarantees are available. Most leather that comes from South America would be graded C. It is usually a harder leather than German leather, for example, and is susceptible to grub holes, but it is a tough, long-wearing leather and perfectly fine for most weekend riders. Moving east and down on the grading scale, leather from Japan is less satisfactory, because it has a poor tensile strength, meaning it rips and stretches easily. Not many saddles from Japan are sold in this country yet. However, you will find saddles from India on sale here, and few experts give them a passing grade. The weakness is not necessarily inherent in the leather as such but in the tanning process used; Indian saddle leather is tanned in clay vats, and as anyone who has worked with clay knows, the substance has a severe drying effect. Leather tanned this way will not absorb grease even when it is heavily applied, so that besides failing to "wear-in" and become

PARTS OF THE ENGLISH SADDLE

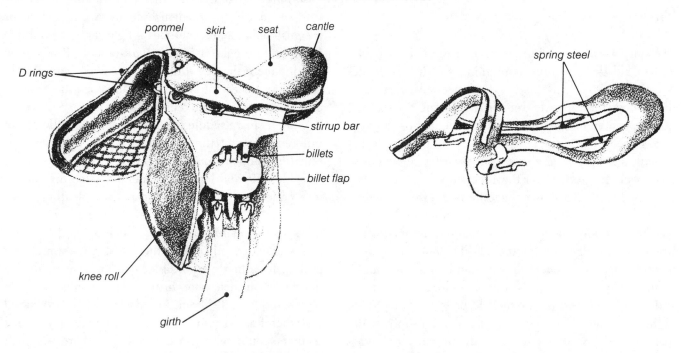

soft and supple, such saddles will begin to crack and break within a short time.

ENGLISH SADDLES

"English saddle" has become a broad term of reference for a number of highly specialized saddles, each of which is as distinctive as the style it is meant to complement: jumping, show ring, racing, dressage, polo, or hacking. Despite its name, the "English saddle" has been used by the Italians, the Germans, the French, the Poles, and the Russians for over a century. The forward-seat saddle, the most popular type in use today, was developed in the late 1800's by Captain Federico Caprilli, an Italian born in 1868 who, to much ridicule and controversy, abolished the classical seat then in fashion. After continued success with his new technique, the "Caprilli system" was adopted by the Italian cavalry in the early 1900's. Soon afterward, English saddlemakers were making forward-seat saddles for home use and export, followed only slightly later by the Germans, who began making a heavier, more stoutly padded version. The forward-seat saddle was such a remarkable success that it is now what most horsemen think of as the standard "English" saddle. Our contemporary "all-purpose" saddle is based on the forward-seat design and should not be confused with older, straight-flapped "general-purpose" saddles.

Parts of the English Saddle

If the tree is of poor construction, then the saddle is worthless, no matter how rich the leather or how fine the fittings. At one time all English-saddle trees were made of solid wood, but now laminated plywood and fiberglass seem to have become equally popular. What these materials have to offer makes infinite good sense—they are lightweight and they will not warp.

There are two basic types of tree construction: the rigid tree and the spring tree. Both are usually reinforced with steel arches over the head and around the cantle. In the spring tree, two strips of steel extend from the head to the rear of the tree directly under the seat where they function as springs (hence the name), and the stirrup bars are inset into the tree just below the head. Since the head of the forward-seat tree is set at a 45-degree angle to the horse's back, the stirrup bars are farther forward than those on the straighter tree. The rigid tree is normally constructed either with a straight head for normal use or with a cut-back head for use in saddle-seat saddles and for wide-back mounts such as Arabians and Morgans.

Whether spring or rigid type, the tree is next fitted

with webbing and padded with such materials as felt, foam rubber, wool, or leather, and that padding is then covered with a saddle leather. (Pigskin, a soft, beautiful, but not particularly strong leather, is often used to cover seats. However, it should not be used on other parts of the saddle if it is expected to be long-wearing.)

All saddles of any value will have well-padded panels under the tree. These panels act as cushions for the horse's back and are divided by a channel above the backbone, ensuring that the weight of the saddle will rest on the muscle pads on either side of the spine. Usually covered in leather, either plain or quilted, the panels are padded with felt, foam rubber, hair, or wool, and if they are well constructed a saddle pad is often unnecessary. Panels can be found in different styles, from a full one which provides padding under the seat and the flaps of the saddle to a short one which pads only the seat. Most forward-seat and all-purpose saddles feature narrow-waisted panels that extend forward to support the knee and include padding in the rear to hold the girth securely.

Forward-Seat Saddle

This was designed to eliminate interference with the horse and give the rider added security in jumping. Adaptable for both the two-point seat (rider's weight on legs and heels) and the three-point seat (rider's weight on legs, heels, and seat), it allows the horseman to lean forward in relation to the horse's speed and gait. The spring tree contributes to the rider's driving seat, and because of the 45-degree angle of the head, the stirrup bars are automatically farther forward. The panel or flap has a padded knee roll to support the thigh and brace the rider as he comes off a jump. The seat dips, supporting the rider in a centered position, and the narrow waist allows the rider a closer grip without stretching his thighs uncomfortably wide. Ideal for jumping, this saddle may be less comfortable on long trail rides.

Jockey Saddle, or Racing Saddle

This is a radical extension of the Forward Seat saddle. It was first developed in America for racing and then adopted in England during the late nineteenth century. British riders traditionally sat way back on the horse's loins, as one can see in old English racing prints. The "new" American style was picked up by the conservative English only after American jockeys,

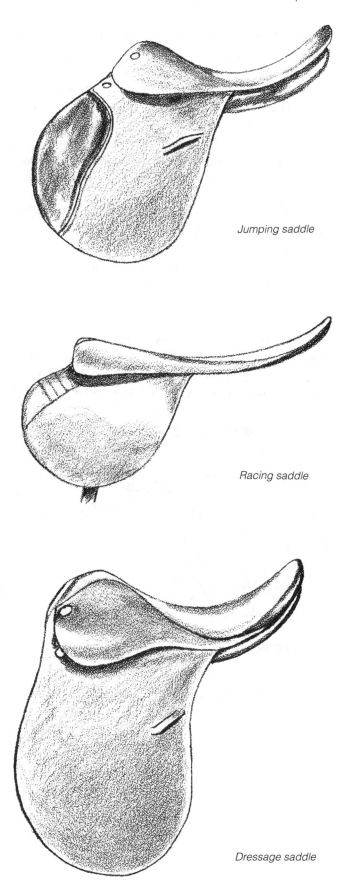

Jumping saddle

Racing saddle

Dressage saddle

riding far forward with shortened stirrups and hands only inches from the horse's mouth, won so consistently that their innovative technique could no longer be ignored. Racing saddles are light in weight, averaging $1^1/_2$ pounds without stirrups. Their seat is relatively unimportant in racing, since the jockey makes almost no use of it, and the stirrups hang far forward so that the jockey is actually doubled over onto his calves when the horse is walking, balancing atop the animal's neck when galloping, and standing up in the stirrups during a canter or trot. American jockeys traditionally ride "acey-deucy" with the left stirrup slightly longer than the right; this allows the jockey to consistently throw his weight into the turn—an advantage since all American racetracks turn to the left only.

Exercise Saddle

For training young horses for racing, it is used in place of the racing saddle, which can, because of minimal padding, hurt the animal's back when used daily. The exercise saddle is a slightly larger and somewhat

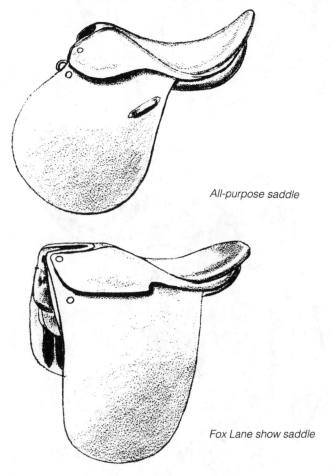

All-purpose saddle

Fox Lane show saddle

heavier version of the racing saddle and includes stuffed panels for better cushioning. Usually this saddle weighs upward of 5 pounds.

Saddle-Seat Saddle

This is designed to show off the animated action and highly arched head carriage of the Three- or Five-Gaited Saddle Horse and the Tennessee Walker. Because of the way in which the head and neck are carried, the center of gravity of a gaited horse is farther back than in either the English or the Western way of going. Therefore, the rider uses a flat seat that will allow his weight to shift back toward the cantle. This saddle features a cutback pommel and straight flaps. Long stirrups permit the rider's heels to drop almost directly below his center of gravity. This saddle is placed 2 or 3 inches to the rear of the all-purpose saddle, and it is normally designed with a short, lightly padded panel.

Dressage Saddle

This could be described as a felicitous cross between the jumping saddle and the saddle-seat saddle. Surprisingly, the dressage saddle as we know it today is a relatively new discovery. Before World War Two, all dressage riders used a straight seat show saddle; after the war a new saddle came into use that was better adapted to this specialized type of riding. Since the dressage horse is trained to collect and move effortlessly off its haunches with its center of balance more to the rear than that of, say, the jumper, the modern dressage saddle needed to have a deeper, shorter seat than the show saddle which would allow the rider to sit with his seat bones well under him. While it has straighter flaps than the jumping saddle it does include the useful knee roll commonly associated with that saddle. The stirrup bars are centered directly under the rider's thighs to help him maintain a straight leg and longer stirrups. All these features enable the rider to keep his weight to the rear, brace his back, and use leg pressure either ahead of or behind the girth to activate the horse's hindquarters.

ALL-PURPOSE AND POLO SADDLE

This is designed to encourage a modified forward seat and allow the rider to rest in the middle of the saddle, supported chiefly by the seat bones. It features a deeper seat and straighter flaps than the forward-seat

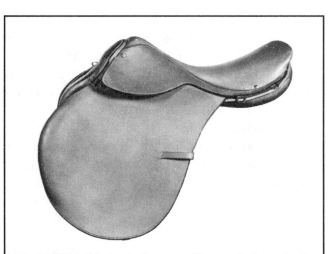

Smith-Worthington Custom Forward Seat Saddle. This is one of the very few English saddles made here. The tree, of hand-forged steel and birch, is guaranteed for the life of the original owner. The seat is pigskin (imported from England), and the panel leather is first chrome-tanned and then glove-tanned, a combination that makes the panels sweat-resistant, strong, soft, and less prone to drying. The all-wool stuffed panels have a high tallow content that wards off moisture. Smith-Worthington will make the saddle in either a forward-seat or hunt-seat style with adjustable length of center. It can be ordered through local tack shops.

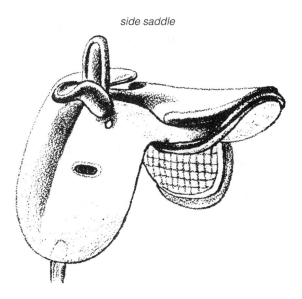

side saddle

Sidesaddles evolved through the centuries from a pad that included a platform on which to rest the left foot to a two- and later three-horned saddle with a single stirrup. (The third horn is also called a "knee rest," depending upon its height.) Most of the sidesaddles available today are antiques, many of them imported from England. The English sidesaddle has three girths: a regulation wide web girth, a thin leather girth which

saddle, and it may have padded knee rolls for additional support. While the forward-seat saddle is intended primarily for jumping, this saddle is more versatile—ideal for trail riding, excellent for use in elementary jumping and dressage work, and especially adaptable to the rigorous demands of polo.

SIDESADDLE

The sidesaddle, although it seems an oddity today, was popular in the East and later in the West for a longer period than is generally recognized. Brought to our country from England, it was still being used as late as the 1920's, when proper women did not fork a horse. Reported to have been made popular by Queen Elizabeth I, who, it was said, wanted to hide her deformed legs, the sidesaddle is still most useful for physically handicapped people who cannot sit astride.

How to Measure a Horse's Back for Proper Saddle Fit

To measure a horse for a saddle, take a soft piece of lead or electrical wire about 18 inches long and heavy enough to hold its shape. Mold the wire over the horse's back just behind the withers where the saddle would sit. Trace the resultant shape onto paper and mark the corresponding sides NEAR and OFF. Take two more "shape" measurements with the same wire—one about 9 inches behind the first; the other to discover the silhouette of the back from the beginning of the withers to the beginning of the croup. This picture will provide the saddler with enough information to determine the proper fit on the horse. It is also useful to let the saddler know such details as your height, weight, and inseam measurements to ensure that the saddle will fit you as well.

goes over the first one, and a balance strap that runs around the girth and attaches to the rear off side of the seat. It is a small, dainty saddle, and the seat of those made before the 1800's is frequently covered in velvet or fabric.

In the 1890's, Colonel Charles Goodnight of Texas designed a sidesaddle for his wife which became the standard for the Western sidesaddle. It was longer, wider, and heavier than its English counterpart, and the balance strap was replaced with a rear cinch. The Goodnight saddle had two leg horns (one a knee rest) and a padded leaping horn. The Goodnight design also included a carpetbag strap and heavily tooled leather skirts.

The proper way to sit a sidesaddle is facing straight forward, so balanced that the impression is given that the rider has only one leg. A whip carried on the right side is necessary to replace the cueing function of the leg.

Military Saddle

The American military saddle, or McClellan saddle, that we know today, the two long bars joined by a high wishbone pommel and rounded cantle tree, was actually influenced by the Hungarian cavalry. Back in

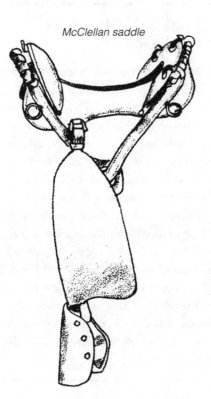

McClellan saddle

the 1850's Captain (later a commanding general of the Union Army) George B. McClellan was serving a tour of duty in Europe as a military attaché. There he observed the Hungarians' distinctive saddle, a hammock-like affair with a heavy leather stretched between the pommel and the cantle to form a seat above an open slit over the horse's spine. McClellan, a horseman of an inquisitive nature, studied the Hungarian design and brought it back to the States, where he married it to the existing Army Ringgold tree. The saddle that resulted from this union retained the opening between the bars but added a high pommel, a deep seat, and squared skirts fastened by brass screws. Heavy girth straps (surcingles) passed over the pommel and cantle and joined on each side in a ring much like our present-day stock saddle's "on-the-tree rigging." However, unlike our stock saddle, the McClellan was a single-cinch, center-fire-rigged saddle.

By today's standards, the McClellan was anything but comfortable; the hard wood tree was simply covered with wet rawhide, which shrank to an iron-hard finish. The rawhide, a seemingly indestructible substance, eventually would crack and erupt into hard, knifelike edges, making the long hours in the saddle often more intolerable than the battles into which it was ridden. After the Civil War, a smooth black leather enveloped the rawhide-girdled tree.

The McClellan stirrup leathers included a separate sweat leather, or fender, whose wide triangular shape helped to protect the rider's legs. The stirrups were heavy, usually made of oak or hickory, and were covered in front by leather hoods which a cowboy would call tapaderos but the Army called leather hoods and stamped U.S. Regulation McClellans always had four brass rings—two affixed to the pommel, two to the cantle—to which had to be attached such necessities as the saber, the canteen, the crupper, the breastplate, and the martingale. The breastplate, used primarily by officers in full-dress outfit, usually carried a brass tack which displayed a picture of the American bald eagle.

Compulsory equipment with the McClellan was a blue wool blanket, 67 × 75 inches, that was normally folded into six thicknesses. The blanket was finished in an orange border and carried an orange U.S. in the center. Officers might have a saddle cloth that either went over the blanket or could cover the entire saddle to shield the rider from leather stains.

The McClellan, used by the Remount Division of the U.S. Army until the beginnings of World War Two, when tanks replaced the horse in warfare, is still used for ceremonial purposes and by mounted police today. The Australian, or Stockman, saddle, is a direct descendant of the McClellan.

Fabric Saddles

Saddles made of synthetic fabrics are a popular innovation. The best-known are manufactured by Wintec and are made of nylon in a variety of styles. The advantage is that they are lightweight, easy to clean (wiping with a damp cloth will do the job), and reasonably inexpensive. On the other hand, nylon has nowhere near the durability of leather; occasional riders have fewer complaints about fabric saddles than people who use them on a daily basis. Moreover, you must use Wintec's own girth and stirrup leathers, since the natural oils found in real leather break down the nylon fabric.

WESTERN SADDLES

These came from Spain via Mexico and entered this country probably by way of Texas. At least one source tells of Juan de Oñate, who, in 1598, crossed the Rio Grande with eighty wagons and thousands of head of livestock including about one hundred head of breeding horses. This early rancher also brought new techniques of herding along with him. The Mexican style of the *vaquero* (cowboy) had taken much from Spanish ancestors, but the open country of Mexico demanded something more than the Spaniard's long prod poles then used to move cattle, and the long *reata* (lariat) was devised for roping. One end of the rope was attached at first to the horse's tail, later to the rear of the saddle; after much trial and error, it ended up on the horn, a squat rounded shape on the top of the fork. From these beginnings the modern horn evolved into a higher, stronger, and essential part of the saddle. The Californians quickly adopted the lariat for their ranches, while the Texans turned to a shorter rope which performed better in the heavy brush country where a quick, accurate throw was essential.

"Western" is, in fact, a broad term for several styles of riding. The type of country where cattle ranged determined the kind of work the horse had to do and, therefore, the kind of tack the wrangler needed.

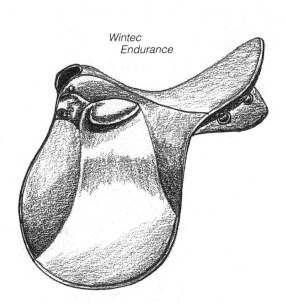

*Wintec
Endurance*

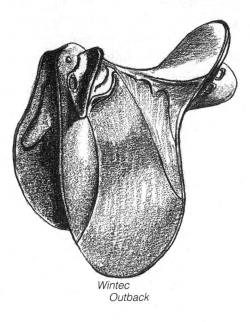

*Wintec
Outback*

1892

Double Seat Chair Saddle.

Styles in each region and even in each town varied greatly, and the smallest detail could pinpoint a cowboy's origins and his skills. In California where the country was open, the cowhorse was trained to line the rider up for a clean throw of the long lariat. Californians were dally men (from the Spanish *dar la vuelta*, "to give a turn"), which meant that they wrapped the end of the rope around the saddle horn, allowing it play instead of tying it fast. This style spared the horse the sudden jolt as the calf's weight reached the end of a slack rope. The heavy brush country of Texas, however, called for a horse with quick responses as it routed out the cattle. This was the country where the cutting horse developed, and a good one was a much-appreciated treasure. Bred to anticipate its quarry's every move, the cutting horse could maneuver the calf, thereby giving its rider a clean throw of the rope. Here the tie-fast horseman reigned, tying his rope firmly to the saddle horn and letting it rip.

Working the Texas range also required that the horse be able to perform sliding stops, quick turns, and rollbacks (because reining was generally rough, the curb was preferred over the spade bit). And because Texas ropers trained a horse to keep up the slack between itself and the calf, the impact of several hundred pounds on the front of the saddle was too great for the

Mexican's single-cinch saddle. Therefore, Texans developed a rear cinch that was worn loose but would keep the saddle from slipping over when they dismounted to approach a calf.

The Western saddle is continuing to evolve today as horsemen are participating in ever-wider varieties of riding events. Western saddles, if you don't count such specialty saddles as the bronc-riding or trick-riding types, may be categorized into three basic styles.

General-Purpose Saddle

This is the most common one, ideal for pleasure and trail riding. It weighs approximately 30 to 35 pounds and features a deep seat with high swells and cantle. The padded seat is built up in front for extra comfort. Since the horn is not needed for roping, it is smaller than the one found on a Roping Saddle—usually 2 inches high with a $2\frac{1}{2}$- to 3-inch cap.

Roping Saddle

The heavy-duty stock saddle is made from stout leather, and everything about this saddle is intended to hold up to stress and hard work. The roping saddle weighs anywhere from 38 to 55 pounds; the horn is large, rarely less than 3 inches high or 3 inches in diameter. Some ropers prefer rawhide-covered horns or will themselves wrap cotton rope or strips of rubber around the horn to prevent the rope from slipping and to ease the friction as it is dallied. The swells and cantle of the roping saddle are usually low and will not interfere with the rider as he speedily dismounts.

Equitation Saddle

This is designed for show, either in the ring or in parades, and is usually elaborately decorated with intricate embossed or hand-tooled designs on the panels and fenders. These, in turn, may be finished with contrasting buck stitching. Nickel plate or silver wire often laces the perimeter of the cantle and Cheyenne roll. Other potential areas for heavy ornamentation include the conches, horn cap, skirt corners, cantle plate, stirrups, and breastplate. The horn is small and low and sometimes inlaid with silver. The padded seat, almost always covered in suede, is built up in front toward swells that are of medium height. The cantle is usually high and the dish of the seat deep. The basic measurement to consider when buying a show saddle is

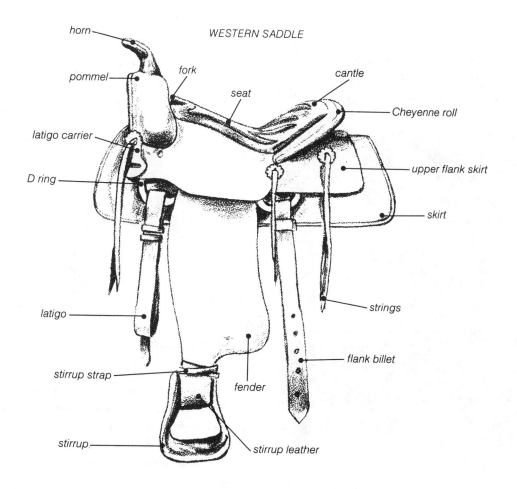

WESTERN SADDLE

horn
pommel
fork
seat
cantle
Cheyenne roll
latigo carrier
D ring
upper flank skirt
skirt
latigo
strings
stirrup strap
flank billet
fender
stirrup
stirrup leather

the dollar measurement. And, needless to say, it can go very high.

Bronc Saddle

Totally Western in origin, this specialty saddle was designed to give the rider the best ride on a bucking horse. In rodeo competition, points are given not only for lasting the full time but for skill and control as well. Judges look to see if the cowboy's spurs are hitting the points of the shoulders when the horse's front feet hit the ground and that the rider's feet are dragged back ready to swing forward when the horse kicks. It is essential, therefore, that the bars of the bronc saddle allow the rider such freedom. The size of the undercut of the swells determines the rider's leg action, and the Rodeo Cowboy Association specifies that the swells may not be undercut more than 1 inch on each side. Most bronc riders prefer a saddle with a low cantle and stirrup leathers that will not accordion. The bronc saddle is always three-quarters double-rigged, with the front rigging ring directly below the center of the swells.

Some bronc-riding contests require a bareback rig instead of a saddle. It is always made of heavy saddle leather and features a "handhold"—a sturdy piece of leather, often three-ply, which loops back to lace in either a center, right, or left position. Some of these rigs also add a soft padding to the area directly under the handhold to protect both the hand and the horse. The "skirt" of the rig is extremely short and ends in heavy rings to which 2-inch latigo straps and a contest-type cinch are attached. The bronc rider sits directly behind the rig with his legs forward over the skirt and the handhold between his legs.

Parts of a Western Saddle

The tree of the basic Western saddle was commonly made from beechwood covered with bullhide or rawhide. Now, with modern materials available, the tree is usually made from laminated wood, often white ponderosa pine fitted together with the grain pointing in different directions and then glued under high pressure. This technique, which is also used by most of the European saddlers, is warp-resistant and less likely to

Artist Gordon Snidow's personal saddle made by master saddlemaker Eddie Bohlin.

Photo by Herb Brunell

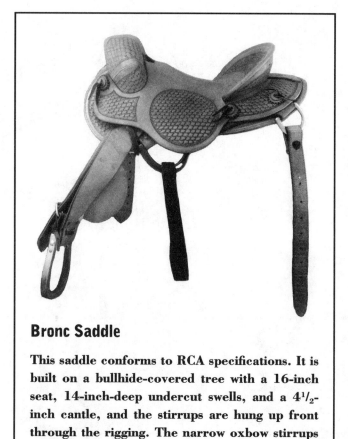

Bronc Saddle

This saddle conforms to RCA specifications. It is built on a bullhide-covered tree with a 16-inch seat, 14-inch-deep undercut swells, and a 4½-inch cantle, and the stirrups are hung up front through the rigging. The narrow oxbow stirrups are uncovered, and the rigging is three-quarters double.

break through stress to certain joints. Trees are also available in aluminum and in fiberglass. Both of these materials are lightweight and strong, and the fiberglass tree is quickly becoming popular for children's saddles. However, horsemen often have a "prove it" attitude about most new materials, and until all the results are in, wood will remain the most called-for material. Certainly this is not true of plied wood, which has replaced solid wood (in repute.)

The tree of the Western saddle is made up of a fork, horn, bars, and cantle. The fork includes the gullet (that space formed by the shaping of the fork) and the swells (the area on either side of the horn mount). The height and width of the gullet may vary, depending on the use for which the saddle is designed, from an average of $5^3/_4$ inches wide, $6^3/_4$ inches high to an average of $6^1/_4$ inches wide, 8 inches high. Measured from swell to swell, the width of the fork averages $10^1/_2$ to 14 inches. A saddle horn can be made of wood, brass, steel, or iron covered in either bullhide, saddle leather,

or rawhide and is either laminated onto the fork or mounted on with bolts and screws. Horns are usually available in a range of shapes, cap widths, and heights (from a low of $2^1/_2$ inches to a high of 4 inches), with these measurements depending on whether it is intended for actual roping, for either tie-fast or dally men, or for grabbing onto for balance during barrel-racing or pleasure events.

The bars are a particularly important part of the tree, and skilled craftsmanship is necessary to angle them for good fit on a horse's back and proper balance for the rider. Bars are categorized as follows: regular (about $5^1/_2$ inches), semi-Quarter Horse (about 6 inches), Quarter Horse (about $6^1/_2$ inches), and Arabian or Morgan (about $6^3/_4$ inches). If wider-spaced bars are desired they must be specially ordered. Many saddletrees come with steel-reinforced bars, and a number of models feature bar slots for stirrup leathers. For those styles with built-up seats, a riser is often added on the bars directly behind the fork.

RCA Contest Saddle Specifications

Rigging: $^3/_4$ double—front edge of D ring must pull not farther back than directly below center of point of swell. Standard E-Z or ring type saddle D must be used and may not exceed $5^3/_4$-inch outside-width measurement.

Swell Undercut: not more than 2 inches—1 inch on each side.

Gullet: not less than 4 inches wide at center of fork of covered saddle.

Tree: Saddles must be built on standard tree.

Specifications:

Fork—14 inches wide

Height—9 inches maximum

Gullet—$5^3/_4$ inches wide

Cantle—5 inches maximum height, 14 inches maximum width

Stirrup leathers must be hung over bars.

Saddle should conform to the above measurements with a reasonable added thickness for leather covering.

No freaks allowed.

Front cinch on bronc saddles shall be Mohair, and shall be at least 5 inches wide.

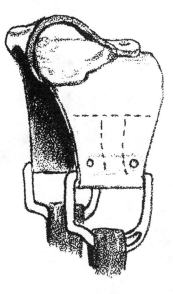

The cantle, basic to any Western saddletree, helps the rider maintain a deep seat. Western cantles are often between $2^3/_4$ and $4^1/_2$ inches high, average $12^1/_2$ to 14 inches wide, and dish approximately $^7/_8$ inch to over $1^1/_4$ inches deep.

Within this century the seat of the Western saddle has been padded with foam rubber and covered with suede, quilted or plain, and has included such extras as the "Cheyenne roll," that extra padding directly behind the cantle that is most welcome if you ever get caught behind the horse and come down hard on the cantle. Many horsemen are finding that this kind of seat is more comfortable and gives them greater grip and security.

The best type of seat for the Western saddle is a subject of raging controversy that this book will attempt simply to describe but not enter. Early Western saddles—those brought here from Mexico, for instance—put nothing between the tree and the rider's seat bones. Shortly thereafter, the tree was covered first with bullhide, then with a layer of saddle leather, and

that was the standard method for a long, long time. Today, the majority of Western saddles have a quilted and foam-rubber-padded built-up seat which slopes downward toward the rear, forcing the rider to sit deep into the cantle. Monte Foreman, a man who is gradually influencing many a Western horseman's way of riding, designed a "Balanced Ride" seat that eliminates the built-up front. Instead, the flatter seat allows the rider to move with the horse, sitting well into the saddle when it walks and getting forward when it travels at a faster gait or goes up and down hills. Stirrups on Monte Foreman saddles also hang farther forward than do those on the conventional saddles.

Rigging

How a saddle is rigged indicates how it is balanced on the horse's back and how the girth attaches to the saddle. All English saddles are "center-fire" rigged, and so was the rigging brought into this country by the Mexicans. Their center-fire rigging consisted of two stout straps, one which passed around the front of the fork and the second which ran over the rear of the tree behind the cantle. The ends of the two straps joined to a large ring centered on either side of the tree. When the rear strap was considerably longer than the front strap, the ring to which they were joined was then balanced further forward and it was known as three-quarter rigging. The early Texas ropers found that neither the center-fire rigging of the Mexicans and Californians nor the three-quarter rigging could adequately hold the saddle in place when they were roping

Saddletrees can be bought precovered with rawhide or bullhide. Trees come in different bar widths and various styles of horns, forks, and cantles. Hand-sewn wet rawhide or bullhide covers a laminated fork made of ponderosa pine and a ductile-iron horn that is bolted into the fork. Many trees come with one of the following types of horn: regular, egg-shaped pelican, two-rope, high dally, and double dally.

a large animal. For when several hundreds of pounds of calf hit the horn, the impact would jerk the saddle forward and badly bruise the horse. Ropers needed a solution, and since necessity is the mother of invention, they quickly found one. They shortened the two straps and finished each in a large ring, so that two rings instead of one appeared on either side of the tree. This was known as "rim-fire" rigging, a name which has since evolved into "full rigging," "double rigging" or "full double."

The full-double rigging was particularly successful, and the design traveled throughout the Southwest and into the Northwest. Today of course, the full-double is found in every state. But it is also beginning to lose some of its popularity. Many nonroping horsemen find that the full-double saddle is too heavy for everyday use and that the forward cinch tends to chafe a horse directly behind the elbow, a problem particu-

larly apparent in steep-shouldered animals. Many horsemen are turning to a seven-eighths double-rigged saddle with the girth to the rear of the full-double but forward from a center-fire rigging. Instead of the usual "on-the-tree" rigging, the rigging rings on other than roping saddles are often sewn into the skirt. This "in-skirt" rigging, while obviously inadequate for calf roping, is excellent for pleasure riding since it is less bulky and allows the rider closer contact with the horse.

BAREBACK PAD

For those who enjoy closer contact with the horse but want some covering to protect the animal's back, the bareback pad is a useful piece of equipment. It comes with either leather, cotton duck, or canvas outer covering and is lightly padded with felt or sponge rubber or fiber hair. Bareback pads are available in English style with a web surcingle and handhold sewn onto the pad and metal D rings for attaching leathers and irons. Western-style bareback pads are practically identical, with a slight difference found in the girth, which ends in a metal D to which a latigo holds a string girth, and in the stirrups, which are usually made of bent wood.

Because these pads are frequently used by less than experienced riders who may, when feeling insecure in their seat, rely on the reins for balance (a habit that encourages heavy hands and a hard mouth to match), we recommend pads with the handhold rather than those without. Neck straps are also useful in this regard.

PACKSADDLE

For those who want to travel away from the well-worn trails and plan to go where McDonald's and Pizza King aren't—at least, not yet—a pack horse or mule may be necessary. Most people think that these animals are much stronger than in fact they are, so you should not expect the horse to carry more than 175 pounds. That may sound like a lot of gear, but remember to count the weight of the feed and the weight of the pack itself. Of course, the feed weight will lighten considerably as each day goes by.

The most common packsaddle is the "saw-buck" type, which is made of two sets of sturdy wooden pieces joined to form a high-slung X. The bottom part of the X is attached on either side to bars which rest on

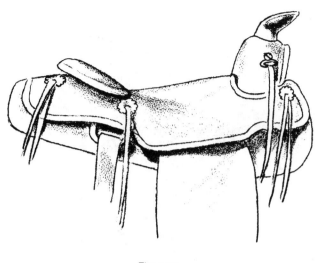

Flat seat

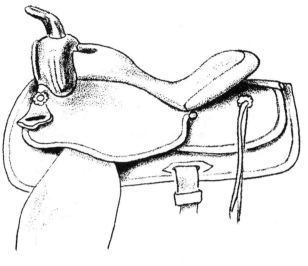

Built-up seat

the muscle pads on either side of the horse's backbone—much like the bars on most saddletrees. The bars are usually rounded on each end, tapered to fit the animal's back and then lined with sheepskin or another type of soft padding. Two leather rigging straps pass up the inside of the X frames to crisscross around the bucks and down the opposite side. The two rigging rings on each side are joined by a cross strap, and two latigos hold the front and rear cinches. A breast collar and breeching are important parts of the packsaddle; a breast collar eases the strain to the girths when the horse is going uphill, and breaching, held in place by a back strap and a strap to the rear X frame, eases the strain when it is going downhill.

Saddle pack bags can be made of canvas, leather, plywood, or any lightweight but sturdy material. They are usually longer than they are deep (approximately 24 inches long and 22 inches high) and are hung on either side of the saddle. Usually the entire pack is then covered with a tarp and secured in place with a diamond or squaw hitch.

Supplements to the Saddle

BREASTPLATES

The Western-style breastplate is most often used to hold the saddle from slipping backward for riding in

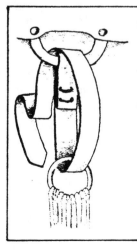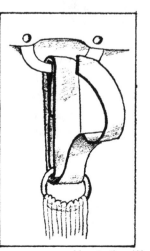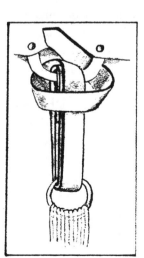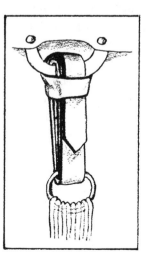

How to tie a Western front cinch

The seat size of any saddle depends a great deal on the type of tree selected and whether there is padding. The average size is from $14^3/_4$ to $15^3/_4$ inches long. Seat size is occasionally misunderstood by the novice saddle buyer. Essentially, what the experienced Western horseman is looking for is a seat large enough to allow him freedom of movement, especially to swing his stirrup fenders forward; short enough, on the other hand, so that he doesn't find himself "riding the cantle," and not so wide that it causes him to stretch uncomfortably.

To measure the seat, place a ruler at the center base of the fork and measure the distance between that point and the center of the top of the cantle. Most manufacturers publish charts which give approximate size ranges, taking into consideration the rider's height and weight. The novice should ask the advice of his local tack shop. Most shops will allow the buyer to sit on the saddle perched atop a rack designed for this purpose. Testing the feel of the saddle in this way is obviously inadequate, but the buyer may have no choice. There are some neighborly tack shops that will throw the saddle being considered onto a horse pastured out back. Short of saddling up the horse for which the saddle is intended, this is the best way to get the feel and the proper fit.

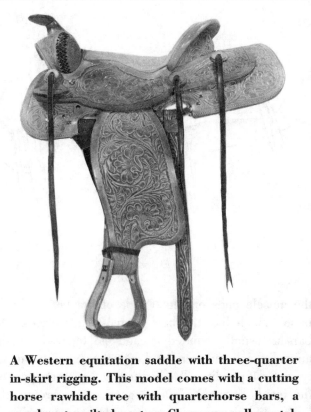

A Western equitation saddle with three-quarter in-skirt rigging. This model comes with a cutting horse rawhide tree with quarterhorse bars, a rough-out quilted seat, a Cheyenne roll, metal-edged wooden visalia stirrups, and skirts and fenders decorated with a deep embossed floral pattern. Saddles of this type usually weigh about 40 pounds.

hilly country. Now, however, it is also used as a place to attach a tie-down strap or a running martingale, and parade riders find it ideal for showing off elaborate tooling or silverwork. The Western breastplate comes in two styles: the standard and the ring type. The former is simply a strap of leather that loops on either end through the cinch rings to buckle back upon itself. A second strap loops around the horse's neck just above the withers. Some breastplates have a third strap which attaches on one end to a small D in the center of the breaststrap and, at the other end, between the horse's front legs to a small D on the cinch. The ring breastplate is made of two pieces of leather (sometimes of cord to match the cinch) joined in the center by a large ring. This permits the straps on either side of the shoulder to move independently of each other and con-

form to the horse's anatomy as it moves. The center ring is often preferred by those who use a tie-down or martingale.

The English breastplates serve a number of the same purposes as their Western counterparts, although they are rarely decorated. English breastplates also come in two different styles: the hunt breastplate and the racing, or polo, breastplate. The former consists of a chest strap attached to the girth which ends in a metal ring near the center of the horse's chest. Two straps connected to this ring pass each on one side of the neck, where they are joined by another strap that crosses the mane just above the withers. Two additional straps, one on each side of the withers, buckle to the metal eyes of the saddle and hold the breastplate firmly in place. A running or standing martingale is commonly attached to the center chest ring. The racing, or polo, breastplate is similar to the standard

If you look hard enough, you can find a Western pleasure saddle for under $300 (with no guarantees about comfort or quality), and for $10,000 you can get a custom-made silver-and-gem-decorated parade saddle. Obviously, for most horsemen the latter price is unnecessarily high and the former price too cheap. A good-quality saddle will more likely range from $500 to $900. Custom-made saddles usually cost more than ready-made ones (but not as much more as one might expect). What changes the price is whether you want hand tooling instead of stamping, buck stitching, silver, built-up seat, a different horn shape, or other details that require special attention.

Bareback pads are made in two or more materials with the underside material absorbing sweat and padding the horse's back against concussion and the top side providing a smooth seat. When selecting a pad, look for one that best cushions against concussion, providing both protection for the horse's back and more comfort for the rider. The top fabric should give the rider good grip with roughout leather offering a particularly nonslipping surface. Pay special attention to the quality of materials and the fastenings used on the girth and stirrup straps. If the way in which they are attached to the pad appears in the least flimsy, pass it by. Many pads are made with a foam underside and a tightly woven fabric upper. Girth and stirrup straps may be found in nylon web, heavy cotton web, or leather.

Western breast collar; however, it is usually lighter in weight and padded with less bulky material, and the neck strap is adjustable.

GIRTHS

There is at least one girth to match every saddle, Western or English. Girths, or cinches, are available in leather, vinyl, web, nylon, cord, linen, elastic, and cotton, rayon or mohair strands. For English hunt-seat riding the girth is usually made of leather or vinyl and may be shaped on the threefold design—a straight piece of leather or vinyl folded over to form three layers about 3 inches wide—or may be the chafeless girth, slightly tapered behind the elbow to prevent chafing, or the Balding girth, in which the center of the leather strap is split into three equal pieces and then twisted

in two places. The chafeless girth often has elastic at one or both ends for easier saddling and, more important, to give the horse more freedom to expand its chest when jumping. The Balding girth is frequently used by hunt members and polo players, who find that the three separate surfaces lie flat under the horse's belly and are less likely to slip. Saddle-seat riders traditionally

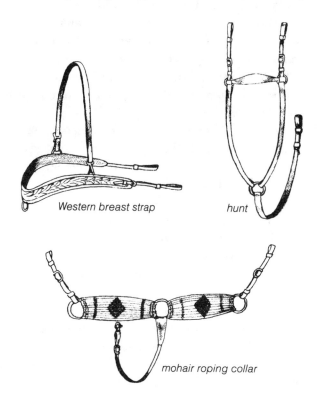

Western breast strap   *hunt*

mohair roping collar

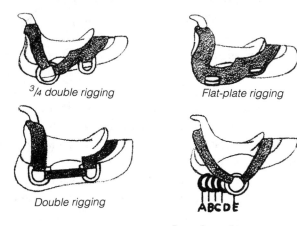

³/4 double rigging   *Flat-plate rigging*

Double rigging   ABCDE

A. Spanish B. ⁷/8 C. ³/4 D. ⁵/8 E. Center-fire

SAWBUCK PACKSADDLE

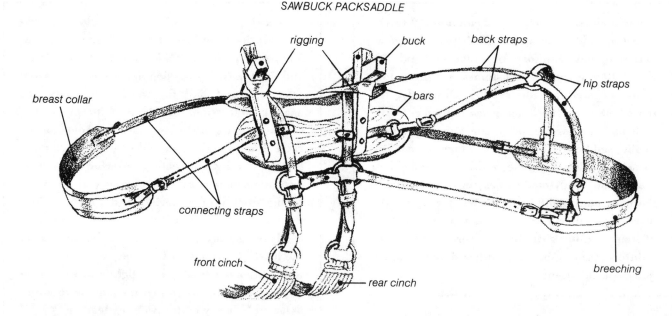

In talking about Western girths, it is necessary to distinguish between front and rear. Almost all front girths are made of cincha cord of pure mohair, pure cotton, or a combination of mohair and rayon—a particularly strong and soft blend. The standard front cinch is generally 30 inches long and made from an average of seventeen braided cords with cords of a different color woven in perpendicularly in anywhere from three to seven places. The cinches are attached to flat metal rings that often have a tongue to buckle. This type of girth also comes with two small D's woven into the center crossbar, the forward D for snapping on a tie-down or a breastplate and the rear D for attaching the connecting strap to the flank girth. A roping cinch is a wider version of the standard one, often made from twenty-four strands of braided cord with a diamond-shaped center made out of either woven cord, a webbing strap, or a leather patch.

use a white canvas, web, or linen show girth usually 5 inches wide. Jumping and dressage riders use a girth made from either mohair, nylon, or Trevira cord. This string girth is normally sixteen strands wide, with eight strands woven into each buckle. Girths for racehorses are similar to those used by hunt riders but are usually much thinner, sometimes no more than 2 inches wide. Elastic webbing is often used, since it allows the horse to expand its chest freely when working.

Several accessories used on English girths are worth knowing about. For instance, a girth extension, a small double strap with buckles on one end and holes to buckle on the other, is particularly useful for horses that have become so fat on summer pasture their girth no longer fits.

A buckle guard, simply a small piece of medium-weight leather with three sets of slits spaced evenly across the top to accommodate the billet straps, helps to hold the billets firmly in place and protect the flap from scarring.

Fleece girth covers made of machine-washable acrylic are tubular-shaped to slip over a leather or elastic girth. Because these covers are particularly soft, they help prevent chafing to the horse's belly.

Racehorses and jumpers, especially those used for open jumping, sometimes carry an Olympic overgirth, or surcingle, to prevent the saddle from flopping forward as the horse comes off the jump. Usually it is used in addition to the saddle's own girth and wraps around over the center of the seat and under the horse's belly.

Western girth accessories include girth covers with the tops of the ends scooped out to accommodate the latigo knot and the cinch, D's, to prevent girth galls. They are available in woolskin or synthetic fleece. There is also a ring chafe made from woolskin or fleece which slips over the back of the ring to cushion the horse against rubbing.

While the front girth on a Western saddle is normally made of cord, the flank cinch is usually made of leather, often about 3 inches wide. The flank cinch should never be drawn up tight but rather left hanging

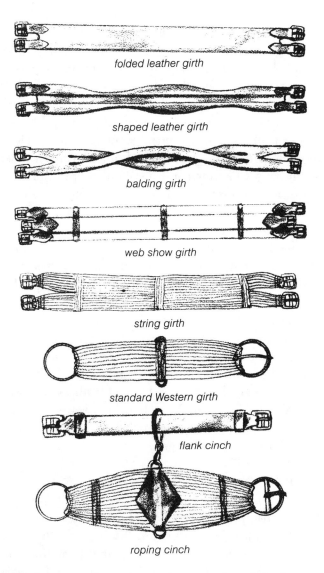

folded leather girth

shaped leather girth

balding girth

web show girth

string girth

standard Western girth

flank cinch

roping cinch

"The dressage seat, the stock saddle seat, the jumping seat and the racing seat, apparently so different, are all basically the same. The only real differences are the lengths of the stirrup leathers and the forward inclination of the rider's torso to enable him to keep his weight as close as possible over his mount's center of gravity. For between a state of balance and a state of unbalance there is no intermediate point, no half of one and half of the other. Either a rider is in balance with his horse (not merely in balance on the horse) or he is off balance."
JOHN RICHARD YOUNG
"The JRY: A Forward Seat Stock Saddle"
American Horseman, *October 1973*

with about 2 inches of space between it and the largest part of the horse's belly. A connecting strap holds the flank cinch to the front girth and prevents it from swinging and interfering with the horse. Most flank cinches are about 36 inches long, and roping cinches are sometimes as wide as 4 inches.

BILLETS

For the Western saddle there are three different styles of billet straps, and all three are used on the same saddle. The front girth is attached on the off (right) side to an "off billet," a strong piece of leather approximately $1\frac{1}{2}$ to 2 inches wide and 33 inches to 8 feet long that is folded in half, with the cinch tongue buckling through matched holes in the double layer. The longer off billet is known as a half-breed off strap, and it wraps through the cinch rings twice for extra strength.

The near (left) side of the front girth is attached to the saddle by a latigo, or tie strap, a long (approximately 5 to 7 feet), pliable "latigo" leather. One end is folded and tied to the rigging ring on the saddle. The other end is looped down through the cinch buckle, up through the rigging D, and back through the cinch buckle, to be secured either by the cinch tongue or more often by a tie knot which loops around the rigging D. The extra length of strap is slipped into the tiestrap holder which can be found directly in front of the fork.

Both rear billets are the same on either side of the saddle. Each is tied into the rear rigging D's and fastens to the flank billet by buckles.

Billets on English saddles extend directly from the tree and are made of stout nonstretchable leather which is tapered into either two or three straps with holes to accommodate the girth buckles. Often the off side of the saddle will have two straps while the near side, which must take the most stress each time the saddle is used, will have three straps. Some riders buckle the girth alternately to any two of the three billets, thereby lessening the wear to one particular strap.

STIRRUP LEATHERS

Stirrup leathers attach the stirrup to the bars of the saddle and allow for a degree of length adjustment. In the Western saddle most stirrup leathers also include a fender, necessary to keep the rider's legs from rubbing raw. The outside of the fender, though it may be left plain, is usually decorated with embossing or hand tooling. Fenders average approximately 17 inches long and 8 inches wide, with the ends quickly tapering to form stirrup leathers about $2\frac{1}{2}$ inches wide.

There are several methods for fastening the ends of

the leathers together, and all of them are strong and dependable. One technique, called the "quick-change buckle," is not really a buckle at all. Rather, it consists of two rectangular pieces of metal, one with prongs, that attach one beneath the other to the same end of the strap so that they are free to slide up and down the leather. It works when the opposite end of the leather, with its sets of punched holes, slips under both loops of metal until the prongs grab into the desired holes and the first loop is lowered over the pronged end to hold it fast. The "Blevins buckle" is similar in theory to the former fastening but slightly different in form. It works this way: the pronged piece of metal is affixed to one end of the stirrup leather, the other end has punched holes and a sliding metal loop. The pronged end grabs into the holes and the sliding loop is brought down over the prongs to hold them securely in place.

There is a third method of holding the stirrup ends together, and this too is not actually a buckle. For this fastening, matching sets of holes are punched through both ends of the stirrup leathers. Two stout metal pins

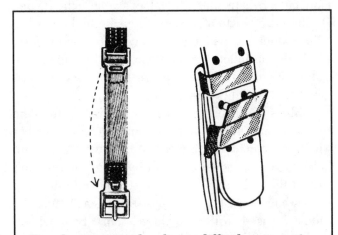

For horsemen who have difficulty mounting 16-hand-plus horses, there is a most useful gadget called the extension leather. The near (mounting) leather is fitted with a slot off of which extends an extra piece of material, usually made of web. The end of the web contains a buckle and a hook; the hook rests in the slot when the leathers are normal length and can be quickly unhooked when the rider mounts.

Quick-Change Buckle. Used on Western stirrup leathers for fast adjustment.

with holes drilled into their ends are inserted through the two layers of leathers until only the ends protrude. A metal clasp (something like a safety pin) is passed through the holes and then closed.

On some Western saddles metal is not used at all; instead, matching holes are punched through the ends of the leathers and a thin piece of rawhide is laced through to tie. This last method, often seen on older saddles, is less commonly used today, probably because it is so time-consuming to undo and retie each time you want to change the length of the stirrups.

An important part of any Western-style stirrup leather is the "hobble strap," a thin strip of leather with either a straight or a shaped body that measures about 12 inches long and $1/2$ to $7/8$ inch wide. Hobble straps wrap around the stirrup leathers just above the stirrup and prevent the stirrup from slipping out of position.

English-style stirrup leathers for hunt and pleasure saddles are often $7/8$ to $1^1/8$ inches wide, with polo leathers often a bit wider and racing leathers narrower, available in $1/2$, $5/8$, and $3/4$ inch and up. Sewn-in heavy-duty buckles fasten through punched and often numbered holes on the other end.

STIRRUPS

It wasn't until after the discovery of the stirrup that horsemanship began to develop from its early inexpertness into a highly polished art. While it was the Huns who were credited with introducing the stirrup into Europe, it was actually adopted in what is now Hungary and didn't come into common use there until as late as the 9th century and in Britain still later.

The English-style stirrup is always made of metal—either nickel-plated steel or stainless steel—and it comes in two basic types, regular and offset. The regular stirrup is designed with the eye centered so that when resting on a flat surface it is perfectly symmetrical, while the eye of an offset stirrup is set to one side so that when the iron is placed on a flat surface it leans appreciably to that side. These irons are keyed to the right or left foot, since it is the tilt that encourages the rider to keep his ankles cocked, his heels down with the force of his weight on the inside ball of his foot. Highly desirable for hunt-seat riding, the offset stirrup would not be acceptable for such riding styles as dressage.

Foot free safety stirrup

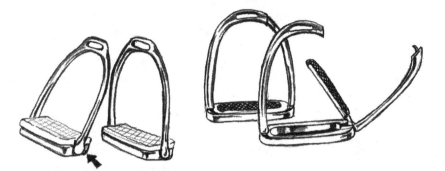

New flex, fills stirrups   *Kwik-out irons*

The center-balanced stirrup is still the more frequently used, and there are many shapes and weights available within this style. There is a safety iron known as the Peacock pattern, a three-sided stirrup open on one side and held together by a heavy rubber band. If the rider falls, the rubber band releases to prevent him from being dragged. A lightweight cradle pattern, which may be described as a squat rounded iron, is most popular with jockeys and is available in aluminum and in small sizes.

Bottoms of irons either are finished with a rough tread or accommodate stirrup pads for better grip. These pads are made from either rough-textured metal or, more commonly, rubber.

When buying stirrups, you should consider the weight—normally the heavier the iron, the easier a stirrup is to regain when lost—and the width: in case of a fall, a too-narrow stirrup can grip the foot too firmly and a too-wide stirrup makes it an easy matter for the entire foot to slip through.

The Western stirrup is made from a wooden form that is covered either with a strap of metal bound along the side or, more commonly, entirely in leather. Some leather-covered stirrups also have a second layer of

leather wrapped around the bottom of the stirrup for better wear and grip.

Western stirrups come in several basic styles: the Visalia, the bell-bottom, the roper, and the oxbow. The last one is a particularly narrow, rounded-bottom stirrup designed to support the arch rather than the ball of the foot; used by horsemen who wear their stirrups driven home, it is frequently found on rodeo and bronc saddles.

Tapaderos, or stirrup hoods, originated with the early Mexican saddle. Called "taps" by Texans, they were tooled, stamped, or decoratively carved but an important protection against the thorny brush. "Taps" were sometimes enclosed and lined with fleece, almost a winter overshoe, certainly most welcome during cold weather. Californians preferred a larger type called a wing tap that extended below the toe and was indeed shaped like one half of an angel's wing. For parades, elaborately tooled, silver-inlaid tapaderos were used, and these designs are visible today during, for instance, the Rose Bowl parade in Pasadena.

While we're on the subject of tapaderos, English-style riders have a small version which they call cups or hoods. Lined with fleece or wool, these cups slip

ENGLISH STIRRUPS

fillis

hunt

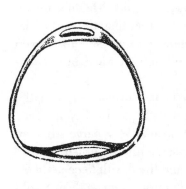

peacock

offset

cradle

foot-warmer

To determine the correct stirrup length for any style of riding, sit in the saddle with legs relaxed and hanging down straight. The bottom of the stirrup should be:

- **Forward hunt seat—just above the anklebone**
- **Balanced English seat—at anklebone or just below**
- **Saddle seat—just above sole of boot**
- **Western—1 to 1½ inches above sole of boot**

over the front of the stirrup to enclose the toe and provide warmth on freezing days.

Halters

From its first day of life, the single item of tack any domestic horse requires is a halter—a simplified bridle without bit or reins. There are any number of good, serviceable all-purpose halters sold through tack shops, and there are also several specialized types as well. Most stables use one of the following materials and styles for general needs: cotton rope or nylon rope (often identical in style, they are normally held together by tiller clamps or may even be of one-piece construction with no hardware); nylon web (usually has a friction buckle; it should be double-stitched at stress points); leather (extremely attractive when properly cared for, it should be stout, with plenty of stitching, and have quality hardware that won't crack the leather). For animals in shipment, there is a jute-fiber shipping halter, a wide, stout halter that includes a thin browband and throatlatch. The halter has little hardware and the lead often cannot be removed. Shipping halters are made to slip off the horse easily when this is needed. On the other end of the halter spectrum is the show halter. More like a bridle, it is often thinner than the other halters, may be rolled or buck-stitched, and is too lightweight to use for anything other than show. Instead of a bit, it has a chain chin strap whose ends slip through the two cheek rings and join under the chin to attach to the lead rope.

When purchasing a halter you should look for one that is not skimpy, with stress points double or even triple and sewn together with small stitches (about ten to the inch); made carefully, with no rough edges and with strap ends that are either beveled or tapered; more heavily stitched than riveted (an abundance of rivets usually indicating cheap manufacturing); and of good-quality materials. Nylon should feel soft and supple, leather smooth; hardware should be rustproof, smooth

WESTERN STIRRUPS

Visalia

bell-bottom

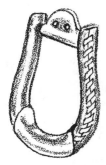

oxbow

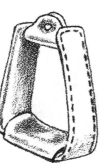

roper

tapaderos

and shaped so that it does not cause undue wear on the halter.

LEADS

Lead ropes or lead shanks are available in most of the materials used to make halters and are often sold to match show halters. Leads average between 6 and 8 feet long, with the 1½ to 2 feet nearest the halter sometimes made of chain, and always hook with a swivel snap. For young, exuberant animals, the lead snap can be hooked to the right halter ring and then passed under the lip and up through the left halter ring; the additional leverage under the chin usually gives a handler a bit more control.

Lunge lines are usually about 25 feet long and normally made of nylon or cotton web about 1 inch wide with a swivel trigger or spring-style snap at one end. Some come with a sewn-in handhold.

Harness

In A.D. 800 the Arabs, returning from such territories as Bokhara and Samarkand, brought the hame collar into northwestern Europe. An invention of the Turkic peoples, it radically affected the harness then in use and with the addition of shafts permitted one horse to pull carts that could previously be drawn only by two bullocks. On the other hand, the breast collar entered Europe from the North, where it was probably adapted from reindeer harness. These two discoveries were far more efficient than the yoke-and-pole technique then in use and, in combination with improved wagons, changed the course of European travel and development.

Today, horses are driven in harness for many purposes, the least of which is transportation. There is a variety of types of driving done in all parts of the country, and clubs gather to encourage and promote their own brand. (See pages 273–79 for more on the subject.)

Huge draft horses are still used by the Amish people in Pennsylvania to plow and cultivate their prosperous farms. In all sections of the country you can find individuals who continue to rely on horses for working the land and pulling heavy wagons. Work harness is made of stout leather, and everything about it is heavy-duty. Special clubs and fairs include draft-horse pulling or plowing contests, and many of the contestants will invest in silver-inlaid patent leather-covered harness for these competitions.

Trotters, as anyone who has bet $2 knows, are bred for speed. Racing harness is designed to help the horse move easily and maintain its gait. Unlike flat-

HALTERS

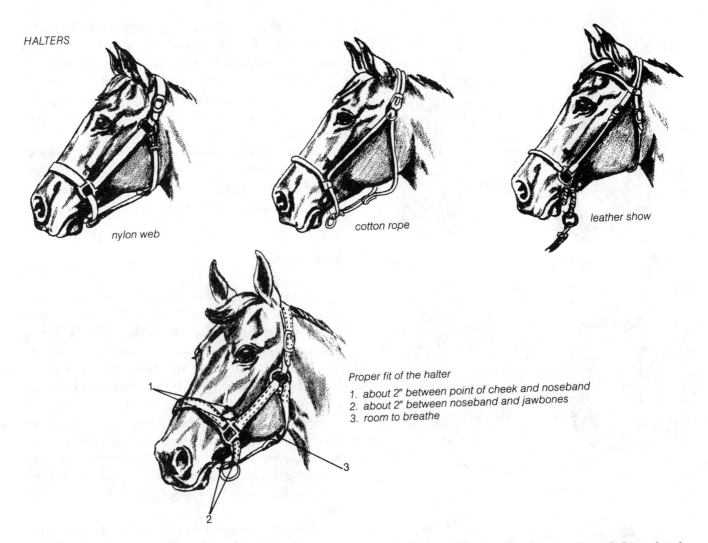

nylon web

cotton rope

leather show

Proper fit of the halter
1. about 2" between point of cheek and noseband
2. about 2" between noseband and jawbones
3. room to breathe

racing tack, a trotter's harness needn't be exceptionally light; it must, however, be strong and may include such specialized tack as a pool cue (a pole to discourage the horse from turning its head to the side) or any of the other pieces of equipment special to the racing trotter.

Show harness or light-carriage harness is designed for one horse to pull a small carriage or cart, and it is the harness used by the majority of horsemen. Light harness is often used in training a young horse, in showing gaited horses, Arabs, and Morgans, and for pulling a buggy or sleigh down the road.*

Harness is specialized tack designed to allow the

* Probably the least-known type of driving today was one of the most widely practiced sports about one hundred years ago. We are talking about coaching, a sport that requires great skill and elaborate equipment. Coaching and even tandem driving now boast a small, highly dedicated group of experts, all of whom know each other and where to find coaching equipment. We will not attempt to

horse to pull either a vehicle or a plow while under the driver's control. With only slight variations, almost all harness is made up of a bridle, a saddle, traces, a collar, and breeching or thimbles that slip over the fills.

The bridle is similar to a basic English-style headstall with the addition of blinders attached to the cheekpiece and to the browband. Blinders were made in traditional patterns, with coachmen-driven horses in square or D-shaped blinders, light-carriage-driven horses in hatchet-shaped or round blinders, and racing trotters in any variety that will work, including half-moon-shaped blinders. Trotters and occasionally light-harness carriage horses will also carry an overcheck—a strap of leather that attaches to each of the bit rings, joins in the center of the horse's face, runs up between the eyes through a loop in the crown-

describe coaching further except to recommend that those interested in learning more see the section on Driving, pp. 273–79.

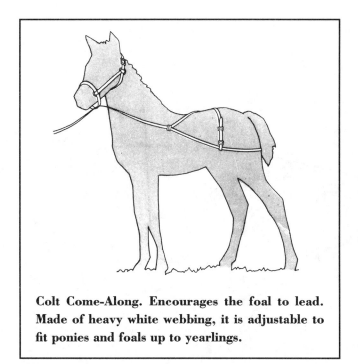

Colt Come-Along. Encourages the foal to lead. Made of heavy white webbing, it is adjustable to fit ponies and foals up to yearlings.

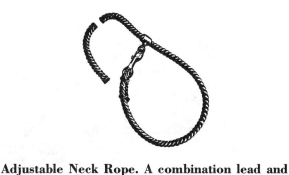

Adjustable Neck Rope. A combination lead and neck rope with a thimble adjusted near the center and a trigger snap at one end of the rope. To secure the rope, the thimble is set so that it joins the snap at the base of the horse's throat where the trigger snap clips into the eye of the thimble.

piece of the bridle, and follows the crest of the neck where it hooks onto the saddle. The overcheck is used to dictate the proper extension of the head as the horse moves along at a fast pace.

The single-harness saddle fits around the horse's girth and has padded panels which rest on either side of the horse's backbone. On top of these panels two ring ferrets serve as guides for the reins. The saddle head usually has a brass hook to which to attach the

overcheck. The bellyband includes tugs—loops, which hang from either side of the saddle, to hold the shaft—and is loosely buckled over the girth. To prevent the saddle from slipping forward, a crupper, a piece of padded leather which encircles the base of the tail, is connected to the saddle by an adjustable backband.

Horses trained to pull may be fitted in either a neck collar or a breast collar, depending on traditional styles and the type of work expected. The neck collar is pear-shaped, designed to lie closely around the base of the horse's neck along the shoulder line. It is heavily

"Every one may not know what breaking in is, therefore I will describe it. It means to teach a horse to wear a saddle and bridle, and to carry on his back a man, woman, or child; to go just the way they wish, and to go quietly. Besides this, he has to learn to wear a collar, a crupper, and a breeching, and to stand still while they are on; then to have a cart or a chaise fixed behind, so that he cannot walk or trot without dragging it after him; and he must go fast or slow, just as his driver wishes. He must never start at what he sees, nor speak to other horses, nor bite nor kick, nor have any will of his own, but always do his master's will, even though he may be very tired or hungry; but the worst of all is, when this harness is once on, he may neither jump for joy nor lie down for weariness. So this breaking in is a great thing."

ANNA SEWELL
Black Beauty

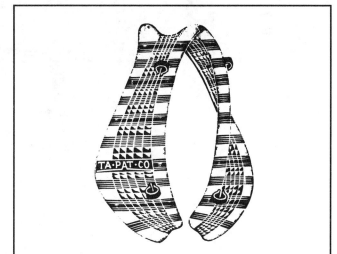

Collar Pads. Quilted awning-stripe drill with composite stuffing and four hooks. Sizes 16 to 30 inches, and it is suggested you order two sizes larger than the collar.

SINGLE HARNESS

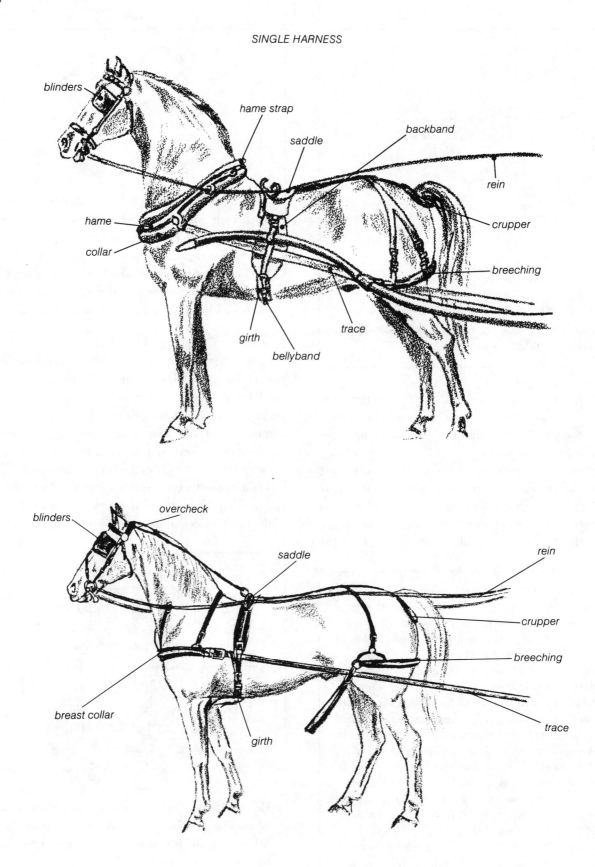

padded. Usually the top of the collar is closed by a strap or a special snap fastening. The hames fit in the groove that lines the outer part of the collar and are joined together at the top and bottom. These two gracefully shaped pieces of metal or wood reinforced with metal help to distribute the pulling pressure across the horse's shoulders. The breast collar is a wide band of stout leather that fits around the horse's chest and is held in place by a strap which passes over the neck just above the withers. Traces, two thick leather straps, attach at one end directly onto the hames or onto the breast collar at the point of the shoulder and, at the other end, onto the carriage or plow.

For most types of use the harness is now complete. However, for single harness used on a cart or carriage, breeching is often a necessity. Consisting of a strap that passes along the horse's hindquarters, it is held in place by a second strap which passes over the croup and across the backband, with the ends of the breeching hooking onto each of the shafts. Breeching should be thought of as a counterpart to the breast collar; when the horse is going downhill, the weight of the carriage is borne by its haunches instead of its shoulders, in hilly country and even for slowing down a carriage on level ground breeching is essential. For horses worked on flatter terrain, a leather thimble extending from each side of the saddle slips over the front of the shafts and bears some of the pressure when the carriage is slowed. The thimbles can also keep the vehicle from plowing into the animal, something that can quickly sour a willing horse.

Saddle Pads

Padding between the saddle and the horse's back exists in a wide variety of materials and styles. Most tack shops stock a large selection of pads, and it is often difficult for the horse owner to know which one will best fill his needs. Saddle pads serve a number of different and important purposes and the final selection will have to address these needs.

One of the first things to consider is whether the pad is needed to help customize the saddle and compensate for an imperfect fit on the horse's back. Following this, the pad should absorb sweat to keep the horse's back cool (certain synthetic fabrics have been found to cause sweating, which can increase the risk of

Putting on a Single Harness

1. Put collar on upside down so that the widest part of the collar is slipped over the horse's eyes. Then reverse it so that the narrow part rests above the horse's withers. If the collar does not slip on easily, remove the hames and undo the collar.
2. Set saddle on horse's back, slightly farther back than normal.
3. Put tail through the crupper and attach the crupper to the saddle by the backstrap.
4. Place saddle in proper position, tighten the girth so that it fits the horse snugly, and buckle the bellyband so that it hangs loosely under the belly.
5. Put on the breeching and hook it onto the backstrap.
6. Put on the bridle, adjusting for proper fit, and adjust length of overcheck if used.
7. Attach reins to bit and pass the reins through the ferrets on the saddle. It is usual for the driver to take up the reins from the off side.
8. Put the horse in front of the cart and raise the shafts above the horse's back.
9. Pull the shafts forward, lower them, and run them through the tugs on either side of the harness.
10. Hook the traces to the cart, so adjusted that when they are pulled tight, the shaft tugs will be in the middle of the saddle's side panels.
11. Buckle the breeching onto the shaft leathers or, if breeching is not used, slip the thimble over the front of the shaft.
12. Attach overcheck, if used, and hook it to the top of the saddle.
13. Pick up the reins.
14. Calmly get into the cart and enjoy the ride.

saddle sores), protect the saddle from excessive dirt and sweat, and help to absorb concussion to the horse's back as the rider moves in the saddle. Which pad is right will depend on the amount of riding that is normally done, whether the type of riding induces sweating, whether the impact of concussion is an important factor due to either the rider's weight or his or her lack of experience, whether it is convenient to launder and care for, and whether it will be needed for ornamentation.

Natural fibers such as wool and cotton are excellent for absorbing sweat and have a tradition of use. Certainly, cotton fiber pads are easy to wash and line dry and are usually long-wearing. Their disadvantage is that they are rarely thick enough to offer protection from an ill-fitting saddle and they do not absorb concussion as effectively as others.

New foam pads, often covered in synthetic fleece, offer better protection from shock but it is necessary to note that thickness of the foam is not a criterion for judging the effectiveness of shock absorption. Look instead at the density of the foam and consider its ability to support weight evenly. Another factor to consider when buying a saddle pad is the amount of rebound highly elastic foams may produce. Rubber and some foams can reverberate the shock from concussion, sending it to the horse's back at the same rate as they absorb it, with a "double bounce" resulting.

English-style saddle pads are usually designed to fit specific saddles, such as the forward-seat, saddle-seat, and all-purpose styles. Western pads are rarely cut to conform to the saddle, but are available in rounded edges for barrel racing and with a cut-back head for a high-withered animal. Materials used for English and Western saddle pads and blankets include felt, cotton, sheepskin, synthetic fleece, hair, foam rubber, nylon, duck, wool, rayon, and jute. Pads used for English saddles are normally made from one layer of wool or cotton felt or sheepskin or from synthetic fleece. There are often sewn-in leather strap loops which slip over a billet strap and hold the pad from slipping out from under the saddle. A piece of wear leather sewn into the neck of the pad is often added to prevent galling a high-withered animal.

Western saddle blankets were traditionally made by Indian weavers. Such patterns as the Navajo, Mojave, and Chimayo were greatly prized and are still valuable today. A number of factories copy their designs in wool or synthetics. Californians used *tirutas*, heavy woven black-and-white blankets made by the Sonora Indians. These blankets normally included tassels extended along the rim of the saddle and are most decorative. Western saddle blankets are usually 30 × 60 inches and folded in half so that the fold crosses the horse's withers. Many horsemen preferred to use two blankets under the saddle; the bottom layer made of cotton, the top blanket of wool. By layering the two blankets sweat was more efficiently absorbed and chafing from the saddle was therefore reduced.

Many of the excellent synthetic fibers on the market are becoming popular with good reason; they are usually available in pads about 30 inches square. Each of the synthetics reacts differently to use, and a few are such good absorbent agents that we heard one horseman complain that his drew out all the moisture from the horse's skin. Other horsemen have found that foam rubber tends to heat up and irritate the skin. Some of the Western blankets come with two pieces of leather—sewn-in along opposite edges. When folded and placed on the horse's back, the leather strips fall directly under the front billet straps and the fender, minimizing chafing from these parts of the saddle.

Horse Blankets

One thing that has become apparent in the consideration of tack is that nothing is simple and there is no

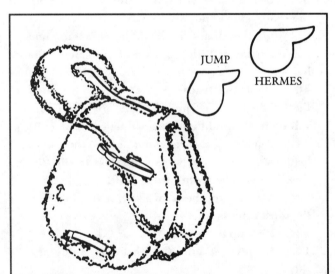

JUMP

HERMES

The Sherpa Fleece® saddle pad is made of a deep pile polyester fleece that is absorbent and machine washable and dryable. The model shown is called the "Back Comforter Pad," and it includes a layer of foam under the cantle, seat, and knees, which helps to distribute the rider's weight on the horse's back. It is available in Hermes, average jump, or large jump saddle styles.

single answer to any question. So you may well expect that if the question is "What kind of blanket should I use?" the answer will be "That depends on the type of animal, the facility in which it is kept, and the work you expect it to perform."

There are blankets to keep a horse from the effects of a cold, drafty stable; there are blankets to keep the horse's heavy winter coat from growing in too quickly; there are blankets to absorb moisture; to repel moisture (rain), and to insulate; and there are blankets to protect the animal's fine skin from flies and mosquitoes.

Horse blankets for warmth are usually made with an outer layer of canvas or duck lined with either wool, flannel, or any number of excellent synthetics. Blanket liners are sold separately, and there are a number of good reasons for acquiring one. Many are made of materials that are easy to wash (an important consideration), and such liners, while necessary for cold nights, can be removed when the day warms.

Cooling sheets are simply blankets designed to be used in warm weather. Usually made of washable cotton and occasionally duck or even lightweight wool, they are used to absorb moisture and to protect the horse against becoming chilled after heavy exercise.

Blankets normally rest over the horse from its

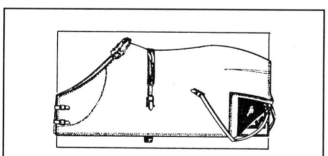

The New Zealand–style blanket is made from tough waterproof and rotproof green cotton canvas with English melton fabric lining. This blanket is designed to be cleaned by vacuuming, brushing, or washing and rinsing with water hose and mild soap. It features acrylic fleece at withers to protect against rubbing, chrome leather strap closures at front, and web surcingle with chrome leather reinforcement to keep the blanket in place. Leg straps are adjustable. This model is available in 72-inch (average horse), 76-inch (large horse) and 80-inch (extra large horse) sizes.

You can make your own "poor man's cooler" by opening and stitching on two large burlap feed sacks and sewing them together along one side of their length. Slip over the horse's back with the seam along the withers and push some baling twine through the weave of the burlap where the two sidepieces meet at the chest. Tie to close. This cooler absorbs moisture as the horse is being cooled out, but don't leave it on when you're not nearby, since it will easily slip off the horse's back and hang down the front of its neck.

withers to the base of its tail. The sides hang to the bottom of the horse's belly, where they are held in place by surcingles (usually two), front and rear straps that wrap around the animal's barrel in either a straight or a crisscross pattern to fasten on the left side. The front part of the blanket wraps around the horse's chest to buckle close. Some blankets also include a full tail flap (or a tail strap with snaps for attaching a tail guard) and front D's for connecting a hood. Some coolers are long, square pieces of material that wrap the animal from the poll to the base of the tail. These coolers sometimes come with browbands and strings to tie in the front.

Surcingles are usually sewn onto blankets, but they may be ordered separately.

Some show and race horses require additional stable clothing in the form of a full hood. Such hoods are made in almost all of the blanket materials and are used for the same reasons you would use a blanket. A

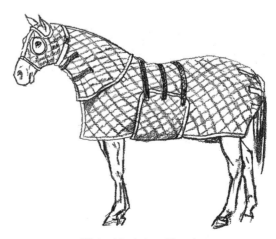

Winter blanket and hood

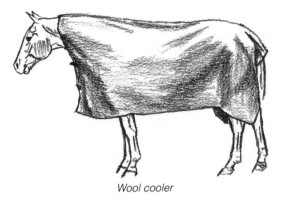

Wool cooler

jowl hood, or sometimes simply a jowl neck strap, is intended to be worn, winter or summer, on those show horses which must keep a trim throatlatch. The jowl strap, made of either wool, rubber, or vinyl-lined duck or a blend of wool and nylon, will cause the horse to sweat off fat before it ever accumulates. Jowl sweat straps are frequently used on Morgans and Arabians that are shown in conformation classes.

Tack for Specialized Training

Before any horse is "finished" there are a number of training phases the young animal must successfully pass through, as a child must complete the first grade before he may enter the second grade and certainly before he receives his graduation diploma. To continue with the school analogy, the young, green horse that has been taught to accept a halter and lead can be said to be ready to start the first grade of training. For some people, a horse is "finished" when it has received just enough training to accept a saddle and bridle and carry a rider (passenger); for others, training continues until the animal qualifies for the equivalent of a Ph.D. in a specialty such as dressage, eventing, or cutting.

No matter what the type of work the horse is being prepared to do, the trainer must begin by teaching the animal to be attentive to cues and to learn to balance itself properly for its physique, its way of going, and ultimately, the work it will eventually be asked to do. An entire wardrobe of training equipment exists, and while the amateur trainer may be able to improvise in making some of the tack necessary to advance his horse from one grade to another, he should have an under-

standing of how such tack works. Following is a description of some of the equipment available.

LUNGING EQUIPMENT

Especially useful for initial training, the lunging cavesson is essentially a halter with a ring in the center of a reinforced and padded noseband. The most versatile type will have three rings, one on each side of the noseband and the third one in the center. For the individual who needs to lunge his horse only occasionally, a bridle or halter, plus a saddle, is sufficient. For the trained horse, usually clipping the lunge line to the halter's D ring under the jaw will permit you to reverse the direction without readjusting the setting. It is used with a lunging rein—simply a long (usually about 25 feet) length of lightweight material (webbing, cotton, or nylon) with a swivel snap at one end and perhaps a handhold loop on the other end.

SURCINGLE AND BODY ROLLER

There are a number of practical uses for this piece of equipment, which, to define it simply, is either a girth strap that goes around the horse's middle or a saddle without seat or stirrups. Web, cotton, and nylon surcingles are used to hold blankets and fly sheets in place. A body roller is a surcingle with two pads that rest on either side of the horse's backbone. Its most common use is as part of a bitting or training harness.

BITTING HARNESS

This flexion-producing device is a common training aid for most English-trained horses, and it has become popular with Western trainers as well. The harness consists of a roller, made of a rubber-based webbing or leather, that has a number of sets of D rings (as many as five sets on the top and two sets at the girth) for adjusting to the bit and such tack as the sidecheek, the overcheck, the crupper, the breastplate, the driving reins, and, for gaited animals, to shackles and the tail set. Most bitting rigs come with elastic side reins and a stout leather bridle. There is a Western equivalent of the bitting rig, basically a running martingale on two side reins which are attached to the curb bit on one end and to the horn of the saddle. It can be used both while the horse is being ridden and while it is standing in its stall. When the horse's head is out of position, the running martingale pulls back on the curb until the an-

An All-Purpose Surcingle is useful for training, lunging, and exercising a horse. It will accept such training aids as side reins, an overcheck bridle, or crupper and harness straps. The one pictured here is made of 4-inch cotton web and nylon web with Dees and rings.

Leather Bitting Harness. Shown here is a bitting harness of full weight russet leather with a $3^3/_4$-inch flexible body roller that has leather-lined back pads. The girth is adjustable from either side and the crupper has self-adjusting side straps to prevent slipping. The bridle is of doubled leather and carries a full cheek snaffle bit.

imal learns to hold its head properly to stop the action of the bitting rig.

SHACKLES

Developed primarily for use with Three- and Five-Gaited animals, it is made of two often weighted front boots that fit over the shoe and are held in place by elastic or latigo leather that either attaches to a riding saddle or a roller or, like a suspender, encircles the horse over the withers.

ANKLE RATTLERS AND ACTION CHAINS

These specialized pieces of equipment are used primarily on horses trained for park riding and on Three- and Five-Gaited horses. Rattlers are ankle bracelets loosely strung with rubber or heavy aluminum beads, and as the horse moves, it learns to work its feet so that the anklet rattles. These come in varying weights, from under 10 ounces to over 34 ounces, with additional weight requiring extra muscle to lift the leg up high. Chains, either plain or soft-rubber-covered, are used to provide weight only and are relatively noiseless. Ankle-chain rattlers are usually made of heavy leather lined with a softer leather. Dangling from the anklet are eight sets of three 1-inch links of chain which

swing freely and are designed to hit the horse's pastern as it moves.

TAIL SET

This item will only be found in the wardrobe of a gaited horse such as American Saddle Horse, the Tennessee Walking Horse, or the Hackney pony. It is designed to be worn by the young horse to "set" the healing surgically treated tail. For those breeders who use this equipment, we do not need to describe it further or indicate where it can be found.

HOBBLES

To the Eastern horseman, hobbles are used solely for breeding mares and for special grooming or medicating needs. For the Western horseman, however, hobbles are an everyday fact of horse care and often the only way to keep a saddle horse from wandering off. Although horses have only four legs, horsemen have managed to invent more than four types of hobbles. They include the breeding hobble (made of either reinforced leather or nylon, it fits around the mare's hocks, with a strap coming off each hobble to pass under the belly and attach to a neck strap); the chain hobble; the Utah hobble; the figure-8; the four-way hobble; extra-long hobbles (can be used to sideline or cross-hobble); pacing hobbles; pawing hobbles (a hanging chain hits the coronet when the horse paws); and kicking chains (usually $1/2$-inch heavy chain links that hit the horse's leg when it kicks).

Protective Equipment

Most of the protective equipment listed here is to protect the horse, some of it is intended to protect the horse's tack, and such equipment as the muzzle is intended to protect the horseman.

A neck cradle is an important item to have around a stable for horses that refuse to understand that the blanket they are wearing will keep them warm or that

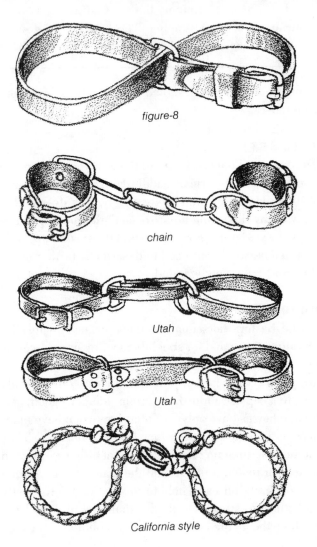

HOBBLES

figure-8

chain

Utah

Utah

California style

the bandage covering a wound is necessary for healing. The most common neck cradle is made from smooth, rounded pieces of wood held together by wooden beads that allow the cradle some flexibility. The wood cradle hangs from the horse's neck by two leather straps.

Some horsemen prefer to use a bib to prevent the horse from tearing its blanket or opening up healing sores. Most bibs are made of leather and are designed to hook onto the two side rings and the chin ring of the halter. Some also come with an adjustable noseband that permits the horse to eat and drink but restricts it from reaching around to grab with its teeth.

For those horses that can't kick the cribbing habit, a problem that can ruin an otherwise good animal, most catalogs sell "cribbing straps." The variety of devices ranges from a plain broad strap that tightly encircles the horse's neck to a French-type strap reinforced with metal to prevent the neck or windpipe from expanding. There is also a spike cribbing strap, a deterrent if we ever saw one, which, to quote the catalogs, has "proved most effective to prevent wind sucking and cribbing." It works in response to the expansion of the neck, forcing metal spikes through holes in a neck strap that prick the horse as it sucks in air. Actually, although it looks like an instrument of torture from the Dark Ages, it doesn't deter many horses at all.

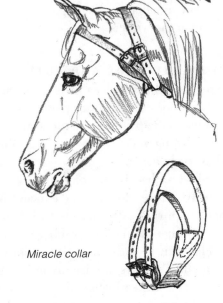

Cribbing straps

Miracle collar

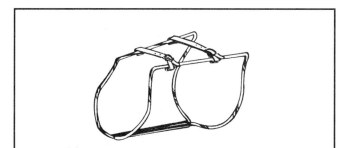

A cradle made of light metal for long wear comes with leather straps for adjustment. It is used to prevent gnawing of blisters or sores or tearing blankets.

BANDAGES AND BOOTS

When rating a horse, knowledgeable riders look at the animal's feet and legs first, and if they aren't in good shape, the rating is "worthless." When you consider that an animal as massive as the horse is supported by four relatively thin legs and tiny feet, you can see that leg and foot problems are common, with lameness a perpetual companion of most of the finer-bred animal's existence. Because it is the fine-boned, thin-legged horses that are the most valuable to racing and jumping enthusiasts, years of experience, money, and intellect have been dedicated to theories behind bandaging and booting horses.

Bandages and boots, although not the same, serve many of the same functions. Bandages, however, do have a greater variety of uses. They are obviously necessary for such health reasons as covering a deep wound, for a wrap over a heating liniment, or as a container to hold ice around the horse's legs. (See page 135 for medicinal uses of bandages.) But bandages are also used regularly on the horse in perfect health, and these bandages serve such important functions as giving support to fine tendons, preventing chafing caused by muddy tracks or rough terrain, keeping the legs warm in a cold stable, holding a tail in shape, preventing a horse from harming itself should it cross-fire or interfere, and finally, protecting the animal's legs in shipment. Stable or standing bandages used for warmth are normally made of wool or flannel and cover the leg from below the knee to below the fetlock. Exercise bandages that fit snugly for support are usually available in elastic, and many catalogs feature elasticized hose that slip over the necessary area; the exercise bandage should cover the area below the knee to the top of the fetlock only. There is also a shipping bandage, similar to the stable bandage except that it is used over cotton batting and protects the animal's legs from cuts and scrapes or worse during shipment.

Because horses are capable of inflicting an incredible number of sores, wounds, or bruises upon themselves, horsemen have retaliated with an equally incredible number of preventives in the form of boots, and there are boots available that cover every part of a horse's legs. There are also boots for teaching or improving gaits or for simply protecting the legs from irritating mud. Catalogs feature boots made of leather that may be lined with foam rubber, with vinyl, with felt, with wool felt, with lamb's wool, or with French calfskin. These boots are designed to cover the shin, tendon, ankle, coronet, knee, and hoof (as standard protection for hunters), to protect the hock during shipping, to protect the heels during cutting and roping, and thick boots to protect the polo pony's legs during a game. Bell boots, which fit over the horse's hoofs, are used on hunters as protection against bruising their

---

Boots are generally available in the following materials: leather-covered, lined with felt, fleece, foam, or rubber; vinyl or plastic-covered boots, which may be lined with the same materials listed above; or rubber boots. The leather-covered boots are hard-wearing yet flexible and repairable. Vinyl or plastic-covered boots are lightweight, flexible, and clean easily. Rubber boots are generally less expensive than the other materials and while they share the good qualities of flexibility and ease of cleaning, they usually do not offer the same degree of protection and are not as long-wearing.

Linings for boots must be soft, absorbent, and easy to clean. Felt and foam rubber linings fulfill the first two requirements but are difficult to wash. Nonporous rubber linings are excellent shock absorbers and clean with ease but do not breathe, neither absorbing sweat nor allowing air to circulate.

Most boots are fastened either by straps with buckles or with Velcro.

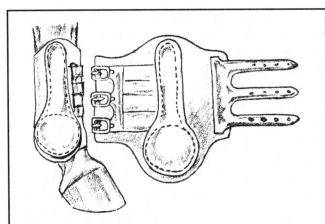

Shin and Ankle Boots

Covering the ankle and most of the cannon, this boot usually has either extra padding or a firm insert panel for protection to the area of the splint and the inside of the ankle. Though it is designed primarily for use on front legs only, rear leg boots are available and some styles will fit both. These are often referred to as splint boots and are so called to differentiate them from shin and ankle boots intended for protection rather than support.

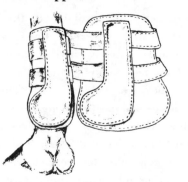

Tendon and Ankle Boots

Used to protect or support tendons as well as the backs and insides of the horse's ankles, they have support panels or extra padding in the back. The open-front style is normally preferred for use on jumpers because it allows the horse to feel contact with a rail, while horses used for eventing will often be found wearing wraparound styles.

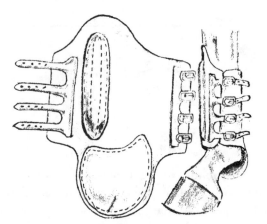

Galloping Boots
These provide protection to ankles, shins, and tendons and are often considered an all-around protection.

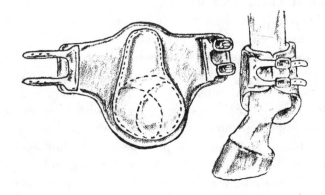

Ankle Boots
Designed to protect both the hind and front feet from brushing the inside ankles.

feet if they knock down a pole. Racing trotters and pacers wear quarter boots to protect them if their feet interfere with each other, and Five-Gaited Saddle Horses wear a hinged quarter boot to improve the action of the legs. Horses that develop a capped elbow will be put into a show boil roll, a padded roll, much like a rubber tire, that fits around the horse's coronet to prevent the horse from bruising its elbow with its shoe as it is lying down. Overreach boots are often necessary protection for many of the gaited horses and trotters that have a propensity toward striking heel or foreleg with the shoe tip of the hind foot. Brushing, or ankle, boots protect that area from hind legs that tend to brush against the inside of the front ankles. Horsemen can easily make a brushing "boot" by taking a piece of heavy felt, wrapping it around the horse's leg, tying it in the center with a ribbon, and then folding the top over the ribbon to form a double layer of material.

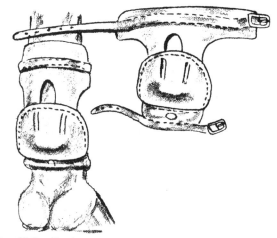

Skid or Sliding Boots
For quarter horses and others that perform quick sliding stops, these boots offer protection to the hind pasterns and fetlocks.

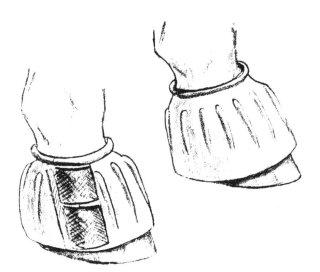

Bell Boots
Covering nearly all of the hoof, these boots prevent over-reaching of the front feet. Quarter boots are simply bell boots that are narrower at the front and wider at the back.

If you are interested in learning more about the subject of tack, the first reference to go to is E. Hartley Edwards, *Saddlery* (Arco Publishing Co., 1963). Although just the slightest bit dated and a little too British at times, it offers the most complete and articulate descriptions of bits, bridles, saddles, and accessories to be found. A useful book for further understanding of the three major groups of bits—the snaffle, double, and Pelham—is *Bit by Bit: A Guide to Equine Bits*, by Diana R. Tuke (Arco, 1974). Over 190 photographs complement the text. Ed Connell's *Hackamore Reinsman* explains how to take a green horse and trainer from the first bosal to sliding stops and whirls on the hackamore. The accent is on making a finished hackamore horse with an untouched mouth, California style. Ed Connell's *Reinsman of the West: Bridles & Bits*, Volume II, gives the how and why of making a spade-bit horse out of the hackamore horse. Both books published and distributed by Longhorn Press, Box 150, Cisco, Texas 76437. *The Illustrated Glossary of Horse Equipment* (Arco, 1976), is just that: 101 photographs of English and Western equipment with clear, concise explanations of what each item is and what it does.

Snow-Proof. Use on saddles and boots to soften and preserve leather while protecting it from snow and rain. Your local hardware or tack shop should carry it, or write to the company directly. The Snow-Proof Co., Livonia, New York 14487.

How to Clean Tack

Equipment

- saddle or glycerine soap
- sponge for applying soap
- towel for removing mud
- soft rag for drying leather
- dandy brush for serge saddle linings
- metal polish
- neat's-foot oil, castor oil, Snow-Proof or Lexol
- toothpicks for cleaning dirt out from holes
- a pail of warm water
- saddle stand and bridle hooks

Tack must be cleaned regularly to prevent drying, rotting, or breaking, and it should always be cleaned after each use. While going through the basic cleaning process, stay alert to such signs of wear as pulled or broken stitching; buckles that bend against the laws of leverage; billets, girth, or bridle parts that are cracked and dry. All tack that is not in storage should be sponged several times a week with a glycerine saddle soap, which not only cleans but leaves a waxy, protective coating for the leather. At least once or twice a week, the saddle and bridle should be taken apart completely for a thorough cleaning. To do this, disassemble the saddle entirely: remove the girth(s), the billets (on the Western saddle), the fenders and stirrup leathers, and the stirrups. Put the bit, along with the metal stirrups, in a basin of cool water to soak.

Begin cleaning by forcefully damp-sponging or brushing with a coarse towel all mud from the saddle and bridle, taking special care that the panels do not retain any clinging clumps of mud. If the saddle has a sheepskin or serge lining, go over it thoroughly with a dandy brush. If the girth is made of washable fabric, brush it out and soak it in cool water with a mild soap. After the leather parts have been cleaned of mud, dry them with a soft, absorbent cloth and set them aside to dry. Don't put them in direct sunlight or near other direct sources of heat or the leather will dry out and become brittle. If the leather seems at all dry (particularly when you're checking the billets, stirrup leathers, and girth), apply a light coat of neat's-foot oil; however, do not if the leather feels soft and pliable. Overapplication of neat's-foot can make tack very tacky and unpleasant to touch or ride. Finish the saddle off with an application of saddle soap. Barely dampen a sponge or soft cloth and rub the soap onto the leather. If it lathers, that means the sponge is too wet.

Before putting the saddle and bridle aside, take a wooden toothpick and poke it through the holes in the stirrup leathers to remove any dirt or excess saddle soap. Buff the leather, if you like, for that wonderful shine that means clean tack.

Before sitting back to relax, remember to take the metal bit and stirrups out of the water in which you left them to soak. Scrub off any remaining mud or crust, dry, and then polish with a metal cleaner. Take the washable girth out of its water bath and if it is not satisfactorily clean, dump it into a washing machine with the saddle pad, using a cold setting and a mild detergent. Ω

chapter 6

Apparel

ost books and catalogs neatly divide riding apparel into two distinct sections—English and Western—as if little knowing or caring that the two can and do overlap in many different ways. True, there is a special "look" worn by people who favor the English style of riding, and there is certainly a familiar cowboy image shared by all those who prefer stock saddles, but curious as it may seem, these two costumes

Two 19th-century English gentlemen, a U.S. Cavalry officer and a Mexican vaquero.

have quite a bit in common. For one thing, apparel for the horseman evolved over centuries of horsemanship, and designs were developed to fulfill specific needs and functions, which may help explain why these styles, once they reached their peak of development in 19th century England and America, tended to stop right there without much concession to popular fashion thereafter. Levi's, Stetsons, hunting "pinks," and top boots still look very much the way they did around the turn of the century, and though this conservatism might bother those who like to change their fashions from one season to the next, the reaction has in fact, in recent years at least, been quite the opposite. Denim has become a universal fabric, and hacking jackets and high boots are as familiar to readers of *Vogue*—even those who are likely never to set foot near a stable—as they are to readers of *The Chronicle of the Horse.*

The History of Riding Apparel

Actually, it is somewhat ironic that riding clothes should be considered fashionable only now, when it was the English riding outfit of the 18th-century country gentleman that set the style for all men's clothing (and some ladies' garb as well) worn throughout the Western world today. When William Coke, Duke of Norfolk, went to court to plead the cause of the American colonies to George III, he wore his riding clothes, which were like those of all aristocratic English gentlemen of the day, and soon launched a revolution of his own. Gainsborough immortalized the costume in paint, and within a generation, everyone but everyone in England was wearing it as well. Hunting and riding for sport had developed late in the 18th century, and the French styles then ruling the world were unsuitable. Riders needed simple materials that could be easily cleaned and were sturdy enough to withstand the wear and tear of the hunting field. Coats had to be shorter and cut away at the front for freedom and comfort. Breeches replaced silk hose; plain linen rather than lace ruffles graced the neck; and high-crowned hats were devised to save the rider's head in case of a fall. Thanks to the Industrial Revolution, which made England the world's leader in the spinning and weaving of cloth goods, and to the sheep business in Australia, which produced fine merino wools for the Empire, not to mention the excellence of British tailors, suitable

materials could be turned into attractive, durable, and well-fitting clothing that exactly met the needs of the sportsman. Once the style became widely popular in England, George (Beau) Brummel and his Regency dandies turned it into an art form—by refining and tightening the clothing and making it an international rage. Since materials were pretty invariable, expert tailoring became something of an art as well; Beau Brummel boasted that he had his coat, waistcoat, and breeches all made by different tailors, each one the master of his particular specialty. An example of Brummel's powerful influence: the Prince of Wales was seen to burst into tears when Brummel told him that his breeches didn't fit properly.

In spite of the overrefined nature of Regency costume—when breeches were tailored very tight (and very uncomfortable, especially in the rain) and made of doeskin and then corduroy—serious English riders came to their senses and demanded breeches that were looser above the knees and a more comfortable single-breasted coat to replace the tight, double-breasted swallowtail (although the latter can still be seen in the hunt field today). Thus English riding clothes for men became fairly fixed in cut by about 1820, and the style continued to exert its considerable strength on men's wear of all kinds—from the formal cutaways and top hats proper for occasions of state and the tail coats still worn in the ballroom (where true chivalry may be said to exist even today) to the everyday suits worn on Madison Avenue. The English were not so rigid, however, as to overlook useful styles from other parts of the world (so long as they were in the Empire). India, where polo was popular, was the source of jodhpurs and the jodhpur boot, as well as the sport itself.

Ladies were not so easily accommodated. In the early 18th century, riding clothes for women resembled masculine garb, but by mid-century, Englishwomen rarely rode astride. Few of them hunted until well into the 19th century, if only because the sidesaddle was uncomfortable, if not dangerous, for cross-country riding. When the third pommel was invented, it became safer for ladies to hunt, but the clothing at least from the waist down, had to be (and still is) specially designed for the saddle (and tailored, in fact, while the lady was sitting *in* her saddle). Even Queen Victoria, who wore a high hard hat, a tailored bodice, and masculine neckwear, kept her long, flowing skirts (which made mounting and dismounting very awkward indeed without help). Tailor-made clothing became fashionable for women by about 1870, and by the end of the century, as women began to ride astride again, it became widespread. (Actually, it was still considered proper in England for women to use a sidesaddle as late as 1930, and nearly half the women equestrians still did so, but the love of cross-country riding won out. The style, which is very elegant indeed if not always practical, is currently enjoying something of a revival.)

In the meantime, riding clothes were adapted throughout the rest of the world from the English styles. America was an eager recipient of English woolen goods as well as fashion. As hunting clothes became simplified for street wear, Americans developed their own versions of riding and military clothing, wearing them West as they explored, exploited, and settled the frontier and built towns where more formal garb was appropriate. Long frock coats, jackboots (or Wellingtons or Napoleons), and Southern wide-brimmed planter's hats or bowlers were the sign of a Western gentleman—not a dude, but a prosperous civilian. ("Dude," incidentally, is a sort of international putdown. It seems to come from the dialectical German word *Dudenkop,* meaning "stupid-head," and in England it indicates a fop.)

Out on the range, work clothing was rougher and more suitable for riding. Much of what eventually became the cowboy outfit was likely to have been produced at first in the East—as the Stetson hat was—or at least designed by an Easterner—as Levi's were. Nevertheless, the influence of the Spanish-American *vaquero,* whose own style derived originally from North African Moors and medieval warriors, was strong.

What the Well-Dressed 18th-Century Equestrienne Wore

"A coat and a waistcoat of blue camlet trimmed and embroidered with silver, with a petticoat of the same stuff, by which alone her sex was recognized, as she wore a smartly cocked beaver hat, edged with silver and rendered more sprightly with a feather, while her hair, curled and powdered, hung to a considerable length down her shoulders, tied like that of a rakish young gentleman, with a long streaming scarlet riband."
The Spectator *(London)*

Since Spanish riding styles were different from those in the East, Westerners made some pretty important changes in their dress for riding purposes. In the brush country of Texas, hats, like the Mexican sombrero, had to be wide enough to keep the sun off the face, and bandanas became standard neckwear to keep the neck and face free of scratches, sunburn, and dust. Pants had to be as stout and as comfortable as possible for long, hard hours in the saddle. Snugness at the knees mattered less, since the combination of the Spanish saddle with long stirrups and horses bred to lope rather than trot made posting unnecessary. Mexican aprons, or *armitas* (little arms or weapons), were refined into leather chaps, which afforded wonderful protection for the leg (against thorns and cold) and a good grip on the saddle as well. Boots were high, like the English type, because they had a protective function too, but they were narrower at the toe to get into and out of the stirrup easily. Heels were raised—not just to keep them from sliding through the stirrup or to dig into the ground for holding a wild calf, but perhaps also to give the cowboy a bit of stature on the ground as well as on a horse (though cowboys were proud, it is said, of having small feet). Spurs had an elaborate look quite different from the modest, stubby English spurs; Spanish and Mexican versions, like those worn by the knights of yore, had long steel shanks with huge rowels, and Texans took to them quickly, scorning the small brass cavalry spurs.

Western styles differed from region to region, depending on climate, strong regional snobbery (Texas vs. Mexico vs. California vs. Oregon, ad infinitum), and the differences in riding and herding techniques and equipment. Californians were more directly influenced by the Spanish than the Texans were, wearing low-heeled shoes and truly enormous spurs. Northern cowmen in the dead of winter could be seen wearing fur chaps, heavy wool shirts, warm vests, and overcoats. And Indians had their influence, too, on beaded gauntlets, horsehair hat bands, fringes for chaps (or leggings), and silver tobacco canteens, as well as many other decorative trappings that would later become important in parade dress.

It seems to be true of all styles of riding clothes, regardless of region or purpose, that a show—whether it be in the hunting field, in the show ring, at the rodeo, on the polo field, or at the racetrack—always brings out the formal, traditional costumes in which rigid con-

The two decades that have elapsed since this catalog was first published have seen a diminishing number of tack shops and tailors catering to the custom-made crowd. New Yorkers especially regret the passing of Knoud's—for horsepeople one of the bright spots on Madison Avenue—and Kaufmann's emporium further downtown at 23rd and Park. However, those of us who shop by mail order should not regret the fact that custom-made breeches are basically a thing of the past. Thanks to the widespread use of spandex, Velcro fastenings, and attractive if artificial suede patches, clothing manufacturers can produce sizes and shapes to fit virtually any figure, no matter how large or unusually shaped. And, thanks to the reintroduction of natural materials such as cotton and wool that enable fabrics to "breathe," riding clothes are once again comfortable to wear as well as stylish and practical. Most riding breeches nowadays are made of a combination of cotton and spandex, while the best-fitting riding jackets tend to be made of wool rather than synthetics, although coats made of the latter are more reasonably priced. Coats are probably the hardest to fit and should probably be tried on rather than purchased by mail (unless you fit standard sizes), and some alterations by a tailor may be necessary.

Another welcome advance is the proliferation of riding gear that keeps the body, especially the extremities, warm in cold weather. The use of Polarfleece and Gore-tex is a particular boon to those of us who have to put up with below-freezing temperatures in wintertime and bone-chilling winds and rains at other times of year. Manufacturers of such clever items as really warm boots, socks, gloves, vests, and such deserve our thanks as well.

One trend that may have some advantages—but not always—is that of casual clothing for all of those hours we don't spend in the show ring. Denim breeches with suede patches are definitely easier on the leg than loose blue jeans, and pull-on breeches certainly prevent stuck zippers or buttons that don't hold. Do watch out for riding sneakers, however, at least if you plan to ride in them. They haven't much of a heel and their soft uppers don't offer much protection against being stepped on. They are good (if expensive) for mucking out and working around the barn, and they do give riders their own sneaker, not a bad thing in this day and age of sneaker supremacy.

There are a lot of items offered in the catalogs that are attractive, especially those with horsey logos and decorations, but perhaps not as practical as gear available elsewhere. A sports bra is probably a good idea for a well-endowed female rider, but probably less expensive if obtained from a regular sporting goods store. Ditto to silk underwear (which helps wick moisture away from the body), rain jackets, fleece vests and jackets, ear muffs, and other clothing worn by hikers.

Riding helmets, of course, are specially designed for riding, and safety features continue to be improved, with sturdier chin harnesses and lighter-weight but tougher helmet shells. Black velvet is still required for hunt-seat classes, but cap covers and plain helmets make it possible for the everyday rider to look cool without sacrificing safety.

servatism plays a heavy role. For when we are preparing ourselves to perform at our best, the old adage about clothes making the man (or woman) is still true. Although we may scoff at the rules for hunting apparel, shudder at the contempt with which a Texan regards a spur-dragging Californio (or vice versa), and wonder at the amounts of money, time, and energy spent on clothing one can wear only on the back of a horse, we may as well relax, enjoy it, and join in. For all of the clothing that horsemen and horsewomen wear developed for specific purposes, and in looking over the products available today, we would do well to keep the practical as well as traditional aspects in mind.

So, starting at the bottom, which as everyone knows is the foundation of a good riding seat, we shall begin with boots and move up the body, stopping now and then for some interesting sidelights of the historical as well as the anatomical sort. After a general discussion of the different types of apparel, we offer up complete costumes for specific equestrian events, and we will drop in along the way some information about manufacturers and distributors of ready-made items and sources for custom-made products.

> ● These boots are made for traveling: jodhpur and Western boots can most easily be worn in transit. Since feet tend to swell during flights, high boots are the least comfortable. Rubber boots, including Newmarkets, can safely and easily be folded in a suitcase. Leather boots toted by hand can be guarded from scratches by carrying bags of either cloth or vinyl. You can protect your headgear either by wearing the hat or by placing a hunt cap in a waterproof zippered vinyl case. All items are available at tack shops.
>
> ● Boots carried by hand provide a surprisingly large amount of packing space. If you're not using boot trees, stuff the footwear with socks, underwear, and other small foldables—you'll appreciate the additional space in your suitcases.

Boots

Sturdy riding boots as we know them today would certainly be unnecessary if it were not for the stirrup. (The carvings on the Parthenon and the paintings of Frederic Remington are testament to the fact that the Greeks and Native Americans had no need for either.) The invention of the stirrup is credited to the nomadic Huns of Asia in the 5th century, but it was not used in Europe until the 9th century, after Charlemagne's wars in what is now Hungary. And it was not until the year 1000 that the stirrup arrived in Britain, thanks to the Scandinavians, who had adopted it a century earlier from the steppe peoples of Eastern Europe. Nevertheless, the development of the riding boot did take place in Western Europe, and the styles that we use today descended directly from medieval long leather boots designed to protect the legs in battle and secure the foot in the stirrup. Jackboots were worn over pants by courtiers in England in the early 17th century, and eventually they were streamlined into military boots such as the *Wellington*, and then into the *Napoleon*. (Ironically, Waterloo notwithstanding, it was Napoleon who won the boot battle, for it is from that style that the *top, or hunt, boot* derived. Wellington, however, can also be said to have triumphed, for variations of his style of boot are still made today.) Fashioned of grain leather, with the inside left brown and the outside blackened with a combination of egg white and lampblack, the boot had a top high enough to cover the knee while its wearer was riding through brush or enemy lines and soft enough to be turned over to reveal a brown cuff.

As riding developed into a sport, this cuff disappeared, leaving a vestigial sewn-on brown top to contrast with the black of the boot itself. (Beau Brummel was said to have polished his boot tops with champagne and peach marmalade—or apricot jam, some say—and the boots themselves with port wine and black currant jelly.) Eventually mahogany became the fashionable color for boot tops, although to this day there is much discussion about the proper shade. In England there were strong regional differences and sets of rules determining same, but in this country, the principal rule is that colored tops may be worn only by members of the hunt and then only with white breeches. Ladies may wear black patent leather tops, presumably because patent leather needs no polish that might stain a lady's breeches. *Jockey boots,* once made with stitched-on tops, are now simply dyed in two colors to create a fake top, which would be frowned on at a formal hunt or in an appointments class. Gentleman hunters who wish to wear top boots some of the time and butcher boots (topless black hunting boots) on other occasions may buy slip-on tops, but they tend to slip around during use and leave a noticeable mark on the boot beneath.

Hunting, or dress, boots, with tops or without, should reach to the small of the knee in back, or—as tradition has it—to the spot just below the second (some say fourth) button of the breeches, or eyelet if the breeches are laced. In these days of buttonless, laceless stretch breeches, the best test of a new boot is to make sure that the back of the boot top touches the back of the upper leg when the knee is bent, for as boots are broken in they will drop, especially if only half lined. Dress boots traditionally have relatively straight tops, but these days the Spanish, or Continental, top—which rises in front and dips behind the knee—is fashionable, presumably because it gives the look of a higher boot. Bootmakers claim that it also affords more freedom for the leg.

Whatever the style, boots must fit snugly at the knee (so that only one finger can be inserted and then

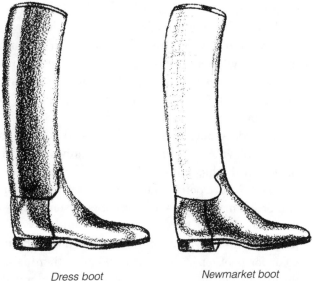
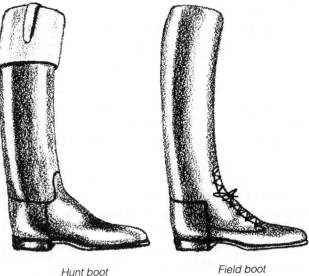

Dress boot   *Newmarket boot*   *Hunt boot*   *Field boot*

with some difficulty), over the calf, and at the heel and instep, but not so tightly that they cut off circulation. People with large calves have often complained that boots were designed only for thin people, and this is generally true where ready-made boots are concerned. Gussets or zippers may be inserted at the top, and the tab that still exists as a decorative element on some boots is said to have been designed as a cover-up for the seam of an inset (though we suspect that it was for pulling on the boot, since insets would weaken the boot's structure). However, none of these measures to widen a boot is recommended; a far more satisfactory solution is a pair of custom-made boots, which will accommodate not only a wide calf but a pair of different-sized feet, or any other irregularity one's foot might have. Custom-made boots will disguise a foot's natural flaws; a double layer of leather at the top, for instance, will make the calf look narrower and more in proportion with the rest of the leg. A boot that is made to measure and then stretched, after soaking, to a proper fit is always superior to a pinching ill-fitting boot. And custom-made boots, which have many other advantages as well, will last a lifetime with good care and can be readily repaired—if necessary by the original bootmaker, who will try to preserve the boot's original shape.

Although several kinds of leather can be used to make boots, the best choice is full-grain calfskin, which is supple, easily shined, and porous so that the leg and foot may breathe. The best calfskin comes from France, where veal is a much-loved dish, but it is becoming increasingly difficult to obtain, as the French learn to love steak *à l'américaine*. Unblemished hides are also rarer now, since hedgerows are being replaced with barbed wire, which will scratch and scar the hide. Scratches may be sanded off the leather, but this spoils the surface; as Hank Vogel, a custom bootmaker, points out, a full-grain hide with minor blemishes is much better than a corrected hide (scar tissue is stronger than normal tissue, for one thing), and we may just have to get used to them in the future. American calfskin—in spite of our enormous beef industry—is not particularly satisfactory for bootmaking; not only is it likely to be badly marked, but there are very few tanners of calfskin around these days, and many people believe that calves raised to do nothing but eat in sheltered barns cannot possibly have skins tough enough to stand up under wear. Baby calf is even finer than calfskin (which can be from an animal of an age up to one year), but it is not very durable. Jockeys, for whom every ounce counts, may order custom-made boots of baby calf, but most other riders find that in spite of its good "feel," it rarely lasts more than a season or two with hard wear. Cordovan, another popular boot leather, although increasingly difficult to obtain, is not simply a dark brown leather (all hides are colorless before being dyed brown, black, or any other shade you like) but the hide of a mature horse. Twice as heavy as calfskin, although not as strong (it will tear, rather like paper, under stress), it is warmer on the foot and won't hold a shine. Scotch grain is calf with a texture stamped on; it is heavy and stiff and doesn't take a good shine, though the stamping will cover up minor, unimportant blemishes in the leather. Patent leather is sometimes used to dress up jodhpur boots for evening saddle seat wear. Porvair is a synthetic material that has enjoyed some popularity in recent years. It is relatively inexpensive and easy to clean and care for, but it is not particularly durable and does not have the feel of genuine leather.

Many people like the look of a leather-lined boot, but an unlined boot made of heavier leather is cooler and more flexible and permits a better feel of the horse. Lined boots give more protection and hold their shape, but they don't wear as long, since the lining at the ankle—the point of greatest stress—will eventually crack and pull away from the outer leather, and for this there is no repair. A German (or three-quarter) lining is a good compromise for those who prefer the sturdiness of the lined boot, since it is fully lined except for a cutout oval area at the inner calf. One custom bootmaker with whom we spoke told us that 90 percent of his boots were ordered without linings and that the German-lined boots were preferred by dressage riders.

Soles and heels are traditionally made of leather, but synthetic material for the former is more durable, and waterproof rubber for the latter is skid-resistant (important for one's dignity on a linoleum or highly polished wooden floor if not in the stirrup). Whatever the material, soles should always be full, since half soles will interfere with the stirrup iron. Spur rests, or wedges attached to the back of the heel, are optional additions to hunting boots but are probably better left off. Spurs should fit properly without slipping down, and a knocked-off spur rest leaves an unattractive heel that will need to be repaired. *Garter straps,* which buckle around the top of the boot with the buckle on the outside, are required in formal hunting attire. They were originally designed to keep the boots themselves from slipping down (inevitable with soft, unlined leather), but their primary usefulness nowadays is a feeling of security, for they can double as pieces of bridle should any become broken in the field. Straps should match the color of the breeches if top boots are worn, although patent leather tops need patent leather garters, and plain black boots need plain black garters.

The *field boot,* usually brown and thus not appropriate for formal hunting, has laces to allow for a high instep. It is probably the best-fitting of all boots, since the ankle can be drawn to a good tight fit no matter how much room the foot may need to get into the boot. Because of this, field boots (whose style takes the name of its inventor, Blucher) are now being made in black for hunting, although some masters still frown on their use. These boots are sometimes reinforced at the toe with a toe cap for extra protection, although the stiffness may be uncomfortable for some people. This is really more decorative than useful, especially when punch marks are patterned on them, as in men's dress shoes.

Waterproof *Newmarket boots* take their name from rainy Newmarket, the famous racing center in England. They are attractive, practical, and a good deal cheaper than hunt or field boots. Traditionally made with legs of box cloth (a linen canvas) lined with leather and water-resistant leather vamps, Newmarkets are now available with more effective rubber feet and waterproof tops. (Box cloth is no longer produced, even in England.) Most Newmarket boots are shaped like dress boots, but there are also a field boot style and a paddock boot (or high shoe) with canvas sides.

Black rubber boots are also made for wet weather in imitation of the dress hunting boot. Although they are cheap and lightweight, they don't allow the boot to break in or to breathe, and in hot weather they may cause an uncomfortable accumulation of perspiration, in spite of woven-linen liners. Plastic materials are also used, but they too are hot, and they never really fit the foot very well. Nevertheless, they are often practical for growing children, because they are inexpensive and provide a certain amount of leg support. Rubber boots with leather linings are a new compromise, but we haven't subjected them to experiment as of this writing. Spur rests are sometimes built into rubber boots, since they have a slicker surface than leather.

A variation of the field boot is the high-laced shoe, or *paddock boot.* Designed to be worn under chaps or jodhpurs, it is quite a bit less expensive than the higher boots. Like other low boots, it gives far less support to the leg and is less desirable for jumping. But paddock boots are more comfortable in cooler weather, especially with insulation, and more easily removed than high boots, and they make fine walking shoes as well. Paddock boots can be made in various designs and in various colors. *Turf boots* are similar but employ zippers instead of laces in front and elastic inserts for maximum comfort and a good fit.

It should come as no surprise that there are sneakers especially designed for riding, as well as for basketball, running, and everything else people do. There are many types of riding sneakers available, although few of them are sturdy enough to protect the foot or have heels deep enough to afford safety in the stirrup. Michael Plumb's testers found that most brands were difficult to put on, thanks to the lacing, and picked up debris because they are open in front. If you like the comfort and don't mind the inconvenience, look for a brand that has a reinforced toe, speed lace hooks, and a heel at least half an inch high.

Jodhpur boots, usually worn by children and saddle-seat riders, were brought to England in the 1920s from India, where they derived from polo boots. Like high shoes, they reach a few inches above the ankle and fit under pants or leggings. They have split sides rather than frontal laces and are closed with straps (one or two) or, more recently, with elastic or zippers. (This style may be referred to as a *gaiter boot* or jodgore shoe.) The elastic-sided boots are easy to remove and are often selected by nervous parents who would rather lose a boot than have their children catch a foot in the stirrup and be dragged. Because jodhpur boots are so popular, they are readily available at reasonable prices in most tack and apparel shops, though these are usually made of cowhide rather than the more desirable (and more expensive) calf.

Traditional *gaiters* (leggings or puttees, as they are called in India) are rarely seen today except on formally dressed ringmasters, coachmen, or chauffeurs,

since boxcloth, the material of which they were always made, is no longer available and the gaiters must be custom-made. A modern version of gaiters, called leg chaps, is now available ready made from some tack shops and catalogs. The gaiter style is very useful, protecting the leg like a boot and giving a better fit on the calf and more support than a pair of trousers. Leg chaps, made of split cowhide like full chaps, are meant to be worn in lieu of boots, covering the lower leg (and trousers) when ankle-height shoes are worn. They are snug at the calf, cover the gap between shoe and cuff, and serve to protect the ankle as well.

Surprisingly, jodhpur boots are popular in the West as well as in the East, because they fit comfortably under long chaps and are easier to walk in than high-heeled *cowboy boots.* But the high-heeled boot is still the most distinctive feature of the Western rider (with the possible exception of the Stetson), and it is undoubtedly the most popular boot worn today anywhere. The boots are manufactured in many styles and used for everything from riding motorcycles to standing around in drugstores. But like hunting boots, they were designed originally for riding horses, and they too derive from the jack, Wellington, and Napoleon boots of the 18th and 19th centuries. (Those were, after all, what Americans wore West, whether they went as soldiers or as civilians.) Early Western boots didn't have much of a heel, but eventually cowboys added them—for various reasons, the primary one being to keep the boot from sliding through the large stirrups of the stock saddle. The first heels were slanted in under the boot and were about two inches high; later, as roping cowboys needed a good way of digging into the earth as they hung on to a struggling calf on the other end of a rope, they demanded straighter, wider *"walking" heels.* Both types of boot are made today for riders and walkers, along with the short Wellington boots, which are only 9 or 10 inches high, unlike the 12-to-13-inch-high cowboy boots. Polo boots, now increasing in fashionability out of as well as in stirrups, are very tall (19-inch) boots similar to old Western cowboy boots with underslung heels and stitched uppers.

Proper cowboys of old—like professional or serious riders anywhere today—avoided the store-bought boot, even though a pair might have run only $3 or $4 a hundred years ago. The best boots, then as now, were custom-made to one's personal measurements and designed to last a good, long time. Bench-made boots

Leather riding sneakers   *Low tops*

JODHPUR BOOTS

strap model	*elastic side*	*paddock boot*	*side zipper*

were a bit less expensive, because there was less hand-work in them, but because they were partially made up ahead, they never fitted exactly right, an important consideration when most of your waking hours were to be spent wearing them. Handmade boots invariably had unique, handmade decorative elements worked into the leather. These designs were used not just for looks or to cover up minor blemishes in the leather, but also to stiffen the leather and increase the amount of leg support and protective value (to leg as well as to boot). Although the old ready-made boot was fairly plain, modern ready-mades are usually dressed up with cutouts, stitched decorations, incised patterns, and inserts of colored leather. These designs go into and out of fashion very quickly (to preserve that indi-vidual, handmade look), and even the basic style of the boot seems to take some surprising turns for the sake of stylishness, especially in the shape of the heel and toe. The latter now tends to be round or pointed rather than square, as the toe always used to be. Toes still are nar-row, however, an important detail for the cowboy who must find the stirrup without looking down. The tradi-tional cowboy boot came up to the knee and was cut straight across the top, with perhaps some leather mule ears (or straps) hanging down the side for pulling-on purposes. These days, straight tops are reserved for the shorter Wellington boots, while the higher boots are scalloped front to back with shorter leather pull straps.

Most good Western boots were and still are made of calfskin, like English boots, although cowhide is more common (and less supple and less expensive) in ready-made styles. Caribou, water buffalo, and sharkskin are exotic work-boot leathers; lizard and other exotics are only for dress boots. They are usually lined with oil-resistant soles of synthetic material or treated leather,

with steel-reinforced toes for extra protection. Soles must be light and flexible, with the arch curved high; the instep may be pegged with wood for extra support.

BOOT WEAR AND CARE

The purchaser of a new pair of riding boots—regard-less of style—must be sure that they are well-fitting. Well-fitting means roomy at the toe, reasonably snug at the heel and ankle, and tight over the calf. Badly fitting ready-made boots may be stretched on a machine or mold, or, if you can bear it, on your foot, but all care should be taken to avoid damaging your feet or unnatu-rally weakening the leather. All boots will relax a bit eventually; the softer the leather, the more they will stretch or drop. Any good rider trying to keep his heels down will cause some flexing and wrinkling at the heel; this part of the breaking-in process is to be expected and worked for. But once they are broken in, boots should be cared for properly to prevent deterioration of the leather and to preserve the original shape of the boot. Boots should be given internal support when not in use. Custom-made *wooden boot trees* are worth the investment for custom-made boots, but ready-made trees are available. Most good bootmakers do not rec-ommend lightweight spring-type trees, which can dis-tort the shape of the boot, but prefer the idea of stuffing boots with rolled-up newspaper or a magazine to fill the entire leg.

Before we store the boot, however, let's get back to the way it fits on the foot. A heavy sock is probably the best form of protection for both foot and boot, even in warm weather, and this should be taken into account in fitting the boot. Socks will absorb sweat, protect the foot from abrasion, and preserve the condition of the leather. As anyone who has ever ridden during the win-ter will know, these socks are not particularly effective

Mule-eared boot   Wellington boot

Riding boot   Polo boot

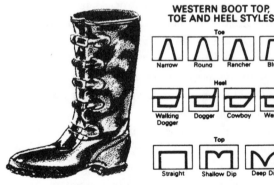

Overshoe

**WESTERN BOOT TOP,
TOE AND HEEL STYLES**

Toe

Narrow   Round   Rancher   Blunt

Heel

Walking   Dogger   Cowboy   Western
Dogger

Top

Straight   Shallow Dip   Deep Dip

Muckers

Western rubber boot

for keeping the foot warm. One can try two pairs of socks—light cotton inside a woolen pair—but these, or extra-heavy long socks, may make the calf uncomfortable. Long underwear that covers the whole foot is often a good solution—and a traditional one as well, for the British were quite accustomed to wear wool or silk mixed with wool from top to toe. Whatever the material, long johns with seams at the seat or inside the leg are to be avoided if one plans to be comfortable in the saddle. Light thermal socks or short heavy socks are warm too, and they will not affect the calf (have them knitted to your specifications, or cut off and hem a long pair). Sheepskin innersoles are helpful, or you might decide to go whole hog and order boots with fleece-lined feet, available in both Western and hunting boots for an extra $15 or $20. Fleece foot warmers may also be attached to stirrups—perhaps a bit more practical for riders who confront different kinds of weather the year around.

All sorts of devices and remedies have been dreamed up to make boots easier to pull on and off. English boots are usually pulled on with jockey, or boot, *lifts* that hook into canvas or webbing loops inside the boot. (These loops, incidentally, once had a double purpose; a button hook attached to them would connect to a button on the breeches to keep them from riding up; some boots even had buttons installed inside for the purpose.) Western boots, like some English boots, have mule ears, or straps for pulling by hand. Some people sprinkle chalk or talcum powder inside the boot before sliding it on; this will also help later on, especially if the foot is wet. For removal, *boot jacks*, some made simply of wood or acrylic plastic and some more elaborate with iron handles for leverage—occasionally designed like beetle antennae or steer horns to fit around and grip the boot—are more efficient and dignified than struggling alone or begging help from a friend. Whatever method you use, however, be sure that your leg and foot are entirely relaxed before you start tugging.

Good leather deserves considerate care, and it will reward the wearer with years of service for the trouble. In the old days when servants were plentiful, hunt boots were waxed as they were blackened, so that scratches could be rubbed down with bone and filled with black wax to make them disappear. The wax also insulated the leather against horse sweat; boots could then be easily sponged off with warm water to eliminate any sweat marks. For cleaning, boning, and waxing, the boots had to be supported by boot trees to give a firm base, and boots properly kept could last forever with no disfiguring marks. Although this kind of boot can still be made by custom bootmakers, most boots are made of unwaxed black-dyed calf, like regular black shoes. Scratch marks cannot be removed, worn areas will lighten in color, and sweat can damage the leather; but they are cheaper, and caring for them does not require a staff of servants and a supply of deer bones.

Because calfskin is more delicate than cowhide saddle soap is too strong. If dirt cannot be brushed off

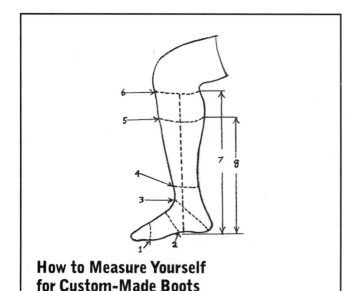

How to Measure Yourself for Custom-Made Boots

Trace the outline of your bare foot on a piece of paper that has been placed on a firm surface (not a carpet). Hold the pencil upright but inclined slightly in toward the foot. Then, with your breeches on and using a tape measure, make a series of measurements of each foot and leg, as follows, rounding off to the nearest quarter inch: ball of foot (1), instep (2), heel (3), ankle (4) calf at the widest part (5), below knee (6). Then measure on the back of the leg the distance between the floor and the top of the boot (7) and from the floor to the widest part of the calf (8). Give the bootmaker your street-show side as well. Be sure to specify the various options: dress or field style, color of leather, cuff, full, or no lining; spur rest; swagger tab or punched toe.

or wiped off with a dry cloth, a mild soap and a cloth dampened with lukewarm water will remove mud and sweat marks. Water dries out the leather and soap pulls the color, so be sparing. Gasoline and isopropyl alcohol will also clean the leather (especially good for built-up polish), but—like water—they are drying agents, and a leather conditioner should be applied after use. Boots that have become soaking wet should be dried completely and naturally (not in front of a fire or radiator) after each wearing and given a leather conditioning to keep them from losing natural oils; do not use too much conditioner or the leather will become too soft, and avoid neat's-foot oil, which will inhibit the shine. Some people like to rub glycerine on the leather lining to keep it supple. Silicone or Sno-Pruf will act as a water-resistant dressing for those who like to ride in the rain; the latter is also a conditioner and will help keep the leather soft.

Once the boot has been cleaned and dried, apply a thin layer of polish—cream polish such as Meltonian cream is best, as paste-wax polishes will crack and flake off—and let it settle. Then buff it up until you can see your face in the shine. Dark polish will help darken boots, although boots that have lost their color, usually on the inner calf, are more difficult to restore, if not impossible. An alcohol-based dye will help—with some leather conditioner to prevent drying—but since the original leather color is very thin and dyes will rub off quickly, the light leather color will wear through sooner or later. But take those marks as a compliment to your riding; at least it will be obvious that you are using your calves properly.

Once the boots are polished, they can be stored (or carried) in *boot bags* or simply put away with boot trees. Take care to keep the boots in a place that is neither too damp nor too dry, for mildew will discolor leather and drying will ruin it. If your boots need repair, don't wait until just before your next ride. Take them back to your dealer or bootmaker, who will make sure that a new sole will not alter the original size and that heels are replaced, not ground down, since that will distort the shape of the boot.

Pants

Although Americans have still not come up with a good substitute for leather, we have managed to develop new

Most tack shops carry basic types of English and Western boots in various price ranges. Because retailers usually stock only the most salable models and sizes, you may not always be able to find what you want at first, but shops can usually order out-of-stock items from their wholesale suppliers. Ordering boots by mail is not always successful, because boots are not as easy to fit as shoes. Most shops require that you send a tracing of your stocking feet, with the desired boot height measured from the floor (still in your stocking feet); your regular shoe size in flat-heeled shoes; and your calf measurement over breeches for English boots and over socks for Western boots. Custom bootmakers usually require more information than that (see page 211); you can write to them directly (or through your tack shop, if it is the distributor for a particular firm) and ask for leather swatches and a measuring chart.

The best-known custom makers of English boots in this country from which one can order direct as well as through certain tack shops are E. Vogel (19 Howard Street, New York, New York 10013) and The Dehner Co., Inc. (3614 Martha Street, Omaha, Nebraska 68105). These companies have retail price lists for their products, which include the standard styles of top boots, dress and field boots, steeplechase boots, Newmarket dress and field boots, Wellington boots, jodhpur boots, paddock shoes, and turf boots. Extras include special materials (such as baby calf, waxed calf, reverse calf), double or stitched soles, special straps and linings, and rush delivery.

Western boots are manufactured ready-made in an extremely wide range of materials, styles, colors, and sizes, and they vary in price accordingly. The cheapest boots are made of cowhide, rawhide, or synthetic leather; the most expensive are handmade from fine French calfskin or any number of exotic leathers (anteater, anaconda, ostrich, sea turtle, and so on). Most tack shops carry boots from several different manufacturers, which also advertise in the horse magazines. The quality of workmanship differs from one firm to another and from one price range to another. If you find a boot that you like and want to order another pair from the same firm, your tack dealer will be able to order it, or you can write to the firm yourself for the names of its distributors. The best-known manufacturers of Western boots are

Ariat International Inc.
940 Commercial Street
San Carlos, CA 94070
This firm is notable for its new line of boots designed for extreme weather conditions.

Justin Industries
Box 548
Fort Worth, TX 76101
(www.justinboots.com)
In addition to making Justin Boots, this company also owns the divisions that make Nocona Boots and Tony Lama boots.

Lucchese Boots
6601 Montana
El Paso, TX 79925
(www.lucchese.com)
Top of the line footwear for real and would-be Westerners.

Nashville Boot Company
3409 Love Circle
Nashville, TN 37212
(www.nashvillebootco.com)
This company manufactures two popular brand names: Acme Boots and Dan Post Boots.

Most of these companies produce relatively inexpensive boots in the basic styles—riding (with underslung heels), walking or utility (with straight heels), Wellingtons, and polo boots. But many of them will have expensive styles as well or can make boots to order; Lucchese boots, for instance, can run as high as $500 or more.

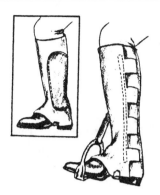

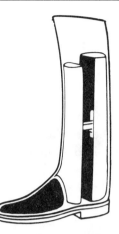

Leg chaps made of durable split cowhide are an informal substitute for boots or full chaps.

Boot accessories are available wherever boots are sold, although even here special items may be ordered by mail from specific manufacturers or distributors. Boot trees in plastic or aluminum are relatively cheap but wooden trees are often preferred by custom bootmakers to preserve rather than stretch the shape of the boot.

Miller's Harness Company distributes English-made Equi-Trees, which are remarkably effective and inexpensive. These are adjustable to fit any width of boot leg and exert firm, even pressure while they allow for air circulation.

Boot bags can be obtained in knit fabrics with a drawstring top, in a suedelike material, and in zippered vinyl or leather double bags with handles.

To get boots on and off, you may want boot hooks or lifts and boot jacks. Hooks are made of metal, usually nickel-plated, with or without wooden handles. Boot jacks can be made at home for the cost of the wood, but simple wooden or acrylic jacks with rubber treads and with or without leather-lined throats are cheap. A club boot jack with a closed circular throat and elaborate iron jacks with designs and special handles to grip the boot can cost as much or as little as you like. If you can't persuade your farrier or a local blacksmith to make you one, try looking in secondhand stores that specialize in Western antiques.

materials for making pants and other cloth garments. No one has improved on cotton denim for Levi's, and most riders agree that wool and cotton have never been surpassed for feel, durability, and appearance. Although cotton and cotton twill went into a period of oblivion during the 1970s and 1980s, as synthetic and

stretch fabrics came into common use, their superiority in cool weather brought them back to the fore, alone or in combination with nylon, rayon, spandex, and other materials that ensure a good fit.

One of the strict requirements of riding an English saddle, in which the rider is forced to post at the trot, is a tight-fitting knee, with no excess material to cause soreness to the rider or wear in the fabric. At the same time one must be able to mount, flex the leg, and dismount—which can put a lot of strain on tight-fitting pants. In addition, the fabric used must be sturdy and easily cleaned, if it is to remain in good condition over any period of time. In the days when tailors were faced with a choice of leather, corduroy, wool, or heavy cotton gabardine, expertise in designing the garment and fitting it to the individual's specifications really deserved to be called an art. Buttons or laces were used to fasten the breeches at the knee and below, leather patches (or "strappings") had to be stitched on inside the knee and at the calf to improve grip and prolong wear, and material had to be relatively loose above the knee for purposes of comfort. And there you have your *traditional breeches*—flaring at the thigh, gripping tightly at the knee, and disappearing smoothly beneath the boot. Fly fronts could be made simply with buttons or with drop

What Victoria Knew

Underwear has only recently become noticeable in tack shops and catalogs, in large part thanks to the development of suitable undergarments for other sports. Sports bras come in various styles—traditional, slip-on, tank top, and so on—and in various materials—all cotton, polyester, spandex, nylon, or a combination. Each rider will have her own preferences, depending on her shape and size, but the most important considerations are comfort, support, and breathability (wicking moisture away from the skin to keep you cool and dry). Although sports bras can be obtained anywhere athletic gear is sold, equestrian underpants are definitely a specialty item, with Polarfleece padding and/or special seams to prevent chafing and discomfort, and kneelength styles to minimize panty lines under snug breeches. Riding shorts, with padding in crucial areas, are also available for men. Cold-weather underwear of pure silk or polyester creates a snug but lightweight layer to help you retain warmth while allowing moisture to escape. Stirrup bottoms keep pants in place; rib-knit cuffs for pants and shirts will help prevent slipping.

fronts buttoning at the sides over a buttoned fly. (Ladies' breeches, when they were worn, had modest side buttons, of course—later replaced, as were men's buttons, by zippers.) It is believed by some experts that the flare of breeches was particularly exaggerated for women—to hide the hip's curve for the sake of modesty.

This distinctive style was practical because sturdy cotton or wool fabrics were not stretchy. Cavalry twill, one of the most popular traditional materials, was developed from a double twill during the early years of World War One (for the cavalry, of course) when it was discovered that a twill running to the left (instead of right) with the yarn twisted against the direction of the weave resulted in a remarkably strong material. In fact, it took 600 miles of woolen or worsted yarn to make a 53-yard piece of the stuff, which was heavy, solid, and attractive at the same time. Cotton or wool whipcord too was strong, even more so than gabardine, and had the advantage of not picking up animal hairs. These were definite improvements over the buckskin or doeskin that Beau Brummel and his dandy colleagues tried to put over on the world in the name of sleek fashion. Worn skin-tight, these leather breeches were terribly uncomfortable, especially in the rain (though they looked wonderful in the drawing room). Even the Prince Regent in those days tried white kidskin but only once, for it was not strong enough to contain his royal person.

Then, in the mid-20th century, thanks to the U.S. Equestrian Team's observation of ski teams at the Winter Olympics, came rayon, nylon, spandex, and the other synthetics, which suddenly made it possible for breeches to stretch—two ways, four ways, and, maybe someday, even eight ways. Thanks to the use of an elastic thread called *spandex* (DuPont's trademark is Lycra), *stretch* breeches could be made well fitting without the help of a custom tailor and, for the first time since the demise of leather breeches, the garment could be designed without the customary flare (or peg) above the knees. These fabrics are also easy to clean, and they hold their shape (even if the wearer doesn't hold his or hers). Breeches of stretch fabrics became so widely popular that for a time it was impossible to buy them in cotton or twill short of applying to a custom tailor. This is, thankfully, no longer the case, as riders quickly realized that stretch breeches weren't without their problems. They are not particularly flattering, for instance, if your figure is imperfect, and they aren't quite as well-ventilated as cotton or wool fabrics. Also, they don't wear as well as the traditional breeches, and one should take care in buying a new pair—by sitting on a saddle—since they tend to pinch behind the knee in a sitting position. But the stretchiness is definitely a good thing, so the synthetics are now combined with cotton—a small percentage of synthetic (usually spandex) to a large percentage of cotton. The development of synthetic suedes for patches at the knee or covering the full seat and of Velcro fastenings helped to complete the evolution of modern riding breeches, although perhaps the most significant change is in the attitude of manufacturers who finally realized that not all riders are reed-slim and began to provide sizes for the full-bodied as well. There are even maternity breeches available for the truly dedicated.

There are strict rules about the proper material and color for breeches worn in the hunt field. Synthetics are frowned upon, only white is permitted with a scarlet coat or formal black riding coat, and then only for the master, the hunt staff, and gentleman members (or entrants in an appointments class at a show). Lady members wear buff or brown breeches; the staff and gentleman members may wear buff or brown, but only if the individual hunt allows it. Other riders in the field may wear buff, canary, or rust; gray, light green, and other colors are available, but should be worn only for cubbing and hacking. Brown and navy are popular now for informal wear—another credit to the U.S. Equestrian Team and its international experience.

Jodhpurs were brought by the English from India because of the greater comfort they afford in hot weather, as well as the ease of wearing the accompanying short boots. Like breeches, jodhpurs usually flared above the knee until recent years, when the stretch fabrics took over. They may or may not flare at the ankle, but all (except Kentucky jodhpurs) usually have cuffs and are reinforced at the knee. As with breeches, colors should be conservative—beige, brown, canary, and gray are most popular—and it is nice, although not necessary, to consider the color of your horse in selecting them. Cotton-denim and wide-wale-corduroy jodhpurs are popular variations, the former for schooling, the latter for winter wear. Pants for saddle-seat suits are sometimes still made of wool, since they must match the coats, which are usually wool worsted. However, polyesters are creeping in here too and are often preferred for warm-weather costumes. The *"Kentucky"*

pants developed by Meyers of Lexington, Kentucky, and worn by saddle-seat riders are actually variations on jodhpurs, reinforced at the knee and flared cuffless over the boot. (They were once shorter, to reveal rather than cover the boot.) Some are made of black or dark-brown material with satin stripes down the sides, like tuxedo trousers, for formal evening classes on gaited-horses. Riding pants of tweed or other materials to match riding jackets are also popular nowadays for informal hacking or afternoon saddle-seat riding. Pants clips can be worn with flared legs to prevent complications with stirrups.

Happily for traditionalists, denim is still made of cotton, and Levi's (or Lees or Wranglers, or the other kinds of dungarees) are still made of denim. Levi Strauss was a New York tailor who went West to find gold in 1849—and instead he found miners wearing the wrong kind of clothes. He panned his own gold by selling them pants made of the cloth that he had expected to sell for tents and quickly ordered as much additional duck and denim as he could get from New York. (Duck, incidentally—from the Dutch word *doek*, meaning cloth or, particularly, canvas—is a closely woven cotton twill, originally a linen canvas; denim is a firm twilled cotton made with a colored warp and white filling threads, the name coming from the French *de Nîmes*, referring to the town in France famous for its manufacture of serge cloth. And if you're interested, "dungaree" is from the Hindi word *dügrï;* meaning pants made of twill, and "jeans" originally stems from the French name for Genoa, the town in Italy known for its production of cloth.)

The pants that Levi Strauss designed were intended for heavy wear and comfort in the mines, and cowboys all over the West quickly found them suitable for riding as well. At first they were made in brown or natural canvas color, but Strauss happened on an indigo-blue dye as the most distinctive and stain-camouflaging color he could find, and he had it woven into the denim that we see today all over the world. As he continued to refine the pants, which became known as Levi's, he used copper rivets for the pockets and strain points, and a great American tradition was born. Cowboys resisted the rivets at first as a low-caste innovation, but by the 1890's they had caught on. At that point, complete with heavy-duty orange thread and an oilcloth ticket identifying the garment, *Levi*'s as we know them now were worn everywhere in the West. The

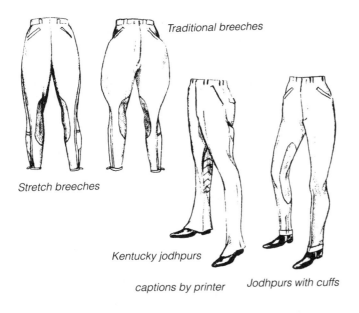

Traditional breeches

Stretch breeches

Kentucky jodhpurs

captions by printer

Jodhpurs with cuffs

patent on the design lasted until 1908, when many other manufacturers got into the act.

Because the stock saddle and the Western cow pony do not require posting at the trot, Western riding pants don't have to be snug at the knee, but legs must be narrow and tapered to fit into boots, and comfort demands close-fitting hips and a low waist. Long hours in the saddle demand the utmost in durability. As they wear and are washed, blue jeans, or dungarees, become a faded blue, soft, and especially well fitting. Because it took time and heavy work to make them so, the faded look was a desirable sign of achievement. Nowadays, of course, one can buy Levi's or other denim pants already softened and faded; where else but in America can you pay someone to do so much work for you, even wearing your own pants! Jeans are also decorated these days with various unnecessary but often attractive designs and features. Flared pants are no good for riders—at least, not without pants clips—and decorations don't matter so much, as long as the material is sturdy; and the rider is fortunate in that for jeans, special catalogs and custom tailors are hardly necessary today. Care should be taken, however, to avoid badly placed or sewn seams at the seat and inseam, which can cause considerable discomfort. Suspenders and belts were not common in the old West, although sashes were occasionally worn, as well as holsters and belts (or whangs) for chaps. In the new West, belts—preferably with a large silver buckle incised with elaborate designs—are an integral part of the costume.

CHAPS

Leggings made of calfskin or pigskin were and are a traditional part of informal British garb. These developed from the "start-ups" worn by peasants in the 16th century—woolen or linen leg wrappings held by a string at the ankle. Because they were not tailored to fit or made from expensive materials, start-ups were practical only as protection, but as they became more sophisticated, leather was used to improve the grip on the saddle. It was more durable and better-fitting as well. Leggings are still available in England today, but in this country, *schooling* and *polo chaps* are relatively common, usually custom-tailored with a tapered zipper leg (often improved with elastic) and an adjustable buckle front or back or both. Made of full-grain natural cowhide with the rough (suede) side out, chaps are long-lasting and comfortable, and make for a wonderfully secure seat. They are also warm in cold weather (and in warm weather too, which may be a disadvantage in some areas). When appearances don't matter, chaps are often preferred to breeches, and certainly to any pants not designed for riding in an English saddle. They are long—to the ankle; and as any Westerner would point out they are plain old shotgun, or wingless, chaps, which are a far cry from English leggings.

Chaps are certainly a more familiar sight in the West, where they have a good long history. In Mexico, riders wore big flaps of leather called *armas* that fastened over the front of the saddle and hung down on each side, tucking over the legs like a robe. These were designed to protect the rider against cactus or mesquite and were extremely useful, except when one dismounted and left them in the saddle. Eventually, armas were made to fit the man rather than the saddle and became known as *armitas*, which were leather shields that hung from a belt around the waist and came down to the boot tops, attaching around the leg with leather thongs. These too were relatively clumsy, and gradual refinement resulted in chaps as we know them. (This word is pronounced "shaps," incidentally. It is short for the Spanish word *chaparejos* or *chaparreras*, meaning leather breeches. This word derives from the root word *chaparro*, or evergreen oak, which referred to the oak thickets that were so abundant in Southern Texas.) These early chaps were closed around the legs, permanently sewn, often with fringe down the outer seam, and resembled Indian leggings except that they had no seat. Just after the Civil War, Texans usu-

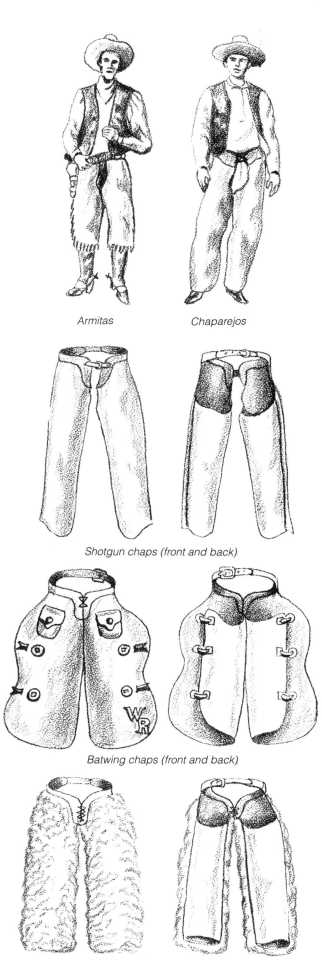

Armitas   Chaparejos

Shotgun chaps (front and back)

Batwing chaps (front and back)

Woolies (front and back)

ally referred to them as leggins, if only to avoid using a Mexican word, but chaps they became in any case, especially as their use spread over the whole West. This type was the *shotgun* variety, since the legs resembled the twin barrels of a shotgun. Because they were hot and difficult to get on and off, wraparound open-leg chaps were devised in the Southern states. Nevertheless, cowboys in the North hung on to their shotguns for the warmth, and that style became associated with mountain men, who called them Texas legs. Lone Star cowboys, in the meantime, refined the open-leg chap into what became known as a *Texas wing.* In this style, a wing, or outer flap, was attached to the inside part of the chap (the part between the leg and the horse) with leather thongs held by conches or rosettes, the flap being left loose to extend back over the leg for additional protection. Some cowboys favored chaps with wide, flaring wings, called *batwing chaps* for obvious reasons, which they could easily pull on and off over boots and spurs simply by unsnapping the conches, loosing the whang around the waist, and backing away. Later on, chap makers cut away the lower part of the inside leg and curved it so that it could not catch on the stirrup (this was the Cheyenne leg). Originally the chap was fastened all the way down to the boot, but now it is generally left open from knee strap down. In some areas, where brush was not thick, half chaps, or chinks, were preferred, because they were cooler. Like the shotguns, chinks derived from *armitas* and came down just to the boot tops. They attached with thongs rather than being sewed together like shotguns.

In most places chaps were made of cowhide, but in cold, brush-free prairies, where chaps were worn for protection against the cold rather than against thorns, they were often made of sheepskin or angora goat hide, with fur intact. *Woollies,* or angoras, were usually worn in the North, although they—like most other chaps— were manufactured in Texas. Like boots and spurs, chaps were usually plain for everyday wear, but cowboys with money and a fancy taste could dress them up as much as they pleased. Conchas of silver or nickel were elaborately patterned or engraved; initials could be spelled out in nailhead brads on the wings; and pockets (in front of the leg) could be made of a different-colored leather. Sometimes the material of the chaps itself could be gussied up; one King Fisher of South Texas even went as far as to "borrow" the hide of a visiting circus tiger. The hides of equally unfortunate

Apparel by Mail
———— Ω ————

TACK-SHOP CATALOGS USUALLY carry a wide range of styles and sizes in riding clothes for English and Western riding, either from name manufacturers or under the name of the shop. In buying clothes by mail, follow very carefully the instructions given on the catalog's order form. Give your regular size for coats, shirts, or pants only if that size always fits you well; if in doubt, buy the larger size and have it altered if necessary. For greater accuracy, enclose with your order your overall height in stocking feet, your weight, and exact taped measurements of your arms (from point of shoulder to one inch above the thumb), back (from midneck to waist), circumference of bust, waist, and hips (over the buttocks), outseam (from natural waistline to the floor in stocking feet), inseam (from crotch to floor), and calf at the widest point. Most catalogs feature measurement charts along with their order blanks.

English riding coats come in all types of material (as with prizefights, in the lightweight, middleweight, and heavyweight divisions), in synthetics, wool, and corduroy; and in conservative solid colors, gaudy patterns, and tweeds. When in doubt, go for the natural material in the conservative, solid color. The selection of material and the quality of tailoring are what make the difference in price, since cuts tend to be traditional. Correct hunting coats and hacking jackets in a Continental (double vent), traditional (single vent), or frock style, and formal cuts, such as the swallowtail or weasel-belly styles, are available ready made or custom made. Saddle-seat suits (with long, regular, or short coats) are also available ready made in double knit, wool worsted, or gabardine. If you are ordering a custom-made coat, ask for a sample of the material and the range of prices before you order. If you order a ready-made coat by mail, be prepared to ask your own tailor to make adjustments so that the coat allows freedom of movement at the shoulders and is well-fitting at the waist.

In ordering pants, be sure to note whether cuffs, belt loops, and pockets (if you want them) are included and that side zippers (if you want them) are used for women's pants; specify otherwise if you want otherwise. In buying Western pants, be sure that the seams at the seat and inseam are properly made so that they won't cause rubbing in the saddle; many Western styles today are designed for people who never ride, so be sure you get what you want.

Chaps are available ready made in three or more standard sizes, depending on the manufacturer, and are usually much cheaper than custom-made chaps. The best chaps are cut to measure from a single piece of top-grain cowhide and, since these will last a long time, they are well worth the investment. Schooling or polo chaps (shotguns) are usually made suede-side out with zippers running down to the ankle; batwing chaps, fringed shotguns, and show chaps can be made in various colors, grain- or suede-side out, with many different stitching designs and ornaments. In ordering chaps, specify your waist size (below the belt at the hipbone), inseam and outseam length (with boots on), length from knee to floor, your height, weight, and the measurements of upper thigh, midthigh, one inch above the knee, and the calf at the widest point, with boots on.

Catalogs offering English (hunt seat and dressage) apparel are: Devon-Aire, 4904 Savarese Circle, Tampa, FL 33634; Dover, Box 5837, Holliston, MA 01746; Eisers, P. O. Box T, Hazleton, PA 18201; Miller's, 235 Murray Hill Parkway, East Rutherford, NJ 07073; State Line Tack, P.O. Box 1217; Plaistow, NH 03865; Tack in the Box (dressage), 2413 82nd Street SW, Salem, OR 97301. The only catalog in which we could find great (and gently) used apparel, as well as gear for side-saddle riders is The Old Habit, 8363 West Main Street, P. O. Box 726, Marshall, VA 22115. Another specialist, in custom-made dressage apparel, is Riding Right, Kardas Road, Valley Falls, NY 12185.

Catalogs offering Western apparel include: Denny Sergeant's Western World, 13600 Stemmons, Farmers Branch, TX 75234 (800-383-3669); Miller Stockman Western Wear, P. O. Box 5127, Denver, CO 80217; and Sheplers, P. O. Box 7702, Wichita, KS 67277. These two Web sites may also be useful: www.cowboytrail.com and www.west-mall.com. Ω

wolves, cougars, and horses were pressed into similar service, though cowhide remained the most practical material for the working cowhand. In addition to their normal function, chaps, or leggings, had a special use: "to give a leggin" meant to punish a cowboy by beating him with a pair of chaps.

Shirts

Although there doesn't seem to be much in common among blue work shirts, polo shirts, and body shirts, they were all originally designed for the same purpose: to be worn by riders. Regardless of style, the most important requirements of a riding shirt are that it be absorbent (horses may sweat, but gentlemen perspire too, and even, as the old expression has it, ladies glow); easily cleaned; warm when necessary and cool when not; shaped at the waist to prevent riding up; and free of restriction at the shoulder. Since English and Western riding shirts were usually worn beneath a vest and/or a coat, appearance was less important than comfort. In England, shirts could be woolen or cotton or silk. In the hunting field they were invariably white, with a soft collar to which a stock could be attached. For informal hunting or hacking, a shirt could be colored or checked, and like the informal tweed riding jacket, it was dubbed *ratcatcher*—implying, no doubt, that the informal hunter was no better than a hunter of rodents, one who traveled on foot accompanied by a ferret or a dog.

Riding shirts originally had a high cravat, probably borrowed from the court, but the detachable white stock, or hunting cravat, has been in common use since the second half of the 19th century. Polo shirts, originating in India for the sport and designed to be comfortable in warm weather, had an open collar and buttoned down to midbreast. Shirts were shaped at the waist for a good fit. Fishtail shirts were particularly effective, since their long tails came between the legs to button onto the front of the shirt, making them remain in place no matter how strenuous the ride. The body shirts fashionable today for women are modern versions of these practical garments.

Western shirts in the 19th century were almost always *pullovers*, usually of wool or flannel (or linsey-woolsey, a combination of linen and wool), with buttons to mid-chest (or none at all) and an open collar. Military shirts were made of gray flannel until 1881, when

Ratcatcher shirt with choker

How to Buy Riding Shirts and Neckwear

Most riding shirts—English or Western—come in regular shirt sizes, but care must be taken to be sure that they are not constricting at the shoulders and that the material can be easily cleaned. Durability and warmth (or coolness) are other important considerations, depending on your particular riding style. Simple ratcatcher shirts with or without straight collars and button-on ties will cost about $15 for cotton and slightly more for knit fabrics. Chokers that can be buttoned onto shirts are made in velveteen, cotton, or silk.

Permanent-press oxford-cloth stocks and silk four-fold stocks can be obtained ready-tied or plain. Stock pins can be as cheap or as expensive as you like.

Western shirts are widely available in any number of styles and prices, in muslin, wool challis, or even velour with sequins or special embroidery.

the Army borrowed blue wool from miners and lumbermen and cowboys, who generally didn't bother about a collar unless they were dressing up. Fancy civilian shirts (or boiled shirts) were usually linen pullovers of the same style, with or without ruffles at the neck and with detachable collars. Montgomery Ward, the famous early mail-order house, advertised around 1870 five boxes of paper collars (with suspenders thrown in) for a dollar, or five linen shirtfronts (or dickeys) for the same price. But cowboys preferred hickory (sturdy cotton) flannel, or wool pullovers with no collar at all but a bandana to protect the neck. The fancy decorated frontier shirts so familiar today (on country-and-Western singers more than on riders) were adapted from the old pullover shirts. The only similarity in style is the tapered waist and the construction of the shoulder, which allowed for free movement of the shoulders and arms.

NECKWEAR

Stocks, which to some may seem an unnecessary frill, actually have a purpose for the rider beyond covering up the neck. Made traditionally of white piqué linen or silk, *stocks* could be made in various widths to be used in case of accident as a bandage or sling for the rider or as a tourniquet or pressure bandage for the horse. Although ready-tied stocks that fasten behind the neck are much easier to put on, they are not allowed in formal hunting or appointments classes. The *stock pin*, usually of gold and measuring $2^{1}/_{2}$ to $3^{1}/_{2}$ inches long, is essentially a plain safety pin, which also can be pressed into service in emergencies, although its primary purpose is to keep the stock from bulging in front. The pin should always be worn horizontally, to avoid lacerating the chin. Informal riders in English saddles often prefer simple *button-on chokers* or ties worn with plain or checked shirts; hacking scarves—worn like ascots—are popular in England, where polka dots are the fashionable design, although Hermès scarves would certainly be appropriate anywhere today.

Because Western pullover shirts had terrible collars or none at all and because riders didn't need or want to bother with detachable collars, *bandanas* were the traditional form of neckwear. These were ordinary farm handkerchiefs made of printed cotton in colorful red or blue designs, although silk was preferred if one could afford it, since it was cooler in summer and warmer in winter. Bandanas (from the Hindi word *bañdhnū*) are usually folded in a triangle to tie at the front or back in lieu of a collar, though they can also be worn inside the shirt to make an open collar look dressier, or tucked into a pocket. On the range, they are still worn close-wrapped around the neck (or tied down over hat brims) to protect the rider from cold, the sun, or brambles. In dust storms, too, the bandana can be pulled up over the face to keep nose and mouth from getting filled up. (It offered another sort of protection to the stagecoach bandit who preferred to remain anonymous.) Like the stock, the bandana can also double as a tourniquet or bandage in an emergency. It can be used as well to strain unclean water, and not surprisingly, it will perform the numerous other services traditionally associated with handkerchiefs. In town, one could wrap a length of black ribbon around the neck under a paper or celluloid collar (the latter only if you didn't smoke, for it was highly flammable) and tie it around your neck in a bow, but the bandana was very much more convenient.

HOW TO TIE A STOCK

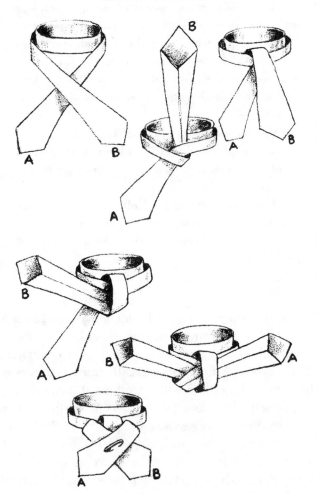

Vests

Although most people think of the vest—or waistcoat, or weskit—as a rather unnecessary part of a three-

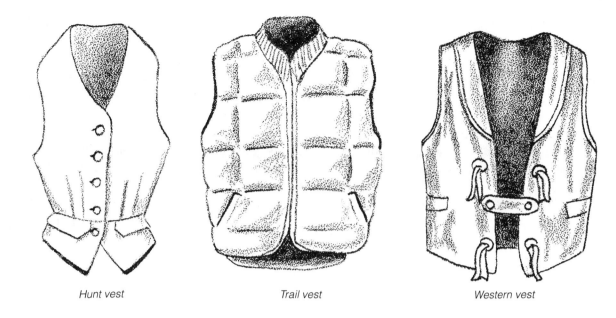

Hunt vest   Trail vest   Western vest

piece suit, it is actually one of the oldest and most useful articles of clothing for the rider. During medieval times, horsemen often wore vests, usually in the form of short, sleeveless leather jerking. Knights wore them as padding under coats of mail; lesser soldiers wore them as the armor itself. Wool-lined leather vests were worn in the U.S. Army as recently as World War One. Furnished with pockets, made of stout, warm material (for protection against weather, slings, arrows, and even musket fire), and sleeveless to allow the rider freedom of arm movement, vests have been equally important in the horseman's apparel in both England and America.

In the hunting field, the vest was refined for the sake of appearance and is traditionally made of plain wool melton cloth in yellow or white or buff, with four pockets (each with flaps) and five buttons. Long enough in the back to cover the kidneys, often with satin insets (now nylon) rather than wool, and seamed at the waist for comfort in the saddle, vests are still practical garments for the sake of warmth and extra pockets. Informal riders often prefer knitted or tattersall-checked vests, named for the famous London horse market.

Western vests are usually sturdier affairs, made of buckskin or stiff duck cloth. They probably derive from the waistcoat of colonial times—really a sleeveless coat with lapels and pockets to be worn under a heavier topcoat. In the old West, yellowish buckskin vests were widely available—conveniently sleeveless for the rider, warm enough when buttoned for a hardy life out-of-doors, and soft for comfort. Lined with fleece, they could be made warmer, and so they are today. Although fancier vests were and still are made, decorated with porcupine-quill beads, elaborate stitching, buckskin fringes or black braid edging, or cloth inlays, most hardworking riders prefer the plain version.

The informal rider, east or west, tends to use the same cold-weather garment—the down-filled nylon *trail vest* that looks like a ski jacket without sleeves. This vest can be worn over a sweater or shirt or under an outercoat. With a roll collar at the neck and throat and 2 inches of extra length at the back, it is wonderfully warm and even more comfortable than a full jacket for riding.

Coats

As we noted earlier, the ordinary suit coats that we know and wear today owe their basic design to the riding coat of the English country gentleman of the 18th century. So does the formal swallowtail coat, which closely resembles the formal riding coat still worn in the hunt field. Rules for proper garb at the hunt are strictly observed in most areas where fox hunting is taken seriously (see the end of this chapter for those rules), although to the casual observer these may seem overly fussy. There are reasons for these rules, one of which is indeed formality for the sake of tradition. More practical, however, are the differences in clothing worn by the master of foxhounds, the huntsmen, the whippers-in, the gentleman and lady members, juniors, guests, farmers, and servants. Obviously, these differences exist to enable everyone in the field to distinguish one category of rider from another and to tell hunters of one locale from another. These variations may be as subtle as the number or design of buttons or as obvious as the color or cut of the riding coat. Before

we get into these distinctions, however, let's look at the basic requirements for the riding coat itself.

For comfort in the saddle and a trim appearance, the coat should be narrow at the waist with the skirts allowed to cut away toward the back to allow for freedom of the leg. Lapels should be short (so that the wind won't flap them around) and equipped with a throat tab (so that the coat may be buttoned at the neck). Side pockets with flaps to keep the contents inside have obvious practical purposes, as does the long center slit at the back—or double slit with a fuller skirt—to allow the skirts to cover the saddle (and not to be sat upon)

Hacking outfit   Hunt wear   Dressage wear   Saddle-seat suit

and a waterproof lining to protect the coat's fabric from the sweat of the horse and saddlesoap stains. Other pockets may also be part of the garment—a breast pocket, a ticket or whistle pocket (on the upper right side), and at least one inside pocket, called a poacher's pocket and made large enough to hold a hare. The material should be sturdy and easily cleaned for long wear. Several traditional cloths are still used today. Melton cloth is a densely woven wool, which is soft and warm and yet keeps its shape. The name comes from the town of Melton Mowbray in England, where it first became popular. Boncloth is like melton but even smoother. Twill is made of wool or worsted yarn, which is twisted to make the fabric more durable. Variations of this include Bedford cord, in which the wool or cotton is given a rounded cord effect in the weaving; covert, or Venetian twill, which is lightweight and has a flecked appearance; and whipcord, which is very strong with a noticeable rib and a resistance to animal hair. Melton and twill are still used these days, although they are very expensive. Polyesters are cheaper and lighter in weight but not so long-lasting; they are often used in combination with wool or cotton. Dacron, silk, rayon, and madras are other materials worn often in warm climates.

Formal hunting—whether in the field or in appointments classes—requires the use of certain traditional cuts for the riding coat. The *frock coat* has long skirts, with square corners and buttons to the waist for the master and rounded skirts for gentlemen members. The *swallowtail* (or shadbelly) coat is a double-breasted garment that cuts straight across at the waist and has long tails extending down the back. This cut is usually preferred by lady members, although others may wear it, and other cuts are also acceptable. *Weasel-belly coats,* which are also called cutaways or Dublingtons, are a variation of the shadbelly. All of these formal cuts must be custom-made, but many kinds of simpler riding coats are available ready made. Olympic jackets are variations of the frock coat, except that the skirts are shorter and the materials usually lighter in weight. These are what one usually sees on riders in open-jumper classes; unlike most riding clothes, they may be quite bright in color—scarlet, green, or blue as well as black. For informal riding and for equitation, hunter, and jumper classes that do not require appointments, brown or gray tweed or conservatively solid-color riding coats are ideal. *Traditional-length* coats have a single vent in back with no pleats or belt, and usually (but not always) a seamed waist. Length depends on the build of the rider; the bottom of the coat generally comes as far down the thigh as the rider's wrist can reach. The more recent and more stylish *continental length* is shorter (if less flattering for wider, less-than-expert riders), because it has a double vent in back, which cannot extend as far up the back as the single vent and thus necessitates a shorter skirt. In the days when breeches and jodhpurs were flared at the thigh, the skirts of the coat were ample to allow for them; nowadays coats are much trimmer, although a long look—especially in saddle-seat suits—is flattering and desirable. Riding coats generally have three or four buttons to the waist (buttons on some old coats came below the waist), a high front, narrow notched lapels, and at least two pockets with flaps.

There is always a good deal of concern about buttons and collars when formal hunting apparel is discussed, mainly because these are the ways in which one hunt distinguishes itself from the others. Hunt colors (on the detachable collar) and insignia (on the buttons) may be worn by members of the hunt only by invitation, and "earning one's colors" is a great honor. (In appointments classes, entrants are required to carry a copy of the letter authorizing the use of colors by the master.) Until one reaches this stage, collars and buttons must match the coat instead of the hunt livery. The number of buttons also varies, depending on one's rank. Six-buttoned coats (four in front and two over the back vent) are traditionally reserved for the master and hunt staff; three or four buttons are worn by everyone else. Gentlemen wear hunt buttons on the front of their coats; ladies wear them on the vest or on the back of the hat to hold the hat guard. The hunt staff may also wear buttons on their sleeves—either a relic of the days when sleeves buttoned closed or a handy way of carrying extra buttons.

The coats of *saddle-seat suits,* unlike hunting coats, must match the pants in color and material. These coats are quite long—about halfway (or more) down the thigh—with rounded flared skirts that may have a center vent or long double-inverted pleats, usually embroidered with silk arrowheads. Made of fine wool worsted or double-stretch worsteds, saddle-seat suits are generally black, navy blue, or brown—sometimes with pinstripes or faint patterns—and silk or nylon linings that may be plain, colored, or handsomely patterned. For evening wear, coats may be designed like tuxedos with satin, nylon, or silk lapels in the same color as the coat. Silk brocades were popular during the 1960s but matte-finish, lighter-colored monotone coats are currently in vogue. Accessories or jacket color are occasionally designed to match the browband and ribbons worn by the horse.

Informal gaited classes are somewhat less rigid about color, and gray, green, beige, and white—in season—are allowed, with plain matching lapels. Saddleseat coats usually have two buttons and semipeak lapels for a stylish appearance.

Fit is very important in a riding coat, especially in the shoulders, which should be restricted as little as possible. This is perhaps the most important reason why a rider should steer clear of the hacking jackets designed and sold for street wear. These fashionable garments often omit pockets and insulated linings for the sake of a trim look, and the material used is generally less sturdy, since nonriders rarely encounter athletic situations or mud splattered up by the hooves of galloping animals. These jackets for nonriders are usually more expensive as well, for the sake of the designer, and it behooves the serious rider to investigate the clothing specially designed for riding. If a readymade garment is not suitable, then one should consider a coat made to order by a tailor familiar with the requirements of riders. With good care, the coat will last for a long time and be well worth the investment.

Happily, good care of the woolen riding coat need not involve the expense of professional attention. Dry cleaning is not necessary and may even cause damage by removing dye from the buttons. Steam pressing will make good cloth brittle, for it extracts natural oils, and the fabric may be damaged by the pressure. Allow a wet and muddy coat to dry naturally (not in front of a fire) and then brush it with a stiff brush (not on a hanger, or the shoulders and collar may stretch out of shape). If dirt still remains, sponge the area with lukewarm water and a detergent until the surface becomes damp but not soaked. Do not rub, and don't use soap, but use that stiff brush again and allow the material to dry slowly. To remove a shine on the surface, rub gently with a warm damp cloth. During periods when a coat is not being used, do not simply hang it in a closet. Lay it flat in layers of newspaper and surround it with Epsom salts (not camphor balls), which are cheap and odorless and will not affect the color of the garment.

Although Western riders often prefer a vest to a coat, *short denim jackets* cut at the waist and often adorned with a brown corduroy collar have been as traditional for years as they are popular now. Made like Levi's with metal rivets and orange thread, they match the pants nicely and made up what was probably the first leisure suit. *Chaquetas* were heavy cloth or leather jackets worn in the Texas-Mexico brush country. As with English riding coats, there are certain features that these short jackets must include for the sake of the rider: full sleeves, at least two button-flap pockets, a waist tab to make the jacket snug around the waist, and—for cold weather—a lining of blanket material or soft fleece, for additional protection, with a collar that buttons across the throat.

FOUL-WEATHER GEAR

Although cowboys in the Far West may have to contend more with weather than the English rider who can always simply turn around and go home, horsemen should always be prepared to deal with the elements wherever they ride. In 1823, Charles MacIntosh of Glasgow received a patent for a solution of naphtha and crude rubber cemented together, and this waterproof material quickly became popular throughout the British Isles. In 1825, the Duke of York wore a blue cape of the stuff, but before long special riding macintosh coats and aprons were designed specifically for the rider. *Riding aprons* were simple affairs that dropped 8 inches below the knee and fastened on the right side with a belt at the waist; a leg strap made certain that breeches were covered. They could be folded easily into a large pocket for carrying, but were somewhat less effective than the *macintosh coat*. With taped and sealed seams, a belt and buckles of a soft finish that would not cause friction, ventilated underarms, a long back vented with a fan of the same material to cover the saddle, knee flaps, and a pommel strap to keep the whole rig in position, this very useful garment still exists today. Now made of rubber, rubberized nylon or cotton, or clear plastic, raincoats of this type are lightweight and easily packed. The three-quarter length is preferred, with generous pleats at the back for easy mounting, raglan sleeves for freedom of movement, elastic or snap closings at the wrist, and straps for the cantle, legs, and pommel.

A Coat of a Different Color

It's about time we debunked a few old myths. For one thing, 19th-century hunting prints aside, scarlet coats were not and are not worn by everyone in the field, but are restricted to the master, the huntsmen, the whippers-in, and invited gentlemen members. (Ladies, juniors, and guests must all wear black.) Even then, scarlet is often replaced by the hunt livery, or whatever is traditional for a particular hunt (which can be almost any color but green, which is reserved for hunt servants). For another thing, scarlet—not pink—is the accurate name for the color. Many believe that the word pink derived from the name of a London tailor who obviously made a fortune while reddening the English countryside, but no evidence has been found that such a tailor ever existed. It is far more likely that the word pink was first applied to the scarlet riding coat as a journalistic slur. It was used as early as 1828 in an Oxford newspaper, perhaps coming from the old expression "Fight in scarlet, hunt in red, dance in pink"—which refers to the fading color of an old field coat whose brilliance would disappear through years of cleaning. The coloring agent used to make the old coats was cochineal dye—made from a paste in which the blood of Mexican cactus beetles was mixed in a solution of tin.

In any event, scarlet undoubtedly became the traditional color for hunting for political reasons. Fox hunting was a Tory sport, and red was the Tory color, having derived from the royal livery worn for deer hunting (all deer in England having belonged to the throne). And even then, the use of scarlet was not simply traditional but practical as well, for it is visible from a great distance, so that fallen or missing persons were less likely to be overlooked in the excitement of the chase. Scarlet is now used as well by Olympic and equestrian-team riders from countries where teams are not dressed in military garb, and this is the only occasion on which women are allowed to wear red.

In the West, *slickers,* or fishskins, voluminous enough to cover the whole saddle as well as the rider, were made of canvas duck treated with oil or paint to keep the rain out. Designed like coats, slickers had sleeves and pockets furnished with slits for easy access to pants pockets. Like the foul-weather gear worn by sailors, slickers are traditionally yellow for good visibility, but the material from which they are made nowadays is usually rubberized cloth or plastic, more durable than oilcloth. Mexican *ponchos,* worn in the South, are like blankets made of finely woven wool or wool and linen with a slit in the middle to accommodate the head. Although they fit less snugly than a coat, ponchos are effective protection, since the material sheds water and is very warm. Both slickers and ponchos are rolled and tied behind the saddle and are used for making bedrolls or covering packs or slapped in the face of cattle to turn them. The slicker could even stop a horse from bucking when tied behind the saddle with its ends hanging down the animal's sides.

Gloves

Like foul-weather gear, gloves have always been worn by riders for protection against weather, but they also serve to prevent rubbing and blisters caused by leather reins. Not only must the material be strong enough to afford such protection, but it must also be supple enough for the rider to maintain a good grip even in the rain and a sensitive feel on the reins or rope. Leather has always been the preferred material and pigskin the preferred leather, for it is sturdy, supple, and soft. Many other materials have also been and are still used. In the West, buckskin, horse or steer hide, and even kangaroo leather are used, and in the East, *string gloves,* knitted in one piece from white cotton yarn, are very popular, because they give a good grip, are cheap, and are easily cleaned. *Rain gloves* for the hunting field, made of white or colored cotton, are carried under the girth, with each glove on its proper side of the saddle, thumb against the palm of the glove and against the saddle, the fingers toward the front.

In recent years, leather-like vinyls have been developed for *riding gloves.* In addition to being cheaper than leather, these gloves are elasticized for perfect fit and reinforced at the palm for long wear, and yet they are thin enough for maximum sensitivity. Variations on

Cold-Weather Apparel

A welcome new line of clothing that has emerged over the last few years is designed to keep the rider warm in spite of winter winds, sleet, and chill. Many specialized items, of course, are available virtually anywhere, not just through tack shops: ear warmers and socks, fleece vests and pullovers, snow boots and warm gloves. Some of these, however, are not intended to be worn under riding helmets or inside riding boots, and the chilly rider must look to tack shops for well-fitting garments that are suitable for use in the saddle and around the stable. Wonderful fabrics—such as Polartec and Polarfleece, Thinsulate, Larsloft, and Pebatex linings and insulation—have enabled manufacturers to produce clothing and boots that are comfortable, long-wearing, and shaped appropriately for riding. Layering is still the best approach, beginning with silk or synthetic long johns or underwear that wicks away moisture while enabling the body to retain warmth. Breeches are now made in waterproof or water-resistant fabrics lined with insulation and equipped with ankle zippers, stirrup straps, Velcro fasteners, and leather seats. There are even fleece stretch breeches with suede patches for casual wear, headbands designed to be worn under a helmet, and gloves lined with fleece and reinforced with leather. There is a wide range of cold-weather riding boots available, from paddock boots and shoes to full boots; in making your choice, be sure to go for a good heel, a removable insole (for drying and cleaning), good support and comfort, a waterproof surface (waxed leather), and a warm lining. If you prefer your regular riding boots, you might try Polar Warmers (from Riding Right), which slip over boots and fasten with Velcro to keep them snug.

the theme include crochet-back gloves with leather palms and mesh gloves with durable nylon palms and rubber strips for a good grip (Leather gloves in England were once made with knitted string inserts for the same reason and to protect the leather from wear.)

Gloves worn for *bull riding,* in which the cowboy's life (or at least the skin on his palm) can depend on the sturdiness of the material, are usually made of strong leather with long sleeves to protect the wrists. These gloves resemble the traditional Western gauntlets—now relatively rare, but very effective in preventing rope burns and in keeping cold wind from blowing up the sleeve. The flaring cuffs were often six inches long or longer and decorated in some way, more or less elaborately depending on taste. Fringed leather, Indian beadwork, nailheads worked into the leather, and colored stitching could be made in a variety of designs, many of them created by Indians and sold at trading

Slicker

Riding raincoat

Insulated winter riding boot and paddock boot

Western jackets are widely available in cotton, denim, or suede leather, and prices vary accordingly. Custom-made leather jackets can, of course, cost as much as you are willing to spend.

Outwear or foul-weather gear designed for riding can be made of clear, light plastic or specially treated fabric, with or without linings. A nylon or plastic jacket may cost very little while an imported Irish MacIntosh riding coat or an Australian wax-fabric coat may top $200.

posts. In spite of their usefulness, however, gauntlets were cumbersome to handle when not in use—they couldn't be fitted into a pocket, for one thing—and this may be the reason they went out of style. Elaborately decorated leather cuffs or bands of leather to fit over shirt cuffs at the wrist would help protect bare wrists against weather and preserve the cuffs of the shirt or coat from wear.

Polo gloves, traditionally worn on the left hand only (the one that gripped the reins), were usually ventilated like golf gloves, but polo players now often wear light full-leather gloves on both hands to avoid blisters.

String gloves

The least expensive riding gloves are made of cotton string, wool, or stretch fabrics; leather gloves or lined string gloves and wool-lined leather and special thermal gloves may run $25 or more. Heavy steerhide bull-rider gloves with long sleeves are useful.

Gloves may be available in standard sizes (4 to 10 for men, women, and children) or simply in small, medium, and large; stretch fabrics may be available in one size only.

Leather riding gloves

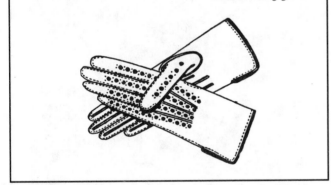

Whatever gloves you select, their usefulness will be extended by good care. Leather gloves may be cleaned with a solvent, but be sure to rinse off any substance, including soap, with a cloth moistened in lukewarm water, and to dry them naturally. Cotton gloves may be washed in mild soap and water; don't wring them out but dry them slowly—on your hands or a form if possible to keep them from shrinking or losing their shape.

Hats

Hats, like gloves, are considered a fashionable accessory in most areas, except when needed for protective purposes. Easter bonnets, straw boaters, and silk top hats hardly have a place in everyday contemporary dress, any more than white cotton or pigskin gloves do.

However, hats should be considered an integral part of the complete riding outfit, and not just an additional expense for the sake of style. Tricorne hats with elaborate feathers have disappeared, but top hats are still used in the hunting field—not the tall silk stovepipes but specially made protective hats designed to keep the rider's head intact should he take a tumble. *Riding top hats* are about $5/8$ inch lower in the crown than the formal silk hat (ladies' hats are lower still). They were once made of laminated twill and calico impregnated with shellac and ironed on a form in layers. The covering was beaver until silk became widely available in England after import duties were lifted many years ago. The brim was shaped and trimmed with a wide leather band. All riders wore adjustable draw cords at the chin and hat guards in back to keep the hat in place; ladies also wore hunting veils to protect their delicate complexions from the ravages of weather and mud. *Hat guards* are still required in formal hunting; they are loops that attach to a ring sewn inside the back of the coat collar, a little to the side.

Because William Coke, Duke of Norfolk (the one who started the revolution in men's clothing, you'll recall), had the unfortunate experience of losing his silk hat in mid-stride, he employed the hatmaking Bowler family of Southwark to design him a smaller, more wind-resistant hat with a rounded crown. First called the Coke hat or Billycock after its original wearer, it eventually took on the name of its maker. Off the hunting field and on the heads of racing enthusiasts, it became known as the *derby*, but for riding purposes it retained the shellacked crown for protective reasons.

In 1780 another design, the *hunt cap*, was introduced. When George III wore one in Windsor Park, it became quite fashionable, and it is still worn today by the hunt master and staff (and no one else in the field except for juniors). The term "capping fee"—the sum paid by nonmembers—evolved because the hunt secretary, who collected the fees, wore a hunt cap. This type of helmet was made in the same way as the top hat—with layers of laminated, shellacked material fashioned over a wooden block. The foundation material was felt, and the covering was velvet or velveteen; only the lining was silk, and that was quilted and padded with felt for further protection. Because the hat was close-fitting, a ventilation hole was necessary; this was placed on the top of the crown, covered with a screw-on button. The ribbon attached to the back of

Hunt cap   Derby   Top hat

the cap is used to distinguish the hunt staff from juniors (as if that were difficult to begin with) and paid wearers from unpaid wearers. Children's caps have one bow with the two tails pointing down. The master and the staff boast two bows and two tails, pointing up if paid, pointing down if not.

These styles have remained unchanged (except that top hats have lower crowns for hunt, dressage, and saddle-horse classes), but materials are now virtually indestructible heavy plastic or fiberglass, which is light as well as strong. Caps give better protection against superficial scalp wounds, and they don't interfere with hearing. Bowlers are better protection against more serious injuries, and they also prevent rain from dripping down the neck and protect ears and cheeks from brush. Collapsible visors, hammock chin straps, or harnesses, with or without protective chin cups, are a good deal more secure than the usual elastic cords that replaced the original adjustable draw cords. Velvet is still traditional for hunt caps, as silk is for top hats and derbies, but for everyday informal wear riders often prefer plain *schooling helmets*, which derive from polo and racing helmets designed more for protection than for looks.

Polo helmets were once made of three-ply natural cork, employing at least thirty pieces of cork laminated over rubber padding and crossed tapes within the crown. As with racing helmets, these were designed to cover the ears and were furnished with sturdy chin straps for additional protection, holes for ventilation, and even face shields like those worn by football players. Nowadays, heavy plastic or fiberglass has replaced cork, and inner cushions to prevent concussion and absorb shock are made of rubber or felt.

As of May 1, 1984, every junior (18 years and younger) exhibitor at American Horse Shows Association-recognized shows must wear a helmet with a safety harness and a collapsible brim whenever the rider is mounted anywhere on the show grounds. This rule puts horse shows in line with combined training and Pony Club requirements that headgear be sturdier and safer than hunt caps are (hunt caps' rigid brims have been known to snap on impact and injure the wearer's face). Some hunter-seat equitation riders use brimless Caliente-type helmets worn with a black fabric cover, although a number of traditional helmets and hats meet AHSA, as well as U.S. Combined Training Association and U.S. Pony Clubs, standards.

Needless to say, helmets do little good unless they are worn, and even then they're not much good if they don't fit snugly. Newspaper may be used as padding in an emergency—as for the casual rider who must borrow someone else's hat. Because head protection is of

Stetson   Schooling helmet   Polo helmet

Lexington lid-blocker safety helmet

extreme importance, especially for children and for beginners, no expense should be spared in acquiring this particular piece of gear.

In recent years a proliferation of lawsuits stemming from riding accidents has made hat manufacturers and retailers more nervous than a day-old foal. Accordingly, hats are now put through rigid testing for durability, but the word "safety" no longer appears in the merchandising of the hats. Lawyers advise that the words "protection" and "safety" create an implication that can lead to manufacturer liability in the event of an injury, so all sorts of disclaimers appear on labels and in tack-shop catalogs. Requiring a particular style of headgear is risky business, and even "recommending" one is suspect (see box on page 231).

Nevertheless, the American Horse Shows Association has mandated hunt caps with flexible peaks and what are popularly called "safety harnesses" (more accurately, solidly affixed leather or clean plastic chin straps) for all hunter, jumper, and equitation riders under the age of 18. Sensible riders of any age can also

be found wearing them, and not just when jumping over fences.

Schooling helmets have become popular for almost all styles of informal riding. Hot-weather riding comfort comes from a lightweight, ventilated model in white, over which a stretch cover can be fitted when the weather turns cooler or for more formal occasions.

Riding caps of tweed, fine wool, or felt have no protective function in falls, but they are good for keeping sun or rain out of the eyes. They must be designed with a snug crown and moderate wings to prevent their flying off at a gallop; in training gallops at the track, it is customary to turn the hat around front to back just to avoid this sort of problem. Men in informal saddle-horse classes nowadays prefer snap-brim felt or straw hats over derbies or top hats.

Like tweed caps, Western hats are no help in an accident, but they are one of the most distinctive features of a cowboy's gear, worn as much for style as for their usefulness in keeping the elements off one's head and out of one's eyes. They can also double as water buckets and as pillows during a night out on the range, and they come in handy for slapping ornery horses or fanning ornery fires. Western horsemen have always taken a good deal of pride in selecting the best available. There have been many different types of Western hats, not all of them of the ten-gallon variety. Soft felt slouch hats, wide-brimmed *planter's hats*, bowlers, and wool or wool-felt hats were all commonly worn in the 19th century, each acting as an index to the identity

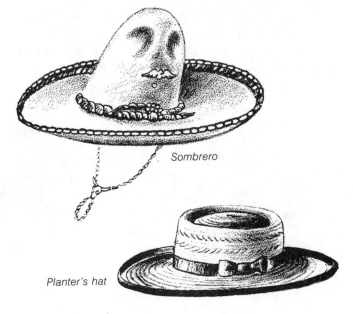

Sombrero

Planter's hat

Traditional silk or beaver top hats for hunting and dressage, with crowns ranging from 4 to 5", in sizes from 6½ to 7¾, will cost between $150 and $300 and are available at most tack shops that specialize in hunting gear. Saddle and hunt derbies will run from $60 to $100. Hat cords or guards in black or red range from $10 to $15.

Hunt caps with black velveteen covering can be had for as little as $30 or $40, but some models are more decorative than protective. Now that protective headgear comes in strong, lightweight materials and in various styles, including schooling helmets and the traditional velveteen cap, riders have few excuses for not wearing hats that meet ASTM standards and are certified by the Safety Equipment Institute (SEI). Be sure to look for these initials on the label before you buy. Troxel, Aussie Rider, Lexington, and Pro-Lite are among the manufacturers of these ASTM/SEI-approved products, which consist of a thin plastic outer shell and a thick inner shell of polystyrene, with a chin harness. Prices range from $50 to $100. Most manufacturers produce removable pads and foam inserts to provide a snug fit, but Lexington makes a helmet with an air pump that inflates the lining, a nice feature for children, who might be difficult to fit. And for those who are difficult to please, helmet covers come in different colors and patterns. Racing and polo helmets may have special face shields and safety harnesses.

In Western hats, safety is not as important a consideration (although some styles are sold with a

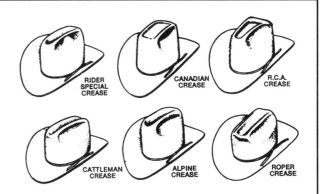

fiberglass lining), but style and material make the difference. Style can mean width of brim, height of crown, or type of hatband, but more important is the type of crease. Hats made by Stetson (St. Joseph, MO 64502) are individually hand-creased in various styles. Tack shops that carry the hats of this and other manufacturers may have several crease styles in stock, but if you are particular, write directly to the manufacturer. Materials rather than style are usually what determine price. Straw hats may cost as little as $30; beaver fur or mink can run $300 or more. Linings may be nylon or silk; sweat bands of synthetic or real leather. Hats in the moderate range—from $30 to $75—are usually of felt made from wool or fur, although synthetic felts may be had for less than $30. Western hat covers vary in price from $3 to $5; carrying cases may be $25 to $100, depending on the number of hats you want to carry; metal hat racks that attach to the ceiling (of your room, car, or truck) cost about $10.

and status of the wearer. Rich men in town tended toward high hats and bowlers—as did gamblers and gunfighters, though one could easily get into trouble for being "duded up" if one ventured out of town. (Butch Cassidy and his famous gang got into a different kind of trouble for wearing bowlers, but only because they were unwise enough to have their photographs taken while wearing them.) Wool hats were worn by poor men, and to be called one of the "woolhat bunch" was to be soundly insulted.

The most familiar Western hat is undoubtedly the Stetson—a name that like Colt or Winchester has be-

come one of the great institutions of the West. Yet this hat, like the rifles, has an Eastern origin. John Batterson Stetson was a Philadelphian who traveled to the West for his health during the Civil War. He noticed en route that no one was making hats that suited the practical needs of the cowboy. Texans wore *Mexican sombreros*, which had very wide brims with high curved edges, a high-peaked crown, and a loose dangling strap (or *barbiquejo*) under the chin. But these were a bit impractical for hard riding, since the wind could pull them off and the chin strap could strangle the rider if the hat got caught in the brush. When Stetson got back to Philadelphia in 1865, he started to manufacture hats of his own design. They became popular immediately and have been called *Stetsons* (or John B's) ever since. Quality was the Stetson trademark from the beginning, and the hats have never been cheap, costing as much as $10 or $20, even before the turn of the century when a cowboy's pay might be only slightly more for a month's work. But they were made to last, and a good hat would be considered a lifetime investment. Cowboys swore they could dance on their hats, soak them, and shoot holes in them without destroying the shape. Stetsons now start at about $30 and come in a wide variety of styles and materials. The original "Boss of the Plains" and the "Carlsbad" are no longer standard items, but one can still feel the old West in names like "Revenger" and "Rider"—to say nothing of the new West in the "Marlboro."

Like the sombrero, the Stetson had a wide brim and a peaked crown, but it was designed to give a better fit and made soft enough to be creased. Hat creasing in the old days was something of a regional specialty and identification; the four-finger Montana peak was a style that affected even the Army, with its traditional fore-and-aft-creased campaign hats. Fancy hats made of beaver-fur felt and standard hats of wool or fur felt are available now, along with synthetic felt and straw for summer wear. Brims vary in width, but they have always been made wide enough so that in cold weather they could be tied down over the ears with a bandana, while in warm weather they were wide enough to keep sun off the neck.

"Ten-gallon," incidentally, doesn't refer to the capacity of the hat but was a slang expression. Cowboys would use the brims—not the crowns—for scooping up water to drink. Hat decoration was another area in which cowboys could show their individuality and region. Hatbands were and are still made of leather rawhide, tooled leather, feathers, and braided horsehair, often of Indian design and manufacture.

In spite of the claims about a hunt derby's strength or the durability of a Stetson, there isn't much point in deliberately damaging these valuable items of apparel. Obviously, good care and occasional cleaning (usually a brushing is sufficient) will keep the hat looking its best. Some people like to carry or store their hats in hat bags; special hat racks, from which Stetsons can hang by the brim, are often installed in the closets of affluent cowboys. For rain, clear-plastic hat covers are available for both English and Western styles.

Now that we have dressed the rider for various styles of riding and in all kinds of weather, let's consider those other items that help to complete the equestrian outfit. They are not clothing exactly but important pieces of equipment that enable a person to become a real horseman, not just someone wearing riding clothes. They do not count as accessories but are real aids to riding—sticks and spurs, specifically—which emphasize and strengthen the effect of natural aids such as the legs and hands.

Sticks

Contrary to popular notions, riding sticks and whips are not instruments of torture but effective and invaluable aids, to be used in conjunction with other aids (such as the legs in riding and the reins in driving). A stick is used to reinforce the others, either by giving additional pressure or by creating a noise to attract a horse's attention. A stick should be applied firmly and immediately after disobedience or a failure to respond; otherwise its use is likely to confuse the animal and may have the opposite effect from the one intended.

Crops are sticks between 2 and 3 feet long with a handle at one end, usually with a wrist loop attached, and a leather tab at the other. Many riders, especially beginners, find the wrist loops handy, but they make switching hands more difficult, and some instructors advise against them (a razor blade will make a neat job of removing the strap). The least expensive crops are made of fiberglass or plastic covered with woven thread, vinyl, or braided leather. More expensive models are leather throughout or steel with a covering of braided flax or tooled leather. Some come equipped with silver handle caps, suitable for engraving. Tradition dictates that the crop's color match the rider's boots: black with black footwear and brown with brown.

Jumping bats are sturdy, short (about 19 inches) but very flexible sticks. They are usually made of rawhide with a braided leather cover, a leather handle, and leather "feathers" which may be arranged in various patterns. Variations include fiberglass centers, tape or rubber handles, and braided-thread covers.

Popular in England are bats made of twisted willow wood with leather handles. Bats do not have wrist loops, and the tabs at the business end are wider than those on crops. These shorter sticks are more suitable for jumping, because of the forward seat and shorter stirrup used by the rider, who needs only to reach the area of the flank just behind the girth. Feathered bats are less likely to hurt a horse and are often recommended for children or adult beginners with bad tempers.

Jockey bats are heavy sticks, made of plastic or fiberglass coated with leather or thread and furnished with leather, tape, or rubber handles. Like jumping bats, these have wide leather "poppers," or flaps, to make a noise when slapped against the horse's flank.

Dressage whips are longer and thinner than crops or bats, long enough (about 3 feet) so that only the rider's wrist need move to apply it. These do not have wrist loops but have leather or steel button heads at the end of the handle to prevent slipping. The other end of the whip, which is usually made of fiberglass covered with braided flax, is a thin tip or lash rather than a noise-producing tab.

Gaited-horse whips, slightly shorter than dressage whips, have the same general shape and features. They are made of fiberglass with a white leather (or black rubber) handle and a black linen-thread covering.

Polo whips are similar to crops in shape, complete with wrist loop, but generally with a larger tip (or "mushroom") on the handle to ensure a firm grip. Once traditionally made of whalebone (now illegal, of course), braided gut, or flax, covered with pigskin and with a rubber handle, they are now usually fiberglass with a waterproof thread cover.

Hunting whips, which are properly carried in the hunt field or in an appointments class, have a crook handle (18 to 19 inches long) for opening gates and a long lash to keep hounds in line. The old-fashioned hunting whip was fashioned of whalebone covered with plaited kangaroo hide, calfskin, or pigskin with a staghorn hook, serrated to prevent slipping when one was pushing the bar of the gate. Nowadays the hook is still serrated but is usually made of ash, while the whip itself is made of fiberglass. There are usually a silver or nickle collar on the handle and a plaited leather thong or lash with a silken tip, the thong attached by a leather keeper to the whip itself. The master's thong is usually longer—about 1½ yards—than that of the other riders—usually 1¼ yards—but never long enough to interfere with horses' legs. The whip is held two-thirds up the stick and carried with the hook up, facing the rider, and the thong is looped (not wrapped around the whip) several times and held next to the whip.

Fly whisks are sticks furnished with long horsehair brushes. They double as riding sticks and as a useful means of keeping flies away from the horse during riding. They can be made of Malacca with horsehair braided over it as a cover, although fiberglass is more common.

Western riding bats are heavier than English crops, with leather flaps and a large loop for wrist or saddle horn. These bats may be made of braided calfskin or rawhide.

Quirts are used like bats; the name comes from the Mexican Spanish word *cuarta*, meaning a horsewhip. They are made of plaited flexible rawhide with no stiff central core—just a leaded butt from which a lash (or several lashes) or slender leather extends for anywhere from a foot to 3 feet. The handle is short and there is always a wrist loop. Quirts used to be made of woven horsehair or stitched buckskin (doubling as a slingshot in a fight). Quirt making was sometimes a prison activity. Indians were expert quirt braiders. Since they wore no spurs (because they wore no boots), Indians would use these in a simple version with a wooden handle and several rawhide lashes about a foot long. Charles Russell's famous painting *Salute to the Fur Trade* shows a Blackfoot with a quirt made from an elk antler.

Driving whips are 4 to 5 feet long and are made of rawhide (traditionally of holly wood) with braided or thread covers and leather or tape handles capped with silver or nickel. They have silk lashes at the tip of the whip long enough to reach the horse's withers from a sulky or carriage.

Lunging whips are even longer than driving whips. They can be 6 or 7 feet in length, with eight- to ten-foot lashes, which can be set in swivels to prevent tangles as one turns. The stocks are usually made of willow wood or steel with a black thread cover, a leather handle, and a rawhide lash. The whips are used in conjunction with the lunging line, reinforcing from behind what the voice and the line command up front.

RIDING STICKS

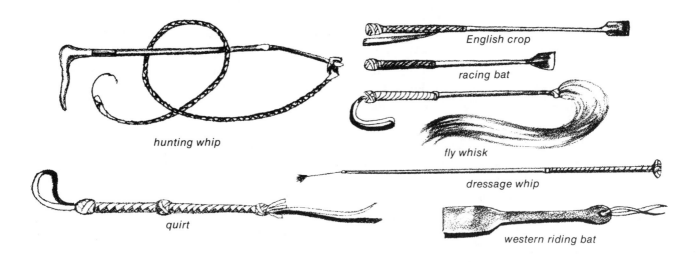

hunting whip

English crop

racing bat

fly whisk

dressage whip

quirt

western riding bat

Spurs

Spurs, like sticks, are usually considered by non-equestrian types to be a cruel means of forcing the horse to obey; but—again like sticks—they are relatively simple aids used to reinforce leg pressure or apply leg aids more precisely, to attract a horse's attention, and to punish disobedience gently but firmly. They are a time-honored accessory to the art of equitation, having been worn since the Middle Ages when boots were invented to deal with the stirrup. Spurs can be overused or abused, and horses that have been mistreated may resent them, even going so far as to move away from active heel with or without a spur on it. Because spurs are practical, however, every rider should learn to wear them at some point, and any rider wearing them should take care to avoid carrying a good thing too far. In some hunting classes and on the formal hunting field, their use is mandatory. They are also required for bucking-horse contests—not for appearances' sake or to stay on, but to goad the animal into action; they are called grappling irons. Western spurs certainly look cruel with their long shanks and sizable rowers, but the construction of the stock saddle requires a larger spur simply to reach the horse's flanks (misused English spurs with single spikes can be far more painful). The basic difference between the English and Western spurs, however, and there are many variations even within these two categories, is in origin as much as in practical application.

ENGLISH SPURS

Because all spurs were originally European, we can't call these European spurs, although they are made in Germany as well as in England; however, since they came to this country via England—and in the West, at least, are referred to as Anglo spurs—we shall call them English anyhow. The most common type is a simple steel (usually stainless or chrome-coated) spur, curved around just above the heel of the boot, with necks to which leather straps attach for fastening around the boot foot and short, blunt, slightly downward-curving shanks. These are *Prince-of-Wales spurs,* and they are preferred for beginners and for riders in the hunt field where unroweled spurs must be worn. *Hammerhead hunt spurs* are usually worn by the hunt staff and gentlemen riders; they are heavier, and their shank has a head at its tip. Ladies' show spurs have flat-sided shanks with a small head on the tip and are somewhat more severe than the simple Prince-of-Wales design. Rowels (or small wheels) are not uncommon on these English (or German) spurs, but they are quite fine and hardly resemble their Western counterparts. *Dressage spurs,* with horizontal rowels, are delicate, to be used for this most delicate of riding styles, in which the rider's motion must be virtually imperceptible. *Side rowels,* or angled shanks (toward the horse, of course), offer unusual control, but these are not to be worn by any but the most experienced riders. Spur straps are russet or black leather, matching the color of the boots. Chains are sometimes used instead of

SPURS

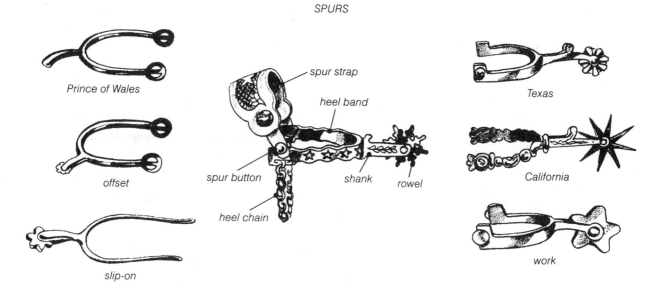

Prince of Wales

offset

slip-on

spur strap

heel band

spur button

heel chain

shank

rowel

Texas

California

work

leather, but these are not allowed in some hunting circles or classes. Most spurs have loop ends to which straps are attached; others are designed with buckle ends and require four straps rather than a pair. "Anglo" spurs are what Westerners called the military type, usually made of brass with a shank curving slightly upward, a small rowel, and straps attaching them firmly to the lower part of the heel. These were worn West by cavalry men, but no cowboy worth his salt would be seen dead in them.

WESTERN SPURS

Horsemen out West got their spurs from Mexico, where they were known as "chihuahuas" and featured large rowels and long shanks. *Texan spurs* were and are usually hand-forged of steel with rowels between 2 and 3 inches in diameter (or smaller) and a heel band about an inch wide. The shank is about 2 inches long and straight, while the rowel wheel is blunt-pointed with anywhere from five to eighteen points. A chapguard barrel or thumb keeps the chaps from getting entangled in the rowers. The leathers attach to buttons at the front ends of the heel band; swinging buttons are attached to a staple, but buttons are often forged directly on the band itself. The leather strap is made in two pieces, with the long piece acting as tongue and the short piece carrying the buckle. The buckle is usually worn on the inside of the leg to avoid catching on brush, and a decorative concho may be applied to the spot where the tongue piece connects with the spur

button on the outside. To hold the spurs down (they are worn higher than Anglo spurs), tie-down straps or chains are worn around the arch just in front of the heel, though the weight of the spur is often enough to hold it in place. Bell clappers or jingle bobs are some times added to clink against the rowels as one rides or walks, which one can actually do in these huge contraptions because they ride high above the heel.

California spurs were actually closer to the Mexican spur in design, with even larger rowels, or cart-

1892

wheels—up to 6 or 7 inches in diameter—which were often equipped with sharp spikes. These spurs were designed to be worn on low-heeled shoes rather than high boots, but even after Californians adopted the cowboy boot they preferred their own spurs, although they could not walk with them on. These highly decorated spurs were usually, unlike Mexican spurs, worn loose, with chains under the instep. This, and the fact that shanks curved downward in quarter, half, or full curves, were what gave the Californians so much trouble when dismounted. *Slip-on spurs* have no straps or chains at all and are designed with blunt-end rowels.

Miscellaneous Accessories

Most catalogs featuring riding apparel and equipment include, along with the workaday breeches, pants, boots, hats, spurs, and such, a bright array of attractive horse-related items that don't fall into any of the categories discussed so far. Some of these things are gift-shop goodies—key chains, handbags, change purses, scatter pins, and other kinds of jewelry—but others are downright useful for the horseman and deserve attention here.

GOGGLES
Drivers of sulkies and carriages use specially designed goggles to protect their eyes from kicked-up turf, mud, or stones, as well as from wind, rain, or horse tails. Although these may be considered specialties for specialists, riders who wear contact lenses on horseback might find them very useful indeed. Wraparound goggles, available with clear or tinted shatterproof plastic lenses, have close-fitting strong plastic frames and are relatively inexpensive. Some styles have cutout pieces over the nose to reduce pressure, and some are equipped with chrome wire frames, a hinged nose, and adjustable earpieces. To keep eyeglasses in place during a strenuous ride, the adjustable elastic straps worn by runners or tennis players are handy. They clip onto the eyeglass frames and fit tightly around the back of the head.

GROOMING APRONS
Unlike the macintosh aprons worn during rainstorms in England, the sidesaddle aprons worn by ladies in the 19th century (and some even today), or the early version of the Western chaps, these aprons are somewhat less elegant but equally useful. Equipped with two roomy pockets, these sturdy hide garments wear forever and give good protection to clothing. The blacksmith's apron is similar in that it is made of hide, but it ties at the waist instead of wrapping around the neck and is chrome-tanned to keep the farrier cool as he works at his forge.

HUNTING HORNS
Expensive copper horns with nickel mouthpieces in fine bridle-leather cases can hardly be considered useful or even necessary equipment for anyone but the professional huntsman in the field, but the idea of a horn—or a whistle—isn't a bad one for riders who do a good deal of cross-country or trail riding. Westerners use highly polished hollow steerhorn, although whistles are more convenient and a good deal easier to blow. If one gets into trouble—because of an accident or getting lost—the high, piercing sound of a horn or powerful whistle might just bring help in a hurry.

ROPES
Although trail riders might find it helpful in an emergency to have a rope in hand (on the saddle, most likely), a belt could serve the same purpose—to repair a piece of broken tack or tie a horse (or its front leg, say, if the animal becomes hurt and is unable to use the limb). Ropes of very specific types are necessary equipment however, for cowboys, who use them to catch horses, rope and tie calves, drive cattle, make temporary corrals, drag cows to safety, haul firewood, rescue drovers at streams, kill snakes, make hackamores, and hang their enemies. Ropes have in the past been made of different materials, each with its own defenders: the *reata* (meaning to tie again) is made of rawhide, or cowhide dried in the sun; grass ropes were made of twisted, not braided, hemp, sisal, and later cotton and were stronger than *reatas* but didn't last as long; and hair ropes, or *mecates*, were made of horsehair (soft), cow tails (stiff), and mohair (silky). A lariat (from *la reata*) or lasso (from *lazo*, meaning noose) was a rope of any sort with a running noose (through a honda or slip ring) used for throwing to catch and bring down animals. It might be 40 to 50 feet long—or even 70 feet in open country; shorter in brush

country. There are two basic styles of roping: hard-and-fast tying and dally roping. The former involves a shorter rope (usually grass) attached to the horn of the saddle with a horn string or thong, and the latter used a longer rope (60 to 100 feet, depending on the kind of country) which was held free in the hands until the target was caught and then turned around the horn (One could always recognize a dally roper by the missing thumb on his roping hand!) The best ropes used for lariats today are made of nylon $3/_8$ to $7/_{16}$ inch thick and 30 to 35 feet long. Shorter strings (all ropes are called strings) of cotton or nylon are used for hog-tying animals, usually calves, by the two hind legs and one foreleg. Hitches are many and varied, their names reflecting their uses or shapes: barrel hitch, basket hitch, bed hitch, double-diamond hitch, half hitch, hex-diamond hitch, pack hitch, prospector's hitch, and stirrup hitch.

WIRE CUTTERS

Like ropes, these useful pieces of equipment are necessary gear for the cowboy and the fox hunter, and like knives they should be considered necessary for any trail rider who expects to be out for more than just an hour or two. Not designed for cutting into someone's pastureland, wire cutters can get a horse or a rider out of a sticky and perhaps dangerous situation, one not to be taken lightly. These can be purchased together with leather cases that can be strapped to the saddle. They are traditional (and required) gear for whippers-in in the hunt field.

Special Notes on Buying Riding Apparel

The charts that follow these notes include dress regulations (or firm suggestions) that apply to specific equestrian events or activities—in the hunt field, in the show ring, on the polo field, and at the racetrack, as well as in the schooling ring, on the trail, and in the backyard. Except where competitions are being judged by a rigid set of rules (such as those listed in the *Rule Book* of the American Horse Shows Association), these charts need not be followed strictly by the beginning rider. But as one acquires experience and develops an interest in competitive events, one should keep them in mind,

since riding clothes are not cheap and any significant purchase should take future use into account. Obviously, one can wear whatever one likes around the stable—and the less fancy the better, since mucking out has never been a particularly dainty job—but even here sturdiness of fabric and comfort should be considered. The moment one gets on a horse, however, appropriate riding clothes become important, not for the sake of appearance so much as for practical reasons. Ill-fitting pants and boots will soon take a toll of the rider, and tight-shouldered, too-long jackets may restrict one's freedom in the saddle. Gloves, hats, warm vests, and rain gear may not be necessary if the weather is always perfect, but even California can't guarantee that sort of climate throughout the year, and one should therefore be sure to get accessories that are designed to stay on, stand up under wear, and avoid interference with one's contact with the horse, as well as protect the rider from the elements.

Even for growing children, a sensible outlay of money is recommended, not necessarily for custom-made apparel, but at least for reasonably well-fitting clothes that are designed to do their job. When one is learning to ride, one needs all the confidence and support one can get, and a good pair of shoes or boots and a protective hat of some sort will be a big help—to both rider and parent. Children's clothing is widely available ready-made in relatively low price ranges, but the wise purchaser may get some real bargains by reading bulletin boards at stables or tack shops, where second-hand clothing is often announced at bargain rates. In the good old days before the population explosion caused a threatening situation, large families often made the purchase of good children's wear a practical investment, for one could hand down boots, pants, and other pieces of garb from one growing child to the next. These days, apparel often has to leave the family to be handed down, but one should not fail to take advantage of the occasional "slightly used" advertisement. And speaking of hand-me-downs, don't scorn a good old pair of breeches or a riding coat because it is out of fashion. Exaggerated "pegs" or flares and wide skirts can be altered, usually at a reasonable cost, by any tack shop with access to a tailor, and the original garment, because of its fine fabric, may be worth its weight in melton for many years longer.

Even if one rides only occasionally and not in competitive events, one should try to perform well—if not for one's own sake, then at least for the horse's—and comfortable, practical riding clothes will help keep one's mind on one's work by eliminating potential distractions caused by blisters, flapping pieces of material, restricted arm movements, or concern about one's cleaning bills.

Although riding clothes come in many shapes and colors, one would do well to heed the following words of George Morris in his book *Hunter Seat Equitation* (Garden City: Doubleday, 3rd ed., 1990).

All in all, a rider entering a show ring should appear elegant in an understated, conventional way. No part of his riding attire should draw attention to itself and under no circumstances should there be any flashiness. Imagination can enter in subtly tailoring clothing to the rider's build and in coordinating colors with the horse.

Although he certainly wasn't concerned here with parade classes, Morris brings up two important points that most riders—Eastern or Western, in the show ring or out—must think about in selecting clothing: well-fitting coats or shirts and pants to display the rider's figure to best advantage and to hide flaws; and overall appearance in terms of the horse-and-rider combination. Short, dumpy riders, for instance, may compensate for their unhorsemanlike build by choosing clothes that emphasize height and slenderness. There is nothing less attractive than a baggy coat, which may affect the rider's posture in the saddle, to say nothing of the impression that a judge may receive. High-heeled boots designed for fashionable street wear may look wonderful but may be just the wrong thing to put into a stirrup. Boot heels for Western stock saddles shouldn't be more than 2 inches high, if that, and on an English saddle, 1 inch is really quite sufficient.

If one cannot find well-fitting ready-made clothing or boots, one should always consider the fact that custom-made equipment can be far more practical in the long run than badly made, cheaper apparel. This may be especially true for people whose individual conformation requires careful tailoring and for those who want specific types of traditional wear for the sake of the rule book or for the love of history and excellent materials.

Now that you have decided to spend some money and have a pretty good idea of what to spend it on, the next step is to find the items you want. The simplest solution—though not always the most satisfactory—is to visit your local tack shop. Most parts of the country in which there is a certain amount of equestrian activity can support a tack shop of some sort (check the Yellow Pages under Riding Equipment and Apparel)—or at least a department in a sporting-goods, hardware, or farm-supply store. If you have trouble locating such a store, check with your feed supplier, your farrier, or a neighboring horse owner. Tack shops usually have a number of ready-made items on hand or can easily order out-of-stock items from their suppliers. Many shops will also have custom tailors or bootmakers on call or even on their staffs to make new apparel or to repair old or damaged equipment.

Some manufacturers—here and abroad—restrict their distribution exclusively to a certain retailer or group of retailers, and if you have your heart set on something that your own tack shop cannot obtain, write to the manufacturer directly—either for a catalog and prices or for the name of the dealer nearest you.

People who live in areas where tack shops are small or nonexistent should get their names on the mailing lists of the big mail-order shops described at the end of this *Catalog.*

Custom tailors and bootmakers, like manufacturers and retail shops, frequently advertise in the horse magazines and will supply catalogs or price lists on request if they deal direct with customers; when they work through distributors, they will give the name of the shop or dealer in your area.

Dress Requirements

HUNTING
(in the field, on hunt teams, and in appointments classes)

The master of foxhounds wears a square-cornered single-breasted frock coat of melton or heavy twill in either scarlet or hunt-livery color with one flap pocket on each side, a whistle pocket (optional), a collar of the hunt's adopted colors, and four buttons ending at the waist seam, two on the back above the vent, and two or three on each cuff. Vests should be plain white, buff, or yellow, and brass buttons on vest and coat must conform to hunt livery, engraved with the insignia of the hunt. Breeches must be white unless otherwise specified, with no more than four small buttons showing at the knee (cotton or silk breeches not permitted). The stock should be plain white with a gold stock pin. The hunt cap must be black; heavy leather gloves are worn, with rain gloves carried under the saddle. Boots must be of black calf with sewn-on brown or colored tops and sewn-on but not sewn-down tabs, and white (or colored) boot garters to match the breeches are to button on the outside of the leg between the two lowest buttons. Heavy spurs with a short neck and no rowels are worn high on the heel, and a regulation hunt whip must be carried (with a hunting horn, sandwich case, and flask attached to the saddle).

Huntsmen and whippers-in wear the same as the master but must carry a pocketknife and wire cutters. Whippers-in can forget the horn but must have a poaching pocket inside the coat and no outer pockets, carrying an extra pair of stirrup leathers (or hound couples), one across the upper body (from right shoulder down to waist) and the other on the off side of the saddle.

Gentlemen members who have been so permitted by the master may wear three-button scarlet coats, the hunt livery, or black in one of the accepted formal cuts (shadbelly, cutaway, or weasel-belly or frock coat with

Riding sidesaddle to hounds

rounded, not square, skirts), and white breeches. (Buff or brown breeches may be worn with black coats, but white is preferred.) With the following exceptions, the gentleman member dresses like the hunt staff: vest buttons may be brass or bone, black bone to be worn with a black coat; high silk hats with hat guards are worn except that a black derby must be worn with a black coat, in which case boots must not have tops and garters must be black.

Lady members riding astride may not wear scarlet but must wear a black or dark-colored hunting coat, or a shadbelly or cutaway cut, with buff or brown (not white) breeches and a black derby or silk hat (required with shadbelly or cutaway) with a hat guard and no veil. Boots must be black, with or without tabs or tops; patent leather tops are permissible for ladies (and for no one else), and garters must be black or made of patent leather if patent leather tops are worn. A lady will carry a light hunting whip (its color the same as the girth), and except for her stock pin, a wristwatch, and finger rings, no jewelry is permitted.

Lady members riding sidesaddle wear habits of black, dark gray, or navy blue, which include a formal one-button jacket, breeches or a full skirt, and an apron over breeches that rides parallel to the ground slightly above the ankle of the left boot and is held by a strap at the waist. Hats may be black derbies or silk hats, and hat guards must be worn (except when a veil is worn). Boots without tops, gloves, a hunt whip, and rain gloves on the off side of the saddle complete this elegant outfit.

Ladies and gentlemen who have not "earned their colors" are considered guests, and they are to wear the same costume as the members except that scarlet is not worn, collars must be of the same color and material as the coat, and buttons are to be plain. Juniors under 18 wear the same except that a hunt cap is permitted.

HUNTER-SEAT EQUITATION (RATCATCHER, CUBBING, JUMPER CLASSES)

Any plain-colored (not scarlet) or tweed riding coat or jacket, with (or without) a vest of a solid color or tattersall checks, over breeches or cuffed jodhpurs of any color except white. Ratcatcher or plain shirt with stock, choker, or tie; turtleneck sweaters may be permitted. A glove of leather or string in any color, and any kind of appropriate riding boot or shoe, without a colored top. Dark blue, brown, or black hunt caps or black or brown derbies are required in hunter-seat classes, and spurs must be unroweled. Ratcatching hats may be of soft felt, porkpie, or tweed, although hunt caps are preferred in case of falls. Equestrian teams wear their regulation team uniforms.

ENGLISH PLEASURE

Coats of any tweed or solid material suitable for hunting in solid conservative colors (black, blue, gray, beige, or brown) with matching breeches or jodhpurs and boots. Dark blue, black, or brown hunting cap or derby. (Conservative wash jackets in season.)

SADDLE-SEAT (formal evening classes for gaited horses and park horses)

Dark gray, dark brown, dark blue, or black tuxedo-type coats with collars and lapels of same color worn over jodhpurs and vests to match, with a top hat and gloves. Unroweled spurs, whips, and crops are optional. Boots may be of black patent leather or calfskin; elastic-sided jodhpur boots are permitted.

SADDLE-SEAT (informal gaited classes)

Conservative solid-colored (black, blue, gray, green, beige, brown) jacket with matching jodhpurs. (White jackets permitted in season.) A derby or soft hat must be worn, along with jodhpur boots of black or brown. Unroweled spurs, whips, crops are optional.

DRESSAGE (formal, third level and up)

Formal-cut black riding coat (shadbelly, cutaway, frock coat with rounded sides) over white breeches, with white stock and gold pin. High silk hats and leather gloves, with unroweled spurs on topless black boots, complete the outfit.

INFORMAL DRESSAGE (up to third level)

Black or dark-colored hunting coat over breeches or jodhpurs of matching color with black boots. A stock must be worn, as must gloves, and a black derby or a

---

The seat on a horse makes gentlemen of some and grooms of others.

CERVANTES

---

dark blue or black hunt cap. Unroweled spurs are optional, as are whips.

RACING (flat or steeplechase)

Racing silks, appropriately colored to identify the owner of the horse, are recommended, the lighter the material the better (silk is not required). Jockey boots are usually black with mahogany tops, sewn on or dyed. Goggles are recommended for rainy days; no spurs are allowed in flat racing, but sticks are essential, and jock (as in jockey) straps are basic equipment for males.

POLO

A lightweight, short-sleeved shirt in appropriate team colors, open at the neck, with a white polo cap or helmet and brown polo boots with brown leather garters. Leather gloves (on one or both hands), a polo whip or stick, and a polo belt made of wide ribbed canvas for support are recommended. Spurs must be blunted, and ribbed knee guards must be as sturdy as possible. In the old days, when these things mattered, polo players were allowed to wear camel-hair coats between chukkers.

WESTERN PLEASURE

Western hat, Western trousers, and a long-sleeved shirt are required. Boots are necessary, too, but rope reata, and chaps may also be requested in some classes, such as those for working cow horses. Spurs are optional.

ARABIAN COSTUME CLASSES

Native-type costume including flowing cape or coat pantaloons, headdress, scarf or sash. Nothing must be in either hand other than reins, a portion of the sash, and a riding crop.

PALOMINO SPANISH FIESTA CLASS

Spanish costume is required, with special tack.

APPALOOSA AND PINTO COSTUME CLASSES

These require authentic Indian warrior costumes.

DRIVING (single sulky or buggy)

A dark tailored costume for men and women with leather gloves and a soft felt hat with plain dark band for men. In evening classes, ladies are permitted an evening dress with a neutral-colored lap rug; men should wear a black lounge suit, black shoes, and a gray top hat.

DRIVING (road coach)

Male drivers should wear black top hats and morning coats in the show ring; ladies may wear dark, tailored suits with skirts and with small hats that will not catch the wind. The coach guard must wear a scarlet coat with gold braid and gaiters. Aprons and gloves may also be required, along with a whole battery of equipment for the coach (an extra collar, reins, brake shoe, blankets, lap robes, tool kit, and so on and on).

COMBINED TRAINING AND THREE-DAY EVENT

The clothing recommended for dressage, polo (or cross-country), and hunter-seat equitation are used in the three phases of this activity. The higher the level, the more formal the apparel in dressage and stadium jumping, especially when one reaches Prix St. Georges and Olympic competition.

TRAIL RIDING (distance and cross-country)

Comfort and protection are the only real rules here, but anyone who plans to ride for more than just a couple of hours should take along some practical items: a knife, a pair of wire cutters, a map, a canteen filled with water, a piercing whistle, a raincoat or blanket rolled behind the saddle, and—in any remote area where help cannot be summoned by yelling or blowing the whistle—a rifle, handgun, or humane killer. This last item, which can be fitted into a special holder for the saddle, is not simply for protection against wild animals or madmen loose in the woods, or even for food gathering, but also for the awful—yet possible—event that a horse should become so badly injured that it must be put out of its misery before help can be expected to turn up.

> *"There are only two classes of good society in England; the equestrian classes and the neurotic classes. It isn't mere convention; everybody can see that the people who hunt are the right people and the people who don't are the wrong ones."*
>
> G. B. *SHAW*
> Heartbreak House

chapter 7

Equestrian Activities

Now that your horse is (1) yours, (2) in its stable, (3) well fed and cared for, (4) in good health, (5) dressed properly, and (6) ridden or driven by an equally well-turned-out person, let's consider activities. Pleasure riding and hunting are great fun, and at some point the lure of trying to compare your horse's abilities or your own against others' will become irresistible. After all, riding is a sport, and sports involve competition.

Outdoor show at Coto de Caza, California

But what if you don't own your own horse? There are ways, as you'll see, to borrow or rent one so that you can compete. You don't even have to be a rider or driver to appreciate equestrian competition. Competition calls for spectators, and you can spend many happy hours watching good horseflesh and riding. Maybe your interest will grow to expertise and you can become an official. The possibilities are limitless.

This chapter is intended as a panorama of activities. Obviously, to discuss horse shows, rodeos, dressage and combined-training trials, endurance riding, or any of the myriad activities that fit under the chapter's heading with any degree of thoroughness would require the book-shelf space of an *Encyclopaedia Britannica* as well as the size and expertise of such a project's staff and consultants. Instead, you'll discover the wide variety of competition, some of which may kindle your interest about using your horse or yourself to see how you'll do against the world. We're grateful to participants who have shared their expertise and experiences with us—and you.

Horse Shows

What is a "horse show"? To most people living in the East it is a place where hunters, jumpers, and equitation riders can win ribbons. In the South, it's for gaited and Fine Harness horses. Westerners think of shows primarily in terms of stock-seat equitation and classes. Breed devotees consider shows as places to exhibit specific breeds.

The answer is that all these people are correct. A horse show is a competition in which many (or few) activities take place. Perhaps the best way to focus on exactly what takes place is by saying a few words about the variety of classes (a class is a group of competitors competing under the same criteria and rules against one another) found at horse shows.

HUNTER DIVISION

These classes judge the horse against certain requirements needed by fox-hunting animals. Conformation classes take an animal's build into consideration; judges look for the kind of build that will carry a rider comfortably and handily across country. Working hunters will be required to perform either on the flat or over fences. Courses approximate the obstacles found in the hunting field, such as brush fences, post-and-rails, and oxers (see pages 220–21 for definitions of jumps). Way of going is an important consideration, taking into account a horse's style, smoothness of pace, and manners. Hunter horses are divided according to experience, from preliminary and notice to first- and second-year green and open. Appointment hunter classes come even closer to hunt-field requirements. Riders must wear or carry appropriate gear, as must their mounts, down to an edible item in the sandwich box and a letter from a Master of Foxhounds authorizing the rider to wear his hunt's colors. Corinthian classes are open only to members of a recognized hunt, and hunt-team classes are for two or three members of such recognized packs.

JUMPER DIVISION

Jumping classes are open to horses of any breed, size, or gender. Preliminary jumpers are animals that have won less than $2,500 in AHSA competitions; Intermediate, $2,500 to $5,000; and Open, in excess of $5,000. Another category is Amateur-Owner, whose owners show their own horses (and may keep any prize money without jeopardizing their amateur status). The height and spread of fences are smaller for horses just starting out in the Jumper Division. Courses are also accordingly less demanding.

The object of jumping is to clear obstacles cleanly; style and grace over fences are irrelevant. Scoring is done in terms of penalty points called faults. In classes where touches (coming into contact with the obstacle without dislodging it) are penalized, one-half fault is incurred when the horse's body behind the stifle touches a fence, and one fault if in front of the stifle. Touches don't count under FEI rules (the Fédération Équestre Internationale is the worldwide ruling body of equestrian sports). Knockdowns (dislodging any element of an obstacle) and refusals do. Each knockdown counts as four faults. A refusal, stopping in front of a fence, is three faults. Three cumulative refusals requires elimination, as do starting a course before the judge's signal, failing to begin within one minute after a warning signal, and jumping obstacles in the wrong order.

Some classes include liability for time penalties. One-quarter fault is assessed for each second or portion thereof in excess of the stated time limit.

Show-jumping action at the International Jumping Derby, Newport, Rhode Island.

A round is concluded after all entrants have performed. In the event of an equality of faults by two or more entrants, another round called a "jump-off" may be called for. One that results in yet another equality of faults may require a second jump-off. In that case, if two or more entrants are still tied in jumping faults, the fastest time around the course will determine the winner. Fences are raised and widened and the course shortened for each jump-off to make the round more demanding.

Two jumping classes never fail to enthrall spectators. In a "Gambler's Choice" (or "Take Your Own Line"), each obstacle is allotted a point value according to its difficulty. Competitors may jump all the obstacles they choose in any order or direction. If a fence is jumped cleanly, the competitor will receive its value. The highest score amassed within a time limit (usually 60 or 90 seconds) will win.

"Puissance" means power, and a Puissance class may end with finalists attempting a "great wall" standing in excess of 7 feet.

Open and International jumping are always the feature attractions of important shows. Sometimes, as in the case of Gambler's Choice and Puissance classes, civilian (including professional) riders will compete against Olympians.

SADDLE-HORSE DIVISION

American Saddle Horses are the "peacocks" of the show ring. They enter in a flurry, then try to attract the judge's attention as being the flashiest in the class. Three-Gaited Horses perform at the walk, trot, and canter, their roached manes setting them off from Five-Gaited Horses. This latter group, with flowing manes and full tails, are judged at the walk, trot, canter, and two artificial paces called the slow gait (or singlefoot) and the rack. Both gaits, natural to the breed and developed through training, hark back to antebellum days when Saddle Horses provided comfortable and hardy mounts for Southern plantation owners as the men inspected their vast holdings. Classes within this category are for amateur and professional riders, women, and, with regard to horses, stallions and geldings and mares.

Tennessee Walking Horses are also Southern-derived flashy movers. Their gaits are a smooth running walk, trot, and what has been described as a "rocking chair" canter. Walkers most commonly perform in Southern shows, especially in Kentucky and in the state whose name they bear.

HARNESS DIVISION

Animals featured in these events pull light vehicles and display a flashy, high-actioned pace akin to that of gaited horses. Indeed, Fine Harness horses are American Saddlebreds—shown, however, at just the walk and trot (or park gait). Manners as well as action are a criterion; since ladies drive the rigs, their horses must be the kind that they could take for a spin through traffic and other distractions.

Hackneys are another breed used for harness classes. These high-stepping ponies are shown either singly or in pairs. Here too judges look for brilliance in way of going as well as manners.

Western Horse Shows

Classes at Western horse shows include any or all of the following divisions:

HALTER

The halter division judges the conformation qualities of a particular breed. Horses are *stood up*, or posed for

Jumps

The types of jumps used in Hunter classes are representative of natural obstacles found in the hunt field. These include the post-and-rails, stone wall, Aiken, chicken coop, brush, plank, and white gate. The Aiken, a split rail over bushes, is named for a famous town in South Carolina. An "in-and-out" duplicates the type of fencing found along either side of country lanes, and the two elements should be separated by the width of a lane. This combination is generally meant to be jumped in one stride and is so arranged at horse shows.

The post-and-rails is a natural rail fence, usually of three cross rails. The chicken coop is a triangular wooden obstacle ranging from perhaps 2 feet 6 inches to 4 feet. It's not that hunters jump real chicken coops in the field; panels in fences are shaped that way because cattle won't jump widths. The Liverpool jump is named after a famed jump at the Grand National Steeplechase in Liverpool, England. This water jump may have a rail or brush element as well. Wings are added to narrow fences to channel the horse to prevent runouts.

It should be noted that whatever the shape or composition of the jump, the obstacle should be constructed to collapse easily to prevent injury to a falling horse or rider. Much of the breakaway characteristic depends upon the type of cups that hold the rail to the jump standards. A shallow cup will permit the rail to roll out with ease. A deep cup and narrow rail will not be dislodged with less than a full impact. The inside dimensions of a cup for a 4-inch pole must be a minimum $1\frac{1}{2}$ inches deep and 5 inches across; the maximum depth must not exceed one-half the diameter of the pole. Metal pins are required to hold the cups (friction or tension devices are banned). While the AHSA prefers metal cups, plastic ones may be used.

These metal cups may be made by your local blacksmith, but are generally purchased from jump suppliers. Jumps may cost thousands of dollars for a supply sufficient to run a Grand Prix, which is why many shows rent or lease jumps rather than make or buy their own. One source of custom jumps is Bert Lytle Associates, 20520 Monacacy Road, Dickerson, Maryland 20842, (301) 428-8861, owned by Chuck Kinney, P.O. Box 450, Newbury, Ohio 44065, (216) 338-6116. They will rent for shows of every size from one-day local events to the major "A" circuit shows. Or you can buy all types of jumps from them, ranging from schooling rails to an entire course. They will sell you used or new fencing, or you can get do-it-yourself parts and build your own.

Many shows use 12-foot, 14-foot, or, rarely, 16-foot lengths. Obviously the longer the pole, the greater the weight and the less the tendency to pop out of the cups when hit.

The jumper-competition fences are not representative of hunt-field conditions, but are really special fences constructed to test a horse's jumping abilities. Jump testing for height are straight rails or poles, stone walls, and series of straight fences used in *barrierspringer* events.

Fences designed to test for horizontal distances are called spread fences. They may include the oxer, double oxer, hogback, and triple bar. While these obstacles are of different configurations, they can all be raised and lengthened, as for jump-offs.

The formidable-looking Puissance walls are generally constructed of light plywood, and the upper elements slide off easily. The solid appearance is only paint-deep.

Paint is employed to create illusions which the horse may find difficult to handle. There are traditional patterns used such as stripes to simulate railroad crossing gates. Bull's-eye are often painted on panels. No "Gambler's Choice" class would be complete without one fence painted to represent the joker in a deck of cards.

The paints used are standard outdoor waterproof formulas. Colors are pretty much left to choice. Very popular are poles painted red and white, with all-white or other variations used at will.

post-and-rail

one-stride

in and out

chicken-coop

Liverpool

brush fence

puissance wall

oxer

deep cup

shallow cup

the judges' inspection then asked to jog so that the animals' soundness can be assessed. The horses that come closest to the breed's conformation criteria will win the top ribbons.

SHOWMANSHIP

Showmanship at halter, a class for youth and amateur exhibitors, tests showmanship skills. The format is identical to a halter class. but here the creature at the other end of the lead shank—the exhibitor—is being judged. The grooming and fitting of the horse and the exhibitor's ability to present his or her horse to best advantage are the criteria.

WESTERN PLEASURE

Horses in this division are judged at the walk, jog, and lope, on the basis of providing a pleasurable ride. Judges look for true and comfortable gaits, an alert yet calm disposition and good manners alone and in the company of other horses.

WESTERN RIDING

Horse and rider execute a pattern that involves passing around pylons and a log, and change gaits at specific points around the course. The ability to change leads at the lope precisely and easily is being tested, as well as prompt responses and good manners.

WESTERN HORSEMANSHIP

Western horsemanship, or equitation, tests the rider's ability. Riders first guide their horses through a prescribed pattern that uses all three gaits and involves combinations of straight and curved lines, circles, and figure eights.

Finalists return to ride as a group. Moving on the rail at the walk, jog, and lope, they are judged on their body position, form, and how well they control their horses.

TRAIL

This class tests horses on how well they cope with the kind of obstacles found on a trail ride. In addition to three mandatory obstacles (opening, passing through, and closing a gate; passing over a series of logs; and backing through logs set in an L-, U- or V-shaped pattern), the course may include a small ditch or a bridge.

In addition, the horse may be asked to stand while the rider puts on a rain slicker or places a letter into or removes a letter from a mailbox.

Scoring is based on the willingness and ease with which the horse completes the course.

REINING

Reining classes, which are always among the most popular events at Western horse shows, require horses to demonstrate the athletic ability and responsiveness needed to be a superior working stock horse. Think of reining as Western dressage, and you won't be far wrong.

The order of movements, all done at the lope, calls for circles and figure eights, as well as the rundown, in which the horse moves down the center line or along the rail from one end of the arena to the other). Another movement is the rollback, a combination stop, a 180° turn on the haunches, and a departure all done in one fluid motion.

In the spin, the horse's inside hind foot acts as a pivot, remaining firmly planted while the horse moves his forequarters around in one or more 360° circles.

The most spectacular part of any reining pattern is the sliding stop, in which the horse drops his hindquarters and "melts" them into the ground while, at the same time, the forelegs keeping going to maintain balance until the horse comes at a complete stop.

Scoring is done on the basis of each movement. Each horse begins with a score of 70, to which one full or half point will added for well-performed movements, and subtracted for those that have been poorly done. The total scores determine the placings.

WORKING COW HORSE

This class tests the horse's reining ability and cow sense. It begins with the so-called *dry work*, a reining pattern that is judged in the same way as a reining class.

In the second phase, a single cow is released into the arena. Horse and rider first hold the cow at the arena's end to demonstrate control over the animal. They then drive the cow down along one side of the arena, turning the animal in both directions. Finally, the horse moves the cow into the center of the ring and turns it again in both directions (a more difficult chore without the arena fencing to help).

Scoring, based on how well the horse reins and then works the cow, ranges from zero to 100, with 70 as the average score.

In addition to these divisions, a Western show may have cutting, calf roping, team penning, and barrel-racing events. It may also be part of a combined show that includes English-style hunter, hunter-seat equitation, and jumper divisions. All of these disciplines are described elsewhere in this chapter.

EQUITATION DIVISION

Riders in the Equitation Division are judged on their horsemanship, or how well they demonstrate the essential form and control for their particular style of riding: hunter-seat for jumping, saddle-seat for Saddlebreds and other breeds ridden in that manner, or stock-seat for Western riding.

Beginning riders first compete in Maiden classes. Winning their first blue ribbon moves them up to the Novice level, a total of three first places puts them into Limit, and six into the Open category. Open riders may then choose to compete for one of the prestigious American Horse Shows Association Medal championships. Each has its year-end Finals: the "Good Hands" for saddle-seat riders at the National Horse Show in East Rutherford, New Jersey; the stock-seat Finals at the Scottsdale (Arizona) Arabian show; and the hunter-seat Finals at the Pennsylvania National in Harrisburg. To qualify, riders must win a designated number of first places in Medal classes throughout the year. As in qualifying classes, the Finals call for work at the walk, trot (or jog), and canter (or lope), and, for hunter-seat riders, jumping a course of 3'6" fences. Riders may also be asked to execute one or more specified tests, such as a figure-eight or dismounting and remounting. The best riders then return for additional work, and on some occasions finalists have been asked to ride each others' horses.

The hunter-seat world has other sought-after national junior equitation championships. The Maclay, as the National Horse Show's ASPCA Maclay class is popularly known, requires not only winning a number of blue ribbons over the year (the precise number depends on the part of the country in which the rider lives), but also making the "cut" in one of four regional elimination events. The United States Equestrian Team Medal title, which calls for more "jumpery" than "huntery" courses, is decided at the USET's training

center in Gladstone, New Jersey, and at a California show. Many of its winners, as with champions in other horsemanship competitions, have gone on to prominence in international riding, as well as becoming leading professional riders and trainers.

Riders over the age of 18 need not feel left out. Adult equitation classes have enjoyed a renaissance in popularity in all disciplines and in all parts of the country.

BREED DIVISIONS

So far, except for the Saddle-Horse Division, we have been talking about events open to more than one breed or type of horse. Quarter Horses compete as jumpers, crossbreds as hunters, and any number of breeds appear in the Western Section. The American Horse Shows Association recognizes other divisions which are limited to specific breeds: Appaloosa, Arabian, Morgan, Paint, Palomino, Pony of the Americas, Shetland, and Welsh (as well as the previously mentioned Saddle Horse, Hackney, and Tennessee Walking Horse). Within each division is a variety of sections and classes all stressing the breed's versatility.

The Morgan Division emphasizes this point. Morgans are shown as harness horses, as English and Western pleasure mounts, and as Western working and English jumping horses. And speaking of versatility, the Justin Morgan class requires its entrants first to trot $\frac{1}{2}$ mile in harness, then run the same distance under saddle, show as an equitation horse, and finally pull at least 500 pounds a distance of 6 feet.

LOCATING A HORSE SHOW

With an estimated 10,000 horse shows held throughout the United States and Canada every year, finding one to ride in or just to watch isn't a difficult job.

More times than not, participation in horse shows begins at the very local level, usually at the stable where you're learning to ride. Schooling shows, so-called because their primary purpose is to educate novice riders and green horses about the ways of the show ring, are informal affairs. The judge may be a local rider or trainer, or someone eager to practice judging in order to qualify for a license.

To ride in a "recognized" show, one sanctioned by the American Horse Shows Association, the ruling body of this country's equestrian sports, is the next step up. Annual AHSA membership dues are $65 for senior members and $40 for juniors (under 18 years of age); other categories include a $1,000 life membership. For further information about membership, which includes a copy of the *AHSA Rule Book* and a subscription to the organization's invaluable magazine, *Horse Show,* contact the AHSA at 22 East 42nd Street, New York, NY 10017 (telephone: (212) 972-2472).

Competing in an AHSA-recognized horse show requires adhering to standards of conduct and avoiding certain prohibited equine medications. Horses are routinely given blood and urine tests as part of the AHSA's enforcement policy; if the horses test "positive," their riders, trainers, and even owners face hearings, suspensions and/or fines.

Depending on length, number, and types of classes, as well as the amount of prize money, AHSA shows are rated C, B, or A, with the last-named the most important. As with schooling shows, most riders start out small and then work their way up to longer, more prestigious events.

That's where the best competition occurs and, accordingly, they are the best places for spectating. If you're interested in a particular kind of activity, consult the calendar of events in the activity magazines listed in chapter 9. The same advice applies to particular breeds (e.g., Arabians or Morgans); see the magazines in chapter 1's list of breeds. A far more comprehensive source of information is the AHSA's own *Horse Show* magazine.

Inveterate and veteran show-goers have their favorite fixtures. This blatantly idiosyncratic roster, listed by breeds or activities, includes many of ours:

One *hunter/jumper* series begins each winter in Florida, first in Palm Beach in January and February and then in Tampa. A rival circuit takes place in February and March in Ocala, Florida. There's also activity at that time of year in Tucson, Arizona.

The Devon Horse Show takes place outside Philadelphia, Pennsylvania at the end of May. Ox Ridge, in Darien, Connecticut, is traditionally a fixture during the week of Father's Day. Lake Placid (New York) is in early July, while shows at several Vermont and New Hampshire ski resorts range across the entire summer.

The American Gold Cup, also at Devon, Pennsylvania, is in mid-September, as is the Eastern States Exposition in West Springfield, Massachusetts, and the

Oaks Classic in Irvine, California. Then come the East Coast's indoor shows: Harrisburg (Pennsylvania) in mid-October, immediately followed by the Washington (D.C.) International, the National Horse Show in East Rutherford, New Jersey, and the Toronto (Canada) Royal Winter Fair.

The Spruce Meadows facility in Calgary, Alberta, is as close as North America comes to duplicating Europe's great horse show grounds. Shows take place there throughout the summer into September.

Western riding is spotlighted at the National Western Stock Show, held in Denver, Colorado, in mid-January; the Del Mar National in Del Mar, California, at the end of April; and the Grand National, at San Francisco's Cow Palace, in November. The Reining Futurity takes place in Oklahoma City, Oklahoma, in December.

For top *Arabians* action, try the Scottsdale (Arizona) Arabian show in February. The Arabian and Part-Arabian Nationals take place in October, alternating annually between Scottsdale and Louisville, Kentucky.

Quarter Horse competition can be found at the All American Quarter Horse Congress in Columbus, Ohio, in October; the American Junior Quarter Horse Championship Show in Amarillo, Texas, in August; and at the AQHA's World Championship in Oklahoma City, Oklahoma, in November.

Saddlebreds strut their stuff at October's Bluegrass Classic in Lexington, Kentucky, followed by a show in nearby Louisville. Kansas City, Kansas, hosts the American Royal in mid-November.

The highlight of the *Tennessee Walking Horse* year is September's weeklong Celebration in Shelbyville, Tennessee.

For *Morgans,* try the Massachusetts Morgan in Northampton in May; the Golden West Championship Morgan in Monterey, California, in July; and the Morgan Grand National in Oklahoma City, Oklahoma, in October.

Appaloosa fans won't want to miss the Appaloosa Nationals in Oklahoma City, Oklahoma, in June and July, and the Appaloosa World Show in Fort Worth, Texas, in November.

A final note for spectators: Many horse shows combine several disciplines. For example, Devon and the National Horse Show hold divisions for hunter/jumpers and for saddle horses, while there's both

Western and English activity at the Arabian Nationals, the National Western Stock Show, and Cow Palace's Grand National. You'll also find such admixtures at the many state and county fairs that include horse shows.

GRAND PRIX JUMPING

What, exactly, is the difference between a "Grand Prix" and any big jumping course? Nowadays all horse shows of whatever size seems to call the final jumper class of the week a "Grand Prix." Unfortunately, the sport has yet to set a valid definition or sufficient standards, but the practitioners seem to know what it is. Generally, a Grand Prix is not merely a show's final event, but a truly featured event, one for which a separate admission charge might be made. Frequently it is the only event of the afternoon. It is marked by a greater degree of difficulty; the fences are bigger and there are more of them. It is clearly a *tour de force* for rider and horse.

No phenomenon has had as much impact on the show jumping scene in the last decade as the rise of Grand Prix events. The first Grand Prix in the United States was held in Cleveland in 1965, and from that point the sport grew slowly, but with steady impetus.

By 1984 the American Grand Prix Association tour had achieved total prize monies of over $1 million. There are, in addition, Grand Prix at other shows. One reason, of course, is the growing maturity of the sport, as shown by television coverage. What used to be an occasional few minutes on a sports magazine format show has grown to a series on ESPN, the sports network. Famed riders and trainers serve as experts, teamed with a "color" person who asks leading questions.

Through the years supporters of televised equestrian events wondered why more was not shown on the home screen. It was felt the sport had everything: action, colorful courses, attractive horses, and the chance of watching an accident to horse or rider. It now develops that the action is quite limited from the point of view of the television audience. Courses are frequently poorly covered with too few cameras, and there is (fortunately) far more mayhem and chance of serious accident in, for example, auto racing.

At this point the growth of the television audience is problematical, but attendance at the events does seem to register a modest yearly growth. The stadia, however, seem embarrassingly empty: 15,000 spectators in a 75,000-seat arena just do not fill in all the blanks.

OFFICIALS OF THE SHOW

Horse shows are not spontaneous or haphazard events. Those sanctioned by the American Horse Shows Association must be run according to the rules and procedures of that governing body, while to coordinate hundreds of horses exhibited in dozens of classes over several days requires attention to other kinds of rules and procedures. Throughout the year and the country, thousands of people are involved in making shows of all sizes work. Most are unpaid volunteers who donate their services. The AHSA prescribes the number and types of officials used at its rated shows, but fixtures will often employ even more people for even smoother operation.

A show's president, vice-president(s), treasurer, and secretary assume ultimate responsibility for its success or failure. The president is spokesman for the show, since actions are taken in his name. He may also be the final arbiter, depending on the table of organization. The president is assisted by vice-presidents who are assigned specific tasks such as publicity, press relations, stabling, and ground crew.

The treasurer's role is clearly defined. He collects fees from exhibitors and through ticket sales, and he issues checks for expenses and prizes. At the end of the show he must render a clear accounting of all financial matters.

The secretary, who bears the brunt of the work, is in closest contact with the exhibitors. Her first task is to prepare the official prize list, a detailed presentation of what the show offers in the way of classes and awards. Exhibitors' response determines the size of classes and the amount of stabling space required (if the show is longer than one day). The secretary also corresponds with officials selected to help run the show in coordination with the AHSA. She can usually be found during the show at a paper-strewn table surrounded on one side by ribbons and trophies and on the other by exhibitors who range from questioning to querulous.

Ribbons, Trophies, and Prizes

Ribbons and trophies are badges of triumph, proclaiming to the world successes of horses, riders, and teams. Usually only the first six places are awarded ribbons, although eight is the number in horsemanship and stakes classes. Each place is given a different color, and this order is uniform through the United States and Canada:

First place	**Blue**
Second place	**Red**
Third place	**Yellow**
Fourth place	**White**
Fifth place	**Pink**
Sixth place	**Green**
Seventh place	**Purple**
Eighth place	**Brown**

The Grand Championship ribbon is a large rosette composed of blue, red, yellow, and white ribbons, while the Reserve (or runner-up) Championship is made of red, yellow, white and pink.

A point system is used to determine the Champion and Reserve recipients. It is based on cumulative points for position in each class within a division during the entire show. First place counts for five points, second is three points, third is two points, and fourth is one point. Equal points are given in case of a tie.

Larger shows frequently employ a show manager, who is not an ASHA official. He coordinates the efforts of various committees and resolves disputes whenever they arise (much as a president would). In addition he acts as referee in such matters as arguments over stall space or jumping order.

The veterinarian is a licensed medical person whose presence, either actual or on call, is required by recognized shows. When requested, he rules on animals' soundness and fitness, and he takes urine samples to test for the presence of drugs. His decisions are "non-protestable."

Many shows also have blacksmiths on hand to replace loose or lost shoes.

Other officials include gatekeepers, who handle In and Out gates and supervise the jumping order. Some shows have "official" photographers or tack-shop displays. They are "official" only in that they have been so designated, frequently after payment of a fee for that exclusivity.

These officials are more or less permanently attached to a particular show. Others, those licensed by the AHSA, rotate from fixture to fixture. They do not work as a team, but are assigned individually after being nominated by a show committee.

More than 2,000 Registered or Recorded judges are on the AHSA roster. The Registered judge has had more experience, having passed rigid testing procedures to demonstrate his (or her) expertise to judge one or more divisions. A Recorded, or junior, judge must work under a Registered, or senior, judge for ten shows, then be highly recommended before he can advance his rating. How many judges of either category a show will have depends on its duration and the types of classes it offers. For example, there may be one for hunter-jumper classes, one for saddle seat, and a third for Western division events. Many, if not most, judges are qualified in more than one division, but where more than one ring will be in use, there must be more than one to assess the classes.

Also either Registered or Recorded, a steward is paid as a member of a show's official staff. As the official representative of the AHSA on the show grounds, he makes sure that events are run as specified, oversees the performance and conduct of exhibitors and other officials, is responsible for drug testing and regulations, supervises weigh-ins where minimum weights are required, and makes sure small and large ponies are accurately measured for appropriate classes. Within three days after the show, the steward files a detailed report with the AHSA commenting on the show, its facilities, and any irregularities or complaints.

The announcer has a dual role. To the public he is the "voice" of the show, informing spectators about which entrant is performing. His official function involves introducing specific horses to the judges, informing exhibitors with regard to which gait and direction to take, and outlining various tests to riders in certain classes.

A ringmaster, usually resplendent in a scarlet coat

Horse Show Public Relations and Press Relations

by Marie C. Lafrenz

1. The old rule of "how, what, why, when, and where" is still valid. When you send out a release, be sure to include all the information. It's surprising how many releases I've received neglect to give the date or the location. Be sure to double space all releases and be sure to have the name, address and telephone number of the sender at the top. If any further information is required, the addressee will know where it is available. If the show is being run for charity, be sure to mention that. Even the most jaded editor is likely to feel a bit more kindly if the event is being staged for some worthy cause.

2. The releases must be interesting and well written. It should sound more like a news story than a commercial. If you want to run an ad, be prepared to pay for it—don't try to pass it off as a news release.

3. A catch phase always helps. For example, the Smithtown Horse Show had an exhibit of hounds at their show for years. It was all rather ho-hum to the press until I started to call it the "Smithtown 11 mini-hunt." The reporters started calling me to ask just what a mini-hunt was. It was the same attraction the show had for years but the shutterbugs and audiences ate it up. Other phrases I coined which still haunt me were "You don't need blue blood to win blue ribbons," "The National-World Series of the Horse Show Sport," and "Snowman—The Cinderella Horse." Sometimes one good slogan can sell an event.

4. Publicity should be geared to the size of the show. As a rule, you can't expect to get the full-scale treatment on a one-day show unless it has some unique feature that makes it outstanding.

5. For local papers use local names. It's always nice to make the big time; but it's the local media that pull in the gate and they are very parochial. They want local names. Even if the world champion is coming to your show and you're all excited about it, the local papers will probably be more interested in the item that Shirley Smith whose father runs the gas station on Main Street is entered in the lead-line class.

6. If you are lucky enough to get the world champion, by all means send that information to the big metropolitan dailies near you, but don't assume that the sports editor knows it *is* the world champion. Tell her. Brag a bit about the importance of the champion. The editor may be a baseball fan who doesn't know or care about horses.

Now for a truly valuable bit of information: the phrases "Olympic rider," "Thoroughbred," and "ex-race horse" seem to have a special magic. If you have any of these competing you're in luck.

7. Sending a prize list to regular horse show reporters is a big help. A reporter can get all sorts of goodies out of it: names of judges and stewards, committee members, which challenge trophies are likely to be retired, names of last year's champions, and so on. Of course, a cub reporter who is doing the show won't be likely to know what a prize list is all about.

8. In dealing with big events, such as the National, Devon, or any of the really important A shows, consider doing special features for special columnists. Study their style and tailor the item to match it. On occasion I've written columns in individual styles and had them used verbatim. Such a column must be an exclusive; it's a lot of work but well worth it. Columnists have their following who read every word.

9. Keep releases for radio use very short. You can get double mileage by using your first brief release for both radio and newspapers. Most radio stations want material weeks in advance, and if you are doing a real publicity campaign, that's a good time to start off with the first general news release. Limit this one to just the basic facts. You can elaborate in subsequent releases.

10. Contact any TV programs that have talk-show formats. For this a very special type of PR is needed. A very racy, dramatic presentation helps to catch their attention. Give them a brief description of possible stars who might be interesting for interviews on TV. A word of caution: be sure the persons you suggest will cooperate. I was ready to commit hara-kiri when I set up an interview for a top-rated TV show and my subject chickened out the day before. I was lucky enough to get a fabulous pinch-hitter, but don't count on it.

11. Are displays in local store windows possible? This is a good form of publicity for the show. It involves quite a bit of work but gets wide attention. For one show, we serviced about 50 leading stores, provided sets of prize ribbon, program covers, and trophies to make attractive window displays. It got a tremendous response.

All of the above are preshow efforts—now for the show itself.

Be sure to have a followup. Nothing is worse than to give reporters a big advance rush, then drop them on the day of the show. I like to start off the day by getting a list of post entries from the secretary and copying enough for distribution. The recorder, announcer, committee, secretary, and any reporters who cover the show will love you for making this list. I then like to make about a dozen copies of full, running summaries. These are good not only for publicity purposes but for AHSA or other organizational records, high-score award records, and for the trophy committee, which likes to have a record of who won the challenge trophies. However, if you are short of manpower or don't have a regular PR person, a marked program will do very well.

Do be sure to have a knowledgeable person on hand who can help set up interviews, explain what's going on, point out local riders, well-known riders and horses, and so forth. Too many shows manage to turn off the press by leaving them to flounder. It's a sad but true fact that very often the greenest reporter is assigned to a horse show. You can make life a whole lot easier for him by taking him under your wing. You'll probably get a lot better coverage of your show, too, and I've even developed a lot of horse-show devotees this way. The next year, last year's beginner comes back feeling like an expert.

There's a widespread belief that you can make reporters write good reviews by plying them with food and drinks. I have nothing against this method, but you can do a whole lot more for your project by plying them with good, solid information as well.

Press badges sent out in advance are helpful, but at least make sure that reporters will have no problem getting in. Never charge the press admission.

Now for some basics that seem very obvious to an old hand but may be helpful for someone new to the field:

Try to compile a list of all communications media in your area well in advance of the show. Get correct deadlines and be sure to meet them. If there is any change of schedule, time, or a cancellation, be sure to get that information out at once.

When possible get the name of editor, sports editor, club editor, or any county reporter of a larger paper assigned to your area. Many big city dailies have suburban editors. If some socialite or celebrity is on a show committee, send that information to the society or feature editor. In all releases put the most important information first. If an editor is short of space and has to cut the last paragraph, you will get some pretty funny results if you saved the best until last.

Sometimes you may follow all the rules, and have a fine release, but it still won't be used. This may just be a matter of hard luck in timing. I've had papers print a full release of a leaky roof show that happened to fall on a rainy January Sunday when not much else was going on, and the sports editor was glad of filler material. On the other hand, one of our major shows fell during World Series week. This is just one of the hazards of the game.

If you can afford to get professional help, here's where it should be used. A good PR director and a good photographer can really put your show on the map. Cut out some of the frills and parties if necessary, rather than try to save money on the PR program. It pays higher dividends. If you have to rely on volunteer help, make sure that the person who takes this job is accurate, dependable, consistent, and diplomatic.

Does all of this sound like a lot of work? Well, it is, but if you really hope to improve anything you've got to be willing to work at it. Maybe horse shows won't turn into America's number-one spectator sport overnight, but you'll sure be helping them move in the right direction. Ω

This piece, written by one of the most well-regarded veterans of the horse show press and public-relations world, is adapted from an article that first appeared in a 1976 issue of Horseman's Yankee Pedlar. *Its advice remains eminently applicable for dealing with today's media.*

and carrying a coaching horn, keeps events moving. He sounds his horn to "call" each class, escorts those who present awards to the center of the arena, and also assists in pinning winners.

One or more timekeepers will be required in classes where excessive time is penalized. They will use stopwatches or supervise the deployment and use of electronic chronometers.

FURTHER READING

Janet Blevins of Knight Equestrian Books recommends the following books about horse shows and showing:

Practical Horseman's Book of Riding, Training and Showing Hunters and Jumpers edited by M. A. Stoneridge (Doubleday).
Saddle Seat Equitation by Helen Crabtree (Doubleday).

Four companies that manufacture not only ribbons but also badges, rider numbers, score cards, and other such show paraphernalia are:

A-1 Awards, Inc.
1530 Sandy Court
Antioch, CA 94501
(317) 542-1900

Imperial Badge Co.
P.O. Box 109
Everett, MA 02149
(617) 343-2941

Stineman Ribbon Co.
Lambs Bridge
South Fork, PA 15956
(814) 495-4686

Cornette Ribbon & Trophy Co.
850 Dunbar Ave.
Oldsmar, FL 34677
(813) 854-2824

If any prize money is offered, it is prorated according to position. In a $1,000 stake class, for example, the division might be first place, $500; second, $250; third, $125; fourth, $75; and fifth, $25. Some state championships are determined simply by a totaling of all the money won by each horse throughout the year at the state association's recognized shows. Each dollar represents one point, and at the end of the year an official audit discloses the order of finish.

Trophies are substantial, at least more so than ribbons, and often quite imposing. The winner of an important class or all winners at important shows may receive, in addition to a blue ribbon, anything from a simple plated goblet or plate to a sterling tray, bowl, or statuette. In challenge classes, the same trophy is awarded year after year until the same rider, horse, or owner wins three "legs" on it, resulting in permanent possession. Other challenge trophies are lent to the winning exhibitor during the year and must be returned prior to the next year's show. Some shows have given up on the involved work of trying to regain trophies; they keep the original and issue a replica or plaque which the winner may keep. On the other hand, some exhibitors do not wish to be burdened with actual possession of a cup or trophy that must be returned suitably engraved and in good condition a year later. Frequent winners find it difficult to keep track of which trophy belongs to which show, and perhaps they don't plan to campaign on a particular circuit the following year. These are people who therefore graciously decline physical possession after the ceremonial presentation.

Popular and frequent prizes at Western shows (including rodeos) and distance rides are silver or bronze buckles. Like ribbons, plates, and cups, buckles are engraved or stamped with the show's name and date and often with the winner's name.

Lest equine participants be neglected, horse blankets bearing the name and date of the show, as well as sometimes the horse's name, are given to champions and reserve winners.

Whether sterling or plated, silver trophies require a fair amount of elbow grease to stay shiny. One way to cut down on polishing time is to keep silver in an airtight cabinet, where tarnishing is much slower. This method is particularly good for cheaper plate, which will wear down to the base metal after a few polishings.

Prize money is distributed in one of three ways. Most common is a check handed to the winner along with the ribbon and/or trophy. Some shows keep running records of winnings, paying the total at the end of the fixture or off-setting the amount against stabling and entry fees. Least satisfactory is mailing checks after the show has ended, since resolving any conflicts or disputes is quite difficult.

Ribbons, trophies, and prizes, along with fading photos and newspaper clippings, attest to the transitory glory of the show ring. But since they represent past recognition, they really never lose their luster.

Western Horsemanship by Richard Shrake (Western Horseman).

The Good Mudder's Guide: A Manual for Horse Show Mothers by Cheryl Seaver (Howell Book House).

Complete Guide to Western Horsemanship by J. P. Forget (Howell Book House).

Natural Horse-Man-Ship by Pat Parelli (Western Horseman).

Ride Western Style, a Guide for Young Riders by Tommie Kirksmith (Howell Book House).

Starting the Western Horse by J. P. Forget (Howell Book House).

Western Horsemanship by Richard Shrake (Western Horseman).

Over 25 and Showing! (A Test of Sanity)

───── ∩ ─────

By Sarijane Stanton

Is there logic when an intelligent, healthy "middle-aged" person wants to embark on a difficult, hazardous, and expensive hobby? Throughout your life, things have fitted into your plan; you have organized your efforts and achieved goals. Possibly you have a family and/or business with their multiple responsibilities. Into this confusion you set out to take up horse showing as a hobby.

The first mistaken idea is that horse showing is not a hobby, but another business. This connotes complete faith that horse showing will be workable and attainable as are other accomplishments. Little do you know at the outset the multiple problems you will be faced with as an amateur.

Here are some of the various obstacles to showing:

1. How liberated can a woman feel while traveling cross country and getting a flat tire on her trailer or truck—hoping at any moment that a gallant knight will stop and help?

2. Traveling across country via airlines and rental cars hoping to find a show in some obscure town. You finally arrive to find that your horse injured himself an hour earlier and can't compete.

3. How the expense of showing is always more than you allotted; will your family eat a lot of rice, or will you do without that special piece of furniture for your home?

Dressage

by Catherine McWilliams

Dressage has been described as "the gradual harmonious development of the horse's physical and mental condition with the aim of achieving the improvement of its natural gaits under the rider and a perfect understanding with its rider." Basic dressage training is the best preparation of a horse for any number of tasks, notably jumping, hunting, and pleasure riding.

Aside from its value in training the riding horse, dressage as an end in itself is increasing in popularity as a competitive sport. Horse shows offering competi-

4. Baby-sitters who call at 11 p.m. to cancel when you were leaving for the show at 4 o'clock the following morning.

5. Family crises: A schooling show is running overtime, you are in the last class, and you are entertaining business associates that evening.

6. You fall and feel as if you had been run over. You return home to little sympathy and much abuse.

7. "Setting up house" in a motel room with all the luxury of coffeepot, ironing board, clothes you did not have time to press, and beverages and food for several days. Also one Suburban filled to the top with enough clothes for months and enough equipment to stock a tack shop.

8. The bitter disappointment of realizing you won't be chosen for the Team (you started too late for this particular goal).

9. The new attitude toward "bookkeeping" as you try to figure out show expenses—did you or not? Which classes? Hauling? Farrier???

10. Your children tell their friends that their mother is a "fireman" because she wears black boots.

11. The awareness of how many divorces occur over horses.

12. What is the equine mystique that you can't outgrow? When you ride you become captivated with the total beauty and excitement of the horse; often this takes precedence over other responsibilities. As an adult you would think you could control this lust. Somehow you can't and you return daily for that "moment." That's what showing is all about, and that's why you will never become "overage" in this sport. ∩

tion in dressage are being held all over the United States. Local dressage organizations in many areas sponsor shows, clinics with expert instructors, and educational meetings. Since dressage is an Olympic sport, the USET has a dressage squad which has made a respectable showing in recent international competitions.

The goal of elementary dressage is to produce a horse that is calm, is obedient to the rider, and moves freely and easily at the walk, trot, and canter. Trained on a simple snaffle bit, it is expected to accept the rider's contact while maintaining a quiet, low head carriage with a certain degree of flexion at the poll. The horse's balance and suppleness are developed so that it is able to make smooth transitions between the gaits, halt on command, lengthen and shorten strides at the trot and canter, and bend its neck and body to follow the curves of simple turns and circles.

Dressage training is the systematic method of producing these desired goals. To be most effective, a rider should be trained in the fundamentals of the dressage seat, sometimes called the "classical," "full," or "normal" seat. Its principal characteristics are a fairly long stirrup, facilitating close leg contact: a deep seat, with all the rider's weight in the middle of the saddle; and an erect upper body, supporting quiet hands that maintain a steady contact with the horse's mouth. Except in the earliest stages of training for a young horse, the dressage rider sits in the saddle at all times, absorbing the motion of the horse's slow and fast paces alike by the suppleness of his body, rather than by knee grip or rising forward out of the saddle.

The purpose of this deep seat is the great control afforded over the horse. The rider can use his legs and weight aids most effectively from this position. (For jumping or cross-country riding, of course, the dressage rider would assume the forward seat.)

A major requirement of dressage training not stressed in most other types of schooling is the way in which the horse accepts the rider's hands through the bit and the reins. Contact in dressage means much more than the horse's merely tolerating a certain amount of pressure on its mouth. A horse correctly in contact, or "on the bit," not only accepts the pressure of the rider's hands but seeks to maintain it. The horse must be relaxed in both its jaw and its poll and be willing to yield at these points if the pressure is slightly increased. If the pressure is gently decreased, the horse should stretch its neck in an attempt to maintain contact. There should be no leaning against or pulling on the bit, nor should the animal try to tuck its chin away. The correct type of contact is not easy to achieve and requires skilled hands and legs to develop.

Because contact is not a characteristic of the horse's mouth alone but is a product of the carefully fostered desire to go forward, impulsion must be painstakingly developed by the rider. The forward impulse originates in the energetic stepping forward of the hind legs, then is transmitted through the horse's relaxed back to a stretching of the neck and a "reaching" for the bit. The most skillful hands can never produce good contact from a horse that does not go forward energetically. Thus the energy of the gaits, contact, and head carriage are inextricably related.

Dressage competition is available at all levels of training. In fact, the requirements of the dressage tests themselves, as written by the AHSA, provide an outline for the correct sequence of schooling. The simplest way to describe the degree of training of any horse is to name the dressage test it is capable of performing well. Saying that an animal is a "second-level horse" or a "Prix St.-Georges" horse produces quite an accurate picture in the mind of anyone familiar with these tests.

A dressage test is a written pattern of exercises which is carried out in a special dressage arena. In competition, each horse performs the pattern individually, while the judge (or judges) assigns a numerical score and makes comments on each individual movement.

There are two or three different tests at each level. Test 1 is always less difficult than Test 2 at any one level.

The simplest test is Training Level, Test 1. At the Training Level, a horse performs clockwise and counterclockwise on the correct leads at all three gaits. The animal should accept contact with the bit, keeping its head quiet and mouth closed. In addition to the walk, it is shown at the "working" trot and canter. The working paces are gaits "in which an individual horse presents himself in the best balance and is most easily influenced and worked" (AHSA). A good working trot or canter involves a regular rhythm, a good length of stride, and a generous degree of energy, or impulsion resulting from lively action of the hind legs. The Training Level horse should be able to bend easily on large (width of arena, or 20-meter-diameter) circles while changing direction. The horse must pick up the correct lead from the trot in both directions, as well as making transitions between halt and walk, walk and trot, and trot and canter.

While an experienced rider with a suitable mature horse that has not been specifically trained in dressage might be able to produce a good Training Level test in a few weeks, a young or difficult horse may require a year or more to attain this standard.

First Level tests require, in addition to the exercises in training level a lengthening of stride in the trot and canter. In this exercise the horse is expected to maintain the rhythm of the working gait while covering more ground with each stride. Circles of 10-meter diameter are performed at the trot, and the transitions and changes of direction are more numerous.

At Second Level, the horse is expected to perform the shoulder-in at the walk and trot. This is one of several lateral, or two-track, movements in which the horse travels simultaneously forward and to the side. Ten-meter circles at the canter and a turn on the haunches from the halt are also required.

While many of the movements in Training, First, and Second levels are similar, the standard of proficiency at which they are judged increases with the level of the test. The same change of rein at the working trot that earns a score of 6 or 7 in Training might barely receive a score of 5 if done during a Second Level test.

Third Level tests are considerably more difficult than Second Level in that they introduce the collected gaits. A correctly schooled horse usually requires at least 2 years of training to produce them. Collection is the ability of the horse to shift its balance toward its hind legs. The results are gaits that are springy, light,

and graceful. Although the strides of the collected paces are shorter than those of working gaits, the horse uses even more energy, which is channeled into upward as well as forward motion. This produces the elevation of good collected gaits.

A Third Level horse must also show the extended paces. Extension is developed from lengthening the stride, but is also characterized by a maximum of energy directed forward. The extended trot is one of the most spectacular dressage movements, in which the horse produces so much push with its hindquarters that the front legs "snap" straight forward at each stride.

Other Third Level exercises are the haunches-in and two-track movements, the simple change of lead at the canter, the rein-back, and the counter-canter. Circles of 6 meters (at the trot) and 8 meters (at the canter) are also required.

Fourth Level tests add flying changes of lead at the canter; pirouettes, or turns on the haunches, at the walk and canter; and two-track and 6 meter circles (volte) at the canter.

Prix St.-Georges and Intermédiaire call for essentially the same exercises as Fourth Level, but in progressively more difficult sequences. For example, repeated flying changes are required after four, three, and two canter strides. Also, the standard against which the horse is judged becomes increasingly high.

The Grand Prix de Dressage is an Olympic test. In addition to all the difficult paces, figures, and transitions of the lower-level tests, it includes three exceptional exercises. These are the flying change of lead at every stride (informally called "onesy"), the piaffe (trotting in place), and the passage (a highly collected trot). The Grand Prix de Dressage is truly an acme of the horse world.

Perhaps the most spectacular form of dressage is noncompetitive. *Haute école* ("high school") dressage is done by such troupes as the Spanish Riding School of Vienna, the Cadre Noir of Saumur, France, and the Andalusian Riding School of Jérez de la Frontera, Spain. There you will see the "airs above the ground"—breathtaking rearing and leaping movements as the horses are guided by riders in the saddle or on the ground.

Dressage is one phase of combined training, taking place on the initial day of a three-day event. Tests range from Training to Third Level, depending on the level of the event.

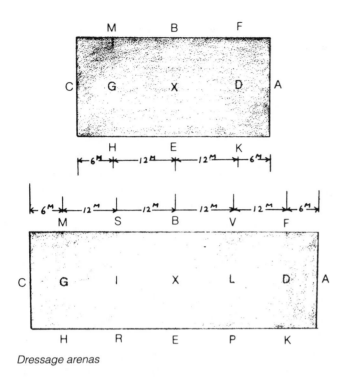

Dressage arenas

Additional information can be obtained from the U.S. Dressage Federation, Box 80668, Lincoln, Nebraska 68501. The magazine *Dressage & Combined Training* (P.O. Box 2460, Cleveland, Ohio 44112) covers the sport's activities and lists dates and locations of dressage events throughout the United States and Canada.

Further Reading

Dressage, by Henry Wynmalen (Arco) explores training techniques up to the most advanced levels. *The Complete Training of Horse and Rider* and *The Art of Dressage* (both published by Doubleday) were written by Alois Podhajsky, former director of the Spanish Riding School. An excellent introduction is *Dressage for Beginners* by R. L. V. Ffrench Blake (Houghton Mifflin).

Common Sense Dressage by Sallie O'Connor (Half Halt Press), *Complete Training of the Horse and Rider* by Alois Podhajsky (Wilshire), *Horses Are Made to Be Horses* by Franz Mairinger (Howell Book House), and *A Classical Riding Notebook* by Michael Stevens (Half Halt Press).

WHERE TO SEE DRESSAGE

One of America's most famous dressage trials, which attracts horses and riders from all over the country, is Dressage At Devon, held at the end of July in Devon, Pennsylvania. Elsewhere in the country are Lake Erie College's Dressage Trials, Painesville, Ohio (February); Central Florida Dressage Classic, Clarcona, Florida (March); Westchester-Fairfield Dressage Association, Westport, Connecticut (September); Potomac Valley Dressage Association, Upper Marlboro, Maryland (September); and Bell Canyon Thanksgiving Dressage, Canoga Park, California (November).

The U.S. Dressage Federation (whose address is given earlier in this section) prepares annual calendars, while the American Horse Shows Association's annual *Rule Book* and its *Horse Show* magazine also list names, locations, and dates for its recognized trials. Calendars in such magazines as *The Chronicle of the Horse*, *Dressage & CT*, and *Horseplay* are other sources of nearby dressage trials.

Rodeos

The word rodeo is Spanish for "roundup," and this truly American sport had its origins in that cowboy activity. Not during roundups, but afterward, when ranch hands gathered to relax, talk turned to who could rope a steer the fastest or ride the meanest bronco. The only way to find out was by trying, and the resulting informal contests became popular throughout the West. In the latter decades of the last century cities began to sponsor events, prize money was offered, and the sport was formally established.

There are now more than five hundred professional rodeos sanctioned by the Rodeo Cowboys Association, ranging from local events to giant pageants. Add to these fixtures unsanctioned rodeos and others conducted on the scholastic and intercollegiate level, and the total swells to more than two thousand every year. Some even take place in penitentiaries, the most famous of which is the Huntsville (Texas) Prison Rodeo.

Five events constitute the most traditional and widely seen activities. Bareback bronc riding requires a combination of brute strength and fine balance. The rider is perched on the horse's back holding only a grip cinched around the animal's belly. He must stay on

Barrel racing

Calf roping

board for 8 seconds. Scoring ranges from none to 100 points; each of two judges awards up to 25 points for the rider and a like number for the horse. The man is judged on his technique, while the horse earns high points for ferocity. Disqualification results from failing to spur the horse at the first jump out of the chute, changing hands on the girth, touching the horse with the rider's free hand, and being bucked off.

Saddle bronc riding is similarly scored, but the equipment differs. The saddle is much smaller than a regular stock saddle and lacks a horn, while the rein is merely a length of braided hemp tied to the horse's halter. Ten seconds is the required time.

Bull riding places entrants on Brahma bulls. Riders may use both hands to stay on board, and spurring isn't called for while cowboys are spinned and bucked around the arena. Eight seconds is the time limit.

Taurine belligerence is also a factor in steer wrestling, also known as bulldogging. An entrant gallops after a longhorn, then jumps from his saddle, plants his feet while grabbing the bull by the horns, and twists the animal to the ground. The fastest time wins.

The fastest time also wins in calf roping. The animal receives a head start; the rider gallops after in hot pursuit and with a flick of the wrist lassoes the calf. He wraps the rope around the saddle horn and dismounts. Then, while the horse backs up to keep a firm tension on the rope, the rider flips the calf to the ground and

ties three legs together with a short length of rope known as a piggin' string. A judge signals when the animal is immobilized, at which point the time is measured.

Several other events are part of a large-scale rodeo. Barrel racing is for the ladies, as each rider traces a cloverleaf pattern around a triangular course marked by three barrels. Chuck-wagon and chariot races are hair-raising affairs. Exhibitions may consist of trick riding or trick roping. And of course, every rodeo includes grand-entry and finale parades.

Professional rodeo riders refer to the countrywide route they take over the year as the "suicide circuit." There are easier ways to make a living. Bruises, sprains, and more serious injuries are accepted as a matter of course. A few turns of adhesive tape, a couple of painkilling aspirins, and the cowboys are ready for the next event. Fatigue also takes its toll, since few rodeo participants can afford to own or charter airplanes as transportation between far-flung shows. More often they'll pack their tack and horses into a trailer, then drive all night to the next competition. To stabling expenses must be added entry fees, and the financial aspect can prove as much a killer as bone-crushing rides and falls on horses and bulls. Why, then, do rodeo riders go through such agony? Part of the answer is the glory, bolstered by amounts of money a successful person can win. Contenders for title of the National All-Around Champion, based on prize money earned over the year, may average in excess of $50,000. Those who are in the public limelight can also receive bonus money for television commercials and product endorsement.

As in other equestrian sports, rodeo riders can start out early in life. There are small-fry events—rodeos for high schoolers and collegians. Further education, rider style, is available from rodeo schools run by former and present stars (many teachers have lost to their pupils who learned their lessons too well).

Rodeoing isn't only for riders and ropers. Stock dealers who own strings of bucking horses and bulls lease them to rodeos. Clowns do more important jobs than perform amusing stunts; they rescue fallen riders from horses' hooves and bulls' horns. Hazers gallop alongside steer-wrestling quarries to keep the bulls on a straight course.

Two popular rodeo and Western horse show events that have spawned their own organizations are barrel racing and reining.

Further Information

The Professional Rodeo Cowboys Association publishes a biweekly tabloid, *Rodeo Sports News*. Information about membership and subscription is available by a letter to 101 Pro Rodeo Drive, Colorado Springs, CO 80919-9989. A monthly magazine, *Rodeo News*, is available from P.O. Box 8160, Nashville, Tennessee 37207. Another organization is the International Rodeo Association, P.O. Box 615, Pauls Valley, Oklahoma 73075.

Undergraduates who want information about their set will find it from the National Little Britches Rodeo Association, 2160 South Holly, Suite 105, Denver, Colorado 80222; the National High School Rodeo Association, 11178 North Huron, Denver, CO 80234 (telephone: (303) 452-0820); or the National Collegiate Rodeo Association, 2925 Isaacs Ave., Walla Walla, WA 99362 (telephone: (206) 529-4402).

Dates and locations of rodeos are available from all the above organizations and also from listings in *Western Horseman* and other Western-oriented magazines.

The National Barrel Horse Association
P.O. Box 1988
Augusta, GA 30903-1988
phone: (706) 722-RACE

The National Reining Horse Association
3000 NW 10 St.
Oklahoma City, OK 73107
phone: (405) 946-7400

CUTTING

Cutting comes from actual ranch work. To separate, or "cut," a specific cow (or steer) from its herd, a cowboy positions his horse between the cow and the herd. Because the cow will then want to rejoin the others, that's when the horse's skill comes into play. Head held low, the cutting horse stays back on its hocks and anticipates the cow's every move, springing from one side to the other to keep the cow from passing, all without any assistance from the rider.

In the sport of cutting, each contestant has three minutes to ride into a herd, select and separate a specific cow (regardless of gender, every bovine is called a "cow"), and then drop the reins and let the horse take over. Whenever the rider thinks the horse has sufficiently worked one particular cow, the rider may elect to "quit" that cow and, time permitting, work another. The judges award points based on the horse's dexterity, also taking into account the cow's enthusiasm toward the proceedings.

Watching a good cutting horse work a cow is an exhilarating sight. Sitting on one is even more exciting, so it's no wonder that the sport is growing rapidly, with

Action during a cutting competition.

big purses and big audiences (and price tags to match on proven horses and young prospects). To find out more about the sport, including where to see it in action, contact the National Cutting Horse Association, 4704 Highway 377 South, Fort Worth, TX 76116 (telephone: (817) 244-6188). Three books are also good sources of information: *Training and Showing the Cutting Horse* by Lynn Campion (Prentice Hall); *Cutting* by Sally Harrison (Howell House); and *The Cutting Horse* by Thomas McGuane et al. (National Cutting Horse Association).

Team penning is something of a first cousin to cutting. The first of a team of three riders separates a specific cow, then hazes the animal up the arena to the second rider. That rider in turn passes the animal to the remaining teammate, who maneuvers the cow into a pen. In some competitions, three cows are cut and penned. The fastest time among the teams determines the winner.

Polo

by CHRISTINE AND W. REID GRAHAM

At midfield, eight horses and riders line up, two abreast. All eyes are on the mounted referee in front of them. The horses are silent, ears forward; the players hold mallets outstretched. The crowd is silent in the bleachers.

"Play!"

The ball is tossed into the middle, and suddenly the horses spring to life. Mallets crack together as the two teams fight for the ball. A horse and rider spring free from the melee, heading toward the goal, and the crowd roars its encouragement.

The game they are watching is in many ways one of the most challenging of all team sports. It demands not only the concentration, timing, and teamwork of the individual player, but also the stamina and handiness of the horse. The polo player must be in complete harmony with both his mount and his teammates if they are to be effective in outscoring their opponents.

The word *polo* comes from the Tibetan word *pulu*, which means "root" or "ball." It was played in Persia as early as 600 B.C. From there it became popular in India and Tibet, where it was played with as many players as the field could accommodate. Paintings depict early polo players as both men and women.

In the 19th century, British Army officers in India took up the sport, and in 1869 polo was first played in England, with more players and at a much slower speed than we know it today.

However, the sport was an instant success, and its popularity quickly spread to the Americas. In the late 1880's the first United States polo clubs were formed in New York City and on Long Island, and the United States Polo Association was organized to sponsor tournaments, publish the rules of the game, and assign ratings, or "handicaps," to the individual players.

The handicap system was a great step forward for the sport. Its purpose is to equalize the competition so that the two teams in a match can start out on the same footing. Each player is assigned a rating (usually between −1 and 10 goals), based on his ability in relation to other players. Obviously, ability on the playing field is determined partially by the quality and number of one's horses, so this factor is also taken into account. In a polo match, the ratings of the individual team members are added to get a total for the team. The team with the lower handicap is allowed to assume the difference between its total and that of the higher-rated team. For example, a 5-goal team playing an 8-goal team would start the game with 3 points already on the scoreboard.

In formulating and publishing the rules, the United States Polo Association provides set standards for the safety of the sport. The game is often divided into four or five periods, or "chukkers," of seven and one-half minutes each. Teams consist of four players in an outdoor game, which is played on a field measuring 300 yards by 150 yards. The outdoor ball is made of wood and is about the size of a baseball, thus allowing players to hit shots ranging over 100 yards. Indoor polo is played by teams consisting of three to a side in an arena measuring 100 yards by 50 yards. The indoor ball resembles a miniature soccer ball and lends itself well to the fast-paced arena game (which is much like ice hockey).

Right of way on the field is determined by the "line of the ball," or the direction in which it is traveling after it is last hit. If a player is riding on the line, for example, and taking a shot on his right-hand, or "off," side, he has the right of way. Any infringement of the rules is a foul. A player crossing the line in front of one having the right of way is causing danger to that player and thus must be penalized. Crossing the line is per-

POLO EQUIPMENT

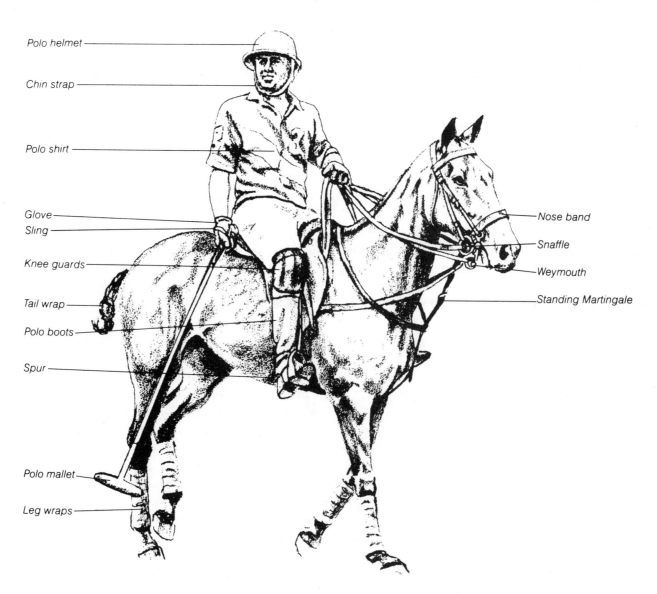

Polo helmet

Chin strap

Polo shirt

Glove

Sling

Knee guards

Tail wrap

Polo boots

Spur

Polo mallet

Leg wraps

Nose band

Snaffle

Weymouth

Standing Martingale

haps the most common foul. Some other examples of riding that endangers others on the field are bumping another player at a dangerous angle, reaching with a mallet in front of a horse's legs, unnecessarily rough bumping, or high hooking of an opponent's mallet. Penalties are assigned a number from 4 to 1, depending upon their severity. A Number 1 penalty, the most serious, is committed when a player knowingly and dangerously fouls in front of the goal he is defending in order to prevent his opponent's shot from entering the goal. In this case, a free goal is automatically awarded to the other team. The other penalties result in a free shot awarded to the team that has been fouled, ranging from a free shot of a set distance at a defended goal to a

free shot of a much shorter distance at an undefended goal. Fouls seem to occur much less frequently among experienced players, who can anticipate the moves of the ball and place themselves and their mounts in the right place at the right time. Those who have taken the time and effort to train a polo pony correctly realize that the safety of their mounts is too important to risk.

The ability to anticipate the play and a good working relationship with horse and teammates are the most important characteristics of an accomplished polo player. Aggressiveness, also important, must be tempered with an ability to sense when and where your presence is most beneficial. It is almost impossible for one player to beat another team singlehandedly. A

Action during a match at the Ox Ridge Polo Club, Darien, Connecticut.

team can work far more efficiently if responsibilities and strategies are designated in advance. This is why each team member wears a number on his jersey. A Number One is basically responsible for receiving passes and scoring goals and for covering the actions of the opposing team's "back," or Number Four, player. This involves "riding off" in such a way as to divert him from interfering with the shots of your teammates.

The Number Two player is more important offensively and is responsible primarily for scoring goals or passing to his Number One. He must be versatile and a strong and accurate hitter, as he often alternates positions with both the Number One and Number Three players if they are not otherwise occupied. He must be able to play both offense and defense.

The Number Three player must also play both offense and defense. Many polo players feel the Number Three must be the strongest member on the team. He not only must stop the attack of his opponents, but also must change the direction of the ball by passing it up to the offensive territory covered by his Number One and Two men.

The Number Four, or "back," primarily defends the goal and attempts to turn the play when his goal is under attack. As any good player knows, these are not rigid guidelines corresponding to the number of his jersey. Positions are interchangeable when circumstance calls for it. Ideally, all players should be capable of assuming any one of these responsibilities when

necessary. All players are also required to guard against the activities of their opponents by riding them off the play or by hooking an opponent's mallet when he is in possession of the ball.

Great physical strength is not always a necessary qualification for a good polo player; a sense of timing is by far more important. If you are sufficiently in tune with the rhythm of your horse to sense the instant in which his foreleg pushes off and lifts from the ground, you can time your mallet to meet the ball at precisely that instant, thereby using the power of the horse rather than relying on your own strength. Many women polo players have used this principle quite successfully.

One does not necessarily have to be an accomplished equestrian to play polo, in fact, many beginners are taught polo and riding simultaneously. Polo represents a unique style of riding. In order to lean over to take a shot, you must be willing and able to lift yourself entirely out of the saddle. The game demands full concentration; little or no thought is given to posture or placement of the legs and hands. The reins are held loosely in the left hand.

However, a sound knowledge of the basic principles of equitation is essential in a sport where so much depends on achieving the best possible performance from your horse. Leg pressure alone must often be enough to stop and turn, or to jump from a standstill into a gallop. These spontaneous responses require a mutual understanding between horse and rider, and patient training of both can usually eliminate the need for anything more severe than a snaffle bit.

Most polo players agree that 75 percent of the game depends upon the horse. As the old polo adage tells us, "It doesn't matter how good a player you are if you can't get to the ball first." Although a horse does not have to be of any particular breed, Thoroughbreds or horses with some Thoroughbred blood seem to excel in the sport because of their speed and stamina. There is constant pressure on the horse to stop, turn, and gallop, and very few breeds can sustain this pressure for too long. Many polo ponies are ex-racehorses, and Arabians and Quarter Horses are often used successfully in arena games, where the length of the playing field is much shorter than it is outdoors.

A good polo pony must also be well balanced and surefooted. In South America, ponies are often taught to execute a 180-degree turn on their forelegs. This

The sport's governing body is the United States Polo Association, 4059 Iron Works Pike, Lexington, Kentucky 40511. Queries on national, regional, and intercollegiate activities will either be answered or referred to appropriate sources.

Twenty-five colleges, universities, and secondary schools are members of the U.S. Polo Association, and you can watch games between them at matches and tournaments during the academic year. The participating institutions are:

California Poly Polo Club at California Polytechnic State University
Colorado State University Polo Club
Cornell University Polo Club
Culver Military Academy Polo Club
Florida Atlantic University Polo Club
Garrison Forest School Polo Club
Georgetown University Polo Club
Harvard University Polo Club
Kent School Polo Club
Lawrenceville School Polo Club
Purdue Intercollegiate Polo Club
Skidmore College Polo Club
Stanford University Polo Club
Texas A&M University Polo Club
Texas Tech University Polo Club
Tulane University Polo Club
University of California at Davis Polo Club
University of Connecticut Polo Club
University of Georgia Polo Club
University of Oklahoma Polo Club
University of Southern California Polo Club
University of Virginia Polo Club
Valley Forge Military Academy Polo Club
Washington State University Polo Club
Yale University Polo Club

takes a great deal of coordination and training and is believed to save time. However, many players in the United States feel that this movement puts undue strain on their ponies' legs. Instead, the horse is trained to wheel on its haunches. The hindquarters can absorb the shock and at the same time provide the drive to start a horse again at a full gallop. Proper balance involves a great deal of schooling as well.

Balance and stamina are to a large degree qualities

that good training can provide. Any player who can't afford the luxury of a full-time trainer must be prepared to spend many hours galloping his mount to develop its wind, trotting to develop muscles and tone, and executing figure-8's and circles for balance and turning ability.

But no matter how much time and patience is spent, a potential polo pony must have an innate sense of aggressiveness and courage. Many horses truly enjoy competition and will keep abreast of the ball without flinching from the mallet or from the physical contact with another horse.

A horse that was donated to the University of Virginia polo team was a magnificent example of this courage and love of competition. To see him in the fields, one would have doubted that he ever could or would play polo. He was a huge animal and stood pigeon-toed when he was not crossing his legs. It seemed that he didn't even have the strength to raise his ears from their usual horizontal position. But when he was tacked up for a game, he would raise his long, thin neck; his ears would come up; and those huge, ungainly hooves became sure and quick. Many inexperienced players were totally unprepared for his speed, his adroit split-second turning, and his deliberate pleasure in riding off another horse. Often he anticipated the movement of the ball more accurately than did his rider; if it took a sudden change of direction, he wheeled on his haunches so quickly that for a few seconds it would seem as though he were actually galloping backward. At the age of 18 he could—and did—show many $5,000 ponies the backs of his heels.

Although it requires much time, as well as financial commitment, on the part of the player, polo in the United States today is a growing sport that offers a great deal of enjoyment to those persons who love horses and competition. There are numerous polo clubs throughout the United States, and the expense and quality of polo vary commensurately. However, anyone who really wants to play the game will undoubtedly be able to do so. If one cannot afford the cost

A canter is a cure for any evil.
B<small>ENJAMIN</small> D<small>ISRAELI</small>
The Young Duke

of a "made" polo pony, he can always train his own. The U.S. Polo Association runs a strong schedule of both high-goal and low-goal tournaments for players of all abilities. Local clubs often hold their own tournaments to determine regional championships.

Perhaps the most important and certainly the fastest-growing polo forum is at the collegiate level. College polo offers the student an opportunity to learn all facets of the game, ranging from basic riding skills and horse care all the way to playing in the National Intercollegiate Polo Tournament. The cost to the student of college polo is kept very low because older players donate horses, time, and money to support the teams. Another significant side of college polo has been the emergence of women's teams at the varsity and junior-varsity levels. At present there are at least eight colleges and universities which sponsor women's teams and provide full-season schedules culminating in a national tournament.

Polo is one of man's oldest sports, and the reasons behind its longevity are numerous. It is a sport that offers something to everyone. To the fan it is a high-risk, fast-paced game full of contact, skill and action, often ending in a breathless sudden-death overtime. To the player, man or woman, it offers the excitement of competition, the camaraderie of teammates, and the overwhelming satisfaction when player and pony merge into one dynamic being intent on only one objective: the Game.

Daphne Bedford on Kilts at "The Kennels" obstacle at The Radnor three-day event.

Combined Training

by CATHERINE McWILLIAMS

Combined training is a competition that tests the all-around training and ability of horse and rider. (The French call it *"concours complet,"* or "complete competition.") At advanced levels in this sport, competitors take part in a Three-Day Event which requires speed, endurance, jumping ability, soundness, courage, obedience, suppleness, and handiness. Three separate tests—a dressage ride, a cross-country ride over obstacles, and stadium jumping—make up the Three-Day Event. At lower levels of competition, these three phases may be offered over one or two days, and the competition called a horse trials, one-day event, combined training, or three-phase event. Some shows offer only dressage and either cross-country or jumping. The rules governing all these competitions are promulgated by the United States Combined Training Association, which publishes a schedule of events held throughout this country, gives a number of year-end awards, and maintains a rating system for horses.

An important characteristic of combined-training events is the great variety of the courses. Unlike ordinary hunter or jumper competitions, where one finds essentially the same types of fences in similar arrangements at every show, each fence on a cross-country course is unique. In addition to the wide variety of materials used (e.g., telephone poles, stone walls, natural hedges, earth banks, streams, ditches, tractor tires, beer barrels, hay bales, log piles, and farm wagons), the positioning of the fences creates both interest and degree of difficulty.

Obstacles may be placed at the top or bottom of steep hills, before or after sharp turns, at the edge of dark woods, and on slopes. The simplest type of jump, which any horse could hop over in the ring, thus becomes a real challenge because of its placement on the terrain. An increasingly popular type of obstacle is the puzzle fence, where the rider has a choice of several routes over a complex obstacle. Usually the puzzle is arranged so that the shortest route over it requires the greatest jumping ability or effort, while the safer or easier routes involve a loss of time.

The most arduous type of combined-training competition is the international- or open-level three-day event. A breakdown of the requirements for each phase shows what is required in this demanding competition.

First Day: The dressage phase consists of a special FEI test approximately equivalent to AHSA Third Level. Working, medium, and extended paces are required, as well as countercanter and two-tracks. The test calls for a great degree of impulsion and suppleness, as well as considerable collection to perform well, even though the true collected paces are not required. The dressage score, converted into penalty points and weighted to give the correct ratio of 3:1:2:1 (dressage, cross-country, stadium jumping, respectively), is added to the penalties for the other two phases to determine final placings. Elimination in this or any other phase is elimination from the entire competition, since no separate awards are given for the three phases.

Second Day: The cross-country day is by far the most-important of the three. It consists of four phases:

Phase A: Roads and Tracks   The distance is usually 2 to 4 miles, taken at a speed of 240 meters per minute (about 9 miles per hour), or the equivalent of a fast trot. It is done over a marked trail that includes all types of terrain, but without jumps. Phase A serves as a warm-up for the remainder of the course.

Phase B: Steeplechase This begins with a standing start immediately following Phase A. The course is about 2 miles long at 550 meters per minute (or 20 miles per hour). Bonus points are given for faster times. The course consists of about ten typical steeplechase jumps up to 3 feet 3 inches in their solid parts, but up to 4 feet 7 inches to the top of the brush portion.

Phase C: Roads and Tracks A route 8 to 10 miles long at 9 miles per hour, run over varied terrain, almost always includes long up and down slopes. No scored obstacles (where jumping-fault penalties are counted) are included, but this phase takes great skill to negotiate while saving the horse as much as possible for the real test to come.

Ten-minute compulsory halt and veterinarian check-

After Phase C, riders dismount, adjust saddlery, and sponge off sweaty horses. A veterinarian inspects each horse and eliminates any that are tired or unfit.

Phase D: Cross Country This course is about 5 miles long at 45 meters per minute (or 17 miles per hour), over about thirty obstacles. The maximum height of the jumps, 3 feet 11 inches, is low by show-jumping standards, but their breadth, construction, and siting make them formidable. They may be 6 feet 7 inches wide at the *top* (!) and 9 feet 10 inches wide at the base. Jumps with a 6- to 7-foot drop on landing are common. Most events feature nearly vertical slides 20 to 30 feet high, often with fences at the top or bottom. Obstacles commonly involve streams or ponds. Each course includes a few multiple obstacles with up to four or five jumping efforts required at each one.

Scoring: Since all the cross-country obstacles are solid, the only jumping faults are refusals, run-outs, and falls. A horse may refuse twice at *each* fence on the course (thereby earning an awesome penalty score) without being eliminated. However, the third refusal at any of the obstacles constitutes elimination, as in the second fall in steeplechase and the third fall in cross-country.

All four phases are timed with stopwatches. Penalties are assessed for going too slowly. In the steeplechase and cross-country, bonus points are given for faster times, up to a stated maximum.

Third Day: The stadium-jumping competition is a test of the horse's ability to recover from the rigors of the second day. First, a veterinary inspection eliminates any unsound horse. Then each remaining competitor negotiates a stadium-jumping course, in which the obstacles are of the same height as in the cross-country phase. The course should be "irregular and winding" and usually includes several combinations and a water jump. This course is not intended to test jumping ability as much as the horse's obedience and suppleness. It rewards handiness and precision, as all the fences can be knocked down easily in contrast to the solid obstacles of the day before. As in horse shows' stadium-jumping competition, refusals, falls, knockdowns, and exceeding the time allowed are all penalized.

The Three-Day Event tests more facets of a horse's

Further reading

Janet Blevins of Knight Equestrian Books also recommends *The USCTA Book of Eventing* by Sallie O'Connor (U.S. Combined Training Association,). *Novice Eventing with Mark Todd* by Todd & Murphy (Trafalgar Square). *Training the Three-Day Event Horse & Rider* by James C. Wofford (Doubleday).

training and abilities than any other single type of competition. Preparing for an event gives the rider a very clear picture of the horse's capabilities in many areas and is an excellent basis for future training. Many good event horses later go on to further success as show jumpers or dressage horses.

Competition in combined training is not limited to grueling advanced events as described above. There are smaller events where the phases are all ridden on the same day, available with intermediate levels of difficulty. A prospective eventer can begin by participating in "Pre-Training"-Level events.

These competitions involve a dressage test of the Training Level variety, a 1- or 2-mile cross-country phase taken at slow speeds over obstacles no higher than 3 feet 3 inches (often much lower), and accordingly lower fences during the stadium-jumping round.

WHERE TO SEE COMBINED TRAINING HORSE TRIALS

The United States Combined Training Association, Inc., 525 Old Waterford Road, NW, Leesburg, VA 20176 (telephone: (703) 779-0440), publishes a semiannual *Omnibus* listing all its recognized horse trials.

Fox Hunting

Although man has hunted from horseback for thousands of years, the sport of fox hunting is a relative newcomer. Its catalyst was the Enclosure Acts passed by the British Parliament beginning in the early 18th century. That legislation required landowners to separate private property from common land, and the fences, walls, hedges, and banks and ditches were inviting obstacles for the squirarchy's sporting set to jump. More serious hunters enjoyed watching packs of hounds finding and following a fox, while farmers were pleased to see the countryside rid of predators on their chicken coops. British colonists brought fox hunting to North America, where it became especially popular in the Middle Atlantic states. Important packs were later established in New England and the South. There are now 146 hunts in the United States and Canada. Most pursue live foxes; some, however, are "drag" hunts (following a scent which has been previously dragged across the countryside), and a few Western hunts chase coyotes.

We asked several fox hunters to list and answer some of the most frequently asked questions put to them about the sport. Their responses provide a nice overview of hunting:

—Q. *Why do people still hunt when there are more effective and efficient ways to eliminate foxes?*

A. The primary purpose is not to kill. Hunting is also known as "riding to hounds," and the canines are the stars. Hunting should be considered a spectator sport, the chance to watch the hounds in action. That's why people continue to wake up before sunrise, travel many miles to where hounds meet (that is, the starting place of that day's hunt), and disregard inclement weather. Many have hunted for years without ever seeing a fox killed, especially if they hunt with a drag pack. Indeed, most American and Canadian hunts try to avoid killing a fox so that it can provide a merry chase on future days.

—Q. *When does hunting take place?*

A. The season is divided into two segments. Cubbing, so-called because young foxes are encouraged to run across country, begins in September. The formal season extends from late October or early November until February or March. Climate determines a season's duration—the warmer the longer, at least until vixens start to whelp and farmers begin to till their land.

Most packs hunt two or three days a week, one of which is usually a Saturday. The time when hounds meet varies from hunt to hunt, from 7 to 10 o'clock in the morning. A hunt may last for only a few hours or all day, depending on the weather, scent, and enthusiasm of the participants.

—Q. *Is hunting one long gallop?*

A. Not at all. There's a fair amount of standing around while hounds explore likely spots to pick up a scent. Even during a chase, you may have to stop and wait your turn to jump a fence.

It should be added that going out hunting is not a license to gallop in all directions or jump everything in sight. Trampling crops, traumatizing livestock, or trespassing on posted property will lead to owners' denying the hunt permission to ride across that land (and there isn't all that much acreage still available for hunting in most places). "Larking," or jumping unnecessarily, is

A meet of foxhounds in front of an 18th-century Virginia mansion.

the mark of an ignorant hunter. Jumping dangerously or trying to clear a fence that's too big for your abilities is plain dumb. There's no shame in taking an alternative route or waiting for a gate to be opened—just be sensible, and you won't need to pack your Blue Cross card in your sandwich case.

—Q. *What does a day's hunting cost?*

A. Hiring and transporting a horse averages at least $50. Some hunts charge a "capping" fee (the cash is deposited in a hunt official's outstretched cap) for a day's cubbing, while others do not. All, however, require a capping fee during the formal session per outing.

In addition, you'll need special apparel during the formal season (see Chapter 6, pages 223, 238, for

chapter-and-verse about what to wear). Cubbing is less formal sartorially; some hunts encourage wearing "rat-catcher" (hacking) clothes, while others permit jeans, chaps, and just about anything else.

—Q. *Then who is permitted to wear those red coats?*

A. Only people so invited by a hunt, and hunt officials. Speaking of officials, the master of foxhounds is in charge of the entire operation. The huntsman (some MFHs assume that function) supervises hounds, assisted by whippers-in, or "whips," who help keep hounds in line. The honorary secretary takes care of finances and paperwork. The field master determines what route members of the field (those following hounds) will take.

—Q. *As a newcomer, where should I place myself?*

A. There is a scrupulously adhered-to order in the hunt field. The master, huntsman, and whips stay in the front with the hounds. Members of the hunt lead the field, with juniors and guests behind them. One advantage of being back is that fences may have been lowered by the time you reach them, and stone walls turned into Kitty Litter by preceding horses' hooves.

—Q. *Should I use my own horse?*

A. Only if it's mannerly and in good condition. You don't want to be mounted on a horse that kicks or is difficult to control (hunt-field activity has been known to turn usually manageable horses into maniacs). Stamina is equally essential, since hunting horses must be able to negotiate trappy (uneven and difficult) terrain for many miles and hours.

—Q. *What is the most important thing a novice fox hunter should do?*

A. Be familiar with hunting etiquette and protocol and adhere to it. Most rules all boil down to "Don't interfere with the hounds or the people who are working them."

—Q. *Where can I learn these rules?*

A. *Riding to Hounds in America* by William Wadsworth, published by *The Chronicle of the Horse,* is something of a Bible on the subject. The best way to be introduced to the sport is in the company of a member of the hunt, and it's also reassuring to be in the company of someone who knows the territory.

If you're not sure that you're quite up to riding to hounds or you'd merely like to watch the proceedings, you can follow the hunt by car or on foot. It's known as "hilltopping," and regular hilltoppers can indicate the best routes and spots to follow and view the action.

The Chronicle of the Horse, published in Middleburg, Virginia, is among other things the official organ of the Masters of Foxhounds Association. *The Chronicle*'s annual Hunt Roster issue provides names and addresses of whom to contact about participating in specific hunts. Most of the following recognized hunts accept guests and visitors, and in some instances a hunt may be able to help you hire a horse.

UNITED STATES

Alabama:
Mooreland Hunt, Huntsville

Arizona:
High Country Hounds, Flagstaff

Arkansas:
Misty River Hounds, Huntsville

California:
Los Altos Hounds, Woodside
Santa Fe Hunt, Temecula
Santa Ynez Valley Hunt, Santa Barbara

Colorado:
Arapahoe Hunt, Littleton
Bijou Springs Hunt, Parker
Roaring Fork Hounds, Aspen

Connecticut:
Fairfield County Hounds, Westport
Middlebury Hunt, Middlebury

Florida:
Four Winds Foxhounds, Delray Beach
Live Oak Hounds, Monticello
Palm Beach Hunt, West Palm Beach
Two Rivers Hunt, Tampa

Georgia:
Belle Meade Hunt, Thompson
Midland Fox Hounds, Midland
Shakerag Hounds, Atlanta
Shamrock Hounds, Rome

Illinois:
Cornwall Hunt, Naperville
Fox River Valley Hunt, Barrington
Mill Creek Hunt, Wadsworth
Oak Brook Hounds, Byron
Shawnee Hounds, DeSoto
Wayne-duPage Hunt, Wayne
Wolf Greek Hounds, Goreville

Indiana:
New Britton Hunt, Carmel
Questover Hounds, Carmel
Romwell Fox Hounds, Romney
Traders Point Hunt, Zionsville

Iowa:
Moingona Hunt, Waukee

The Blue Ridge Hunt point-to-point races, Berryville, Virginia.

Most hunts sponsor related activities in which spectators are as welcome as participants. Hunter paces require teams of riders to complete a course in as close to a predetermined optimum time as possible. Hunter-trial participants are judged according to how well they emulate the pace, handiness, and manners of a perfect field hunter. Hound shows focus on canines, with individuals and groups assessed in terms of foxhound conformation. Dates and locations are available from individual hunts or *The Chronicle of the Horse*'s Sporting Calendar pages.

Steeplechase racing originated as an adjunct to hunting when riders with excess energy raced each other home (the most visible finish line was usually a church's steeple, hence the name). Many hunts sponsor hunt races which feature events for professional and amateur riders, many of whom ride horses they ride to hounds. Hunt races tend to be informal affairs for spectators, who enjoy tailgate picnics and watch jumping and flat races from hillsides overlooking the course. For dates and locations, check local newspapers, look in *The Chronicle of the Horse*, or write to the National Steeplechase and Hunt Association, 400 Fair Hill Drive, Elkton, MD 21921.

Kansas:
Fort Leavenworth Hunt, Fort Leavenworth
Mission Valley Hunt, Stilwell

Kentucky:
Camargo Hunt, Burlington
Iroquois Hunt, Lexington

Long Run Hounds, Louisville
Woodford Hounds, Versailles

Maryland:
De La Brooke Foxhounds, Mount Victoria
Elkridge-Harford Hunt, Monkton
Goshen Hunt, Olney

Green Spring Valley Hounds, Glyndon
Howard County-Iron Bridge Hounds, Ellicott Cty
Mr. Hubbard's Kent County Hounds, Chesteron
Marlborough Hunt, Upper Marlborough
New Market-Middletown Valley Hounds, Middletown
Potomac Hunt, Potomac
Wicomico Hunt, Salisbury
Wye River Hounds, Easton

Massachusetts:
Myopia Hunt, South Hamilton
Nashoba Valley Hunt, Princeton
Norfolk Hunt, Dover
Old North Bridge Hounds, Concord
Tanheath Hunt, Norfolk
Winnimusset Hounds, New Braintree

Michigan:
Battle Creek Hunt, Augusta
Metamora Hunt, Metamora
Waterloo Hunt, Grass Lake

Minnesota:
Long Lake Hounds

Mississippi:
Chula Homa Hunt, Bolton
Whitworth Hunt, Jackson

Missouri:
Bridelspur Hunt, Defiance
Meramec Valley Hunt, Chesterfield

Nebraska:
North Hills Hunt, Omaha

Nevada:
Red Rock Hounds, Reno

New Hampshire:
North Country Hounds, Lyme

New Jersey:
Amwell Valley Hounds, Hopewell
Essex Fox Hounds, Peapack
Hidden Hollow Hounds, Red Bank
Monmouth County Hounds, Moorestown
Spring Valley Hounds, Allamuchy

New Mexico:
Juan Tomas Hounds, Corrales

New York:
Genesee Valley Hunt, Geneseo
Golden's Bridge Hounds, North Salem
Hopper Hills Hunt, Victor
Limestone Creek Hunt, Fayetteville
Millbrook Hunt, Millbrook
Old Chatham Hunt, Old Chatham
Rombout Hunt, Staatsburg
Smithtown Hunt, Aquebogue
Windy Hollow Hunt, Port Jervis

North Carolina:
Green Creek Hunt, Tryon
Mecklenburg Hounds, Matthews
Moore County Hounds, Southern Pines
Red Mountain Foxhounds, Rougemont
Red Oak Hounds, Red Oak
Sedgefield Hunt, Greensboro
Triangle Hunt, Raleigh
Tryon Hounds, Tryon
Yadkin Valley Hounds, Cleveland

Ohio:
Chagrin Valley Hunt, Gates Mills
Miami Valley Hunt, Dayton
Rocky Fork Headley Hunt, Columbus

Oklahoma:
Artillery Hunt, Fort Sill
Lost Hound Hunt, Edmond

Pennsylvania:
Abington Hills Hunt, Dalton
Beaufort Hunt, Harrisburg
Brandywine Hounds, West Chester
Huntington Valley Hunt, Furlong
Mr. Jeffords' Andrews Bridge Hounds, Christiana
Oley Valley Hounds, Limekiln
Pickering Hunt, Phoenixville
Plum Run Hunt, Gettysburg
Radnor Hunt, Malvern
Rolling Rock Hunt, Ligonier
Rose Tree Foxhunting Club, Brogue
Saxonburg Hunt, Saxonburg

272 | THE WHOLE HORSE CATALOG

Sewickley Hunt, Sewickley
Mrs. Shoemaker's Weybright Hounds, Felton
Mr. Stewart's Cheshire Foxhounds, Unionville

South Carolina:
Aiken Hounds, Aiken
Camden Hunt, Camden
Greenville County Hounds, Columbus
Middleton Place Hounds, Charleston
Whiskey Road Foxhounds, Aiken

Tennessee:
Charing Fox Hounds, La Grange
Hillsboro-Cedar Knob Hounds, Nashville
Longreen Foxhounds, Collierville
Mel's Fox Hounds, Nashville
Oak Grove Hunt, Germantown
Tennessee Valley Hunt, Maryville

Texas:
Col. Denny's Cloudline Hounds, Celeste
Hickory Creek Hunt, Argyle
Kenada Fox Hounds, Waller
Stonebroke Hunt, Conroe
Vineyard Hounds, Commerce

Virginia:
Bedford County Hunt, Bedford
Blue Ridge Hunt, Boyce
Bull Run Hunt, Manassas
Casanova Hunt, Casanova
Deep Run Hunt, Manakin-Sabot
Fairfax Hunt, Great Falls
Farmington Hunt, Charlottesville
Glenmore Hunt, Staunton
Keswick Hunt, Keswick
Loudon Hunt, Leesburg
Middleburg Hunt, Middleburg
Old Dominion Hounds, Warrenton
Orange County Hunt, The Plains
Piedmont Fox Hounds, Upperviile
Princess Anne Hunt, Williamsburg
Rappahannock Hunt, Warrenton
Rockbridge Hunt, Lexington
Smith Mountain Hounds, Pennock
Southampton Fox Hounds, Franklin
Warrenton Hunt, Warrenton

Washington:
Woodbrook Hunt, Tacoma

CANADA

British Columbia:
Fraser Valley Hunt, Surrey

Manitoba:
Springfield Hunt, Dugald

Ontario:
Bethany Hills Hunt, Keene
Eglinton and Caledon Hunt, Terra Gotta
Ennisclare Hunt, Campbellville
Frontenac Hunt, Kingston
Hamilton Hunt, Hamilton
London Hunt, London
Ottawa Valley Hunt, Stittsville
Toronto and North York Hunt, Wellington Waterloo
    Trollope Hunt, Hespeler

Quebec:
Lake of Two Mountains Hunt, Hudson Montreal Hunt,
    Bromont

Gymkhanas

Gymkhanas is a Hindu word rhyming with "Ghana" and meaning "field day." The event originated among

Parade of foxhounds at a horse show.

Since riding to hounds can be an all-day activity, a spot of sustenance along the way will be welcome. A sandwich case (or box) and a flask are traditionally carried attached to the saddle (although jacket pockets are often pressed into service). Less expensive are lunch kits or canteens with room for both liquid and solid refreshment.

Ham or beef sandwiches are traditional fare, and tidbits of cheese and raisins are excellent quick-energy snacks. Go easy on complicated victuals, because holding the pickles and the lettuce will be hard to do when the field is preparing to gallop away. Flasks traditionally contain brandy or port, and remember what alcohol's effect on a less-than-full stomach can do to you.

British cavalrymen stationed in India, and it now describes a morning or afternoon of games for horses and riders.

A typical event is "Musical Tires," adapted from that old parlor favorite "Musical Chairs." One fewer automobile tire than contestants is all the equipment that's required, along with a portable tape recorder, radio, or phonograph. The tires are placed around the field or ring in a circular pattern, spaced about 25 feet apart. When the music starts, riders canter their horses in a counterclockwise direction. As soon as the music is stopped, they dismount and, leading their horses, run to the nearest unoccupied tire. A rider "occupies" a tire by standing (with both feet) inside it. Contestants are required always to move forward; even if they are only several feet in front of a tire, they may not move clockwise. When the dust settles, one rider will be "untired," and that person is eliminated. One tire is removed before the next round begins, and rounds continue until all but one contestant—the winner—are eliminated.

Gymkhana events may be included in horse shows or rodeos, or they can be combined in a separate activity. More than fifty competitions for individuals and teams are described in the book *Gymkhana Games* by Natlee Kenoyer, published by The Stephen Greene Press.

Driving

by ROBERT G. HEATH

For 3,000 years horses have served as driving animals in agriculture, transportation, battle, and sport. While the other uses have all but died away, the sport of driving flourishes. In fact, interest in pleasure driving is so strong that as recently as 1975 a need was recognized for an organization that would bind together, inform, and aid persons interested in this fascinating aspect of the equine sports, and the American Driving Society was formed.

Driving calls for a refined style of horsemanship, with the horses moving quietly and under complete control of the driver, called the whip. In the show ring, the judges like to see a touch of flair and brilliance in movement, and these skills accrue to the whip and his horse, as in any other activity, as experience is gained and potential fulfilled.

In modern driving, several combinations of horses or ponies may be put to a variety of carriages.

One horse, or a single, can comfortably convey four people in a four-wheel surrey, but more commonly a single horse is put to a two-wheel vehicle such as a Meadowbrook or Road cart, or if you're going "fancy," a Stanhope gig. Two horses can be driven side by side, a pair, or one in front of the other, a tandem. Except when utilizing a rather unusual two-wheel vehicle called a curricle, or a Cape cart, a pair is driven to a four-wheel vehicle. The tandem, which is almost always driven to a two-wheel carriage, is considered the most sporting of the driving turnouts and perhaps the most difficult to drive.

The lead horse in the tandem does not have shafts at its side to restrain it, and it must share the confidence of its driver to stay out there on its own and not waver. It is not unusual for a tandem's lead horse, whether from lack of training or because it shied at a strange object, to turn completely around and face the driver! At this point, the groom, who is essential to the safe driving of a tandem, has to jump down and correct the situation.

Three horses can be hitched in any one of three ways. Most commonly they are put together as a unicorn, a pair in the wheel and one out front of his own. The same problems faced by the tandem driver come into play here. Three horses hitched abreast are called a trandem, and though this is seldom seen, three in line, one in front of another, are called a randem.

The epitome of driving thrills comes in handling the four-in-hand. Two pairs of horses, one in front of the other, make up this turnout. It is particularly suited to pulling a road coach, which was both a commercial and a private means of transport from 1874 until the railroads eclipsed its commercial use in the early 1900's.

The early training of a driving horse is essentially the same as that for any other horse. Assuming the animal is entirely unbroken, he must first be handled and made to feel at ease around the stable. He must lead into and out of the barn without resisting. Then a progressive program, using quiet voice aids, is instituted. Lunging is done first with a cavesson or halter; then with a roller pad around the girth; then with a crupper under the tail. An open bridle with a light bit is put on in the stall and is worn while the horse is on the lunge, though the line still goes to the cavesson and not the bit. Next, "long lines" are attached to each side of the cavesson and our young driving horse has his first experience at being driven from behind. All of the work thus far should be done in a ring, so that if there is a problem the horse has the confidence that the ring imposes on him. Once the horse moves freely and comfortably, the "long lines" are attached to the bit, and the trainer moves nimbly behind the animal at the walk and trot, maintaining a light contact with the mouth.

A five- to ten-pound object, such as a five-foot piece of two-by-four, is attached by way of two lines that go through the roller pad to a breastplate. And now, for the first time, our pupil learns what it is like to have something dragging behind it. A blinker bridle replaces the open bridle, and for a while the horse will be unsure of itself because its vision is restricted. I want to stress here that all of these formative training stages must be gone through easily and quietly; progress is to come only when the horse is entirely comfortable at each stage of the training.

The conclusion of the preliminary training is al-

Robert Heath driving his Thoroughbred horse to a Norfolk cart.

most complete. The horse stands quietly, responds to the voice, and moves away without diving into the collar or breastplate, and the entire picture is one of ease and unhurried activity. We can now put the horse to a two-wheel jogger, or breaking cart.

The trainer, still on the ground. asks the horse to move off, and here it is desirable to have an assistant on either side of the animal, with lead shanks attached to a halter over the bridle. The assistants may have to help the animal around corners, since the shafts and the restrictions caused by them are new to it. In a short time, the trainer may quietly get into the cart. and at this point we should have the makings of a good driving horse.

It is strongly advisable to have any driving horse go well in single harness before it is asked to drive in pairs or tandem.

Subtlety of aids is the goal of almost all equestrian pursuits, and so the accomplished whip uses the voice aids as quietly as he can and makes his adjustments smooth and unobtrusive. The right hand, which should at all times carry the whip, must be ready to use it to enforce a voice aid. Adjustment of the reins, if slight, may be done by backward and forward turning of the left hand. To shorten the reins, to go downhill, for example, the right hand pushes them back through the left hand; likewise, the reins should be drawn through the left hand for lengthening. The whip must become completely familiar with the position of the reins so that by using the right hand he can make any single adjustment or multiple adjustments without looking down. Not only does this manner of handling the reins convey the appearance of complete ease on the part of the driver, but it also maintains an even contact with the horse.

Four-in-hand or tandem driving brings with it a real challenge. Now four reins must be handled in the left hand, in this order: between the thumb and first finger, the rein of the near-leader; between the first and second fingers, the off-leader and near-wheeler; and

A four-in-hand competes in a coaching competition at the Devon Horse Show.

between second and third fingers the off-wheeler—quite a handful, especially in the case of a "four" if they lean on their bits.

Two further techniques must be mastered. The use of the brake, particularly on heavy carriages, is important to overall driving skill. The driver puts on the brake with the right hand and, if it is properly adjusted, can release it by knocking it off with the right elbow. The application of the whip is another facet of driving that takes a measure of skill, particularly when it is to be used on the front of the leaders in a "four" or tandem who are almost 15 feet away from the driver. It is necessary, of course, that the whip be that long, and it requires considerable practice to be able to use it neatly at this distance and flick it back onto the stick out of the way.

The groom's role in driving should not be overlooked; it requires a great deal of knowledge. He must first of all be a good horseman; he must know how to fit a harness to various combinations of horses; and he must be aware of the simple yet profound mechanics of a carriage. In addition to these responsibilities, he must be of sharp personal appearance so that he will dress appropriately for the vehicle that is being used.

Were it not for the important contribution that horsedrawn carriages made to commercial transportation in the mid-1800's, we might not enjoy such a varied sport today.

The Concord coach was developed in the 1820's by an enterprising New Hampshire firm led by Lewis Downing, who was joined by an expert coach builder, Stephen Abbot. The Concord was a popular long-distance vehicle, which eventually achieved worldwide renown, and such was the demand for it that the men worked 14-hour days and produced coaches with scrupulous attention to detail. This stagecoach was pulled by four or six horses and was designed to carry up to nine passengers within, plus the same number on top, at an average speed of 10 miles an hour. Luggage and mail completed the load, and directly under the driver's seat—or box, as it is still called—was a compartment in which was placed the "treasure box."

Most of the trips covered about 100 miles, but imagine the coordination and organization, not to mention the durability of vehicle and harness, that made the longest stagecoach route in history a reality. In 1858, the famous Overland Stage carried the mail from Missouri to California—a distance of 2,795 miles. It took 24 days and 165 changeovers to complete, and

the fare was $150 per person. Despite enormous difficulties, the Overland's Concord coaches, so expertly built, so skillfully driven, and with the trips so completely organized, made a significant contribution to the conquest of the West.

At the same time in England, the Royal Mail was already running 1,500 coaches a day out of London. Road coaches made their appearance as early as 1784, but evolved into much finer and lighter vehicles than the Concord coach because of the invention of the paved road by Messrs. Telford and Macadam. The government leased various mail routes to enterprising individuals; the operators supplied coaches, horses, and coachmen, while the government provided a uniformed guard for each coach. He was responsible for the coach's keeping its schedule and for the safety of its cargo. The Royal Mail, which ran with near split-second timing, primarily carried postal matter, although when the mail bags constituted less than a full load passengers were permitted aboard—as many as five on top and six inside the vehicle. So intense was the competition among the various operators of these coaches that, with the sound of the coach horn (blown by the guard) as forewarning, the changeover of teams at a relay point was accomplished in less than thirty seconds from the time a coach stopped until it was on its way again. Punctuality was a source of pride to these operators, whose precision was such that coaches at a full gallop passed each other going in opposite directions at exactly the same place on the road day after day after day. One might wish the same could be said of our present-day public transportation!

This exceedingly professional commercial operation took on an aspect of sport in England when "dandies"—dashing young men who were always looking for excitement—would pay the coachmen to be allowed to sit on the box and take the reins. In the late 1800's private coaches became fashionable to own and drive, though the only persons able to equip themselves with a stable of horses and a carriage house full of vehicles were the very wealthy. As the railroads came into prominence in the United States and in England, so the number of commercial coaches declined, though the gentry continued to drive these and smaller vehicles for pleasure.

In the early 1900's, the sport of coaching really took hold, along with the pleasure driving of smaller two- and four-wheel carriages of all sizes and shapes.

A typical Sunday afternoon in New York's Central Park and along Fifth Avenue would see a parade of elegant barouches with grooms in formal livery riding on the back, ladies driving fine horses to George IV phaetons, and gentlemen driving single horses to Stanhope gigs.

The National Horse Show at New York's Madison Square Garden in the early 1900's was dominated by Hackney-horse and pony-driving classes. On several occasions no fewer than twenty park drags—a relatively light and formal road coach—entered the ring to be judged. Great whips such as Alfred Vanderbilt and his famous coach Venture, horsed by four grays. were known across the country. He took his team to England to compete and won the championship at the world-famous Olympia horse show, the only American ever to win this top coaching prize.

World War One interrupted the growth of driving, but the sport rebounded strongly during the 1920's, only to go into a steady—and understandable—decline after the stock-market crash of 1929 and the Depression that followed on its heels. The economic recovery from the Depression coincided with World War Two, and the driving sports continued to be dormant. In fact, no recovery came about until well after the war, in the 1960's. But once it began, it grew in quantum leaps. The Devon (Pennsylvania) Marathon for driving turnouts started in 1965 and drew twelve entries; in 1975 ninety-six entries from all over the Eastern Seaboard came to compete.

The American Driving Society was formed in 1975 to encourage all those persons interested in driving, regardless of the breed of horse they drove. However, various breed clubs, particularly the Morgan, Arabian, Hackney and American Saddlebred organizations, have encouraged driving for a long time. The emphasis that the breed societies place on their driving animals is more toward performance in the show ring and, therefore, often requires a professional trainer. The American Driving Society, on the other hand, places its emphasis more on the complete turnout and the pleasure of driving a horse or pony to various vehicles, most of which date back to the early 1900's.

A typical driving show has pleasure-driving classes wherein the judges take into account the complete picture presented by the driver, his whip, his horse, and his vehicle. The judge observes the way the animal moves at the walk, trot, and extended trot, or trot-on, and whether it stands quietly and backs under control.

1892

Then the judge will turn his attention to the harness and vehicle, looking for safety, cleanliness, and appropriateness. This last consideration allows a hunter type of horse driven to a sporting two-wheel natural-wood meadowbrook cart with russet harness to compete against a well-bred Hackney driven to a two-wheel Stanhope gig complete with patent leather harness and a groom in full livery. Each turnout is equally appropriate if presented properly, and therefore the competition is open to many more persons than might be the case if a different set of requirements were applied.

Tests of a driver's skill are always popular, and two types of show-ring classes measure whips' competence—those judged primarily on the basis of time and those requiring the driver to execute a number of difficult maneuvers.

Time classes can be extremely exciting; cantering is allowed, although it requires a real expert to move through the obstacles that are placed only 8 to 12 inches wider than the widest part of the vehicle. Plastic traffic cones often serve as obstacles so that even if the vehicle dislodges one, no damage will result. The usual obstacle class consists of a course through twenty or so sets of cones.

Gambler's Choice classes are great fun, as much for the spectators as for the participants. Eight or so obstacles are each given a point value of 20 to 100, dependent on their degree of difficulty. Obstacles take such forms as bridges, farmyards, a water splash, a serpentine and a T—perhaps the most difficult. Here the whip is required to drive into the top portion of the T from its side, back up into the vertical portion of the letter, and drive out the same way he came in—not much room for error. A supple, well-schooled horse and a skilled whip are required to accomplish this quickly, since time is also a factor. Each competitor is normally given 2 minutes in which to complete as many obstacles in a Gambler's Choice class as he can in whatever order he chooses, the winner being the entry that accumulates the most points during this time period.

In classes not judged against the clock, obstacle courses are also driven. Here the whip is asked to execute movements similar to those in the timed classes, but a qualitative judgment is made on the basis of the ease of the horse's maneuvers and the ability of the whip to drive through the obstacles without apparent effort. Judges look for smooth performance, subtle aids, and no resistance from the horse—in fact, for the sort of animal we would all like to own and drive.

Combined driving events host divisions for training, preliminary, intermediate, and advanced drivers and horses. At entry-level divisions, one carriage may be used for all three phrases. Many vehicles can now be adapted so they can be used in both the formal presentation phase and as a safer and more functional vehicle required for the marathon. However, upper levels necessitate two vehicles: one for dressage and cones and another for the marathon.

The marathon's demands require a driver to be fully aware of the inherent dangers involved and the need for safety for horses and humans. Every person on board—drivers, grooms, and navigators—should wear protective headgear at all times. Protective vests of the variety that three-day eventers now wear when going cross-country are also a good idea. In addition, the driver should wear a safety seat belt.

Harnesses are now available in traditional leather or more sophisticated synthetic materials. Weight becomes a factor in the marathon, which can range up to 22 kilometers (14 miles), and synthetic harnesses offer greater strength than leather at less weight. They can also be cleaned easily by simply being hosed off. Whichever material you choose, make sure the harness fits properly with no missing stitching or worn places.

Among other gear that any well-prepared marathon vehicle and its personnel should carry are spare traces, a roll of duct tape, leads ropes, and extra bell, shin, and ankle boots.

For many persons, the long hours of preparation that are demanded of competitors and the rigors of the show ring are too much to contemplate; the simple pleasure of driving behind a horse is reward enough. In addition to the fun of driving, many enthusiasts enjoy restoring carriages during the long winter evenings and then putting their horses to the finished vehicles in the spring. Sleighing is a winter sport still enjoyed, of course, by drivers who don't mind the cold, and the sound of jingling bells has a magic of its own.

The Sunday drive through the country reminds one of the unhurried way of life of years gone by, whether you're driving a "horse and buggy" or a carriage to a pair of high-stepping Hackney horses. The joy is timeless!

The following American Driving Society (P.O. Box 160 Metamora, MI 48455) events include ADS-approved shows.

February	Florida State Fair Pleasure Driving Show Tampa, FL (813) 484-4687
March	Arizona Combined Driving Event/ USET Pairs Selection Trial Coolidge, AZ
February	Cherry Valley Carriage Assn. Sleigh Rally Cazenovia, NY (315) 682-1871
March	Live Oak Combined Training Event Ocala, FL (813) 677-3040
March	Welcome VI USET Pair Selection Trial Newnan, GA (706) 253-1201
April	L.A. County Fair Spring Horse Show Pomona, CA (714) 623-3111
April	Aiken Driving 1993 CDE Aiken, SC (803) 648-1696
April	Fair Hill Driving Event Middletown, DE (302) 378-4520

April	Santa Ynez Valley Carriage Classic Los Olivos, CA (805) 965-6588
May	Michigan HSA Spring Horse Show State Fairgrounds Detroit, MI (313) 628-3489
May	Myopia Driving Event/USET Pairs Selection Trial Hamilton, MA (508) 468-3156
May	Vermont Spring Classic Northampton, MA (413) 962-7735
May	Mid-Hudson Driving Association CDE Ledge Farm Stormville, NY (914) 832-6215
May	Nebraska's Pioneer Combined Driving Event Lincoln, NE (402) 789-2545
June	Gladstone Spring Driving Event Hamilton Farm Gladstone, NJ (908) 234-0151
June	Cobleskill College Combined Training Event Cobleskill, NY (518) 993-4092
June	USET Festival of Champions Hamilton Farm Gladstone, NJ (908) 234-0151
July	Fox River Valley Hunt Barrington HS Barrington, IL (708) 697-7091
August	Fairfield Driving Show Fairfield County Hunt Club Westport, CT (203) 378-4520
August	Snoqualmie Valley Combined Driving Event Redmond, WA (206) 622-3720
October	Middletown Pony Club CDE Warwick, MD (302) 378-4520
October	Fair Hill International Fair Hill, MD (302) 378-4520

Anyone attracted to the sport of driving should seek the advice of a knowledgeable person when selecting a suitably trained horse or pony, a vehicle, and a harness that is safe and fits well. (Safety is a factor that should never be underestimated in any aspect of the driving sports. A broken strap can partially separate the horse from the vehicle and may frighten the animal sufficiently to cause it to run away—with most unpleasant consequences. Anybody who takes up driving should beware of "Grandpa's old harness." It may look all right, but almost certainly it is rotting at crucial points.) With proper guidance, a whip will quickly become familiar with the techniques that have been mastered by the experienced international competitor driving a team of four horses or the owner driving his finely tuned show horse. But even more important, every whip, regardless of the level of skill he or she aspires to, will share equally in the thrill of driving a horse or pony to a vehicle.

Distance Riding

The sport of distance riding encompasses two distinct but similar activities. Competitive riding asks contestants to cover a specified span of overland country within a stipulated time; arriving too soon or too late results in penalization. An endurance ride is more of a race, in which the goal is to cover the distance under a maximum time allowance.

In addition to prizes given to those riders who finish closest to the optimum time in a competitive ride or at the head of the pack in an endurance ride, there are awards for horses that demonstrate the best physical condition.

Condition and conditioning are of utmost importance, when one considers that distances from 25 to 100 miles must be covered in three or two days or even one day. Horses must be of breeds and types whose conformation and stamina qualities are up to the de-

Winkers and Blinkers and Shafts—Oh My!

A BEGINNER'S APPROACH TO DRIVING

———————— Ω ————————

by STEVEN H. SIMENOWITZ

ALTHOUGH I HAVE BEEN driving for only about a year, I have always found driving fascinating. Driving appealed to my romantic side, evoking images of feisty, fat ponies prancing down the tree-lined avenues that run through the French countryside, wicker picnic baskets, and Victorian finery. Furthermore, driving seemed like an intensely practical use for a horse, in stark contrast to the pseudodemocratic "one horse, one rider" credo adhered to of necessity by so many horse people, thus enabling family members, children, and other assorted nonriders to experience equally equestrian ecstasy. Moreover, a near disaster with a client who "knew how to ride," coupled with my own broken bones gained during the course of nearly four decades in (and off) the saddle, convinced me that driving warranted a closer look.

Yet, despite my family's involvement in horses for more than four generations, I had never really been exposed to driving. To be sure, a friend of mine once had a Standardbred gelding he had adopted from the race track and hitched to a Meadowbrook cart. Another acquaintance did weddings with a draft horse and a vis-a-vis. Still, nobody had all the answers to the evermounting pile of questions I accumulated in my efforts to get started.

A voracious reader by nature, I pored over every book and article about driving that I could get my hands on. Although I was a quick study, I began to realize that I needed some overall guidance and direction to avoid potentially costly mistakes, as driving is perhaps the only sport in which putting the cart before the horse can have literal as well as figurative consequences.

I quickly discovered that driving even has its own language. Until I began driving in earnest, I thought that *breeching* was something that one did to get out of a contract and that a *singletree* was all a developer left on a heavily wooded lot before construction began. Similarly, where else but in driving could the otherwise unwanted and superfluous fifth wheel assume such a noble stature?

I searched for a driving guru and finally found one in Bob Willumsen, whom I met at a local county fair, where he was in charge of the horse-drawn events. His magnificent teams of Belgians stood contentedly in their slipstalls, oblivious to the throngs of envious onlookers. Bob and I began to talk, and before long the dam burst and the torrent of questions that had been building up inside me gushed out.

He was kind enough to take the time to answer each one thoughtfully and, at last, it all started to make sense. Bob invited me to his farm in Southampton, Long Island, which he operated with his wife, Doris.

I just "happened" to be in their neighborhood a few days later, and he and Doris gave my wife and me a grand tour of their magnificent facility, proudly displaying their collection of horses, harness, and vehicles. I asked Bob to keep his eyes open for the perfect driving/riding horse and told him my aspirations were limited to taking a cart out in the park on Sundays with a single horse. At the time, I didn't quite understand why Bob just shook his head and laughed goodnaturedly.

About two weeks later I received a call from him, telling me that one of his gurus, a logger in Maine, had located the perfect horse, a three-year-old Belgian-Morgan cross whose original owner had taken ill. We immediately set out for Belfast just to look, although I took my four-horse trailer and some money just in case. We arrived in Belfast after dark, but I prevailed on Bob to take me to see the horse before dinner. When we entered the barn, the horse stood patiently looking at me with big, rheumy eyes. Despite a big wormy belly and a bad haircut, it was love at first sight.

Cautiously inquiring about his health, I was presented with a veterinary certificate that read more like a New England poem than a health document. "To whom it may concern: I have examined a three-and-one-half year old sorrel grade gelding and found him to be sound of wind and limb as can be ascertained by physical diagnosis. He travels well—needs to be wormed. Look at his frogs; they are superb. Seems kind and intelligent."

The next morning we took a test drive, hitching the gelding to a forecart with one of the owner's massive Belgians. For an unmatched pair they worked remarkably well together, and it became abundantly clear that Litchfield, as I called him, was coming home with me, superb frogs and all.

After we got Litchfield home, we wormed him and began to train his mane. Meanwhile, Doris started training me with an incredible amount of patience and poise. In ground driving and cart driving, I tried to keep my lines short, maintain contact with Litch's mouth, and keep my elbows flexed while trying to remember that *Gee* meant right and *Ha* left. (I painted G and H on my right and left shoes just in case.)

After achieving minimal proficiency, the subject of buying harness arose. I learned that harness, like furniture, comes in two types: painted and unpainted. Unlike furniture, however, the unpainted harness, which is called *russet* (probably a Pennsylvania Dutch word meaning 20 percent more expensive) is more costly. The theory is that since nothing is covered by black dye, the russet harness requires a better grade of leather, free of blemishes. It stands to reason that black harness is sort of the chef's surprise of driving—you really don't know what's under all that shiny black polish.

Until you work with it, harness seems like a web of disjointed pieces, but once you get the hang of it, you quickly realize that it is in fact a web of disjointed pieces perpetually crying out to be left unbuckled, unhooked, and unsnapped.

Bob recommended a draft express harness with a breast collar until Litch finished growing. We then discussed saddle and collar pads, and I innocently asked what color I should get. [A brief word here about farm colors. Figure out the most expensive thing you will ever buy, see what colors it comes in, and work backward from there. It is far easier to find a piece of fabric for an apron than have your shiny new dually custom-painted to match your tie.]

I chose burgundy and gray, to match my handmade imported charcoal tweed jacket. Pretty soon it was burgundy tie, gray derby, burgundy apron with gray trim, and burgundy sheets and boots, with gray piping. Then the barn (gray stain), the driveway (burgundy stone), the Suburban, and the house. Gift giving was easy so long as it was burgundy or gray. At my local tack shop, if I held up a teal halter and asked its color, the automatic response was "Burgundy and gray, Steve."

Likewise, I discovered that vehicles come in a dazzling array of shapes, sizes, configurations, styles, and colors. As a general rule, stripped vehicles are not all that expensive, so I decided to get a Meadowbrook cart. When I added brakes, half-moon fenders, dash holder, extrawide tires, heavy-duty springs, brass rein rail and whip holder, brass shaft tips, tug stops, upholstered seats (in burgundy and gray), spare kit, tool box, brass hubs, stain, pinstriping, detailing, CD player, and cellular phone, however, the price tag only slightly exceeded the national debt.

Nevertheless, the turnout came together nicely, and Litch is moving smoothly and flexing at the poll (like a vacillating voter on Election Day). Maybe I'm not an accomplished whip, but I'm not bad.

The other day I saw a notice in one of the magazines for a pair of Haflinger geldings. I wonder where area code 802 is. . . . Ω

©*1993, 1997 by Stephen H. Simenowitz. Editor's note: A longer version of this article originally appeared in* Hoofprint *magazine, January 1993. Although the author is now an accomplished whip, this article remains unmodified to keep the flavor of the beginner's perspective.*

mands (Arabians, Appaloosas, and Morgans have been consistent winners). Riders build up their mounts' wind, tone, and circulation gradually through short, then longer, rides. Not only must they be convinced of their horses' condition; a panel of lay judges and veterinarians assesses all equine entrants before, during, and at the conclusion of each ride. They conduct their judging in competitive rides by basing it 100 percent on condition, then deducting points for time penalties.

Distance riding takes place in all fifty states and Canada. Among the most important events are the Woodstock 100 Mile in Three Days Ride in Vermont, a competitive ride, and two endurance fixtures, Virginia's Old Dominion 100 mile and California's Tevis Cup.

Further information:

North American Trail Riding Conference
P.O. Box 2136
Ranchos de Taos, NM 87557
(505) 587-1661

American Endurance Riding Conference
701 High Street
Auburn, CA 95603
(916) 823-2260

FURTHER READING
Janet Blevins of Knight Equestrian Books recommends the following:

"*The New York State Police were first forming and the horses for the various troops were in White Plains, New York. As the horses were assigned into the troops they were loaded into railroad cars and taken to their various assignments. There was one particular stallion, Big Red, that was assigned to B Troop Malone. The horse refused to load in the car. They tried every trick in the book, but Big Red refused. The captain of B Troop called Trooper Harmodue and asked him to saddle and mount Big Red, which the trooper did. The captain handed the trooper a checkbook and said, 'He's assigned to B Troop Malone. Ride him up there.' Trooper Harmodue rode Big Red from White Plains, New York, to Malone. He put a new set of shoes on Big Red at Blue Mountain Lake. Big Red arrived in B Troop Malone in fine shape, and trooper and Big Red were friends for years; the horse would whinny each time Trooper Harmodue entered the stable. Both Big Red and Trooper Harmodue served in B Troop Malone until the trooper's retirement many years later.*"

WILLIAM P. BRAYTON

America's Long Distance Challenge by Karen Paulo (Trafalgar Square).

Long Distance Riding by Marcy Drummond (Houghton Mifflin).

Carriage Driving, a Logical Approach Through Dressage Training by Heike Bean with Sarah Blanchard (Howell Book House).

Driven Dressage for the Single Horse by Sandy Rabinowitz (American Driving Society).

Endurance Riding by Claire Wilde (Half Halt Press).

Riding for the Handicapped

An activity that has been sweeping the country lately in a small but significant way involves the use of horses in working with handicapped children and adults. The therapeutic benefits of animals for humans can be considerable, especially for people who cannot relate to society in usual ways. Riding programs for those who are physically or emotionally disadvantaged have proven to be very rewarding indeed—not only providing pleasurable activity but also helping to build up confidence and improve physical coordination. Although handicapped-riding programs require money and personnel, horse people have responded well by lending horses and assistance (each student normally

Matthew Mackay-Smith, D.V.M., in Vertain, winning the Old Dominion (Virginia) One Hundred Miles in Twenty-Four Hours Ride.

needs at least three people as well as a horse) and by donating funds to local causes. If you are interested in knowing about riding programs in your area, starting one, or volunteering your services, write to North American Riding for the Handicapped Association, P.O. Box 33150, Denver, CO 80233 (telephone: (313) 452-1212).

Riding for the Handicapped— Special Equipment

by CAROL PARKER

Therapeutic horseback riding programs are designed to offer the benefits of riding to handicapped people. In order to provide a safe, enjoyable, and productive program, special equipment is often used. When choosing special equipment, safety is the prime concern. Thoughtful design, quality construction, and use at appropriate times only are important. Many handicapped equestrians require no adaptive equipment. Others have specific needs that require accommodation or use special equipment to enhance the therapeutic value of horseback riding.

The North American Riding for the Handicapped Association, Inc., (NARHA) has published in its "Handbook" the following lists of guidelines for the use of special equipment:

1. It should be used only where absolutely necessary.
2. It must not be used beyond the rider's need.
3. It must not be attached to the rider and horse at the same time.
4. It should not restrict or interfere in any way with the rider's balance, movement, or contact with the horse.
5. It should not cause the rider discomfort or embarrassment.
6. It should not cause the horse discomfort or risk of injury.

Other considerations by the therapist and instructor at the initial assessment will determine the use of special equipment.

These are:

1. The type and extent of the disability. Whether it is a stable, progressive, or improving condition.
2. The age, health, weight, and height of the student.
3. The student's knowledge, experience, and reactions to horses, the instructor, and volunteers, and so forth.
4. The frequency, length, and form lessons will take.
5. The type, width, height, and variety of mounts that will be ridden.
6. The inevitable extra cost involved.

STANDARD EQUIPMENT

English or Western tack may be used in a therapeutic riding program. However, the use of English tack is much more common. Exercises are done more freely in an English-type saddle. Mounting and dismounting are easier. The rider has closer contact with the horse and gains more of the benefits from the horse's movements. However, the deep seat of a Western saddle does offer greater support and security to the rider, especially helpful for the beginner handicapped rider or one who is just starting to ride independently. (Many disabled riders are accompanied by a "sidewalker." This is a person who walks alongside the rider, offering whatever assistance may be necessary or desired.)

Hard hats or helmets with a full chin harness are also considered standard equipment. Fitting a helmet may be difficult because of small head size (microcephaly) or large head size (hydrocephalus), but a helmet should still be required.

SPECIAL EQUIPMENT

Numerous items of special equipment have been designed for handicapped equestrians. Other pieces of tack or common equipment can be used without further adaptation. Specifically designed special equipment includes mounting ramps, Devonshire boots, hand holds, ladder reins, bit leads, and safety belts. Conventional pieces of equipment often used in therapeutic riding programs are Peacock safety stirrups, fleece saddle covers, neck straps, bareback pads, web or rubber reins, overhead check reins, and vaulting surcingles. These lists are not exhaustive, and some programs may use equipment not mentioned here.

Mounting ramp. A mounting ramp is used to facilitate the mounting and dismounting of disabled riders. It is often impractical or impossible for the instructor to lift a rider from the ground onto his or her horse. Some riders will not be physically able to actively assist the instructor in the mounting process. Others will be able to help on a limited basis only. Still others will be able to mount independently from a platform, but not from the ground.

A mounting ramp is the largest and most expensive piece of equipment a therapeutic riding program is likely to have. It is perhaps the most essential piece of special equipment as well. Numerous plans exist, each modified to suit the needs and budget of existing programs. Basically, a mounting ramp consists of a ramp 16 to 18 feet long, leading to a 3-by-4-foot (or larger) platform. Stairs may also lead to the platform for those riders able to negotiate them. A railing should be provided on one side of the ramp, stairs, and platform, so that riders can steady themselves as they walk up the ramp and may mount from partway up the ramp, as well as from the platform. The ramp and platform should be covered with rubber matting or some other nonskid surface. The height of the platform varies. A good standard height is 32 inches. Generally, the height of the average horse used in the program should be equal to the height of the platform plus the height of the seat in your average rider's wheelchair. This makes transferring from the wheelchair to the horse easier. Most mounting ramps are made of wood, although other materials have been used. Some come in sections that can be connected, others are built as permanent, single units.

Devonshire boots. Devonshire boots are a special kind of stirrup, with leather enclosing the front, sides, and bottom, they are used to prevent a rider's foot from sliding all the way through the stirrup. The floor of the stirrup also gives greater support and stabilization to the rider's foot and ankle. Thus, a rider with impaired or weakened control may be able to position his or her feet correctly or at least keep his or her feet in the stirrup irons. A cerebral palsy rider with tight heel cords (natural "heels up" position) would find the Devonshire boots useful.

Hand-holds. A hand-hold helps the rider maintain his or her balance. It offers security to the rider by providing something to hold on to, which is better than grabbing at the reins and abusing the horse's mouth or hanging on to the pommel of the saddle and pinching fingers. Hand-holds are leather straps that can be attached to the dee rings in the front of the saddle. They can also be made larger and attached to the billets on either side of the saddle. In either case, they must be comfortable to grip, somewhat flexible, and sturdy.

Ladder reins. Ladder reins are designed to aid riders with poor hand grasp or poor arm coordination, or those who have the use of only one arm. At regular intervals, the reins are bridged by a supplemental piece of leather or webbing. The rider can then hold on to one of the rungs, enabling him or her to keep the reins the proper length and to steer.

Bit leads and cavesson leads. In many cases, the handicapped rider is assisted by a "leader," a person who controls the horse from the ground and actually leads the horse through his paces. To give the leader control of the horse, a bit lead may be used. A bit lead is a specially designed lead rope that splits in two at one end to form a "Y" shape. At the tops of the "Y" are buckles or snaps that attach to the rings of the bit. Additions can be made to a regular lead rope to construct a bit lead. A cavesson lead may also be used to control the horse. This is a lead rope with a buckle or ring at the end that can be attached to the underside of the horse's cavesson or noseband.

Safety belts. A safety belt is a wide belt with handholds sewn into its back or sides. The rider wears it around the waist or pelvis. His or her sidewalkers hold on to the hand-holds, thus helping the rider maintain balance in the saddle. This way the sidewalkers don't have to grab the rider's clothing, which might slide or cause embarrassment.

Peacock safety stirrups. Many therapeutic programs use the Peacock safety stirrups as a precaution. They are designed to prevent a rider's foot from getting caught in the stirrup. The innerside of the stirrup is the same as a regular stirrup iron, but the outer side has a heavy rubber band attached to the top and bottom. Should the rider press against the rubber band, as his other foot starts to slide through the stirrup or in a fall, the rubber band releases. These stirrups are usually available at any tack shop.

Fleece saddle cover. Some handicapped riders are prone to pressure sores because of decreased sensation, lack of muscle tone, or thin skin. Riders with spinal cord injury or spina bifida would have this problem. A fleece saddle cover should prevent riders from developing pressure sores. Commercial "seat savers" are available that cover just the seat portion of the saddle. A regular saddle pad can also be used so that the rider's legs are cushioned against the flaps of the saddle. Slits can be made in the saddle pad to run the stirrup leathers through and to secure it to the saddle.

Neck straps. A neck strap is a stirrup leather buckled loosely around the horse's neck. Its function is similar to that of a hand-hold. Should a rider need extra support for balance, he or she can grab the neck strap. To hold the neck strap, the rider must lean forward. This is desirable for riders learning how to post and perform the half-seat.

Bareback pads. A bareback pad is basically a soft felt or fabric saddle with no tree. Often small children or cerebral palsy riders with tight adbuctors (the muscles on the inside of the thighs) cannot stretch their legs around a regular saddle. Bareback pads offer a solution. Also, they allow the rider to get closer to the horse's warmth and movements, which actually has a massaging effect on the rider's tight or spastic muscles and helps him or her to relax. Bareback pads are easily found in local tack shops.

Web or rubber reins. These are reins made out of webbing or rubber instead of the normal leather. Riders with poor hand grasp find these useful. When trying to teach an equestrian to ride with equipment as normal as possible, web or rubber reins can be used as a step between ladder reins and leather reins. Web reins and rubber reins are common items in most tack shops.

Overhead check reins. Overhead check reins are also called antigrazing reins. They consist of a piece of cord with a snap at one end. The snap is attached to the ring of the horse's bit. Then the cord is run through the loop in the browband and finally attached to the dee ring on the saddle. This prevents the horse from lowering his head to eat grass. Overhead check reins are helpful to the handicapped rider who, for various reasons, cannot cope with such a sudden action on the horse's part.

Vaulting surcingle. A vaulting surcingle looks like a large belt with two rigid handlebars built into it. The hand-grips should be well sprung from the girth portion, so the rider's hands can slip in and out easily. There is padding around the withers to protect the horse. Vaulting surcingles may be made of webbing or leather. The leather ones are sturdier.

For the physically disabled, exercises may be performed in a vaulting surcingle. The mentally handicapped may enjoy the sport of vaulting. In the case of emotionally disturbed riders, a sense of teamwork can be fostered by asking two or three riders to perform various exercises together on a horse equipped with a vaulting surcingle. Many handicapped riders may be introduced to the canter when being lunged with a vaulting surcingle.

Bells or beepers. Although bells or beepers are not attached to the horse in any way, they still can be considered special equipment for the blind equestrian. Various noise-making devices can be positioned around the riding arena to help a visually impaired rider develop a sense of spatial orientation.

For further information about riding for the handicapped write: NARHA (North American Riding for the Handicapped Association, Inc.), Leonard Warner, Executive Director, P.O. Box 100, Ashburn, VA 22011.

Books on riding for the handicapped (available from addresses listed):

It Is Ability That Counts by Lida L. McCowan, executive director, Cheff Center for the Handicapped, Box 171, RR1, Augusta, Ml 49012.
Reins of Life by John Anthony Davies, published by J. A. Allen & Co., 1 Lower Grosvenor Place, Buckingham Palace Rd., London, U.K., S.W. 1W, OEL.
Riding Across the Silence Barrier: Teaching Riding to the Deaf by Robin Hulsey; Riding High, Inc., 609 Thunderbird Court, Chesterfield, MO 63017.
Riding for Rehabilitation—A Guide for Handicapped Riders and Their Instructors by Joseph Bauer. CANRIDE, 209 Deloraine Ave., Toronto, Ont., Canada M5M2B2.
Therapeutic Riding—Medicine, Education, Sports by Dr. Wolfgang Heipertz, with G. Heipertz, A. Kroger, Werner Kuprian. Published in English by Greenbelt Riding Association. Write Canadian Equstrian Federation, 333 River Rd., Ottawa, Ont., Canada K1L8B9.

Horse Transportation

If you're going to compete or fox-hunt or take your horse along on a vacation, some form of equine transportation will be necessary. Although renting a trailer or hiring a professional horse-transportation company is a possibility, chances are you'll end up owning your own trailer or van.

The primary consideration involving what kind to buy depends on the number and the size of your animal or animals. A van (a "trailer" with a built-in truck) is necessary for more than two animals; otherwise a trailer will serve for one or two. The proper length, height, and width are functions of the horse's or pony's size. Smaller breeds and types can fit into smaller spaces, but it is never desirable to cram an animal into a small vehicle (chafing and poor posture will result).

Regardless of size, a trailer or van needs to meet certain requirements. Proper ventilation is important, both when the vehicle is at rest and when it is in motion. Air flow should be available, but indirect; a steady blast of air on a horse's head can lead to serious medical problems.

You will also need easy access to the front of the

Devon two-horse trailer

Devon two-horse trailer, interior view

Devon eight-horse "gooseneck" trailer

vehicle. Horses should be led into a trailer, and front doors allow the handler to make the safest exit, as well as permitting access should the horse become unruly. The space near the front door is very useful for storing a day's supply of feed, hay, water, and tack.

A two-horse trailer requires a removable divided bar or panel, which should be heavily padded to protect against injury. The partition should be kept in when you are transporting only one horse, since it will act as a restraint to support the horse when the vehicle is in motion. The partition can be removed if you need to transport bales of hay or another bulk load.

Tail chains should also be padded so they won't rub hide or hair when horses rest against them.

Trailers with tandem axles are far more stable than the single-axle variety. The axles should be independently sprung so that they can ride at different heights. If they are not sprung, the height of the hitch is of paramount importance. Rear wheels will not ride on the ground if the towing point is too low, while the front wheels will leave the ground when a hitch is too high.

Trailers are usually fitted with an electric or hydraulic brake system, which automatically operates in conjunction with the towing vehicle's brakes.

A 2-ton trailer is a formidable load for a car, and many small models should not be expected to play Percheron. Larger cars, station wagons, and jeep-type vehicles, as well as pickup trucks, should encounter no difficulty. Whatever you use, make sure that the hitch is welded as well as bolted to the towing vehicle. This job is not for an amateur mechanic, since the safety of your horse, as well as your car or truck, depends on the solid foundation of the hitch.

Driving a trailer requires some training, and a bit of practice with an empty vehicle is a good idea. Avoid jackrabbit starts and quick stops; anticipate your braking needs, then apply the brakes gradually. When passing other vehicles, remember the additional length because of your load. Be especially careful at high speeds or in high wind; a trailer seesawing across a road is hazardous to both occupants and others on the highway. Backing up presents certain problems, which can be overcome by practice. Remember: to turn right, steer left and to turn left, steer right. These principles apply to a one-horse trailer or an eight-horse rig. Some larger trailers have a "fifth wheel" construction whereby the hitch its fastened to a pivot mounted on the towing pickup truck.

Driving a van is somewhat easier, since the cargo area is an integral part of the vehicle. Vans are handled like any truck, although novices will need to become familiar with the transmission's special gearing (designed to carry great weight under different road conditions).

The additional weight of a loaded trailer will also take some getting used to, and you'll want to practice locally with your horse in the back before setting out to drive a long distance.

An experienced horseman was heard to remark as he watched an animal walking quietly up a trailer ramp. "That's worth a few hundred dollars right there."

Anyone who's ever struggled to load a recalcitrant horse into a trailer or van knows what he meant. A well-schooled horse should include as part of its education learning to accept vehicular transportation. It's a matter of practice, patience, and tact on your part, and the lesson should be completed well in advance of shipping. Two hours before your event is scheduled to begin several miles away is not the time.

Loading a stubborn or frightened horse is also a matter of practice, tact, and cooperation. As you entice the animal gradually with a bit of its favorite feed or a treat, have someone (or several people) push its rump with a broom or a rope behind the horse. Watch out for rearing or flying hooves. If a horse absolutely refuses, there's little to be done except wait awhile, then start over (blindfolding can sometimes help).

Before any animal is loaded, it should be outfitted in protective shipping boots or bandages. Padded head bumpers protect against injuries to the poll.

Trailers and van can be bought new or used. Among leading trailer manufacturers are

Sooner Trailers
1515 McCurdy
Duncan, OK 73533

Jiffy tandem trailer jack

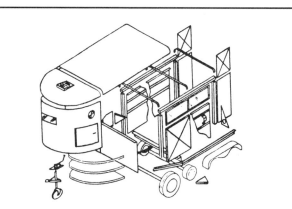

Cotner Manufacturing Co.
Route 611, Box 42
Revere, Pennsylvania 18953

Hartman Trailer Manufacturing Co.
7 Walnut Street
Perkaskie, Pennsylvania 18944

Cherokee Manufacturing Co.
Industrial Park Road, Box 344
Sweetwater, Tennessee 17874

Devon Trailers
Ragged Hill
West Brookfield, Massachusetts 01585

Their vehicles, as well as those of other manufacturers, are sold through distributors. Check Yellow Pages or ask around at tack shops and horse show parking lots.

Used trailers and vans can be bought at considerable savings, but only if the vehicle is worth the price. As in the purchase of any used auto or truck, a thorough mechanical inspection is a prerequisite. Look particularly, in addition, to see that the roof, sides, floor, electrical system, and tires are in satisfactory

Planning to take a trip with your horse in tow? If so, you might want to consider joining the Equine Travelers of America. That organization's directory lists overnight stabling opportunities in (to date) 36 states and three Canadian provinces, giving ETA members' locations and phone numbers and descriptions of boarding facilities, as well as nearby motels, feed dealers, and veterinarians.

Membership entitles members to receive the directory and to be listed in it.

Equine Travelers of America, Inc., P.O. Box 322, Arkansas City, Kansas 67005 (316/422-8131).

condition. Better still, have someone familiar with trailers do the inspecting for you.

Long-distance transportation, hundreds of thousands of miles, requires considerable preparation. If you're not going to make the trip at one clip or you have no one to spell the driving chore, arrange in advance where both you and your horse can bunk down for the night. Take along enough hay, feed, and water for your animal, and punctuate the trip every several hours by stopping and letting the horse out to stretch its legs.

Many long-distance transport vehicles now have Citizens Band radios. They're worth their weight in gold if you have an accident and need to summon assistance, or to learn about traffic and weather conditions from your fellow voyagers. Pick yourself a suitably horsey CB "handle," and "Ten-four to you, good, buddy."

Few people put as many miles on their vans over a year as Billy Robertson, a former member of the U.S. Equestrian Team's stadium-jumping squad and now a successful trainer and exhibitor of hunters and jumpers. Whom better to ask to say a few words on the subject?

How to Photograph Your Horse— or Someone Else's

You've seen many photos of horses. Some animals have been in repose, while others were in action. Some photos were appealing, while others made you wince.

For wide-angle shots, be sure to stand far enough back to capture all the action.

Positioning yourself at the "right" spot permits capturing the horse, the rider, the jump, and the spectators.

A Five-Gaited Saddle Horse taking a conformation pose at the National Horse Show.

Some Considerations in Buying Your Trailer

by WILLIAM G. ROBERTSON

IF YOU ARE GOING to haul your own horses, then the only way to go is to buy a _____!" I so often hear that statement, and it always tickles me. For when I hear the blank filled in with one noted make of trailer or another I always have the desire to reply, "That's true—they're nice; but have you ever tried to (1) drive one all day? (2) drive one on ice? (3) haul a bad shipper in one? (4) load a tough horse into one? (5) repair or sell one?—or, all too often, (6) have you ever tried to afford one?

Buying the perfect trailer as a means of transportation for your horse or horses and being happy with it is like buying the perfect horse. It takes a lot of thought and planning to acquire it, and an equal amount of hard work and "luck" to be happy with it.

With regard to forethought and planning, certain questions must be answered. Once they are, there's an endless list of manufacturers eagerly waiting to sell you your dream machine. But first beware that the dream is not a nightmare! Let me pass along certain basic misconceptions: Basic Misconception Number 1: Hauling your own horse is really fun. Basic Misconception Number 2: Hauling your own horse is a lot cheaper. Basic Misconception Number 3: Hauling a friend's horse is even more fun and can save you money. (But wait until the horse tears your equipment apart, it tears itself apart, and your "friend" hauls you into court and proves that because of your negligence his valuable show animal is now a total financial loss.) Basic Misconception Number 4: Nothing beats pride of ownership.

'Nuff said. Now you must put pencil to paper and labor over the pros and cons of "To buy or not to buy," remembering that your alternatives are to ship with a friend in his van, to use your stable's van, or to go commercial. To make an intelligent decision, you'll have to answer the following questions in order:

1. What will be the cost of the original equipment, the cost of maintenance, and the cost of operation?

2. How frequently will it be used, and who will use it?

3. How many horses will I be hauling most of the time?

4. How long will the trips be, and how much loading and unloading will be involved?

With respect to Question 1, I'm always amazed how someone can justify a purchase of an $8,000 pickup truck and a $2,800 trailer just to avoid that horrible $60 shipping bill incurred every other month or so. Question 2, frequency of use and who will be using the trailer, bears on accessory equipment. When I was delivering horses for dealers, I drove trucks that lacked air conditioning, AM-FM stereos, power steering, and other amenities. They do make life more pleasant when it's my rear end behind the wheel all day but decide whether the accessories are needed for your groom/driver.

On the third point, most people *undertruck* themselves. That is, don't buy a two-horse trailer if you'll need one for four animals, and be sure your engine is strong enough to haul the load it will be required to pull. Undertrucking is both false economy and dangerous.

Ending with Question 4, long distances require major equipment, and there's very little loading and unloading. Let me suggest a floor plan I've used for years. A van stopped at my ranch on its way from New Mexico to Florida one year, and ten polo ponies filed out of that dinky vehicle after a long 14-hour drive. I was amazed; I thought you might get away with small ponies, but not expensive competition horses. However, as I learned, "Horses don't know how much they cost," and cheap ones tend to ship the same as expensive ones—hopefully, with all four feet on the floor. And the best way to keep all four on the floor is to ship them standing at an oblique angle.

This theory is certainly not original with me. Horses were shipped for years loose in boxcars, and mares and their foals are always shipped in large boxes in vans. I just noticed how these animals always positioned themselves to travel at an angle (I've found that standing that way on subways or buses provides the most comfortable position for humans too). In my 24-foot-long and 6-foot-wide eight-horse trailer, I've shipped such nationally known horses as Circuit Breaker and Fur Balloon without any incident, and these are physically big animals.

Such an arrangement is clearly unsuitable for one-day shows where the trailer must also be a portable stall. That is, to remove seven other horses to get to the first one is impractical and difficult. But for cross-country shipping, to my mind nothing beats this system, and as proof, it's being copied by other shippers. ∩

When it comes time for you to snap a shot, you'll understand how difficult equestrian photography can be.

Let's start with taking a photo of a horse standing still. The best angle is a side view, especially if you want to show it to a prospective purchaser who can thereby discern all the strengths (and few, if any, of the weaknesses) of the animal's conformation. First, be certain to include the whole horse. Too many pictures crop off the animal's knees or feet. On the other hand, don't step so far back that excessive background is included to detract from the subject.

There's a real trick to posing a conformation shot. The hind leg closest to the camera should be the farthest back, and the foreleg on the same side should be farthest forward, both framing the legs on the other side. This posture provides the most balanced perspective. Alertness is equally important. Ask the person holding the animal's lead line or reins to attract the horse's attention by whistling, waving a rag, or going through any sort of contortion that forces the subject to raise its head and prick its ears forward. A simple background—a solid barn or empty field—will be least distracting from the horse. Avoid shadows, especially that of the photographer or handler.

Action photographs are more difficult, if only because you're no longer in control of the subject. If you don't want the action to pass you by, plan your shots in advance. Station yourself at a fence and, if you're not planning to shoot one of the first entrants, determine the pace and angle you'll need by watching a few of the early riders and horses. When your subject comes into view, pan the camera (following the subject's movement through the viewfinder) and shoot at preselected moments. Time your shutter release: capturing an early takeoff seems to diminish a fence's height and a horse's performance, while a picture of a horse landing shows the animal in an awkward position. Although head-on pictures can often be effective, side or three-quarter head-on views are better, especially if the photographer stays low to give the illusion of a formidable fence.

Lighting is a problem, but it can be simplified through today's films with their fast emulsions. Sometimes a blur gives the effect of speed and motion. If you don't want that effect, use Kodak's Tri-X black-and-white film. Its 400 ASA rating (speed quotient) can be pushed during developing from twice to three or four times with only a moderate occurrence of graininess.

Confer with your camera shop salesman and processor. The same can be done with color film, both slides and prints, although some loss of color values may occur.

Unless you have a very sophisticated camera, shooting indoors will compound the lighting problem. Flashcubes, lights, and strobe units can be distracting and dangerous if used close up. Moreover, their efficiency is reduced by the square of the distance to the subject. Physicists understand that technical talk, but we should know only that beyond 20 feet, bulbs, cubes, and strobes are less than useful.

Telephoto lenses are a way to move close to the action. A fixed focal length (from 100mm to 300mm) is one choice, while a zoom lens which by a flip of a lever can be changed from 85mm to 210mm is a more useful alternative. A high shutter speed and steady hand (or tripod) are essential in this case, since magnification will translate vibrations into blurs.

You may wonder (and marvel) at how professional equestrian photographers always seem to have the right shot "in their pocket." A motor-driven camera is of great assistance. They merely point and shoot up to five frames per second, an equivalent of freezing frames through a movie camera. The gear, it should be pointed out, is expensive—up to $300 above the cost of a good 35mm single-lens-reflex camera.

At the other extreme are pocket cameras. The most important consideration is to keep both photographer and subject still while the shutter is snapped. Pocket Instamatics or their equivalents won't provide the sharpest slides or prints, but they have their advantages in portability during trail rides, hunts, and other cross-country activities.

Videotaping Your Horse (or Someone Else's)

by SAM SLATER

Since watching videos of your equestrian activities can enhance your enjoyment, at some point you're going to want to take videos of your horse, your child's horse, or even yourself riding. In the following paragraphs, I'll give you some tips on equipment, shooting, and postproduction that should help even the person who doesn't know one end of a camera from the other to produce clear, concise videos that are devoid of technical embarrassments. For, as we all know, equestrian activities themselves can often be embarrassing enough!

EQUIPMENT

People are constantly asking, "What kind of video camera should I buy?" My standard response is that it isn't the make of the camera but its features that are important.

What you first have to determine is how you'll be using the camera. Will you use it constantly, either for schooling, sales, or going to lots of shows or competitions? Or, will you be just bring it out of storage every so often? And, when you use it, will you be shooting for hours and hours, or just one or two short classes or rounds? The answers to these questions will determine what sort of camera you should get.

If you're using a camera constantly and for long periods on a given day, I recommend two things: a fairly lightweight camera and several extra batteries. Currently, there are two main home video formats: 8-millimeter and VHS. The lightweight cameras are more prevalent in the 8mm format, but they also are available in VHS (usually the smaller VHS-C format). The big advantage to VHS is that you can pop your tape out of the camera and stick it right in your VCR to watch it (VHS-C tapes need an adapter that is usually included with the camera). With 8mm cameras, however, you must attach a video line from the camera into a VCR or television, and run the tape in your camera (not a big disadvantage, though).

The main reason for my recommending lightweight cameras is that after an hour or so of shooting, your arms and shoulders can get very tired under a heavy camera. In fact, if you're really going to be doing a lot of videoing, you might consider purchasing an inexpensive tripod. The tripod will not only relieve your fatigue, but will make your shots much smoother.

Regarding smooth shots, many of the newer home video cameras are equipped with internal image stabilizers that do smooth out unsteady shots. This is a helpful feature, along with automatic iris and focus (standard in almost all current cameras), and manual zoom control. The zoom, especially one with a fairly long focal zoom length (at least 10:1 is recommended), is important if you're videoing anything at a long distance, such as eventing cross-country rounds or steeplechase races. Incidentally, long-distance shots are even more sensitive to unsteady camera operation, so image stabilizers and tripods are especially important.

Since most horse sports are conducted in daylight, low-light capacity is not necessarily important, but if you ever shoot at night, increased low-light capacity might be helpful. All of these features can be discussed with your camera salesman, who should be familiar with the various options.

Extra batteries are essential if you're going to be doing a lot of filming. Find out their time capacities, which do vary, and learn to keep track of the time as you shoot. Also, some sort of soft-material case is helpful to hold camera, batteries, tape, chargers, and other accessories. The case will keep all the gear together and, to some degree, protect the equipment, especially from the dust and straw that are so prevalent in horse environments.

Your best bet may be to try using cameras belonging to friends before purchasing one to find out which features specially appeal to you.

COMPETITIONS

The one big rule about shooting competitions is that there are no second takes. The competition occurs at a specific time, and you have to be ready to video then, not necessarily when it's convenient to you. Prepare ahead of time.

Start with your batteries. Before you go to a competition or even before shooting at home, make sure they are fully charged and that you have plenty of them. Nothing is more annoying—or more easily avoidable—than running out of batteries.

Arrive at the competition site early. Test your camera and video tape well before the competition starts so you are thoroughly ready. As the time for videotaping nears, turn the camera on a minute or so early and record some extraneous footage. You can always get rid of it or fast-forward through it, but if your camera's not on in time, you can't recreate footage you've missed!

So you're ready to shoot, the camera is on, and the competition is about to start. You look through the viewfinder, but instead of an image, all you can see is black. That's right—you forgot to remove the lens cap! (You'd be amazed how many professional camerapeople occasionally make this mistake.)

Once you've solved that problem, and you have an image in the viewfinder, you're ready, but you should make sure you're shooting from the right place. Try to avoid filming where your view, even for a small part of the competition, will be blocked. A good general rule is to get some sort of elevation, either on a hill, a grandstand, or on top of a vehicle parked close enough from which to shoot. If you have to shoot from ground level and someone steps in front of you, either politely ask them to move or as smoothly and steadily as possible shift your position.

If at all possible, avoid shooting too much sky in your background. The camera's auto iris tends to darken the action in the foreground when there's too much sky, another good reason to get some elevation when shooting.

Always try to position yourself so you're not shooting into the sun. Whenever possible, keep the sun behind your back, especially early in the morning, late in the day, or in winter when the sun is low in the sky.

When it comes time for the actual shooting, your automatic iris and focus should take care of the light level and focus, while your camera's zoom feature should help keep the horse or horses you're filming easily in frame. If you're concentrating on one horse, a good general rule is to let that horse fill about two-thirds of your viewfinder's frame. As the horse goes farther away or comes closer, you can adjust the zoom accordingly. However, constant zooming in and out can be distracting to your audience.

When filming a horse jumping, leave a little room in the frame in front of the horse so that you can see the animal's forward movement as well as the landing on the far side of the fence.

It's also a good idea to shoot a little more (ten to fifteen seconds) at both ends of the competition, as camcorders can sometimes "roll over" on footage you've just shot, and you may lose several seconds of important stuff.

When the competition is over, especially if it's been a successful one for the person and/or horse you're videoing, don't hesitate to include such features as ribbon-presentation ceremonies, victory gallops, and perhaps even a quick interview with the rider. These can often be the most fun to watch at the end of a good effort.

HOME/SALES

When videoing a horse at home, especially one that is for sale (where a positive impression is essential), remember that in this case, it's *you* who control the time

and the action, so there's no need to rush things. Use the same general shooting rules that apply to competitions, but consider these suggestions specifically for home use.

Although avoiding shooting into the sun is sometimes impossible at competitions, it can always be done at home. You can also choose the time of day when the light is most flattering.

Keep conversation to a minimum. Extraneous noise can be very distracting. It also can interfere with a planned, live voiceover that you might want to do for identification and information purposes (an especially good idea when showing more than one horse in the same video).

In general, a sales video should be kept as simple as possible. Sometimes, it's better to show a young horse loose rather than being ridden, as you can get too hung up on the details of the riding. With an older, more experienced horse, you might do better to send a competition video, either one you have shot or a one by a professional, rather than go to elaborate lengths to get the horse ridden properly for your video.

Remember that you're showing a horse on video. You don't want the horse to look shabby or dirty, but a small amount of dirt probably won't show up on the video, so don't spend hours sprucing the horse up. Also, if you're trying to impress a customer with how high your horse jumps, remember that video tends to make all things bland and moderate, so no jumps will look either terribly high or low. If you're determined to try to impress a prospective buyer about your horse's jumping ability, there is one trick: position a very small person to stand near the jump—the fence will look big!

It bears emphasizing that you should always accentuate the positives. A video of a good mover should contain lots of shots of him moving. If you have what you consider to be a good rider on the horse, the video should show the animal under saddle. If the horse makes a mistake or does something you don't want to show, don't panic—you can edit it out later.

The Hollywood term *continuity* applies to sales videos. If you are doing several takes of a horse doing its thing, be sure the animal looks the same throughout. For instance, don't remove a tail bandage halfway through the shoot. Changes like that just call attention to the fact that you have edited the tape, and could cause viewers to suspect that you have left a lot out.

Even if you do a voiceover, you'll still want to include written information about your horse when you send the tape, since people tend to pay more attention to what they're watching than to what's being said. Again, you are probably better off keeping your voiceover narration very simple, mainly for identification.

The main point to remember about homemade sales videos even more than competition footage is that you as producer and director are in control not only of what gets filmed, but of how it is shot and especially of what ultimately gets shown. Which brings us to . . .

POSTPRODUCTION

You've finished shooting, you've arrived home from the competition or finished shooting at home, and now you're ready to show your video. If you're showing a video to other people, especially someone you want to impress, there's a very good rule for showing *raw* (unedited) footage: have your finger on the remote-control fast-forward button and be ready to use it! This way you can fast-forward through anything you don't want to show. Better still, when possible, view the footage by yourself ahead of time so you can anticipate when the fast-forward is needed.

I strongly recommend dubbing (selectively duplicating) or editing a tape before showing it, and certainly before sending it to anyone you wish to impress. This fairly simple process can be done usually by just running a video line from your camera (or another VCR) to a recording VCR. If you anticipate doing a lot of dubbing, you should obtain a VCR with four heads (fairly standard nowadays), which makes a much cleaner dub. Basically, to make a dub, all you have to do is play your original tape in your camera (or second VCR) and record it onto your recording VCR, keeping the recording VCR in *record* and pushing the *pause* button on the recording VCR whenever you see footage you don't want. The video salesperson, VCR manual, or a knowledgeable friend will explain how to dub, but the process really is very simple.

There are two reasons for dubbing footage before you show it or especially before you send it to someone: one, you are showing an edited tape that only has what you want the viewer to see. Two, you can retain the original, so if anything happens to the copy, you can always make another one.

Many of this article's recommendations apply to videotaping any activity, not just equestrian matters. But I think it is important to remember the basic rules

of horse videos: be on time for the competition! allow room in the frame for the horse to jump or move forward, accentuate the horse's (and rider's) positives, and—most important of all—keep it *simple.* These all can add up to a video production that is useful and informative but, more important, a pleasure to watch. ∩

Sam Slater, whose Hunt Cup Productions is based in Coatesville, Pennsylvania, is a longtime follower—with and without a video camera—of the equestrian scene.

All in the Mind: The Rise of Sports Psychology

Those of us of a certain generation recall with often less than great fondness certain aspects of our early riding lessons. "Up–down, up–down" we were told. "Heels down . . . lower your hands," the instructor continued, issuing a nonstop series of commands from often drill-sergeantlike instructors. And when our heels or hands didn't stay, we were just as often corrected at an increased volume and in a more exasperated tone of voice.

Competition was, if anything, more of the same. As we sat on our horses at the gate waiting to enter the ring, our stomachs full of butterflies and our faces the color of new-mown hay, we were ordered to relax. And when our expressions didn't change, we were simply told, "Didn't you hear me? I said *relax!*"

Even though *The Whole Horse Catalog* isn't a riding manual, an innovation in equestrian training has become so important that not to include even a brief essay would be a real sin of omission. The subject is sports psychology or, more specifically, improving riding by improving the rider's mental and physical awareness. To some degree or another, the "mental game of riding" has all but replaced learning-by-rote/military command styles for basic instruction and preparing for and taking part in horse shows and other equestrian competitions.

The first and still the most important guru is Sally Swift, whose *Centered Riding* (Trafalgar Square Press) introduced the approach to the horse world in the mid-1980s (other sports had already discovered it, through such books as *The Inner Game Of Tennis*). As Swift uses the word, *centered* refers as much to a mental as to a physical process, describing inner awareness as well as body balance. An important concept is *soft eyes,* that shift attention away from visual stimuli to allow the mind and body to focus more on feeling what the rider's and the horse's bodies are doing.

Swift also provides a thought-provoking array of images intended to help visualize or sense what various aspects of riding are meant to feel like. For example, the rider's hands should hold the reins as if they were holding little birds: too tight a grip will hurt the birds, while one that's too loose will permit them to fly away.

Centered Riding is now also available as a series of videos. Both formats are best sellers, and deservedly so: few people have delved into what Sally Swift offers without discovering something that has enhanced their riding—and in the process provided a better understanding of how our minds and bodies learn.

In *The Natural Rider,* (Summit Books) British trainer Mary Wanless makes much of the difference between the hemispheres of the human brain. The left side of the brain is the verbal and linear side that processes information in a logical fashion. The right side is nonverbal and feelingly automatic; it accounts for how we learn by what can be described only as intuition, as in when something just comes to us. Wanless suggests many ways to develop right-side feeling, then sets forth awareness questions and imagery that test readers' and riders' techniques and, equally important, their perceptions. Some questions are specific, others are more abstract. All require considerable thought and honesty. For example:

* Do you feel satisfied with your ability to ride horses on the bit, or are you still struggling with this? Is it the end point or the beginning point of your work? How much do you know about what you do to the horse and what the horse does to you? How do you deal with your own frustration? How does this differ when you are working alone and when other people are watching you?
* Do you tend to blame the horse as a scapegoat, or defer to him?
* Do you blame him, or do you blame yourself? Are you threatened by the horse, or challenged by him?

A second book by Wanless, *Ride With Your Mind Masterclass,* takes this approach even further (it's subtitled *An Illustrated Guide to Right Brain Riding*). Case studies of the author's students examine their problems and describe how Wanless worked them through the difficulties. One such study, set forth in the chapter "Becoming Casual," talks about the effects of fear on the human body. An emphasis on human and equine biomechanics throughout this book particularly recommends it to instructors.

Images are at the heart of *That Winning Feeling!* by Jane Savoie (Trafalgar Square Press). The author calls her approach *psychocybernetics,* a mechanism that uses visualization and positive thinking to succeed. Although some readers may raise an eyebrow at the cheerleader pep-talk tone, others will find such basic concepts as learning by reward and reinforcement helpful. The chapters on mental rehearsals and other forms of preparation for competition are particularly good.

Readers of *Practical Horseman* are familiar with columns by the magazine's resident psychologist, Dr. Janet Sasson Edgette. Her book, *Heads Up! Practical Sports Psychology for Riders, Their Trainers, and Their Families* (Doubleday), will earn the good doctor even more fans. She stresses the processes whereby we can make changes. Such changes need not be upsetting, or even require learning new skills: a child who had the positive experience of working on a school project with a classmate can use the same feeling of partnership with a pony with whom she had formerly been at odds. The book's forthright and sensible discussions of interpersonal relationships, especially between students and instructors, make it a highly recommended addition to the literature.

Thanks to the authors of these books, together with other trainers, writers, and sports psychologists, the horse world has discovered the value of meditation, self-hypnosis, mental rehearsal, and rituals and symbols. Mental rehearsal is a particularly prevalent technique: the rider visualizes the perfect equitation round or dressage test or reining go-round, then tries to duplicate in the arena what she has seen and felt in her mind's eye.

Sports psychology as applied to riding is a growing field, largely because it's been shown to work. In the words of Kip Rosenthal, who is both a successful hunter-jumper trainer and a trained psychologist, "We have always had systems to develop a horse's physical ability, as well as to help horses mature mentally. We've also had systems to teach riders the physical aspects of form and control. And now, finally, there are techniques designed to help riders deal with the mental demands of training and competition."

Sherlocks And Fetlocks: Mystery Novels and Horses

∩

by STEVEN D. PRICE

IT SHOULD COME AS NO surprise that of all the horse-related themes in mystery fiction, the odds-on choice has always been racing. With vast sums of money riding on the outcome of races and with Thoroughbreds bought, sold, or syndicated for millions of dollars (pounds sterling in the case of our British cousins), there's no lack of motive or opportunity for skullduggery. Accordingly, let's begin this brief survey of equine whodunits with the sport of kings—and cons.

Mention horses to any mystery buff, and five'll get you ten that the response will be "Dick Francis." The British ex-steeplechase jockey not only was the first of several riders to swap their tack for typewriters, but Francis's track record also shows him to be not only the most prolific (a book a year for the past three decades) but among the most successful contemporary mystery writers of any genre.

Francis's early efforts remain, to many minds, his best. In addition to well-plotted and fast-paced stories, such books as *Nerve, Odds Against, Bonecrack,* and *Forfeit* had as protagonists jockeys who provide vivid insights into the rigorous physical and mental demands of racing over fences.

One early book, *Flying Finish,* was as much about small-aircraft piloting as about racing. That provided a foretaste of what might be described as Francis's middle period, in which story lines included other subjects. For example, *In The Frame* dealt with the art world, *Reflex* with photography, *Banker* with high finance, and *Proof* with the wine and spirits business. Although readers learned a goodly amount about these subjects, we did so at the expense of horses, which was, after all, the reason many of us so eagerly awaited his books.

Francis's most recent books show a skill at writing novels that almost transcends the genre. Characters and characterizations have become more complex and more deftly and convincingly handled, as *Longshot, Comeback, Decider* and *Come to Grief* (marking the reappearance of a favorite protagonist, Sid Halley) show. His most recent novel—*10 Lb. Penalty*—combines particularly deft characterization with horsey interludes that any reader, or rider, will enjoy.

Mark Daniel, whose credentials include being raised in a training yard and editing a racing journal, demonstrates a knowledge that can only be gained firsthand. And the man knows how to write: *Unbridled, The Devil to Pay,* and *The Bold Thing* belong in the same field as early Dick Francis with regard to conveying the race-riding experience; *Unbridled*'s chapter on winning the Grand National mirrors descriptions by people who have actually ridden around the Aintree course. High marks also go to Daniel's ear for dialogue and his earthy descriptions.

Another British entry in the field is John Francome, the successful National Hunt jockey. His credits, with collaborators, include seven books, among them *Outsider, Rough Ride, Blood Stock,* and *Declared Dead.* Although the plotting tends to be pedestrian and the writing often florid, there's an authentic aroma of horses and racetracks throughout.

Alas, the same cannot be said for an American entry in the Rider-Turned-Writer Sweepstakes. The legendary jockey Bill Shoemaker is the putative author of *Stalking Horse* and *Fire Horse.* The plots are adequate, but it's a shame that whoever wrote under Shoemaker's name failed to convey any of the sense of "horse"-ness that the previously mentioned British books do.

Not all crimesolvers come from the backstretch. Railbirds find occasions for such chores, and the best of them is Shifty Anderson, the protagonist of William Murray's entertaining novels. A professional magician when he isn't trying to pull winners out of his hat, Anderson can be found in, among other titles, *The Getaway Blues, The Hardknocker's Luck,* and *When the Fat Man Sings.* Murray earns bonus points for his characters and for his dialogue, too.

Let's not forget that the racing-mystery genre began with the classic Sir Arthur Conan Doyle's Sherlock Holmes tale *The Mystery of Silver Blaze.*

Speaking of classic mysteries, let's begin a brief survey of other disciplines than racing with Josephine Tey's *Brat Farrar,* which concern a mysterious young man who may or may not be the heir to an English riding school. *Airs Above the Ground* is Mary Stewart's equally venerable espionage effort that involves Spanish Riding School Lipizzaners.

Contemporary authors include Carolyn Banks, whose protagonist, Robin Vaughan, is a transplanted Texan and a dressage enthusiast. *Death by Dressage* takes good advantage of the author's obvious familiarity with the enter-at-A-halt-at-X crowd, while *Groomed for Death* finds a vacationing Vaughan snooping around Manhattan's Claremont Riding Academy. Other titles in the series are *Murder Well Bred, Death on the Diagonal,* and *A Horse to Die For* (and there will no doubt be others by the time you read this, given the pace and impulsion with which Banks produces books).

The hunter-jumper world is well served by Jody Jaffe. Her heroine, Natalie Gold, a reporter on a North Carolina newspaper when she isn't riding in amateur-owner hunter classes, first appeared in *Horse of a Different Killer.* Other novels, *Chestnut Mare, Beware* and *In Colt Blood,* delivered more of the same: Gold glitters in snappy dialogue, Jaffee knows horse shows and their denizens, and despite a leit-motif of kvetching that tends to become tedious, mystery buffs will look forward to more from this talented writer.

Finally, a word about unearthing these books. Nothing succeeds like success, and Dick Francis's mysteries have found eternal paperback life beyond their original hardcover form. Ditto William Murray, Carolyn Banks, and Jody Jaffe. As for the others, locating those that are out of print or even out of stock (the publisher hasn't gotten around to reprinting copies) takes as much work as picking a winner in a field of eight-year-old maidens. Bookshops that specialize in mysteries should be your first stop, since these places often have out-of-print and secondhand sections (they also have proprietors and sales help that will be aware of other horsey mysteries). Public libraries are another likely source.

Like handicapping a horse race, looking for books can be a time-consuming and frustrating procedure, but also like handicapping, the payoff is worth the effort. Or, to switch equestrian metaphors, happy hunting. Ω

Steven D. Price is the author of a mystery set in the horse-show world Riding For A Fall *(Tor Books, 1987—and very much out of print). This essay is adapted from one first published in* The National Sporting Library Newsletter *and is reprinted here with the NSL's kind permission.*

Hollywood Goes to the Horses, or "Cue The Pinto"

Think of horses in the movies, and the image of cowboys galloping through the purple sage and across the silver screen comes to mind. But before we talk about *oaters* (as Westerns were once familiarly known), let's look at flicks that contain other riding styles and activities.

Some of these movies can be easily rented or purchased at your local video store. Others are harder to come by, so keeping a close eye on newspaper TV listings, especially AMC and other old movie channels, is necessary. Still other movies are almost impossible to find, but since they're so good, at least from a horsy point of view, we just couldn't leave them out.

Dressage calls to mind the Spanish Riding School Lipizzaners. The story of how General George Patton arranged for their rescue at the end of World War Two is told in Disney's *Miracle of the White Stallions*, starring Robert Taylor as the School's commandant. For other scenes with Lipizzaners, *Patton* contains a brief segment that shows George C. Scott riding one, while in *The Seven Per Cent Solution* (Sherlock Holmes meets Sigmund Freud) there's a sequence of Lipizzaners galloping loose around their Vienna riding hall.

Three-day eventing has been well served in two movies, both of which include footage from actual horse trials competition. *International Velvet* takes Tatum O'Neal to the British Olympic squad where the sharp-tongued coach is played by Anthony Hopkins (perhaps, some might argue, excellent training for his subsequent role as Hannibal Lecter). *Sylvester* (1985) stars Melissa Gilbert who discovers and then excels at eventing, making her mark at a competition at the Kentucky Horse Park.

Something to Talk About, a relatively recent movie that peripherally deals with show jumping, stars Julia Roberts. Robert Duvall appears as her father, who runs a hunter/jumper training and sales barn. The height of the fences in the finale look suspiciously low for a so-called Grand Prix, but—hey—that's show biz.

In *This Happy Feeling,* Curt Jurgens rides in an old-style jumper class in a movie that also starred Debbie Reynolds and Alexis Smith. Ms. Smith also stars in *Stallion Road,* in which Ronald Reagan plays a veterinarian who vies with Zachery Scott for her affections. The jumping here includes a six-bar competition, which shows the flick's age almost as clearly as the pegged breeches worn by the riders.

Will a youngster on an inexpensive pony named *Danny* win the big equitation class? Is there any doubt? It's a sweet story anyway, authentically made and with no well-known actors.

Two old Disney live-action movies are very much worth seeking out. *The Horse in the Gray Flannel Suit* shows Dean Jones trying to tie in an advertising campaign to his daughter's show jumping, while the documentary-style *The Horse with the Flying Tail* is the story of Nautical, the palomino that ended up jumping for America on the U.S. Equestrian Team.

Many people remember *Tom Jones* for its rousing foxhunting scene, but Albert Finney, Susanah York, and the others were actually chasing a stag, not a fox. For real foxhunting, try *The List of Adrian Messinger*, a murder mystery set in Ireland's Galway Blazers country. Frank Sinatra, Tony Curtis, and several equally well-known actors play cameo roles, but the real excitement for the horsy set comes from George C. Scott and Kirk Douglas (that's Michael Douglas's father, for you youngsters) riding to hounds. Director John Huston was a hunting man, and the film shows it.

Rosalind Russell takes hunting (sidesaddle, no less) to new heights of hilarity in *Auntie Mame*. There's far more shuddering than laughter in Alfred Hitchcock's *Marnie*, in which Sean Connery and Diane Baker spend a sequence galloping across Maryland's countryside.

Foxhunting suggests steeplechasing, a category led by *National Velvet*, one of the great horse flicks of all times. Elizabeth Taylor and Mickey Rooney star. The Grand National is also in the conclusion of *Champions*, the story of British race rider Bob Champion's miraculous comeback from cancer. The jockey is played by John Hurt, and the steeplechase footage is equally impressive.

For a race over fences of a different sort, try *A View to a Kill* (the title, incidently, is a phrase from the foxhunting song, "John Peel"). Roger Moore as James Bond is pursued by bad guys over what looks like an eventing steeplechase course. The fences grow in size just as Bond's horse gets to the take-off spot, which makes seeing distances a somewhat dicey proposition (however, let's remember that he's James Bond).

Thoroughbred racing figures in many movies. Among the best-known are *Kentucky Derby*, for which Walter Brennan won the 1938 Best Supporting Actor Oscar (he appeared with Loretta Young and Richard Greene); *Riding High*, with Bing Crosby; and, of course, the Marx Brothers' *A Day At The Races*.

There's Quarter Horse racing in *Casey's Shadow* with Walter Matthau, and Standardbred harness racing in *Phar Lap*, about the legendary Australian trotter who mysteriously died while in the United States, and *April Love*, a saccharine Pat Boone learns-to-drive saga.

Polo has the reputation of being an upper-crust sport, so it's no surprise to find polo scenes in film depictions of the good life. One example is *Pretty Woman* with Julia Roberts and Richard Gere. Another is the big-bucks caper, *The Thomas Crown Affair*, in which Steve McQueen dazzles Faye Dunaway with his fancy mallet work.

For a wilder contact sport, there's *The Horseman*, with Omar Sharif and Jack Palance. *Buzkashi*, in which Afghanistani riders vie to drag a goat carcass across the goal line in a no-holds-barred contest, is not for the fainthearted. Neither is the movie.

A far safer activity is *ring-spearing*, a form of jousting, in which Warren Beatty competes in the otherwise-forgettable *Lilith*.

Although it doesn't fit neatly into any category other than "quaint", *Murder at the Gallop* is one of a series of British adaptations of Agatha Christie's Miss Marple mysteries. The formidable Margaret Rutherford plays the snoop sister detective at a riding resort (*The Gallop* of the film's title).

Rodeo fans will be happy to learn, if they haven't already found out for themselves, that there are lots of good movies about that sport. Three in particular capture the atmosphere of life on the road, and in and out of the chutes and arena: *Junior Bonner* with Steve McQueen and Robert Preston; *The Lusty Men*, with ex-champion Robert Mitchum taking newcomer Arthur

---

The National Archives in Washington, D.C., promulgates four "regulations" with regard to the positions of horses and riders depicted in equestrian statues.

- A horse standing on all four legs with rider mounted designates the rider to be a "national hero."
- A horse with three legs on the ground with rider mounted indicates that the rider died as a result of wounds suffered in battle.
- A horse with two legs on the ground with rider mounted indicates that the rider died during a battle.
- With the horse in any of the above positions, the rider standing beside the horse indicates that the horse was also killed.

Kennedy under his wing; and, most recently, *Eight Seconds*, in which Luke Perry plays Lane Frost in the story of the legendary young bull rider's life.

Rodeo takes us back to the West, as in *westerns*. Although there have been tens of thousands of cowboy movies, few have considered horses as anything more than a mode of transportation, except for such razzle-dazzle equine stuntwork as Trigger's untying Roy Rogers's bound hands. Therefore, let's confine ourselves to those flicks that treat horses as an essential part of their storylines.

The Rounders stars Glenn Ford and Henry Fonda in a funny love-hate relationship with an ornery horse. *Smoky*, with Fred McMurray, is based on the classic Will James tale of devotion. *My Friend Flicka* shows Roddy McDowell's rescuing a rogue horse (a sequel, *Thunderhead—Son of Flicka* was followed by yet another, *Green Grass of Wyoming*). And, for sheer excitement, the sequence in an Australian western in which Tom Berlinson as *The Man from Snowy River* rides down a steep mountainside in pursuit of a herd of wild horses is among the great moments in horse flicks.

Several classic horse stories have also been turned into classic films. The first version of John Steinbeck's *The Red Pony* with Robert Mitchum is considered the best—Steinbeck himself wrote the screenplay and Aaron Copeland wrote the score. Of the several versions of Anna Sewell's *Black Beauty,* the one with Mark Lester and Walter Slezak is considered most worth seeing. *The Black Stallion*, the first of the many Walter Farley novels, came to the screen with Kelly Reno, with Mickey Rooney as the boy's mentor and the horse's trainer. *Misty* is Marguerite Henry's *Misty of Chincoteague*, the tale of the Virginia island pony.

Finally, *Into the West* is a contemporary story about two Irish youngsters who steal a magical horse of mythical proportions and head west to act out their cowboy-wannabe fantasies. It's a charming film for horse lovers of any age.

Calorie Count: According to the American College of Sports Medicine, a 150-pound person burns 250 per hour calories while saddling a horse, 430 calories while grooming, 286 calories during general riding, and 465 calories while riding to the trot.

chapter 8

Holidays on Horseback

A good indication of how equestrian sport has grown is in the area of vacations. Like other sportsmen, riders are traveling far and wide to spend time at favorite places or to discover new and unusual facilities. And even if someone isn't able to devote an entire holiday to riding, it's quite possible to spend a few hours in the saddle or to be a spectator at a racetrack, a horse show, or a more exotic exhibition of horsemanship.

Whether at home or abroad, a horseback vacation is a nice way to meet people. Other guests at a riding resort, and the staff too, share at least one interest with you, and common experiences and *après-cheval* conversations can lead to instant camaraderie and often lasting friendships.

The United States and Canada

PLEASURE RIDING

The simplest form of vacation riding, even if it involves only a trip across town, is to hire a horse for an hour or more of hacking. To locate public stables, look in telephone directories' Yellow Pages under "Riding Academies" or "Stables." Questions at tack shops may lead to public stables that do not advertise or some private places that will rent horses.

Telephoning in advance is always a good idea, to inquire about style of riding (English or Western), facilities (ring and/or trails), and cost. If an establishment's policy doesn't permit strangers to ride on the trail alone, you may have to pay for the services of a guide. Even if you learn that a stable doesn't rent horses, consider taking a lesson; you never know what nuggets you'll pick up from the resident instructor.

You may arrive at a place only to discover it's a

dump or, worse, its conditions can be dangerous to equine health and human safety. Chances are you won't enjoy a ride at a stable where horses are kept in dirty stalls in a poorly ventilated barn. Another indication is the quality and condition of tack. Saddles don't have to be made by Hermès, but tack that's dirty or held together with baling wire is both unattractive and potentially dangerous. So is a stable owner who permits his animals to be abused by their riders. Note whether riders come galloping back to the barn, their horses dripping with sweat. Sad to say, some owners tolerate such behavior.

Although this book doesn't intend to offer advice about riding techniques, a few words might be appropriate here, starting with common sense. First, don't get carried away and overestimate your ability, or you might find yourself literally carried away. When you're asked about your riding ability, don't be embarrassed about admitting you've ridden only in rings or that you'd like a well-mannered quiet animal if that's the case. Many owners insist on observing for a few minutes how strangers ride before allowing them to leave the ring. Don't make a scene if you're remounted on a more placid horse or refused permission to go out on the trail; the decision is for the owner's—and your own—good.

If you do ride outside by yourself, be sure you're

wearing a watch to keep track of time (some stables allow five or ten minutes grace at the end of an hour, while others go by a time-clock philosophy and charge accordingly). Stick to trails. Even better, go out with someone who knows the area. The other person may be glad of the company, and the stable owner won't have to worry about having to send out search parties.

The life of hack horses is no bed of roses. Different riders with varying abilities and attitudes toward horsemanship all try to get their money's worth out of them, so it's little wonder that insensitivity to rein and leg aids are the rule, not the exception. In defense, hacks have learned how to take advantage of riders. Their tricks range from bucking and rearing to stopping, with goodies like trying to rub off riders against trees thrown in. Accordingly, treat an unfamiliar horse with respect, and don't permit the animal to get you into a potentially dangerous situation (for example, moving within biting or kicking range of another horse). Of course, if you find yourself on a real problem, take it back for another horse.

One way to get the most out of an hour's hack, especially if you're riding in a ring, is to try to school your horse. Work on collection, extension, bending, and smooth transitions between gaits. Although you shouldn't expect to work miracles, every little bit will help both the horse and you.

Your attitude toward other riders is also important. Courtesies in ring riding include calling out "Rail!" before overtaking another rider along the outside track and "Heads up!" to call attention to yourself under other situations. Cutting off another person is bad manners, as is interfering with an instructor and student who may be having a lesson at the same time you're riding. The fact that you have paid a few bucks doesn't mean you own the place.

"Rules of the road" on the trail are essential. Don't gallop past others, and when passing another rider, slow down to the slower gait (if you're cantering and he's trotting, you trot too). If you stop along the way, don't tie your horse by its reins. At worst the animal may injure his mouth, and at best you risk the possibility of a long solitary walk back to the barn. If you have a serious accident, wait for help; your horse knows its way home, and someone will come looking for you. Along the same lines, don't go galloping after another rider's loose horse, for you'll only frighten the animal.

The better play is to try to help the person. Finally, walk the horse for the first five minutes (longer if it's a cold day) to loosen equine and human muscles, and walk the last mile back. If your horse is sweaty, offer to walk it until it's cooled off. (Asking whether you can remove the tack is also a nice gesture.)

Thousands of national, state, and county parks and forests have riding facilities or are serviced by nearby stables. A complete listing appears in the *Rand McNally Guidebook to Campgrounds* (published by Rand McNally).

Like golf courses, bridle paths have become places where business deals are negotiated. When one advertising executive went on a business trip to Philadelphia, his host asked about his sports interests. He said he enjoyed riding. So, as it turned out, did his host. One morning, as they trotted around Fairmont Park, a substantial commercial arrangement was successfully concluded. Moral: Even captains of industry like to ride.

A Checklist for Packing

- boots
- spare laces for field boots or paddock shoes
- boot pulls and a folding boot jack
- breeches or jodhpurs (including an extra pair), or
- jeans or riding pants (including an extra pair)
- cap, helmet, or hat
- spurs
- whip or crop
- gloves
- boot-height socks
- raingear

And a Few Words About Rider Fitness

Do yourself a favor and prepare for your vacation by making yourself as "riding fit" as possible. That's no problem for anyone who rides on a regular basis, but if you haven't been in the saddle in a while or do so only on an infrequent basis, invest the time and effort to get into shape.

That's especially sound advice for those of us who spend their time desk-bound and/or who will be going to spend many hours in the saddle. Although consecutive days of riding tend to eliminate the sort of rigor mortis that a nonriding next day seems to bring, any unaccustomed strain on muscles and joints will produce unwanted discomfort to some extent.

A Few Notes on Shopping and Packing for Your Horseback Holiday

What to take in the way of clothing and riding tack depends primarily on where you're going and what you'll be doing. In that regard . . .

* Make an effort to find out what's considered proper apparel at the place you're going. Some English-style facilities require only boots and breeches or jodhpurs, while jeans and chaps are acceptable alternatives at other places. Hard hats are often mandatory, especially for jumping, and you can't count on the resort to provide protective headgear that's in your size or in a wearable condition.

* If a riding facility doesn't provide a list of recommended apparel, take the initiative and ask. That advice holds true not only for riding but for *après-cheval* wear, since certain resorts still encourage their guests to "dress" for dinner and evening activities.

* No matter what you bring, comfort is an overriding consideration. You won't want the hassle of breaking in stiff new apparel like jeans, chaps, and boots. It's more than just not looking like a "dude" in new duds. If, for example, you're planning to treat yourself to new pair of boots, buying them in plenty of time to break them in at home is sensible not only for the comfort factor, but to ensure proper fit.

* Most riding resorts have no objection to guests bringing their own saddles, but, to be on the safe side, inquire about that too. If you require a special kind of saddle or pad, explain the reason why if you encounter any reluctance about bringing your own tack.

* Whatever you decide to take, make sure everything fits and is in good working order. Check to see whether your boots need new heels or soles, or whether the laces on paddock or field boots need replacing (take along a spare pair just in case). If the canvas pull-on straps inside your high boots are frayed, take them in to a tack shop or bootmaker to be replaced. Is the safety harness on your hunt cap or helmet in good shape? Do the suede knee patches on your breeches flap in the breeze? Are there any holes in your riding socks or your gloves? Could your felt or beaver Western hat use a cleaning and reblocking?

Similarly, the same critical eye that you'll cast over your riding gear should also extend to your nonriding wardrobe, especially any clothes that you might not have worn since last season.

* Experienced travelers avoid taking bulky clothing whenever possible. Instead of taking thick sweaters to colder climes, consider the "layered look" of a turtleneck, polo shirt, and crewneck wool sweater or sweatshirt. Layering clothing provides more warmth than one heavy garment (something to do with the insulation factor of layers of air), and you can always shed the sweater or sweatshirt if you're too warm.

* Experienced travelers also prepare for the unexpected. An extra pair of jeans or breeches will be welcome in case your primary pair is soaked in a rainstorm or lingers in a pile of laundry that somehow failed to be laundered in time for the next day's riding. Ditto a spare pair of gloves in case one becomes lost or torn. Eyeglass-wearers should take along an extra pair.

* Extended hours in the saddle, such as while trekking or fox hunting, increase the chances of breeches or jeans chafing your legs raw. "Long john" underwear is an antidote, especially the lightweight silk or polypropylene variety that "wicks" perspiration away from the skin.

* Nobody likes to think about inclement weather on vacations, but unless you're planning to pony-trek across the Sahara, some type of raingear will be a necessity. Riding "mac" raincoats are designed to keep rain off rider and saddle, and wax jackets are becoming universally popular (floppy ponchos can cause your horse—or someone else's—to spook). A vinyl cover will keep a hunt cap's velvet from becoming soaked. As for footwear, many people routinely use rubber riding boots instead of leather ones, but if you prefer leather boots, invest in a pair of riding rubbers. Rubbers are also good protection against the muck and mud that seem to be a permanent fixture around stables even on dry days.

• Nobody likes to think about aches and pains either, but they happen to the best of us. Accordingly, your toiletries should include such items as aspirin or another kind of analgesic in case of sore muscles, Band-Aids in various sizes and shapes, medicated powder, self-adhesive "corn pads" in case your boots rub your toes, heels, or instep, and a small roll of Ace-type bandage in case a stirrup leather rubs against your calf. If you care about rough, chafed and/or burned skin, pack sunscreen and lip balm too.

• Serious photographers don't need to be reminded about cameras, accessories, and film, but the rest of you might want to include a "point-and-shoot" camera (*and*, lest we forget, several rolls of film). Even smaller are the disposable cameras that consist of a roll of film with a built-in lens; don't expect to take great panoramic or stop-action pictures, but they do provide acceptable souvenir-type snapshots.

• With regard to packing, cramming boots, breeches, a hat, a crop, and other riding paraphernalia along with other garments and items into a formal-size suitcase is often a problem. Boot and helmet carrying-cases are a good alternative. So is all-in-one luggage specifically designed for riding gear. One such item is the Equestri-All, a sturdy canvas tote with zippered compartments for high boots, a separate detachable case for a hunt club or helmet, and Velcro strips on the handles to hold a crop or whip. The bag's main compartments are roomy enough for chaps, breeches, gloves, spurs, raingear, and whatever else you need for riding.

A packing hint: If you don't plan to take your boot trees with you, such small, crushable items as socks and gloves can be stuffed into your boots. So can, on your way home, other small items of clothing destined for the laundry. In that way, you'll have more room in your luggage for souvenirs or other goodies you've picked up during your trip.

The best preparation for riding is riding, so try to do as much as you can in advance of your trip. But if you can't get into a saddle at home, treat your body to stretching exercises.

A popular exercise that stretches calf muscles and ankle joints requires only a flight of stairs. Stand with just the soles of your feet on one step as if you were walking upstairs. Letting your heels hang over the step, slowly sink into your heels as if sinking into stirrups (hold on to the banister if you wish). Don't force your weight down—just allow it to sink. Repeat until you feel your muscles stretch.

Another stretching exercise is to stand about three feet away from a wall. Place your palms against the wall, then lean into the wall in a slow "vertical push-up," keeping your heels and soles flat on the floor. You'll feel your calf muscles stretch.

To stretch the "jockey muscles" that run along the inner thighs, stand with your legs stretched about three feet apart. Keeping your feet flat on the floor, slowly bend your right knee while simultaneously extending your left leg. You'll feel the muscle of your left leg stretch. Then, reverse the position to bend your left knee and stretch your right leg's muscle.

Any kind of exercise—deep knee bends, sit-ups, and even walking more than you normally do—will pay dividends in terms of increased flexibility and stamina. Have a nearby errand to run? Take a walk instead of taking your car. You'll be better off.

SUMMER CAMPS

One of the people who assembled this book counts among his happiest hours the time he spent riding at summer camp. Although the camp did not specialize in the sport, enough campers took part to warrant a half-dozen horses supplied by the instructor, a local horseman who, assisted by his teenage children, taught the rudiments of "survival-seat" English and Western riding. Once campers mastered these basic skills, they went on to take twice-weekly hour-long group hacks through the countryside. Special events included breakfast and or dinner picnic rides, overnight expeditions to the instructor's farm, and—very much the equestrian highlight of one memorable summer—the chance to ride the instructor's horse, as well as to go on a day-long ride to another camp several towns away. Hours in the saddle (including unscheduled "free rides" on available horses) provided the foundation for a lifetime of enjoying horses, including a summer as a riding instructor at a camp down the road from the one he attended for many years.

Campers at "specialty" riding camps are usually assigned their own horses, which they feed, groom, and ride daily in lessons that offer concentrated instruction. Such camps hold at least one horse show (often several) over the summer, sometimes inviting another riding camp to compete. Some places even offer the chance to compete at a "recognized" horse show or a dressage or combined-training trial in the area.

To the amount of tuition must be added such extras as canteen purchases and laundry. Parents also need to take into account the expense of visiting their children on designated weekends.

Camps that have riding programs advertise in equestrian magazines as well as in regional and national newspapers (the Camps pages of *The New York Times Magazine* is a very good source). The American Camping Association, 12 E. 31st St., New York, NY 10001 (telephone: (212) 268-7822 or (800) 777-CAMP), will refer inquiries to its member-camps; if you have a preference, indicate the part of the country and whether you wish an all-girl, all-boy, or coed camp.

Don't despair if you're no longer of camping age (generally, 18 and younger). Anyone with the available time and the riding and teaching skills may be able to spend a summer as a riding counselor or "instructor," as those people usually style themselves. It's not a soft job—teaching for at least five hours a day, six days a week, plus taking groups for picnic and overnight rides, and planning and staging a horse show or gymkhana or two. Although some camp riding programs have more than one instructor and/or grooms, you should be willing and able to do stable chores and management. A working knowledge of veterinary medicine is also useful. But look at it this way: You'll have a golden opportunity to spend an entire summer around—and on—horses. Another benefit, especially to those who spend their winters behind a desk, is that you'll work yourself into great physical (and emotional) shape.

The American Camping Association may be able to point you in the direction of a camp that's in the market for a riding instructor. You should also check the ads in equestrian magazines and general-circulation newspapers. Inquire too at riding academies and dealer barns, since many such establishments provide horses to summer camps, often furnishing instructors as part of the package. With regard to negotiating a job once you find a camp looking for a riding counselor, a letter of recommendation attesting to your riding and stable-management abilities and your sense of responsibility is always a plus.

Whether you're interested in becoming a camper or in working as an instructor, start making your inquiries in autumn or early winter. Camp directors like to fill their rosters and hire their staff as soon before the summer as possible.

A tip for instructors: Serving as judge at your own horse show is the quickest way to start World War Three. Everyone will be much happier if you hire someone from outside.

DUDE RANCHING AND PACK TRIPPING

Ask any group of people what comes to mind at the mention of the phrase "horseback vacations," and the majority will reply, "Dude ranches." Spending vacations "out West" has been going on since before the turn of the century, and people who have tried it report that it's a wonderful way to spend a holiday.

The word "dude" has been around for many more years than such vacations have. It originally meant a stylish dresser (the meaning endures in hip vocabularies); strangers who appeared in Western towns wearing either non-Western or brand-new cowboy clothes were so labeled by the locals. By extension, those ranches that began to supplement their income by taking in paying summer guests earned the name "dude ranches."

Dude ranches now exist not only in Western states and Canadian provinces, but throughout the country. Some, especially those in the East near large cities, are open throughout the year, although the majority have seasons that begin after Memorial Day and last through September or October.

Choices for such vacations range from real working ranches where guests stay in the family's spare bedroom to posh resorts that are about as authentically Western as Ralph Lauren advertisements. Something that all have in common, however, is riding, and plenty of it. Don't expect bucking broncos, though. Traumatic experiences are not souvenirs that ranch owners are eager for guests to take home with them, so dude-ranch horses tend to be placid, follow-the-leader mounts, although better riders can be assigned more challenging horses once the wranglers see that you know what you're doing.

Another of dude ranching's strong selling points is that it's an ideal family vacation. Mothers or fathers who haven't been on horseback in years find that placid horses provide undemanding transportation, and there's always basic instruction from ranch hands for people who don't know which end of the horse gets the carrot. Some ranches have separate daytime or evening programs for youngsters, who then join their parents for meals and other activities.

A typical week at a "typical" (that is, one based on the experiences of vacationers we spoke to) dude ranch begins with your arrival. You'll be welcomed, shown to your accommodations, and given a chance to change into ranch clothing. Then, depending on the time of day, you may be given a quick tour of the ranch's facilities or a meal or else an invitation to plunge into whatever activity is scheduled at the moment.

Your first full day will begin, like all days, at daybreak. Following a hearty breakfast, you'll be given a little time to digest the meal. Then it's off to the corral and into the saddle.

Guests who know how to ride will be asked to demonstrate their skills for the instructor, who's usually known as the "wrangler." He'll then be able to match you with a horse of suitable ability and temperament or, if you need instruction, assign you to a group of people at your level.

If you do know how to ride, you'll go off on a group trail ride through whatever kind of scenery the area offers: forests or mountain trails with vistas of craggy mountains in the distance, the stark majesty of a desert, or perhaps through a wildlife preserve where you may well encounter deer, elk, eagles, and other fauna.

A morning ride will bring you back in time to clean up for lunch, followed in most instances by a rest period. There may be more riding in the afternoon, or the chance to swim, play tennis, fish (many Western ranches provide excellent trout fishing), or just sit and do nothing. Depending where the ranch is located, there may be sightseeing at a nearby town, state or national park, or some other local attraction.

Evening entertainment can be a barbecue, a square dance, a hayride, or a talent show or more professional entertainment (every dude ranch seems to have at least one "singing cowboy"), or any combination. If, however, you find yourself plumb tuckered out, just watching TV and turning in early is not considered being a spoilsport. Such informality is one of dude ranching's charms; there are no social directors hounding guests to sign up for tango lessons or "Simon Sez" tournaments. In that regard, several single men and women have commented that they're grateful for the lack of social pressure that's so often found at other kinds of resorts, although romances have been known to blossom under the prairie moon.

Subsequent days will be filled with more riding, including day-long expeditions further afield from the ranch once your muscles have become acclimated. Sustenance—and the chance to dismount and stretch your legs—will come in the form of a sandwich lunch packed in saddlebags or an encounter with the ranch's chuck wagon somewhere along the trail. The itinerary may be just a "great circle route" swing across the countryside, or there may be a specific destination in mind.

Many of the larger ranches feature weekly "rodeos" for their guests. Events include goat-roping or -tying, barrel racing, and gymkhana games like musical chairs (you dismount when the music stops and, leading your horse, scurry to the nearest available bale of hay).

Playing cowboy won't be make-believe if a *working ranch* is your vacation choice. Depending on the time of year and the ranch's work schedule, you'll actually participate in branding and vaccinations, cattle roundups, and drives from winter to spring and summer pastures. As in the movie *City Slickers*, you can count on being more than a spectator; it's hard, dusty, and (in the case of rain) wet work, but you'll come away with a healthy respect for ranching, ranchers—and yourself for having taken part in the process.

What Will It Cost? A week's dude-ranch vacation ranges anywhere from $500 to four times as much. The price includes accommodations, meals, riding, and other activities, although some ranches add a surcharge for more than one ride per day. Remember also to figure in the cost of getting to and from the ranch from wherever you call home.

What to Take: Although the precise kind of clothing depends on the specific ranch's formality, certain items are necessities. Heading the list are a couple of pairs of jeans and at least one pair of Western boots. Everything should be well broken in, and not just so that you don't look like a "dude"; new jeans and boots lead to chafing and blisters. A felt or straw ten-gallon hat of the Stetson variety are equally suitable and useful, depending on the weather; the wide brim keeps the sun and rain off your face. However, some ranches insist on protective helmets, so be sure to ask. Since Western evenings tend to be cool, a denim jacket is a good idea, as is a raincoat or slicker. As for the rest of your wardrobe, check with your host.

Where to Locate a Ranch: More than seventy ranches in ten Western states belong to the Dude Ranchers Association. A letter of inquiry to P.O. Box 471, LaPorte, CO 80535 will result in a stampede of brochures from many of the members. The DRA's annual magazine/directory lists thumbnail descriptions of the establishments.

Other sources of information include the state tourist offices listed in this chapter, as well as ads in such magazines as *Western Horseman* and the travel sections of major newspapers.

Grand Cypress Equestrian Center: Riding With Style

Although dude ranches abound, English riding resorts are few and far between. One such facility, however, can be found on the grounds of the Grand Cypress Resort complex in Orlando, Florida.

The Grand Cypress Equestrian Center has a wide range of lessons, clinics, and other activities (including trail rides) for riders at the novice up to the advanced level. The facility takes particular pride in offering instructorship certification from the British Horse Society; toward that goal, a training program will prepare candidates for the exams that are given several times a year.

Judging from its calendar of events, the Equestrian Center makes every effort to present as wide a range of participatory and spectator events as possible. These include hunter paces, dressage clinics, and dressage trials and hunter/jumper horse shows throughout the year.

And for those family members or companies whose interests don't extend to riding, there's tennis, golf, and other resort sports to be found elsewhere in the complex. Then too, Orlando is also the home of Disney-World, SeaWorld, and other tourist attractions.

For further information, see your travel agent or contact the Equestrian Center at (800) 835-7377, or fax (407) 238-6322.

International Trekking and Other Cross-Country Riding Opportunities

The world abounds with trekking opportunities. In the rugged and inviting Connemara region in the west of Ireland, riders mounted on surefooted hunter-type horses and native ponies explore the undulating countryside, with its occasional stone walls to be jumped (or gone around, depending on one's preference). Connemara's proximity to the Atlantic Ocean affords chances for galloping along sandy beaches too. Lodgings are in farmhouses or small hotels, and anyone with the energy after a full day in the saddle to stay up after dinner will be welcomed like a long-lost relative in the local pub.

One highly recommended Connemara trek is organized and led by Willie Leahy. Mr. Leahy can be contacted at his home address, Aille Cross, Loughrea, County Galway (telephone: 41216).

Across the Irish Sea in Scotland, Highland Horseback offers a series of rugged trips from mid-May until October. The trips encompass all or part of a 200-mile stretch from Aberdeen west to the Atlantic Ocean. The so-called Long Ride lasts eight days, the Halfway Ride four days. Contact Highland Horseback, Auchinhandoch, Glass, Huntly, Aberdeenshire, Scotland AB5 4YJ.

France's Loire Valley is the setting for 12-day trips that, like Spain's Rutas a Caballo, follow public pathways. Scheduled during May, June, September, and October (July and August are deemed too hot), the trips pass along vineyards and through forests that, in your imagination, make you feel one-for-all-and-all-for-one with D'Artagnan and his pals. For information, contact Les Cavaliers, 2412 Harrison Street, San Francisco, CA 94110 (telephone: (415) 641-6291).

Trekking in France is particularly well organized. ANTE an acronym for the Association Nationale pour le Tourisme Équestre (National Association for Equestrian Tourism), is a federation of organizations and facilities that specialize in cross-country riding. It publishes *Tourism Équestre en France*, a 112-page booklet listing member stables and clubs that offer the activity; the booklet, which is in French, is available

The pause during a cross-country ride through Spain.

through the French National Tourist Office or from ANTE, 15 rue de Bruxelles, Paris 75009.

For similar information about several other European countries, get in touch with the following other members of FITE (Fédération Internationale de Tourisme Équestre):

Austria: Bundesfach Verband für Reiten und Fahren, Prinz Eugenstrasse 14/1/6a, A 1040 Vienna.
Belgium: Association Belge de Tourisme Équestre, Avenue Hamoir 38, B 1180 Brussels.
Great Britain: British Horse Society, National Equestrian Centre, Stoneleigh, Near Kenilworth, Warwickshire CV8 2LR.
Hungary: Magyar Looms Szovetseg, Kerepesi Ut 7, H Budapest VII.
Italy: Associazione per Il Turismo Equestre e per L'Equitazione di Campagna, Largo Messico 13, 00198 Rome
The Netherlands: Nederlandse Ruitersport Vereniging "Joyeux", P.O. Box 3039, NL 6093 ZG Heythuizen.
Switzerland: Association Nationale Suisse de Tourisme Équestre, rue de l'Industrie 19, CH 2316 Les Ponts de Martel.
Germany: Deutsch Reiterliche Vereinigung, Freiherr-Von-Langerstrasse 13, D 1410 Warendorf 1/West.

Iceland doesn't normally spring to mind when the subject of horseback holidays comes up, but that's only because much of the world isn't aware of that island nation's trekking activities. An organization called Hestasport offers a number of both short- and long-distance tours through the northern Iceland region of Skagafjordur. Hestasport's promotional material promises a range of scenery, from lush green, wildflower-dotted valleys to hot springs and geysers to bleak lava fields. Riders are mounted on native Icelandic ponies, a shaggy and small but sturdy breed noted for its smooth, racklike *tolt* gait. Trekkers change ponies several times a day, so herds of up to 100 ponies (that's right, 100 ponies) accompany treks.

Tours take place over seven- to nine-day periods. Accommodations are in farmhouses, or, if you choose a trip through highland wilderness areas, in cabins or tents. For further information, contact Hestasport's U.S. representative: Hestasport, 41 B Clove Rd., Monroe, NY 10950.

The widest selection of international trekking opportunities is found in Equitour's temptingly detailed "Worldwide Riding Holidays" brochure. Destinations range from a jungle ride through Belize to—for all you "Man from Snowy River" wannabes—treks through Australia's outback. Other destinations include Kenya, Hungary, Morocco, and India, as well as the U.S., Canada, and other countries mentioned elsewhere in this chapter. For a copy, contact Equitour, Bitterroot Ranch, Box 807, Dubois, WY 82513 (telephone: (307) 455-3363 or (800) 545-0019).

Camping with Your Horse

At some point in your trail-riding career, you're likely to look forward to more than a few hours or even an entire day in the saddle at one stretch. When that happens, you start to think longingly about the prospect of camping out, of spending two or more consecutive days away from home (and in the case of your horse, away from barn).

Opportunities for such extended excursions are varied and plentiful, from private and public campgrounds to maximum roughing it experiences in pristine parts of state and national parks and other wilderness areas.

Let's begin with the universal truth that things that should just go without saying need to be said anyway: please be sure that your horse is physically and temperamentally suitable for consecutive days of work through unfamiliar surroundings and terrain. With regard to temperament, you'll need a horse that stands quietly while tied; one that doesn't object to streams, logs, ditches, and other obstacles encountered along a trail; and especially one that doesn't lose its cool at the sudden appearance of other animals (especially deer, squirrels, and low-flying birds). If your horse lacks any of these essential behavioral traits, you'd do well to consider further training, or to borrow or rent another mount.

An established campground, particularly one that's reasonably close to home, makes a sensible base for your first experience. The first step in the plan-ahead department is to contact the facility for answers to the following questions: Are horses allowed on the grounds? Are they permitted to graze, and are there pasture areas for safe foraging? What kinds of hays are and aren't permitted to be brought in (with regard to weed seeds that may or may not be present)? Are there streams, ponds, and/or lakes both at the campsite and along the trails where horses are permitted to drink? Is there sufficient shade where a horse can be tethered? Is there permanent stabling, or must you use a portable corral or a picket line, or be obliged to hobble your horse at night or tie it to your trailer?

(A *picket line*, if you haven't encountered the phrase outside a seminar on labor law, is a rope hung between two trees at a height of at least seven feet, high enough so that horses will not become entangled. One end of a lead rope that's long enough to allow a horse to lie down is tied to the line. The other end (with a swivel snap) goes on the horse's halter. Horses seem to accept this method of overnight tethering, seldom pulling against the picket line hard enough to upset the arrangement.)

The list of horse-related items to take along should be checked and double-checked before you leave home (to paraphrase insurance salesmen, you won't need them until you need them, and by then it's too late if you don't have them). These items include halters and lead ropes; a portable corral, hobbles or rope for a picket line; the horse's tack; feed and water buckets; grain and hay; insect repellent; and an equine first-aid kit (see chapter 4 for recommendations in that regard).

Once you're reached the camp grounds is the time to establish your horse's home-away-from-home. A shady spot is essential, and that's where you should set up your portable corral or picket line if you're using one or the other (horses that are hobbled need a pasture where they can graze, preferably in the company of other hobbled horses).

According to experienced campers and campsite operators, the cardinal sin that equestrian overnighters can commit is to tie their horses to trees. Not only will horses cause irreparable damage to the tree by chewing whatever bark and foliage they can gets their teeth on, but pawing hooves dig up and trample roots while urine seeps into and destroys root systems.

Also with regard to equine by-products, it's only good manners to remove all manure and any bedding material and dispose of it properly. Although the idea of riding ol' Paint down to the communal swimming hole may seem like a good one, especially on a hot summer day, you really don't want to take the chance of fouling the water and spoiling the spot for others.

Once you've become accustomed to horseback overnights close to home, you're ready to expand your horizons. Camping is a wonderful way to see the world and enjoy nature 24 hours at a time.

Comprehensive advice about what horses and riders need to take, as well as where-to and how-to information, is available from the following organizations:

Back Country Horsemen of America
22815 168 Ave.
East Graham, WA 98338
(360) 803-5161

Back Country Horsemanship Program
Hocking College
School of Natural Resources and Ecological Sciences
3301 Hocking Pkwy
Nelsonville, OH 45764
(614) 753-3591 ext. 2512

Two publications that together thoroughly cover the subject are:

Back Country Horsemanship Guidebook
available from: P.O. Box 597 Columbia Falls, MT 59912

Mountain Manners
available from: Back Country Horsemen of Montana
P.O. Box 5431 Helena, MT 59604

Museums

Whatever your particular interest in horses and horse sports, there's a museum (usually with an accompanying library) devoted to it. They make wonderful destinations or stopoffs on vacations or business trips around the country.

For breadth of scope and activities, the Kentucky Horse Park has no rival. Set in the heart of the Bluegrass country, the park is a working horse farm of more than 1,000 acres. Its International Museum of the Horse, the largest of its kind in the world, includes interactive displays and a Horse in Sport gallery that shows horses in competition and recreation activities. (The superlative website supervised by the Museum's curator and found at http://www.imh.org/khp/ should not go unrecognized.)

A Walking Farm Tour takes visitors to a farrier's smithy and a harness-making shop. The Breeds Barn features 24 of the park's more than 40 breeds of horses. From April to October, a Parade of Breeds presents different breeds put through their paces by authentically costumed riders and handlers. The park is also the retirement home for several well-known horses, including Thoroughbred racers Forego and John Henry, American Quarter Horse superhorse Sgt. Pepper Feature, and CH Imperator, the world champion five-gaited Saddlebred.

The park is the setting for competitions throughout the year, including the Rolex Kentucky Three-Day Event (the first American horse trials to receive a five-star rating), the High Hope Steeplechase, and a series of polo matches on summer and fall Sundays.

If seeing so much equestrian activity makes you yearn to climb into the saddle, there are pony and horseback rides, as well as many miles of trails.

Campgrounds have more than 250 camper and RV sites, areas for tent camping, tennis and games courts, and a junior-Olympic–sized swimming pool.

Kentucky Horse Park, 4089 Iron Works Pike, Lexington, KY 40511. (606) 233-4303. Fax: (606) 254-0253

For information about any in the following sampling of specialty museums, write or phone for details, including upcoming exhibitions and visiting hours.

Permanent and temporary exhibitions and a time line trace the history of the American Quarter Horse at the American Quarter Horse Heritage Center and Museum, 2601 I-40 East, Amarillo, TX 79104. (806) 376-5181. Fax: (806) 376-1005.

The Appaloosa Museum and Heritage Center is devoted to that breed, the Nez Perce tribe that created the breed, and the Appaloosa Horse Club's registry and activities. Appaloosa Museum and Heritage Center, 5070 Hwy. 8 W, P.O. Box 8403, Moscow, ID 83843. (208) 882-5578. Fax: (208) 882-8150.

The three- and five-gaited American Saddlebred are featured at the American Saddle Horse Museum, 4093 Iron Works Pike, Lexington, KY 40511. (606) 259-2746. Fax: (606) 259-1628.

For books and other items concerning the oldest of the popular breeds there's the Arabian Horse Trust, 12000 Zuni St., Westminster, CO 80234. (303) 450-4710. Fax: (303) 450-4707.

The Morgan breed originated in Vermont, and that's where to find The National Museum of the Morgan Horse, P.O. Box 519, Shelburne, VT 05482. (802) 985-8665. Fax: (802) 985-5242.

Exhibitions of general interest, although the majority of which have a Western bent, are the hallmark of The Museum of the Horse, P.O. Box 40, Ruidoso Downs, NM 88346. (505) 378-4142. Fax: (505) 378-4166.

Spotlighting Western horsemanship and competition is the The Pro Rodeo Hall of Fame and Museum of the American Cowboy, 101 Pro Rodeo Dr., Colorado Springs, CO 80919. (719) 528-4761. Fax: (719) 548-4874.

Located across the street from one of America's venerable Thoroughbred racetracks is the National Museum of Racing, Union Ave., Saratoga Springs, NY 12866. (518) 584-0400. Fax: (518) 584-4574.

In the town that's closely associated with trotting and pacing Standardbreds is The Harness Racing Museum and Hall of Fame, 240 Main St., P.O. Box 590, Goshen, NY 10924. (914) 294-6330. Fax: (914) 294-3463.

Further Information

UNITED STATES

These state agencies will provide general-interest brochures, and, if specifically requested, more detailed information about equestrian holiday opportunities.

Alabama Bureau of Tourism and Travel
532 S. Perry St.
Montgomery, AL 36104
800-ALABAMA

The National Sporting Library: Horses from A to Z

—————— ∩ ——————

by LAURA ROSE

THE NATIONAL SPORTING LIBRARY, located in Middleburg, Virginia, may be the best-kept secret in the horse world. The library has been amassing books about horse and field sports since 1954, when its first donations were stored in a barn. Today the collection numbers around 14,000 volumes, some dating back to the 16th century, covering such subjects as dressage, the horse in art, horse breeding, racing, veterinary care, polo, show jumping, carriage building, foxhunting, and horseshoeing. Books on related field sports include those on shooting, angling, cockfighting, and falconry.

A steady flow of scholars, horsemen, students, and pleasure readers finds its way to the National Sporting Library to explore a wide variety of topics. Visitors have included a teacher researching sidesaddle riding for her work with a living-history group; a college student researching therapeutic riding for her work with mentally challenged patients; an architect researching the construction of riding arenas; an author researching the history of horsemanship; a college professor researching the ethics of hunting; a people dentist researching equine dentistry; and many, many more.

The National Sporting Library, a nonprofit organization, was founded in 1954 under the direction of Alexander Mackay-Smith and George L. Ohrstrom Sr. Guidance for the Library's growth came from Mr. Mackay-Smith, a well-known scholar, author, and magazine editor. Mr. Ohrstrom, a horseman and executive who owned *The Chronicle of the Horse,* provided fiscal leadership. Upon Mr. Ohrstrom's death in 1955, George L. Ohrstrom Jr. accepted his father's responsibility.

Today the NSL collection includes books, art, memorabilia, and films. A highlight is the rare-book collection, which features hundreds of titles representing the great names in the history of horsemanship and veterinary medicine. The Library's earliest book, *Artis Veterinariae* (Baser: Johann Faber, 1528), was written by fifth century Roman writer Publius Vegetius Renatus, and is considered the first book on veterinary medicine ever printed. Another treasure is William Cavendish's *Methode et Invention Nouvelle de Dresser les Chevaux* (Method and New Way to Train Horses), published in 1657, and considered the epitome of all horse books.

The scope of the NSL's collection was greatly enhanced by donations in recent years by the Ohrstrom Foundation of New York and Mr. and Mrs. John H. Daniels of Minnesota and South Carolina. The Ohrstrom Foundation presented the NSL with the von Hunersdorf Library, an extremely rare and valuable collection of over 200 books on classical equitation and veterinary care. The Daniels donated their 5,000 volume collection of sporting books, one of the finest private libraries in the country.

The recent donations underscore the library's greatest need: more space. At present, the Library shares Vine Hill, an historic 1804 brick mansion, with *The Chronicle of the Horse.* However, plans are in the works for a new 15,000-square-foot building to house the NSL's world-class collection. The new building, which will resemble a carriage house, will be on the same seven-acre site as Vine Hill.

When the library staff is not helping visitors with their research queries, they are often found working on the next issue of the library's quarterly newsletter, sent around the world to members of "The Friends of the National Sporting Library." In addition, each fall the Library holds a duplicate book sale for the hundreds of sportsmen and book lovers who are members of the Friends. The sale, which is run like a silent auction through the mail, is the library's main fundraiser.

The National Sporting Library is open to the public weekdays from 10 A.M. to 4 P.M.

For more information, contact:
National Sporting Library
301 West Washington Street
P.O. Box 1335
Middleburg, Virginia 20118
(540) 687-6542
http://www.nsl.org

Laura Rose is librarian of the National Sporting Library.

This beautiful illustration appears in the Duke of Newcastle's Méthode et Invention Nouvelle de Dresser les Chevaux *(Antwerp, 1657), one of the highlights of the National Sporting Library's collection.*

Alaska Division of Tourism
3333 Willoughby St.
Juneau, AK 99801
(907) 465-2010

Arizona Office of Tourism
1480 E. Bethany Home Rd.
Phoenix, AZ
(602) 255-3618

Arkansas Dept. of Parks and Tourism
One Capital Mall
Little Rock, AK 72201
(800) 643-8383

California State Office of Tourism
1121 L St., Ste. 103
Sacramento, CA 95814
(916) 322-2881

Colorado Tourism Board
1625 Broadway, Ste. 1700
Denver, CO 80202
(303) 592-5410

Connecticut Dept. of Economic Development
210 Washington St.
Hartford, CT 06106
(203) 566-5638

Delaware Tourism Office
99 Kings Hwy., Box 1401
Dover, DE 19903
(302) 739-4271

Florida Division of Tourism
107 W. Gaines St.
Tallahassee, FL 32301
(904) 488-7300

Georgia Dept. of Industry and Trade
Tourist Division
P.O. Box 1776
Atlanta, GA 30301
(404) 656-3590

Hawaii Visitors Bureau
2270 Kalakauua Ave., Ste. 801
Honolulu, HA 96815
(808) 923-1811

Idaho Travel Council
Room 108, The Statehouse
Boise, ID 83720
(800) 635-2820

Illinois Office of Tourism
State of Illinois Center 3-400
100 W. Randolph St.
Chicago, IL 60601
(312) 814-4732

Indiana Dept. of Commerce
Tourism Development Division
1 North Capitol, Ste. 700
Indianapolis, IN 46204-2288
(317) 232-8860

Iowa Dept. of Economic Development
200 E. Grand Ave.
Des Moines, IA 50309
(515) 281-3100

Kansas Dept. of Commerce Development
400 W. 8th, 5th floor
Topeka, KS 66603
(913) 296-2009

Kentucky Dept. of Travel Development
Capital Plaza Tower, 22nd floor
Frankfort, KY 40601
(502) 564-4930

Louisiana Office of Tourism
P.O. Box 94291
Baton Rouge, LA 70804-9291
(800) 535-8388

Maine State Development Office
State House Station 59
189 State St.
Augusta, ME 04333
(207) 289-2423

Maryland Office of Tourist Development
45 Calvert St.
Annapolis, MD 21401
(301) 917-3517

Massachusetts Office of Travel and Tourism
100 Cambridge St.
Boston, MA 02202
(617) 727-3201

Michigan Dept. of Commerce
Travel Bureau
P.O. Box 30226
Lansing, MI 48909
(800) 248-5700

Minnesota Office of Tourism
375 Jackson St.
St. Paul, MN 55101
(800) 328-1461

Mississippi Dept. of Economic Development
Division of Tourism
P.O. Box 849
Jackson, MS 39205
(800) 647-2290

Missouri Division of Tourism
P.O Box 1055
Jefferson City, MO 65102
(314) 751-4133

Montana Dept. of Commerce
Travel Montana
1424 9th Ave.
Helena, MT 59620
(800) 541-1447

Nebraska Travel & Tourism
P.O. Box 94666
Lincoln, NE 68509
(800) 228-4307

Nevada Commission on Tourism
Capitol Complex
Carson City, NV 89710
(800) NEVADA-8

New Hampshire Office of Vacation Travel
P.O. Box 856
Concord, NH 03301
(603) 271-2666

New Jersey Division of Travel and Tourism
20 West State St., CN 826
Trenton, NJ 08625
(609) 292-2470

New Mexico Tourism & Travel Division
1100 San Francisco Dr.
Santa Fe, NM 87503
(800) 545-2040

New York State Dept. of Economic Development
Division of Tourism
One Commerce Plaza
Albany, NY 12245
(800) CALL-NYS

North Carolina Division of Travel & Tourism
430 N. Salisbury St.
Raleigh, NC 27611
800-VISITNC

North Dakota Tourism Promotion
Liberty Memorial Building
State Capitol Grounds
Bismark, ND 58505
(800) 437-2077

Ohio Office of Travel and Tourism
P.O. Box 1001
Columbus, Oh 43266-0101
(800) BUCKEYE

Oklahoma Tourism and Recreation Dept.
500 Will Rogers Bldg.
Oklahoma City, OK 73105
(405) 521-2406

Oregon Economic Development Dept.
Tourism Division

26 S.W. Salmon
Portland, OR 97204-3299
(503) 222-2223

Pennsylvania Bureau of Travel Development
416 Forum Building
Harrisburg, PA 17120
(800) VISIT-PA

Rhode Island Tourist Division
7 Jackson Walkway
Providence, RI 02903
(401) 277-2601

South Carolina Dept. of Parks, Recreation and Tourism
1205 Pendleton St.
Columbia, SC 29201
(803) 734-0218

South Dakota Tourism
711 Wells Ave.
Pierre, SD 57501
(800) 843-1930

Tennessee Tourist Development
P.O. Box 23170
Nashville, TN 37202
(615) 741-2159

Texas Travel and Information Division
11th and Brazos
Austin, TX 78701
(512) 463-8583

Utah Travel Council
Council Hall, Capitol Hill
Salt Lake City, UT 84114
(801) 533-5681

Vermont Travel Division
134 State Street
Montpelier, VT 05602
(802) 828-3236

Virginia Division of Tourism
202 N. Ninth St., Ste. 500
Richmond, VA 23219
(804) 786-2051

West Virginia Dept. of Commerce
Travel Division
Capitol Complex
Charleston, WV 25305
(800) CALL-WVA

Wisconsin Dept. of Development
Division of Tourism
P.O. Box 7970
Madison, WI 53707
(608) 266-2147

Wyoming Travel Commission
Interstate 25, College Park
Cheyenne, WY 82002
(800) 225-5996

U.S. TERRITORIES:
Puerto Rico Tourism Co.
11 E. Adams St.
Chicago, IL 60603
(312) 922-9701

also:

2995 L.B.J. Freeway
Dallas, TX 75234
(214) 243-3737

3575 W. Cahuenga Blvd.
Los Angeles, CA 90068
(213) 874-5991

1290 Ave. of the Americas
New York, NY 10020
(212) 541-6630

200 S.E. 1st St.
Miami, FL 33131
(305) 381-8915

U.S. Virgin Islands Tourist Information Office
343 S. Dearborn St.
Chicago, Il 60604
(312) 416-0180

also:

3450 Wilshire Blvd.
Los Angeles, CA 90010
(310) 739-0138

7270 N.W. 12th St.
Miami, FL 33126
(305) 591-2070

1270 Ave. of the Americas
New York, NY 10020
(212) 582-4520

1667 K St., NW
Washington, DC 20006
(202) 293-3707

FOREIGN COUNTRIES
The following tourist offices of countries and regions mentioned in the text are the primary sources of travel information. Consulates in American cities can also furnish such data as visa and currency requirements and restrictions.

Argentina Tourist Information
330 W. 58th St., Ste. 6K
New York, NY 10019
(800) 722-5737

Consulates are located in Baltimore, Chicago, Houston, Miami, and New Orleans.

Australia Tourist Commission
2121 Ave. of the Stars
Ste. 1200
Los Angeles, CA 90067
(310) 552-1988

also:

489 Fifth Ave.
New York, NY 10017
(212) 687-6300

Consulates are located in Chicago, Honolulu, Houston, and San Francisco.

Austria National Tourist Office
500 N. Michigan Ave., Ste. 544
Chicago, IL 60611
(312) 644-5556

also:

4800 San Filipe St.
Houston, TX 77056
(713) 850-8888

3440 Wilshire Blvd.
Los Angeles, CA 90010
(213) 380-3309

500 Fifth Ave.
New York, NY 10110
(212) 944-6880

Consulates are located in Atlanta, Boston, Chicago, Cleveland, Denver, Detroit, Honolulu, Houston, Los Angeles, Miami, New Orleans, New York, Philadelphia, St. Paul, San Francisco, San Juan, and Seattle.

Bahamas Tourist Information Office
1950 Century Blvd. N.E.
Atlanta, GA 30345
(404) 633-1793

also:

875 N. Michigan Ave.
Chicago, IL 60611
(312) 787-8203

3450 Wilshire Blvd.
Los Angeles, CA 90010
(213) 385-0033

150 E. 52nd St.
New York, NY 10022
(212) 758-2777

Consulates are located in Miami and New York.

Brazil Tourism Authority
551 Fifth Ave., Ste. 210
New York, NY 10165
(212) 916-3200

Consulates are located in Atlanta, Chicago, Dallas, Houston, Los Angeles, Miami, New Orleans, New York, and San Francisco.

Danish Tourist Board
655 Third Ave.
New York, NY 10017
(212) 949-2333

also:

150 N. Michigan Ave., Ste. 2110
Chicago, IL 60601
(312) 726-1120

8929 Wilshire Blvd.
Los Angeles, CA 90211
(213) 854-1549

Behind the scenes at the Spanish Riding School, Vienna, Austria.

Consulates are located in Chicago, Cleveland, Honolulu, Houston, Los Angeles, Miami, New Orleans, New York, Philadelphia, San Francisco, and Seattle.

Dominican Republic Tourist Information Center
485 Madison Ave.
New York, NY 10022
(212) 826-0750

Egyptian Government Tourist Office
630 Fifth Ave.
New York, NY 10020
(212) 246-6960

also:

313 Geary St.
San Francisco, CA 94102
(415) 781-7676

Consulates are located in Chicago, Houston, New York, and San Francisco.

French Government Tourist Office
9401 Wilshire Blvd.

Beverly Hills, CA 90212
(213) 212-2661

also:

645 N. Michigan Ave.
Chicago, IL 60611
(312) 337-6301

P.O. Box 58610
Dallas, TX 75258
(214) 742-7011

610 Fifth Ave.
New York, NY 10020
(212) 757-1125

Consulates are located in Boston, Chicago, Detroit, Houston, Los Angeles, New York, San Francisco, and Washington, D.C.

German Tourist Office
440 S. Flower St., Ste. 2230
Los Angeles, CA 90071
(213) 688-7332

The French Cavalry School at Samur.

also:

747 Third Ave.
New York, NY 10017
(212) 308-3300

Consulates are located in Atlanta, Boston, Chicago, Detroit, Houston, Los Angeles, Miami, New Orleans, New York, San Francisco, Seattle, and Washington, D.C.

British Tourist Authority
2580 Cumberland Pkwy.
Atlanta, GA 30339
(404) 432-9635

also:
875 N. Michigan Ave., Ste. 3320
Chicago, IL 60611
(312) 787-0490

2305 Cedar Maple Plaza
Dallas, TX 75201

350 S. Figueroa St., Ste. 450
Los Angeles, CA 90071

40 W. 57th St.
New York, NY 10019
(212) 581-4708

Consulates are located in Atlanta, Boston, Cleveland, Dallas, Houston, Los Angeles, New York, and San Francisco.

IBUSZ Tourist Office (Hungary)
630 Fifth Ave., Ste. 2455
New York, NY 10020
(212) 582-7412

Iceland Tourist Board
655 Third Ave.
New York, NY 10019
(212) 949-2332

Consulates are located in Atlanta, Boston, Los Angeles, Miami, Minneapolis, New York, Norfolk (VA), Portland (OR), San Francisco, and Seattle.

Irish Tourist Board
757 Third Ave.
New York, NY 10017
(212) 418-0800

Consulates are located in Boston, Chicago, New York, and San Francisco.

Israel Government Tourist Office
5 S. Wabash Ave.
Chicago, IL 60603
(312) 782-4306

also:

4151 S.W. Freeway
Houston, TX 77027
(713) 850-9341

6380 Wilshire Blvd.
Los Angeles, CA 90048
(213) 658-7462

420 Lincoln Road
Miami Beach, FL 33139
(305) 673-6862

350 Fifth Ave.
New York, NY 10118
(212) 560-0620

220 Montgomery St.
San Francisco, CA 94102
(415) 775-5462

3514 International Dr., N.W.
Washington, D.C. 20008
(202) 364-5699

Consulates are located in Atlanta, Boston, Chicago, Houston, Los Angeles, Miami, New York, Philadelphia, and San Francisco.

Italian Government Tourist Office—ENIT
500 N. Michigan Ave.

Hunting in Ireland, with the Rock of Cashel (County Tipperary) in the background.

Chicago, IL 60611
(312) 644-0990

also:

630 Fifth Ave.
New York, NY 10020
(212) 245-4822

360 Post St.
San Francisco, CA 94108
(415) 392-5266

Consulates are located in Boston, Chicago, Detroit, Houston, Los Angeles, Newark (NJ), New Orleans, New York, Philadelphia, and San Francisco.

Jamaica Tourist Board
36 S. Wabash Ave.
Chicago, IL 60603
(312) 346-1546

also:

8411 Preston Rd.
Dallas, TX 75225

3440 Wilshire Blvd.
Los Angeles, CA 90010
(213) 384-1123

1320 S. Dixie Hwy.
Coral Gables, FL 33146
(306) 665-0557

866 Second Ave.
New York, NY 10017
(212) 688-7650

Mexican Ministry of Tourism
233 N. Michigan Ave., Ste. 1413
Chicago, IL 60601
(312) 565-2785

2707 North Loop West
Houston, TX 77008
(713) 880-5153

10100 Santa Monica Blvd.
Los Angeles, CA 90067
(213) 203-8151

405 Park Ave., Ste. 1203
New York, NY 10022
(212) 755-7212

Moroccan National Tourist Office
20 E. 46th St.
New York, NY 10017
(212) 557-2520

Netherlands Board of Tourism
355 Lexington Ave.
New York, NY 10017
(212) 370-7364

also:

605 Market St., Rm. 401
San Francisco, CA 94105
(415) 543-6772

New Zealand Tourist and Publicity Office
10960 Wilshire Blvd.
Los Angeles, CA 90024
(213) 477-8241

also:

630 Fifth Ave.
New York, NY 10020
(212) 586-0060

1 Maritime Plaza
San Francisco, CA 94111
(415) 788-7404

Norwegian Tourist Board
655 Third Ave.
New York, NY 10017
(212) 949-2333

Consulates are located in Chicago, Houston, Los Angeles, Minneapolis, New York, and San Francisco.

Polish Travel Bureau, Inc.—Orbis
500 Fifth Avenue
New York, NY 10036
(212) 391-0844

Consulates are located in Chicago and New York.

Portuguese National Tourist Office
548 Fifth Ave.
New York, NY 10036
(212) 354-4403

Consulates are located in Boston, Honolulu, Houston, Los Angeles, Miami, Newark (NJ), New Bedford (MA), New Orleans, New York, Philadelphia, Providence (RI), and San Francisco.

Intourist (Russia)
630 Fifth Ave.
New York, NY 10111
(212) 757-3884

Consulates are located in San Francisco and Washington, D.C.

South Africa Tourist Corp.
9465 Wilshire Blvd., Ste. 721
Beverly Hills, CA 90212
(213) 275-4111

also:

307 N. Michigan Ave.
Chicago, IL 60601
(312) 726-0517

747 Third Ave.
New York, NY 10017
(212) 838-8841

Consulates are located in Chicago, Houston, Los Angeles, and New York.

Alvarito Domecq performing at the Andalusian Riding School, Jérez de la Frontera, Spain.

National Tourist Office of Spain
845 N. Michigan Ave.
Chicago, IL 60611
(312) 944-0215

also:

5805 Westheimer
Houston, TX 77056
(713) 840-7411

8383 Wilshire Blvd.
Los Angeles, CA 90211
(213) 658-7188

665 Fifth Ave.
New York, NY 10022
(212) 759-8822

Consulates are located in Chicago, Houston, Los Angeles, Miami, New Orleans, New York, and San Francisco.

Swedish Tourist Board
150 N. Michigan Ave.
Chicago, IL 60601
(312) 726-1120

also:

655 Third Ave.
New York, NY 10017
(212) 949-2323

Consulates are located in Chicago, Houston, Los Angeles, New York, and San Francisco.

Swiss National Tourist Office
104 S. Michigan Ave.
Chicago, IL 60603
(312) 641-0050

also:

608 Fifth Ave.
New York, NY 10020
(212) 757-5944

220 Stockton St.
San Francisco, CA 94018
(415) 362-2260

Worldwide Horseback Vacations by Arthur Sachs (The Complete Traveler, 1996, paperback) devotes a page to each of almost 200 riding facilities and treks around the world. Those in the U.S. tend to be dude ranches, although other types of riding resorts are listed. Foreign destinations range from trekking in Wales, Hungary, and New Zealand to horseback safaris in Africa and Asia. The author promises an enlarged revision by the end of 1998, one that will include hints on safety and pretrip preparation; the new edition will be worth waiting for.

Saddle Up!: A Guide to Planning the Perfect Horseback Vacation by Ute Haker (John Muir Publications, 1997, paperback) is especially helpful on the subject of wilderness rides throughout U.S. National Parks and other public venues. Other types of horseback holidays are presented, as are checklists of what the well-travelled horse and rider need to take along. An appendix lists where to obtain information about specific parks and other areas.

Gene Kilgore's Ranch Vacations, fourth edition

A Note On Equestrian Travel Agents

—————— ∩ ——————

SOME TRAVELERS ENJOY PLANNING their trips from start to finish, making their own arrangements by gathering information from state or national tourist offices and then booking their transportation and ground accommodations with airlines, car rental agencies, hotels, and recreational providers.

Other people prefer to leave the planning and execution to travel professionals. In the case of equestrian vacations, several agencies specialize in horseback holidays. In addition to listing and detailing trips, their catalogs provide powerful fodder for fantasies.

Equitour Fits, Box 807, Dubois, WY 82513
   (800) 545-0019. Fax: (307) 455-2354

Since the merger of Equitour and Fits Equestrian, this agency offers a larger and more varied (and imaginative) menu of horseback vacations than any of its competitors. The range is literally worldwide: from the "Gaucho Ride" in Argentina and "Pub Crawl" in Australia to the "Cappadocia Ride" in Turkey and "Mavuradonna Wilderness Trails" in Zimbabwe. Other trips take vacationers through European, Asian, and Central and South American countries. The U.S.A. is represented by tours in California, Vermont, and the agency's Wyoming home base. Some trips are so-

called *stationary programs,* which involve a base location. There are also opportunities for instruction in dressage, combined training, and western horsemanship.

Cross Country International Equestrian Vacations
   P.O. Box 1170, Millbrook, NY 12545
   (800) 828-8768. Fax: (914) 677-6077

Cross Country International focuses on England, Ireland, Scotland, Wales, France, Italy, and (closer to home) Canada. Offerings include trail riding in those countries, as well as fox or stag hunting where available. Dressage training is available at facilities in England's Yorkshire or Fontainebleau, outside Paris; combined training instruction takes place in England's Devon and at County Limerick in Ireland. Younger riders may be interested in a riding camp in north Wales.

Eastern Trekking Associates
   2574 Nicky Lane, Alexandria, VA 22311
   phone: (703) 845-9366 fax: (703) 379-4059

Eastern Trekking Associates positions itself as offering week-long "affordable horseback holidays." These take place in Ireland (cross-country in the Dingle Penninsula, and training in Cavan), Wales (pony trekking, a medieval castles ride, and a historic inns ride), and Austria (including tours of ancient castles and one that crosses the border into the Czech Republic). Other trips include Hungary, Mexico, and the Caribbean island of St. Croix. ∩

(John Muir Publications, 1996, paperback) devotes a page each to hundreds of guest and resort ranches. In addition to riding, many offer (depending on the season) fly-fishing, cross-country skiing, and other sports. The photographs alone will make you want to drop everything and head for the hills.

Dan Aadland, author of *Horseback Adventures* (Howell Book House, 1995, paperback) shares his true-life—adventure reminiscences about vacations that have involved working ranches, pack tripping, and solo trekking in the U.S. and abroad. It's a good introduction to what to expect.

chapter 9

Organizations

Now that you have acquired your horse, your stable, your management routines, your equine health regimen, your tack, and your apparel and have become involved in one or more equestrian activities—perhaps even including a horseback vacation—you will feel ready to meet other horse people, or at least to read about them. The following chapter includes information about magazines to which you may want to subscribe, organizations you may want to join, and catalogs you may want to order and order from.

Magazines

Name a breed or activity or a region of the country, and there's sure to be at least one magazine that covers the subject or area. Since there's no absolutely complete list of equestrian periodicals, we used various sources to compile this one (and no doubt we missed a few).

Some of these periodicals are sold at large newsstands, many more at tack shops. Others are available only through membership in their breed or activity organizations. Another way to become familiar with magazines devoted to specific breeds, sports, or areas is simply to ask around. If you're becoming interested in, say, rodeoing or Appaloosas or if you've just moved to a new part of the country, ask people who are already involved or who live there what they read. Magazines tend to pile up in tack rooms, stable offices, and home coffee tables, so it's just a matter of asking, then reading around.

A RACK OF FAVORITES

Among the leading magazines of which we have personal and professional knowledge and can wholeheartedly recommend are:

- *The Chronicle of the Horse.* This weekly is the magazine of record for the hunter/jumper, combined training, dressage, driving, hunt racing, and the rest of the English-riding world. It's especially useful for competition results and other news of the show world. P.O. Box 46, Middleburg, VA 20118. (703) 687-6341.
- *Equus.* This monthly is veterinary in orientation, with articles for the layman on equine health and related subjects. You don't need a DVM degree to profit from its contents. 656 Quince Orchard Rd., Gaithersburg, MD 29878. (301) 977-3900.
- *Horse & Rider.* Western enthusiasts will find articles on training, showing and horse health in this monthly. 12265 West Bayaud, Lakewood, CO 80228. (303) 914-3000.
- *HorsePlay.* Profiles of horse-world personalities, how-to instruction, and general features that appeal to English-style riders mark this breezy, well-designed monthly. 656 Quince Orchard Rd., Gaithersburg, MD 29878. (301) 977-3900.
- *Michael Plumb's Horse Journal.* The *Consumer's Report*-style approach of this monthly analyzes

and rates equestrian products. Other articles focus on stable management, horse health, and riding instruction. If the name isn't familiar, Mike Plumb is a seven-time Olympic three-day eventer. Box 2626, 75 Holly Hill Lane, Greenwich, CT 06836. (203) 661-6111.

• *The Quarter Horse Journal.* Because of the size of the American Quarter Horse Association (which publishes this monthly) and the many activities with which the breed is associated, the *Journal's* coverage of activities provides a panoramic view of the country's equestrian scene. PO Box 32470, Amarillo, TX 79120. (806) 376-4811.

• *Practical Horseman.* Just what its name suggests, this monthly focuses on detailed how-to articles on riding, stable management, and horse health. Its target audience is the hunter/jumper, eventing, and dressage world as well as noncompetitive pleasure riders. Box. 589, Unionville, PA 19375. (610) 380-8977.

• *Western Horseman.* Coverage of Western breeds, activities, and the cowboy lifestyle is the hallmark of this monthly. PO Box 7980, Colorado Springs, CO 80933. (719) 633-5524.

BREEDS
In addition to the magazines published by the breed associations and registries listed in chapter 1, the following national magazines are devoted to particular breeds:

America's Horse (American Quarter Horses)
Arabian Horse Digest
Arabian Horse Express
Arabian Horse Times
Arabian Horse World
The Draft Horse Journal
The Hackney Journal
Horse World (Saddlebreds and Morgans)
Miniature Horse News
National Show Horse
Palomino Horses
Paso Express (paso fino)
Paso Fino Horse World
POA Magazine (Pony of the Americas)
Quarter Horse News
The Racking Review (Racking Horses)
Saddle & Bridle (Saddlebreds)
Saddle Horse Report (Saddlebreds and Morgans)
Walking Horse Report

ACTIVITIES AND OTHER SPECIAL INTERESTS
These national magazines deal with specific and specialized activities:

American Cutting Horse News
American Farriers Journal
The Blood-Horse (Thoroughbreds)
The Carriage Journal (driving)
Dressage & CT (dressage and combined training)
The Driving Digest Magazine
dvm—The Newsmagazine of Veterinary Medicine
Endurance News (endurance riding)
Equine Images (equine and equestrian fine arts)
Hoof Print (competitive trail riding)
Horse Show (American Horse Shows Association)
Journal of the AVMA (American Veterinary Medical Association)
The Journal of the Ride and Tie Association
NHSRA Times (rodeo)
NHRA Reiner (reining)
Persimmon Hill (Western art and history)
Polo
Side-Saddle News
Team Penning USA
USCTA News (combined training)
USDF Bulletin (dressage)
USET News (U.S. Equestrian Team)
The Whip (driving)
Women's Pro Rodeo News

Books and Videotapes

As megacorporate publishers concentrate on pursuing bestsellers, equestrian books are among those special-interest areas that are now almost exclusively the domain of specialty imprints or smaller niche publishing firms. This isn't such a bad thing: rather than become lost in the shuffle or forced into an early out-of-print grave, the books are far better looked after and in a more appreciatative way (so for that matter, are their authors).

The following publishers have extensive horse-book lists, and they will be happy to send you their catalogs:

- Breakthrough Publications, Millwood, NY 10546
- Half Halt Press, PO Box 67, Boonsboro, MD 21713
- Howell Book House, Macmillan Publishing USA, 1633 Broadway, New York, NY 10019
- The Lyons Press, 31 West 21 St., New York, NY 10010
- Trafalgar Square Press, Box 257, North Pomfret, VT 05053
- Large bookshops, especially branches of national chains like Barnes & Noble or Borders, stock horse books in their sports or animals sections. Tack shops of all sizes are likely sources for videos as well as books, and their catalogs often devote several pages to viewing as well as reading material.

An enviably comprehensive selection of books on all aspects of horses and horsemanhip can be found at Knight Equestrian Books, PO Box 78, Edgecomb, ME 04556. (207) 882-5494. Fax: (207) 882-9826, E-mail: knight@clinic.net.

The following firms specialize in out-of-print or hard-to-find horse books. Their catalogs are delights:

Larimar Animal Books
13 Springbrook Rd.
Morristown, NJ 07960
(201) 538-1853

Robin Bledsoe, Bookseller (formerly Blue Rider Books)
1640 Massachusetts Ave.
Cambridge, MA 02138
(617) 576-3634

Second Story Bookshop
PO Box 1384
Lexington, VA 24450
(540) 463-6264.

For hard-to-find videos as well as books, try

The Russell Meerdink Company, Ltd.
1555 South Park Ave.
Neenah, WI 54956
(800) 635-6499

THE AMERICAN ACADEMY OF EQUINE ART

The American Academy of Equine Art was formed in 1980 at the suggestion of Alexander Mackay-Smith, noted historian, and Dr. Joseph Rogers. Both men were board members of the Westmoreland Davis Foundation, at Morven Park in Leesburg, Virginia. The idea was to assemble the finest equine artists in the country to exhibit together, share creative ideas, and eventually establish a teaching organization. The academy was to be modeled after the Royal Academy in England. World-renowned equine artists Jean Bowman and Else Tuckerman were consulted. They suggested a core group of ten distinguished painters and sculptors who formed the American Academy of Equine Art, based in Middleburg, Virginia.

The mission of the academy is to establish a standard of excellence in the field of equine art, and to broaden public recognition of equine painting and sculpture through education, demonstration, exhibition, and critique.

The academy's first exhibition was held in the spring of 1980 at the Museum of Hounds and Hunting at historic Morven Park, Virginia. Throughout the years as the academy grew and more artists joined, the annual exhibition moved to a variety of locations, including Arkansas, Massachusetts, Florida, Ohio, South Carolina, and Kentucky.

The AAEA was granted tax-exempt status in 1992. At that time, the academy entered into an agreement with the Kentucky Horse Park in Lexington, Kentucky, to offer an annual series of art workshops in drawing, painting, and sculpture, taught by AAEA members. The workshops fill a void not addressed by any other art school in the country. They provide a unique opportunity for students to study the horse and equine-related subjects at the Horse Park, and to study with some of the best equine artists in the country.

The agreement also called for the academy to hold at least two exhibitions at the Park's International Museum of the Horse each year. In the spring, an invitational show features the work of Academy members and invited artists and is held in conjunction with the Rolex Three Day Event, there. In the fall, the academy holds an annual juried exhibition that showcases the work of a select group of artists that has been chosen from hundreds of entries.

Today the AAEA has exhibiting artists from four

countries and all parts of the U.S. and their Annual Invitational Exhibit tours fine art museums across the country. Many of the academy members are among the finest and most recognized equine painters and sculptors working today. AAEA annual exhibitions are looked upon by collectors and dealers as a source for the best in contemporary equine art.

For more information about the academy or the workshops, write to:
American Academy of Equine Art
P.O. Box 1315, Middleburg, Virginia 20118
Web site: htt://www.imh.org/imh/aaea/home.html

Your Half of the Partnership

FITNESS, PERFORMANCE AND THE FEMALE EQUESTRIAN
By MARY D. MIDKIFF

Body awareness and conditioning will not only make a difference in your approach to riding, but it will make a tremendous difference in the way the horse approaches his time with you. Do you know as much about the human body as you do about the horse's body? Since you live in a human body you should be familiar with all aspects of how it functions and moves, especially as it relates to you and your horse.

Not only is body awareness important to our safety and ability to partner a horse; we also have a responsibility to maintain conditioning for the level of activity we perform with our horse. Whether it be riding competitively or trail riding at a walk, we owe it to our horses to be prepared for any level of activity on his back. Do we feel like a concrete block or a sack of feathers to him? I'm not referring to your weight—your position and ability to remain flexible and rebalance with movement can change the amount of density and pressure the horse feels.

It became apparent to me several years ago that the rider's fitness was as important as the horse's conditioning. Why? Because the objective between horse and rider is a long-lasting partnership. We don't just sit on the horse, look pretty, and hope for the best. Riding is one-on-one communication, a working, moving, lasting partnership.

If you are tight or rigid, unfit and out of balance and rhythm with the horse's movement, you and your horse will wear out much sooner than necessary. He will tighten, begin to build up defenses toward you and become sour about his work or, possibly, lame. Some horse's put up with our shortcomings despite their own pain and discomfort; other, more sensitive types will let you know when they are uncomfortable in a violent way or by simply shutting out all stimuli.

I was inspired to write *Fitness, Performance and the Female Equestrian* (Macmillan) and produce the *Get Fit To Ride* videos mainly because of my own wear-and-tear injuries, not from falls, but from a lack of preparation and understanding of the requirements of my body for riding and work around the horse.

Additionally, through market analysis, I discovered that over 80 percent of the participants in horse sports today are female and, yet, there was little information geared toward her issues and requirements. Gender differences play a large role in the techniques, methods, instruction, and equipment geared toward horse activities. One sex does not ride any better than the other, we are simply different, and require a specific approach to our body mechanics, structure, and weight distribution. I also gained a great deal of insight from working with and interviewing girls and women through my Women & Horses™ national workshop tour.

Through research and consulting with a number of medical and scientific experts, I was able to begin to understand why so many of us (mainly women) are uncomfortable, sore, and frustrated in riding. Riding can

American Academy of Equine Art, Workshop in Lexington, Kentucky.

be the greatest joy in our lives or the most discouraging. Through understanding of the female structure and the way it moves, and the equipment necessary for support we can achieve freedom of movement and balance in the saddle. It also will give us years and years of riding ahead.

I was also puzzled by the fact that through every riding instruction and training program I had been through, no preparation was required, you just get on and go. In all other sports, teachers and coaches not only suggested that I warm up and cool down but required it. Riding is certainly an athletic endeavor and yet there were very few, if any, rider resources of this sort available.

In my book, I take a look back at where we have come from in riding traditions and address where we are today and what we can look forward to. I plan to ride for a lifetime and I know you do, too.

The best way to ensure longevity in riding is through stretching and strengthening exercises on a regular basis, and incorporating a cross-training activity, such as walking. Whether it is in the gym, on a machine, or a walk across the field or through the woods, use this activity to support your love for riding.

Areas we specifically need to isolate and stretch for the best results are the inner thighs, the hamstrings, the quadriceps, and the back. If you can spend a few minutes every day stretching these areas at home, you will notice positive results in your ability to balance while the horse is in motion. Stretching regularly will also greatly decrease overall soreness, saddle sores, and chafing.

I recommend at least five days per week (everyday if possible) of a 10–15 minute stretching session with at least three days per week of strengthening. Also, add a couple of quick stretches right before you get in the saddle such as the hamstring stretch and the quadriceps stretch (quad stretch may also be performed in the saddle).

Strengthening is key to the female rider's upper-body protection. Because women are lighter in the upper body and carry less muscle mass than men, we need to concentrate on the shoulders, the abdominal muscles, and the arms to minimize injury and increase effectiveness. Gaining strength in your upper torso also improves posture, breathing, and, once again, improves your balance while in motion.

I created the Equestrian Ball and Band™, which is an exercise tool, teaching aid, and riding simulation device to assist in rider fitness. By sitting on the large ball and using the band as the reins, you and your instructor or friend can begin to better understand what is happening with your body as you try to move with the bounce of the ball, simulating the swing in the horse's back and belly. You may also sit on the ball and stretch, work on your range of motion with pelvic rolls and side-to-side hip swings, learn to relax in the saddle by holding the ball between your calves, and walk around without clinching your buttock muscles. The use of this tool is unlimited for riders and adds a new dimension to riding in a controlled environment.

Other considerations include your diet or nutrition, and bone health. These are important not only in your day-to-day life but as they relate to riding. The proper food and supplemental balance can make the difference in the ability to respond in an emergency and minimizes down time from injuries.

Start thinking about what you bring to the partnership. Are you holding up your end of the deal? Body awareness, flexibility, and being prepared for riding and work around the horse are not only helpful but necessary to ride for a lifetime.

1. Evaluate your conformation. One area we particularly need to focus on as females is knee position and the hip-joint relationship. Most women are knock-kneed (picture an old Jerry Lewis movie where he runs "like a girl") due to the position of their hip joints and the way they connects to the femur or upper leg. This connection tends to send our knees together instead of facing straight ahead or out to the sides as in a bowlegged position.

A knock-kneed tendency in the saddle can create pain, discomfort, and frustration if it is not addressed and understood. Using a saddle to support the female pelvis, becoming aware of what is going on anatomically, and stretching and strengthening the muscles which surround your pelvis and upper leg are key to preventing knee and hip pain issues.

Learning to ride with body awareness in a balanced position is the only way to find maximum movement in your body, which frees the horse's body for peak performance.

2. Recognize gender differences. Females tend to be lighter muscled in the top part of their body, with most of their weight and strength based below the waist. She has a pelvis designed to give and nurture life, which a male does not. His pelvis is shaped more vertically with a flat sacrum and a channel through the pubic area that prevents friction problems.

The female pelvis has a birth canal and a sacrum which extends more outwardly to allow a baby to pass through. Therefore, the female has difficulty with tucking underneath her hips, as a man can do without much effort. The female, however, does not have topheavy rebalancing issues that the male does.

The point here is that one sex is not better than the other at riding, just different. These differences require gender specific techniques, exercises, and equipment to achieve maximum performance from the horse.

3. Address aging as a part of riding. It's inevitable that we are going to change in many ways as we age. When we are forty-something we do not move or are as coordinated as we were when we were twenty. Wear and tear, chemical and hormonal fluctuations, and lack of flexibility become more apparent as we age. This does not mean stop riding. It means we have to look at it as an activity requiring preparation and prevention.

Osteoporosis is a major issue for aging women. Nutritional considerations, supplements in your diet to ensure bone density, maintaining condition, stretching everyday, wearing supportive undergarments, and using equipment that supports our structure, aids in the aging process. If you are passionate about riding, you will live this program so you can ride into the sunset years feeling good about it.

4. Stretching and strengthening are key to riding forever with comfort and safety.

For flexibility and balance in the saddle you must stretch your body. Stretching brings oxygen, circulation, and awareness to every area while it releases tension, acid, and toxin buildup. When you stretch, you sit in the saddle with a relaxed, draped leg (stirrup length doesn't matter here) and a spine that can bend freely with you and your horse.

Strengthening is also important, especially for women, because of our lighter upper body and the probability of injury to this area. Rotator-cuff tears are more common to female equestrians because of this

lack of preparation to meet riding's strength requirements. I've had shoulder surgery for a rotator-cuff tear, not due to a fall or falls, but simply from wear and tear over many years of training horses.

As often as possible, walk as an excellent cross-training exercise to riding. Get on a treadmill, a stair machine, walk across a field or around the block a few times. While you're out and moving, think about your form and use good body mechanics.

I learned that I must get fit to ride in order to be safe, sound, and protected.

5. Learn how to ride in balance no matter what the breed or discipline.

We so often are conditioned to think that we must ride in a certain way or with a certain look to be successful. The stirrups might be shorter or longer; the saddle may be a different shape, size, or color; and the clothing may vary. But being a successful rider means being in balance throughout your body, no matter what the riding style or breed of horse. The style of riding you prefer can be achieved easiest if your body is correctly aligned to move in the saddle.

These tips all apply to benefit the horse, their condition, attitude, ability to move and stay sound. It is time to fulfill your half of the partnership.

For more information about *Fitness, Performance and the Female Equestrian* (Macmillan) and Women & Horses™ products and programming contact: Equestrian Resources, PO Box 20187, Boulder, CO 80308 (303) 544-0333. Fax: (303) 544-0331

Equine Humane Movements

Because horses are legally considered farm animals in the United States, they are ignored by the Animal Welfare Act of the U.S. Government, except under exhibition conditions or when they are transported interstate. In other words, no federal legislation exists to protect a horse that is being abused or kept in bad condition by its owner. Thanks to the hardworking members of the American Horse Protection Association, there are laws against the exhibition of any horse that has been "sored" or is forced to wear chains, boots, or other devices that affect its gait while causing pain. This Section 11.2 of the Animal Welfare Act came about because of the heavy abuses suffered by Tennessee Walking Horses, although it does, of course, apply to any and all horses exhibited in the United States. (Wild mustangs are also protected by the Federal Government—but because they are wild animals, not because they are horses.)

State laws, too, are not generally concerned with the welfare of horses, except as they are shipped into the state—and in this case the goal is not to protect the individual horse but to keep resident animals free of disease. Such regulations vary from state to state, but usually involve the presentation of a health certificate signed by a veterinarian and a negative Coggins test dated within the previous year or six months.

With the single exception of the state of Maryland, no set of state laws exists to protect horses from abuses caused by cruel handling or negligent stabling. The Maryland law concerns horses rented to the public. Although it was promoted by the Maryland Humane Association for the sake of the horses, we can't help feeling that it was passed primarily because of the potential danger that ill-used animals present to the un-

The American Medical Equestrian Association

By DORIS BIXBY HAMMETT, M.D.

THE EQUINE INDUSTRY IS made up of a very heterogeneous population. The demands of individual sports, and the risks to the rider or driver vary greatly. Regardless of the level of the challenge, there will always be some inherent potential for injury. These concerns cannot be eliminated, but they can be minimized, which is the purpose of the AMEA.

Founded in 1986, the American Medical Equestrian Association (AMEA) is a nonprofit organization whose members are primarily physicians and health-care professionals with an interest in equestrian activities, and equine organizational representatives with a focus on safety. The primary mission of the AMEA is to emphasize safe participation, while maintaining a sense of tradition.

The AMEA addresses these issues in the following areas:

The AMEA serves as a medium through which various equestrian sports and organizations share ideas and experience to mutual benefit. Its resources of information, knowledge, and expertise in various aspects of equestrian competition and participation place a special emphasis on injury prevention and injury management.

Ongoing epidemiological research focuses on injury risks and injury patterns. Only through a more factual understanding of these trends can appropriate and effective changes be made.

AMEA representatives participate in the development of standards for safety equipment, research safety equipment design, and study the efficacy of existing safety equipment.

The AMEA has developed protocols for emergency services to handle injuries. This is critical to prevent lesser injuries from becoming more severe, and to properly handle severe injuries, minimizing fatalities.

An emphasis on education and awareness is important to understand and properly manage these issues. The AMEA achieves these goals through educational programs, informational materials, and position statements.

For a health-care professional interested in the equestrian industry, the AMEA provides a vehicle through which to contribute effectively and efficiently. For an organizational representative, it provides a voice for direction and influence within the AMEA. For an individual with an interest in safety and welfare of the equestrian athlete and the horse industry, it provides an opportunity to contribute.

If participants do not emphasize safety within the horse industry, and outsiders deem the industry risky, more inappropriate legislation affecting us will be passed. Appropriate safety programs and risk management will influence not only the cost of liability coverage but, ultimately, its availability.

Annual AMEA membership includes a quarterly newsletter, an invitation to our annual fall meeting, interim spring meetings, access to all AMEA resource material, and opportunities to contribute to ongoing projects.

For further information, contact the AMEA's Secretary, Doris Bixby Hammett, M.D. at:

American Medical Equestrian Association
103 Surrey Road
Waynesville, NC 28786
(704) 456-3392. E-mail: dhammett@primeline.com

wary riders who rent them. Although these regulations—which involve the licensing and inspection of the stables—seem a bit overprotective, this kind of legislation is sorely needed not just in Maryland but in every state in the country. There is some humane activity going on in other states—California, Pennsylvania, and New York, for example—thanks to the efforts of local animal organizations. States also regulate against the use of unacceptable drugs in race horses—but again, we can't help suspecting that this has to do with protecting bettors and other owners rather than with keeping horses healthy. It is true, of course, that the doping of horses was originally made illegal because Thoroughbred racing (and indeed the breed) in the United States was thought to be in real danger of deterioration as a consequence of the practice. Thanks to the Thoroughbred Racing and Protective Bureau, the use of drugs has been severely curtailed.

If you are interested in putting through legislation in your own state—or even just in reporting single instances of abuse—several avenues are open to you. Keep in mind that it will be difficult to do much about even the most obvious cases of abuse. Nevertheless, it is worth trying, even if all your efforts result only in a bit of adverse publicity for the abuser. First, be sure that you are not the only person to witness the bad conditions. Take photos if possible. Get an affidavit signed by one or more veterinarians attesting to poor conditions and—if it exists—the presence of untreated diseases or injuries. Starvation, poorly ventilated and/or filthy stables, and any other obvious wrongs should also be noted. Once you have put your dossier together, get in touch with the officials of your local humane society or a local branch of one of the national organizations (the Humane Society of the United States, the Fund for Animals, and others). If there is no such organization in your community or area, find out whether there is a state organization where you live. If not, call or write your local law-enforcement agency and be sure that the local newspapers are notified. Many times the pressure of public opinion alone will be enough to force the issue. It was in New York City, where a carriage horse had to be destroyed right in front of the Plaza Hotel. The incident aroused so much indignation that investigations were immediately undertaken into the stabling of carriage horses.

If you are concerned with legislation on a higher level—not simply the improvement of one or two situations—you may try working with others who are similarly concerned. The League for American Protection in New York State managed to have peace officers elected to investigate cruelty cases and to make arrests. It might be worth writing for advice concerning your own state to Mr. and Mrs. Warren Abrams, 147 Daly Road, East Northport, New York 11731. You can also express your interest to the American Horse Protection Association, Inc., 1000 29th Street, N.W., Washington, D.C. 20007.

Future Farmers of America

The Future Farmers of America includes among its activities horse proficiency awards. Sponsored by the American Morgan Horse Association, Inc., they are intended to encourage FFA members to explore careers in the horse industry, such as breeding, training, feeding, and showing.

Among recent winners are youngsters who established a successful stable, bred new strains of horses, and exhibited animals at fairs and shows. They all worked through their state programs under the supervision of local Vocational Agriculture Instructors.

For further information, contact your county extension agent or write to Future Farmers of America, National FFA Center, P.O. Box 15160, Alexandria, Virginia 22309.

THREE OTHER ORGANIZATIONS WORTH KNOWING ABOUT
American Horse Council
1700 K St., NW
Washington, DC 20006-3805
(202) 296-4031. Fax: (202) 296-1970.
E-mail: AHorseC@aol.com

A national federation for the entire horse industry, the Council is a major force in legislative activities, especially with regard to economic matters, land use, and animal welfare. Its annual *Horse Industry Directory* is the single most comprehensive source of names and addresses of equine and equestrian organizations.

American Association of Equine Practitioners
4075 Iron Works Pike

Pony Clubs

—— Ω ——

by CATHERINE MCWILLIAMS

THE BRITISH PONY CLUB, inaugurated in 1929, was the model for the United States Pony Clubs, Inc., which was formally incorporated in 1954. The purpose of the pony club is "to produce a thoroughly happy, comfortable horseman, riding across a natural country, with complete confidence and perfect balance on a pony equally happy and confident and free from pain or bewilderment." The term "pony" is loosely used to refer to any mount, regardless of size or breeding, of a junior rider (the latter considered by the Pony Club to be anyone under the age of 21).

The Pony Club realizes its goals through education in riding skills as well as in teaching the responsibilities and techniques of horse ownership and stable management, such as grooming, feeding, stabling, shoeing, and first aid.

Organization is through local chapters, usually centered in a town or county and often sponsored by a recognized hunt. Local officers are all volunteers, and each chapter decides on its own programs.

The unifying factors that are decided at the national level are, more importantly, the rating system for each level and competition rules. Every pony-club member is rated on a scale from D, the most elementary, to A. While local officers and instructors within a chapter assign D and C ratings, a rider must pass an extensive test conducted by a nationally sanctioned examiner before becoming a B or an A. The requirements for becoming a Pony Club A are so demanding that only a few dozen members in the entire country each year receive this designation.

The rally is the heart of Pony-Club competition. It is available at all levels and designed to test all phases of horsemanship. Few individual awards are offered; most pony clubbers compete in teams of five, with only the group score taken into account. Rallies last over one to three days, and there is little assistance allowed from coaches and other adults.

There are five phases at every rally. First comes a written test covering all aspects of horsemanship and stable management. The second, stable management, begins when competitors arrive at the event and continues throughout the entire rally. Along with formal inspections of stabling and tack, judges continuously patrol the area to note any infractions of safe and correct procedures.

The next three phases, which all involve riding, are modeled after a Combined Training event. Each competitor rides a dressage test ranging in difficulty from a modified Training Level test for D's to the AHSA Second Level Test 1 for A's. A cross-country course is followed by a round of stadium jumping, also varying in difficulty according to riders' abilities.

Local clubs usually sponsor many other activities. Most chapters provide regular expert instruction at minimum cost, as well as horse shows, lectures, demonstrations, films, and mounted and unmounted practice sessions. In all cases, sportsmanship, teamwork, and paramount concern for a horse's welfare are always emphasized.

United States Pony Clubs, Inc.
303 South High Street
West Chester, Pennsylvania 19380 Ω

Lexington, KY 40511-8434
(606) 233-0147. Fax: (606) 233-1968

Among the organization's features is an emergency toll-free number (800-DIAL-A-VET) through which callers will be directed to the nearest veterinarian.

US Department of Agriculture Extension Service
14th St. and Independence Ave., SW
Washington, DC 20250
(202) 720-2677

This government agency coordinates cooperative state research and education services. If your horsekeeping questions can't be answered here (usually via government pamphlets or other printed material), you'll be referred to other agencies either at the federal or state level.

Intercollegiate Horse Show Association

The purpose of the Intercollegiate Horse Show Association is to provide a framework for competition on the collegiate level.

Classes range from Walk-Trot, for first-year competitors, to those able to handle Open division courses.

These competitions are unique in that riders may not use their own horses or tack, and schooling is not permitted. Thus each rider is tested upon his equestrian abilities without benefit of personal mounts of whatever quality. Instead, animals are obtained from nearby stables and riding academies, and these loaners are assigned by lot.

These competitions range throughout the school year with the regional finals in the late spring. Regional high-point champions compete against each other in the national finals.

The IHSA was established in 1967, and the founder, Robert E. Cacchione, remains at its head. Further information may be obtained by contacting the Executive Director at Box 741, Hollow Road, Stony Brook, NY 11790, or by calling (516) 751-2803.

The following, by zone, are the 1998 member colleges.

ZONE 1 (NEW ENGLAND: CONNECTICUT, MASSACUSETTS, NEW HAMPSHIRE, RHODE ISLAND, VERMONT)

REGION 1

Brown University
Community College of Rhode Island
Connecticut College
Johnson & Wales University
Roger Williams College
Salve Regina University
Stonehill College
Teikyo Post University
University of Connecticut
University of Massachusetts–Dartmouth
University of Rhode Island
Wesleyan University
Wheaton College

REGION 2

Bates College
Boston University
Colby Sawyer College
Dartmouth College
Framingham State College
Harvard University

Middlebury College
Mount Holyoke College
Mount Ida College
New England College
Tufts University
University of Massachusetts–Lowell
University of New Hampshire
University of Vermont

REGION 3

American International College
Amherst College
Becker Junior College
Clark University
Elms College
Hampshire College
King Oak Farm
Landmark College
Smith College
Springfield College
University of Massachusetts
Williams College
Worcester Polytechnic Institute
Worcester State College

ZONE 2 (NEW YORK: UPSTATE NEW YORK, WESTCHESTER, NEW YORK CITY; NORTHERN NEW JERSEY; CANADA)

REGION 1

Barnard University
Centenary College
College of St. Elizabeth
Columbia University
Cooper Union
Drew University
Fordham University
Manhattanville College
Marist College
Marymount College
New York University
Pace University
Sarah Lawrence College
United States Military Academy
Vassar College
William Paterson College

REGION 2

Alfred University
Cazenovia College
Clarkson University
Colgate University
Cornell University
Rensselaer Polytechnic Institute
Russell Sage College
Siena College
Skidmore College
St. Lawrence University
State University of New York–Albany
State University of New York–Binghamton
State University of New York–Geneseo
State University of New York–Oswego
State University of New York–Potsdam
Syracuse University
University of Rochester

ZONE 3 (DELAWARE, NEW YORK: LONG ISLAND, PENNSYLVANIA, SOUTHERN NEW JERSEY)

REGION 1

Adelphi University
C. W. Post
Dowling
Fairfield University
Hofstra University
Molloy College
Nassau Community College
Sacred Heart University
St. John's University
St. Joseph's College
State University of New York–Stony Brook
Suffolk Community College
Yale University

REGION 2

Beaver College
Bloomsburg University
Bucks County Community College
Cedar Crest College
Delaware Valley College

Kutztown University
Moravian College
Princeton University
Rutgers University
Temple University
University of Delaware
University of Pennsylvania
West Chester University

REGION 3

Bucknell University
California University of Pennsylvania
Carnegie Mellon University
Indiana University of Pennsylvania
Keystone Junior College
Pennsylvania State University
Seton Hall College
West Virginia University
Wilson College

ZONE 4 (MARYLAND, NORTH CAROLINA, VIRGINIA, DISTRICT OF COLUMBIA)

REGION 1

Christopher Newport University
College of William and Mary
George Washington University
Georgetown University
Goucher College
Longwood College
Lynchburg College
Mary Washington College
Randolph Macon Women's College
Sweet Briar College
Towson State University
University of Maryland
University of Richmond
University of Virginia

REGION 2

Averett College
Duke University
Ferrum College
Hollins College

North Carolina State University
Radford University
Saint Andrews Presbyterian College
Southern Virginia College
University of North Carolina–Chapel Hill
University of North Carolina–Greensboro
University of North Carolina–Wilmington
Virginia Intermont College
Virginia Polytechnic Institute and State University

ZONE 5 (ALABAMA, FLORIDA, GEORGIA, KENTUCKY, LOUISIANA, MISSISSIPPI, MISSOURI, SOUTH CAROLINA, SOUTHERN ILLINOIS, TENNESSEE)

REGION 1

Maryville College
Midway College
Morehead State University
Pellissippi State Community College
Tennessee Tech University
University of Kentucky
University of Louisville
University of Tennessee
University of the South

REGION 2

Berry College
Clemson University
Converse College
Queens College
University of Alabama
University of Georgia
University of South Carolina

REGION 3

John A. Logan College
Middle Tennessee State University
Murray State University
Northeast Missouri State University
Rhodes College
Southern Illinois University
Southwest Missouri State University
University of Memphis
Western Kentucky University

REGION 4

College of Charleston
Florida State University
Georgia Southern University
University of Florida
Wesleyan College

ZONE 6 (ILLINOIS, INDIANA, IOWA, KANSAS, MICHIGAN, OHIO, WEST VIRGINIA, WISCONSIN)

REGION 1

Columbus State University
Hiram College
Kent State University
Lake Erie College
Miami University
Oberlin College
Ohio State University
Ohio University
Salem–Teikyo University
University of Cincinnati
Xavier University

REGION 2

Ball State University
Earlham College
Indiana University
Iowa State University
Indiana University
Purdue University–
    Indianapolis
Parkland College
Purdue University
St. Mary of Woods College
Taylor University
University of Illinois
University of Minnesota–Crookston
University of Notre Dame

REGION 3

Denison University
Michigan State University
Ohio Wesleyan University

Otterbein College
University of Findlay
University of Michigan
Western Michigan University

ZONE 7 (COLORADO, KANSAS, LOUISIANA, NEW MEXICO, OKLAHOMA, TEXAS, WYOMING)

REGION I

Arapahoe Community College
Colby Community College
Colorado State University
Larimer Community College
Laramie County Community College
New Mexico State University
South Dakota State University
United States Air Force Academy
University of Colorado
University of Denver
University of Wyoming

REGION 2

North Central Texas College
Northwestern State University of Louisiana
Oklahoma State University
Sul Ross State University
Tarlton State University
Texas A & M University
Texas Tech University
University of Texas–Austin
West Texas A&M University

ZONE 8 (CALIFORNIA, NEVADA, OREGON, WASHINGTON)

REGION 1

Bakersfield College
California State Polytechnic University–
    San Luis Obispo
California State University–Fresno
Fresno Pacific College
Kings River Community College
San Jose State University
Sierra Nevada College

Sonoma State University
Stanford University
University of California–Davis

REGION 2

California State Polytechnic
    University–Pomona
California State University–San Marcos
University of California–San Diego
University of Southern California

REGION 3

College of Southern Idaho
Oregon State University
University of Oregon
University of Washington
Washington State University

Catalog Shopping

When we started assembling this book's first edition more than twenty years ago, our resources included only a handful of tack-shop catalogs because, as nearly as we could discover, that's all there were. Not so today: hundreds of stores present their wares that way. Some also do so via Internet web sites.

Thanks to overnight-shipping facilities, catalogs have become a very popular way to shop. They're also a good way to keep up with new products.

What follows are some of the more important and/or most interesting catalogs we've come across:

Back In The Saddle
570 Turner Drive, Suite C
Durango, CO 81301
(800) 435-3633
Apparel for pleasure and endurance riding, novelty apparel and gift (including toys) items, and books.

Beval Ltd.
Park Avenue
Gladstone, NJ 07934
(800) 524-0136
and
50 Pine Street

New Canaan, CT 06840
(800) 783-PONY
Lavishly photographed catalog of selected English tack, apparel and stable furnishings with an emphasis on items for horse showing.

Blue Ribbon Leather Co.
737 Madison St.
Shelbyville, TN 37106
(615) 884-8799
Specializing in tack and apparel for Saddle Horses, Tennessee Walking Horses, and other saddle-seat activities. Here's also a line of racing equipment.

BMB
3100 S. Meridian Ave.
Wichita, KS 67217
(888) BMB-TACK
Handcrafted halters, tack and blankets, as well as stable and apparel-storing items, all in sturdy fabrics and a range of colors.

Chamisa Ridge
P.O. Box 23294
Santa Fe, NM 87502-3294
(800) 743-3188
New age and natural items for the dressage-minded include books and videos, selected tack, and homeopathic and herbal remedies.

Chick's
P.O. Drawer 59,
Harrington, DE 19952
(800) 444-2441
Styling itself "America's True *Discount* Store," Chick's features a tabloid-format catalog in which primarily western tack and apparel range from entry-level (the majority) to better goods.

Country Reins
3342 Melrose Ave. NW
Roanoake, VA 24017
(800) 791-1144
A limited selection of upscale tack, rider apparel and sportswear, gift items and home furnishings in a handsomely produced catalog.

Dover Saddlery
P.O. Box 5837

Holliston MA 01746
(800) 989-1500
A comprehensive and well-illustrated selection of hunter/jumper, dressage, and combined training gear, together with equestrian-inspired sportswear and gift items.

Eisers
360 Kiwanis Blvd.
Hazelton, PA 18201
(800) 526-6987
fax: (717) 455-1593
The first edition of *The Whole Horse Catalog* listed Eisers as a New Jersey tack shop. Times have changed, and so has Eisers, which now calls itself the country's largest wholesaler of equestrian and equine products. Eisers' 300-page catalog lists the range of items it distributes to tack shops around the country. Although Eisers doesn't sell retail, an inquiry to its toll-free number will result in the name of the nearest place to buy its products.

Horse Country
60 Alexandria Pike
Warrenton VA 22186
(800) 882-HUNT
Tack, apparel and other items of interest to the fox-hunting and hunt racing (as in steeplechase) set.

Libertyville Saddle Shop
P.O. Box M
Libertyville, IL 60048
(800) 872-3353
A full range of English and Western products, tending toward the grass-roots function (as opposed to upscale, elegant) end of the spectrum. The catalog reflects this approach.

Meyer's
113 Walton Ave.
Lexington, KY 40507
(606) 252-2004
A venerable name in saddle-seat circles, Meyers offers tack and apparel for those disciplines.

Miller's Harness Co.
235 Murray Hill Parkway
East Rutherford, NJ 07073
(800) 553-7655

Miller's remains the tack industry's major player through a nationwide distribution network that supplies several hundred saddlery shops (listed in Miller's catalog) with hunter/jumper, dressage, and combined training tack and apparel. Miller's omnibus catalog is supplemented with specialty brochures, all of which are notably well designed and produced.

Nasco
901 Janesville Ave.
Fort Atkinson, WI 53538
(920) 563-2446
and
4825 Stoddard Rd.
Modesto, CA 95356
(209) 545-1600
A farm and ranch catalog that includes basic riding, stable, breeding, and farrier equipment, as well as a wide range of supplies for agriculture ventures of all types.

Pard's Western Shop
306 N. Maple St.
Urbana, IL 61801
(800) 334-5726
A very comprehensive roster of western tack and apparel, with helpful explanatory descriptions of many of the tack items.

Riding Right
P.O. Box 341
County Road 59
Cambridge, NY 12816
(800) 545-7444
In addition to elegant clothes (with an emphasis on dressage) and tack, Riding Right features imaginative gifts for humans and horses, and interior decorating items.

Schneider's Saddlery
8255 E. Washington St.
Chagrin Falls, OH 44023
(800) 365-1311
Offering just about all things to all breeds and disciplines, Schneider's is especially strong in the western, saddle-seat, and Arabian departments. Its very complete catalog reflects the firm's broad-spectrum view.

Shepler's
P.O. Box 202
Wichita, KA 67201
(800) 835-4004
In keeping with its supermarket-size retail outlets in several western cities, Shepler's offers a hefty catalog of western wear. If the look you seek is anything from working rancher to rhinestone cowboy, this is the catalog for you, partner.

State Line Tack Inc.
P.O. Box 935
Brockport, NY 14420
(800) 228-9208
The firm's direct approach of no-frills discount merchandising is reflected in its catalog and frequent tabloid-style coupon-shopping supplements. Judging by State Line's rapid growth, its concentration on low- to mid-priced tack, apparel, and stable supplies seems to have struck a responsive chord with consumers.

Tack in the Box
2413 82nd Ave. S.E.
Salem, OR 97301
(800) 456-9225 or (888) GET-TACK
A generous selection of English tack, apparel, stable accessories, and books.

Wiese Equine Supply
Wiese Way
P.O. Box 1308
Atkinson, NH 03811-1308
(800) 869-4373
A mixed bag of clothing (equine and human), tack, novelty and gift, and veterinary items comes from this offshoot of a veterinary supply house.

The Wise Old Nag
PO Box 1140
Ignacio, CO 81137
(800) 788-5307
The catalog reflects the firm's focus on fitness and natural health for horse and rider, specializing in natural foods, herbs and supplements, as well as books and items on so-called alternative health subjects.

Horses on the Web

As with every other subject under the sun, just about anything about horses and horse sports is just a click away—but only if you're on-line. Whether you want to find information about stable management or a particular sport, shop for an equestrian-related item, or share ideas or experiences with others through chat room correspondence, you'll find it on the Internet.

Two leads for links (which are directory/connections to other sites) are worth knowing about. One is Hay.net, a links-only site run by Karen Pautz at *Bloodhorse Magazine,* that can be found at http://www.haynet.net. The other, and perhaps even more comprehensive, is the Equestrian Links page maintained by Bill Cooke, curator of the Kentucky Horse Park's International Museum of the Horse. It can be reached via http://www.imh.org.

To get some idea of what's available out there in cyberland, here's the Museum's Equestrian Links pages (as of mid-1998). The sites' http addresses don't appear, but once you're on the pages, you can click your way to whatever appeals to you. Or get there by means of any decent search engine.

LISTING SITES
Australian Equestrian Internet Resources
Cindy Pierson's List of Horse Racing Web Sites
Cowboy Resources
Equestrian Links all Over the World
Hay.Net
Horse Racing Information, University of Ky.
Janet's Horse and Rodeo Links
Lisa and Mike's Equestrian Web Pages
National Horseman's Directory
World Equestrian Resources

HISTORICAL AND EDUCATIONAL SITES
The American West
American Saddlebred Horse Museum
Anna Jane White-Mullin's Equestrian Info Site
The Audie Murphy Memorial Website
The Institute for Ancient Equestrian Studies
Area 3 Quarter Horse Club (Ontario, Canada)
Buffalo Bill's Wild West Show
Cindy Pierson's Calumet Farm Trophy Page

The Canadian Cowboy
The Cowboy Lexicon
Chuck Pritchard's C Bar T (Cowboy poetry and Western history)
Domestic Animal Diversity Info. System
Egyptian History
Endurance Net
Enduro Online (Endurance Riding from Brazil)
The Equine FAQs
Equine Protozoal Myeloencephalitis (Univ. of MO–Columbia)
Equestrians Around the World
Equine Discoveries
Equine Heros
Equine Transitional Training Alliance, Inc.
Fox Den Equestrian Guide
Halt@X (Animated Guide to Dressage)
Horses (Photos of English Horses)
Horse Country
Horsing Around
The Horseman's Advisor
Horse Genetics from UC Davis
The Horse Industry in the US (Statistics)
Horse Interactive (Health Care)
HorseNet Europe
Hunting and Polo Sporting Page
Janet's Horsin' Around on the Web Pages
Kentucky Derby Museum
Leave No Trace
Lone Star Hitch
Mr. Horse (from Italy)
National Sporting Library
National Cowboy Hall of Fame
National Museum of Racing
NetVet
The Perseus Project (Ancient Greece)
Pferde Museum (Germany)
PoloNet
New Pony Discovery in Tibet (From CNN)
British Riding Stables
Royal Ontario Museum (Chinese chariot info under "curatorial research")
Those Interesting Equines
Texas Horseman's Directory
Tilly's Tale (Welsh Pony)
The Ultimate Horse Site
Xenophon: Treatises on Horsemanship (From the MIT Classics site)

CLUBS AND ORGANIZATIONS
Aberdeen University Riding Club
Alberta Equine Industry Development Council
Alberta Equine . . . On-Line
American Assoc. of Equine Practitioners
American Assoc. for Horsemanship Safety
American Driving Society
Amer. Miniature Horse Assoc.–Send a "Gift Horse"
American Riding Instructors Association (ARIA) (E-mail only)
American Riding Instructor Certification Program (ARICP) (E-mail only)
American Farrier's Association (E-mail only)
Association Internationale des Estudiant Cavaliers
Assoc. for Horsemanship Safety & Education
Australian Dressage Home Page
BLM—Wild Horse Adoption Program
British Horse Society
Canadian Driving Assoc.
Carriage Assoc. of Amer.
Central KY Riding for the Handicapped
Colorado Horse Rescue
Corolla Wild Horse Fund Home Page
The Endurance Net
Equine Rescue Network, Inc.
Equine Rescue Internet Canada
Georgia Equine Rescue League, Ltd.
German Horse Riding Club
High Country Driving Club
New Hampshire Equine Humane Association, Inc.
North American Riding for the Handicapped Assoc.
Norcal Miniature Horse Club
The Hunter-Jumper Network
Kathy's Cowboy History and Rodeo Page
Midwest Dressage Assoc.
PoloNet
Professional Rodeo Cowboys Assoc.
Project Hope Home Page (Australia)
National Reined Cow Horse Association
ReRun (placement for ex-racehorses)
Kentucky-Rolex Three-Day Event
The American Saddlebred Horse Museum
International Side-Saddle Organization (ISSO) (E-mail only)
World Sidesaddle Federation
Southern Farm Network
Special Equestrian Riding Therapy, Inc.
Springbank Equestrian Society

Team Penning Assoc. of America
Trail Riders of the Canadian Rockies
United States Equestrian Team
United States Pony Club
United States Dressage Federation
US Combined Training Assoc.
USCTA Area VIII
Volvo World Cup
Women's Professional Rodeo Page

BREEDS
Horse Breeds (OK State University)
Horse Breed Listings
Akhal-Teke
Akhal Teke: The Complete Compendium
Andalusian Horse Association of Australia
International Andalusian and Lusitano Horse Association
Appaloosa Horse Club
Arabian Horse Interactive
W. K. Kellogg Arabian Horse Library
Belgian Draft Horse Corp. of America
Brindle Horses
Cleveland Bay Horse Society of North America
American Cream Horse Association
The Canadian Curly Horse (Bashkir Curly)
Northwest Curly Horse Assoc. (Bashkir Curly)
British Donkey Breed Society
The Draft Page
Brewster's Home Page (Draft Horse)
The Dutch Horse
The Endurance Horse & Pony Society
The Exmoor Pony Society
The Fjord Horse Page (Norwegian Fjord Horse)
The Friesian Horse Assoc. of North America
Haflinger Registry of North America
Western Haflinger Association
Lipizzan Assoc. of North America
US Lipizzan Registry
Lipizzaners at the Spanish Riding School
"Diddi" Icelandic Horse Network
Icelandic Horses On line
My Icelandic Horses
Irish Horses
National Miniature Donkey Assoc.
International Miniature Donkey Registry
American Miniature Horse Assoc.
Falabella Miniature Horses (Argentina)

Amer. Morgan Horse Association
Missouri Foxtrotters
The Canadian Morgan Horse Association
British Morgan Horse Society
The Morab Horse Association
The North American Morab Horse Association
The Morab Horse Registry
The British Mule Society
Palomino Horse Breeders of America
The Paint Horse Association
Paso Fino Horse Assoc.
Paso Fino Horse Home Page
The Performance Horse Registry
Amer. Assoc. of Owners and Breeders of Peruvian Paso
    Horses
The Colorful World of Paints & Pintos
The Pinto Horse Assoc. of America
American Quarter Horse Association
US Quarter Horse Registry
Pacific Coast Quarter Horse Association
Natural Gait News (Rocky Mountain Horses)
American Saddlebred Horse Assoc.
The American Saddlebred Horse
The American Shetland Pony Club
Shetland Pony Home Page (British)
American Shire Horse Assoc.
Pace-way for Standardbreds
The Tennessee Walking Horse Breeders' and Ex-
    hibitors' Assoc.
The Tennessee Walking Horse Celebration
The TN Walking Horse Exhibitors' Assoc. of Oregon
American Trakehner Assoc.
The Jockey Club (Thoroughbred)
American Warmblood Society
Welsh Pony and Cob Society of America, Inc.
Wild Mustangs of the Pryor Mountains

TRACKS & SHOW FACILITIES
Aintree Racecourse
Churchill Downs
Del Mar Thoroughbred Club
Hastings Park Racecourse
Keeneland Racecourse
Louisiana Downs
Newmarket Racecourse, England
Quarry Park, Ontario
Santa Anita Home Page
Turfway Park

RACING
AusRace (Australia)
The Bloodhorse Magazine
The Breeders' Cup
Cindy Pierson's Racing Memorabilia Pages
Cyberspace Racing Team
ESPNET SportsZone Horse Racing
Equibase Company
Harness Racing in Australia
Japanese Classic Races
Japanese Steeplechasing
Pedigree Query Site
Official Southern Africa Thoroughbred & Racing
    Home Page
The Running Horse
Samsung Nations' Cup (Korea)
The Texas Thoroughbred
Thoroughbred Sports Network
The Thoroughbred Times
Thoroughbred Owners and Breeders Assoc.
Trotto e Galoppo
Canadian Trotting Association
United States Trotting Association
University of Ky. Horse Racing Archives

HORSE FARMS
Brightstone Farm
Blue Moon Farm (TN Walkers)
Castleton Farm
Clear Creek Stud Farm
Cottonwood Farm
Fairwinds Farm
Flying F Arabians
Good Shepard Farm and Carriage Co. (Halflingers)
Houvenin-Gold Farms (TN Walkers)
Irish National Stud
JFF Miniature Horse Farm
Jumper's Appaloosa Sport Horses
The Karr Ranch
Kismet Farm (Aps & Amer. Warmbloods)
Lane's End Farm
L'il Beginnings Miniature Horses
Maxwell Arabians
MCR Quarter Horses (Canada)
Oak Hill Ranch
Paintbrush Miniature Horses
Regalia Saddlebreds
Sunnyland Racing Arabians

SunRae Miniature Horse Stable
Three Chimneys Farm
Trillium Morgan Horse Farm
Whistlin' Wind Appaloosas
White Raven Appaloosas
Yeguada Alba Ranch (Spanish Thoroughbreds)

MAGAZINES AND PUBLICATIONS

The American Cowboy (pay site)
Anvil Online (Farrier and Blacksmith info. and supplies)
Arizona Equine Classified
The Bloodhorse Magazine
Conquistador Magazine
The Equine Image
Equijournal
Harness Horse.com *(Horseman Mag.)*
Mane Points (from Southern States)
Natural Gait News (Rocky Mountain Horses)
Owner–Breeder
The Thoroughbred Times
Trail Rider Magazine

ARTISTS AND GALLERIES

Original Art by Nancy Alcott
Equine Art by Tami Bassler
Douwe Blumberg Bronze Sculptures
Photos by Arnd Bronkhorst
Cortez Art
Creart
Retired Jockey, J. R. Dailey—Western Art
Western Art by Randy Follis
Gallatin Fine Art Gallery
Steve Lofty Equine Art
Mark Photographic
Model Horses
Equestrian Portraits by Olva Stewart Pharo
The Horse and Hound Gallery
Rodeo in America (Photos)
Sam Savitt Art
Old West Saddle Shop & Seeger's Art
Unicorn Originals
The Vavra Collection of Equestrian Photos
Western Imprints Photos by Thomas Casper
Francis Eustis Gallery
Lynn Wade Art
Sculpture by Cindy Wolf

COMMERCIAL AND MISCELLANEOUS SITES

Angel House Publishing
Arabian Horse Shopping Mall
Autotote Corp.
The Barn
Boojum Expeditions (Vacations, many on horseback)
Buy a Horse
California on Track Handicappers
Carriage Works
Chicago Stables Directory
Chuck Pritchard Saddlery
The Circle 2 Ranch
Compendia!, Inc.—Software for the Equine Industry
Corton Animal Accomodations (Dutch)
The Cowboy Trail
Diamond Lu Horse Videos for Children
Dr. Benson's Nutritional Supplements
Elite Equines Ltd. (Dressage horses)
Equinet
Equus '97
Equine Affaire
Equine Directory
Equinomical Horse Supply, Inc.
Equi-Site
Equitana (USA)
Equitronics
The Farnam Company
Fleniken Quarter Horses
Forest Ranch Equestrian Center
Guidon Books (Western, Military, etc)
Horses of the Dutch
Horses Galore!
The Horseman's Advisor
The Horse Exchange
The Horse Mall
HorseMad
Horse Net
Horse Worldwide
Horsesales, Inc.
Houston Livestock Show and Rodeo
Icelandic Horses and Products
LHA Bookstore (England)
Internet Horse Classified
Irish Horses.Com
Let's Rope Page
Little Filly's Stall
Lone Star Horses
Circle 2 Live Online Horse Chat

Horse Words

Philip (or Phillip)—from the Greek words philos *and* hippos, *meaning lover and horse, respectively— means, obviously a lover of horses, as in Philip of Macedonia or Prince Philip of England.*

Hippalectryon—a four-legged beast with the foreparts of a horse and the hind parts of a rooster

Hipparch—a cavalry commander

Hippia—referred to Athena, as the "horse goddess"

Hippiatrics—equine veterinary medicine

Hippocampus—a sea horse in classical mythology

Hippocurius—referred to Poseidon and meant "horse tending"

Hippodrome—an arena for equestrian spectacles

Hippogriff—a creature with the foreparts of a griffin and the hind parts of a horse (which should obviously be griffohip)

Hippology—the study of horses

Hippophagist—one who eats horseflesh, or practices hippophagy

Hippophile—one who loves horses

Hippopotamus—a "river horse"

Meandaur, Inc. (Horse Gear)
Middleburg (VA) On-line
Monty Robert's Home Page
National Insiders Network (Thoroughbred)
Naturally Equine (Feed)
The Neogen Corp.
The Old West Museum & Saddle Shop
Premier Horse Network

The Professor's Thoroughbred Racing Page
A Ride in the Park
Rodeo Steakhouse
The Russell Meerdink Company
Serious Sports (Includes Horseback)
Software Exchange (Handicapping)
Stallions
Surf the Murf (Handicapping)
Unbridled
Vicki Wall Dressage Training
Virtual Horse City
Awhitehorse.com
WALLOPWare Educational Software

GENERAL INTEREST & SEARCH SITES

The Starting Point
Yahoo
Lycos City Guide
Infoseek
City Net
Internet Yellow Pages
New Riders' WWW Yellow Pages
Ky. Horse Park Trip Planner
Official Ky. Vacation Guide
Lexington Visitor Info (Univ. of Ky.)
Lexington, Ky. (city's official site)
The Kentucky Horse Park

Index

———— Ω ————

Page numbers in *italics* refer to illustrations.